PROCEEDINGS

OF THE

SEMINAR FOR ARABIAN STUDIES

VOLUME 54

2025

Papers from the fifty-seventh meeting of the
Seminar for Arabian Studies
held at the Institut national d'histoire de l'art, Paris,
27–29 June 2024

SEMINAR FOR ARABIAN STUDIES

ARCHAEOPRESS
OXFORD

Orders for copies of this volume of the *Proceedings* and all back numbers should be sent to
Archaeopress Publishing Ltd, 13–14 Market Square, Bicester, Oxfordshire OX26 6AD, UK.
Tel +44(0)1865-311914 Fax +44(0)1865-512231
e-mail info@archaeopress.com
http://www.archaeopress.com
For the availability of back issues see http://www.archaeopress.com
For more information on the Seminar for Arabian Studies and the *Proceedings* please visit the International Association for the Study of Arabia (IASA)'s website: https://www.theiasa.com/seminar/

Seminar for Arabian Studies
c/o Department of Archaeology, University of Durham
Lower Mount Joy, South Rd, Durham DH1 3LE
e-mail psas@theiasa.com
The International Association for the Study of Arabia (formally the The British Foundation for the Study of Arabia): https://www.theiasa.com/

MEMBERS OF THE STEERING COMMITTEE OF THE SEMINAR FOR ARABIAN STUDIES

The Steering Committee of the Seminar for Arabian Studies is currently made up of twenty-one academic members. The Editorial Committee of the *Proceedings of the Seminar for Arabian Studies* includes nine additional members as follows:

Opinions expressed in papers published in the *Proceedings* are those of the authors and are not necessarily shared by the Editorial Committee.

ISSN 0308-8421
ISBN 978-1-80583-060-3
ISBN 978-1-80583-061-0 (e-PDF)

Contents

Guidelines and Transliteration

Guidelines for Authors

For details on the submission of papers and the preparation of papers for publication, authors are requested to consult and follow the latest *Guidelines for Authors.* These are available on the International Association for the Study of Arabia website at https://www.theiasa.com/seminar/publication/. Please contact the editors on https://www.theiasa.com/seminar/publication/ for further information.

Formatting

Electronic versions of papers being submitted for publication should be set in Times New Roman 12-point typeface if at all possible, with double-line spacing on A4-paper size and 2.45 cm margins all round.

The IASA System of Transliteration of Relevant Characters

Quotations, single words, and phrases from Arabic or other languages written in non-Roman alphabets, are transliterated according to the systems set out below.

- We firmly encourage authors to use the correctly transliterated form of any place name, but the names used for types of pottery, archaeological periods, and cultures which have become archaeological standards should be used in that form: Umm an-Nar, Julfar ware, etc. If any place name needs to be given in a non-standard format, the correctly transliterated form should be added in the first instance in any paper (see *Guidelines for Authors* for more details).
- Personal names, toponyms, and other words that have entered English or French in a particular form, should be used in that form when they occur in an English or French sentence, unless they are part of a quotation in the original language, or of a correctly transliterated name or phrase. In the latter cases, they should be correctly transliterated, even when they occur in an English or French sentence.

1. Arabic

ء	M	ج	j	ذ	dh (dh)	ش	sh (sh)	ظ	Ξ	ق	q	ن	n
ب	b	ح	ḥ	ر	r	ص	ṣ	ع	K	ك	k	ه	h
ت	t	خ	kh (kh)	ز	z	ض	ḍ	غ	gh (gh)	ل	l	و	w
ث	th (th)	د	d	س	s	ط	ṭ	ف	f	م	m	ي	y
Vowels		a i u ā ī ū		Diphthongs		aw	ay						

The underlined variants can be used to avoid any ambiguity, e.g. *lam yushir* vs. *lam yushir.*
Initial *hamzah* is omitted.
Alif maqṣūrah is transliterated as ā.
The *lām* of the article is not assimilated before the 'sun letters', thus the form should be *al-shams* but not *ash-shams.*
The *hamzat al-waṣl* of the article should be shown after vowels except after the preposition *li-*, as in the Arabic script, e.g. *wa-ʾl-wazīr*, *fīʾl-bayt*, but *li-l-wazīr*.
Tāʾ marbūṭah (ة) should be rendered *-ah*, except in a construct: e.g. *birkah*, *zakāh*, and *birkat al-sibāḥah*, *zakāt al-fiṭr*.

2. Persian, Urdu, and Ottoman Turkish

Please transliterate these languages using the system set out for Arabic above with the additional letters transliterated according to the system in the *Encyclopaedia of Islam* (http://referenceworks.brillonline.com/entries/encyclopaedia-islamica/system-of-transliteration-of-arabic-and-persian-characters-transliteration) except that *ž* is used instead of *zh*. There is a useful table to convert Ottoman Turkish to modern Turkish characters on http://en.wikipedia.org/wiki/Ottoman_Turkish_language.

3. Ancient North and South Arabian Consonants:

ʾ	b	t	ṯ	ḥ	g	ḫ	d	ḏ	r	z	s^1	s^2	s^3	ṣ
ḍ	ṭ	ẓ	ʿ	ġ	f	q	k	l	m	n	h	w	y	

4. Other Semitic languages

Please use the transliteration systems outlined in the *Bulletin of the American Schools of Oriental Research* (BASOR) 262 (1986), p. 3. (www.jstor.org/stable/i258780).

Editor's Foreword

The Seminar for Arabian Studies is the longest-running academic forum dedicated to the presentation of research on the cultural and natural heritage of the Arabian Peninsula. Since its first meeting in 1968, the Seminar has covered a wide range of subjects including archaeology, epigraphy, history, ethnography, art, architecture, linguistics, and literature from prehistory to the present. In 2019 the Seminar changed from being a British-based forum to an international setting, starting with a meeting at the University of Leiden and continuing with other European institutions. This year marks another turning point, as the meeting is being organized for the first time in the Arabian Peninsula, at the Zayed National Museum, Department of Culture and Tourism (Abu Dhabi), bringing this increasingly important international meeting to the region.

The 57th Seminar for Arabian Studies, held in Paris in 2024, was a particularly memorable event, bringing together scholars from a broad range of disciplines to discuss the archaeology, history, epigraphy, and philology of the Arabian Peninsula. In 2024, the Seminar took place from 27 to 29 June within the elegant architectural setting of the Institut national d'histoire de l'art, located in a remarkable 19th-century covered passage. The Steering Committee was especially grateful for the strong institutional support provided by the International Association for the Study of Arabia, AFALULA, Sorbonne Université, Université Paris 1 Panthéon-Sorbonne, CNRS, Musée du Louvre, and the Senate of the French Republic.

Participation continues to grow annually, and in 2024 over 230 attendees joined the event both online and in person — the largest number ever. The academic programme was particularly rich, comprising eighty-eight papers and twenty posters, organized across several thematic sessions. In an effort to accommodate a broader range of contributions, two new presentation formats were introduced: a short rapportage format (15 minutes long) for fieldwork updates and a longer format (25 minutes long) allowing for synthetic overviews. Both were well received and reflected a desire to balance detailed case studies with broader interpretive syntheses.

The geographical breadth of the contributions was notable, with research presented from across the Arabian Peninsula. While continuing to highlight the evident and growing significance of research conducted in the north-west of the Peninsula, we are also pleased to note that, for the first time in many years a dedicated session 'Ancient South Arabia' was held, focusing on the south-west of the Peninsula. In addition, the programme embraced new thematic directions, such as heritage and community building, highlighting the growing recognition of the role of archaeology in cultural preservation and sustainable development.

As in previous years, special sessions provided a platform for focused discussions on timely topics. Two such sessions were held alongside the plenary. The first addressed Zaydi governance in Yemen, reflecting the Seminar's ongoing commitment to expanding its coverage of lesser-explored areas, particularly in the medieval and modern periods. The papers of this special session form part of this volume. The second, entitled 'Late Antique Arabia (4th–8th centuries): a changing landscape', gathered eleven specialists in archaeology, environmental studies, history, and epigraphy to examine the dynamic transformations of the region during this pivotal period. This session concluded with a keynote lecture by Martina Müller-Wiener and Martin Gussone, entitled *More than the Lakhmid capital — The late heyday of al-Hira in the early Islamic period*. The papers from the Special Session on Late Antique Arabia will be published in a Special Issue of *Arabian Archaeology and Epigraphy*.

In sum, the 57th Seminar was an intellectually stimulating and collegial gathering, and sincere thanks are due to the organizing team in Paris for their dedication in making the event such a success.

This volume of the *Proceedings of the Seminar for Arabian Studies* includes seventeenen papers presented in the ordinary sessions and three papers presented in the special session 'Zaydi governance in Yemen', held in Paris. Our thanks go to all the authors who submitted papers and to the anonymous reviewers who contributed to the academic robustness of the result. The publication of the volume within a year of the event itself is possible thanks to the efforts of a team which includes myself as Editor, and the Assistant Editors Irene Rossi, Akshyeta Suryanarayan, José Carvajal López, Daniel Eddisford, and Orhan Elmaz. We are also thankful for the support of Patrick Harris and Erin McGowan, the dedicated Archaeopress team, who worked hard to facilitate timely publication. Finally, we wish to thank Helen Knox, our copy-editor, whose indefatigable work and exceptional efforts have helped to bring this volume to completion. The Seminar for Arabian Studies and the *Proceedings* are organized by the Steering Committee of the Seminar for Arabian Studies and the International Foundation for the Study of Arabia (IASA). For additional information on the Seminar, please contact Kate Ayres-Kennet (seminar@theisasa.com). The IASA (formally the British Foundation for the Study of Arabia) is a charitable organization that promotes research on the cultural and natural heritage of the Arabian Peninsula. The IASA produces two annual bulletins. For further information about IASA, please write to contact@theiasa.com or visit the IASA website at www.theiasa.com.

Silvia Lischi

May 2025

Society of Antiquaries of London, Beatrice de Cardi keynote lecture

This year's lecture, generously supported by the Society of Antiquaries of London, entitled *More than the Lakhmid capital — The late heyday of al-Hira in the early Islamic period*, was given by Dr Martina Müller-Wiener and Dr Martin Gussone.

The Beatrice de Cardi Awards are administered by the Society of Antiquaries of London. The grants are worth up to £15,000 for archaeological research on the United Arab Emirates, the Sultanate of Oman, Saudi Arabia, and the Pakistan province of Balochistan.

The deadline for applications is 15 January annually.

More information available at https://www.sal.org.uk/what-we-do/grants/our-grant-programmes/

In Memoriam

Walter Wilhelm Müller (1933–2024)

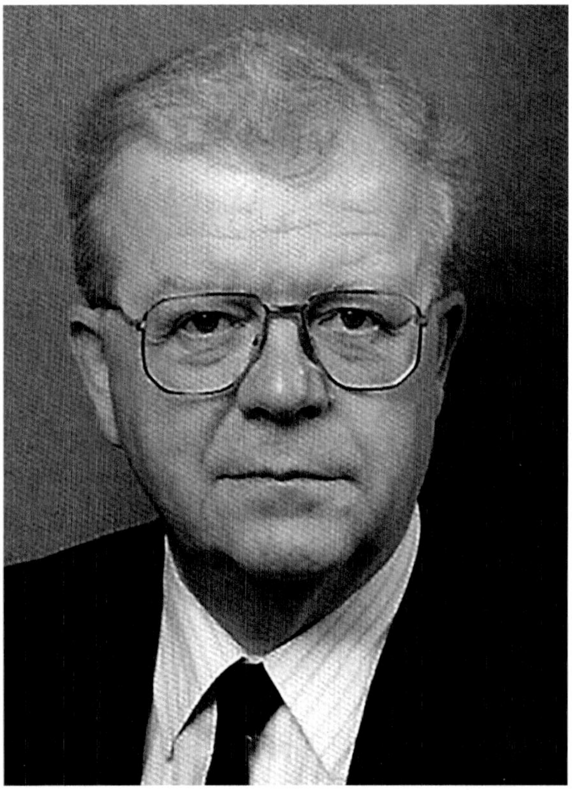

A few weeks after his 91st birthday, Walter W. Müller, Professor Emeritus of Semitic Studies, died in Marburg. His name is inextricably linked with the post-war history of the study of ancient South Arabia and, like few others in his field, he has had a lasting influence on it. Walter Müller was born in 1933 in Weipert-Neugeschrei, then part of Czechoslovakia, in the Bohemian Ore Mountains. After being expelled in 1946, he attended the Realgymnasium in Beerfelden and Michelstadt in the Odenwald, where he passed his *Abitur* in 1955. Having graduated from high school, he initially studied Catholic theology in Mainz. Inspired by Hebrew, he took additional language courses in Syriac-Aramaic and Arabic in the first few semesters and began to turn to Semitic languages. Despite a tempting offer to continue his theological studies at the Germanicum in Rome, which would have relieved him of all future financial worries, he switched to Semitic Studies at the Mainz Seminar for Oriental Studies and continued his research in Tübingen with the internationally renowned South Arabian expert Maria Höfner, who at the time held the only professorship in the German-speaking world in Semitic Studies with a focus on Sabaic. This was even less of a career-conscious decision than it is today and was not without considerable risk if one wanted seriously to embark on an academic career. As he often mentioned with pride, Maria Höfner then became his doctoral supervisor, and in 1962 he wrote his dissertation which was a lexicographical and etymological work on the roots *mediae* and *tertiae* w/y in Ancient South Arabian.

Walter Müller's decision to move to Tübingen, however, was also significantly encouraged by the fact that this university offered the largest range of Middle Eastern subjects at the time and provided a unique opportunity to study Sabaic and the other Ancient South Arabian languages in a comparative linguistic environment. Otto Rössler, who was still teaching in Tübingen at the time, provided the methodological tools for this important work on Semito-Hamitic grammar, opening up the subject beyond the traditional relationships between Semitic languages; Müller always referred to him as one of his teachers. Before completing his doctorate, he took advantage of a Fulbright scholarship to spend a year as a research assistant to the Islamic scholar Gustav E. von Grunebaum at the newly founded Near Eastern Centre in Los Angeles, where he also had the opportunity to deepen his knowledge of the spoken Ethio-Semitic languages with Wolf Leslau. During his years as an *assistant* at Rudi Paret's Chair of Islamic Studies in Tübingen he completed a lexicographical and etymological thesis on Mehri which earned him his *Habilitation* in Semitic philology. A brief glance at the literature on linguistics at the time shows that Modern South Arabian was a much-neglected field in Semitic studies. Müller's examination of this language group produced results that are still valid today. In a nutshell, they can be summarized as follows: Modern South Arabian is closely related to the Ethiopic languages. Ultimately, this finding leads to the implicit conclusion that Modern South Arabian is not to be regarded as the historical continuation of Sabaic or — probably — of the other Ancient South Arabian languages, a conclusion that was further confirmed by subsequent research a few decades later.

In addition to philology and linguistics, Tübingen also focused on another area, promoted by the geographer Hermann von Wissmann, 'one of the last pioneers in the history of the discovery of our earth', as Müller described him in his obituary. It is difficult to underestimate the importance for epigraphy of the opening up of South Arabian regional studies. Although philology, and in particular the greater understanding of lexicon and grammar, is an indispensable prerequisite for the correct translation of ancient South Arabian texts, a deeper understanding of an epigraphic document requires a clear idea of how it is embedded in its environment, for which geographical and topographical knowledge of the terrain often provides invaluable assistance. Müller's collaboration with Hermann von Wissmann therefore provided him with an excellent preparation for the occasion when, after the end of the civil war in 1970, he was given the opportunity to lead the first German Yemen expedition in post-war history with two colleagues. This expedition, which had set itself the goal of epigraphic, archaeological, and linguistic exploration, opened up not only the epigraphic exploration of pre-Islamic southern Arabia but paved the way for scientific institutions, such as the German Archaeological Institute, to enter Yemen.

Even though Müller always described his years in Tübingen as his best and most productive, his full impact was in Marburg, where he was appointed full professor and successor to Otto Rössler in 1975. It was in Marburg that he trained the majority of his students who, after graduating, visited him again and again to work with him. He was particularly fortunate with his students from Arab countries. Many of them came to Marburg from Yemen, Saudi Arabia, and Jordan to study the languages and cultures of pre-Islamic Arabia with him, and he maintained personal contact with them after they had completed their doctorates. They are now either professors or in leading positions in antiquities administrations in their home countries. It was in Marburg that the *Sabaic Dictionary* (1982) was created through many years of collaboration with his colleagues A.F.L. Beeston, Jacques Ryckmans, and Mahmud Ghul. This has provided a solid basis for understanding the corpus of inscriptions that has since grown immensely through archaeological excavations and surveys in Yemen. Written in cooperation with Jacques Ryckmans and Yusuf M. Abdallah, his student from Tübingen and later president of the Yemeni Antiquities Administration, the *Textes du Yémen antique inscrits sur bois* (1994) laid the foundations for the decipherment of the Ancient South Arabian minuscule inscriptions, a new form of text carved on sticks that emerged in Yemen in the 1970s. It is sometimes difficult to read and, in contrast to the monumental inscriptions, was used for texts from everyday economic and legal life.

Müller was a giant in his subject. He investigated every aspect of it, to which his 200 publications bear eloquent witness, and in his extensive review activity he went far beyond the actual boundaries of the discipline. He repeatedly returned to the Old Testament and its environment in smaller works. In addition to ancient South Arabia, the cultural landscapes of pre-Islamic central and northern Arabia are also the subject of his numerous contributions to handbooks and encyclopaedias. It was always a major concern of his to make accessible their cultural history which, as in the case of South Arabia, stretches from the early first millennium BC to the advent of Islam, and to bring the latest state of research to those working in neighbouring disciplines and an interested public. An impressive example, which also provides an insight into the author's working method, is his article '*Weihrauch* [Frankincense]' — published in 1978 as a separate publication — in the supplement volume of *Pauly's Realencyclopaedie der Classischen Altertumswissenschaft*. With his extensive knowledge of the sources, including classical literature, Müller was the first to trace the significance of frankincense for the ancient Near East and the ancient world and recognized the central role played by the South Arabian communities of Sabaʾ and Maʿīn, Qatabān, and Ḥaḍramawt in the cultivation and trade of this indigenous product.

The interpretation and editing of South Arabian inscriptions formed the core of his work, in which he set high standards for the next generations. He published large numbers of newly discovered inscriptions, each of which provides a further piece of the mosaic of knowledge of the language and culture of ancient South Arabia and, in particular, its religious history, which differs significantly from that of the rest of the ancient Near East and of Islam. He is also to be thanked for his numerous new interpretations of the great Ancient South Arabian texts, which every generation tries to tackle anew. He translated and annotated a representative selection in *Texte aus der Umwelt des Alten Testaments* (Texts from the world of the Old Testament) (1982–1988), which demonstrates the immense progress that has been made in the understanding of Ancient South Arabian inscriptions. But he was not above doing time-consuming research work, which included the bibliography with commentary *Südarabien im Altertum* (2001; 2014), published in two volumes which, according to him, is often used but never cited. His concern was never to approach a matter with hypotheses. Rather, his work is characterized by an almost encyclopaedic knowledge of material, facts, and literature and above all by the extensive use of source texts and their critical evaluation.

Müller received numerous honours and honorary memberships. To name just a few: he was associated with the Mainz academy as a full member from 1987 and for many years as chairman of the Oriental Commission. The German Archaeological Institute elected him a corresponding member in 1977 and a full member in 1983. On his 60th birthday, he was honoured by his colleagues and students with a Festschrift entitled *Arabia Felix. Contributions to the language and culture of pre-Islamic Arabia* (1994). In 1998 he was presented with the highest honour of Yemen — for whose country and people he had a sincere, but not uncritical, affection — in the form of a gold medal, which was minted on the occasion of the unification of the two Yemens on 22 May 1990. He was an honorary member of the German Oriental Society and was particularly pleased when he was elected a Corresponding Fellow of the British Academy in 2001, the year of his retirement. Even after his retirement, he continued to play an active role in academic life and continued to publish right up to the end. With him, the study of ancient South Arabia has lost one of its most renowned representatives, who exerted a lasting influence on it for half a century.

Norbert Nebes

Müller first attended the Seminar for Arabian Studies in 1975 and from then on was a regular attendee and speaker for four decades. Together with A.F.L (Freddie) Beeston and Jacques Ryckmans, he was an essential part of each Seminar until he became too ill to attend. He was always amiable but did not hesitate to correct an error and was therefore an extremely valuable member of the meetings. Over the years, he contributed numerous times to PSAS on a wide range of subjects, all of which extended our knowledge by clarifying difficult areas of Ancient South Arabian and wider Semitic philology, and the pre-Islamic history and societies of Arabia. He was always elegantly dressed and had a professorial dignity, but occasionally showed sparks of humour, particularly after some excellent wine. In a moving tribute after the death of Freddie Beeston — who was the very opposite of him in terms of appearance (T-shirt, jeans, and shoulder-length white hair) — Walter (as he was known at the Seminar) told how after one session of the Seminar, Freddie invited him for a drink and they went to a local pub. Unfortunately, it was extremely crowded and there was nowhere to sit, so Freddie said, 'Oh well, we'll just have to sit on the floor.' This they did and it was probably the first time since his youth that Walter had done so, especially in the company of someone who looked like Freddie! All those who knew him will miss Walter Müller, his brilliant work, and all he contributed to the Seminar.

Michael Macdonald
April 2025

References

Beeston A.F.L., Ghul M.A., Müller W.W. & Ryckmans J. 1982. *Sabaic Dictionary (English-French-Arabic).* (Publication of the University of Sanaa, YAR). Louvain-la-Neuve: Peeters/Beirut: Librairie du Liban.

Müller W.W. 1978. Weihrauch: Ein arabisches Produkt und seine Bedeutung in der Antike. (Columns 700–777 in Supplement-Band xv der Realencylopädie von Pauly-Wissowa). Munich: Alfred Druckenmüller. [Offprint.]

Müller W.W. 2001. *Südarabien im Altertum. Kommentierte Bibliographie der Jahre 1973 bis 1996.* Rahden/Westf.: Leidorf.

Müller W.W. 2014. *Südarabien im Altertum. Kommentierte Bibliographie der Jahre 1997 bis 2011.* (Epigraphische Forschungen auf der Arabischen Halbinsel). Tübingen: Wasmuth.

Nebes N. (ed.). 1994. *Arabia Felix: Beiträge zur Sprache und Kultur des vorislasmischen Arabien. Festschrift Walter W. Müller zum 60. Geburtstag.* Wiesbaden: Harrassowitz.

Ryckmans J., Müller W.W. & Abdallah Y.M. 1994. *Textes du Yémen antique inscrits sur bois.* Louvain-la-Neuve: Université catholique de Louvain, Institut Orientaliste.

In Memoriam

Khaldūn Hazzāʿ ʿAbduh Nuʿmān (1967–2024)

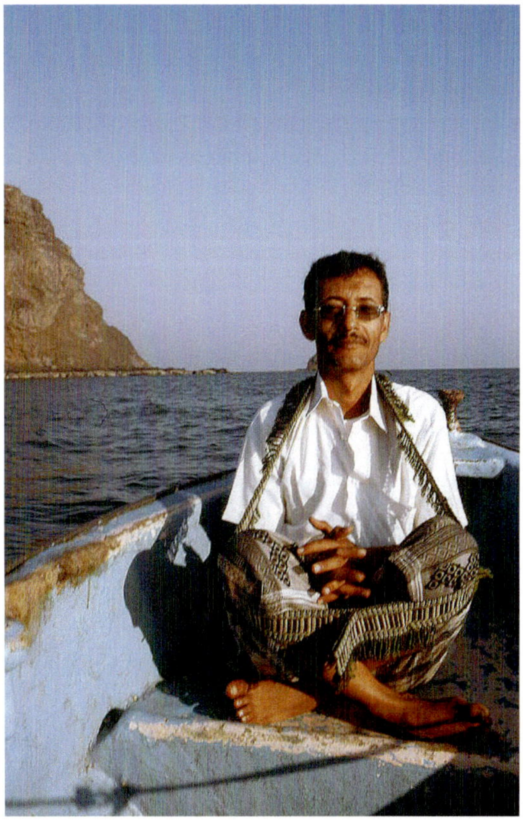

Aden, 2008. Photo by Alessandra Lombardi.

It is with profound sorrow that we commemorate the premature passing of Prof. Khaldūn Hazzāʿ ʿAbduh Nuʿmān, a distinguished Yemeni epigrapher and historian, whose scholarly dedication and human qualities left an indelible mark on all who knew and worked with him.

Born in Taʿizz Governorate, Khaldūn began his academic journey at Ṣanʿāʾ University, where he earned his MA in 2003. His thesis on the reign of the Himyarite king Shammar Yuharʿish, supervised by ʿAbdallah al-Shayba, was soon published as a monograph under the title *Al-awḍāʿ al-siyāsiyya wa-l-iqtiṣādiyya wa-l-ijtimāʿiyya fī ʿahd al-malik Shammar Yuharʿish* (Ṣanʿāʾ, 2004).

Most of Khaldūn's historical and epigraphic research was dedicated to a crucial area of the Ancient South Arabian territory: the Yemeni highlands stretching between Ṣanʿāʾ and Ẓafār, with a focus on the region of Dhamār. He tirelessly trekked this region's mountains to reach remote sites and record inscriptions. We owe him the knowledge of new texts that he published over the years and which have substantially contributed to rewriting the history of the area in the first centuries AD. It was precisely at Dhamār University that Khaldūn made his career in higher education, beginning as a teaching assistant.

Deeply committed to the preservation and valorization of Yemeni antiquities, he also actively worked in museums to organize and catalogue their rich collections, such as at the Baynūn Museum under the direction of Ahmad al-ʿAzizi. Since 2007 Khaldūn had supported Italian researchers in a cooperation project aimed at the digital cataloguing of Ancient South Arabian inscribed objects preserved in Yemeni museums (CASIS). This collaboration opened the way to his enrolment as a doctoral fellow in the Oriental Studies PhD programme at the University of Pisa in January 2009, under the supervision of Alessandra Avanzini. He eventually moved to Italy, joined for a time by his wife Afriqiya.

I had come to know Khaldūn through the CASIS project, but the years of the PhD, which we shared side by side until our dissertations in October 2012, allowed me more closely to appreciate him both as a scholar with immense and passionate knowledge of Ancient South Arabian history and as a delightful companion in our studies. Khaldūn's dissertation, *A Study of South Arabian Inscriptions from the Region of Dhamār* (Pisa, 2012), presented dozens of unpublished texts that he had personally discovered in fifty sites across the area, and was exceptional in both the quantity and quality of new data.

During his Italian years, Khaldūn also became a collaborator of the *Digital Archive for the Study of pre-Islamic Arabian Inscriptions* (DASI), for which he contributed editions of hundreds of texts and translations into Arabic, significantly broadening the accessibility of this resource. He continued to provide updates and corrections to the archive even after his return to his beloved homeland, where he had long envisioned resuming university teaching and expanding his family. This indeed happened soon, with his professorship at the University of Dhamār and the joyful birth of his two children, Shammar and Taif, born to his wife Nahed.

Driven by a vision to establish a permanent space for the study and training of archaeology students at the university, Khaldūn also spearheaded the creation of the Dhamār University Museum, hosting a range of artefacts spanning prehistoric to historic times. As early as 2015 he had played a key role in the recovery and reassembly of artefacts from the Dhamār Regional Museum, which had been destroyed by an airstrike. No doubt, most scholars of ancient Yemen saw the chilling photographs he shared of the museum's ruins. Indeed, Khaldūn always carried his inseparable camera to document antiquities, landscapes, people, and events.

While unpretentious about his scholarly achievements, his career progressed rapidly after his return to Yemen, encompassing directorial responsibilities at the University of Dhamār. Despite the difficulties he had to face in recent years, Khaldūn remained deeply committed to his teaching at Dhamār University and to publishing the results of his epigraphic surveys. He leaves behind a legacy of scholarship in Arabic, English, and French, by his own pen and in collaboration with both Yemeni and European colleagues.

Among his last contributions in European languages, we should include here the article on new early Sabaic inscriptions discovered on the Somali coast, published in 2021 in *Arabian Archaeology and Epigraphy* and co-authored with CNRS colleagues. A contribution to the studies in honour of Christian Robin, published in 2023, focused on new inscriptions from the site of Maṣnaʿat Māriya, administrative centre of the Muhaqraʾum tribe. The same volume also included an article from the *Dhamār Epigraphical Series*, a publication initiative dedicated to the Dhamār region that Khaldūn carried forward with Alessia Prioletta over the years in different editorial venues. In 2024 he contributed several epigraphic articles in Arabic journals, culminating in his final piece entitled 'Janūb al-Jazīra al-ʿArabiyya wa-shamālu-hā fī nuqūsh Ḥuṣn Kuḥlān (al-Yaman)' (*South and North Arabia in the Inscriptions from Ḥuṣn Kuḥlān (Yemen)*) — published posthumously in the inaugural issue of the journal *Athīrat* in February 2025, following careful editing by Mohammed Maraqten and Mounir Arbach.

His sudden death at the age of 57, on 19 August 2024 following a heart attack, came as a shock to all who knew and appreciated him — for his intellectual curiosity and passionate rigour, as well as his deep generosity and delightful companionship, always marked by a brilliant sense of humour that brought relief even in the most difficult situations. Our heartfelt thoughts go to his beloved family.

Irene Rossi

June 2025

Proceedings of the Seminar for Arabian Studies 54 (2025): 1–16

Interconnected buildings in the Old Town of AlUla and their social significance

Aljohara AlModarra, Marek Z. Barański & Apolline Vernet

Summary

Many traditional Islamic towns display a clear connection between their urban structure and the social groupings that define their communities. This complex relationship is fundamentally anchored in a strong sense of place as studies demonstrate that it is common for clusters of buildings to be inhabited by direct or extended family members. However, attempts to reconstruct this distinctive socio-spatial pattern pose a significant challenge in the case of abandoned historical urban centres, despite the fact that they have been deserted for only a few decades.

The Multiscalar Documentation of Urban Dynamics (MuDUD) project's interdisciplinary research on the Old Town of AlUla in the Kingdom of Saudi Arabia serves as an example of a non-invasive and successful method for investigating the impact of social dynamics on architectural space. This paper delves into the subject by examining archaeological building data pertaining to clusters of residential buildings, which are physically interconnected through various architectural means, in addition to engaging in targeted interviews with former town inhabitants. Consequently, it explores the mechanisms behind the creation and transformation of clusters of buildings, offering a new perspective on the town's historical context and urban dynamics through the ages, with a specific focus on the last 200 years.

Keywords: Saudi Arabia, AlUla, social organization, neighbourhoods, interconnected buildings

Introduction

Various studies on traditional Islamic towns (e.g. Alnaim 2022; Correia & Taher 2015; Dabbour 2021; Eben Saleh 1995; King 1998) have underlined a direct relationship between urban structure and social groupings. This complex interplay is deeply rooted in a strong adaptation to climatic conditions along with a pronounced sense of space, as evidence shows that neighbouring buildings often used to be occupied by family members, whether immediate or extended (Alnaim 2022: 294). This results from strictly defined and well-known organizational principles regarding social structure, laws on buying and selling property, access to space, privacy, etc. (Hakim 1986: 15–54).

In the context of AlUla and Saudi Arabia, the right of a neighbour to purchase an adjacent property or a structure when offered for sale by another neighbour is worth highlighting. This concept helps people to maintain, in the long term, the unity of their private neighbourhoods and prevents strangers from breaking the homogeneity of the social structure and family relationships (Alnaim 2022: 304). It also creates an opportunity for reconstruction of social groupings based on archival, architectural, and ethnographic data.

This paper presents preliminary results on the social organization of the historic town of AlUla in the Kingdom of Saudi Arabia. It examines the issue of social groupings through in-depth archaeological building research on groups of neighbouring residential units, which used to be physically interconnected through various architectural means. Furthermore, the paper draws upon several dozen targeted interviews conducted with former inhabitants of the Old Town of AlUla, thus describing the process of the creation and transformation of clusters of buildings and shedding new light on the social history of the town as well as the urban dynamics through time, with particular emphasis on the last two centuries.

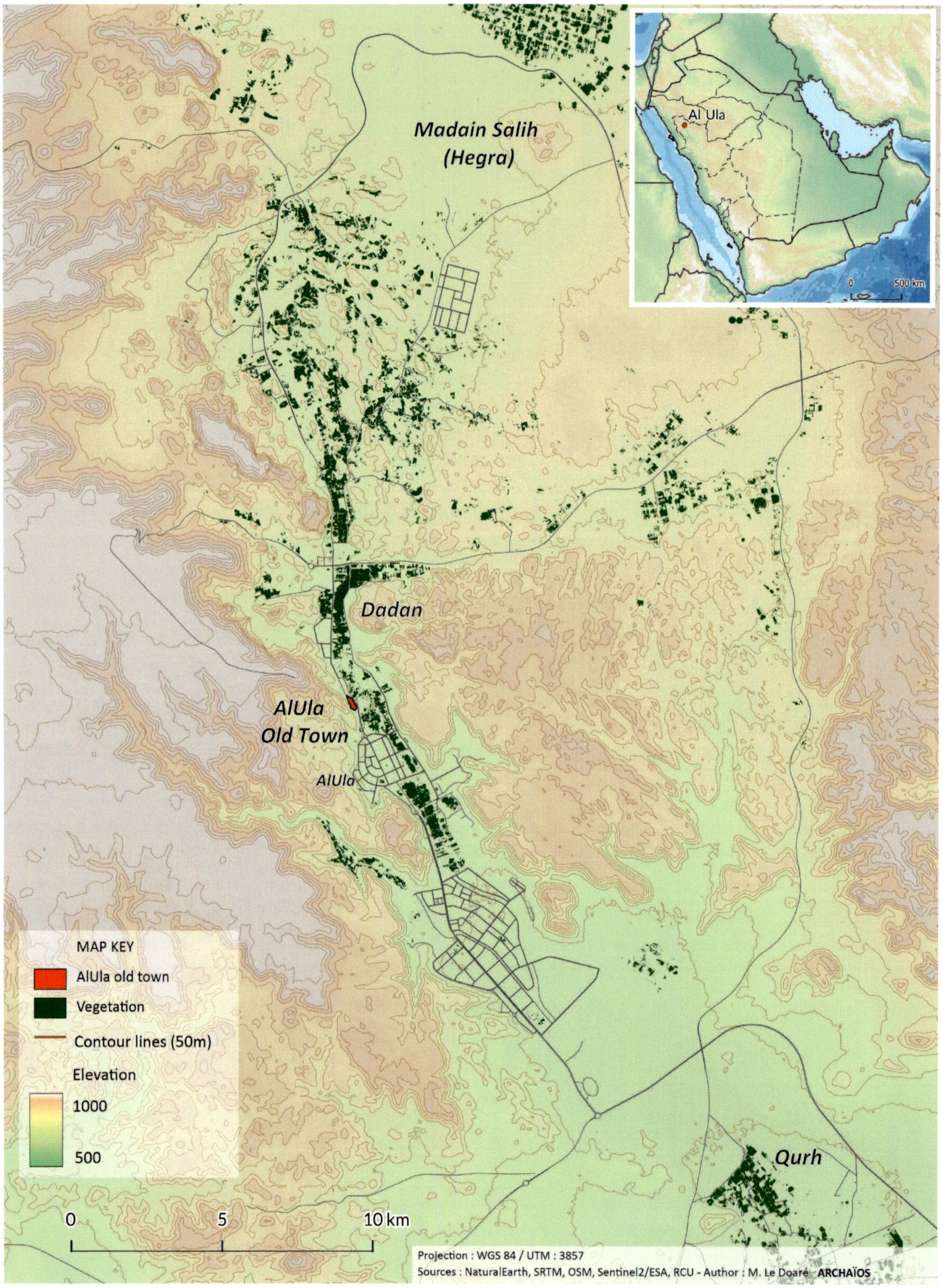

Figure 1. *AlUla Old Town location map (sources: NaturalEarth, SRTM, OSM, Sentinel2/ESA, RCU; author: M. Le Doaré).*

The Old Town of AlUla and its inhabitants

The Old Town of AlUla is located in the north-west of Saudi Arabia within the fertile oasis of Wādī al-Qurrah (Fig. 1), which has served since ancient times as a trade route between the eastern coast of the Red Sea and the Levant. Written sources suggest the existence of an inhabited settlement of the Old Town of AlUla from the eighth century AD until the end of the twentieth century (Nasif 1988: 135–137).

The town grew up along the western mountain range delimiting the valley, most likely around the free-standing rock formation called Umm Nasir with a watchpoint built on top of it. The fortified hill, overlooking a vast palm grove, served as a prominent landmark and strategic location at what has become since the early Middle Ages, the main Darb al Sahmi pilgrimage route between Damascus and Mecca as well as, during the Ottoman period, an important collection place of major taxes due to the central government (Nasif 1988: 129–132).

The Umm Nasir hill divides the settlement into two distinct districts stretching along the north–south axis of the valley, which originally were probably inhabited by two different leagues, the Shuqaiq clans in the north and the Hilf clans in the south (Battesti & Marty 2023: 16–17). It is believed that most of the latest inhabitants of AlUla originated from these clans, which — in many cases — one can associate with current family names (Nasif 1988: 133).

Over the nineteenth and twentieth centuries, the town witnessed a significant growth in population from around 1500 to over 7500 inhabitants (Nasif 1988: 133), some of whom came from outside the town and the region. Changes in population size led to the development of an increasingly dense and interlocking layout of houses and consequently to the extension of the town to the north and to the introduction of more spacious residential units both within and outside the Old Town (Battesti & Marty 2023: 19–21).

Since the 1930s the socio-economic and urban changes related to the exploration of oil deposits in Saudi Arabia (Al-Hathloul & Anis-ur-Rahman 1985) as well as the general deterioration of living conditions within the historical urban centres, resulted in the gradual process of depopulation of many towns, including the Old Town of AlUla. Additionally, the introduction of diesel-powered pumping systems, which caused a significant drop in water levels, contributed to the deterioration of the *qanat* system and a large part of the oasis (Nasif 1980; also Daniel Eddisford, pers. com., 20/01/2024). The residents started to abandon their houses in favour of new residential districts, modern dwellings, and a better quality of life (Battesti & Marty 2023: 21). The construction of a modern road in the 1970s led to the demolition of several dozen historical buildings located in the immediate vicinity of the oasis and, consequently, to the Old Town being cut off from its natural base, along with its area being limited to 5.352 ha (Fig. 2). This time frame yielded an official list of individuals (or their heirs) owning buildings, as documented by the municipality (Royal Commission for AlUla archives). The presence of incomplete and inconsistent data types imposes restrictions on the overall usability of the list. Nevertheless, the dataset comprises more than 140 family names, which facilitates a broader understanding of the town's social organization before its final abandonment in the 1980s (Al-Budair 2021: 14).

For several years now, the historical urban centre of AlUla, which still contains more than 900 cadastral units,[1] has seen significant restoration activities. The outcomes of these endeavours include the formation of a distinctive hotel complex and the alteration of one of the major streets in the Old Town, which is evolving into a popular venue for community members and tourists (Prior+Partners & Royal Commission for Alula 2020: 64–71).

The MuDUD project

The aspiration to gain a deeper insight into the multifaceted history of the Old Town of AlUla, including its spatial, functional, and social organization, led in 2020 to the implementation of the Multiscalar Documentation of Urban Dynamics (MuDUD) project. This research has been carried out by the French archaeological company Archaïos and steered by the French Agency for AlUla Development (AFALULA) on behalf of the Royal Commission for AlUla (RCU). It forms a component of a

[1] In the majority of cases, cadastral units indicate individual residential buildings characterized by their load-bearing walls, a front entrance, a staircase that connects the ground floor to the upper floor, a set of linked spaces, and a latrine tank.

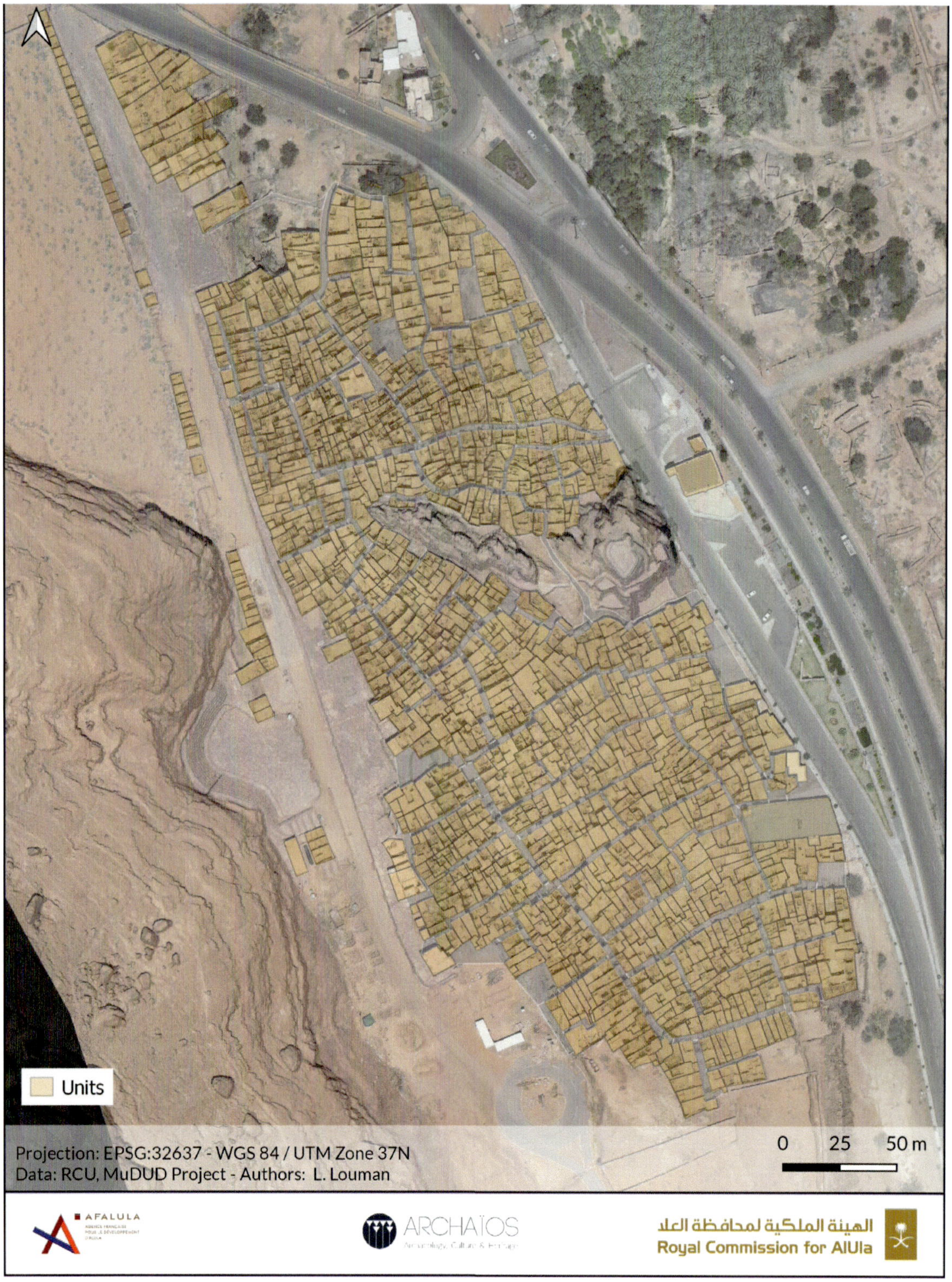

FIGURE 2. *An orthophotographic aerial view of AlUla Old Town (RCU, ARCHAÏOS — MuDUD project; author: L. Louman).*

broader research agenda that covers the entirety of the AlUla Valley and entails numerous investigations of its archaeological sites (AlMadani 2021).

The MuDUD project was able to set a comprehensive time frame for the Old Town of AlUla, starting from the pre-Islamic time until its abandonment in the twentieth century. Furthermore, it provided some evidence of the late Mamluk (*c.*1450–1517) and early Ottoman phase (*c.*1517–1650), which were only partially known until recently. Additionally, it allowed for better identification of the middle Ottoman phase (*c.*1650–1850) during which most of the currently standing buildings and structures were either built or rebuilt, as well as of the late Ottoman phase (*c.*1850–1918) and modern Saudi Arabian phase (1918–1980s) representing the most recent transformations during this last period of the town's occupancy (Gilento et al., forthcoming).

These and other important outcomes arise from the meticulous contributions of a multidisciplinary team that includes archaeologists, architects, art historians, epigraphists, and a variety of other specialists. Consequently, the MuDUD project specifically integrated archival research, archaeological excavations, GIS analysis, and laboratory analyses, along with the examination of architectural features and ethnographic inquiries, including interviews with former residents of the Old Town of AlUla.

Building archaeology

The MuDUD research on architecture focused on direct observations of architectural features specific to building archaeology. The primary subject of these analyses was building techniques and strategies concerning walls, ceilings and roofs, structural and stratigraphic relationships between these and other architectural features, as well as properties of building materials. Detailed architectural documentation methods were adopted from traditional archaeology and historic building-recording practices (Brogiolo & Cagnana 2012; see also Dallas 2003; Massalski 1982a; 1982b). These methods were applied using both analogue and digital tools as well as integrated 2D- and 3D-graphic documentation of architectural elements and features. They have therefore significantly contributed to reconstructing the history of buildings and their relative timelines and in some cases, absolute chronological sequences (Gilento 2020; Gilento et al., forthcoming).

Over 80% of units within the Old Town of AlUla were analysed by the MuDUD team. Most of these units are small, two-storey residential buildings built with stone and mud bricks as well as palm-tree and tamarisk trunks and palm leaves. Their ground floors were often divided into three spaces: an assembly hall dedicated to receiving guests, a smaller side space for sleeping or storing items and products, as well as an above-ground latrine tank, which used to be emptied cyclically through an opening in a wall at ground-floor level. The upper floor, accessed by a staircase, was frequently characterized by an open area — *mirbd* — surrounded by two to three spaces employed for sleeping, meal preparation, washing facilities, and various family-related activities (Fig. 3) (AlModarra, in preparation). Another characteristic, although much smaller, group of buildings comprises large units mostly from the late Ottoman phase with central and open courtyards at ground-floor level as well as multiple and diverse spaces both at ground- and upper-floor level.

Another distinguishing architectural feature of many houses is a *tayyara* (pl. *tayyarat*) — a roofed space above the street at the upper-floor level (Al-Abodi 2012: 12). It leans onto the front walls of the opposite houses and was predominantly utilized for resting or for storing bedding items, contingent upon the time of year (Hafiza Awad, pers. com., 18/02/2024). Consequently, the construction of a *tayyara* depended entirely on a mutual accord between neighbours (Ibrahim Abdulkarim, pers. com., 24/11/2023).

Tayyarat seem to have appeared at the turn of the nineteenth and twentieth centuries and have quickly dominated AlUla's townscape (*tayyarat* account for as much as 50% of the total area of the street network). Unfortunately, the upper floors, *tayyarat* included, are in a bad state of repair as a result of abandonment and various acts of nature. Thus, producing a full set of their architectural documentation is often unachievable.

Ethnographic research

The ethnographic study aimed at a deeper understanding of the history of the Old Town of AlUla and the lives of its residents (AlModarra, in preparation). This research,

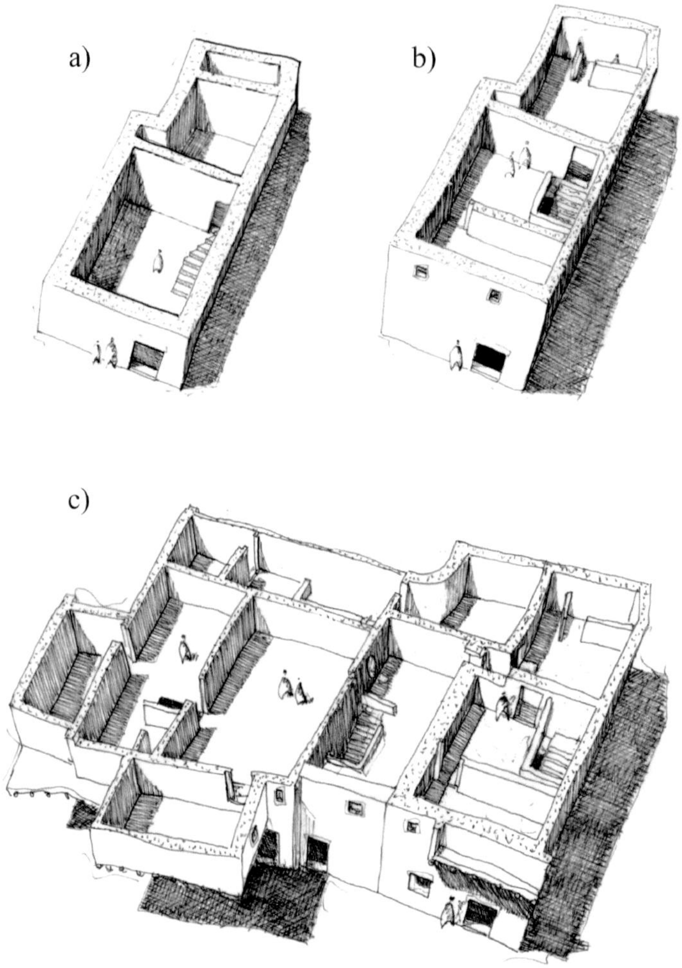

Figure 3. *Drawings in perspective of residential buildings from AlUla Old Town:* **a.** *ground floor of U30;* **b.** *upper floor of U30;* **c.** *a group of interconnected units, U27 & 30 (ARCHAÏOS — MuDUD project; author: M.Z. Barański).*

carried out in parallel with other activities within the MuDUD project, consisted of three interrelated stages.

The first stage included an initial and comprehensive assessment of AlUla and its urban fabric. The preliminary results of the archaeological and architectural surveys of the town and its direct surroundings were used to address the most important questions. The inquiries were related in particular to architectural, functional, and socio-economic issues, such as the division of space, differences between private and public spaces, agricultural practices, house construction and use, uses and functions of architectural features, the purposes of selected tools and objects, and the meaning of various symbols and signs. These issues, along with others, were analysed and described in the MuDUD scientific and field reports (e.g. Vernet, Khan & Giraud 2021; Vernet et al. 2022) that laid the groundwork for further research activities.

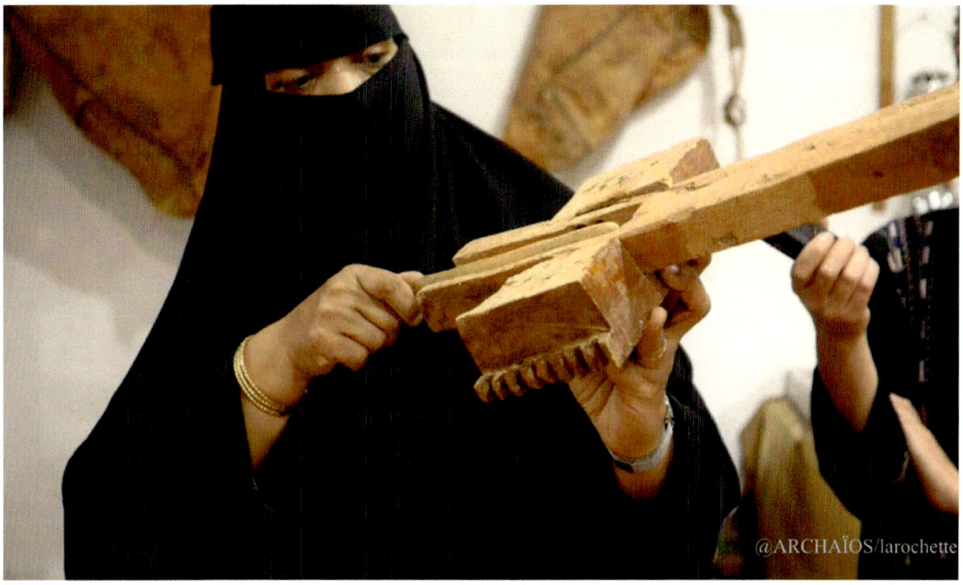

Figure 4. *Gaining insights into everyday habits and practices (ARCHAÏOS — MuDUD project; author: J. Larochette).*

In the second stage of the research, an online questionnaire was developed and a comprehensive social survey was conducted based on face-to-face interviews. This initiative aimed to provide answers to the questions outlined in the first stage of the research and to acquire more insights into the various daily activities undertaken by the town's residents (Fig. 4). Furthermore, the study sought to analyse the ways in which social and economic factors affect urban planning and architecture. While the objective was largely met, the study encountered numerous obstacles, such as challenges in contacting former inhabitants due to the COVID-19 pandemic, the demise of many older individuals who had lived in the town for an extended period, issues related to memory decline, along with a significant outflow of residents to nearby towns and cities. The number of individuals surveyed was notably affected by these factors. Ultimately, a group of twenty-five women and twenty men, all within the age range of 60 to 90 years, participated in the interviews. Audio recordings were made of every interview, and these were further enriched with comprehensive notes (AlModarra, in preparation).

The third stage of the research involved synthesizing the data gathered in prior stages, alongside an attempt to elaborate on the information relevant to the defined case-study areas and the issues deemed most important. One significant topic addressed involved the organization of social groups and the interconnections between neighbouring units, as discerned through the analysis of building archaeology.

Interconnected buildings

As a part of the MuDUD project, 139 groups of interconnected units (Fig. 5) were defined, encompassing a total of 235 units (Vernet et al. 2023; 2024). The distribution of these groups extends beyond a single district, neighbourhood, or sector, as they are dispersed throughout the Old Town area. Notably, these groups comprise a range of two to ten units that are interconnected through various types of wall openings, particularly including doors and windows, which may be categorized as clear or blocked, regular or irregular, narrow or broad, etc. (Fig. 6). *Tayyarat* served as another distinct feature linking the buildings. Furthermore, a variety of well-documented examples demonstrate the interconnections between different buildings and floors, especially between those constructed on sloping terrain or in areas of rock faults. Additionally, certain buildings were formerly linked by means of staircases or ladders.

A significant majority (66%) of the documented interconnections among units occurs at the upper-floor level. If the considerable destruction to the upper floors of the buildings had not taken place, this percentage

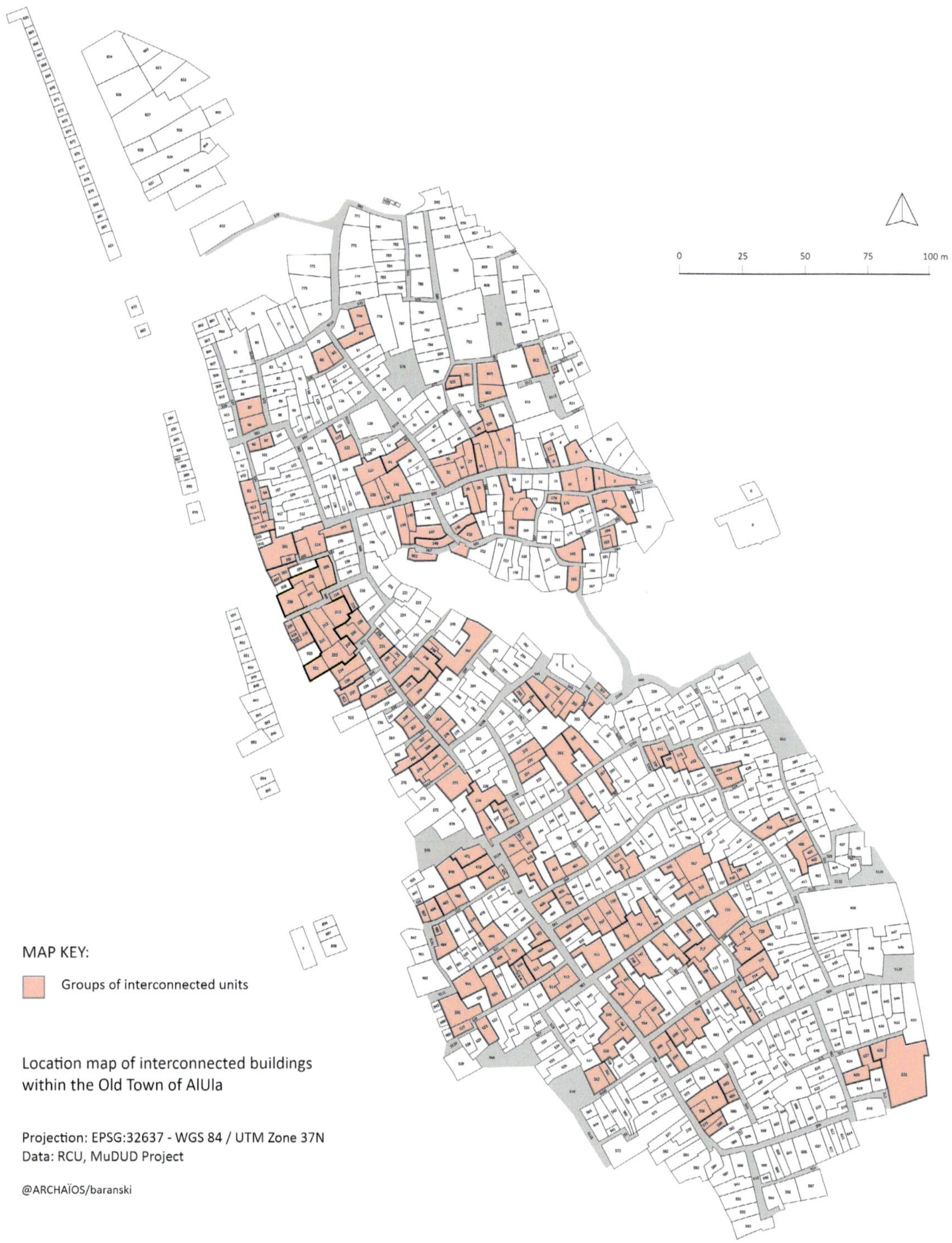

FIGURE 5. *Location map of interconnected units from AlUla Old Town (ARCHAÏOS — MuDUD project; author: M.Z. Barański).*

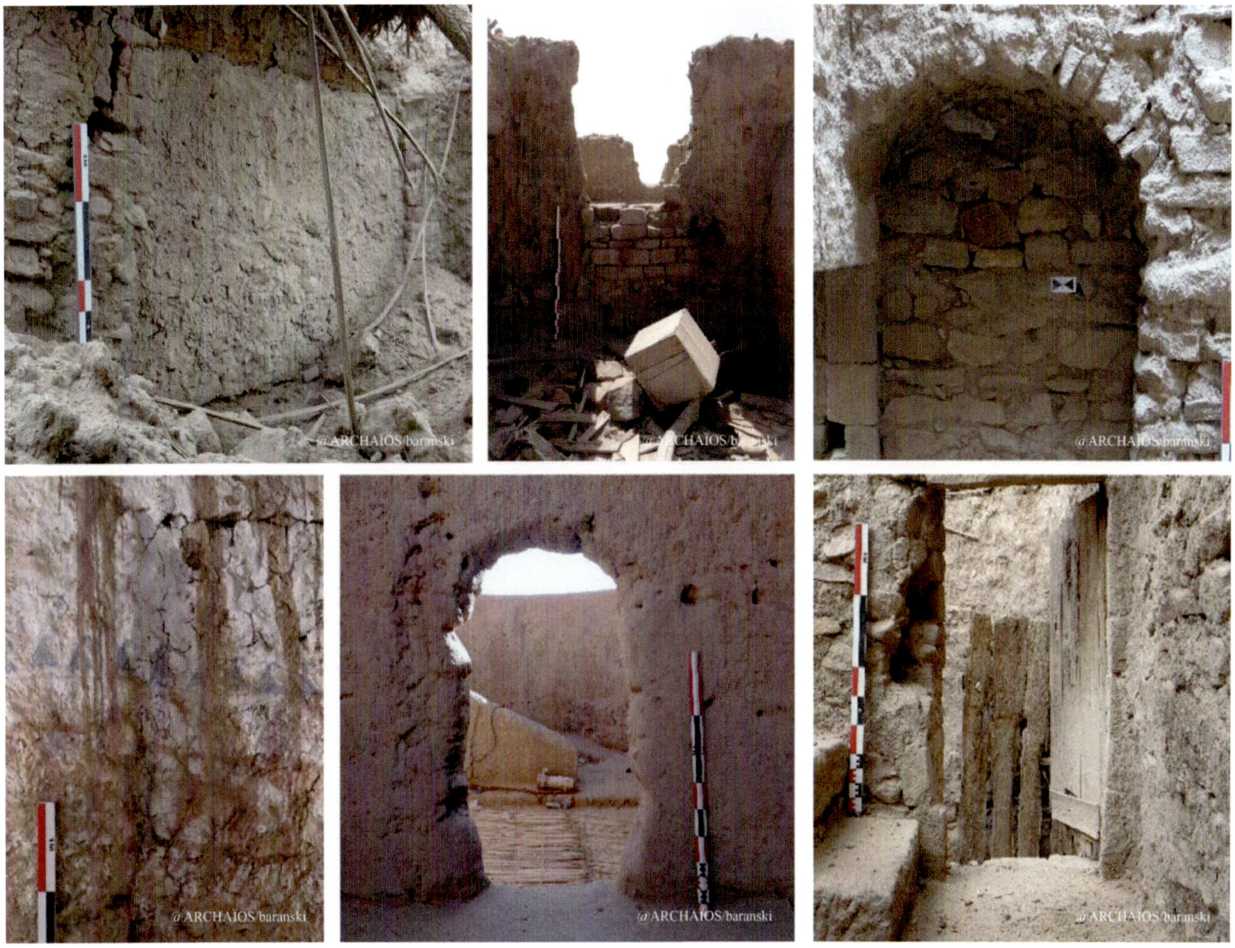

FIGURE 6. *An overview of various types of door openings from AlUla Old Town (ARCHAÏOS — MuDUD project; author: M.Z. Barański).*

would probably be higher. Moreover, it is essential to highlight that many identified wall openings, even when situated within the same unit or among the same group of interconnected units, were constructed or used at different times. This indicates very good social and functional dynamics within households and neighbourhoods. Additionally, it further supports the notion that architecture embodies a continuous and evolving process, wherein buildings function in various independent yet interconnected ways — structurally, environmentally, socially, culturally, and economically (Till 2008). The following section provides a brief overview of the complexity surrounding this matter, illustrated through three case-study areas and four associated groups of interconnected units.

Case study 1

The first case study area is situated in the central part of the northern district. It encompasses four neighbouring and residential units, U27, U30, U31, and U35 (Fig. 7). All these units make up one group of interconnected buildings.

U27 used to be interconnected with U30 and U35 through regular and clear openings at the upper-floor level. Interestingly, a connection through a staircase between the ground floor and the upper floor within U27 was blocked. This complete closure of the pathway must have resulted in spatial and functional integration of the upper-floor areas within U27 and U35. In this case, shared use of space may be explained by the fact that

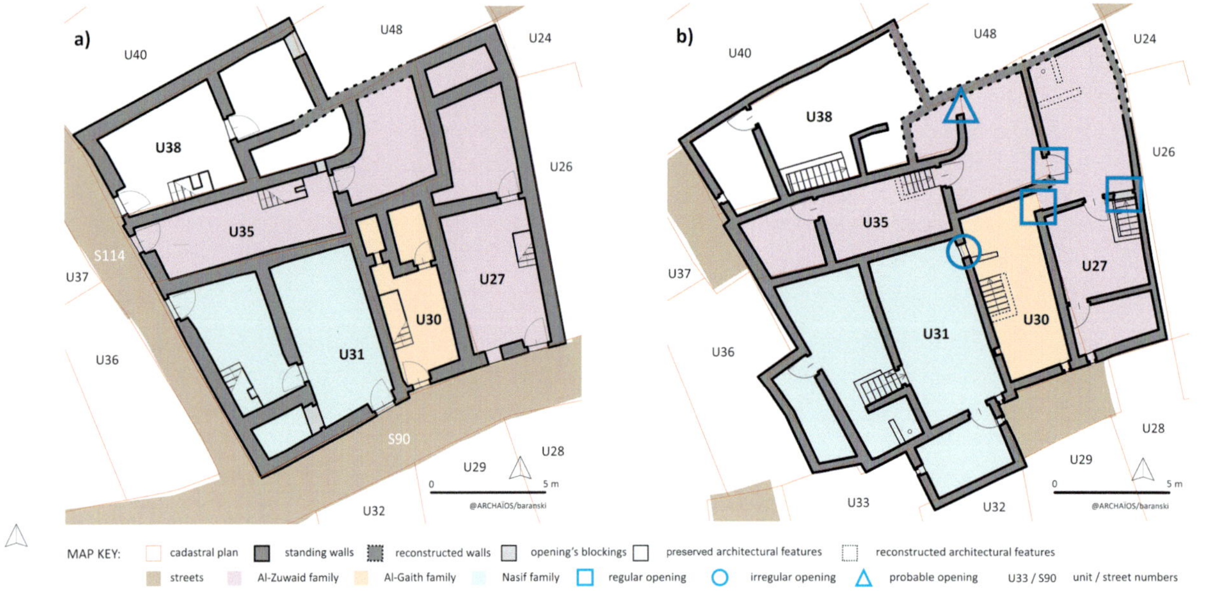

FIGURE 7. *An outline of a group of interconnected units, U27, U30, U31 & U35:* **a.** *ground floor;* **b.** *upper floor (ARCHAÏOS — MuDUD project; author: M.Z. Barański).*

both these units belonged to the same owner from the Al-Zuwaid family. Interviews with a former inhabitant reveal that U35 was purchased by the owner of U27. After the transaction, the ground floor of U27 functioned as a reception area for guests while the ground and upper floors of U35 were used for sleeping, meal preparation, and other household activities. By way of contrast, an interconnection between U27 and U30 can be attributed to the situation in which a widow living in U30 married a man who was a resident of U27. Once she had moved into U27, a passageway between U27 and U30 was created to enable her to visit her daughters (Aisha Al-Duraihim, pers. com., 18/05/2024).

U30 and U31 were also connected, in this case through an irregular and unobstructed wall opening at upper-floor level. Interestingly, the two units belonged to different families. The owners of U30 were members of the Al-Ghaith family, while U31 was inhabited by members of the Nasif family. The Al-Gaith, Nasif, and Al-Zuwaid families are associated with northern clans (Nasif 1988: 133–134).

Case study 2

The second case-study area is also situated in the central part of the northern district, although in the immediate vicinity of the Umm Nasir hill. It comprises six units, U139, U140, U147, U148, U149, and U903 (Fig. 8). These buildings are organized into two separate but adjacent groups of interconnected units, comprising the first three and the last three of the units referenced earlier.

U139 used to be connected with U140 and U147 through unobstructed and irregular wall openings at upper-floor level. Each of those units served a residential function and were inhabited by three different families, Nasif (U139), Ateeq (U140), and Al-Dhiyab (U147). Interestingly, U140 shared a wall with U146. Both these buildings belonged to a member of the Ateeq family, although the architectural analysis did not reveal any documented interconnections between the entities in question.

The spatial and functional relationships within the second group of interconnected units were more complex. To begin with, U148 and U149, as well as U149

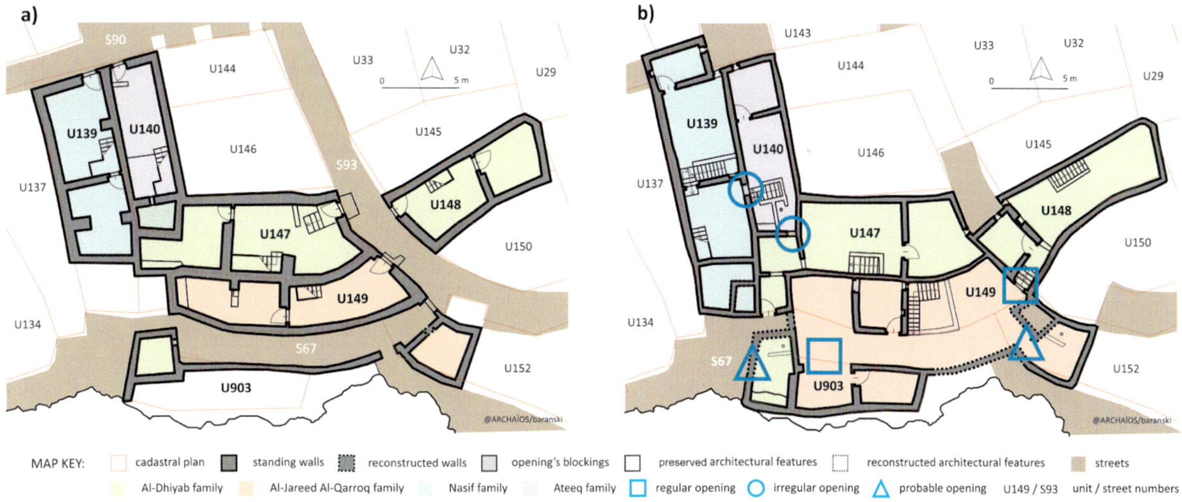

FIGURE 8. *An outline of two groups of interconnected units, U139, U140 & U147 and U148, U149 & U903 respectively:* **a.** *ground floor;* **b.** *upper floor (ARCHAÏOS — MuDUD project; author: M.Z. Barański).*

and U903, were linked through a *tayyara*. This clearly proves that building groups could have been created regardless of the boundaries determined by the street layout. Furthermore, U148 and U147 were owned by the same person from the Al-Dhiyab family. These two buildings are situated on opposite sides of the same street. They are linked neither via a *tayyara* nor through a part of the same group of interconnected units.

The owner of U149 was a member of the Al-Jareed Al-Qarroq family. According to former inhabitants, this building was rented out to the Qurʾān teacher and served as a school (Abdulrahman Al-Za'ir, pers. com., 17/06/2021). As for U903, it was remembered as an uninhabited space or a ruin and served as a dumping area for building materials and brushwood (Aisha Al-Duraihim, pers. com., 18/05/2024).

Case study 3

The last case-study area is located in the south-western part of the northern district, near today's Incense Road. It encompasses eleven units, U205, U206, U207, U208, U211, U212, U213, U232, U233, U836, and U921, which all constitute one group of interconnected units (Fig. 9). Most of these buildings served a residential function. However, U921 was at least a partly unroofed space divided into two, which could have served as a workshop, storage space, or animal pen. U205, on the other hand, was formerly a coffee house where family members assembled for council meetings. The management of a coffee house fell under the jurisdiction of a shaykh, selected by the family to oversee and conduct their affairs. Consequently, a coffee house was located next to the shaykh's house or constituted a part of his house (Saleh Al-Dhiyab, pers. com., 29/11/2023).

The majority of the documented wall openings, which interconnected units within this group, are not only blocked but also situated at ground-floor level. This is the case for U206 and U208, U207 and U208 (connection through two wall openings), U211 and U212, as well as U232 and U233 (connection through two wall openings). The only three examples of clear interconnections come from U205 and U206 (connection at ground-floor level), U207 and U213 and U233 and U921 (both connections at upper-floor level). It is also worth noting that U207 and U212, as well as U207 and U213, used to be linked via a *tayyara*.

The owners of the eleven units represent five families, Al-Boshi, Al-Dhiyab, Najdi, Sogair, and Suqeer. U207, U208, and U213 used to be inhabited by the nuclear families or heirs of three brothers from the Al-Dhiyab family (Abdulaziz Al-Marai, pers. com., 30/11/2023).

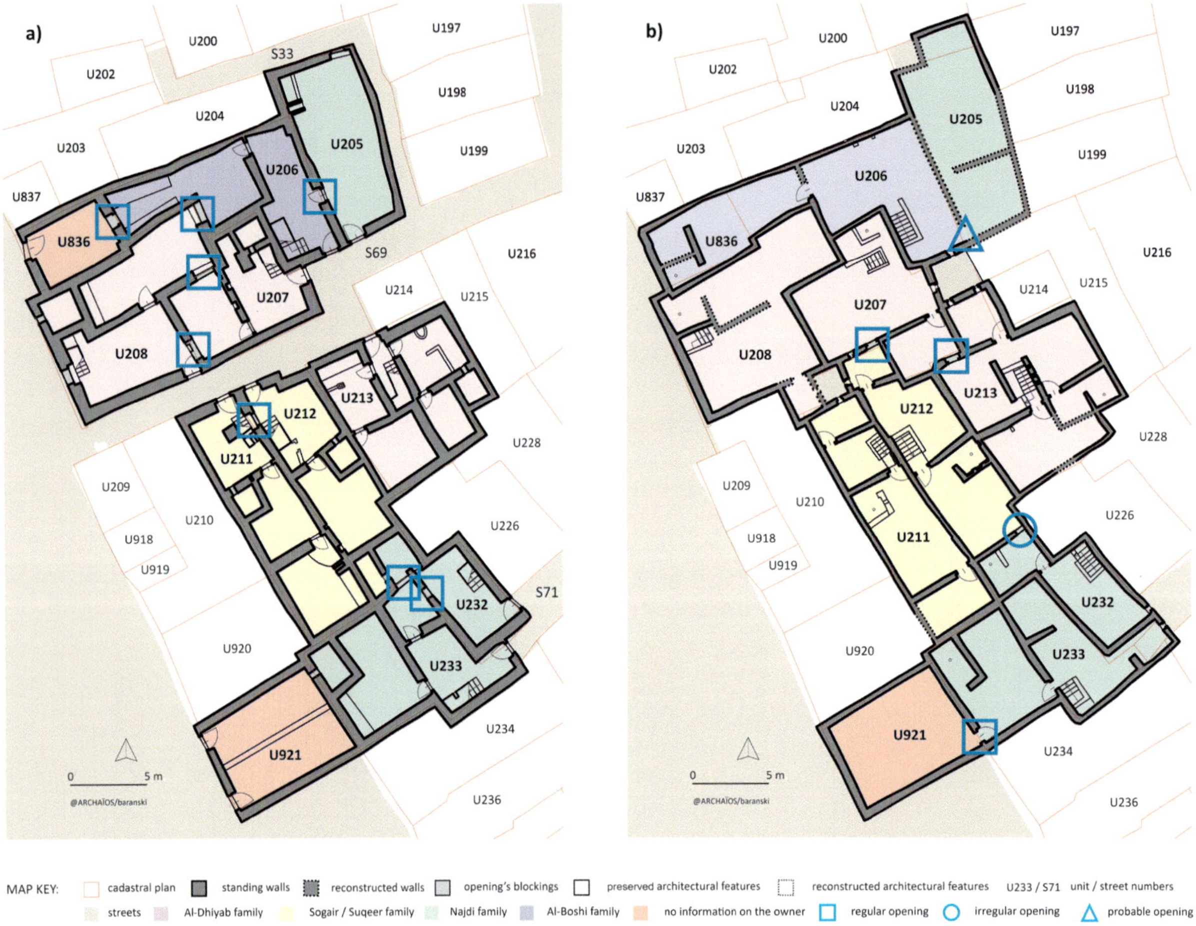

FIGURE 9. *An outline of a group of interconnected units, U205, U206, U207, U208, U211, U212, U213, U232, U233, U836, and U921:* **a.** *ground floor;* **b.** *upper floor (ARCHAÏOS — MuDUD project; author: M.Z. Barański).*

The owners of U211 and U212, as well as U232 and U233, were cousins from the Sogair/Suqeer and Najdi families respectively (Saleh Al-Dhiyab, pers. com., 29/11/2023). U205 served as the residence for the Najdi family, whereas the Al-Boshi family lived in U206. Interestingly, at least three of these families — Al-Dhiyab, Najdi, and Suqeer — represent the Al-Badanah sub-clan of the northern clans (Saleh Al-Dhiyab & Abdulaziz Al-Marai, pers. com., 29/11/2023 and 30/11/2023 respectively).

Reconstructing social groupings

Ethnographic studies on connected units in the Old Town of AlUla indicated several reasons for interconnections, highlighting their complexity. The transformation and integration of buildings stem from long-standing customs, relationships between and within families, as well as economic influences that have developed over time (AlModarra, in preparation).

In most cases, houses were passed from one generation to another. Adult and married sons and their families usually remained in the parental houses in order to help with daily activities, particularly those associated with agriculture and trade. As families expanded and the need for more living space increased, house owners either enlarged their residences or combined them with adjacent properties. One of the most popular forms of such an extension were *tayyarat*, which was often shared between neighbours on a rotational basis or used to connect two units (Ibrahim Abdulkarim, pers. com., 24/11/2023).

Overall, connections between houses seem to indicate a strong intention to foster enduring bonds among extended family members. Furthermore, they contributed to the support of community members, particularly women, who engaged in mutual cooperation and shared diverse responsibilities such as childcare duties. It is worth mentioning that the advancement of communal bonds was achieved by creating passages and upper-floor window features.

At the same time, one can observe the presence of either temporary or permanent divisions within buildings, along with the blocking off of established passages, arising from a multitude of factors. For example, some houses were converted into community gathering centres (e.g. coffee shops) or semi-private council spaces when the owner of the house became the clan representative. Furthermore, at a time when more residents were increasingly leaving the Old Town, the practice of selling or renting out houses or parts of them became widespread. Usually, these transactions concerned family members or neighbours, which contributed to maintaining family or clan control over a certain cluster of buildings. Additionally, there are several examples of turning ground-floor locations into shops or small retail spaces, as well as adapting buildings into other non-residential facilities such as schools (Abdulrahman Al-Za'ir, pers. com., 17/06/2021).

Accounts provided by former residents reveal some discrepancies, illustrating a notable feature of living memory (Samuel 1994; Wertsch & Roediger 2008). The focus of individual and collective memories generally rests on specific viewpoints and interpretations, rather than offering a complete and factual narrative of past events (Roediger & Abel 2015). Nevertheless, the testimonies of former residents of the Old Town of AlUla should be considered as highly valuable and informative. They all suggest that both cultural aspects and practical purposes were fundamental in creating connections among various units. The ongoing transformation of individual buildings and clusters of buildings over time illustrates the changing dynamics of social organization at the levels of households, neighbourhoods, and the town as a whole. Conversely, the arrangement of space, whether utilizing conventional solid partitions or alternative methods, significantly impacted social interactions and played a crucial role in shaping the identity of the Old Town of AlUla throughout history.

Regardless of the underlying reasons that lead to links between buildings, a significant part of the groups of interconnected units seems to reflect family or clan relationships. At least forty-one out of ninety-one of these groups were owned by the same person or members of the same family.[2] However, mapping social groupings through clan names rather than family names tends to yield more favourable outcomes when attempting to reconstruct the socio-spatial organization of the town.

An experiment was implemented as a key element of the mapping project (Fig. 10). It drew upon the documented groups of interconnected units, a comprehensive list of clans and sub-clans of the Old Town of AlUla (Nasif 1988: 133–135), as well as insights gathered from previous residents. Consequently, the units owned by people with the same family name were marked with the same colour (Fig. 10/a). Furthermore, cold colours were used as a reference to the northern clans, and warm colours to the southern clans. Units with no or unclear information on the owners and their family names or affiliation to certain clans were left uncoloured.

As presented in case study 3, units within a group of interconnected units could have been owned and inhabited by different families. By situating this information within the broader context of the town, one creates a dynamic mosaic that limits the capacity to make overarching conclusions. However, when families are organized into distinct clans, the overall perspective shifts slightly (Fig. 10/b). For example, it seems very likely that the Al-Badanah clan (Al-Dhiyab, Al-Farahin, Al-Huwaikim, Al-Jumah, Al-Najdi, and Suqairat families among others) originally resided in the south-western part of the northern district. Additionally, clusters of houses belonging to the Al-Quruq (e.g. Al-Duraihim, Al-Ibrahim, Al-Jabur, and Al-Salih families) and the Al-Tayaminah (e.g. Al-Ghadfa, Al-Ghaith, Al-Haddad, Abu Uwaidah families) clans become clearer, although these concentrations

[2] It is likely that the figure would have been higher had the owner registry been more accurate and had it had been possible to positively identify the owner's full family names.

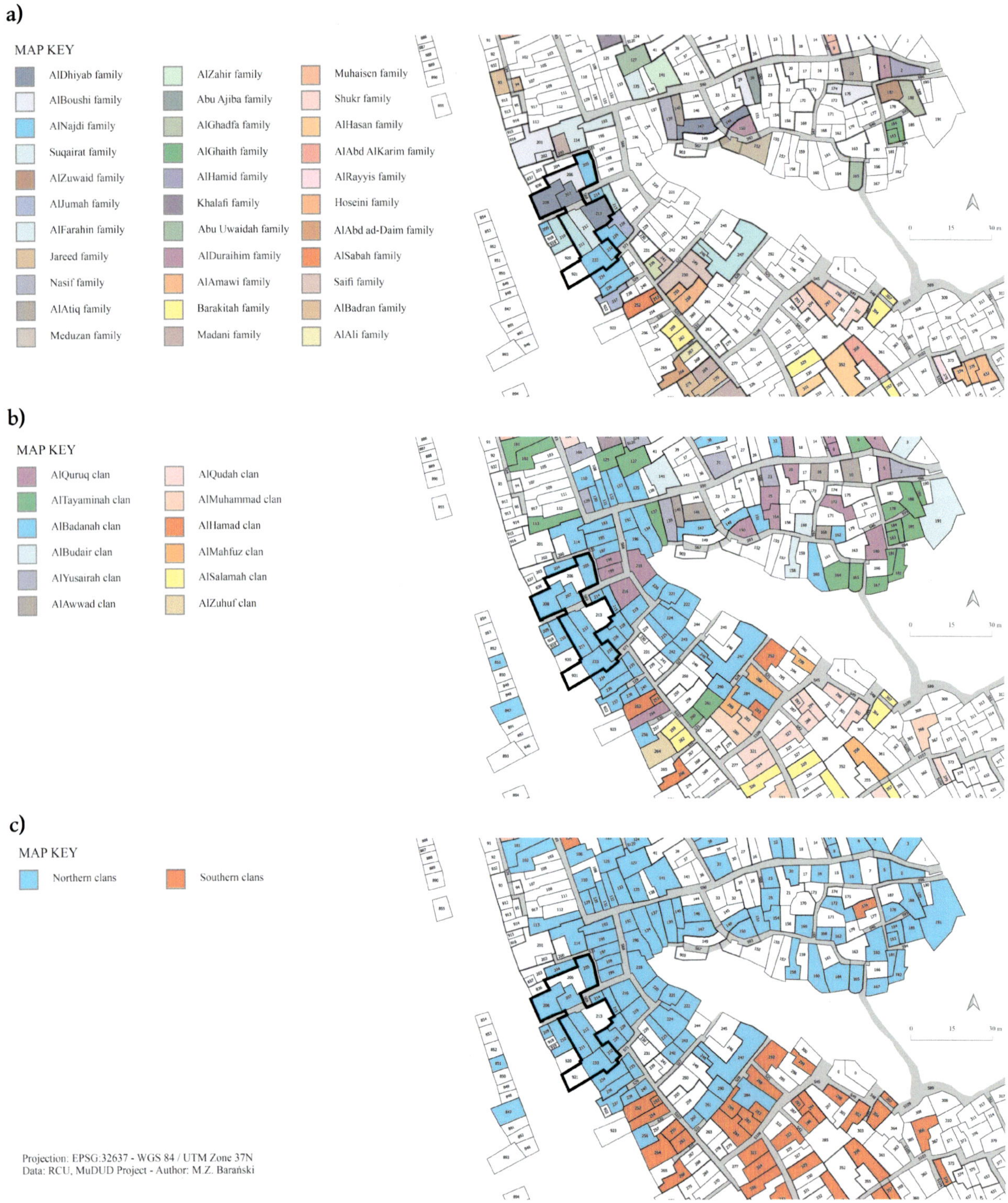

FIGURE 10. *An illustration mapping out social groupings of AlUla Old Town at the level of:* **a.** *the family;* **b.** *the clan; and* **c.** *the league (ARCHAÏOS — MuDUD project; author: M.Z. Barański).*

are smaller and occur in several places within the northern district. Given this context, establishing the likely initial habitat of these clans has proved to be challenging.

The most captivating insights emerge from the analysis of units owned by either northern or southern clan members (Fig. 10/c). One can easily identify the spatial division between these clans, which has only been roughly outlined so far. Interestingly, this division does not extend along one of the main streets of the Old Town of AlUla but along a secondary street that is also partially blocked.

Last but not least, it is important to highlight the fact that there are at least a couple of units (U104 & U176) located in the northern district which are owned by members of families affiliated with the southern clans. The reason for this situation may be linked to the purchase of these properties by a representative of a southern clan or to the marriage between members of two clans (Mouna AlBoushi, pers. com., 20/11/2023).

Conclusion

The Old Town of AlUla provides a remarkable opportunity for detailed research into the interplay between social dynamics and architectural space. The process of collecting, compiling, and integrating archival, architectural, and ethnographic data related to the MuDUD project proved essential for enhancing our understanding of both the town's history and, more significantly, the intricate community that inhabited it. Furthermore, it highlighted a potential and effective means of delineating social connections tied to local familial and clan groups.

Considering the nature of the accessible data, these preliminary findings shed light on the urban and social dynamics that have unfolded over the past two centuries. Nonetheless, certain interpretations regarding social organization appear transferable to earlier times. In this framework, it is essential to conduct additional studies aimed at identifying the owners of particular units, establishing connections between other families and their clan names, identifying shaykh and coffee houses, examining the town's gate and street names linked to certain family names, and analysing street layouts alongside space syntax data.

Acknowledgements

We would like to thank all the MuDUD project team members, Archaïos, AFALULA, and RCU. We extend particular thanks to Hanadi Abokadejah, Maxime Bonnal, Pietro Caciagli, Gabriela Camargo-Méndez, Anaëlle Lesaicherre, Laura Louman, José Ignacio Murillo Fragero, Maria-Paola Pellegrino, Thomas Soubira, and Manon Torre-Guibert. We are especially grateful to the former residents of the Old Town of AlUla, in particular Abdulrahman Al-Za'ir, Abdulaziz Al-Marai, Aisha Al-Duraihim, Saleh Al-Dhiyab, Mouna AlBoushi, Hassan Abu Al-Hassan, Ibrahim Abdulkarim, Abdulkaliq Bin Noah, Saud Abu Odeh, Hafida Abdulrahim Awad, and Abdulrahman Al-Imam, for their willingness to engage in interviews and to share their valuable memories.

References

Al-Abodi A. 2012. The architectural features of the traditional house of Al-Ula town (Al-Deerah). *Journal of Studies in Archaeology and Heritage* 4: 73–126.

AlMadani A. 2021. *The Journey Through Time Masterplan is built on a deep knowledge of the people, the heritage and the landscape of AlUla*. Available at www.linkedin.com/pulse/journey-through-time-masterplan-built-deep-knowledge-people-almadani/

AlModarra A. (in preparation). Traditional residential architecture in the Old Town of Al-Ula, 'Deira' (Ethnoarchaeology). Riyadh: King Saud University.

Alnaim M.M. 2022. Understanding the traditional Saudi built environment: The phenomenon of dynamic core concept and forms. *World Journal of Engineering and Technology* 10: 292–321.

Battesti V. & Marty L. 2023. Bedouins and sedentaries today in al-'Ulâ (Kingdom of Saudi Arabia): al-diyâr and al-Dîra in the rear-view mirror. *Arabian Humanities* 17 [no page numbers]. doi: https://doi.org/10.4000/cy.10103

Brogiolo G.P. & Cagnana A. 2012. *Archeologia dell'architettura — Metodi e interpretazioni*. (Metodi e temi dell'archeologia medievale 3). Sesto Fiorentino: Floregilio.

Al-Budair S. 2021. *From Al-Ula to the end of the world – Excerpts from the biography of a diplomat*. Riyadh: Al-Obeikan.

Correia J. & Taher M. 2015. Traditional Islamic cities unveiled: The quest for urban design regularity. *Revista Gremium* 2/04: 21–36.

Dabbour L.M. 2021. Morphology of quarters in traditional Arab Islamic city: A case of the traditional city of Damascus. *Frontiers of Architectural Research* 10: 50–65.

Dallas R. (ed.). 2003. *Measured survey and building recording for historic buildings and structures, Guide for practitioners 4*. Edinburgh: Historic Scotland.

Eben Saleh M.A. 1995. Al-Alkhalaf: The urban history of a traditional settlement in southwestern Saudi Arabia. *Habitat International* 19/1: 29–52.

Gilento P. 2020. Building archaeology. Pages 100–161 in A. Vernet, A. Baaklini, C. Marquqire, P. Gilento & R. Mèreuze (eds), *MuDUD. Old Town investigation project for AlUla. Scientific report. Phase 0. s.1.* Paris: Archaïos.

Gilento P., Pesce G., Vernet A. & Pesce C. (forthcoming). Development of an interdisciplinary approach to the radiocarbon dating of earth mortars from Alula Old Town (Saudi Arabia). Integration of building archaeology, mortar analysis and radiocarbon dating. *Radiocarbon*.

Hakim B.S. 1986. *Arab-Islamic cities. Building and planning principles*. London: Routledge/Taylor & Francis Group.

Al-Hathloul S.A. & Anis-ur-Rahmaan S. 1985. The evolution of urban and regional planning in Saudi Arabia. *Ekistics* 52/312: 206–212.

King G. 1998. *The traditional architecture of Saudi Arabia*. London: I.B. Tauris & Co.

Massalski R. 1982a. Graficzna metoda badania zabytkowych murów. *Zeszyty Naukowe Politechniki Gdańskiej* 347, *Architektura* 22: 101–114.

Massalski R. 1982b. Problemy metodologiczne badań architektoniczno-archeologicznych. *Zeszyty Naukowe Politechniki Gdańskiej* 347, *Architektura* 22: 115–157.

Nasif A.A. 1980. Qanats at Al-Ulā. *Proceedings of the Seminar for Arabian Studies* 10: 75–80.

Nasif A.A. 1988. *Al-'Ula: A historical and archaeological survey with special reference to its irrigation system*. Riyadh: King Saud University Press.

Prior+Partners & Royal Commission for AlUla 2020. *AlUla zoning rule book. The Journey Through Time*. AlUla: RCU.

Roediger H.L. & Abel M. 2015. Collective memory: A new arena of cognitive study. *Trends in Cognitive Sciences* 19/7: 359–361.

Samuel R. 1994. *Theatres of memory. Past and present in contemporary culture*. London: Verso.

Till J. 2008. Three myths and one model. *Building Material* 17: 4–10.

Vernet A., Khan B. & Giraud J. (eds). 2021. MUDUD. Historical investigation of AlUla Old Town. Multiscalar documentation for urban dynamics. Scientific report, 2021. Archaïos, Paris. [Unpublished report.]

Vernet A., AlModarra A., Khan B. & Giraud J. (eds). 2022. Historical investigation of AlUla Old Town. Multiscalar documentation for urban dynamics. Field report phase 4, 2022. Archaïos, Paris. [Unpublished report.]

Vernet A., AlModarra A., Khan B. & Giraud J. (eds). 2023. Historical investigation of AlUla Old Town. Multiscalar documentation for urban dynamics. Field report phase 6, 2022. Archaïos, Paris. [Unpublished report.]

Vernet A., AlModarra A., Khan B. & Giraud J. (eds). 2024. Historical investigation of AlUla Old Town. Multiscalar documentation for urban dynamics. Field report phase 7, 2022. Archaïos, Paris. [Unpublished report.]

Wertsch J.V. & Roediger H.L. 2008. Collective memory: Conceptual foundations and theoretical approaches. *Memory* 16/3: 318–326.

Authors' addresses

Aljohara AlModarra, Archaïos/King Saud University, Riyadh 11451, Kingdom of Saudi Arabia.
e-mail aljohara.almodarra@archaios.fr

Marek Z. Barański, Archaïos/Academy of Fine Arts in Gdańsk, Targ Węglowy 6, 80-836 Gdańsk, Poland.
e-mail mzbaranski@gmail.com

Apolline Vernet, Archaïos/UMR 8167 Orient et Méditerranée, 27 Rue Paul Bert, 94200 Ivry-sur-Seine, France.
e-mail apolline.vernet@gmail.com

Proceedings of the Seminar for Arabian Studies 54 (2025): 17–31

Preliminary report on the epigraphic survey in Yanbuᶜ, Saudi Arabia: first season (2023)

AJAB ALOTIBI, RISA TOKUNAGA, MAJED DAHASH & MUZHIRA ALQAHTANI

Summary

This paper presents the findings from the first season of the Saudi Heritage Commission's epigraphic survey in Yanbuᶜ, conducted in 2023. The survey's primary objective was to systematically document inscriptions and rock art that remain unrecorded despite their considerable significance. The survey covered 128 sites across sixteen areas surrounding Jabal Raḍwā, including key areas such as Wādī ᶜArᶜar, Wādī ᶜAbāthir, and Wādī Buwāṭ. A total of 991 Islamic inscriptions, 151 Ancient North Arabian inscriptions, and 1367 rock art and petroglyphs were registered. Among the notable discoveries is the possible first-known depiction of a warthog in Arabia, which may date to a period before the onset of aridification in the early fourth millennium BC. The ancient inscriptions are written in Ancient North Arabian, showing features of Thamudic D. The majority of the early Islamic inscriptions, which include an inscription dated 76/695–696, contain religious texts and are tentatively dated to the seventh and eighth centuries based on the letter shapes, while some show letter shapes from much later dates. The recurrent reference to the same individuals in early Islamic inscriptions suggests that many were written by people who routinely passed through. The paper also presents an overview of several significant archaeological structures found during the survey.

Keywords: Saudi Arabia, Yanbuᶜ, early Islamic inscriptions, Thamudic, rock art

Historical background of the area

The Yanbuᶜ governorate, located west of the holy city of Medina, is the only Red Sea coastal region within Medina Province. Although little is known about this area's ancient history, it is conceivable that it served as the maritime gateway for Yathrib, a key caravan city on the Incense Route that existed by the mid-first millennium BC. Ptolemy, in the second century AD, mentions a port named Iambia (Ptolemy 1932: 6.7.3), which is considered to refer to the port of Yanbuᶜ from its phonetic resemblance to the modern city's name.[1] During the early Islamic period, the region played a significant military and economic role due to its strategic location. The Prophet Muḥammad and his army are said to have stayed there for a month during the Battle of al-ᶜUshayrah in 2/623, to intercept a Quraysh caravan (Ibn Kathīr 1998: 239–240). The fertile inland region of Yanbuᶜ al-Nakhl served as a water resource for the Juhaynah tribe. Later, during the Rashidun caliphate, ᶜAlī ibn Abī Ṭālib revitalized the area by developing additional water springs, transforming it into a vital stop for caravans and pilgrims. Since then, Yanbuᶜ has been associated with ᶜAlī's descendants as well as the Juhaynah tribe and Anṣār (supporters of the Prophet Muḥammad), and was reported to have had nearly one hundred springs.[2] In the tenth century, it was described by al-Muqaddasī as a fortified city with two gates. He also stated: 'It is more flourishing than Yathrib, and has more groves of date palms. The fortress is well-built, the markets bustling' (al-Muqaddasī 2001: 75). Furthermore, Yanbuᶜ was recognized as a key stop along commercial and pilgrim routes from the Levant and Egypt. It was connected to Medina to the west and al-ᶜĪṣ to the north via the foothills of Jabal Raḍwā, as well as to the al-Hawrāᵓ port (north of Umluj) to the north-west and the al-Jār port to the south (al-Wohaibi 1973: map of northern Hijaz 800–1150). Additionally, Jabal Raḍwā, a prominent mountain in the region, was renowned for its stone and mineral resources. Consequently, the area's

[1] The ancient port site of Yanbuᶜ is unknown but was possibly located in present-day Yanbuᶜ al-Bahr. See Power 2012: 232–233 for the bibliography of the historical sources for Yanbuᶜ.

[2] Al-Bakrī mentioned this as a claim made by Muḥammad ibn ᶜAbd al-Majīd (al-Bakrī 1983, ii: 656).

wadis probably experienced heavy traffic from ancient times through the Islamic period.

Research history

Despite its historical significance, only a few epigraphic surveys have been conducted in the Yanbuᶜ area. The comprehensive rock-art and epigraphic survey of northern Saudi Arabia in 1987 covered Yanbuᶜ and registered eight rock-art and inscription sites. Nevertheless, the area's importance in terms of rock art and inscriptions was underestimated in its report due to the area's granite rock being unsuitable for carving (al-Kabawi et al. 1989: 44).[3] However, in 2022 during the archaeological mission by the Middle Eastern Culture Center in Japan led by Kawatoko, 138 early Islamic inscriptions were registered in this area (Kawatoko 2005: 57). These included the Salamah inscription of Wādī al-Muthallath, dated 23/643–644, which is considered the oldest dated Islamic inscription.[4] After that, no epigraphic survey was officially conducted for two decades, but independent researchers published early Islamic inscriptions and the area's archaeological sites in books and through social media (see e.g. al-Sayyid 1425/2004, ii; al-Maghdhawī 2023).

In November 2022 the Saudi Heritage Commission launched a project to survey and document ancient mining sites in Yanbuᶜ and al-ᶜĪṣ governorates. The survey of this project confirmed the existence of many Islamic and ancient inscriptions and rock art in the mountains, necessitating another project to document them systematically. Thus, this epigraphic survey project began and its first phase started in the Yanbuᶜ governorate in 2023.

The Heritage Commission's epigraphic survey in Yanbuᶜ 2023

The first season of the Heritage Commission's epigraphic survey in Yanbuᶜ was carried out for a month from 30 October 2023.[5] The survey was conducted using both exploration on foot and vehicles. The rock art, inscriptions, and other archaeological features were documented through photography, and their locations were recorded using a handheld GPS device. The survey covered 128 locations in sixteen areas surrounding Jabal Raḍwā (Fig. 1). The area to the north-east of Jabal Raḍwā includes Wādī Ḍās, Wādī al-Hayam, Wādī Bār, Jabal al-Fudayfid, and Wādī Buwāṭ; the area to the south-east includes Wādī ᶜAbāthir, Jibāl al-Sutayḥah, Wādī Ḥarīr, Wādī Julayjilah, Wādī Yanbuᶜ al-Nakhl, Wādī Īlah (Liy), and Wādī Abū Qarn; and the area north-west of Jabal Raḍwā includes Wādī Dūrīt, Wādī Riᶜ al-ᶜIlqah, and a lower part of Wādī ᶜArᶜar. A total of 2509 Ancient North Arabian (ANA) and Islamic inscriptions and examples of rock art were registered (Fig. 2).[6] In the following sections, the most significant findings of this season will be selected and overviewed by category: rock art, ancient inscriptions, Islamic inscriptions, and other archaeological features.

Rock art

The survey identified 1367 rock art elements in twelve areas, with notable concentrations observed in the north-eastern areas of Jabal Raḍwā (Wādī al-Hayam and Wādī Bār) and to the east (Wādī ᶜAbāthir). In addition to the prehistoric rock art, many *wusūm* (tribal brands) and symbols were observed.

---

[3] The description by al-Rāshid, Abu al-Ḥasan and al-Muraykhī (2003: 85) also seems to follow this comprehensive survey report. However, the Yanbuᶜ area has a rather complicated geological setting and contains rocks well suited for carving, such as fine-grained sandstone. The Yanbuᶜ al-Nakhl basin and the area from the northern foot of Jabal Raḍwā toward the north ('As Sard basin') are part of the 'Hadiyah group' consisting of layers of sandstone, siltstone, and igneous rocks, surrounded by mountains of layered intrusive rocks (Johnson et al. 2013: 403–408).

[4] In 2022 Ajab Alotibi revisited the site and revised the reading of the second line of the Salamah inscription. The new reading is: 1. *Kataba Salmah* 2. *bi-thalāth* (instead of '*thalāth*') *wa ᶜishrīn* (Heritage Commission 2022).

[5] The project is headed by Ajab Alotibi. In addition to the present authors, the survey of the first season was carried out by five officials of the Saudi Heritage Commission, Saad Alzmami, Mohammed Alangari (GIS specialist), Khaled Almahri, Ali Salih Alghamdi, and Samer Ali Aljohani; Yosef Saleh Alroujaye (archaeologist, Majal Alenjaz Constructing Co.); students from the Princess Nourah Bint Abdulrahman University, Danah Almokhatieb, Latifa Ben Okail, and Jood Alzahrani, with the collaboration of a local informant, Mr Faraj Alrifai.

[6] These provisional numbers and the numbers given in Figure 2 are subject to change with further detailed study.

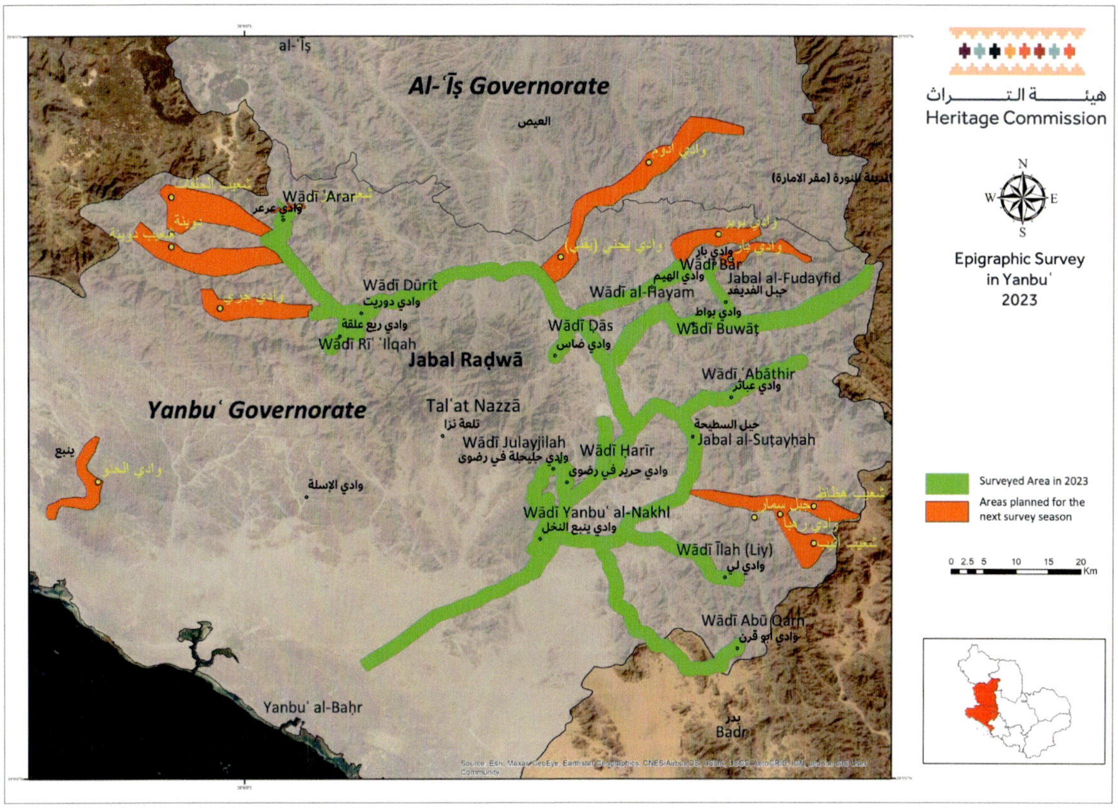

FIGURE 1. *A map of the areas surveyed in 2023 (and showing future survey areas).*

Area number	Area name	Number of locations	Number of inscriptions		Rock art, wusūm and symbols
			Islamic inscriptions	ANA inscriptions	
1	Wādī ᶜAbāthir	20	57	17	244
2	Wādī ᶜArᶜar	35	665	26	29
3	Jibāl al-Sṭayḥah	2	0	2	66
4	Wādī Dūrīt	1	14	10	0
5	Wādī Riᶜ ᶜIlqah	5	11	9	79
6	Wādī Julayjilah	6	33	10	289
7	Wādī Abū Samrah	1	8	0	0
8	Wādī Ḍās	1	4	0	14
9	Wādī Ḥarīr	1	0	0	0
10	Wādī Īlah (Liy)	14	31	15	199
11	Wādī Buwāṭ	17	45	18	144
12	Wādī al-Hayam	9	18	23	172
13	Wādī Abū Qarn	4	6	9	22
14	Wādī Bār	4	11	7	94
15	Jabal al-Fudayfid	2	30	3	15
16	Wādī Yanbuᶜ al-Nakhl	6	58	2	0
Total number		**128**	**991**	**151**	**1367**

FIGURE 2. *Surveyed area names and number of registered inscriptions and rock art.*

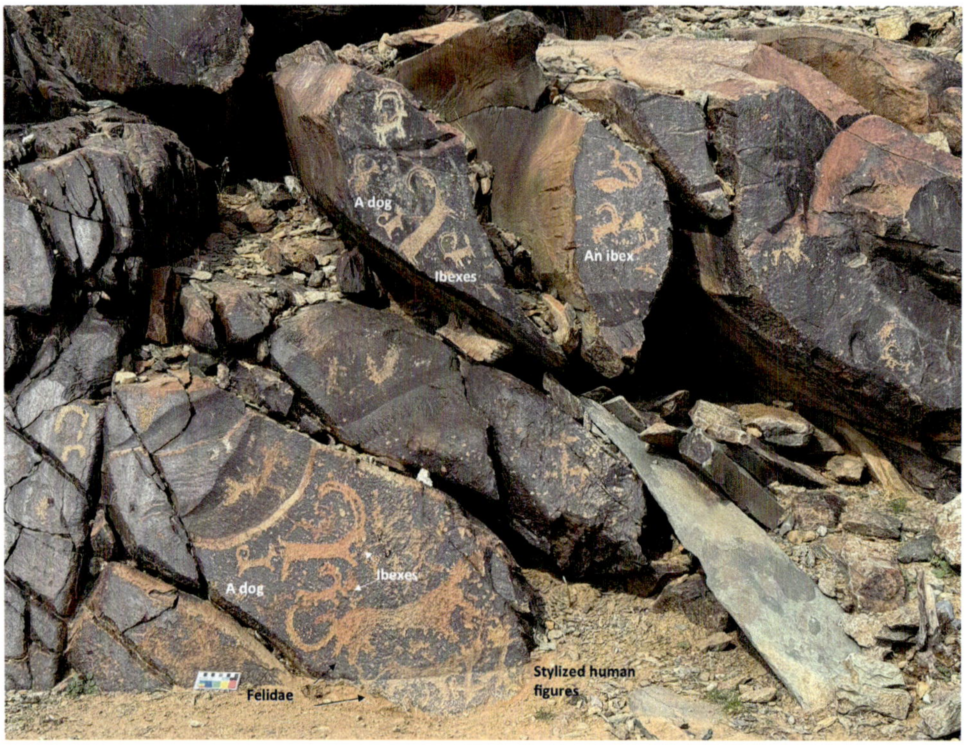

FIGURE 3. *Rock art of Wādī al-Hayam, after soil removal.*

Wādī al-Hayam

In Wādī al-Hayam, ibexes, a hunting dog, two Felidae and two highly stylized human depictions were found (Fig. 3).[7] Judging from the colour of the varnish on the carved surface, a similar depiction of ibexes and a dog on a nearby rock panel seems to be a later imitation, but the rock art of both panels is created using the pecking technique and in both cases, the bodies of the animals are fully pecked.

Another notable finding in Wādī al-Hayam is *dalw wa ḥabl* ('bucket and rope') symbols accompanied by ANA inscriptions. This symbol consists of a circle representing the bucket, with a vertical line above symbolizing a rope.[8] The length of this line varies, ranging from roughly the diameter of the circle to about seven times its length. This symbol has also been observed in the southern Tabuk Province, especially near water features, and is said to represent the presence of water.[9] While some of these symbols seem to have been carved even in the early modern period, three examples from Wādī Hayam were found to be distinctly associated with ANA inscriptions, suggesting that the symbol has existed since antiquity, although whether the meaning remains consistent across time is uncertain (Fig. 4). These examples will be further discussed in 'Ancient inscriptions' below.

Wādī Bār

In Wādī Bār, highly artistic and unique rock art was found. The rock panel illustrated in Figure 5 contains a potential depiction of a warthog or wild boar, a possible wild ass accompanied by its foal, three Grant's gazelles with forward-curving horns, and what appears to be a hunting dog positioned between two of them, with a lion at the bottom of the panel. Furthermore, at the very top of the

[7] A felid and the two human depictions on the lower part of this rock panel appeared after soil removal.

[8] This type of symbol has been documented by Khan in the Mecca region (Khan 2021: 61, 192).

[9] Observed by Tokunaga during the hinterland survey of the Saudi Japanese Archaeological Project in al-Ḥawrāʾ in 2023. The symbol's meaning is based on information from a local informant in the Umluj governorate, Tabuk province.

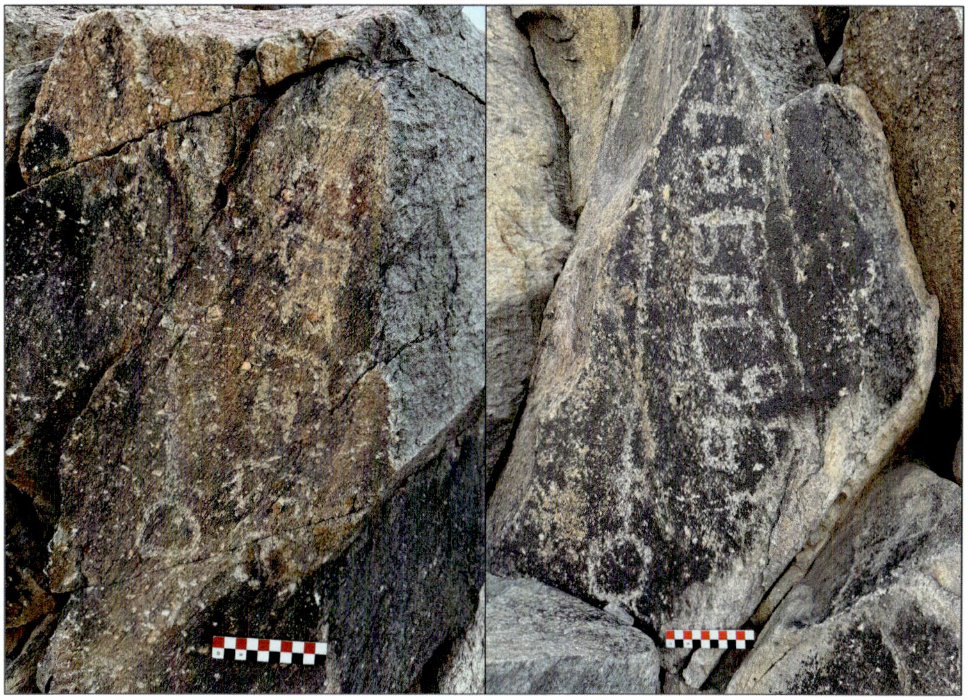

Figure 4. *The 'bucket and rope' symbols associated with ANA inscriptions in Wādī al-Hayam.*

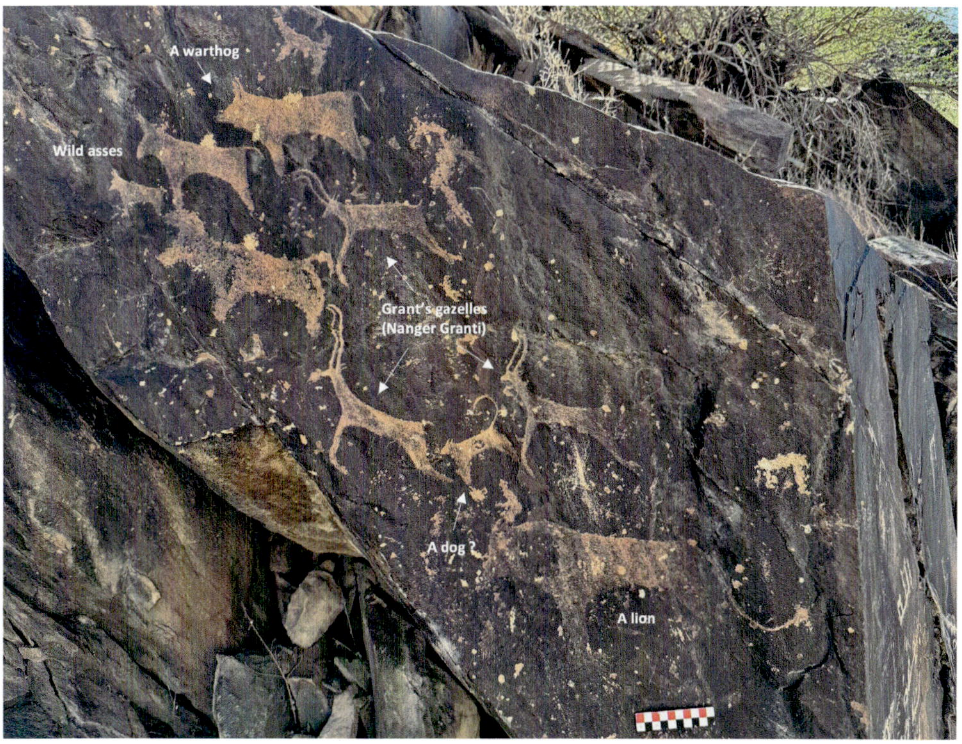

Figure 5. *A rock-art panel including a depiction of a warthog in Wādī Bār.*

panel two small, roughly carved and unidentified animals are faintly visible.

Of particular interest is the representation of the warthog or boar, both of which are suids characteristic of the sub-Saharan environment. This suid, along with the two possible onagers to its left and Grant's gazelles below, exhibits intricate engraving, suggesting the same artisan created them. While the legs of these animals are stylized and relatively simplified, the robust body, thick neck, and detailed rendering of the facial features, ears, and tail are consistent with the morphological traits of a male suid. These characteristics leave little doubt that the animal belongs to the family Suidae. No rock art depicting a warthog has been discovered in Arabia to date, and the example of Wādī Bār seems to be the first attestation in Arabia.[10] The existence of this animal shows that the depiction can be dated before the onset of aridification at the beginning of the fourth millennium BC.

The animal to the left, while similar to the suid, is slightly slenderer in build and features a rounded nose distinct from that of a suid, leading to its identification as a wild ass. To its left is a smaller animal of similar form, probably its foal. The wild ass (*Equus africanus*), which originally inhabited North Africa, is known to have reached western Arabia during the Holocene.[11] Depictions of wild asses are not uncommon in the rock art of the Hijaz, and similar representations have also been identified in the southern part of Tabuk Province (Hasegawa et al., forthcoming).

Additionally, the gazelles, particularly the leftmost individual being pursued by the dog, exhibit the characteristically curved horns typical of Grant's gazelles. A preliminary sketch of a similarly curved horn and head, likely of another gazelle, can also be observed to the right of the uppermost gazelle. The animal depicted at the very bottom of the panel was identified as a lion because of its thick, muscular neck and chest, as well as a long tail tipped with a tuft.

Wādī ʿAbāthir

In the middle reaches of Wādī ʿAbāthir, depictions of ibexes, possible wild asses — similar to those depicted in Wādī Bār — a lion and other felids, a hunter using a bow and arrow, dogs, and some unidentifiable animals were found on a panel high on a rocky outcrop (Fig. 6). The assemblage of depicted animals associated with a Savanna climate, along with the absence of camel depictions, suggests a date between the Neolithic and Bronze Age, although further study is needed for reliable dating. This panel appears to have been used at one time for target practice and a significant amount of damage was observed.

Ancient inscriptions

A total of 151 ancient inscriptions were registered in thirteen areas, all being ANA, mainly Thamudic C and D.[12] Over twenty inscriptions were concentrated in Wādī ʿArʿar and Wādī Hayam. ANA and early Islamic inscriptions tend to be found in the same locations. Most of the ANA inscriptions are written vertically, and the existence of three formulae are discernible: 1) *ʾn PN* ('I am PN'), a typical Thamudic D formula; 2) *wdd (f) PN* ('Greetings be with PN') (cf. al-Jallad 2018: 27, n. 71), characteristic of Thamudic C; 3) a combination of the former two formulae, *wdd (f)* PN1 *w-ʾn* PN2. In two inscriptions in Wādī Rīʿ ʿIlqah, instead of *w-ʾn* ('and I am'), its phonetic spelling *w-n* was observed, indicating the disappearance of inter-vocalic glottal stop (Fig. 7). The two two-line inscriptions in Figure 7 read from the left column to the right.

[10] We would like to express our gratitude to Dr Abdullah Masry for pointing this out at the 57th Seminar for Arabian Studies in Paris. Near the Arabian Peninsula, wild boar is attested in the Fertile Crescent (Guagnin et al. 2016: 7–8).

[11] Grigson (2012) gave an overview of studies on the wild ass in her work on the date of its domestication in the Middle East.

[12] Thamudic C is one of the undeciphered groups of ANA, 'characterized by an introductory formula with *wdd*' (al-Jallad 2018: 27). Although Tsafrir (1996) has examined this formula, its interpretation has yet to be definitively established. Thamudic D likewise constitutes a group whose nature is not yet fully understood. Nevertheless, a comprehensive examination of the existing material by al-Jallad (forthcoming) has considerably advanced the progress in deciphering its script. Thamudic D's characteristic formulae include *ʾn* PN, which is frequently followed by an expression of affection directed towards another individual, as well as *w*-PN *ḥbb* ('with PN, a friend') (al-Jallad, forthcoming).

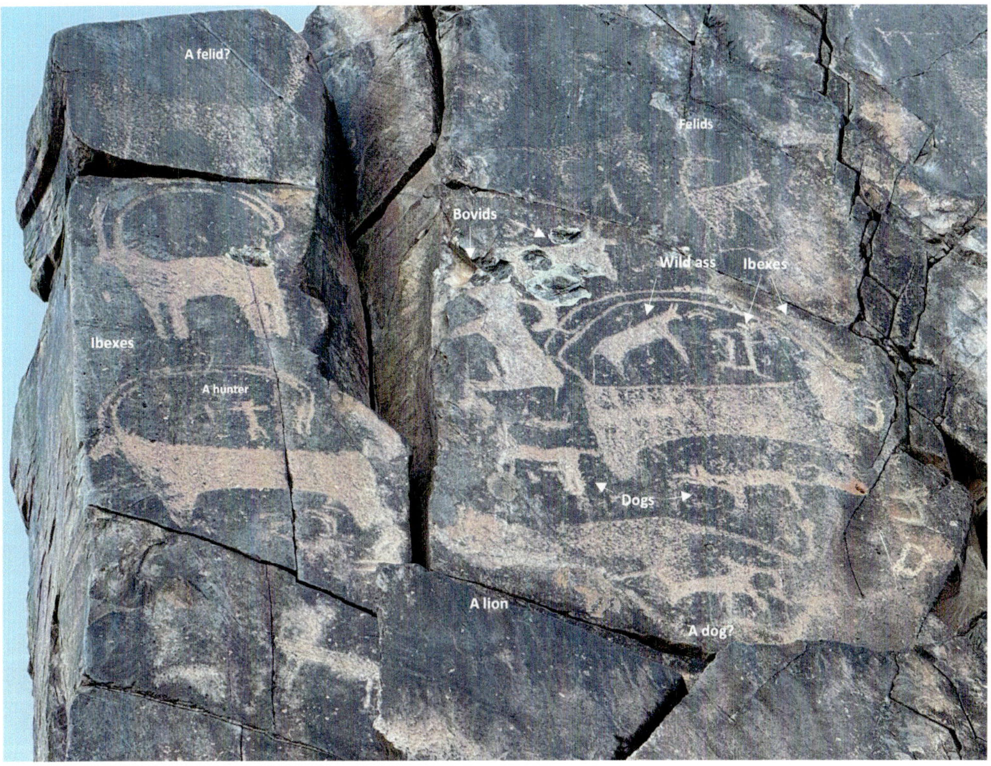

Figure 6. *A rock-art panel high on a rocky outcrop of Wādī ᶜAbāthir.*

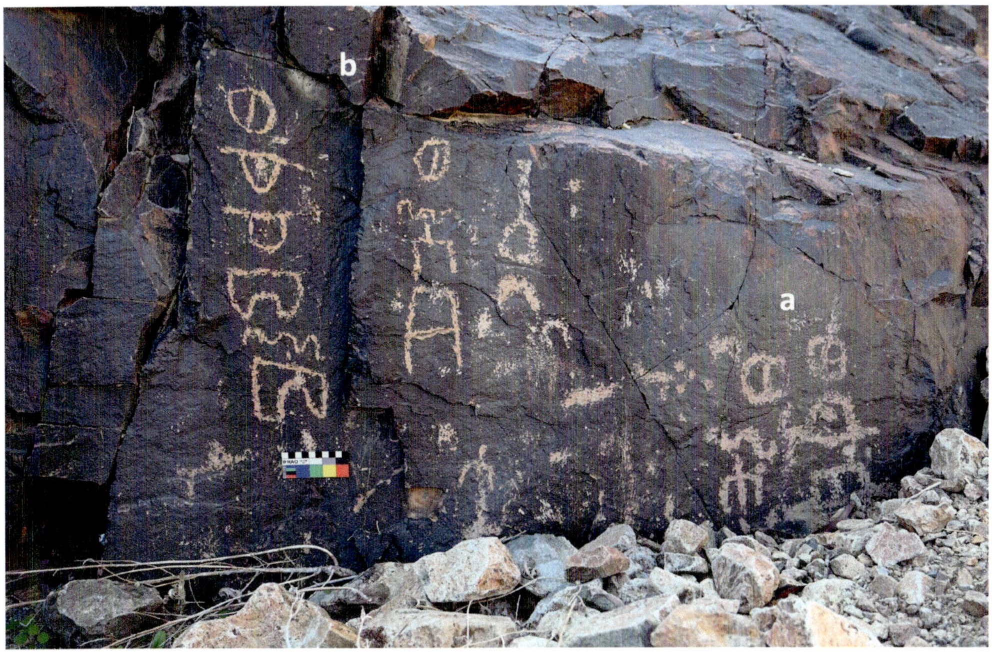

Figure 7. *Thamudic D inscriptions showing the formula* wdd *PN1* w-n *PN2 in Wādī Rīᶜ ᶜIlqah.*

Inscription 1 (Fig. 7/a) is only partially exposed. The text reads:

1. *wdd* ---
2. *w-n* (=*w-ʾn*) *ḥ* ---

'Greetings ... and I am ...'

The text of Inscription 2 (Fig. 7/b) can be read tentatively:

1. *wdd mnm*
2. *w-n* (=*w-ʾn*) *sbb*

'Greetings be with *Mnm* (PN) and I am *Sbb* (PN)'.

Furthermore, a few instances were identified in which what seems to be personal names follow the preposition *l-* (*lām auctoris*), showing authorship. Two of the three ANA inscriptions with the 'bucket and rope' symbols from Wādī Hayam are examples of this (see above 'Wādī al-Hayam', Fig. 4). The letter forms and the degree of weathering of these inscriptions do not differ significantly from the Thamudic C inscriptions found nearby.

In Wādī ʿArʿar, Wādī Riʿ ʿIlqah, and Wādī Īlah, ANA inscriptions tended to be carved lower on the rock faces than Islamic inscriptions. Some Thamudic D inscriptions were only partially exposed, with the lower portions buried beneath the ground. In north-west Arabia, heavy rainfall often brings significant sediment into wadis, and the surface can shift several metres after a single rainfall.[13] The surface level of the wadi at the time of the inscription was probably lower than it is today, and more inscriptions are expected to be uncovered by sediment removal.

Additionally, it is notable that Thamudic C and D inscriptions were often found alongside depictions of camels, ibexes, and ostriches.

Islamic inscriptions

Islamic inscriptions far outnumber ANA inscriptions, with a total of 991 inscriptions registered across fourteen areas during this season's survey. The largest number of Islamic inscriptions was found in Wādī ʿArʿar, followed by inscription sites in the area on the eastern side of the mountain — Yanbuʿ al-Nakhl, Wādī ʿAbāthir, and Wādī Buwāṭ. Most inscriptions are written in Hijazi and Kufic script,[14] presumably dated to the first/seventh and second/eighth centuries. However, other examples, likely dating to much later periods, often exhibit a more casual, handwritten style, blending features of Thuluth, Naskh, and Kufic scripts. After introducing the dated materials, the discussion will focus exclusively on these three major sites.

Dated inscriptions

Despite the large number of inscriptions discovered, only three of them were dated with the following: 76/695–696, 704/1304–1305), and 898/1492–1493) (Fig. 8). The first example, located in Wādī Abū al-Qarn, is a five-line commemorative inscription by a person named Muḥammad bin Ziyād (Fig. 8/a).[15] Due to weathering, the first three lines of the inscription are almost indiscernible. However, with on-site observation and image processing, the inscription was read as follows:

1. *Anā Muḥammad bin Zi-*
2. *yād* [... ...]
3. *kataba hādhā*
4. *yawm al-jumʿah*
5. *min sanat sitt wa sabʿīn*

'I, Muḥammad bin Ziyād, wrote this on Friday in the year seventy-six'.

This self-introductory formula, free from religious elements, features the earliest phase of Islamic inscriptions, as discussed by Imbert (2011).

The second and third examples, dated to the Mamluk period, are found on a rock panel in Wādī ʿAbāthir (Fig. 8/b). Arabic rock inscriptions of this period are quite rare. Both show a mixture of casually handwritten scripts. While 704 is spelt out, 898 is written in Hindu

[13] This information was provided by informants from multiple areas in north-western Arabia.

[14] Hijazi script, developed in the early Islamic period in Mecca and Medina, is primarily defined by its rightward slant and primitive orthographic characteristics. The script shows considerable variation. In contrast, Kufic is geometrically structured. The transition from Hijazi to Kufic occurred in the early eighth century AD, although for rock inscriptions, the boundary is often unclear (George 2010: 31–32, 55–58).

[15] The partial photograph and date of this inscription were first published by Muḥammad Al-Maghdhawī (2023) in his X (formerly Twitter) account.

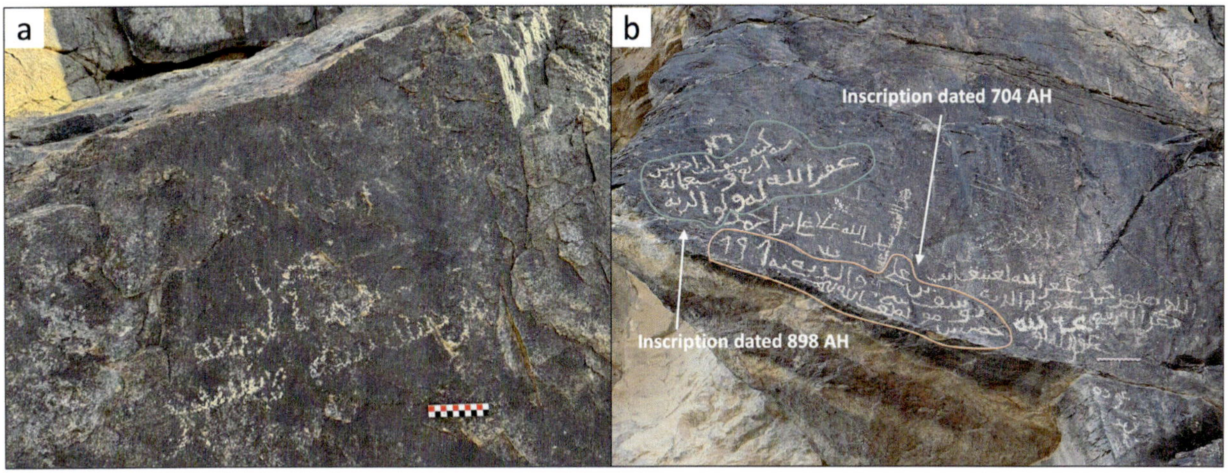

FIGURE 8. *Dated inscriptions from:* **a.** *Wādī Abū al-Qarn;* **b.** *Wādī ʿAbāthir.*

numerals. The tentative reading of these two inscriptions is given below.

Inscription dated 704 AH:

1. *Kataba-hu Munīf ibn Idrīs*
2. *sanat arbaʿ wa-sabʿimiyah* (sic: *sabʿimiʾah*)
3. *ghafara Allāhu la-hu* [*wa-li-*]*wāliday-hi*

'Munīf ibn Idrīs wrote it in the year seven hundred and four. May Allah forgive him and his parents'.

Inscription dated 898 AH:

Ḥaḍara Yūsuf bin ʿAlī bin Mūsā { ? } *Allāh la-hu wa-wāliday-hi sanat 898*

'Yūsuf bin ʿAlī bin Mūsā came. May Allah { ? } him and his parents. In the year 898'.

Wādī ʿArʿar

This season's survey of Wādī ʿArʿar covered the lower half of this long wadi, and a total of 665 Islamic inscriptions were documented in thirty-five locations. The inscriptions are carved on dark, flat patinated rock surfaces, enhancing the visibility of the incisions in light colour. As for the text, almost 60% of the inscriptions are supplications asking for Allah's forgiveness, *Allāhumma ighfir li*-PN ('O Allah forgive PN'). Remarkably, in this formula many inscriptions show the phonetic spelling with the omission of the letter *alif* of *ighfir* (imperative, masculine, singular of the verb *ghafara* 'forgive'). The second largest category was supplication, asking for Allah's forgiveness (*tawbah*) (12%).

On a rock panel at location 24 of this wadi, around a large inscription with repeated *Allāhumma* ('O Allah') following *basmalah*, a dense cluster of much smaller inscriptions containing prayers and declarations of faith was observed (Fig. 9). These inscriptions written in small script are also found in the neighbouring southern part of Tabuk Province, but Wādī ʿArʿar appears to have the higher concentration. The use of small script might have been a regional feature of the area north of Jabal Raḍwā in some period around the second/eighth century. Further research is needed to determine their precise distribution, content, and date.

Although the number of inscriptions in Wādī ʿArʿar is exceptionally large, it is notable that many were repeatedly left by the same individuals. Among 586 inscriptions accompanied by personal names, an unknown person, Hārūn bin Mawhūb, is mentioned in sixty-six inscriptions, ʿUmar bin Wahb in fifty-three, and Mawhūb bin ʿAbdullāh in fifty-nine. Inscriptions by the same individuals are dispersed across various locations along the wadi. Ten other personal names were mentioned in more than ten inscriptions. In addition, inscriptions left by brothers or fathers and sons were

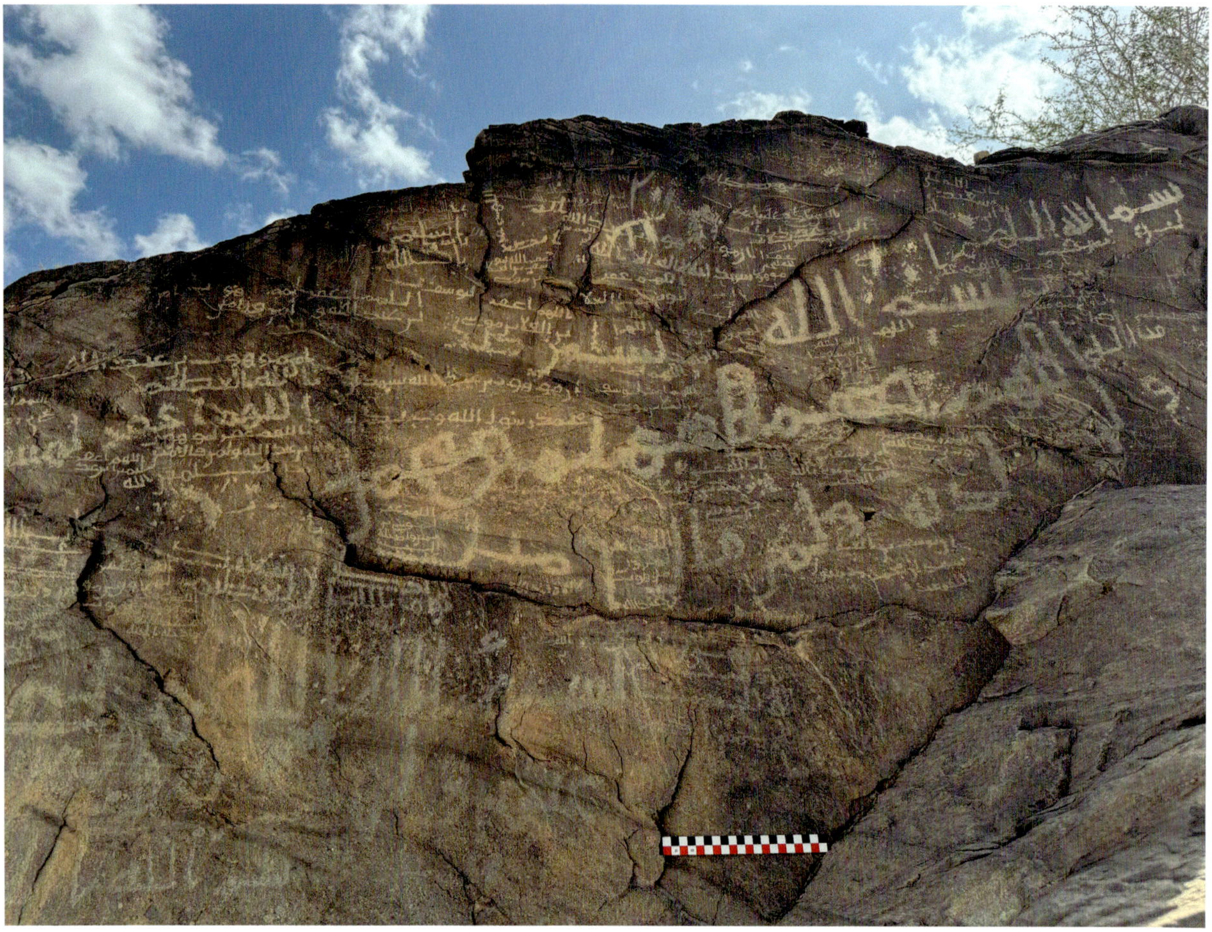

FIGURE 9. *A rock-panel densely carved with early Islamic inscriptions in Wādī ʿArʿar.*

found, and no personal name was accompanied by a *nisbah* (pl. *nisab*) showing the person's attribution (tribe, family, etc.). Considering these features, it is highly probable that most of these inscriptions were carved by local inhabitants.

Wādī Yanbuʿ al-Nakhl

Among the areas surveyed this season, Wādī Yanbuʿ al-Nakhl ranks as the second-largest for the number of inscriptions, with fifty-eight Islamic inscriptions recorded across six locations. Of these, at least thirty are supplications asking for Allah's forgiveness. Although many inscriptions are obscured due to weathering, the inscriptions in this wadi exhibit somewhat more diversity in terms of date and inscribers than other sites. Two of the inscriptions include a *nisbah* in the names. One of them is al-Anṣārī, indicating origins in Medina. However, this does not preclude the possibility that the individual resided in Yanbuʿ, given the presence of a local Anṣār population in the early Islamic period (al-Bakrī 1983, ii: 656). The other seems to be al-Qaṭīyʿī,[16] indicating the person was from al-Qaṭīʿah (present-day al-Muṭayʿah) in Asyūṭ, Egypt.[17] The inscription reads (Fig. 10):

[16] Based on the letter shapes this could also be read as al-Muṭayʿī, but this *nisbah* is not found in early sources.

[17] Al-Muṭayʿah is situated about 12 km south-east of Asyūṭ, on the western bank of the Nile River.

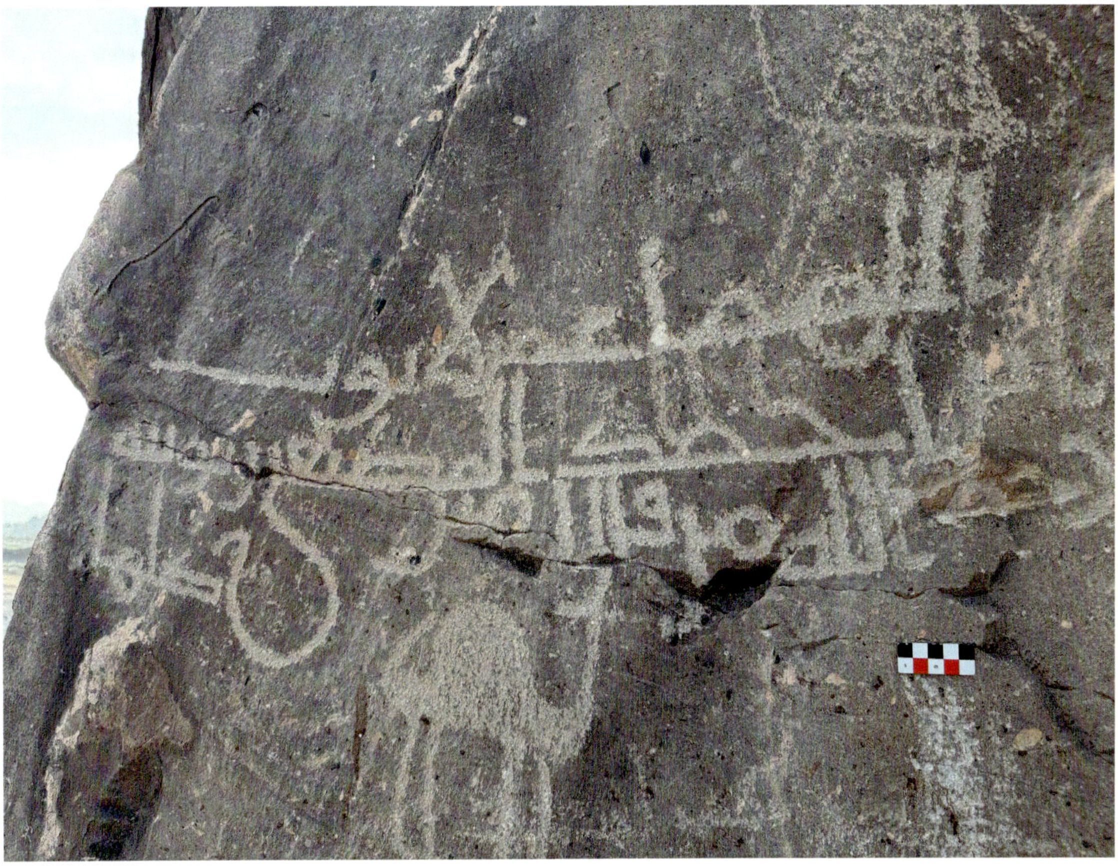

FIGURE 10. *A decorative Kufic inscription in Wādī Yanbuʿ al-Nakhl by a person possibly from al-Qaṭīʿah in Asyūṭ, Egypt.*

1. *Allāhumma ighfir li-Ayyūb*
2. *ibn Aḥmad al-Qaṭīʿī zunūba-hu* (sic: *dhunūba-hu*)[18] *kulla-hā*[19]
3. *Raḥima Allāh man qāla āmīn*

'O Allah, forgive Ayyūb bin Aḥmad al-Qaṭīʿī all of his sins. May Allah have mercy upon whoever said amen!'

Al-Qaṭīʿī could also be a *nisbah* of the al-Qaṭīʿah district, which existed in medieval Baghdād.[20] However, judging from the location of the inscription and the clear influence of decorative Fatimid Kufic,[21] the inscriber is likely to have originated from Egypt. This Egyptian location was a small village documented only from the eighteenth century onwards, but it could have existed earlier (al-Damardāshī 1989: 102). In line 2, 'sins' is spelt *zunūb* instead of *dhunūb*. The sound shift from *ḏ* to *z* is already attested in Middle Arabic, probably reflecting colloquial pronunciation (Blau 1965: 76; 1980: 36). This word is also pronounced /zuˈnu:b/ in modern Egyptian Arabic, and the spelling with *z* gives us glimpse of the inscriber's pronunciation.

[18] The redundant 'tooth' (a vertical or slanted stroke characteristic of certain letters) is observed at the end of this word, making it resemble *zunūbata-hu*. The presence of an extra tooth in this developed stage of Arabic inscriptions may be due to an error by the inscriber.

[19] This word is located below '*dhunūba-hu*'.

[20] For example, this *nisbah* is known through its association with the renowned tenth-century scholar Abū Bakr al-Qaṭīʿī al-Baghdādī.

[21] This feature is particularly observed in the last letter (*y*) of al-Qaṭīʿī.

Wādī ʿAbāthir

Wādī ʿAbāthir has fifty-seven Islamic inscriptions in twenty locations. Judging from the script's shapes and the two dated materials mentioned in 'Dated inscriptions' above, the inscriptions of this wadi appear to have been carved over several centuries since the seventh century. The texts show various formulae, including six inscriptions in *anā PN* formula, which is rare in other surveyed areas. In addition, prehistoric rock art, ancient inscriptions, and numerous modern depictions of camels, *wusūm*, and other symbols can also be observed in the same locations, showing the wadi's significance in regional traffic throughout the ages.

Wādī Buwāṭ

Wādī Buwāṭ is a wadi that connects the north-east of Jabal Raḍwā to Buwāṭ, to which the Prophet Muḥammad travelled seeking the Quraish caravan in 2/623 (Ibn Kathīr 1998: 238–239). An asphalt road runs through this wadi, along which forty-five early Islamic inscriptions were registered in seventeen locations, often found near ANA inscriptions. Most inscriptions in this wadi are religious supplications, with the most common asking for Allah's forgiveness, comprising over 35% of the total. As with Wādī ʿArʿar, multiple inscriptions by the same individual were found in this wadi: ten inscriptions bear the name Ḥulays bin Mawhūb; three the name ʿAbdulmalik bin Kardam; two the names ʿAbdullāh bin Ṭurayf al-Juhanī (*thumma* 'and then') al-Mālikī, ʿUmar bin ʿAbdullāh, and Mawhūb bin Ṭammāḥ. The recurrence of inscriptions bearing the same names means that these people were travelling between Yanbuʿ al-Nakhl and Buwāṭ multiple times, probably to Medina. Also, as ʿAbdullāh bin Ṭurayf's tribe, Juhaynah, shows, these people are probably local inhabitants. Another inscription by Ḥulays bin Mawhūb was found in Wādī al-Hayam, immediately north of Wādī Buwāṭ, and two more inscriptions by ʿUmar bin ʿAbdullāh were found in Wādī Īlah, located east of Yanbuʿ al-Nakhl, showing their mobility.

Other archaeological features

Although not the primary focus of this survey, four archaeological features were identified. This section focuses on two prominent features discovered in Wādī Bār and Wādī Abū Qarn.

Standing stones of Wādī Bār

Dozens of standing stones were discovered at the lower stream of the rock art site of Wādī Bār (located at 24.690200°N, 38.630805°E) (Fig. 11). These are unworked natural stones and after cursory observation, no traces of carving were found. Parallels of these standing stones can be found in north-western Arabia, all linked to the Neolithic period. However, their function remains ambiguous, whether they served as support for dwellings or were used in religious rituals. In Harrat ʿUwayrid in AlUla County, although the arrangement of the standing stones differs, several similar examples have been discovered. One such example yielded Red Sea shells, suggesting mobility between the region and the Red Sea coast during this period (McMahon et al. 2024). The standing stones at Wādī Bār, given their analogy with Neolithic examples and the existence of skilled rock art of the same wadi that could be contemporaneous, warrant specialized research.

Fort-like structures of Wādī Abū Qarn

A group of stone structures was discovered at the mouth of Wādī Abū Qarn (located at 24.164436° N, 38.662331° E). There are three almost square structures, with the largest (*c.*30 x 30 m) on the lower level. The northern half of the structure consists of multiple small rooms, while the southern half remains an open, undivided space. A comparable example can be found at the early Islamic *qaṣr* in Wādī Muhalhal, also in Medina Province, which similarly features a structure with half of its interior as an open space (al-Rāshid 2000: 199–202). The remaining two structures are situated on a north–south ridge to the east, although they have not been confirmed on site. However, based on satellite imagery,[22] the northern structure appears to share similarities with the first structure. The smallest of the three structures features a series of stone alignments along its north–south axis on the ridge, and multiple rooms can be observed in the centre of the building.

[22] The satellite image observation was made on a Google Earth satellite map.

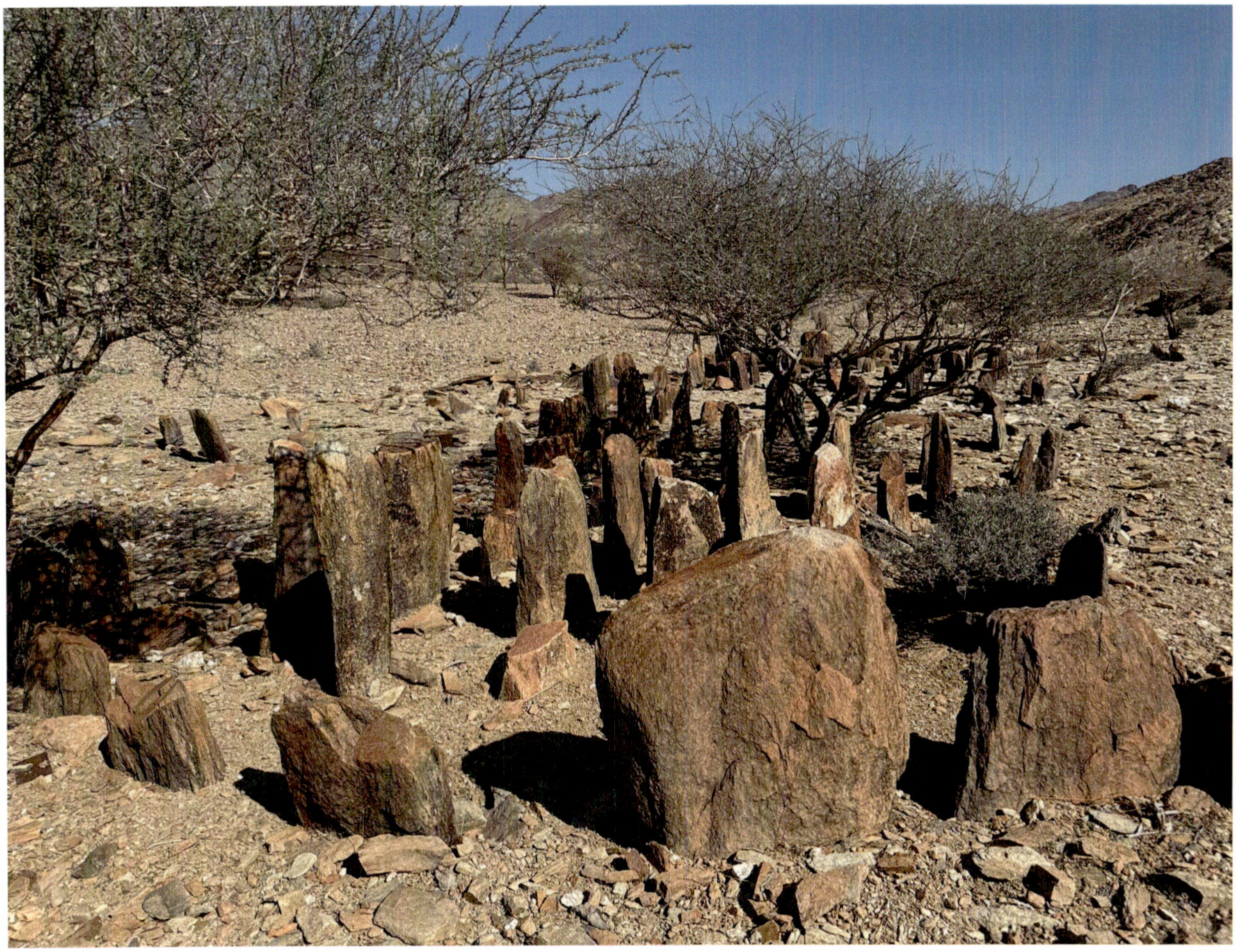

FIGURE 11. *A group of standing stones in Wādī Bār.*

Conclusion

This paper has provided an overview of the results from the first season of the Yanbuᶜ epigraphic survey. The findings revealed the existence of highly developed rock art, probably created by hunter-gatherer communities and dating to the Neolithic period and the Bronze Age, based on the combinations of animals depicted. Future research would benefit from employing XRF analysis, allowing for a more precise determination of the rock art's chronology. Additionally, the prehistoric structures in Wādī Bār require urgent documentation and further investigation.

Regarding ancient inscriptions, both Thamudic C and D were the primary scripts used in this region, although the distinction between the two categories in this region remains unclear. In addition to the presence of mixed formulae discussed above ('Ancient inscriptions'), no significant differences in letter forms are observed. However, the advanced weathering of Thamudic C inscriptions suggests that they predate Thamudic D. This is reasonable, given that Thamudic D was used during the final phase of the ANA inscriptions.[23] Our survey revealed that both Thamudic C and D inscriptions share an almost identical distribution with early Islamic inscriptions, suggesting that key routes used during the ancient period were carried over into the early Islamic

[23] A recent discovery demonstrated that Thamudic D inscriptions coexisted with pre-Islamic Arabic (Developing Arabic) in late antiquity (Tokunaga & Altarib 2024).

period. However, many inscriptions probably remain buried beneath wadi sediment, and the actual total number of inscriptions is yet to be determined.

Islamic inscriptions significantly outnumber ancient ones in this region. The frequent recurrence of inscriptions by the same individual and the rare occurrence of *nisab* with personal names indicate that the majority of the inscribers were local inhabitants. This suggests the presence of a community capable of producing well-formed inscriptions during the first two centuries of the Islamic era. Yanbuʿ's abundant water resources probably made it a hub, connecting important nearby centres such as al-ʿĪṣ, Medina, and the port of al-Jār, as well as the mines and quarries of Jabal Raḍwā. In addition, inscriptions from Yanbuʿ al-Nakhl provide evidence that it was part of a broader network, possibly including pilgrimage routes.

The second phase of the survey, planned for 2025, will focus on the upper reaches of Wādī ʿArʿar and other areas highlighted in orange in Figure 1. Alongside a detailed analysis of the inscriptions and the mapping of early Islamic remains, we expect to gain further insight into the region's transport networks, linguistic features, and other aspects from antiquity through the Islamic period.

References

al-Bakrī, Abī ʿUbayd ʿAbd Allāh b. ʿAbd al-ʿAzīz/ed. M. al-Saqqā. 1983. *Muʿjam mā istaʿjam min asmāʾ al-bilād wa al-mawāḍiʿ.* (4 volumes). Beirut: ʿĀlam al-Kutub.

Blau J. 1965. *The emergence and linguistic background of Judaeo-Arabic: A study of the origins of Middle Arabic.* Oxford: Oxford University Press.

Blau J. 1980. *Grammar of mediaeval Judaeo-Arabic.* (Second enlarged edition). Jerusalem: The Max Schloessinger Memorial Foundation, the Hebrew University. [In Hebrew.]

al-Damardāshī, al-Amīr Aḥmad/ed. ʿA. ʿAbd al-Raḥīm. 1989. *Kitāb al-Durrat al-Muṣāna.* Cairo: Institut Français d'Archéologie Orientale.

George A. 2010. *The rise of Islamic calligraphy.* London: Saqi.

Grigson C. 2012. Size matters — Donkeys and horses in the prehistory of the southernmost Levant. *Paléorient* 38/1–2: 185–201.

Guagnin M., Jennings R., Eager H., Parton A., Stimpson C., Stepanek C. ... Petraglia M.D. 2016. Rock art imagery as a proxy for Holocene environmental change: A view from Shuwaymis, NW Saudi Arabia. *The Holocene* 26/11: 1–13.

Hasegawa S., Alrasheed S., Tokunaga R., Nishimoto S., Koiwa M., Etaya M. ... Fujii S. (forthcoming). Excavations at al-Ḥawrāʾ and the Hinterland Surveys 2018–2023. *Atlal* 34.

Heritage Commission 2022. X (formerly Twitter) account. 30 September 2024. https://x.com/mocheritage/status/1546913303934500865?s=48

Ibn Kathīr/transl. T. Le Gassick. 1998. *The life of the Prophet Muḥammad.* ii. Reading: Garnet. [Reprint, 2006.]

Imbert F. 2011. L'Islam des pierres: l'expression de la foi dans les graffiti arabes des premiers siècles. *Revue des mondes musulmans et de la Méditerranée* 129: 57–78.

al-Jallad A. 2018. What is Ancient North Arabian? Pages 1–44 in D. Birnstiel & N. Pat-El (eds), *Re-engaging comparative Semitic and Arabic Studies.* Wiesbaden: Harrassowitz.

al-Jallad A. (forthcoming). Towards the decipherment of Thamudic D: An identification of new phoneme-glyph values and letter shapes. *Bulletin of the School of Oriental and African Studies.*

Johnson P., Halverson G., Kusky T., Stern R. & Pease V. 2013. Volcanosedimentary basins in the Arabian-Nubian Shield: Markers of repeated exhumation and denudation in a Neoproterozoic accretionary orogen. *Geosciences* 3: 389–445.

al-Kabawi A., Khan M., al-Mubarak A., al-Tamai M., al-Ubaid S. & al-Subhan I. 1989. Preliminary report on the fourth season of comprehensive rock art and epigraphic survey of northern Saudi Arabia 1408 AH/1987 AD. *Atlal* 12: 41–51, pls 33–41.

Kawatoko M. 2005. Archaeological survey of Najran and Madinah 2002. *Atlāl* 18: 45–59, pls 8.1–8.14.

Khan M. 2021. *Wusum: The tribal symbols of Saudi Arabia.* Transl. A. al-Zahrani. Riyadh: Heritage Commission.

McMahon J., Stileman F., Shipton C., Strolin L., Nassr A., Porr M. ... Thomas H. 2024. New evidence for Neolithic occupation in north-west Arabia: Standing stone circles on the Harrat ʿUwayrid. *Levant* 56/2: 185–203.

al-Maghdhawī M. 26 July 2023. https://x.com/mohammed93athar/status/1684307365418369029?t=ogvghrySpifc5FHqSTDAKg. *X*. 30 September 2024.

al-Muqaddasī/trans. B. Collins. 2001. *The best divisions for knowledge of the regions (Aḥsan al-taqāsīm fī maʿrifat al-aqālīm)*. Reading: Garnet.

Power T. 2012. *The Red Sea from Byzantium to the caliphate, AD 500–1000*. Cairo/New York: The American University in Cairo Press.

Ptolemy/trans. E.L. Stevenson. 1932. *The Geography*. New York: New York Public Library.

al-Rāshid S.ʿA. 2000. *Dirāsāt fī al-āthār al-islāmiyyah al-mubakkira bi al-madīnat al-munawwarah*. Riyadh: Muʾassasat al-Ḥuzaimī li al-Tijārah wa al-Tawkīlāt.

al-Rāshid S.ʿA., Abu al-Ḥasan Ḥ. & al-Muraykhī M. 2003. *Āthār minṭaqat al-Madīnat al-Munawwarah*. Riyadh: Deputy Ministry of Antiquities and Museums.

al-Sayyid Ṣ.ʿA.ʿA. 1425/2004. *Malāmiḥ min Tārīkh Yanbuʿ*. (2 vols). Yanbuʿ al-Ṣināʿiyyah: Maṭbaʿah al-Hayʾah al-Malakiyyah.

Tokunaga R. & Altarib A. 2024. A pre-Islamic bilingual inscription of ʿAlaqān, northwest Saudi Arabia. Poster presented at the 57th Seminar for Arabian Studies, Paris. [Unpublished poster.]

Tsafrir N. 1996. New Thamudic inscriptions from the Negev. *Le Muséon* 109: 137–167.

al-Wohaibi A. 1973. *The northern Hijaz in the writings of the Arab geographers 800–1150*. Beirut: Al-Risalah.

Authors' addresses

Ajab Alotibi, Heritage Commission, 2908 King Saud St., Al-Murabba District, Riyadh 12631 – 8569, Saudi Arabia.
e-mail aalotibi@moc.gov.sa

Risa Tokunaga, Heritage Commission, 2908 King Saud St., Al-Murabba District, Riyadh 12631 – 8569, Saudi Arabia.
e-mail rtokunaga@moc.gov.sa

Majed Dahash, Heritage Commission, 2908 King Saud St., Al-Murabba District, Riyadh 12631 – 8569, Saudi Arabia.
e-mail MDahash@moc.gov.sa

Muzhira Alqahtani, Heritage Commission, 2908 King Saud St., Al-Murabba District, Riyadh 12631 – 8569, Saudi Arabia.
e-mail m.halqahtani@moc.gov.sa

Proceedings of the Seminar for Arabian Studies 54 (2025): 32–48

The Yemeni mummies: a brief report and comprehensive bibliography

Mohammed A. Atbuosh & Amgad E.M. Abdulmughni

Summary

Yemen developed a technique for preserving and mummifying the bodies of the deceased with the use of aromatic plant materials and resins found in the local environment. However, these mummies are currently in poor condition, with many of them on the verge of total disintegration. Regrettably, the ongoing illegal excavation and continuous destruction of burial sites, especially the rock tombs containing several mummies, pose a significant threat to this unique scientific treasure. The preservation of the mummies has not been scientifically sound in several aspects. They have fallen into a precarious state due to a lack of ideal environmental conditions, appropriate treatment, and adequate care.

This report aims to provide a comprehensive overview of the published literature on Yemeni mummies and their current condition, updated photographs, and a complete bibliography of the literature, which is mainly in Arabic and has thus escaped the attention of the international academic community.

Keywords: Yemen, mummies, mummification, grave robbing, rock-cut tombs

Introduction

Since the tenth century AD, Yemenis have recognized the significance of the ancient tombs. The Yemeni antiquarian, al-Hamdānī, dedicated the eighth volume of his work, *al-Iklīl*, to Yemen's tombs and their ancient treasures. In describing his own observations of the tombs, he wrote:

> 'It is as if these holes are *nawāwīs* (i.e. tombs)[1] for their dead people, and still they are inside until today; I have seen their bodies … most of them have become disjointed bones, yet they are hard. The more recent ones have bones that are greasy, while the older ones have white bones. Some of their shrouds, made of fine linen, have remained.' (al-Hamdānī in Faris 1938: 45; see also al-Hamdānī 2004: 97 for the Arabic).

Other descriptions by al-Hamdānī often carried a mythical tone, and served as a literary device about the pre-Islamic past (Mahoney 2021: 146–153). Meanwhile, the Yemeni author Wahb b. Munabbih mentioned numerous tombs dedicated to the kings of Himyar. He also pointed out instances of the digging and plundering of these graves, along with the seizure of some of their treasures (Wahb 1979: 74), a widespread practice that can be found in various cultures.

Grave robbing and reuse constitute acts that violate the scientific and cultural significance of these burial sites. It results in the destruction of historical and archaeological evidence, especially artefacts crucial for the study and understanding of ancient history. This phenomenon is deeply rooted and recurrent. It is reflected in the curse formulas on the funeral monuments, which usually implore the deity to overthrow the one who will destroy it, *yḫrs²n* (e.g. CIH 445; CIH 452; RES 4156; RES 4536; cf. Yemeni Arabic *ḫaraš* 'to hoe, dig'). Recently, Stein and Weninger published a newly discovered minuscule inscription, dating to *c.* AD 300, in which a female sender reports on a looted tomb in Sana'a city. This unique text is the first to explicitly mention grave robbing. It is also an important indication of the use of coffins in ancient Yemen to preserve the dead, and provided us with the coffin name in Ancient South Arabian as *ʾrn* (Stein & Weninger 2024: 89; cf. *ʾarōn* Gen. 50: 26).

The phenomenon of grave looting has been explicitly mentioned in Islamic sources since the tenth century, with numerous anecdotes demonstrating the exposure of many tombs and burial sites in Yemen to looting, robbery, or reuse in different historical periods. Al-Hamdānī ascribed a poetic verse regarding the graves of king Asʿad that were found to be stuffed with jewels when looted

[1] *nawāwīs* (sing. *nāʾūs*, burial place), from a Greek loanword, ναος.

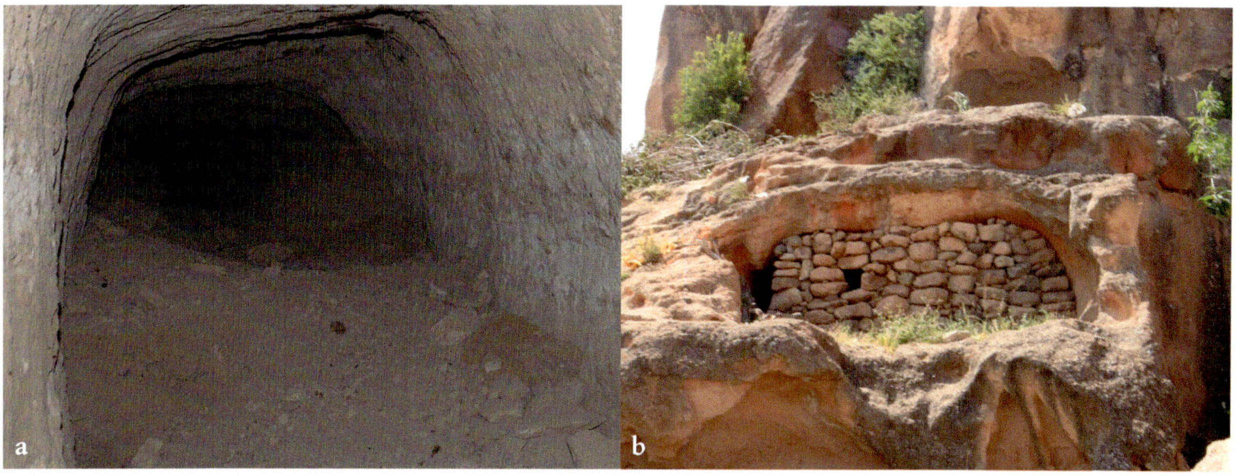

FIGURE 1. **a.** *Illegal excavation of one of the rock-cut tombs in search of its treasures, Hirrān, Ḏamār;* **b.** *use of tombs as dwellings for Bedouins or as storage for livestock feed (photographs J.M. al-Ḥudayjī, 2023).*

(al-Hamdānī 2004: 104). He also stated that 'people are mining gold' from the graves, and called the gold extracted from graves *al-ḏahab al-qubūrī* (lit. grave gold) (2004: 139). This reflects how established the phenomenon had become in developing its own terminology. Examples of such reports include:

1. A certain Yaḥyā b. Sinān said: 'When my grandfather was the governor of Yemen, he used to ransack pre-Islamic tombs to acquire their treasures' (al-Hamdānī: 2004: 173; English translation after Faris 1938: 90)
2. A certain Mujālid al-Marrāni [d. AD 761] said 'I was with the governor of Yemen when a man came and said, "shall I lead you to a treasure?" I said, "Yes". He said, "Send an escort with me". So, I informed the governor, who sent people with me. We dug in a place until we reached the gate of the cave. We opened it and entered, finding a gold-lined coffin' (al-Hamdānī 2004: 175–176; Faris 1938: 92).
3. 'Muḥammad b. Yūsuf, the brother of al-Ḥajjāj [d. AD 714], was in charge of Yemen. He used to send people to dig up graves and search for money because they used to bury their wealth with them' (al-Hamdānī 2004: 174; Faris 1938: 91).

The last text suggests that grave robbing was not limited to individuals but had become an organized practice encouraged by the elite. In recent years, several national and foreign archaeological missions have documented instances of tombs and rock-cut graves being violated (Pirenne 1978: 81–82; Šāyif 2023). They had been reused by the locals as storage facilities for agricultural products and livestock feed, especially in Šibām al-Ġirās and its surroundings. Some residents in other areas had turned them into dwellings, particularly among Bedouin tribes (Bāsalāma 1990: 98) (Fig. 1).

The French expedition noted that most of the rock-cut tombs in Šabwa were used by farmers to store their tools and animal feed. Jacqueline Pirenne also mentioned that one day, in January 1975, she saw a farmer carrying a pickaxe-like tool with protrusions resembling teeth, showing signs of soil and a kind of mortar surrounding it (Pirenne 1978: 81). This farmer may have been one of the treasure hunters searching for treasures in the rock-cut tombs. Instances of such acts persist to the present day, with dozens of rock-cut tombs destroyed, their mummies and treasures stolen. Some mummies were even discarded on the roadside, like the Bayt al-Sayyānī mummy in Ibb Governorate, which fell victim to thieves (*Arabnews* 2023). In March 2023 another mummy was found inside a garbage container in Sana'a, which was handed over by security forces to the General Organization of Antiquities and Museum (GOAM) (Fig. 2).

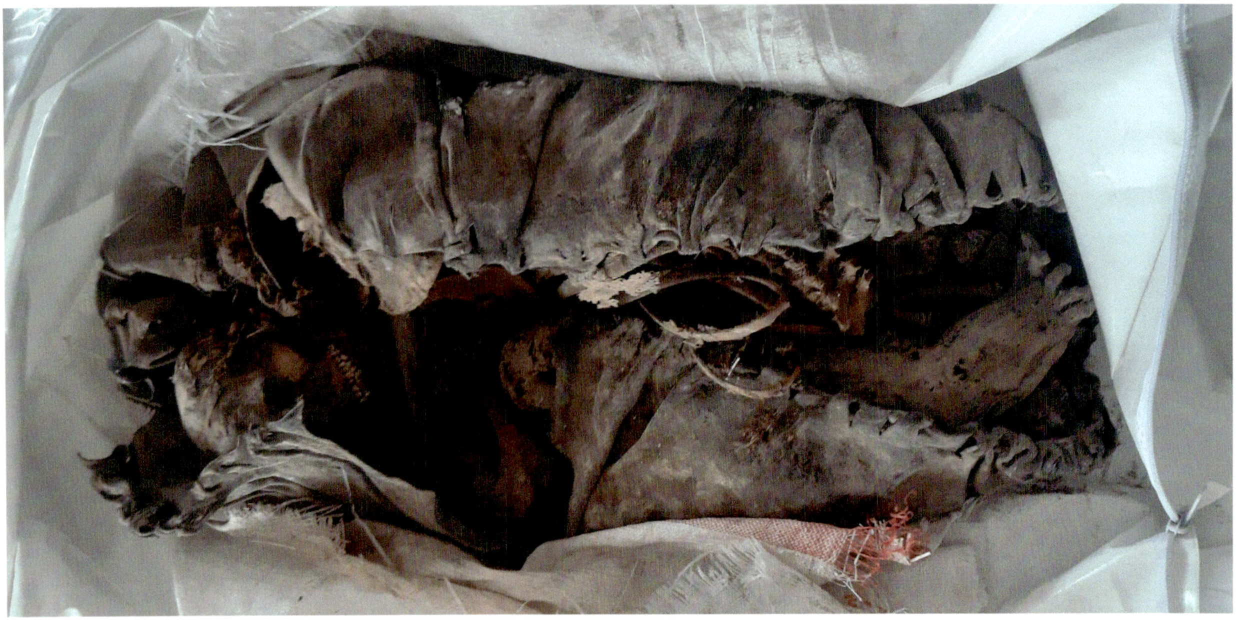

FIGURE 2. *Mummy found inside a garbage container in Sana'a (photographs A. Abdulmughni, 2024).*

Mummification in ancient Yemen

The funerary customs in pre-Islamic Ancient South Arabia indicate a belief in the afterlife. This is evident in the inclusion of grave-goods, such as miniature objects that replicate common and practical items used in everyday life (Mancarella 2018: 122; Gerlach 2002: 58). Consequently, Vogt and de Maigret (1999: 181) had no doubt that the ancient South Arabians believed in the afterlife based on archaeological observations alone. However, from an epigraphic point of view Christian Robin concludes that 'Ḥimyarite Jews did not believe in an afterlife or were not in the habit of mentioning it in their grave inscriptions' (Robin 2021: 207). Although not explicit references to the afterlife as such, some hints to this belief can be found in the inscriptions, such as X.BSB 96, which emphasize *hnʾ hnʾ-h* 'to ensure his [i.e. the deceased's] care' possibly reflecting the author's afterlife beliefs (Stein 2010: 340); the Minaic text MṢM 116/3 reads: *kl ʾḫrm kl-s¹ ymt qbrn* 'all the days to come (?), in its entirety (and) for the duration of the tomb' (DASI); the monotheistic inscription dated AD 464 emphasized the idea of *ḥyw ṣdqm w-mwt mwt ṣdqm* 'to live righteously and to die a righteous death' (Ry 520), a striking parallel to the Quranic expression *mudḫala ṣidqin ... muḫraǧa ṣidqin*;[2] the monotheistic inscription (CIH 539/2) that mentions *w-b-ʿlmn bʿdn w-qrbn* 'and in the far and present world' (DASI); another example is a Jew who asked his Lord *mrʾ ḥyn w-mwtn* 'Lord of life and death', although an explicit concept of the afterlife remains absent in South Arabian inscriptions (Robin 2021: 206). This belief in an afterlife necessitated the preservation of the deceased's body for eternity, along with the soul, which would reunite with the body on its journey to the next life. This is confirmed by an empty wooden sarcophagus found in Egypt, engraved with an Ancient South Arabian script (RES 3427; al-Saʿīd 2003: 69–70) (Fig. 3). An ancient Egyptian loanword, *ba*, appears in the text as *bʾ* (Coptic *bai*), referring to the soul of the deceased (Müller 1988: 628, FN 3, a), while the mummy was called *kṣy* (Coptic *kaise*) (Beeston 1984: 90; Avanzini 2016: 167). It is thus possible that the practice of mummification in South Arabia was influenced by Ptolemaic Egypt (Mancarella 2018: 127).

[2] *rabbi ʾadḫilnī mudḫala ṣidqin wa-ʾaḫriǧnī muḫraǧa ṣidqin* 'My Lord, make me go in [the grave] righteously, and come out [for resurrection] righteously' (Qurʾān 17. 80).

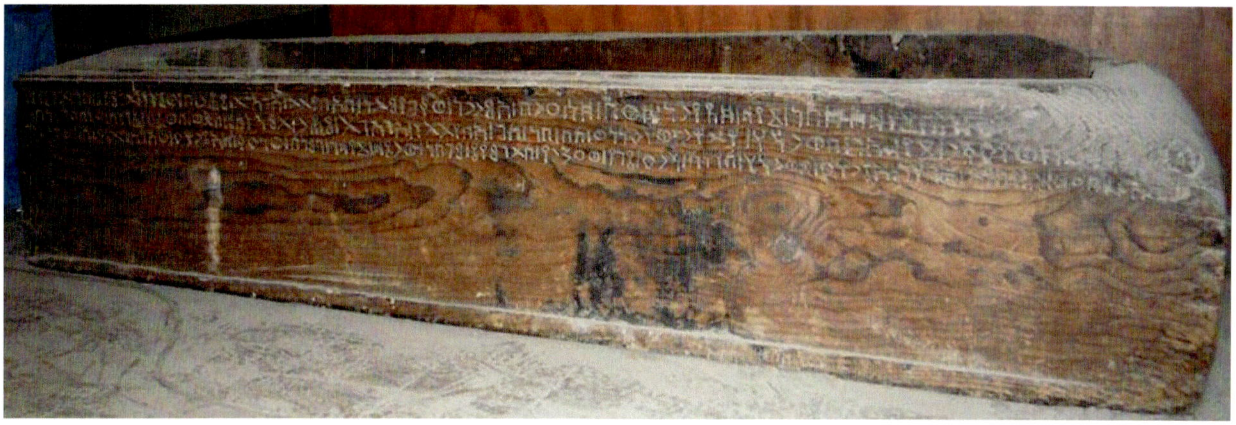

FIGURE 3. *Ancient South Arabian sarcophagus — The Egyptian Museum (by kind permission M. Al-Athori).*

The oldest known evidence of mummification in ancient South Arabia was discovered in the Sabaean tombs at Awām Temple in Marib, where remnants of textile treated with resinous materials were found (Hitgen 1998: 120; Šāyif 2005: 228; Mancarella 2016: 187), along with a few imported Egyptian objects such as a sphinx[3] (Gerlach 2002: 55, 58). Additional evidence of mummification included 'some oxidized cloth and wood' found in the Qatabanian tombs at Ḥayd Bin ʿAqīl in Wadi Bayḥān, Šabwa (Phillips 1955: 113).

The first complete mummies were discovered on 20 October 1983, during a rescue excavation by the Department of Antiquities at the Faculty of Arts and Humanities of Sana'a University, following a report received by Dr Yusuf M. ʿAbdullah on 10 October (ʿAbdullah 1990: 176–181). They were later examined and restored by Egyptian experts in November 1983. Later discoveries included the mummies of Ṣayḥ in al-Maḥwīt (Šāyif 1994) and the mummies found in Mōṯ Valley (Šāyif, al-Sayyānī & Sunnah 2022). Several local newspapers covered these discoveries along with later ones (NewsBriefs 1984; Glanzman 2005; al-Šammāʿ 2011; Anon. 2012; *Saba* 2021). In 2001–2002, the archaeologist Howard Reid collaborated with Juniper TV (a UK company), UK's Channel 4, and National Geographic to produce a 60-minute documentary 'Sheba's Secret Mummies: The Immortals of Ancient Sheba', broadcast in 2002 and later, on 13 April 2016, by National Geographic (al-Ḥusaynī, ʿAli & Rājiḥ 2002).[4]

The mummies were discovered in Šibām al-Ġirās, known in the ancient inscription as *ḏ-hgrn* S^2*bmm* or *ḏ-*S^2*bmm* (Bāsalāma 1990: 202). The two tombs (A and B) were cleared, revealing a mummy wrapped in linen bandages (*Linum usitatissimum*). After lengthy research and X-ray examinations, it was revealed that a metal ring was present on one foot of the mummy, and the deceased wore shoes specially made for the burial (Bāsalāma 1990; Basalama 1998) (Fig. 4). Some tools and pottery vessels were also found buried nearby, as well as a spearhead. There were also rumours about a local child who unearthed a small dagger from the site, which might be another spearhead (Nūr ad-Dīn 1985: 182). Radiocarbon analysis of samples taken from the Šibām

[3] A sphinx was called *ʾb-ʿwtn* (MIbb 4) and *ʾb-ʿwty* (UAM 523), which may provide the basis for the medieval Arabic form *abū l-Hōl* (lit. Father of Dread). Etymologically, *ʿwtn* can be compared to *ʿwt* (RES 3880/6; ATM 869/2–3; al-ʿĀdī 4/4), as a kind of stone, cf. Tigre *ʿawtē* 'victory' (Littmann & Höfner 1962: 477), and Arabic *ʿawwat* 'a way-mark that is set up, composed of stones', a meaning that may have led to a phono-semantic matching with the Egyptian Sphinx **ʾabu al-ʿawt* (al-Ḥājj 2015: 138–139) (lit. the one of the *ʿAwt* stones) and might have modified into *abū l-Hōl*. Al-Hajj wonders whether *ʿwt* was borrowed into Arabic as *ʿatw(ā)* with metathesis (2015: 138–139), cf. Safaitic *ʿty* 'to behave arrogantly'. Alternatively, the Egyptologist Selim Hassan (1949: 156) suggests that Arabic *abū l-Hōl* 'is simply a corruption of an ancient Egyptian name Per-Ḥwl or Bw-Ḥwl meaning the Place of Ḥwl'; others suggest Coptic *balhouba* (Zivie-Coche 2004: 16) or Arabic *ḥourroun* [*sic*] 'falcon' (Wyatt 2007: 162).

[4] https://junipertv.co.uk/portfolio-item/shebas-secret-mummies-the-immortals-of-ancient-sheba

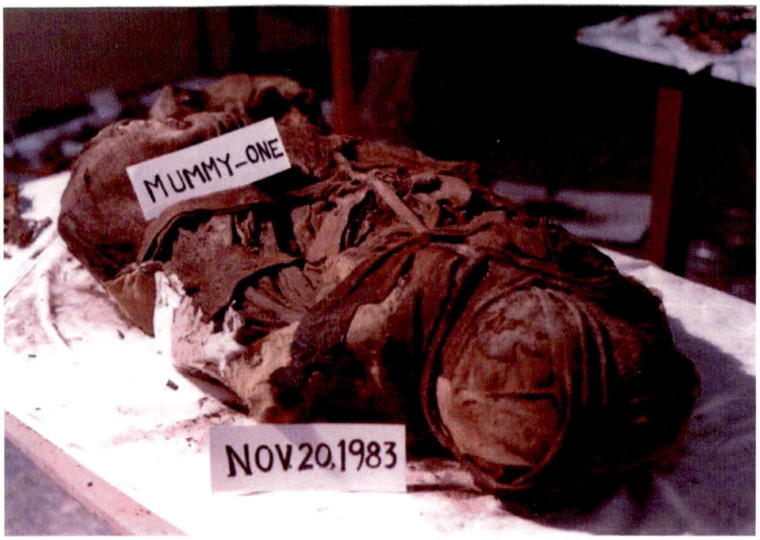

Figure 4. *Mummy One of Šibām al-Ġirās (after Šāyif 1997: 185, pl. 6).*

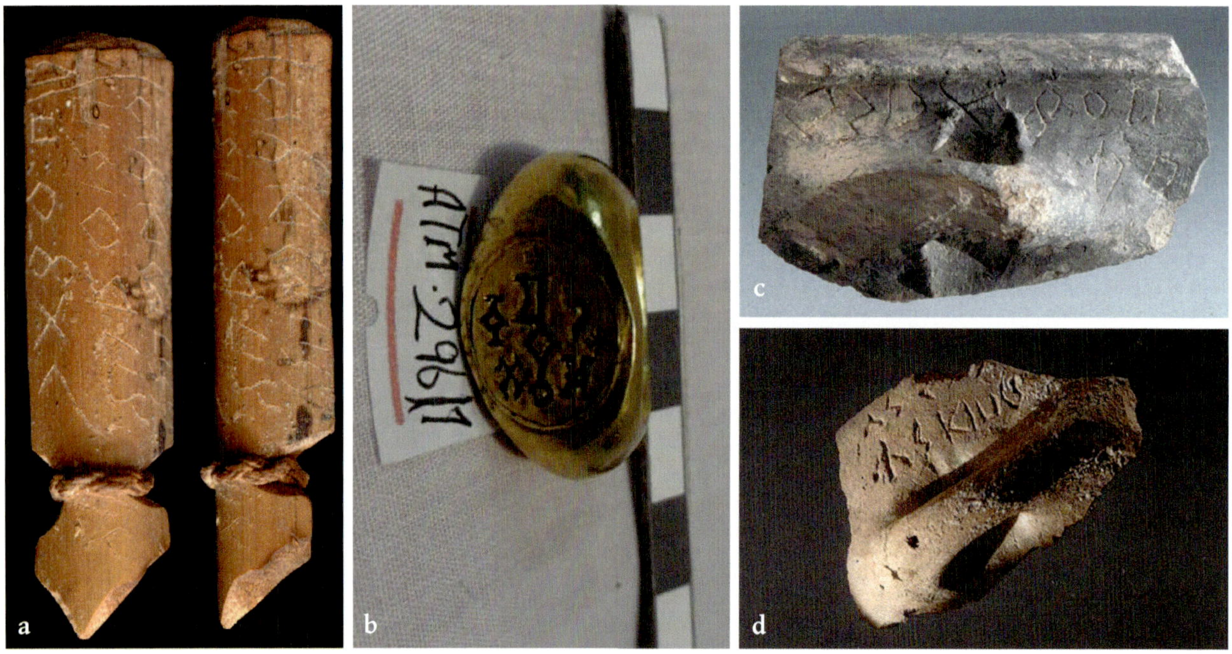

Figure 5. a. *Bāsh 24 on two wooden sticks (DASI, by kind permission GOAM);* **b.** *ATM 296-1 = Wādī Ḍuraʾ 8 on gold ring (by kind permission J. al-Ḥasanī);* **c.** *ostracon (by kind permission I. Gerlach);* **d.** *ostracon (after Gerlach 1999: 123).*

al-Ġirās mummies was undertaken in the laboratories of Beta Analytic Inc. in Florida, dating them to *c.*280 BC (Blakely & Ghaleb 1983: 6; Nūr ad-Dīn 1995: 256, 263), or more securely to the second half of the first millennium BC (Basalama 1998: 253). They cannot be precisely compared to Egyptian mummies, so they are termed rudimentary or primitive (Buckley et al. 2007: 1), but this should not underestimate their scientific value.

Only a single inscription was found with the first mummy, the inscription Bāsh 24 (Fig. 5/a), on a 1.5 × 6.5 cm wooden stick, which reads *Bʿṯtr bn ʿmbʾl* [or: *ʿs^{1}bʾl*] *Hdrn Bns^1* (Bāsalāma 1990: 116, 118, 162; Bāsh 24)

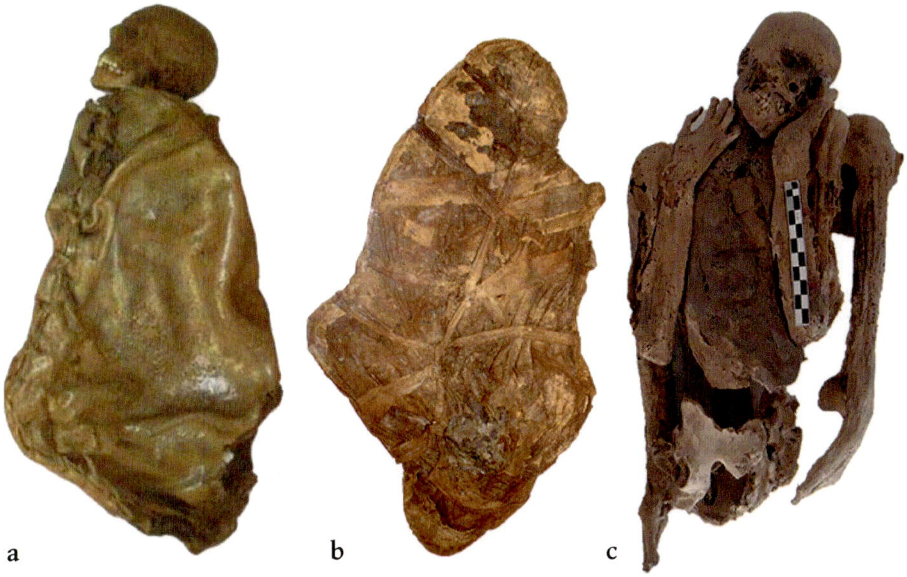

Figure 6. a. and b. *Mummies from Šibām al-Ġirās wrapped in leather, both exhibited in the Museum of Antiquities and Tourism;* **c.** *desiccated mummy from Bayt al-Šāṭir, displayed at the National Centre for Mummies in al-Maḥwīt (photographs A. Abdulmughni, 2024).*

or *Bʿṯtr bn ʿqbʾl ḫdrn* (Maraqten 2014: 137). The text was interpreted by Y.M. ʿAbdullah as a personal name of the deceased. Similarly, a golden pendant was found in the Šuʿūb[5] cemetery inside a child's grave (DAI Šaʿūb 1; Nebes 2002), a gold ring seal inscribed with the deceased's name discovered in Wādī Ḍuraʾ tomb 3 (Wādī Ḍuraʾ 8; Gerlach & Hitgen 2005: 452) (Fig. 5/b), and some 200 inscribed ostraca uncovered in the cemetery of the Awām temple; these were probably attached to a handle or through a vessel neck, by which the name could be affixed to the deceased (inscription 'Gerlach 1999: 123, Abb. 19'; Aw 99 B 62; Gerlach 2002: 57) (Fig. 5/c & d).

In 1996 a French team from the University of Bordeaux conducted excavations that included the analysis in Paris of samples of animal bones and skins from shaft tombs (unpublished report, see Šāyif 2005: 227). The results indicated the presence of linen fabric remnants and tar, as well as microscopic animal remains, straw, and other materials. Textile dating by radiocarbon dating placed them in the seventh century BC. Meanwhile, the results of the Šuʿūb cemetery, discovered in 1999 and which contained several mummies, dated to the first century AD (Gerlach & Vogt 2004; Gerlach & Hitgen 2005) (Fig. 6/a–c).

[5] Šuʿūb is the correct form, as vocalized by al-Maqḥafī, but appears in the literature as Šaʿūb.

The basic stages of mummification can be defined as follows (see al-Safargal 2024: 190–191):

1. Drying the body with lime or salt: by studying the total dissolved solids (TDS) in soil samples from the Šuʿūb burial site, it was observed that the salt index in the soil of the gravesite gradually increases when going downwards. This increase was not in line with the original soil level but rather in the burial container (coffin), which may have several interpretations:
   a. The salt content may be attributed to the layer of gypsum plaster (calcium sulphate) covering the body;
   b. Alternatively, it may be attributed to the original body, subjected to treatments aimed at expelling fluids and drying it out by immersion in salt (al-Marṣad 2023: 25).
2. Treating the body with aromatic substances, oils, fats, and henna (for more on the substances found on the Yemeni mummies, see al-Miḫlāfī 2013: 111). These substances were applied to the entire body to preserve it and prevent decomposition. This is clearly observed on the hair and body of one of the mummies from Šibām al-Ġirās displayed in the Museum of Antiquities and Tourism at Sana'a University.

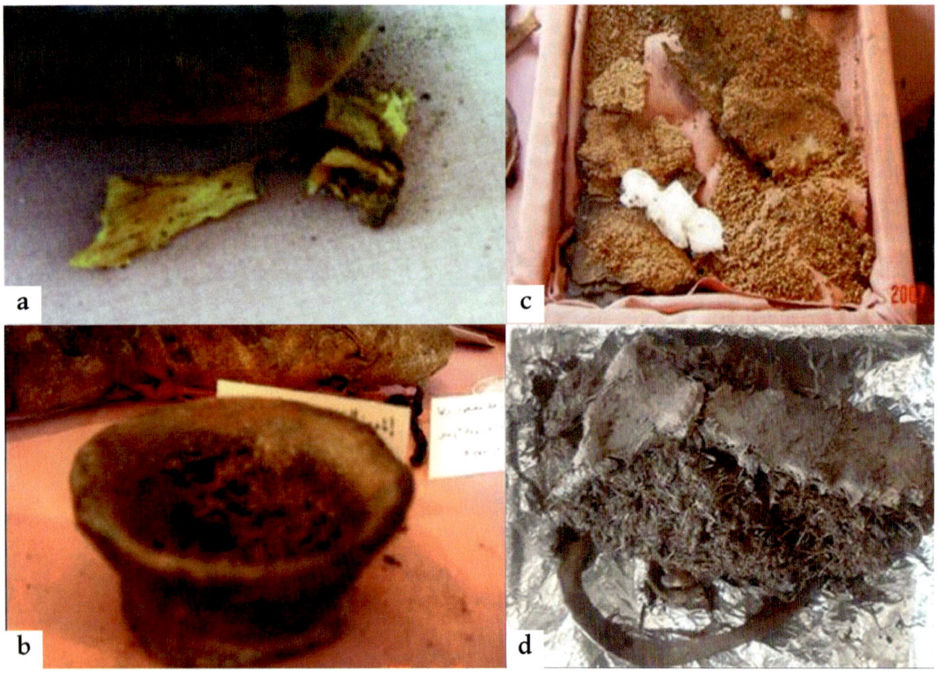

Figure 7. *Materials used in mummification:* **a.** *aloe vera;* **b.** *remnants of chemical substances found beside the mummy;* **c.** *Aerva plant;* **d.** *stuffing of resin-treated straw. (Museum of Antiquities and Tourism at Sana'a University (after Abdulmuġnī, al-ʿAlīyī & Šāyif 2022).*

3. After the incision of the mummy's abdominal cavity and removal of the perishable organs, the cavity was treated with aromatic substances using a piece of linen. The abdominal and thoracic cavities were then refilled with the hygroscopic Aerva plant, which has the ability to absorb moisture, or with resin-treated straw.
4. Use of Aloe vera: perhaps mixed with aromatic substances or with henna to inhibit the action of bacteria and fungi that decompose the body. According to the Islamic sources, the people of Thamud shrouded themselves with skin (*al-ʾanṭāʿ*), and applied aloe vera (*wa-tuḥannaṭ bi-l-ṣabir*). Interestingly, an aloe vera leaf was found with the mummies from Šibām al-Ġirās (Fig. 7/a–d).
5. The body was wrapped with multiple layers of fine linen fabric treated with fats and oils, then covered with Aerva plant or treated straw. The deceased is then dressed in new clothes, as seen in the mummies from Šibām al-Ġirās.
6. The initial bandage layer was topped with a layer of thin-tanned leather, followed by four to five layers of embossed linen fabric, and then a layer of treated straw or Aerva plant (Gerlach & Hitgen 2005).
7. Subsequently, the body was placed in a thick leather sack in a foetal position and the sack secured with leather ropes braided from above and below, with the ends finished in curled patterns (Gerlach & Hitgen 2005).
8. Fumigation: although there are no burial texts about funerary rituals, it is inferred from data and observations that fumigation rituals involving the burning of incense were practised. A censer containing charred materials was found in the graves of Ḥayd Bin ʿAqīl in Šabwa (Šāyif 2002). This is considered a fundamental procedure accompanying the purification of the body and its preparation for mummification. Fumigation may have been extensively conducted within the tombs to purify them and repel vermin, as evidenced by dense soot on the surfaces of some crevices inside the caves and their ceilings.

In her ethno-archaeological study, Amida Šuʿlān (1992: 70–71) documented the burial customs in modern Ḥaḍramawt, particularly in Ḥurayḍa, Šabwa, and Wādī Ḍurā. These included orienting the deceased towards the north-east (qibla) with the body anointed with

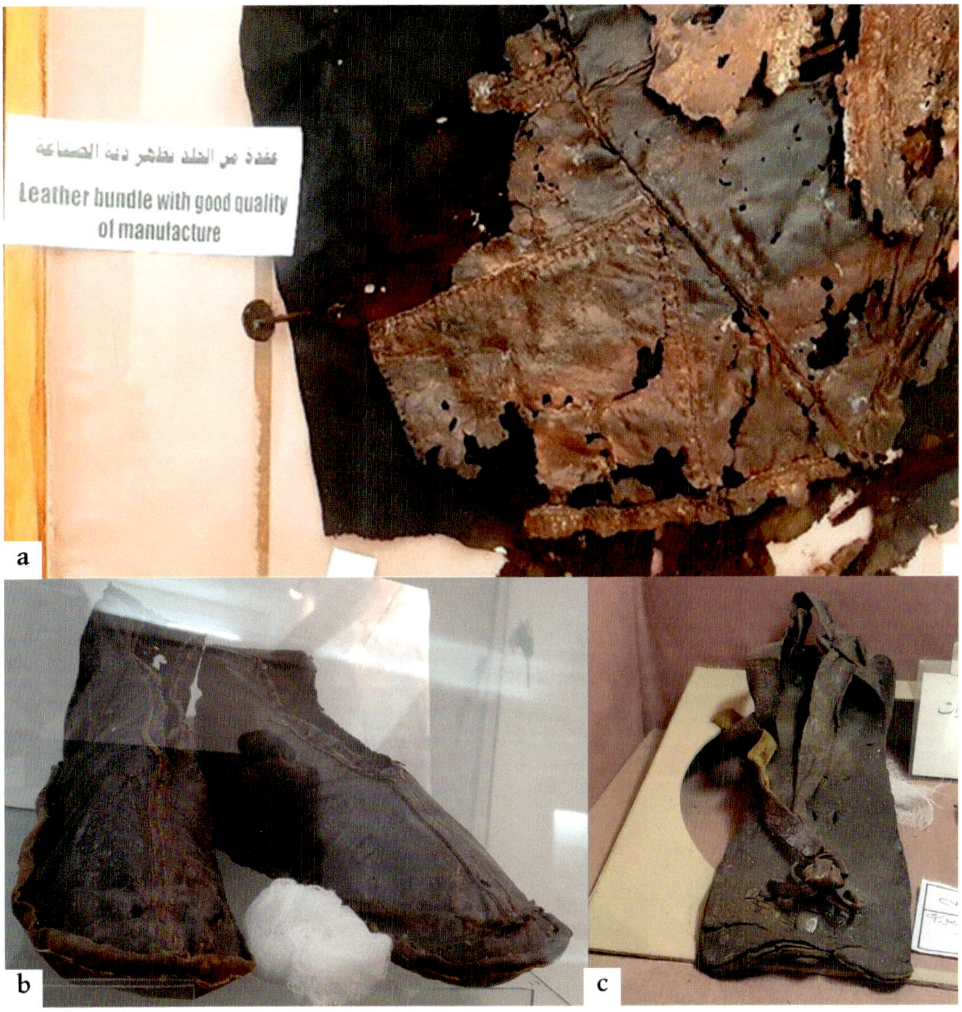

FIGURE 8. **a.** *Remnants of a skin vest with buttons (Museum of Antiquities and Tourism Department at Sana'a University). Funerary shoes:* **b.** *pair worn by the deceased;* **c.** *pair placed beside the deceased (Museum of Antiquities and Tourism Department at Sana'a University) (photographs A. Abdulmughni, 2024).*

sesame oil several times before 'washing' to prevent bone contraction. The body was then fumigated with frankincense and covered with a cloth. Later, the body was placed on a wooden washing platform and washed three to five times with water and *sidr* (jujube). Finally, it was shrouded in cloth, with cotton placed in the ears, eyes, between the fingers, under the armpits, and in excretion orifices. During the final washing of the body, camphor was used instead of acacia. This may show a continuity between the ancient practice and the modern one, and explains the presence of acacia wood with a mummy in the Department of Archaeology and Tourism at Sana'a University. Today, Yemeni women use camphor to repel insects in storage.

Funerary furniture

In 1983 the Egyptian mission, through examination and analysis of the mummies, demonstrated that the bodies were buried wearing new leather garments (mummy no. 4). The legs of the mummy had remnants of dyed leather, indicating that it was wearing leather trousers (Sana'a & Egyptian 1984). Additionally, remnants of a skin vest were found beside one mummy, no. 3), which served as an upper outer garment resembling a jacket with buttons on the upper side. It was finely tailored, and the mummy still wore a meticulously crafted funerary leather shoe measuring 25.5 cm in length, currently displayed in the Museum of Antiquities (Šāyif 1997) (Fig. 8).

After the body was treated, it was dressed in a skin garment, possibly made from ibex or cow (sacred animals) skin for the preservation of the deceased's body. Pirenne recorded observations of carved drawings on the walls of some rock-cut tombs in Ẓafār, the capital of the Himyarites, depicting the head of a bull and another of a serpent (al-Garw 1989: 143–193). This suggests that the idea of preserving the body in ancient Yemen was not only for physical preservation but also aimed to protect the deceased from evil spirits encountered during the journey to the afterlife. One might wonder if there were any specific funerary rituals related to mummification in Ancient South Arabia.

Tombs

Ancient tombs varied in form and materials used in their construction. They could be a pit dug into the ground, a sepulchral building above the ground surface or hewn into the rock (Šāyif 2005). This diversity can be attributed to the varied terrain, which shaped these burial practices. Additionally, successive historical periods had a major impact on enriching the cognitive perspective and diversifying the worldview and beliefs in ancient Yemen (al-Ḥusaynī 2013: 21). For example, cave tombs in the mountains exhibited a wide variety of forms, which can be classified as follows:

1. Hanging cave burials: natural rocky caves on the faces of nearby rocky slopes or elevated ground, often containing irregular natural cavities.
2. Rock shelters: natural rock shelters located in areas that are difficult to access but somewhat protected from rain.
3. Carved rock tombs: also known as rock architecture, they were carved by humans into the faces of cliffs near cities and settlements established on the slopes of mountains. These tombs consist of multiple chambers and niches, clearly visible in the tombs of the Šibām al-Ġirās mountains (al-Ḥusaynī 2013: 43). This was noted by Wahb b. Munabbih, in his account on the legendry king Šaddād, '... then Šaddād son of ʿĀd died after living for five hundred years, and a cave was dug for him in Mount ŠMĀM [Šibām?], and he was buried in it, with all his wealth' (Wahb 1979: 74).

These tombs have provided evidence of the practice of mummification dating back to the second half of the first millennium BC. However, deliberate acts of excavation and destruction by tomb raiders have disrupted its scientific study (al-Ḥusaynī 2013: 43). It is worth noting that there are rock tombs discovered in the Quhāl, Kawkabān, Nāʿiṭ, and Bayt al-ʾAḥraq mountains where inscriptions were found indicating the name of the tomb's owner buried there (al-Garw 1989: 143–193). This corresponds with al-Hamdānī's description of the ancient Yemeni kings, and their treasures.

Funerary temples

Necropolises were found within the South Arabian temples. Considering the nature of the lands where these tombs were built, in mountainous areas with rocky geological formations, we find cave tombs and rock-cut tombs separated from the secular world. However, this is not always the case as, for example, the royal tombs of Šabwa were found within the walls to the east of the city, which is among the valley cities (Pirenne 1978). Additionally, tombs were constructed near buildings and residential areas, close to the temples. Many graveyards were within the temples, especially the large *extra muros* temples, such as the Temple of Awām in Maʾrib (Roux 1998: 170), the temple *Wdm ḏ-Ms¹mʿm* in the Qaṭūṭa Valley in Radāʿ, al-Bayḍāʾ, and al-Masāgid Temple in al-Gūba; they functioned not only as funerary temples but also as centres of pilgrimage.

The site of Šukaʿ near al-Ḍāliʿ provides a similar example to what was found in many areas. It consists of a temple dedicated to the deity *yʾs¹r*, attached to stone cist graves (Fig. 9). These tombs provide a unique style of grave furnishings, composed of marble and limestone votive offerings in the form of human limbs, such as hands, legs, feet, and breasts (Roux 1998; see also Vogt 2002). Perhaps these pieces were intended to replace actual sacrifices at the temple.

The current condition of mummies in the museums

Due to capacity limitations and the lack of expertise, especially in the current tragic situation in Yemen

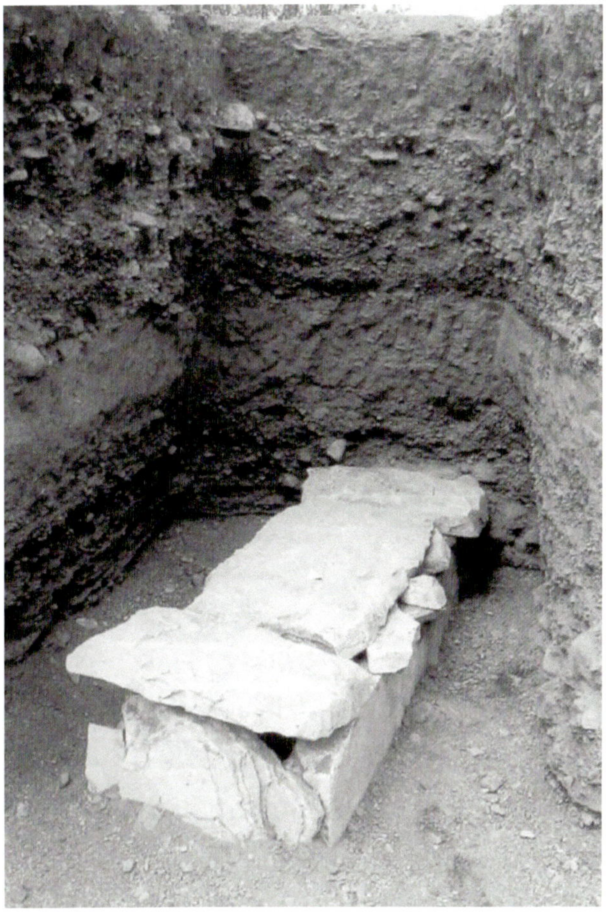

Figure 9. *Stone cist grave (after Gerlach & Vogt 2002: 211).*

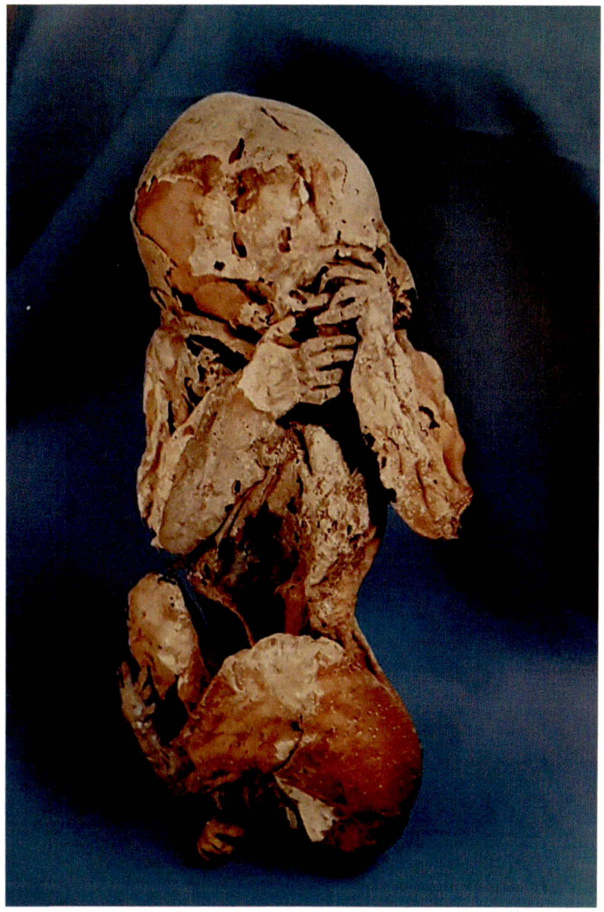

Figure 10. *Mummy of an infant (by kind permission A. al-Ghabri, shared on Facebook, 3 April 2019).*

(al-Siyani 2019; Al-Ḥājj 2024), museums face significant challenges in preserving cultural and archaeological artefacts. This is especially true for mummies, which suffer from various forms of damage resulting from poor display and improper storage, amid a complete absence of regular maintenance or treatment. These facilities are not suitable for preserving and storing such rare cultural artefacts. The National Museum houses around ten mummies, including a unique mummy of an infant (Fig. 10).

Similarly, the Museum of Antiquities and Tourism Department at the University of Sana'a houses six mummies and remnants of others, while the Regional Mummy Museum in al-Ṭawīla, al-Maḥwīt Governorate, possesses one complete naturally preserved 'mummy' (Ṣāliḥ 2004) (Fig. 11) and several fragmentary ones stored in iron boxes (Abdulmuġnī, al-ʿAlīyī & Šāyif 2022) (Fig. 11). These mummies are subjected to inadequate display and storage conditions. They require regular maintenance, which is difficult in the absence of local experts in organic restoration.

Physicochemical deterioration

Mummies are exposed to climatic changes, fluctuations in humidity, sudden temperature increases, and the direct impact of ultraviolet sunlight, which can cause thermal degradation, tissue delamination, and the destruction of resinous materials on the mummies. These damage various linen shroud tissues,

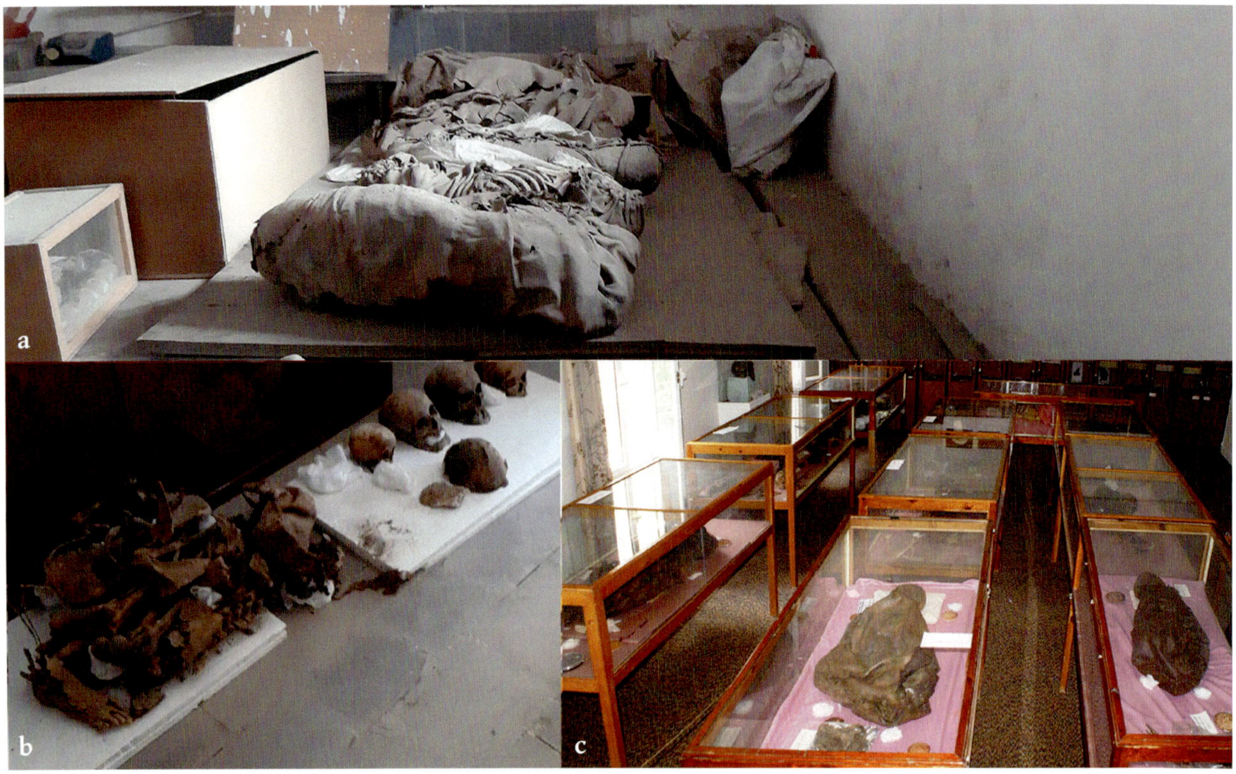

Figure 11. *The condition of the mummies:* **a.** *National Museum in Sana'a.* **b.** *Regional Mummy Museum in Al-Maḥwīt;* **c.** *Museum of Antiquities and Tourism Department at the University of Sana'a (photographs A. Abdulmughni, 2024).*

experiencing what is known as environmental shock. Gases such as sulphur dioxide, nitrogen oxides, ozone, carbon monoxide, ammonia, and hydrogen sulphide not only affect the mummies' wrappings, but also penetrate the mummy's body and internal stuffing, resulting in a total weakening and deterioration of the mummy. Additionally, the impact of suspended solid particles and airborne dust further exacerbates the destructive effects on the mummies.

Biological deterioration[6]

Biological deterioration factors are associated with the biological activity of insects and micro-organisms and the extent of their impact on mummies, as they produce enzymes that digest organic matter (Fig. 12). Fungi represent a significant threat to organic archaeological materials in general and mummies in particular. Not only for the mummies, but also for individuals, fungi can be dangerous as they pose a major health hazard and cause zoonotic superficial infections. The total number of fungi contaminating the indoor air of the mummy hall in the Yemeni museums was found to be 512 colonies/three Petri dishes, belonging to six genera, representing twelve fungal species. The most frequent fungi were Aspergillus (35.5%) and Cladosporium (21.04%), including two species, *A. niger* (16.7%) and *C. herbarum* (8.9%). Forty-seven fungal isolates were obtained from selected samples of Yemeni mummies, with detailed results for the Department of Archaeology and Tourism Museum at Sana'a University and the National Museum (al-Zaqri 2013: 104).

[6] This section summarizes the study by al-Zaqri (2013).

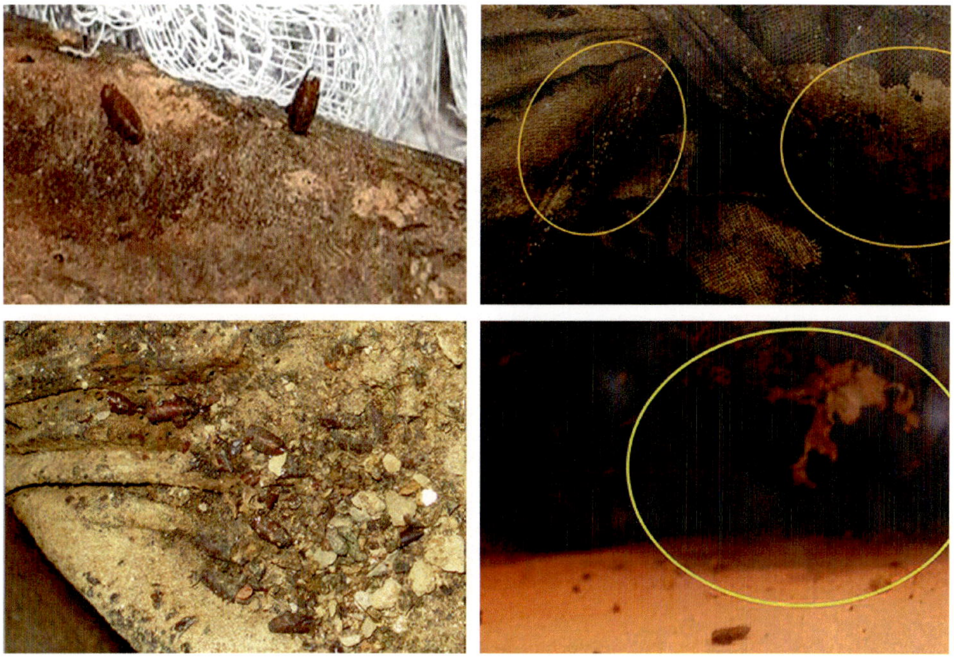

FIGURE 12. *Damage to the mummies includes the biological activity of insects, and tears in the linen tissues and in the skin of the mummies.*

1. Fungi extracted from samples of mummies displayed in the Museum of the Department of Archaeology and Tourism at Sana'a University

Six fungi species belonging to four genera of mummified specimens from the Department of Antiquities were isolated using the conventional methods of swabbing and streaking on potato dextrose agar (Naji et al. 2014: 2). The total number of fungi in all samples was thirty. *Penicillium* was the most common fungus among the isolated mummified specimens, comprising 54.8% of the total count, while the fungus *P. citrinum* was the most isolated fungi from mummies, accounting for 29% of the total fungal count, followed by Corylophilum fungus at 16.1%. This was followed by Aspergillus, represented by two species, *A. niger* at 22.5% and *A. fumigatus* at 6.4% (al-Zaqri 2013: 104).

2. Fungi extracted from samples of mummies preserved in the National Museum in Sana'a

Six species belonging to four genera of mummified specimens from the Department of Antiquities were isolated on potato dextrose agar medium. The total number of fungi in all thirty samples was thirty. Sixteen species belonging to ten genera of mummified specimens from the National Museum were isolated on potato dextrose agar medium. The total number of fungi in all samples was forty-seven, with Aspergillus being the most common isolated from the surfaces of mummies, comprising 48.9% of the total number of samples taken from mummies. The percentage of *A. niger* fungi was the highest among the isolated species from mummified samples, representing 25.5% of the total fungi count. Additionally, *A. flavus* was found in only one sample, representing 10.63%, as well as *A. fumigatus*, *A. candidus*, and *A. ustus* isolated from one sample each at a percentage of 4.25% each. Cladosporium fungus was isolated from three samples, accounting for 14.89% of the total sample count, in addition to filamentous fungi extracted from four samples at a percentage of 8.51% (Naji et al. 2014). The results showed that there are four major enzymes produced by the fungal strains collected, playing a significant role in the deterioration of organic artefacts, especially mummies, namely: cellulase, pectinase, chitinase, and protease (al-Zaqri 2013: 153). As for bacteria and Actinomycetes, they are organisms that grow on the surfaces of mummies and cause severe damage to them. They appear as tears in the linen tissues preserving the mummies and the skin, or in the form of holes, thus destroying the tissue structure of the mummy as a food source (see Fig. 12).

Recommendations

The practice of mummification in ancient Yemen, while significant, appears to be an isolated phenomenon. Further interdisciplinary research and discoveries are necessary to contextualize these practices within the larger cultural frameworks. Given the importance of preserving Yemen's mummies currently in museum collections or storage elsewhere and the challenges facing such preservation in Yemen today, several recommendations are in order.

1. Enhance cooperation between Yemen and international organizations and institutions concerned with the protection of cultural heritage to provide financial, technical, and training support.
2. Secure archaeological sites through local councils in all regions of Yemen, and provide monitoring and protection for tombs containing mummies to minimize tampering and theft.
3. Raise public awareness about the importance of cultural heritage, especially Yemeni mummies, and promote museum outreach, spreading awareness among local communities and residents through educational campaigns, lectures, and workshops.
4. Train human resources workers in the fields of maintenance and restoration to enhance proficiency and technical knowledge in this area.
5. Provide modern technologies and devices, such as X-ray imaging and DNA analysis, for studying and documenting Yemeni mummies.
6. Activate legislation and laws related to the protection of cultural heritage, imposing deterrent penalties on theft operations or the trafficking of artefacts and contents of rock-cut tombs.
7. Foster collaboration between academic institutions and local and international researchers studying Yemeni mummies, exchanging knowledge, experience, and conducting joint research.
8. Utilize international cooperation programmes in preserving and protecting Yemeni mummies and cultural heritage. The Yemeni government can collaborate with organizations such as UNESCO, International Council on Monuments and Sites (ICOMOS), museums, and others to obtain financial and technical support and enhance local expertise.

Acknowledgements

We would like to thank Dr Amida Sholan for her guidance in preparing this report, and Dr Daniel Varisco for proofreading the English. We also extend our thanks to Dr Joann Fletcher and Dr Stephen Buckley of the University of York Mummy Research Group for kindly providing photographs and valuable information that contributed to this study.

Sigla

al-ʿAdi 4/4	cited in al-Ḥājj 2015.
ATM	ʿAtaq Museum.
Aw	Inscription from the cemetery of the Awām temple, published in Gerlach 2002.
Bāsh	Inscription published in Bāsalāma 1990.
CIH	*Corpus inscriptionum semiticarum.* iv. *Inscriptiones himyariticas et sabaeas continens.* Paris: 1889–1932.
DAI Šaʿūb	Inscription published in Nebes 2002.
DASI	Digital Archive for the Study of pre-Islamic Arabic Inscriptions, https://dasi.cnr.it/
MIbb	Museum of Ibb.
MṢM	Inscription in Ṣanʿāʾ Military Museum.
RES	*Répertoire d'épigraphie sémitique.* v–viii. Paris: Imprimerie Nationale, 1928–1968.
Ry	Inscription published in Ryckmans 1954.
UAM	Aden University Museum.
X.BSB	Inscription published in Stein 2010.
Wādī Ḍuraʾ	Inscription published in Breton 1993.

References

ʿAbdullah Y.M. 1990. *Awrāq fī tārīḫ al-Yaman wa-l-ʾāṯār.* (Second edition). Beirut: Dār al-fikr al-muʿāṣir.

Abdulmuġnī A.I. 2023. *al-nuzūl al-maydānī li-l-markaz al-waṭanī li-l-mūmyāwāt, bi-mudīrīyat al-Ṭawīla — al-Maḥwīt* (Visit to the National Centre for Mummies in Tawilah – Al Mahwit Governorate). *ʾĀzāl* 5: 151–162.

Abdulmuġnī A., al-ʿAlīyī M. & Šāyif ʿA. 2022. Mašrūʿ taʾhīl wa-taṭwīr matḥaf wa-maʿmal al-tarmīm wa-l-ṣiyāna bi-qism al-ʾāṯār wa-l-siyāḥa (Project of rehabilitation and development of the museum and the restoration and maintenance laboratory in the Department of Antiquities and Tourism). Sana'a University. [Unpublished.]

Anon. 2012. Farīq ʾaṯrī yakšif maqbara ṣaḫrīya li-l-mūmyāwāt fī wadī Ẓahr. *Al-Thawra* 17242: 17.

Arabnews. 2023. Anger in Yemen after '2,000-year-old' mummy found in trash. Available at https://arab.news/wrd8g

Avanzini A. 2016. *By land and by sea. A history of South Arabia before Islam recounted from the inscriptions.* (Arabia Antica, 10). Rome: L'Erma di Bretschneider.

Bāsalāma M.ʿA. 1990. *Šibām al-Ġirās.* Sana'a: Muʾssasat al-ʿAfīf al-ṯaqāfīya.

Basalama M. 1998. Die Mumien von Shibâm al-Ghirâs. Pages 252–253 in W. Seipel (ed.), *Jemen. Kunst und Archäologie im Land der Königin von Sabaʾ. Ausstellungskatalog des Kunsthistorischen Museums.* Vienna: Kunsthistorisches Museum.

Beeston A.F.L. 1984. Further remarks on the Zayd-ʾil sarcophagus text. *Proceedings of the Seminar for Arabian Studies* 14: 100–102.

Blakely J. & Ghaleb A. 1983. Sana'a 2300 year old mummies discovered. *News Letter*, American School of Oriental Research, Jordan: 6–8.

Breton J-F. 1993. Les objets de luxe. Pages 23–41 in J-F. Breton & M.ʿA. Bāfaqīh, *Trésors du Wādī Duraʾ (République du Yémen). Fouilles franco-yémenites de la nécropole de Hajar am-Dhaybiyya.* Paris: Librairie orientaliste Paul Geuthner.

Buckley S.A., Fletcher J., Al-Thour K., Basalama M. & Brothwell D.R. 2007. A preliminary study on the materials employed in ancient Yemeni mummification and burial practices (summary). *Proceedings of the Seminar for Arabian Studies* 37: 37–41.

Faris N.A. 1938. *The Antiquities of South Arabia being a translation from the Arabic.* Princeton: Princeton University Press.

al-Garw ʾA. 1989. al-madāfin al-yamanīya al-qadīma maṣdar hām li-dirāsat tārīḫ al-yaman al-qadīm (The old Yemeni cemeteries as a source for studying ancient Yemen history). *Majallat dirāsāt yamanīya*: 143–193.

Gerlach I. 2002. Der Friedhof des Awam-Tempels in Marib. Berichte der Ausgrabungen von 1997 bis 2001. Pages 41–58 in DAI Ṣanʿāʾ (ed.), *Archäologische Berichte aus dem Yemen.* (ABADY). Mainz am Rhein: Philipp von Zabern.

Gerlach I. & Hitgen H. 2005. *ʿādāt* al-dafn fī al-fatra al-Ḥimyarīya al-mubakkira, ḥafriyyat maqbirat *Šuʿūb* (Ṣanʿāʾ) (Burial traditions during the Early Himyarite period: Shu'ub cemetery excavation (Sana'a)). Pages 169–171 in Bāṣurra, ṢʿA. (ed.), *Ṣanʿāʾ al-ḥaḍāra wa-l-tārīḫ* (Sana'a. History and cultural heritage). *Proceedings of the fifth International Conference on Yemeni civilization.* Sana'a: [n.p.]

Gerlach I. & Vogt B. 2004. Šuʿūb: ḥafrīya ṭāriʾa fī maqbara ḥimyarīya qadīma bi-Ṣanʿāʾ (Shu'ub: Rescue excavation in an ancient Himyaritic cemetery in Sana'a). *al-Musnad* 2, GOAM, Sana'a: 64–68. [A brief translation of Vogt & Gerlach 2002, originally published in German].

Glanzman W.D. 2005. Intentionally mummified remains of the pre-Islamic period in South Arabia. *Canadian Association for Physical Anthropology Newsletter* 1: 2–7.

Al-Ḥājj M. 2015. *Nuqūš qatabāniyya min Hağar al-ʿĀḏī (Maryama qadīman). Dirāsa fī dalālāti-hā al-luġawiyya wa-l-dīniyya al-taʾriḫiyya.* (Series of Refereed Studies, 4). Riyadh: King Saud University.

Al-Ḥājj M. b. ʿAlī. 2024. *wāqiʿ al-turāṯ al-ṯaqāfī al-ʾaṯrī fī muḥāfaḍat Naʾrib - al-Yaman* (The reality of archaeological cultural heritage in Marib Governorate – Yemen). Cairo: Dār al-kutub al-Yamanīya.

Al-Hamdānī Abū Muḥammad al-Ḥasan/ed. M.ʿA.A. al-Ḥawālī. 2004. *al-Iklīl.* viii. Sana'a: Wizārat al-ṯaqāfa wa-l-siyāḥa.

Hassan S. 1949. *The sphinx: Its history in the light of recent excavations.* Cairo: Government Press.

Hitgen H. 1998. The 1997 excavations of the German Institute of Archaeology at the cemetery of Awām in Marib. *Proceedings of the Seminar for Arabian Studies* 28: 117–124.

al-Ḥusaynī Ṣ. 2013. *ṭuruq al-dafn wa-l-ʾaṯāṯ al-janāʾizī fī maqābir mawqiʿ al-Ḥuṣama, Šuqra* (Burial methods and grave goods in Al-Hosamah Site – Shoqrah). Riyadh: al-Jamʿīya al-saʿūdīya li-l-dirāsāt al-ʾaṯarīya.

al-Ḥusaynī Ṣ., ʿAli ʿI. & Rājiḥ M. 2002. taqrīr ʿan ziyārat al-biʿṯa al-tilfizyūnīya al-tābiʿa li-jāmiʿat Ṣanaʿāʾ wa-Yōrk al-barīṭānīya wa-jamʿiyyat ʾiʿlāmīyiy al-bīʾah wa-al-tanmiya li-baʿḍ al-muḥāfaḍāt (Report on the visit of the TV mission affiliated with Sana'a University, the British University of York, and the Association of Environmental and Development Media, to some governorates). [Unpublished.]

Littmann E. & Höfner M. 1962. *Wörterbuch der Tigrē-Sprache: Tigrē-Deutsch-English*. (Akademie der Wissenschaften und der Literatur in Mainz. Veröffentlichungen der Orientalischen Kommission, xi). Wiesbaden: Franz Steiner.

Mahoney D. 2021. The formation of South Arabian identity in *al-Iklīl* of al-Hamdānī. Pages 137–156 in W. Pohl & D. Mahoney (eds), *Historiography and identity, IV: Writing history across medieval Eurasia*. (CELAMA 30). Turnhout: Brepols.

Mancarella C. 2016. The Awām Temple cemetery in Marib (Maʾrib) revisited. *Proceedings of the Seminar for Arabian Studies* 46: 179–194.

Mancarella C. 2018. Pre-Islamic South Arabian burial rites in the context of social change. MA thesis, Freie Universität Berlin, Fachbereich Geschichts- und Kulturwissenschaften.

Maraqten M. 2014. *Altsüdarabische Texte auf Holzstäbchen: epigraphische und kulturhistorische Untersuchungen*. Beirut: Orient-Institut.

Al-Marṣad I.A. 2023. Dirāsa tajrībīya li-taqwiyat al-ʿiẓām al-ʾaṯarīya al-mustaẖrajah min al-bīʾāt al-raṭiba, dirāsa ḥālah min mawāqiʿ muẖtārah min al-Yaman (Šuʿūb) – al-ʾUrdun (Nāṭifa). (An experimental study on strengthening archaeological bones excavated from wet environments: A case study from selected sites in Yemen (Shu'ub) and Jordan (Natifa)). MA thesis, Department of Heritage Resources Conservation and Management, Faculty of Archaeology and Anthropology, Yarmouk University. [Unpublished.]

al-Miẖlāfī ʿĀ.ʾA.ʾI. 2013. al-Ṭibb fī al-Yaman al-qadīm (Medicine in ancient Yemen). *The Gulf Journal for History and Archaeology* 8: 93–130.

Müller W.W. 1988. Altsüdarabische und frühnordarabische Grab-, Sarkophag-, Votiv- und Bauinschriften. Pages 621–640 in C. Butterweck (ed.), *Grab-, Sarg-, Votiv- und Bauinschriften. Religiöse Texte*. 4. Otto Kaiser (ed.), *Texte aus der Umwelt des Alten Testaments*. 2. Gütersloh: Gütersloher Verlagshaus Gerd Mohn.

Naji K.M., Abdulla Q.Y.M., Al-Zaqri A.Q.M. & Alghalibi S.M. 2014. Evaluating the biodeterioration enzymatic activities of fungal contamination isolated from some ancient Yemeni mummies preserved in the national museum. *Biochemistry Research International*: 1–9. doi: https://doi.org/10.1155/2014/481508 (Accessed 30/1/2025.)

Nebes N. 2002. Ein beschrifteter Goldanhänger aus dem Friedhof von Šaʿūb. *Archäologische Berichte aus dem Yemen* 9: 227–231.

NewsBriefs. 1984. Mummified bodies found in North Yemen. *Archaeology* 37: 83.

Nūr ad-Dīn ʾA-Ḥ. 1985. mūmyāwāt Šibām al-Ġirās, kašf ʾaṯarī muṯīr" (Mummies of Šibām al-Ġirās, an interesting archaeological discovery). Pages 178–191 in ʾA-Ḥ. Nūr ad-Dīn, *Muqaddima fī al-ʾāṯār al-Yamanīya* (Introduction to Yemeni archaeology). Sana'a: Sana'a University Press.

Nūr ad-Dīn ʾA-Ḥ. 1995. mūmyāʾ Šibām al-Ġirās – muḥāfaẓat Ṣanʿāʾ (Mummy from Šibām al-Ġirās in Sana'a). *al-Iklīl* 23: 255–263. [In Arabic & English]. https://archive.alsharekh.org/Articles/294/20751/473075

Phillips W. 1955. *Qataban and Sheba. Exploring ancient kingdoms on the biblical spice routes of Arabia*. London: Victor Gollancz Ltd.

Pirenne J. 1978. allaḏī taʿallamnāh min ṯalāṯat mawāsim ḥafrīyāt fī Šabwa ʿāṣimat Ḥaḍramawt al-qadīma (What we learned from three seasons of excavations in Shabwa, the capital of ancient Hadramawt). *Raydan* 1: 73–88.

Robin Ch.J. 2021. The Judaism of the ancient kingdom of Ḥimyar in Arabia: A discreet conversion. Pages 165–270 in G. McDowell, R. Naiweld, D. Stökl & B. Ezra (eds), *Diversity and Rabbinization: Jewish texts and societies between 400 and 1,000 CE*. (Cambridge Semitic Languages and Cultures). Cambridge: Openbook.

Roux J-C. 1998. La diversité des tombes. Pages 169–171 in Ch.J. Robin & B. Vogt (eds), *Yémen, au pays de la reine de Saba', Catalogue d'exposition, Institut du Monde arabe, 25 octobre 1997 au 28 février 1998*. Paris: Institut du Monde arabe/Flammarion.

Ryckmans G. 1954. Inscriptions sud-arabes. Onzième série. *Le Muséon* 67: 99–119.

Saba. 2021. al-kašf *ʿan ʾaʿmāl* tadmīr li-l-mawāqiʿ al-tārīḫīya bi-*ʾibb* (Revealing acts of destruction of historical sites in the province of Ibb). *Saba News Agency*, 31 January. Available at www.saba.ye/ar/news3126701.htm

al-Safargal T. 2024. al-Ṭibb wa-l-taḥnīṭ ʿind al-Yamaniyīn al-qudamāʾ - dirāsa li-l-šawāhid al-ʾaṯarīya (Medicine and mummification of the ancient Yemenis: A study of archaeological evidence). PhD thesis, University of Sana'a. [Unpublished.]

al-Saʿīd S.F. 2003. *al-ʿalāqāt al-ḥaḍārīya bayn al-Jazīra al-ʿArabīya wa-Miṣr fī ḍawʾ al-nuqūš al-ʿarabīya al-qadīma* (The cultural relations between the Arabian Peninsula and Egypt in light of ancient Arabian Inscriptions). Riyadh: King Fahad National Library.

Ṣāliḥ A.Ṣ. 2004. mūmyāʾ min jabal Milḥān (Mummy from Mount Milḥān). *al-Musnad* 2, GOAM, Sana'a: 22–27.

al-Šammāʿ ʿĀ. (ed.). 2011. Māfyā al-ʾāṯār tutājir bi-huwīyatinā (The antiquities mafia trades in our identity). *al-Jumhūrīya* 15124: 12–13.

Sana'a & Egyptian. 1984. barnāmaj al-taʿāwun al-muštarak bayn jāmiʿat ṣanʿāʾ wa-hayʾat al-ʾāṯār al-miṣrīya (The joint cooperation program between the University of Sana'a and the Egyptian Antiquities Authority). *Dirāsāt yamanīya* 16: 105–199.

Šāyif ʿA. 1994. taqrīr ʿan mūmyāwāt Ṣayḥ fī al-Maḥwīt (Report on the mummies of Ṣayḥ in Al-Mahwit Governorate). Available on request from authors of present article. [Unpublished.]

Šāyif ʿA. 1997. Al-ʾAnṯurūbūlūjīyā aṭ-ṭabīʿīya wa-ʾAhammyyatihā li-ʿilm al-ʾāṯār, dirāsa taṭbīqīya (Physical anthropology and its importance to archaeology: An applied study). MA thesis, Department of Archaeology, University of Khartoum. [Unpublished.]

Šāyif ʿA. 2002. Al-dalālāt aṯ-ṯaqāfīya wa-l-ḥaḍārīya li-l-madāfin fī janūb al-jazīra ḫilāl al-ʾalf al-ʾawwal B.C dirāsa taṭbīqīya li-madāfin Ḥayd bin ʿAqīl (Cultural and civilizational significance of tombs in the south of the Peninsula during the first millennium BC: An applied study of the tombs of Hayd bin Aqeel). PhD thesis, University of Khartoum. [Unpublished.]

Šāyif ʿA. 2005. al-taḥnīṭ fī al-Yaman al-qadīm (Mummification in ancient Yemen). Pages 169–171 in ṢʿA Bāṣurra (ed.), *Ṣanʿāʾ al-ḥāḍāra wa-l-tārīḫ, Proceedings of the fifth International Conference on Yemeni civilization.* Sana'a: [n.p.]

Šāyif ʿA. 2023. al-ḥafrīya al-ʾinqāḏīya li-mūmyāwāt maqbarat al-Ḥayd Wādī Ẓahr (Salvage excavation of the mummies in al-Ḥayd Cemetery, Wadi Zahr). *Raydan* 10: 218–246.

Šāyif ʿA., al-Sayyānī M. & Sunnah M. 2022. Mūmyāwāt maqbarat wādī mōṯ - mudīriyyat Juban (Mummies from the cemetery of Wadi Moth, Juban District). *Raydan* 9: 127–151.

al-Siyani M.A. 2019. Risks of war on Yemeni cultural heritage. Pages 259–264 in J-F. Breton & F. Villeneuve (eds), *La guerre en Arabie antique. Actes des 22ème Rencontres sabéennes, Paris, 21–23 juin 2018.* (CEFAS 2019). Paris: Geuthner.

Stein P. 2010. *Die altsüdarabischen Minuskelinschriften auf Holzstäbchen aus der Bayerischen Staatsbibliothek in München.* i. *Die Inschriften der mittel- und spätsabäischen Periode.* Berlin/Tübingen: Wasmuth.

Stein P. & Weninger S. 2024. Aus altsüdarabischer Korrespondenz: Wie man einem Grabräuber auf die Schliche kommt. *Zeitschrift der Deutschen Morgenländischen Gesellschaft* 174: 77–96.

Šuʿlān ʿA. 1992. ʿĀdāt al-dafn fī ḥaḍramawt, dirāsa ʾiṯnū-ʾaṯarīya (Burial customs in Hadhramaut: An ethnoarchaeological study). MA thesis, Yarmouk University. [Unpublished.]

Vogt B. 2002. Death and funerary practices. Pages 180–209 in StJ. Simpson (ed.), *Queen of Sheba. Treasures from ancient Yemen.* London: British Museum Press.

Vogt B. & de Maigret A. 1999. Tod und Jenseits im antiken Südarabien. Pages 170–182 in W. Seipel (ed.), *Jemen. Kunst und Archäologie im Land der Königin von Saba 3.* Vienna: Kunsthistorisches Museum.

Vogt B. & Gerlach I. 2002. Bericht über die Notgrabungen im Friedhof von Shaʿūb (Sanaʿa). Pages 185–204 in DAI Ṣanʿāʾ (ed.), *Archäologische Berichte aus dem Yemen* (ABADY). Mainz am Rhein: Philipp von Zabern.

Wahb b. Munabbih. 1979. *Kitāb al-tījān fī mulūk Ḥimyar.* (Second edition). Ṣanʿāʿ.

Wyatt N. 2007. *Word of tree and whisper of stone and other papers on Ugaritian thought.* Piscataway, NJ: Gorgias Press.

al-Zaqri A.Q.M. 2013. al-talawwuṯ al-fiṭrī li-l-mutḥaf al-waṭanī wa-maktabāt al-maḫṭūṭāt al-tārīḫīya fī ṣanʿāʾ wa-ʾanšiṭat al-taḥallul al-ḥayawī lahā (Mycological contamination in the National

Museum and Manuscript Libraries in Sana'a City and their biodeterioration activity). MA thesis, Sana'a University. [Unpublished.]

Zivie-Coche C. 2004. *Sphinx: history of a monument*. Trans. from the French by D. Lorton. Ithaca, NY/London: Cornell University Press.

Authors' addresses

Mohammed A. Atbuosh, Independent researcher, International Black Sea University, 2 David Agmashenebeli Alley 13th km., Tbilisi 0131, Georgia.
e-mail m@atbuosh.com

Amgad E.M. Abdulmughni, Restoration and Conservation of Antiquities, Sana'a University, Western Ring Road, Sana'a 1247, Yemen.
e-mail amgadabdulmughni@su.edu.ye

Proceedings of the Seminar for Arabian Studies 54 (2025): 49–56

The ‘cupola’ of the Ṣanʿāʾ cathedral: it still exists

Werner Daum

Summary

Abraha’s cathedral in Ṣanʿāʾ was the predecessor of the Great Mosque. When the church was demolished in the mid-eighth century AD, much of its material (columns, capitals, beams, painted ceilings) was reused for the mosque. These elements have been known and recognized for quite a while. To them, we must now add a recent discovery: the alabaster ‘cupola’, which al-Azraqī describes as the great wonder of the church. However, for technical and Byzantine architectural and historical reasons, the church’s *qubbah* cannot have been ‘one’ cupola. Only an ensemble of small dome-like skylights inset with alabaster plaques is imaginable. From the point of view of style and size, these are clearly the five small domes near the Great Mosque’s mihrab. The mosque’s recent restoration by the Istituto Veneto per i Beni Culturali has exposed the alabaster plaques of these cupolas; they can be dated to the sixth century AD. They are not just another element of spolia from the church but had been what could be termed its spiritual heart, transposed with the same meaning.

Keywords: Ṣanʿāʾ cathedral, cupola, Great Mosque, Byzantine, alabaster plaques

A brief outline of the history of the church and mosque

Abraha’s church, *al-qalīs*, built in *c.* AD 540 (in *c.* AD 560 according to Robin [2015: 126]), stood where the southern colonnades of the Great Mosque are today. East of the church (and, consequently, east of the mosque) was the famous palace of Ghumdān (b. Duhaysh 1424/2003: 213).[1] The mosque is thus the successor of the church, but the church was also preceded by an earlier cultic building — a small sanctuary of the ancient Arabian (and Yemeni) water and fertility religion. It consisted of a small cubicle that has survived as the ground floor of the western minaret. Around the tenth century AD, tradition had it that it was the grave of the prophet Ḥanẓala b. Ṣafwān, also known as Shuʿayb (al-ʿAmrī & Zakkār 1974: 205). The other element of the sanctuary were two tall poles (named *Kuʿayb* and *imraʾat Kuʿayb*) considered male and female, symbolizing a ‘sacred marriage’. They were physically absorbed into the Christian building (b. Duhaysh 1424/2003: 216) and only removed from it when it was demolished in or after 136/753–754. Their original location was, however, preserved in the mosque, in the third row of the southern prayer hall (al-Wāsiʿī 1345/1929: 12). The pre-Christian sanctuary stood in the middle of the flood bed of Wādī Ṣanʿāʾ, shortly before it flowed into the Saylah (Sāʾilah) river. Its precarious location (i.e. a place not safe from floods) was in common with other pre-Islamic sanctuaries in Yemen and the much more famous Kaʿba in Mecca.

The architectural development of the Great Mosque

The earliest Muslim prayer site, erected in year 6/627–628 on the orders of the Prophet, joined the cathedral at its northern edge. This must have been a relatively insignificant and makeshift construction. It was enlarged and endowed with fine ashlar walls under Caliph al-Walīd (86–96/705–715) by his governor Ayyūb b. Yaḥyā al-Thaqafī, who gave the mosque the courtyard form that we still see today. The western and northern walls date to these years, but there were no colonnades yet, as in the other very early (time of the Prophet) Ṣanʿāʾ mosque, the Jabbānah (al-Ḥajarī 1361/1942–1943: 39; al-ʿAmrī & Zakkār 1974: 90). The recent archaeological survey has revealed that the southern wall (called ‘early south wall’ by the archaeologists) ran along a line approximately following the northern edges of the two (later) minarets (Edens & Edens 2022: 30, 34, 50). It

[1] For al-Azraqī see b. Duhaysh 1424/2003; for al-Rāzī see al-ʿAmrī & Zakkār 1989; for al-Ṭabarī see Nöldeke 1881–1882.

could not, of course, have been more southerly because the cathedral was still standing. A few decades later, in or after 136/753–754, the governor, ʿAlī b. al-Rabīʿ, demolished the church (b. Duhaysh 1424/2003: 217–218), used its material as spolia for repair and building works (*ʿimārāt*) of the mosque, and commemorated his activity in an inscription (photograph and translation in Canova 2022: 145–146). Most of the columns and capitals do indeed come from the church (the best overview can be found in Costa 1994) — six are recognizably Christian or in the Ethiopian style; the Sabaean and Himyarite columns and capitals also come from the church (Abraha is reported to have plundered temples and palaces). The wooden ceilings must also be from the church, especially in the northern and western prayer halls, particularly their painted coffers. The restorers (Istituto Veneto per i Beni Culturali) took numerous ^{14}C samples. Their dating varies considerably but point to a sixth-century AD date or earlier, and the Italians describe them as reused older beams preserved in government stores as precious raw material (Ravagnan et al. 2022: 108, 114). It is interesting to note that, according to al-Rāzī (al-ʿAmrī & Zakkār 1974: 82–84), the Prophet had ordered that the new mosque's qibla should point towards Jabal Ḍīn. Neither Jerusalem nor Mecca are mentioned in this context. Jabal Ḍīn is a majestic mountain with a pre-Islamic sanctuary on its summit, north of Ṣanʿāʾ. Al-Rāzī (al-ʿAmrī & Zakkār 1974: 84) says that Jabal Ḍīn, together with Jabal Ḥaḍūr (Yemen's and Arabia's highest peak), was one of the two holy mountains of Yemen.

The eastern colonnade of the mosque was added (or was shifted eastwards) under the Yuʿfirids; two inscriptions provide the dates 265/878–879 and 270/883–884 for the start and completion of the works respectively. When the mosque was thus extended eastwards, the mihrab was installed in the centre of the northern wall. Costa (1994) had already established that the five small cupolas, which will be discussed below, are not in the centre of the qibla wall (marked by the mihrab) but about 2 m left of it and must therefore have been installed earlier, marking the previous central axe.

The dating of the church's demolition and the use of the spolia for substantially rebuilding the mosque depends primarily on al-Azraqī, but also on the ʿAlī b. al-Rabīʿ inscription. In line 9, the inscription says that the caliph gave orders to his governor, ʿAlī b. al-Rabīʿ, *bi-iṣlāḥ al-masājid wa-ʿimārati-hā*. The text does not expressly mention the Great Mosque but its inclusion in the programme must be concluded from the location of the inscription in the Great Mosque itself (cf. Lewcock et al. 1983: 347; 'We can safely assume that the Great Mosque would be included'). With regard to the content, the two genitives must be understood as 'ordered the repairs of the mosques and (ordered) building activities'; not, as has been suggested, 'repairs of the mosques and (of) the buildings' (D. Behrens-Abouseif, pers. com., 2022). Therefore, the church's demolition and the governor's subsequent building activity in the second century AH were responsible for transferring the pre-Islamic spolia from the church, and for extending the mosque southwards to where the church had been. Yemeni historians and Western scholars have never doubted this.

No 'cupola' in the Ṣanʿāʾ cathedral

In my three previous articles on the church (Daum 2018; 2021a; 2021b), I have provided a detailed analysis and reconstruction of the cathedral based on al-Azraqī's (d. 222/836–837) description (b. Duhaysh 1424/2003: 212–215). The church was of basilica-type with the two 'pagan' poles in the forecourt. I will not return to these papers or quote myself here but will deal only with al-Azraqī's *qubbah*, literally 'a [i.e. one] cupola', at the church's eastern end. However, church cupolas were invented only with the building of Hagia Sophia in Byzantine architecture. Over the following centuries, they spread throughout the empire. Consequently, St Catherine's in the Sinai, a church contemporary with Ṣanʿāʾ, does not have a cupola but an apse. This speaks against the Ṣanʿāʾ church having a true cupola. The new Byzantine model had the cupola in the centre, where the clergy served and the emperor sat enthroned, expressing a new political and religious conception. As al-Azraqī credibly reports for Ṣanʿāʾ, the sanctum was no longer at the eastern end (as it was in the Ṣanʿāʾ church). The third argument against understanding al-Azraqī's word 'cupola' in the modern sense also comes from his description — according to him, the 'cupola' was topped by a very large alabaster plaque, which is technically impossible. Alabaster plates cannot be larger than *c.*1 m². When al-Azraqī described the structure at the church's eastern end as a *qubbah*, 'cupola', he must therefore have thought of the Eastern churches of his own time, when they usually had domes. That there were alabasters in the Ṣanʿāʾ cathedral cannot be doubted. Al-Azraqī is very explicit and admiringly reports how truly wonderful it is to see the sun- and moonlight come through the alabaster. In what follows, I will argue that what al-Azraqī meant by *qubbah* referred to a group of small domes (i.e. in the plural), each one topped by an alabaster sheet; the whole structure was transferred in its entirety to the Great Mosque and installed in its roof, after the demolition of the church in the mid-eighth century AD. This group of skylights in the mosque is held together by a solid wooden frame, thus forming a single installation. In the church, their purpose was to let the light into its eastern section, its holiest part. Here is al-Azraqī's description (b. Duhaysh 1424/2003: 215):

> *Wa-kān al-madkhal min-hu ilā bayt* [i.e. from the western part of the cathedral, which I have defined as a courtyard or atrium] *ṭūluhu thamanūn dhirāʿan fī arbaʿīn dhirāʿan. Thumma yadkhul min al-bayt ilā īwān ṭūlu-hu arbaʿūn dhirāʿan ʿan yamīni-hi wa-ʿan yasāri-hi ... thumma yadkhul min al-īwān ilā qubbah thalathūn dhirāʿan fī thalathīn dhirāʿan, jidāru-hā bi-al-fusayfasā ... wa-fīhā rukhāmah mimmā yalī maṭlaʿ al-shams min al-balaq, murabbaʿah ʿasharat adhruʿ fī ʿasharat adhruʿ tughshā ʿayn min naẓar ilayhā min baṭn al-qubbah, tuwaddī ḍauʾ al-shams wa-l-qamar ilā dākhil al-qubbah wa-kān taḥt al-rukhāmah minbar min khashab al-labakh ... wa ... al-abanūs*
>
> 'The entrance led into a *bayt* — its length being eighty ells by forty ells ... Then one enters the *īwān;* its length was forty ells to the right and to the left. Then one enters from the *īwān* into a *qubbah* which is thirty ells by thirty, its walls being covered by mosaics. And in it, where the sun rises, is a *rukhāmah*, or *balaq*. It is square, ten ells by ten ells. (It is so bright that the eye of) whoever looks at it from the bottom of the *qubbah* gets overwhelmed. It directs the light of the sun and the moon inside the *qubbah*. Under this *rukhāmah* stood the pulpit, made of *labakh*-wood ... and of ebony'.

A discussion of the words *rukhāma* and *balaq*

The difficulty here is with the words *rukhāmah* and *balaq*. In my recollection, both mean 'alabaster' in the Ṣanʿāʾnī dialect. The *Tāj al-ʿArūs* lexicon has two words under the lemma b-l-q, *al-bulqah* and *al-balaq*, and has the following to say:

> *al-bulqah: (sawād wa-bayāḍ), ka-al-bulqah, ... fīhā khuṭūṭ min sawād*
>
> 'a whitish stone with black stripes'
>
> *al-balaq: ḥajārah bi-al-Yaman tuḍīʾu mā warāʾihā, ka-al-zujāj, tusammī al-balaq*
>
> 'a stone in Yemen which shows what is behind it, the same as glass, it is called al-balaq'

The *Lisān al-ʿArab* has a similar definition:

> *wa-l-balaq: sawād wa-bayāḍ; wa-l-balaq ḥajar bi-l-Yaman, yuḍīʾ mā warāʾi-hi kamā yuḍīʾ al-zujāj*
>
> '*balaq* is black and white; *balaq* also means a stone in Yemen that shows what is behind it, the same as glass'

I think the first of these two meanings refers originally to one of the most famous marbles of antiquity, the Proconnesian marble (so named after the island which today is called Marmara in Turkish), which Justinian used for his buildings in Constantinople and around the Mediterranean (several sunken ships carrying columns of this marble have been found). The most exclusive variety of Proconnesian marble is whitish-grey with black stripes.

Yemeni alabaster skylights in the Kaʿba

The second definition in both lexica refers to the Yemeni alabaster. This is confirmed by the usage made by al-Azraqī himself in his description of the restoration of the Kaʿba under Ibn al-Zubayr, the anti-caliph (r. 63–73/683–692):

> *wa-arsala Ibn al-Zubayr ilā Ṣanʿāʾ fa-atā min rukhām bihā yuqāl lahu al-balaq, fa-jaʿla-hu fī l-rawāzin allatī fī saqfi-hā li-l-ḍauʾ ...*

> ʻIbn al-Zubayr sent to Ṣanʿāʾ for the kind of marble (*rukhām*) that is called *al-balaq*, and used it for the skylights in the roof (of the Kaʿba) to let the light in (b. Duhaysh 1424/2003: 304; in n. 7, he explains the word *rawāzin* as square/rectangular, *murabbaʿ*, roof openings for allowing the light into the Kaʿba's interior);
>
> *ṣifat al-rawāzin allatī li-l-ḍauʾ fī saqf al-Kaʿba: wa-l-rawāzin murabbaʿa fī-aʿlā-hā, rukhām yamānī yadkhul min-hu al-ḍauʾ ilā baṭn al-Kaʿba*
>
> ʻdescription of the *rawāzin*, which were for the light, in the roof of the Kaʿba: the *rawāzin* were square/rectangular and at its highest point/very top. They were of Yemeni *rukhām*, through which the light enters the bottom of the Kaʿba (b. Duhaysh 1424/2003: 408)'.

The parallel with the Ṣanʿāʾ church/mosque alabasters is evident in relation to the function (i.e. transparent window panes in the roof) as well as the nobility of the material, fitting for a sacred building. I would even dare to suggest that Ibn al-Zubayr, dealing with Islam's most significant place of worship, deliberately imitated the Ṣanʿāʾ cathedral, which still stood in his day, as he did not choose the easy way of importing glass from Constantinople or Egypt — conveniently obtainable by sea — but instead ordered Yemeni alabaster that necessitated difficult transport by camel.

Therefore, *rukhām* (or *rukhāmah*) refers to the raw stone (be it marble or alabaster), while *balaq* is the word for a thin transparent sheet of alabaster. This confirms what older Ṣanʿāʾnīs told me when I asked how they named the few remaining traditional alabaster window panes in the old town.

A description of the five alabaster domes in the Great Mosque

They are so-called ʻfalse cupolas', that is to say, a concentric structure where layers of small wooden planks are laid upon each other in decreasing diameters to create a kind of cupola. An alabaster plaque is inserted at each one's upper end (four remaining). A wooden frame holds the five-cupola structure together which can thus be described or understood as a single object measuring 5.91 by 3.09/3.36 m (see Fig. 1, an isometric drawing showing the structure after restoration and stabilization). The individual wooden frames have been compared by Lewcock et al. (1983: 338–339) with similar constructions in Turkmenistan (third to first century BC) and Afghanistan (*c.* AD 500). For many centuries, the intricate carvings of the alabasters were not visible due to the soot and pollution accumulated over a millennium and a half. Beautiful abstract and foliate carvings were revealed when the Italian restorers cleaned the alabasters.

Can one imagine a cupola topped with a flat square alabaster pane, measuring *c.*5 by 5 m (ʻten ells by ten ells')? To clarify what al-Azraqī's informants meant, we will now compare their and his description with the reality of the five-dome structure in the Great Mosque.

What exactly did al-Azraqī's informants pass on to him? Three things: first, that there was a *qubbah*; second, that a transparent square alabaster sheet covered it, measuring *c.*5 by 5 m in total; and third, that this was above the sanctum at the church's eastern end, following the congregation's gaze. How should we understand this? Could it plausibly describe the five domes in the mosque?

As previously stated, the five-cupola structure in the mosque measures 5.91 by 3.09/3.36 m. While this is not identical to what al-Azraqī's sources remembered for the church, it is sufficiently close, considering an oral tradition passed on over 100 years ago or so. A single alabaster sheet of this size is impossible. I have been to one of the still active quarries in eastern Yemen (near Ṣirwāḥ) where alabaster has been mined since antiquity. It is evident that it was never possible to extract a pane measuring 5 by 5 m. Something of this enormous size could only have been made up of several smaller panes framed together. I mentioned above the installation of Yemeni alabaster windows in the Kaʿba by Ibn al-Zubayr. Had very large panes technically been feasible, the caliph, with his unlimited financial means, would have chosen one large panel for the Kaʿba. In the same way, the Ṣanʿāʾ cupola must have consisted of several smaller panes, an ensemble of small domes covered with alabaster sheets. The five small cupolas in the mosque's roof, located in the central axe of the pre-Yuʿfirid building, fit these conditions very well. The informants used the word ʻ*qubbah*' and said that

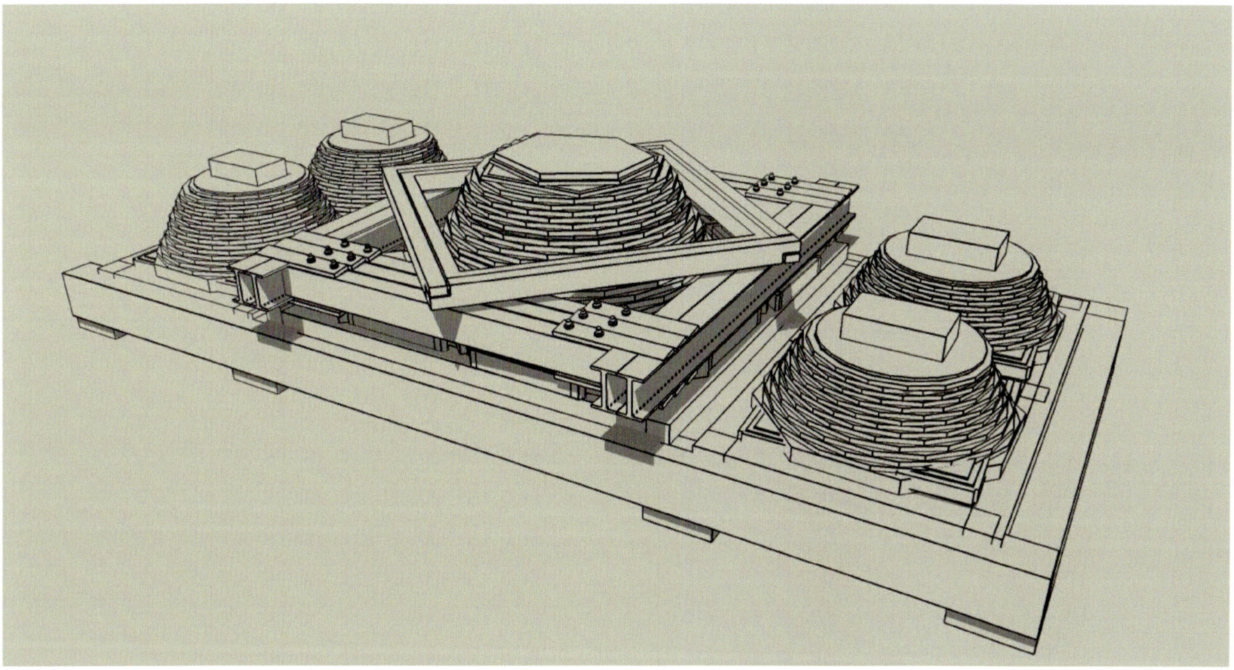

FIGURE 1. *Isometric drawing of the framed five-cupola structure, Great Mosque, Ṣanʿāʾ (courtesy and ©Istituto Veneto per i Beni Culturali).*

the dome was covered with one flat piece of alabaster. It is easy to understand how, over 100 years, the plural became a singular, and the group of five domes (set in a single solidly constructed, removable wooden frame) became one. This minor misinterpretation may even have resulted from al-Azraqī's own pen.

An art-historical approach to the alabaster reliefs

Until the Italian restoration, no one had noticed the five domes. Even those who acknowledged the domed structure, such as Lewcock et al. (1983: 337), could not see the reliefs due to a millennium and a half of pollution. When the Italians dismantled the frames and took the alabasters out, the cleaning process brought to light works of art of exceptional quality and beauty (Ravagnan et al. 2022).

The slab inserted in the central skylight is plain; the other three (the fourth one is lost) are decorated in relief (Fig. 2/a–c). Despite their fragmentary character, there can be no doubt that these are the most accomplished works of art from late antique Yemen. One immediately thinks of sixth-century Byzantine work, such as the reliefs from H. Polyeuktos (the famous Pilastri Acritani near the southern side of San Marco in Venice).

While there is some similarity with earlier Yemeni scrollwork or vines — in particular with a decorated alabaster plaque from Ẓafār, attributable to the rebuilt Ẓafār church, *c.* AD 530, after its destruction by king Yūsuf — the Ṣanʿāʾ alabasters differ not only in quality but also in their motifs. I am not aware of other Yemeni knot-work motifs or indeed scrollwork evoking acanthus leaves (reliefs of the late Himyarite period show vine leaves and grapes, as catalogued by Japp in her survey [2021]).

I was certain that scholars of Byzantine art would be able to link the Ṣanʿāʾ alabasters with other works of art of the Empire and date them accordingly. I contacted most specialists in Germany but with no apparent results. They positioned the motifs in late antique Byzantium or, occasionally, Sasanian art. Jens Kröger suggested — with detailed arguments — the early Islamic/Umayyad period (pers. com., 2022). To my

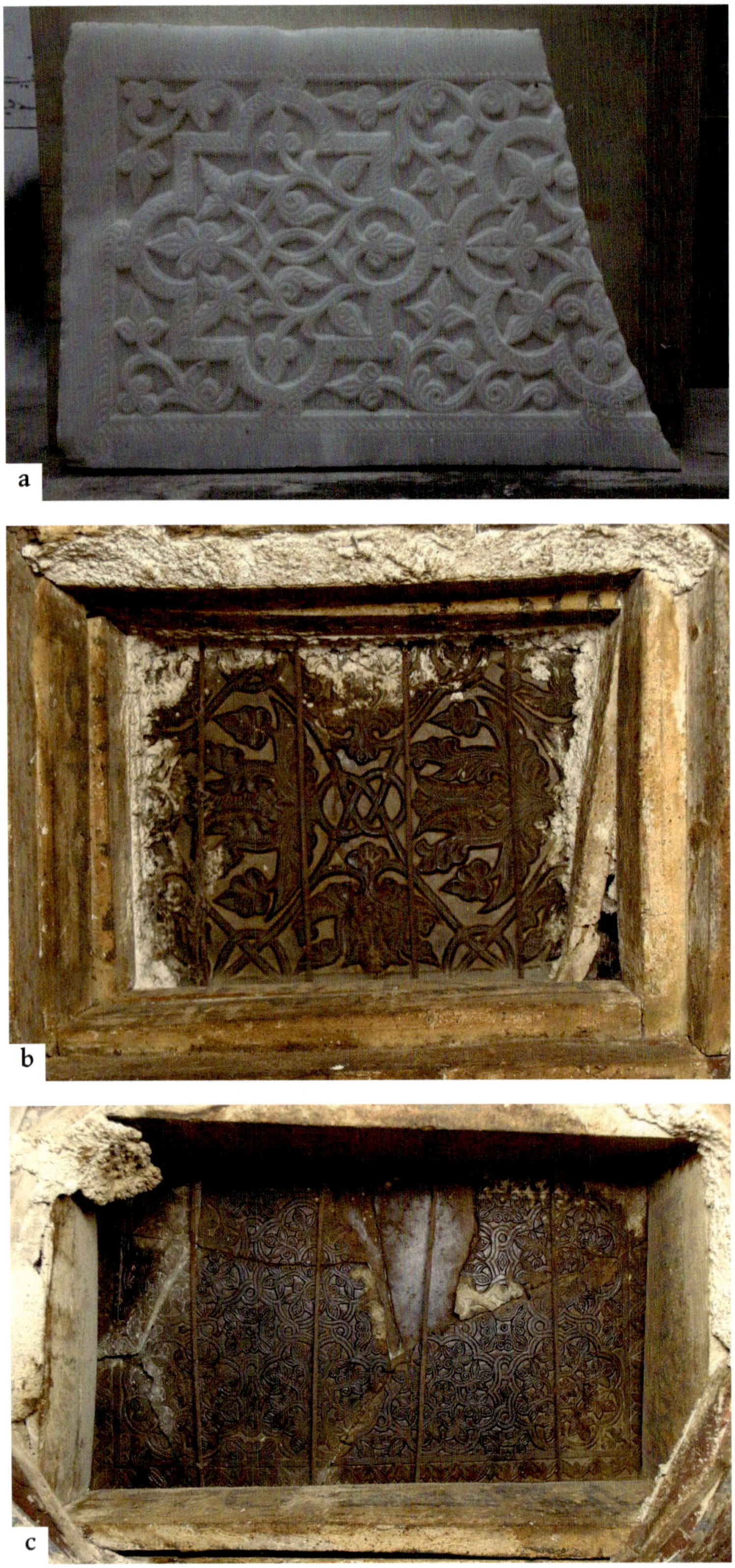

Figure 2. *Three alabaster plaques from the five-cupola structure, Great Mosque, Ṣanʿāʾ:* **a.** *c.30 x 22 cm (when complete);* **b.** *c.40 x 30 cm (when complete);* **c.** *c.60 x 40 cm (when complete) (photographs courtesy and ©Istituto Veneto per i Beni Culturali).*

surprise, I learned that a firm chronology of the stylistic development within late antique Byzantine art has not yet been agreed. As to dating, suggestions ranged from the fifth to the seventh century.

One reviewer was of the opinion that the reliefs should be compared with plant motifs in Sasanian stucco work, as catalogued by Arzhangi (2024). But stucco, as a craft, is very different from reliefs in stone — stucco is moulded while the Ṣanʿāʾ reliefs are carved. From a stylistic point of view, I can't see any similarity between those Sasanian plant motifs (single flowers, mostly buds) and the Ṣanʿāʾ alabasters. The latter have vines and acanthus leaves, which are Mediterranean. This does not mean that there are no Sasanian or Sasanian-inspired elements in the decorative schemes of the Great Mosque. There are, especially in the carved woodwork and painted decoration. A convincing example is the carved wooden bracket from the northern prayer hall, illustrated in Lewcock (2022: 100, fig. 5). In my opinion, the Ṣanʿāʾ reliefs reveal the hand of a master from Constantinople, made accessible to a Yemeni craftsman through a drawing, with the actual carving executed locally. This fits with al-Ṭabarī's report (Nöldeke 1881–1882: 935) that Justinian sent not only material (such as mosaic tesserae and *rukhām*) but also skilled artisans to Ṣanʿāʾ: *bi-l-ṣunnāʿ* ('workmen') *wa-l-fusayfasāʾ* ('mosaics') *wa-l-rukhām. Rukhām* here can only mean 'marble' (correctly translated by Bosworth [1999: 221]).

The Ṣanʿāʾ cathedral is not the only case of Justinian's interest in church building beyond the Empire's frontiers. In recent decades, shipwrecks carrying 'churches in a box', complete with columns, decorative material, etc. have been found around the Mediterranean. The first of these finds was the Marzamemi shipwreck, discovered off the coast of Sicily by Gerhard Kapitän (1980). It has since been the object of groundbreaking archaeological work and has generated a vast corpus of publications, as have other finds, mainly from North Africa. Transportation of this kind was operated on a giant scale — to Ravenna alone, an estimated 1500 tons of marble were sent from Constantinople (Boldini 2020: 83).

The structural and material support for the Ṣanʿāʾ church did not include columns (how would such a heavy load have been transported from Alexandria to the Red Sea?), but the massive bronze door, the mosaic tesserae and other decorative material, the technique of coffered ceilings including, of course, the general plan and, as we can now confirm, the drawings for the alabaster panes that formed the 'cupola'. Abraha, supported by Byzantine artisans, thus created the most splendid building in the Arabian Peninsula, anchored in the civilization of late antiquity. We can still see, touch, and admire much of it through the spolia preserved in the Great Mosque: the columns, the coffered ceilings, their painted decoration and, last but not least, the five domes that continue to open our eyes to the light of the divine. The quiet and measured dignity of the Great Mosque united all of this into a new majestic and, at the same time, restrained splendour.

The direction of prayer and the spiritual meaning of the cupolas

It is not only material remains from the church that are preserved in the Great Mosque, but also its spiritual idea, transposed from its Christian symbolism into a new meaning consistent with the new revelation. This becomes evident when considering the location of the five domes in the mosque, bearing in mind al-Azraqī's description of the cupola's function in the cathedral. Costa (1994: 11) had already interpreted it correctly in 1974. He noticed that the five skylights are not in the centre of the qibla wall, where the mihrab is, but 2 m west of it. Costa concluded convincingly that the domes marked the earlier (pre-Yuʿfirid) central axe, that is, before the transfer of the eastern prayer hall. Costa argued, therefore, that the Umayyad mosque did not yet have a mihrab but that the five domes constituted the earliest physical and spiritual axe of the mosque, attracting and directing the congregation's gaze towards Mecca. This is structurally and symbolically identical to the position of the five-dome structure in the church, where they shone light on its eastern section onto which the congregation gazed — a promise of heavenly glory. There, in the east, where the sun and the moon rise, symbolizing the divine light of Christ's resurrection, was the symbolic centre of the church (as well as its altar). Christian architecture had adopted the 'orientation' of their places of worship against the mostly opposite direction of pagan temples ('I am the Light of the World', John 8: 12; the *āyat al-nūr*, Qurʾān 24. 35, also comes to mind). In the mosque, the five-dome structure was installed in the same position, with the same function and with the same meaning at the farthest field of vision of the assembly, illuminating and highlighting the sacred direction towards Mecca.

Conclusion

In conclusion, we can say that the Great Mosque is not only the material successor of Abraha's cathedral incorporating the tangible legacy (spolia) from the church: its wooden ceilings (arguably the largest extant coffered ceilings from late antiquity), columns and capitals and, last but not least, five domes, which al-Azraqī calls *qubbah* in the singular, were installed in the mosque with a spiritually identical meaning and a spiritually similar location. The transfer took place in the mid-eighth century AD, commemorated in the inscription set by the governor, ʿAlī b. al-Rabīʿ.

References

al-ʿAmrī Ḥ. & Zakkār ʿA. (eds). 1974. *al-Rāzī, Tārīkh madīnat Ṣanʿāʾ*. Ṣanʿāʾ. [n.p.]

Arzhangi S. 2024. Plant motifs in architectural stucco of the Sassanid period in Iran related to the 7th and 8th centuries AD. *Oriental Art and Culture* 5: 356–364.

Boldini I. 2020. The toilsome journey of marbles and stones. Pages 83–113 in S. Cosentino (ed.), *Ravenna and the traditions of late antique and early Byzantine craftsmanship*. Berlin: De Gruyter.

Bosworth C.E. (trans.). 1999. *The history of al-Ṭabarī*. v. Albany: State University of New York Press.

Canova G. 2022. The Great Mosque of Ṣanʿāʾ: The Qurʾānic inscriptions. Pages 133–184 in Ravagnan & Merlo 2022.

Costa P.M. 1974. La Moschea Grande di Ṣanʿāʾ. *Annali dell'Istituto Orientale di Napoli* 34: 487–506.

Costa P.M. 1994. *Studies in Arabian Architecture*. Aldershot: Variorum. [Containing a translation of Costa 1974.]

Daum W. 2018. Ṣanʿāʾ: the origins of Abrahah's cathedral and the Great Mosque — a water sanctuary of the Old Arabian religion. *Proceedings of the Seminar for Arabian Studies* 48: 67–74.

Daum W. 2021a. Abraha's cathedral: change and continuity of a sacred place. Pages 245-259 in G. Hatke & R. Ruzicka (eds), *South Arabian long-distance trade in antiquity: 'Out of Arabia'*. Newcastle upon Tyne: Cambridge Scholars Publishing.

Daum W. 2021b. Abraha's cathedral in Ṣanʿāʾ: when was it built and why? Pages 279-288 in Chr. Darles, L. Khalidi & M. Arbach (eds), *Contacts between South Arabia and the Horn of Africa, from the Bronze Age to Islam. In honor of Rémy Audouin*. Toulouse: Presses Universitaires du Midi.

b. Duhaysh ʿA. (ed.). 1424/2003. *al-Azraqī, Akhbār Makka wa-mā jāʾ fi-hā min al-āthār*. Mecca: Maktaba al-Assadī.

Edens Chr. & Edens B.Y. 2022. Foundations of the Great Mosque in Ṣanʿāʾ. Pages 27–93 in Ravagnan & Merlo 2022.

al-Ḥajarī M. 1361/1942–1943. *Masājid Ṣanʿāʾ*. Ṣanʿāʾ: maṭbaʿ wizāra al-maʾārif. [Reprint, 1398/1977–1978.]

Japp S. 2021. Late South Arabian and Aksumite relief art: Local traditions, foreign models and autonomous transformations. Pages 181–192 in Chr. Darles, L. Khalidi & M. Arbach (eds), *Contacts between South Arabia and the Horn of Africa, from the Bronze Age to Islam. In honor of Rémy Audouin*. Toulouse: Presses Universitaires du Midi.

Kapitän G.1980. Elementi architettonici per una basilica dal relitto navale del VI secolo di Marzamemi (Siracusa). Pages 71–136 in *XXVII Corso di cultura sull'arte Ravennate e Bizantina*. Ravenna: Edizioni del Girasole.

Lewcock R. 2022. The architectural decorations. Pages 95–112 in Ravagnan & Merlo 2022.

Lewcock R., Rex Smith G., Serjeant R.B. & Costa P. 1983. The architectural history and description of Ṣanʿāʾ Mosques: The Great Mosque. Pages 323–350 in Serjeant R.B. & Lewcock R., *Ṣanʿāʾ. An Arabian Islamic city*. London: World of Islam Festival Trust. [Reprint, 2013.]

Nöldeke Th. 1881-1882. *Annales quos scripsit Abu Djafar Mohammed ibn Djarir at-Tabari*. (Prima Series, 2). Lugduni Batavorum: E.J. Brill.

Ravagnan R. & Merlo M. (eds). 2022. *The Great Mosque of Ṣanʿāʾ — Conservation intervention (2005-2015)*. Venice: Istituto Veneto per i Beni Culturali. Available at www.monumentaorientalia.org/wp-content/uploads/2023/09/The-Great-Mosque.pdf

Ravagnan R. et al. [the team]. 2022. The domes. Pages 323–335 in Ravagnan & Merlo 2022.

Robin Chr.J. 2015. La grande église d'Abraha à Ṣanʿāʾ. Pages 105–129 in V. Christides (ed.), *Interrelations between the peoples of the Near East and Byzantium in pre-Islamic times*. (Semitica Antiqua). Cordoba: CNERU, DTR, Oriens Academic.

al-Wāsiʿī ʿA. 1345/1929. *Al-badr al-muzīl li-l-ḥuzn fī faḍl al-Yaman wa-maḥāsin Ṣanʿāʾ dhāt al-minan*. Cairo: al-Maktabah al-Salafīyah.

Author's address

Werner Daum, Leipziger Str. 43, 10117 Berlin, Germany.
e-mail daum.werner@gmx.de

Proceedings of the Seminar for Arabian Studies 54 (2025): 57–71

The nature of post-Bronze Age human occupation at Tell Abraq (Umm al-Quwain): archaeological insights from the 2023 field season

Michele Degli Esposti, Maria Paola Pellegrino, Federico Borgi, Francesca Barchiesi & Rania Hussein Kannouma

Summary

Renewed excavations at Tell Abraq, begun in 2019 by the Italian Archaeological Mission in Umm al-Quwain in collaboration with the Tourism and Archaeology Department of Umm al-Quwain, have transformed our understanding of the site after the Bronze Age. After the erection of a large platform during the Iron Age I (*c*.1300–1100 BC), and the absence of domestic structures broadly between 1100 and 800 BC — perhaps not insignificantly coinciding with the foundation of a new settlement at nearby Muweilah — a very limited domestic occupation is witnessed in the second part of the Iron Age II (*c*.800–600 BC). The site was reoccupied in the final Iron Age III (*c*.600–300 BC) or early in the late pre-Islamic period (PIR.A *c*.300–150 BC) and continued until the PIR.C period (*c*. AD 0–150) when a shrine was erected, but evidence for domestic buildings is absent. Remarkable finds from this period include human statues with parallels to those found at Palmyra (Syria) and Hatra (Iraq), an Aramaic inscription with possible Palmyrene palaeographic influence and gold imitations of Tiberius' aureus. The site developed into a burial ground during the PIR.D period (*c*. AD 150–300) and clearly later, with shaft burials characterized by a lower side chamber which anticipated Islamic practices. This paper will summarize the previously little-known post-Bronze Age occupation of Tell Abraq and highlight the significant discoveries of the Partho-Sasanian period, emphasizing the changing nature of human occupation at the site through the different periods.

Keywords: settlement dynamics, United Arab Emirates, Sasanian graves, pre-Islamic shrine, Persian Gulf connections

Introduction

Renewed, extensive excavations in the eastern part of Tell Abraq (Umm al-Quwain) were conducted by the Italian Archaeological Mission in Umm al-Quwain (IAMUQ), in collaboration with the Tourism and Archaeology Department of Umm al-Quwain (TAD-UAQ) between 2019 and 2023, with a total of nine trenches excavated to different depths, covering an overall area of 1950 m^2 (Fig. 1). Despite this massive undertaking, contexts which could be dated (based on the collected pottery) to the initial Early Bronze Age phase of the site (Potts 2000) were only encountered inside a small test trench dug in 2019 and later discontinued (Degli Esposti et al. 2022: 144–145).

On the other hand, evidence was collected for the prolonged human presence at the site, with material culture bearing witness for almost all the periods into which the south-east (SE) Arabian protohistory is articulated, from the Middle Bronze Age to the so-called late pre-Islamic period, including some not previously reported from (or only vaguely attested at) the site (Degli Esposti et al. 2024).

The nature of the human occupation at the site appears to have changed through time, with phases characterized by a normal residential function, others with a cultic one and still others associated with funerary use.

An outline of this evolution will be presented here, starting from *c*.1300 BC, the conventionally accepted date for the transition between the Late Bronze Age and the Early Iron Age (EIA). This means that the most impressive structure discovered so far, the massive stone building named Building I (B-I), representing a *unicum* in the region, will not be discussed as its construction seems better placed around the mid-second millennium (Degli Esposti et al. 2024: 191–193).

The site apparently developed rather rapidly after B-I's construction, and its first restructuring probably took place soon after its foundation, possibly very slightly earlier than the first phase discussed here.

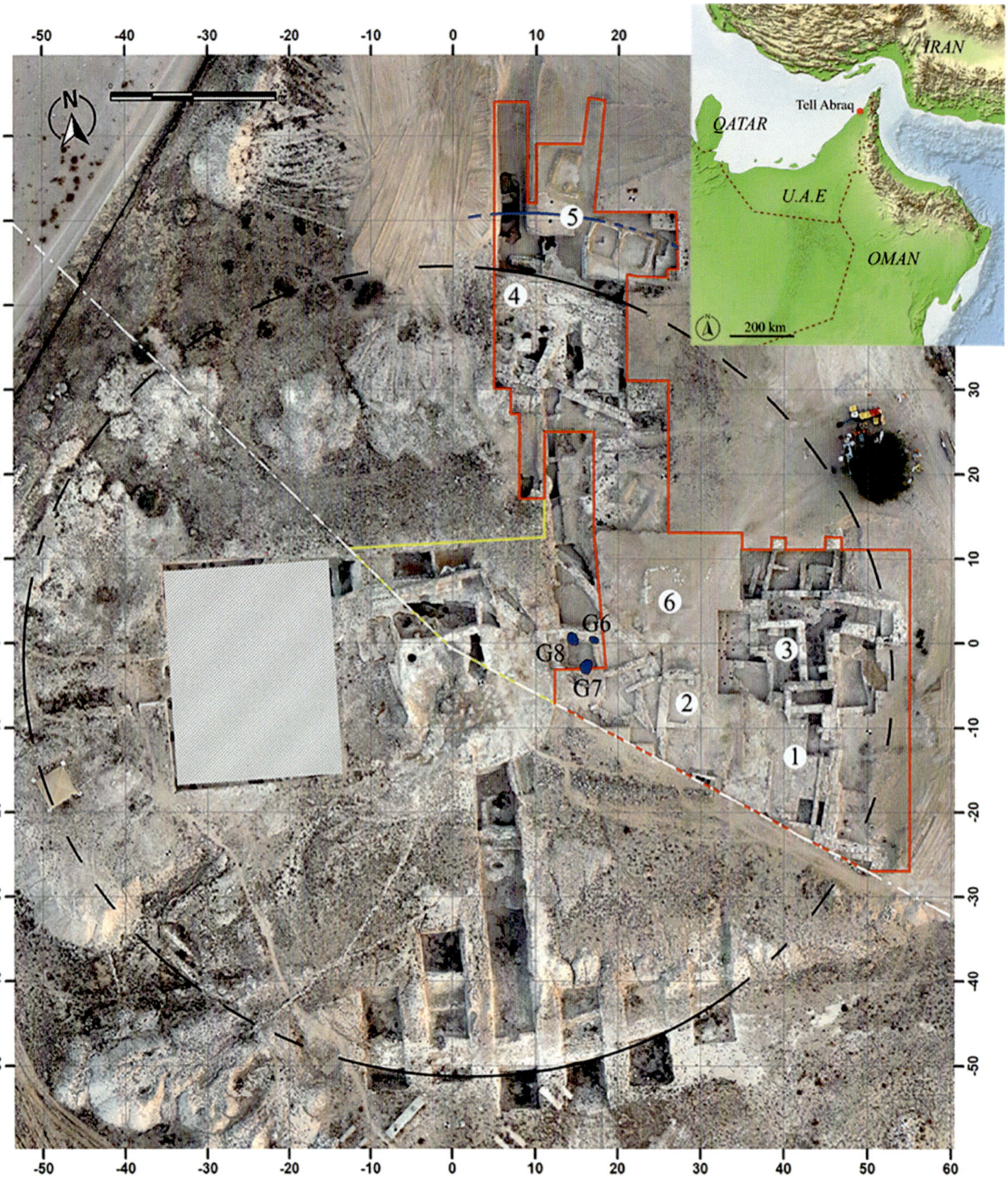

Figure 1. *The location of Tell Abraq in north-eastern UAE and a rectified orthophoto of the site with the location of the features discussed in the text.* **1.** *The main EIA I platform;* **2.** *the later terrace system covering an earlier one;* **3.** *EIA II domestic spaces (now removed);* **4.** *the massive retaining wall of the huge late second-millennium terrace (black line shows its presumed plan; blue line the likely associated ditch);* **5.** *EIA III/LPI mud-brick buildings;* **6.** *LPI shrine; G6, G7 and G8 Sasanian graves. The red line encloses the excavated area and the yellow line the area where only initial cleaning has been carried out. The filled-in rectangle obscures the area cleaned and excavated by the Sharjah Authority, which is still unpublished.*

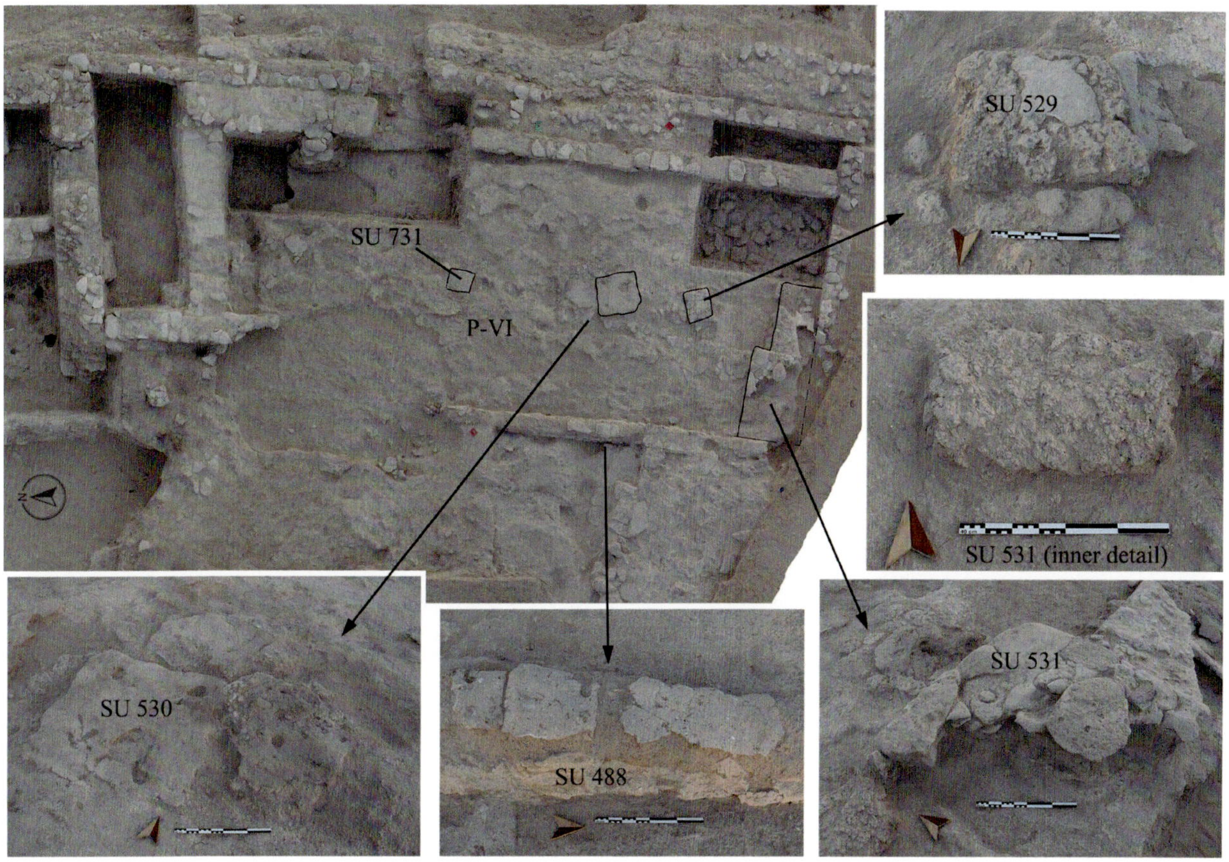

FIGURE 2. *A bird's-eye view of P-VI with close-ups of the features discussed in the text and their building technique, including detail of a mud brick used in the construction of platform SU 531.*

A large platform system of the Early Iron Age I (*c*.1300–1100 BC)

This chronological proximity seems to be confirmed by the techniques utilized in the construction of a large platform (*c*.13 x 6 m) located immediately south of B-I, discovered during the October–November 2023 field season and named Platform VI (P-VI) (Fig. 2).

The platform's northern boundary is defined by the surviving crest of B-I's southern wall. However, it might also have been partially dismantled by later occupation (see below). P-VI comprised a plaster floor framed by low walls, more accurately described as ridges or kerbs, suggesting that it was meant to be an open space. Notably, several of these ridges were constructed using a pinkish clay mortar with abundant small black gravel to obtain the core structure, capped by a hard, probably gypsum-based whitish mortar (Fig. 2). The latter closely resembles the one used in B-I's construction, a technique for which parallels in SE Arabia are currently unknown to the authors.

A few small installations constructed directly above P-VI do not contradict its interpretation as an open-air structure. They comprise three small squared bases (SU 529, 520, 731) built either with mortar-bound stones or a simple layer of a harder mortar resembling the one used for the perimeter ridges. One (SU 530) also displays three sub-circular lacunae that could be suggestive of the original presence of a now-removed moveable item (see Fig. 2).

A fourth feature (SU 531) is located against the south-western corner of the platform. It consists of a

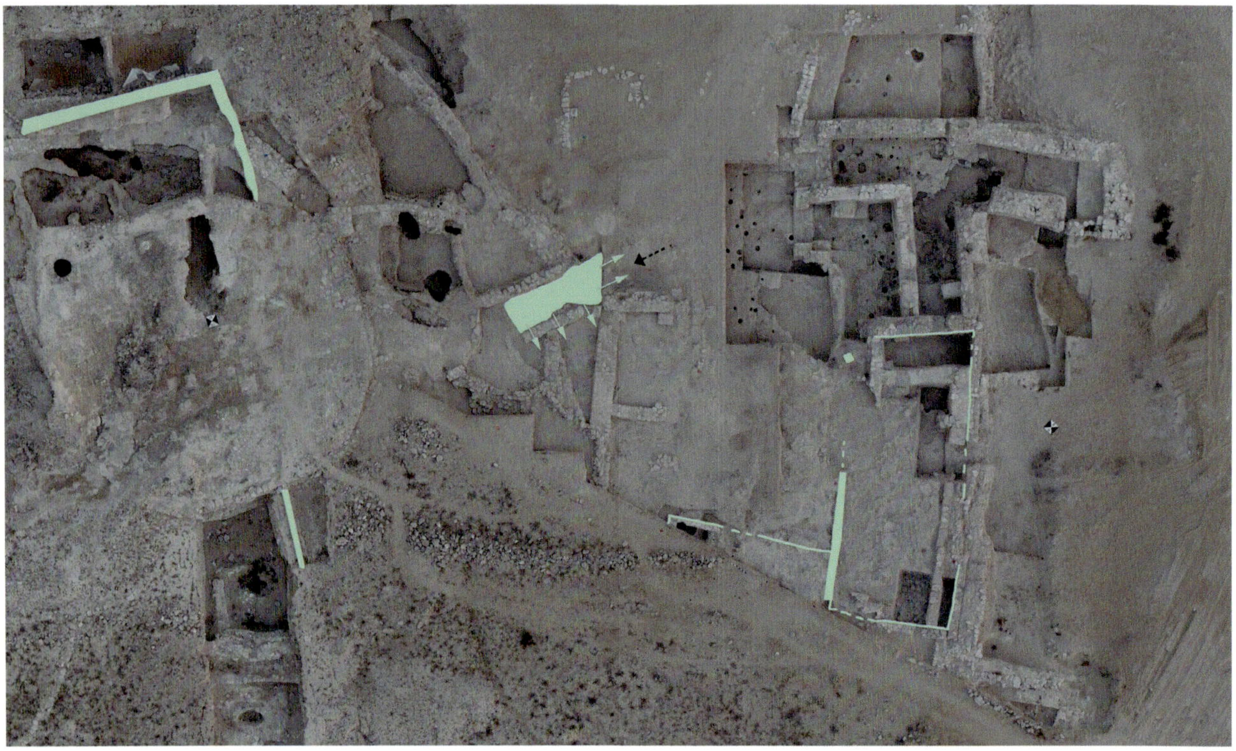

Figure 3. *A bird's-eye view (orthorectified) highlighting the structures that display the use of the same hard plaster as P-VI, possibly indicating a shared chronology. The arrow corresponds to the one in Figure 4.*

sort of podium comprising two juxtaposed rectangular parts made with a combination of stones and possibly bricks, bound with the same hard mortar used for the capping of the perimeter ridges. The possible bricks were made with the same mix of pinkish-brown clay and black gravel used in the perimeter ridges. While a few shaped bricks are evident (see Fig. 2), the combined use of a pisé technique cannot be ruled out.

These techniques are not documented in later structures at the site and appear quite distinctive. Moreover, to date no other site is known to the authors where such a hard plaster was used, with the notable exception of the burial ground of Abraq 2, investigated by the IAMUQ and TAD-UAQ some 700 m west of Tell Abraq (Degli Esposti & Borgi 2023).

The apparent unicity of the building techniques instils more confidence in using them as possible chronological indicators. This relative reliability is supported by the preliminary study of the available radiocarbon dates for B-I mentioned above, which indicate proximity between its construction and the erection of P-VI, despite the numerous building phases that clearly occurred between the former and the latter.

Building techniques allow proposing the contemporaneity of P-VI with other features at the site, including some only partially unearthed by our excavations and some left exposed by earlier works but not discussed in the available literature (Fig. 3).

During the 2023 field season, a large portion of the site immediately west of P-VI was also excavated. A network of stone walls, totally unexpected on such a scale and built with such intricacy was brought to light (see below and Fig. 4). Of particular relevance is the fact that these walls are stratigraphically later than P-VI and also cover at least another structure built using the same techniques as P-VI (Fig. 4, top left). Only partially exposed, this structure comprises at least four large steps, the lower one resembling a kind of small platform.

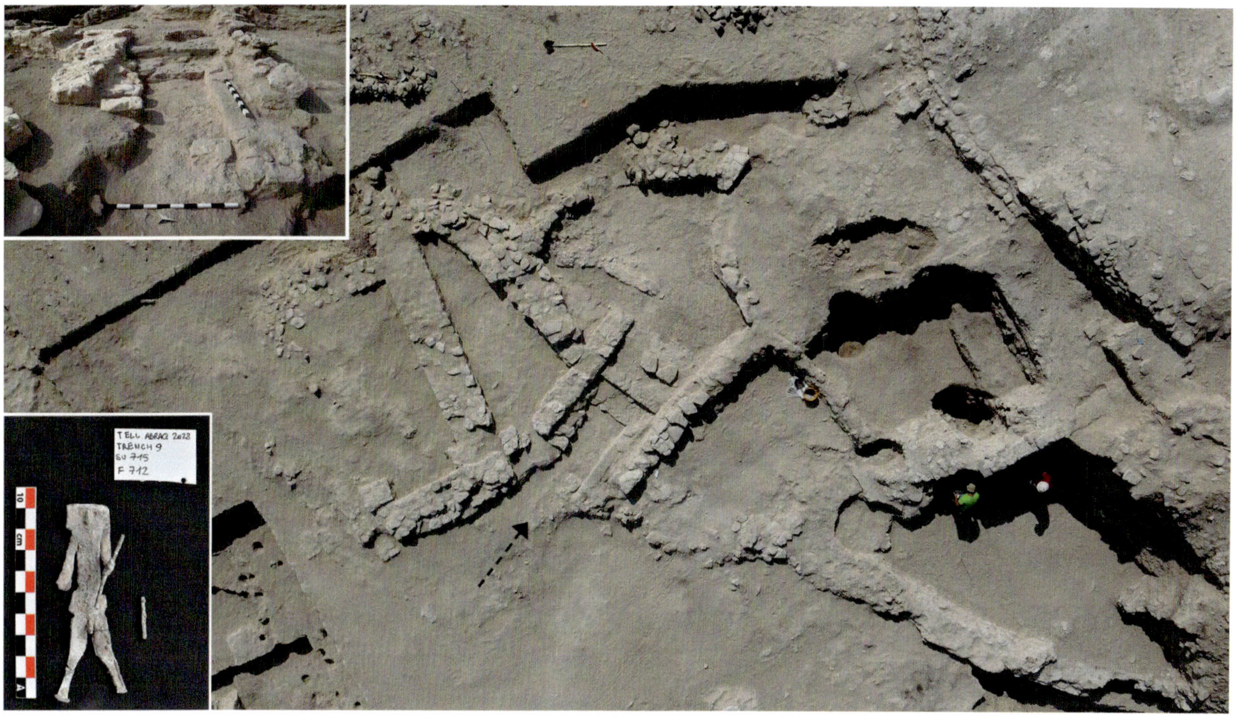

FIGURE 4. *An aerial view of the second phase of the wall network and platform system ascending the eastern slope of the site. Top left, a detail showing the second phase walls (lighter shade) overlaid on the earlier, hard-plastered structures. The dashed arrow indicates where the detailed photo was taken from. Bottom left, the anthropomorphic metal-sheet figurine discovered in association with these later walls.*

The impression is that of a monumental staircase or platform system ascending the slope of the artificial hill that had formed above the ruins of earlier structures (see also Magee et al. 2017 for a reconstruction of the large second-millennium terrace system that extended over the site).

It is, therefore, significant that similarly built structures are found further uphill, in previously investigated areas. Apart from a short straight wall abutting the upper stone-revetted and mud-brick-core platform occupying the top of the site and running south, a more substantial U-shaped wall was interpreted as containing an extension of that same platform, initially tentatively dated to the IA (Potts 1993).

This complex architecture seems not to be paired with consistent structures in the plain surrounding the site. Previous excavation in the western part of the site had already highlighted the predominance of contexts dated to the Iron Age I period but consisting of post holes, dumps and pits, interpreted as evidence for non-permanent occupation (Magee et al. 2017: 223). It appears, therefore, that during this period the elevated (eastern) part of the site hosted a remarkably well-built structure — possibly a platform system — with a likely communal destination, while the surrounding lower land was the place of ephemeral occupation, providing evidence to tentatively suggest a scenario in which the site represented a gathering place for the communities scattered along the coast. While such a role would be consistent with the attraction that the artificial hill would have exerted in the middle of the flat coastal landscape, the scarcity of the associated materials does not enable us to put forward more specific hypotheses about the nature of this occupation.

Restructuring and limited domestic occupation during the Early Iron Age II (*c*.1100–600/500 BC)

The plastered structures described above were subsequently replaced by the more rudimentary stone walls currently left *in situ* west of P-VI (Fig. 4). While they were likely built in the EIA or later, dating these walls more precisely remains challenging as they were directly covered by the reworked topsoil.[1] However, an initial very broad suggestion is that they were abandoned before the first century AD, as the tumble deriving from their decay lay beneath structures that can be dated around that time, as discussed below.

Remains of domestic occupation discovered during previous field seasons north-east of these walls, above the buried structures of B-I (and also later than P-VI), are dated to the second half of the EIA II, based on a reliable radiocarbon date ranging 807–541 cal BC at 2σ (Degli Esposti et al. 2022: fig. 3; 2024: 195–196).

The newly discovered wall network is open to interpretation. These walls do not appear to be part of residential structures. No hearth or post hole has been identified in the area, differentiating it from the small domestic spaces mentioned above. The overall impression is that they could represent a second phase of the earlier platform system but displaying a less accurate building technique.

Pottery was generally scarce in the area; a few relevant finds, however, contribute to the impression of a non-domestic purpose. Among these are a miniaturist dagger currently under restoration and an anthropomorphic figurine made out of a metal sheet (Fig. 4, bottom left) that has several close parallels at Saruq al-Hadid, where they are dated to the first half of EIA II (i.e. *c*.1100–800 BC) (Valente et al. 2019: 290).

Supposing one accepts this parallel as a basis to tentatively date the later phase of newly unearthed walls at Tell Abraq, in which case, the architectural differences between them and the domestic area to the north-east might reflect a chronological gap. This would indicate a shift in the nature of the site's occupation between the early and later part of EIA II.

The absence of domestic structures at Tell Abraq during the first part of EIA II might be seen in correlation with the development of the prominent, fortified site of Muweilah, some 20 km to the south-west (Karacic et al. 2018), possibly replacing Tell Abraq as the pivotal site of a diffuse occupation along the western coastal region of the UAE. Likewise, the presence of a very small area of domestic activity in the succeeding period can mirror the fragmentation of human occupation between several smaller villages after the sudden end of Muweilah's occupation soon after 800 BC (Magee 2003).

The huge terrace and associated ditch, from the end of the second to the second half of the first millennium BC

Another relevant feature that was erected in the last centuries of the second millennium is the huge wall surrounding the site (see Fig. 1). A burnt deposit discovered beneath it provides a *terminus post quem* for its construction between 1397 and 1127 BC (Degli Esposti et al. 2024: 186–188), in agreement with the date proposed in the last quarter of the second millennium, based on excavation in the western part of the site (Magee et al. 2017: 222). It is extremely probable that this wall, built above an earlier, backfilled ditch, coexisted with a second ditch, a portion of which was excavated during the last two seasons. This, in turn, could correspond to the outer ditch identified in the western part of the site. It is worth pointing out here that EIA III pottery was recovered from the deposits backfilling this ditch, both during our excavation and during the international project investigating the western part of the site (Degli Esposti et al. 2024: 195; Magee et al. 2017: 224), suggesting it remained open for a long time, although a gradual natural backfilling has to be considered.

Two mud-brick buildings, Early Iron Age III/initial late pre-Islamic period (*c*.350–after 150 BC)

Despite the apparent remarkable contraction, the occupation at Tell Abraq did not cease with the EIA II occupation. This season a new building (B-IV, 5 x 4 m) was discovered that pairs a previously exposed one (B-

[1] For years, cars climbed the hill passing just above part of these walls.

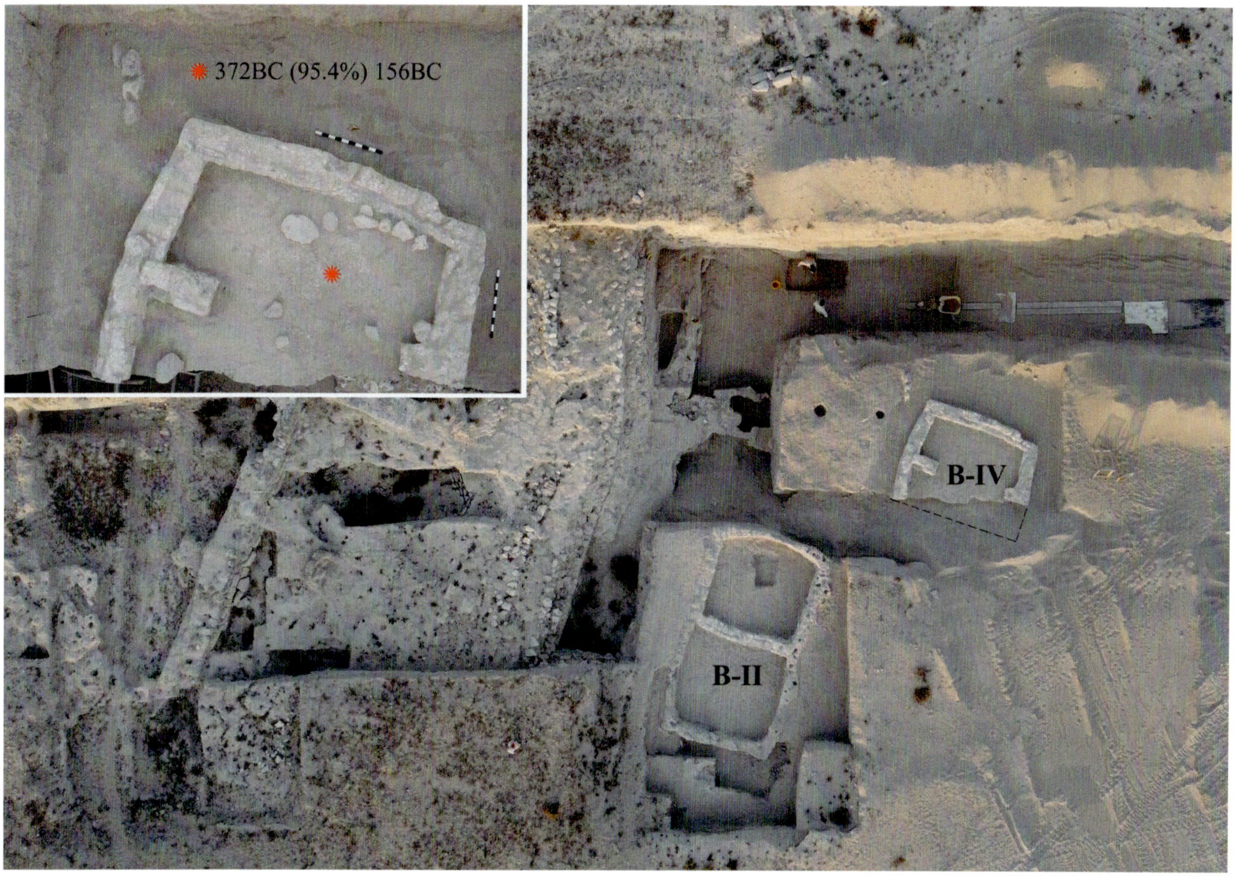

FIGURE 5. *An aerial view of the northern part of the excavated area showing the mud-brick buildings B-II and B-IV. Top left, a detail of B-IV with the location of the date seed sampled from the use surface of B-IV and submitted for radiocarbon dating. A hypothetic integration of B-IV's plan is proposed but we cannot exclude it was meant to include a room with a large entrance facing a simple open area only delimited by one short wall.*

II, 8 x 4 m), both built using a particular type of white mud bricks (Fig. 5). It has already been suggested (Degli Esposti et al. 2024: 196–197) that these mud bricks were made by mixing sand and clay with the carbonate-rich deposits that characterize the coastal sabkha environments typical of the coastal belt, a technique that somehow recalls that attested at the inland site of Thuqaibah, dated to the EIA II/III period (Cordoba 2013). While previous radiocarbon dates (Degli Esposti et al. 2024) did not exclude a possible chronological consistency between the Tell Abraq buildings and the Thuqaibah examples — with the regrettable absence of well-stratified pottery — a newly acquired radiometric date of 372–156 cal BC (2σ)[2] rather places Buildings II and IV between the final part of the EIA III period and the first part of the so-called LPI period, generally dated between 300 BC and AD 300. These buildings sit on the backfilled ditch mentioned above. This new date is also more consistent with the proposed final date for the ditch indicated by the mentioned EIA III pottery discovered in its upper infill. Buildings II and IV can be interpreted as small residential (domestic) units based

[2] From a charred date seed collected from the floor of B-IV. Lab code FTMC-PE64-1; ^{14}C date 2188±32; pMC 76.16±0.31; calibrated with Oxcal 4.4.4 (Bronk Ramsey 2021), atmospheric data from Reimer et al. (2020).

on their unspecific architecture, with the previously mentioned absence of stratified pottery hampering any further discussion of their use.

A late pre-Islamic shrine (first–second century AD)

It is likely that Buildings B-II and B-IV had already been abandoned when another significant change in the ways of human occupation at the site took place. During the past field seasons, a remarkable assemblage of goods was collected midway along the eastern slope of the mound (Degli Esposti et al. 2022; 2024), where a flattened area was evident, which is now known to have been determined by the presence of the buried structures of B-I. The possible presence of a shrine was put forward to explain their presence, although the hypothesis of plundered graves appeared to be more probable (Pavan & Degli Esposti 2023), based on the example of nearby Ed Dur, the reported presence of LPI graves at the site (Potts 1991: 105–119) and the possible identification of other, extremely decayed, similar graves during our previous work (Degli Esposti et al. 2022: 145–146 and fig. 6; 2024: 200–201).

During the 2023 field season, however, the excavation of a poorly preserved building named Building III (B-III) — initially uncovered during the 2022 fieldwork — was completed (Fig. 6), and this discovery has changed the picture.

Despite its poor preservation, with only the bottom row of stones surviving, the roughly square shape of B-III is still visible. Its sides measure *c.*4.8 x 4.5 m. The absence of the southern wall does not seem to derive from a preservation issue but rather indicates it was meant to be open. Another unusual feature discovered south of B-III lends support to this reconstruction. It consists of a relatively limited heap of tumbled stones topped by a huge, now broken, slab (Fig. 6/B). Remarkable is the discovery of an inscribed stone among this rubble (see below, Fig. 7/A). The inscription, written in Aramaic, is currently being studied by M. Moriggi (University of Catania), after a preliminary observation by R. Hoyland (New York University), who identified possible connections with the Palmyrene style (pers. com., February 2024). The placing of this feature raises the hypothesis that these stones are the ruins of an open-air altar or similar small structure, recalling those found in the proximity of the Shamash temple at Ed Dur (Haerinck 2011), although that building cannot be compared with the much simpler one at Tell Abraq. Besides, the suggested association of the Ed Dur temple with Shamash is based on the reading of an inscription, also written in Aramaic (Teixidor 1992: 699 n. 3), incised on the sides of a rectangular basin significantly placed on top of one of the mentioned structures (Structure 4; see Haerinck 2011: 13, pls 71–75).

Overall, the presence of the probable altar and the range of collected artefacts, among which one should recall several bronze figurines (Pavan & Degli Esposti 2023), two stone statues (Degli Esposti et al. 2024: fig. 13), and the fragment of a limestone incense burner that find close parallels at Ed Dur (Haerinck et al. 2021: 116–117 and pls 87–90) (Fig. 7/B), is consistent with the interpretation of B-III as a small shrine.

Recent discoveries have significantly expanded the assemblage of artefacts associated with this building. Apart from a few more terracotta figurines, the most notable discovery has been that of four imitations of Tiberius' aureus — the first coins from a controlled excavation in coastal emirates — three of which were associated with a few coins of the Abiel series and a bronze bracelet (Fig. 7/C).

The gold coins, which find very close parallels at Mleiha (Callot & Mouton 2015), are also important in establishing a date for B-III, as they indicate it was certainly in use after the first quarter of the first century AD. The original aurei of Tiberius were actually minted in ancient Lugdunum (Lyon) during his reign (AD 14–37) (Sutherland 1984: 95 no. 29). A substantial number of Roman gold coins, notably including Tiberius' aurei, have been discovered in India, and it has been speculated that they could have reached eastern Arabia from there; however, the strong links with Characene witnessed at Ed Dur suggest they could have also been redistributed from there alongside other Mediterranean objects (see Haerinck 1998: 292).[3]

Other materials, such as the terracotta figurines (Abric, Pellegrino & Degli Esposti 2024), might indeed indicate an earlier date for the beginning of its occupation. However, although there is no strong

[3] The gold coins are being studied by D. Williams (Austrian Academy of Sciences), and we leave the discussion of this important find to the specific publication. The local Abiel issues are under restoration.

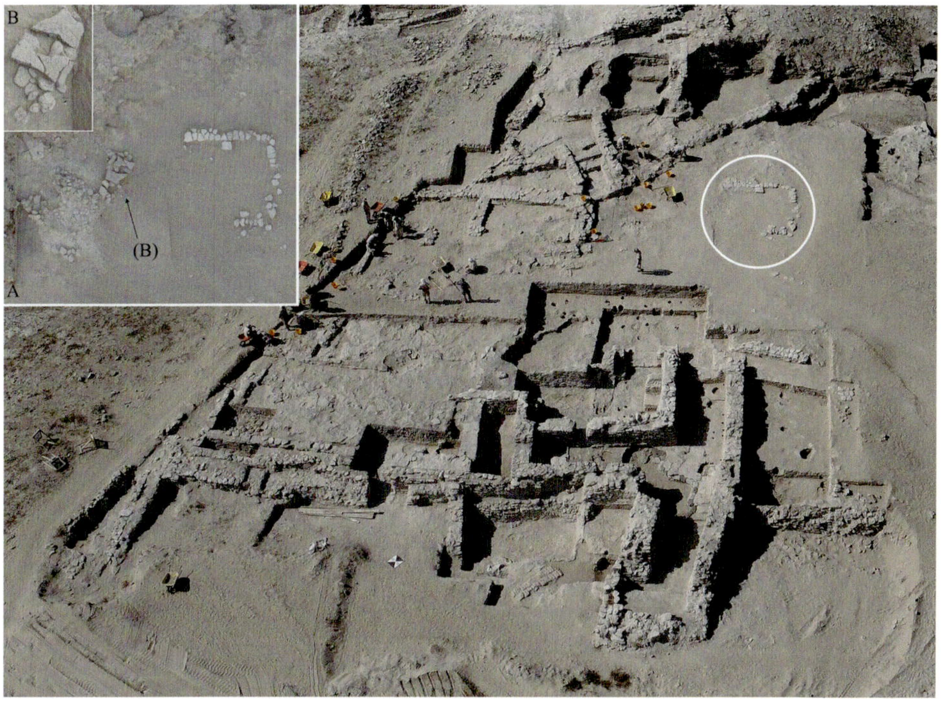

FIGURE 6. *The small shrine B-III (circled) sits on the levelled dune that formed above the remains of B-I (in the foreground).* **A.** *A closer bird's-eye view of the shrine with the adjacent large broken slab belonging to the decayed probable altar — note that the altar's remains cover the adjacent rubble from the wall-network structures;* **B.** *a close-up of the altar's remains. The shrine's sides measure c.4.8 m.*

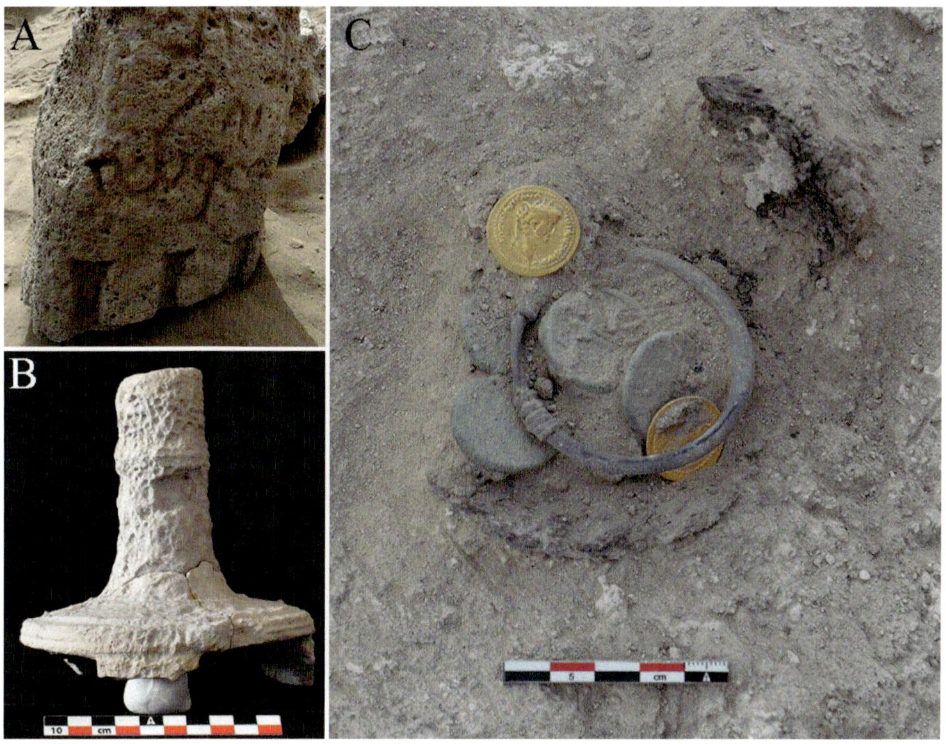

FIGURE 7. A. *The inscribed stone found among the altar rubble (width 25 cm; depth 13 cm; height 40 cm);* **B.** *the fragmentary incense burner discovered near B-III;* **C.** *the probable offering comprising the gold aurei imitations, local Abiel coins and a bronze bracelet, placed inside what remains of a very poorly preserved ceramic bowl.*

argument to rule out the construction of the shrine predating the foundation of Ed Dur, we are more inclined to connect its construction with the life of that large centre which obtained goods from several distant regions (Haerinck 2003). Consequently, we suggest dating the shrine no earlier than the late first century BC or early first century AD. Although it has been recently suggested that Tell Abraq could have hosted harbour activities before the establishment of Ed Dur (Haerinck et al. 2021: 3), there is currently no evidence to support this. One might further posit it was used during the heyday of Ed Dur, until the mid-second century AD. Unfortunately, the amount of pottery collected from contexts associated with the shrine is too small to suggest a date based on ceramic typology.[4]

This date (late first century BC–early second century AD) is consistent with the presence of the two statues, which display a clear southern Mesopotamian influence in the iconography (Degli Esposti et al. 2024: fig. 13),[5] and also with the suggested similarity of the newly discovered inscription with Palmyrene palaeography. The expansion of Ed Dur has been correlated with the Characenian domination over the Gulf trade and its decline was consistently associated with the defeat of the Characene by the Roman legions of Emperor Trajan in the second decade of the second century AD (Haerinck et al. 2021: 3).

The fact remains that a not negligible quantity of coarse LPI pottery was discovered, which does not seem to correlate with the non-residential context of the shrine (and graves) but might now find an explanation in the presence of the mud-brick buildings in the northern part of the site.

As previously stated, however, the construction technique of these buildings, which find no parallel at Ed Dur, suggests they are not contemporary with the shrine and belong to an earlier phase of the LPI period or date immediately before it.

Late Sasanian graves (fourth–seventh century AD?)

The shrine is so far the most recent building we discovered at the site and the last vestige of a non-funerary use of the area.

Apart from extremely decayed features that in a previous publication were suggested might be the remains of LPI graves (Degli Esposti et al. 2022: 145–146 and fig. 6), four other confirmed graves discovered so far clearly date to a later period. After the first of these, Grave 5, was discovered in 2022 near the buried remains of B-I (Degli Esposti et al. 2024: 200–201 and fig. 14), work in the southern end of the 1990 stepped trench excavated by the team headed by Dan Potts led to the discovery of three more graves (labelled 6, 7 and 8; see Fig. 1).

These three graves had an entrance shaft cut through older sediments and structures. At the bottom of the circular shaft, an undercut side-chamber hosted the individual body, so that it would be even more hidden. This lower niche would have been covered with stone slabs and the upper shaft backfilled with sand and debris or other stones. The bodies were lying on one side, with the legs flexed in a crouching position. The arms were usually flexed in a way that one hand was placed almost in front of the mouth, while the other was flexed above the torso. These burials are of further interest in that they seem to anticipate Islamic practices, specifically the *lahd* type which has a rectangular niche cut into the side of the main pit where the deceased is placed (Petersen 2013: 247).

Grave 6 was identified along the eastern margin of the 1990s trench, where a discontinuity in a poorly made stone and mud wall, SU 723, was noted (Fig. 8/D). This wall corresponds to Locus 52 in the old excavation record (Potts 1991: figs 182–183). The discontinuity turned out to be the cut for the grave's shaft, ending in an undercut side-chamber to the south where the body was laid (Fig. 8/C). The deceased was buried with two iron spearheads of different shapes, one placed to the right of the body in front of the flexed arms (F618) and the other above the skull (F619; Fig. 8). Two spherical, well-polished beads made in carnelian and possibly rock crystal, were also found, probably

[4] It might be worth recalling here, however, the presence at Tell Abraq of 'Early Namord' ware dated to the first and second century AD (Potts 1998). At the same time, Tiberius' aurei discovered at Mleiha were dated to the first half of the third century AD on the basis of the context of discovery (Callot & Mouton 2015: 248). Further study of the artefacts connected with the shrine is ongoing which, it is hoped, will help to clarify the final date of its use.

[5] I. Bucci, pers. com., June 2024. The detailed publication of the two statues is in preparation by I. Bucci and M. Degli Esposti.

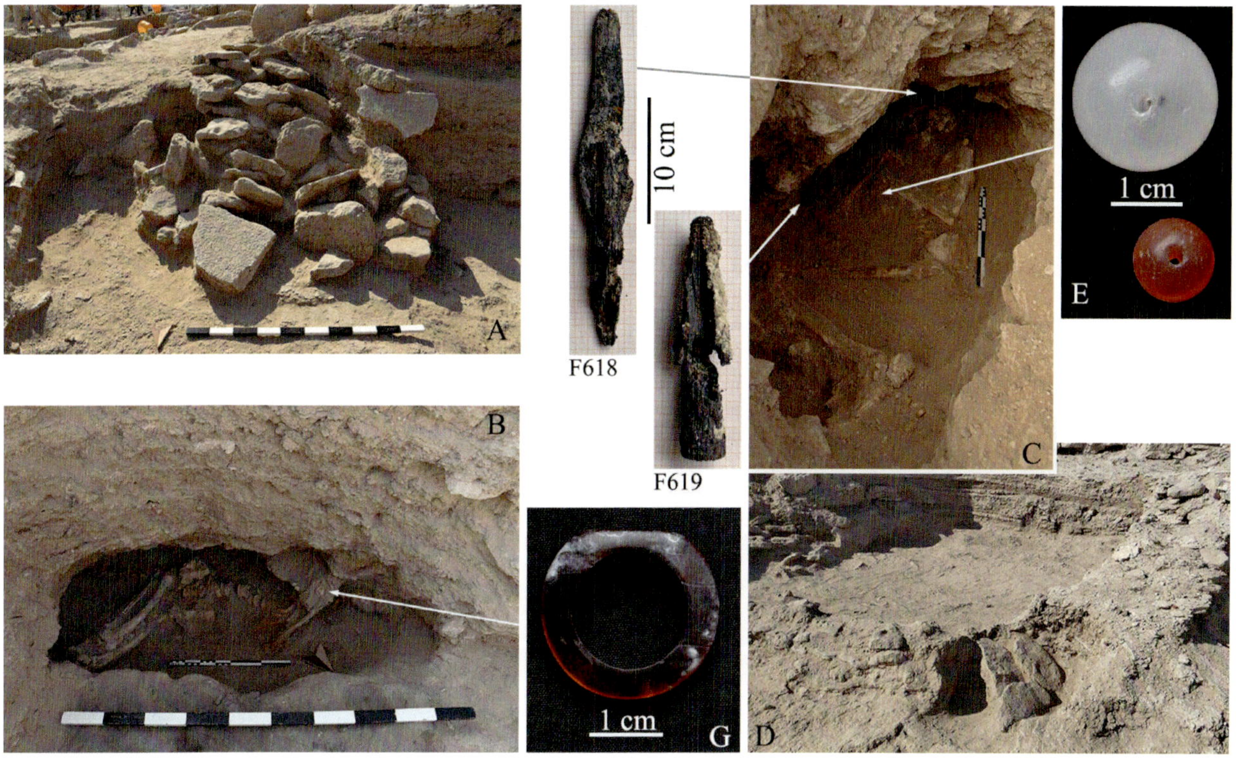

FIGURE 8. *The stone-filled shaft (**A**) and the southern undercut chamber (**B**) of Grave 6, with the carnelian ring found on the body (**G**). The upper part of the shaft of Grave 7 (**D**) and the undercut chamber with the interred body (**C**), with the discovered grave-goods from both graves (E, F618, F619, G).*

held in one hand (Fig. 8/E). This grave was discovered below the area identified as Locus 46 by Potts and said to be a plundered grave that, interestingly, allegedly comprised two iron spearheads (Potts 1991: 114). Only a few, disarticulated human bones were discovered at the time.

Grave 7 is the same grave as the one identified by Potts as Locus 64, excavated at the southern end of the stepped trench. The shaft with its stone fill (Fig. 8/A) was also represented in the southern section of the corresponding square of the grid established at the time (Potts 1991: 112–114). While the skeleton unearthed during the 1990 season occupied a side chamber north of the shaft, the IAMUQ's excavations emptied the grave shaft to discover a second undercut chamber to the south, where another interment was revealed (Fig. 8/B). A carnelian ring was found on one of the left-hand fingers (Fig. 8/G).

Grave 8 also corresponds to a feature that had been identified in 1990 but not properly understood or fully excavated. Earlier excavations (Potts 1991: fig. 182) had brought to light a pit (Locus 51, now renamed SU 663) cut through two ancient stone walls, the upper one named Locus 50 (now SU 673) and the lower one apparently not labelled (now SU 652). After cleaning, it became evident that the pit's fill had not been completely removed and its excavation was restarted. This led to the discovery of a distinctive cemented vault made with flat stones bound in a grey mortar (Fig. 9/A) that bore impressed finger grooves. This vault, for which the authors do not currently know any parallel, sealed a low chamber at the bottom of the main shaft, where a skeleton was found with no associated artefact (Fig. 9/B).

An absolute date for these graves has still to be obtained (sample processing is awaited) but a broad chronology between the fourth and seventh centuries AD

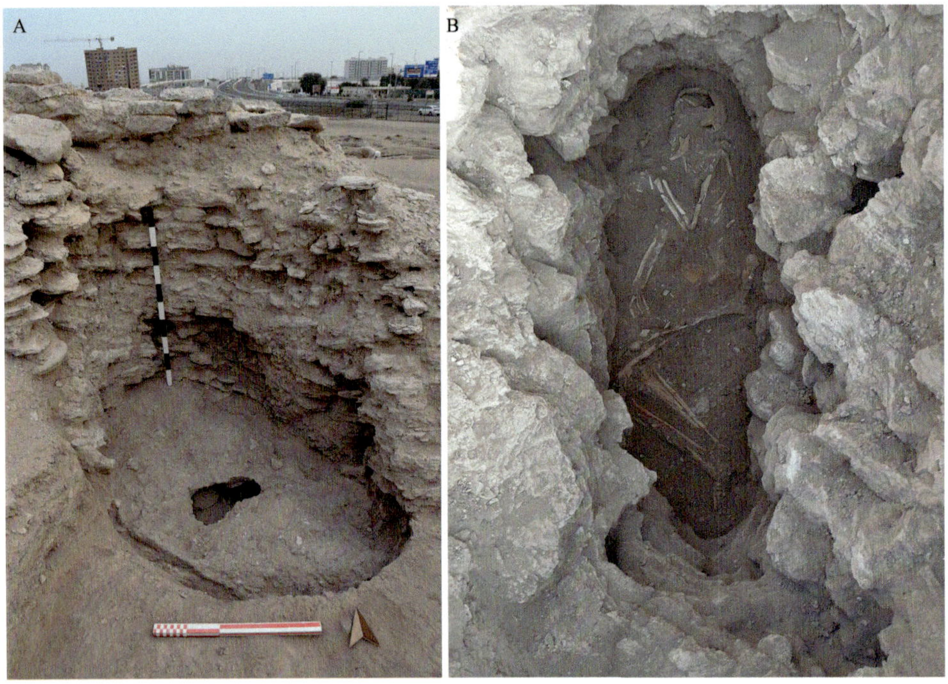

Figure 9. *The shaft of Grave 9 cutting through earlier walls* (**A**) *and the body interred at the bottom* (**B**).

can be suggested based on the morphological similarity between the spearhead found in Grave 6 (Fig. 8/F618) and that from Tomb III at Jabal Emalah (Potts 1997: figs 6–7) that was also placed in front of the body, likewise resting on the right side with flexed legs and arms. Tomb III at Jabal Emalah, as well as another secondary interment in Tomb I, were radiocarbon dated between the third/fourth and seventh/eighth century AD. Nevertheless, they are clearly pre-Islamic and can therefore be dated to the late Sasanian period (Potts 1997: 128, 130). This date would also be consistent with the *terminus post quem* for the end of human presence at Tell Abraq provided by the discovery of a Sasanian drachm attributed to Shapur II (r. AD 309–379) (Potts 1993: 119; 2000: 115).

Concluding remarks

The data gathered during the first five seasons of renewed excavation in the eastern sector of Tell Abraq now enable us to sketch out a preliminary reconstruction of human occupation at the site from the final centuries of the second millennium BC to the first centuries AD, as suggested by the diachronic changes in its layout and architecture (Fig. 10).

The antecedent for the period discussed here is marked by the presence of a substantial building, B-I, probably erected around the mid-second millennium and soon struck by a large fire that led to its rapid and repeated restructuring. Providing space for this building required the removal of a considerable quantity of earlier archaeological stratification, an issue that will be investigated specifically during the 2024 field season.

The presence of B-I illustrates the case of a non-domestic building probably dominating the eastern flank of the site, possibly coexisting with humbler dwellings both in the surrounding plain and potentially along the terraced hill slopes.

Be that as it may, the following phase, corresponding to what is commonly referred to as the EIA I period (1300–1100 BC) and to the first part of the EIA II period (until *c.*800 BC), does not so far show any evidence of dwellings on the mound itself. The eastern flank sees the development of two consecutive, extensive terrace systems, the first of which was built using a distinctive technique, to our knowledge not witnessed elsewhere, that constitutes a reliable link with other features excavated previously at the site. The nature of these structures is consistent with communal use, possibly ceremonial or cultic. No evidence of additional structures was collected, but work

Period	Use	Main structures
c. 1500–1300 BC (?)		*Construction of Building I with the removal of earlier deposits*
		Fire, restructuring and abandonment
1300–1100 BC	Communal (cultic)?	Large platform (B VI) above buried Building I and associated platform system along the eastern slope, reaching the top of the site. Construction of the huge surrounding wall and ditch
1100–800 BC (?)	Communal (cultic)?	New wall network and platform system along the eastern slope
800–600/500 BC	Residential	Domestic occupation in a limited area, above B VI
350–150 BC (?)	Residential	Mud-brick buildings in the northern part of the site above backfilled ditch — end date to be defined
c.50–150 AD	Cultic + funerary?	Shrine (possibly extending later). Reported LPI burials
300–650 AD (?)	Funerary	Burials

FIGURE 10. *A summary of the proposed broad phasing for the site with an indication of the different uses over time. Light blue lines highlight major hiatuses in the sequence. Italicized text indicates phases preceding those discussed in the text.*

in the surrounding plain by the international Mission working in the Sharjah part of the site reports abundant human activity during the EIA I period (Magee et al. 2017: 223). Indulging in a speculative narrative, one may suggest these are the traces left by people visiting the ceremonial site.

Around the beginning of the eighth century BC, the site seems to have undergone a transformation. While the terraces fell into disuse, evidence of domestic activity emerged within a limited area. This suggests a small community may have re-established itself at the site during this period, potentially echoing a broader dispersal following the abrupt destruction of the nearby fortified settlement at Muweilah (Magee 2003).

Domestic activity in this part of the site continued, albeit with the construction of new structures using distinct building techniques, into the early phases of the LPI period. It appears that the site was later destined for uses other than residential.

At least by the mid-first century AD, a shrine was erected above the buried structures and the tumbled stones of earlier periods. Despite its small dimensions, it could attract prestige artefacts some of which are unparalleled in the region. The broader context of this shrine is most likely represented by the blooming of the nearby site of Ed Dur and its participation in a long-distance trade network that connected the whole Gulf and, indirectly, the societies lying beyond its shores.

Probably due to its prominence in the landscape, the site became a burial ground, possibly attracting a community of newcomers during the period of Sasanian influence beginning in the third century AD. The newly discovered graves presented here offer a promising avenue for exploring the movement of people within the region during the period of Sasanian rule, pending the results of radio-chronometric and bioanthropological analyses, for which samples have already been submitted.

At a complex, multi-layered site like Tell Abraq, where human activity spanned nearly three millennia, successive occupations, coupled with erosion and deflation, have inevitably obscured traces of earlier periods. While substantial structures deserving *in situ* conservation are valuable, they also further limit the scope of extensive archaeological investigation necessary to comprehend the site's layout and infer its use beyond the less informative data obtained by examining stratigraphic sequences in small trenches.

While the archaeological record still requires further investigation and breaks in the broad chronological sequence are evident (see Fig. 10), the IAMUQ's strategic approach at Tell Abraq, informed by the above considerations, has proved fruitful. Excavations have successfully begun to reveal the dynamic history of human occupation, shedding light on changes in settlement density, architecture and site usage. Future field seasons will continue to utilize this approach, with a specific focus on earlier contexts to enhance our comprehension of the site's evolution and the broader historical significance of human activity at Tell Abraq through time.

Author contributions

MDE as field director of the IAMUQ planned the research, carried out survey and excavation, analysed data, wrote the first draft and edited the paper; MPP carried out survey and excavation and analysed data; FBo as head surveyor of the IAMUQ carried out aerial photogrammetry, survey and excavation; FBa carried out survey and excavation; RHK assisted in the fieldwork and managed logistics; all authors reviewed the paper.

Acknowledgements

The 2023 field season at Tell Abraq was funded by the TAD-UAQ, which also supports the IAMUQ for accommodation and field logistics. Special thanks are due to its Chairman, Shaikh Mājid b. Saʿūd b. Rashid Āl Muʾallā, for his passionate interest in our research and Haythan Sultan Al Ali, Director General of the TAD-UAQ, for allowing us to publish this work.

References

Abric C., Pellegrino M.P. & Degli Esposti M. 2024. A pottery study approach to small find analyses: The zoomorphic clay figurines from Tell Abraq (Umm Al-Quwain, UAE). Pages 29–57 in A. Kilian, M. Zöller-Engelhardt & A. Pruß (eds), *Excavating the extra-ordinary 2. Challenges and merits of working with small finds. Proceedings of the International Interdisciplinary Workshop at Johannes Gutenberg-University Mainz, 25–26 November 2022*. Heidelberg: Propylaeum.

Bronk Ramsey C. 2021. OxCal v.4.4.4 [software]. https://c14.arch.ox.ac.uk/oxcal.html Accessed 5 May 2024.

Callot O. & Mouton M. 2015. Deux séries monétaires d'Arabie orientale dans un contexte bien daté du IIIe s. apr. J.-C. à Mleiha (Arabie). *Revue numismatique* 6/172: 243–255.

Cordoba J.M. 2013. New perspectives about Iron Age and the oasis culture in the Oman peninsula. Two conclusive seasons at al-Madam (Sharjah, UAE). *Isimu* 16: 139–152.

Degli Esposti M. & Borgi F. 2023. Life and death at Tell Abraq during the 2nd and 1st millennium BC: The Abraq Research Project's 2022 season. *Bulletin of the International Association for the Study of Arabia* 30: 15–17.

Degli Esposti M., Borgi P., Pellegrino M.P., Spano S. & Abric C. 2022. Renewed excavations at Tell Abraq, Umm al Quwain, 2019–2020. Insights into the site's occupation from the mid-2nd millennium BC to the late pre-Islamic period. *Proceedings of the Seminar for Arabian Studies* 51: 141–156.

Degli Esposti M., Borgi P., Pellegrino M.P., Abric C., Barchiesi F. & Houssein Kannouma R. 2024. Another side to the story. Preliminary results from the renewed excavations on the eastern side of Tell Abraq (Umm Al-Quwain). Pages 183–207 in *Advances in UAE Archaeology: Proceedings of Abu Dhabi's Archaeology Conference 2022*. Abu Dhabi/Oxford: Zayed National Museum — Department of Culture and Tourism/ Archaeopress.

Haerinck E. 1998. International contacts in the southern Persian Gulf in the late 1st century B.C./1st century A.D.: Numismatic evidence from Ed-Dur (Emirate of Umm Aa-Qaiwain, U.A.E.). *Iranica Antiqua* 33: 273–302.

Haerinck E. 2003. Internationalisation and business in southeast Arabia during the late 1st century B.C./1st century A.D.: Archaeological evidence from Ed Dur (Umm al-Qaiwain, U.A.E.). Pages 195–242 in D.T. Potts, K. Al Naboodah & P. Hellyer (eds), *Archaeology of the United Arab Emirates: Proceedings of the First International Conference on the Archaeology of the U.A.E.* London: Trident Press.

Haerinck E. 2011. *The University of Ghent South-East Arabian Archaeological Project: Excavations at Ed Dur (Umm al-Qaiwain, United Arab Emirates).* iii. *A temple of the sun-god Shamash and other occupational remains at Ed Dur (Emirate of Umm al-Qaiwain, UAE).* Leuven: Peeters.

Haerinck E., Overlaet B., De Waele A. & Delrue P. 2021. *The University of Ghent South-East Arabian Archaeological Project: Excavations at Ed Dur (Umm al-Qaiwain, United*

Arab Emirates). iv. Small finds from Ed Dur, Umm Al-Qaiwain, U.A.E. (late 1st cent. BCE to early 2nd cent. CE). Leuven: Peeters.

Karacic S., Händel M., Hammer E. & Magee P. 2018. The architecture of the Iron Age II fortified settlement at Muweilah (Sharjah, United Arab Emirates). *Arabian Archaeology and Epigraphy* 29/1: 27–54.

Magee P. 2003. New chronometric data defining the Iron Age II period in south-eastern Arabia. *Proceedings of the Seminar for Arabian Studies* 33: 1–10.

Magee P., Händel M., Karacic S., Uerpmann M. & Uerpmann H.P. 2017. Tell Abraq during the second and first millennia BC: Site layout, spatial organisation, and economy. *Arabian Archaeology and Epigraphy* 28/2: 209–237.

Pavan A. &. Degli Esposti M. 2023. Copper-alloy figurines from Tell Abraq (Umm al-Quwain, UAE) and the circulation of Hellenistic motifs in late pre-Islamic Arabia (300 BC–300 AD). *Arabian Archaeology and Epigraphy* 34: 87–101.

Petersen A. 2013. The archaeology of death and burial in the Islamic world. Pages 241–259 in L. Nilsson Stutz & A. Tarlow (eds), *The Oxford handbook of the archaeology of death and burial.* Oxford: Oxford University Press.

Potts D.T. 1991. *Further excavations at Tell Abraq. The 1990 season.* Copenhagen: Munksgaard International Publishers.

Potts D.T. 1993. Four seasons of excavation at Tell Abraq (1989–1993). *Proceedings of the Seminar for Arabian Studies* 23: 117–126.

Potts D.T. 1997. Late Sasanian armament from southern Arabia. *Electrum* 1: 127–137.

Potts D.T. 1998. Namord ware in south-eastern Arabia. Pages 207–220 in C.S. Phillips, D.T. Potts & S. Searight (eds), *Arabia and its neighbours. Essays on prehistorical and historical developments presented in honour of Beatrice de Cardi.* (Abiel. New research on the Arabian Peninsula, 2). Turnhout: Brepols.

Potts D.T. 2000. *Ancient Magan. The secrets of Tell Abraq.* London: Trident Press.

Reimer P.J., Austin W.E.N., Bard E., Bayliss A., Blackwell P.G., Bronk Ramsey C. ... Talamo S. 2020. The IntCal20 Northern Hemisphere radiocarbon age calibration curve (0–55 cal kBP). *Radiocarbon* 62: 725–757.

Sutherland C.H.V. 1984. *The Roman imperial coinage.* i. *From 31 BC to AD 69.* (Revised edition). London: Spink and Son.

Teixidor J. 1992. Une inscription araméenne provenant de l'Émirat de Sharjah (Émirats Arabes Unis). *Comptes rendus des séances de l'Académie des Inscriptions et Belles-Lettres* 136/4: 695–707.

Valente T., Contreras F., Mahmud A., Al Ali Y.Y.A. & Boraik M. 2019. Anthropomorphic figurines from Area 2A of Sārūq Al-Ḥadīd, Dubai, UAE. *Proceedings of the Seminar for Arabian Studies* 49: 283–292.

Authors' addresses

Michele Degli Esposti, Director of the Italian Archaeological Mission in Umm al-Quwain, Institute of Mediterranean and Oriental Cultures, Polish Academy of Sciences, Nowy Świat 72, Room 327, 00-330 Warsaw, Poland.
e-mail michele.degliesposti@gmail.com

Federico Borgi, Director of the Italian Archaeological Mission in Umm al-Quwain, Tourism and Archaeology Department, Government of Umm al-Quwain, PO Box 1500, Umm al-Quwain, UAE.
e-mail federico.borgi@gmail.com

Maria Paola Pellegrino, Archaïos, 20 rue des Gravilliers, 75003 Paris, France.
e-mail mariapaola.pellegrino@archaios.fr

Francesca Barchiesi, Dipartimento di Storia Culture Civiltà, Università di Bologna, Piazza San Giovanni in Monte 2, 40124 Bologna, Italy.
e-mail francesca.barchiesi4@unibo.it

Rania Hussein Kannouma, Tourism and Archaeology Department, Government of Umm al-Quwain, PO Box 1500, Umm al-Quwain, UAE.
e-mail rania.kannouma@tad.uaqgov.ae

Proceedings of the Seminar for Arabian Studies 54 (2025): 72–87

Dating early narratives of the Hijra

Adrien de Jarmy

Summary

This study examines the progressive development of early Hijra narratives within Islamic tradition. Using a novel method for dating semantic units within hadiths or motifs, it demonstrates that Hijra narratives were constructed over several decades, shaped by diverse transmitters and evolving historical contexts. An SQL (Structured Query Language) database was programmed to collect and trace these motifs, allowing for precise tracking of their transmission. The analysis identifies three key stages in the construction of the narrative: the early layers of narratives circulating at the end of the first/seventh century; the addition of various anecdotes of persecution and divine protection during the first half of the second/eighth century; and a distinctive interpretation of the 'constitution' of Medina (*ṣaḥīfat al-Madīna*) by Ibn Isḥāq in the *Sīra*. The findings underscore the role of political factors, particularly the rise of the Abbasid state, in shaping a canonical version of the Hijra story to present a unified Muslim community. This approach offers a dynamic, multi-layered analysis of the evolution of Islamic historiography, challenging static interpretations and illustrating how these narratives were adapted to serve political purposes across centuries.

Keywords: Muḥammad, Hijra, Sīra, hadith, digital humanities

Introduction

According to Islamic tradition, the Hijra refers to the migration of Muḥammad and his followers from Mecca to Medina in AD 622. It marks the beginning of the Islamic calendar and symbolizes the formation of the *umma*, the first community of believers. In their study of the narratives reported by ʿUrwa b. al-Zubayr (d. 94/712–713), Gregor Schoeler and Andreas Görke have identified a series of early traditions (hadiths) concerning the Hijra that were circulating in Medina at the end of the first/seventh century (Schoeler & Görke 2008: 38–77; Görke 2005). Applying the *isnād-cum-matn* method — a technique for analysing hadiths by examining the chain of transmission (*isnād*) alongside the content (*matn*) of the narrative — has made it possible to highlight the central role of this transmitter in the dissemination of the first accounts relating to the life of Muḥammad (Motzki & Schoeler 2012). However, by focusing on a single transmitter and his followers, this approach presents limitations for the dynamic analysis of the development of the narratives. The objective of this article is not so much to focus on a single transmitter as to understand when and where early Hijra narratives were put into circulation, and when these narratives began to gain authority within the Islamic tradition.

In order to overcome this difficulty, I have adopted what I call the pattern-dating method, already tried and tested in my earlier work on the controversy related to the identification of the collective of the *sābiqūn* in the Islamic tradition (de Jarmy 2025). The foundations of this method go back to the work of Joseph Schacht and G.H.A. Juynboll and the identification of *common links* (CL), *partial common links* (PCL), and *inverted common links* (ICL) (Schacht 1979: 77–81, 315–328; Juynboll 1993; 1994).[1] The approach I propose is in line with this continuity, while differing in certain respects. In the Islamic tradition, the basic unit is the hadith. The methodological revolution initiated in Iraq led Muslim scholars to associate chains of transmission with texts. This only developed in the second/eighth century, which poses a real problem for going back to the first/seventh century and leads Schacht to consider that any attempt to go back to this period is futile (Schacht 1949). With the aim of partly breaking the mould imposed by the Islamic tradition,[2] I suggest that, instead of being strictly limited to the hadith, the analysis focuses on examining recurring literary motifs in the Islamic

[1] The list of supporters and critics of Schacht and Juynboll has already been summarized; see Berg 2003 and Pavlovitch 2020.

[2] For a first attempt to circumvent the structure of the Islamic tradition, see Tillier 2022a and 2022b.

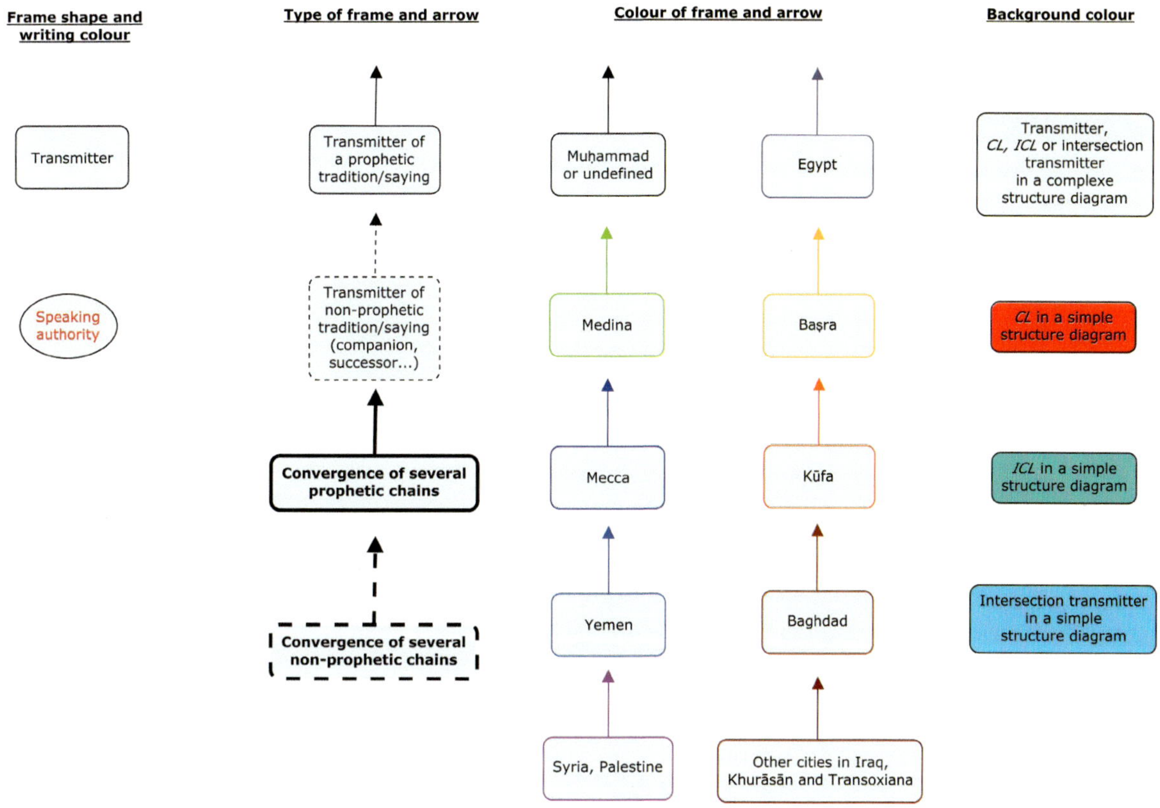

Figure 1. *Key to the diagrams.*

tradition. A motif may correspond to a hadith or to only part of a hadith, and may include variants of the text. This approach offers a more flexible perspective for dating and analysing the moment when a word or text acquires authority. I propose to consider the motif as a semantic unit, manifesting as a coherent narrative or story dispersed across multiples texts. Occurrences of a motif and its associated transmitters within the corpus are then recorded in a relational database programmed in SQL language[3] using the MySQL management system. The database is organized around three interconnected tables: one for the sources, one for the transmitters, and one for the motifs.[4] The corpus includes sources from historiography (*Sīra* and *maghāzī*), biographical dictionaries (*ṭabaqāt*), as well as Islamic jurisprudence (*fiqh*) and Quranic exegesis (*tafāsīr*), from the earliest texts up until the classical hadiths compilations of the third/ninth and fourth/tenth centuries. The database is used to generate diagrams through the CmapTools software (https://cmap.ihmc.us/) to identify transmission patterns. Each diagram is systematically accompanied by a record of all occurrences of the motif and their placement within the corpus.

Figure 1 presents a key of diagrams, which fall into two categories: diagrams with simple structures, where one or more chains of narrations trace back to a single speaker, and diagrams with complex structures, where chains are attributed to multiple speaking authorities.

[3] SQL (Structured Query Language) is a declarative query language. It is a programming language created by Donald D.D. Chamberlain and Raymond R.F. Boyce (1946–1973), two colleagues of Edgar F. Codd at IBM. SQL was designed solely to provide a simplified means of querying a relational database based on the model invented by Codd.

[4] The SQL database was programmed during my PhD dissertation and contains around 3000 hadiths linked to 1200 transmitters. The database is not accessible to the public, but its structure is detailed in de Jarmy 2023: 67–74.

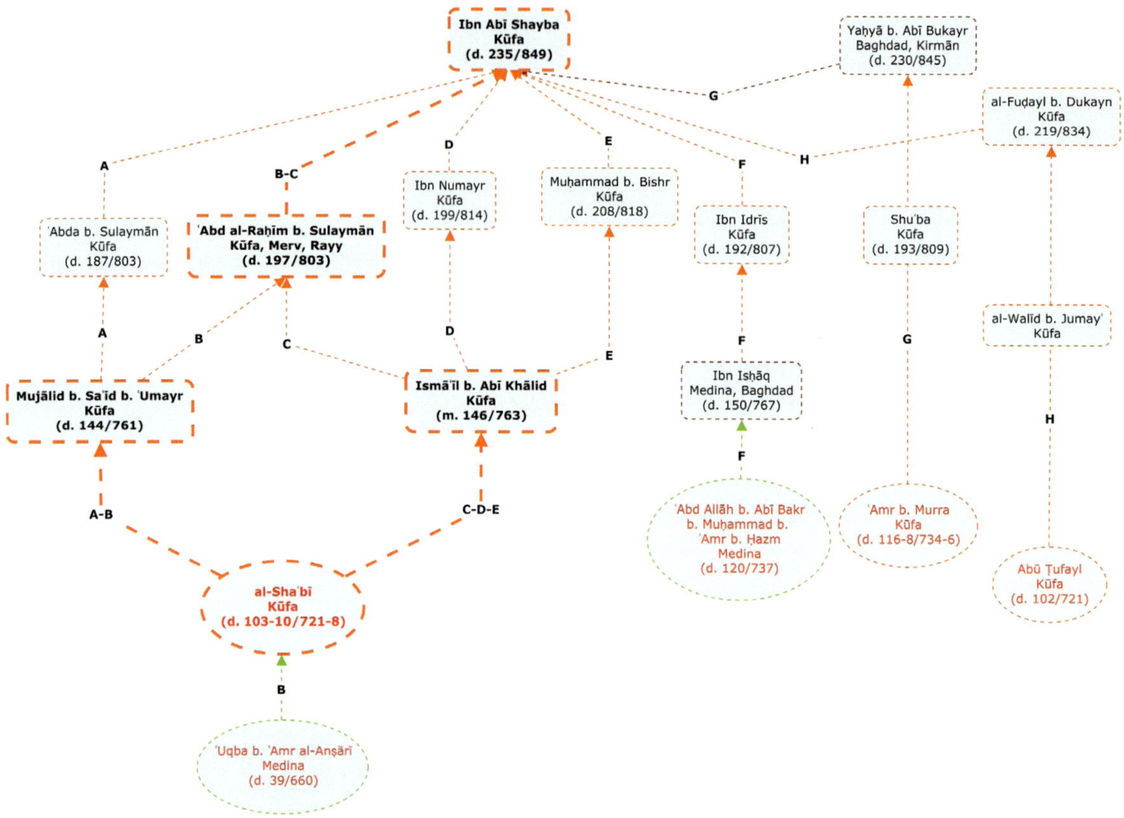

FIGURE 2. *The oath of al-ʿAqaba according to Ibn Abī Shayba.*

Where possible, the dating provided by the diagrams is also compared with data provided by external sources such as the Qurʾān and commentaries, biographical information about the transmitters, data conferred by material sources, and even academic literature. Generally speaking, the approach is to establish the dating of the motif by going back up the chronological thread of the data; based either on the indications of the material sources or on the dating proposed by the diagram, these two starting points may be interchanged.

As far as the Hijra is concerned, it is clear that this is not a story told all at once or by a single speaker, but rather a gradual, polyphonic construction over several decades. This process of narrative enrichment contributed to the growing importance of this narrative within the Islamic tradition, until Ibn Isḥāq made it a founding moment of the *umma*. This study thus aims to highlight three distinct strata in the construction of the Hijra narratives.

The first layers of Hijra narratives

The oaths at al-ʿAqaba

The accounts of the two oaths sworn at al-ʿAqaba by the first *anṣār*[5] to Muḥammad, in anticipation of welcoming him to Yathrib, are among the earliest strata of Hijra narratives. Two versions can be identified.

In the Iraqi version reported by Ibn Abī Shayba (1989, vii: 444–445), the transmitters make no distinction between the first oath — also known as the women's oath in Islamic tradition because the *anṣār* do not yet promise to engage in combat against the Quraysh — and the second oath.

Figure 2 presents a diagram with a complex structure, illustrating a motif attributed to several

[5] Inhabitants of Yathrib/Medina who welcomed Muḥammad and his companions from Mecca during the Hijra.

authorities or speakers. The majority of the connections trace back to the Kūfan scholar al-Shaʿbī (d. 103–110/721–728) as well as to authorities from the generation of the companions (*al-ṣaḥāba*). Al-Shaʿbī is both speaker[6] of chains A, C, D, and E and exchanger,[7] chain B being attributed to ʿUqba b. ʿAmr al-Anṣārī (d. 39/660). The reattribution of the motif to the companion is probably the work of Mujālid b. Saʿīd b. ʿUmayr (d. 144/761), or his disciple ʿAbd al-Raḥīm b. Sulaymān (d. 197/803). Whatever the case, the testimony of al-Shaʿbī is confirmed by Mujālid b. Saʿīd b. ʿUmayr and Ismāʿīl b. Abī Khālid, respectively PCL of chains A and B, and C, D, and E, as well as by the presence of complementary chains G and H which go back to two authorities contemporary with Kūfa: ʿAmr b. Murra (d. 116–118/734–736) and Abū Ṭufayl (d. 102/721).

We can now turn our attention to the groups of traditions that clearly distinguish the first from the second oath of al-ʿAqaba. These are shown in Figures 3 and 4 respectively (Ibn Hishām 1987, ii: 86; Ibn Saʿd 1990, i: 170; al-Ṭabarī 1879–1901: 1213–1218): both diagrams reveal motifs with multiple attributions. In Figure 3, chains A, B, and C are attributed to the companion ʿUbāda b. al-Ṣāmit (d. 34/658). The Egyptian transmitter Marthad b. ʿAbd Allāh (d. 90/708) appears at first sight to be the CL of chains A–B and C, but the Medinese ʿAbd al-Ḥamīd b. Jaʿfar (d. 153/770) reports chain C through his father. This is a common procedure in hadith when a transmitter wishes to attach a chain to an authority in the town from which he comes from. As a precautionary measure, it is therefore best to refer to Marthad's disciple Yazīd b. Abī Ḥabīb (d. 127/745), PCL of chains A and B.

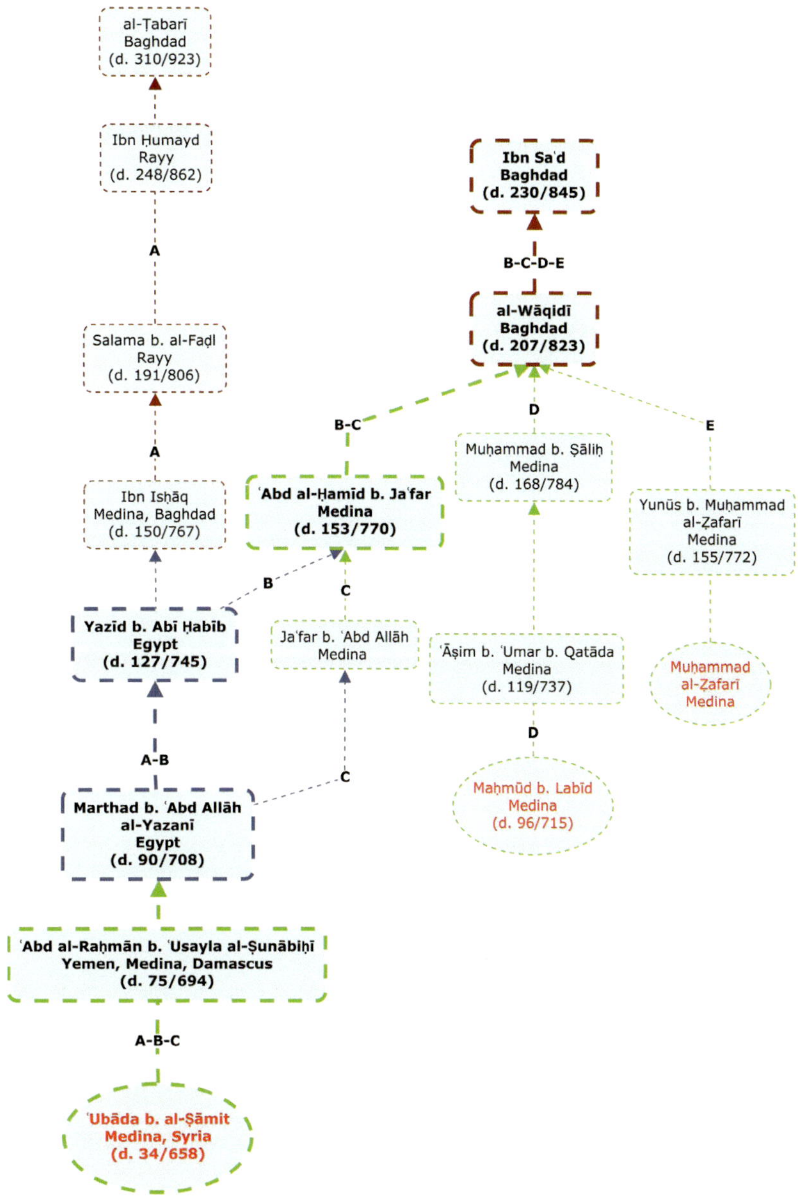

FIGURE 3. *The first oath of al-ʿAqaba.*

In Figure 4, ʿUbāda b. al-Ṣāmit also appears as the speaker of strings E and H reported by his grandson ʿUbāda b. al-Walīd, CL of both strings. Here too we

[6] Speaking authority of a word, or at least the person to whom a word is attributed.
[7] Speaker relegated to transmitter status by a late transmitter.

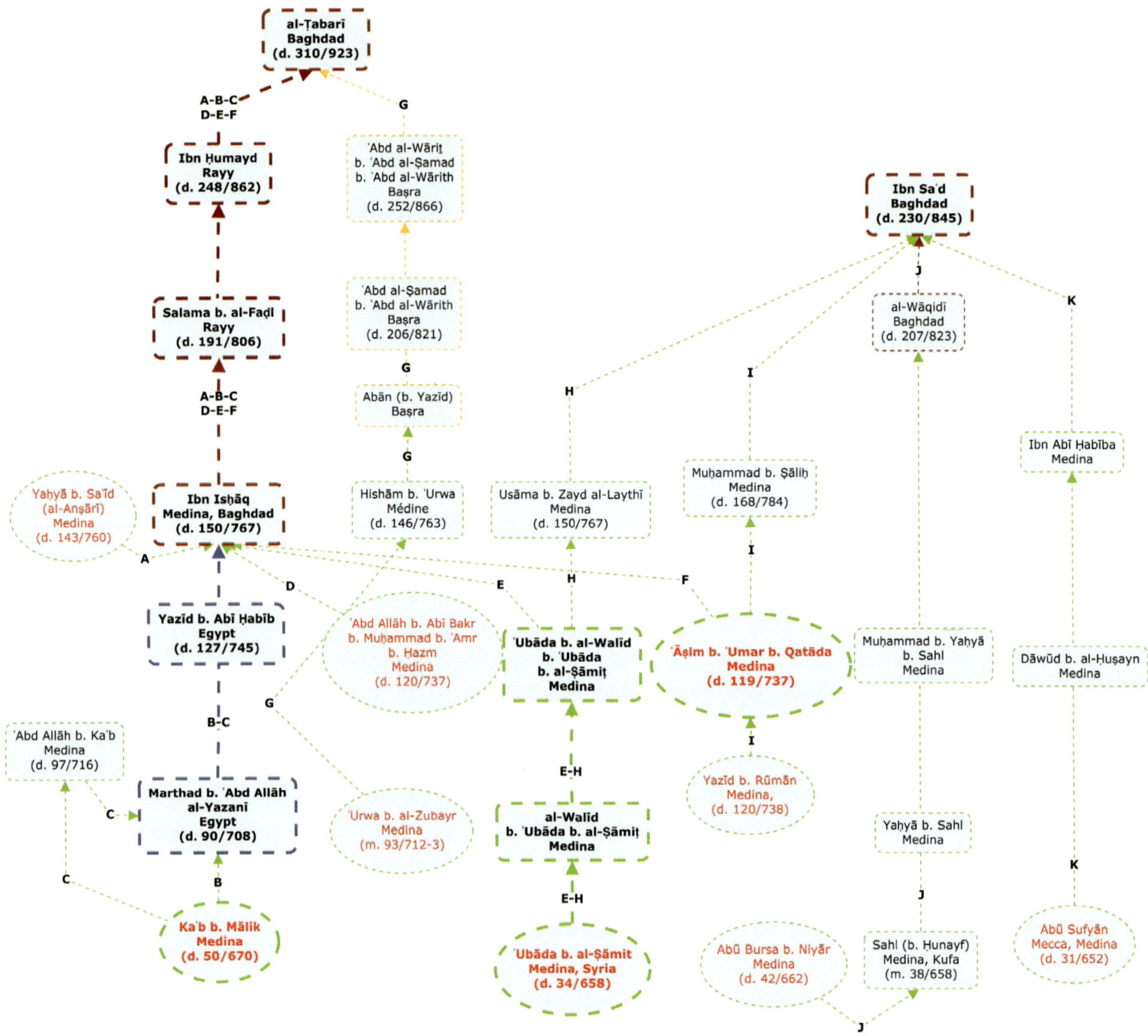

FIGURE 4. *The second oath of al-ʿAqaba.*

can identify a process of reassigning the motif to an ancestor. Marthad b. ʿAbd Allāh and Yazīd b. Abī Ḥabīb are also present in Figure 4, but the latter loses his PCL status here. The main transmitter towards whom most of the chains converge is none other than Ibn Isḥāq (d. 150/767), ICL of chains A, B–C, D, E, and F. The following hypothesis must then be deduced. The motif would first have appeared in this form from the mouth of ʿAbd Allāh b. Abī Bakr (d. 120/737) and ʿĀṣim b. ʿUmar b. Qatāda (d. 119/737) in Medina (chains D and F). Indeed, as Schacht noticed, broken chains (*mursal*) are older because they express a time when chains (*isnād*) had not yet been attached to texts (*matn*) (Schacht 1979: 39). In a second stage, the motif would have been reattributed to companions such as Kaʿb b. Mālik (d. 50/670), ʿUbāda b. al-Ṣāmit, Abū Bursa b. Niyār (d. 42/662), and Abū Sufyān (d. 31/652), potentially at the time of Ibn Isḥāq's compilation of the text.

The convergence of the transmitters mentioned in the two diagrams thus leads us to identify their circulation in Medina and Egypt in the years 100–120/710–730. It is possible that the stories were already circulating a little earlier in this form in Medina via the teaching of ʿUrwa b. al-Zubayr (d. 93/712–713) and Maḥmūd b. Labīd (d. 96/715), the speaker of channels G and D, but this cannot be confirmed without the presence of CL. Thus, while this episode is already well known at the end of the first century of the Hijra (see Fig. 2), the narrative of the two oaths only really begins to be structured in the Islamic tradition at the beginning of the second/eighth century (see Figs 3 and 4).

Muḥammad and Abū Bakr hide in the cave of al-Thawr

The story of the cave is another ancient literary motif in the Islamic tradition, recounting the escape of Muḥammad and Abū Bakr who find refuge for three nights in the cave of al-Thawr to escape the Quraysh. Protected by a spider's web at the entrance, they escape their pursuers. ʿĀmir b. Furayra, the *mawlā* of Abū Bakr, comes to graze his flock of sheep near the cave once the early evening hours have passed, allowing the two fugitives to feed on their milk. After these three nights, they hire a guide to lead them towards Yathrib along the coast (ʿAbd al-Razzāq 1973, vii: 384–390; Ibn Hishām 1987, ii: 127–128; al-Ṭabarī 1879–1901: 1234–1235; al-Ṭabarī [n.d.], xiv: 258–260).

Figure 5 also features a motif with multiple attestations. The motif is attested very early in Mecca and Medina when Miqsām b. Burja (d. 101/719–20), Mujāhid b. Jabr (d. 104/722), and ʿUrwa b. al-Zubayr (d. 94/712–713) appear as the speakers of chains A, F–G, J, and I. ʿUrwa b. al-Zubayr also plays the role of exchanger, since his speech is then reattributed to ʿĀʾisha (d. 58/678) in chains C, D, and E. In any case, the convergence of the chains towards ʿUrwa b. al-Zubayr and Mujāhid b. Jabr tends to suggest that the motif was indeed in circulation in these places at least by the end of the first century AH, before it was also reported by Qatāda b. Diʿāma (d. 117/735) in Baṣra at the beginning of the following century. Moreover, in all the texts retained in the corpus, this episode is unanimously understood as a reference to verse 40 of Sura 9 *al-Tawba* (*Repentance*):

> 'If you do not help him, yet God has helped him already, when the unbelievers drove him forth the second of two, when the two were in the cave (*humā fī l-ghār*), when he said to his companions, "Sorrow not; surely God is with us". Then God sent down on him his *sakīna*, and confirmed him with legions you did not see; and He made the word of the unbelievers the lowest; and God's word is the uppermost; God is All-mighty, all-wise'.

The cave (*ghār*) mentioned in this passage is identified by all scholars as a reference to the cave of al-Thawr. Mujāhid b. Jabr (d. 104/722) is also known to be one of the very first commentators on the Qurʾān in Mecca. We would therefore have traces here of a narrative constructed as one of the first exegeses of the Quranic text, and it is indeed this sense that Mujāhid b. Jabr and ʿUrwa b. al-Zubayr would have retained. However, the motif was probably enriched by other anecdotes not attested in the first stratum of the narrative. Thus Mujāhid b. Jabr and ʿUrwa b. al-Zubayr make no mention of the anecdote of the spider (*al-ʿankabūt*) which, at the behest of God, is said to have woven its web in front of the cave of al-Thawr to deceive the Quraysh who had gone in search of Muḥammad. This particular anecdote, based on the interpretation of the end of the verse, therefore seems rather to appear later during the second/eighth century.

The arrival in Yathrib

The flight of Muḥammad and Abū Bakr concludes when the two men arrive in Yathrib. For several days, the town's inhabitants had made a habit of waiting for Muḥammad's arrival on the lava fields near the town. According to the Islamic traditions, a Jew posted on a tower spotted them first and announced it aloud to the others. At first, the Medinese cannot distinguish Muḥammad from Abū Bakr, until the latter raises the cloak with which he protects the Envoy of God (ʿAbd al-Razzāq 1973, vii: 395; Ibn Hishām 1987, ii: 133–134; al-Ṭabarī 1879–1901: 1242).

In Figure 6, ʿUrwa b. al-Zubayr (d. 94/712–713) appears as the CL of chains A, B, and C. We can therefore conclude that the motif was in circulation at the end of the first/seventh century in Medina.

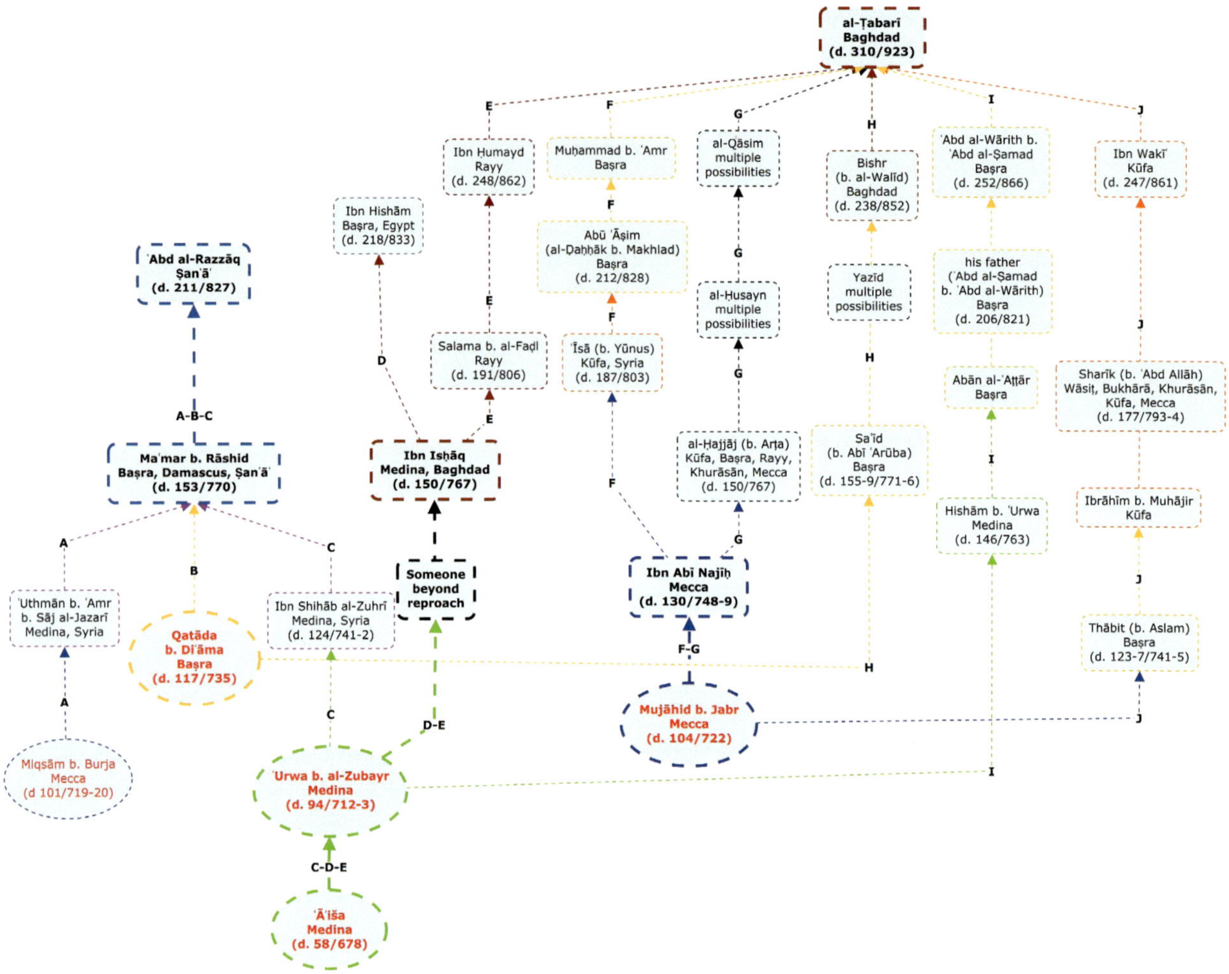

FIGURE 5. *Muḥammad and Abū Bakr hide in the cave of al-Thawr.*

The building of the Prophet's mosque in Yathrib

Before arriving in Yathrib, Muḥammad stays three nights in Qubāʾ with the Banū ʿAmr b. ʿAwf, a village 3 km south of the city, and founds the first mosque there. Muḥammad then travels just under 1 km north to the Banū Sālim b. ʿAwf, at the bottom of the Wādī Rānūnāʾ, where he leads the first Friday prayer. Finally, he decides to go to Yathrib, where, according to the story, several tribes offer their land for the construction of the Prophet's mosque. Muḥammad declines them all and lets his camel wander, guided by God, until the beast stops on land used to dry dates belonging to Sahl and Suhayl, two orphans of the Banū Mālik. Muḥammad pays them to set up his mosque there and moves in with Abū Ayyūb for the time it takes to build it. Bilāl is finally chosen to be the community's first muezzin. The foundation of Muḥammad's mosque thus concludes the emigration (ʿAbd al-Razzāq 1973, vii: 395–396; Ibn Hishām 1987, ii: 133; Ibn Saʿd 1990, i: 184–185; al-Ṭabarī 1879–1901: 1258–1260).

Figure 7 again reveals a pattern with multiple attributions. Maʿmar b. Rāshid (d. 153/770) appears as the CL of chains A, C, and D, and Ibn Isḥāq (d. 150/767) as the speaker of chain G and the transmitter of chain B. The pattern is therefore attested at least in the middle

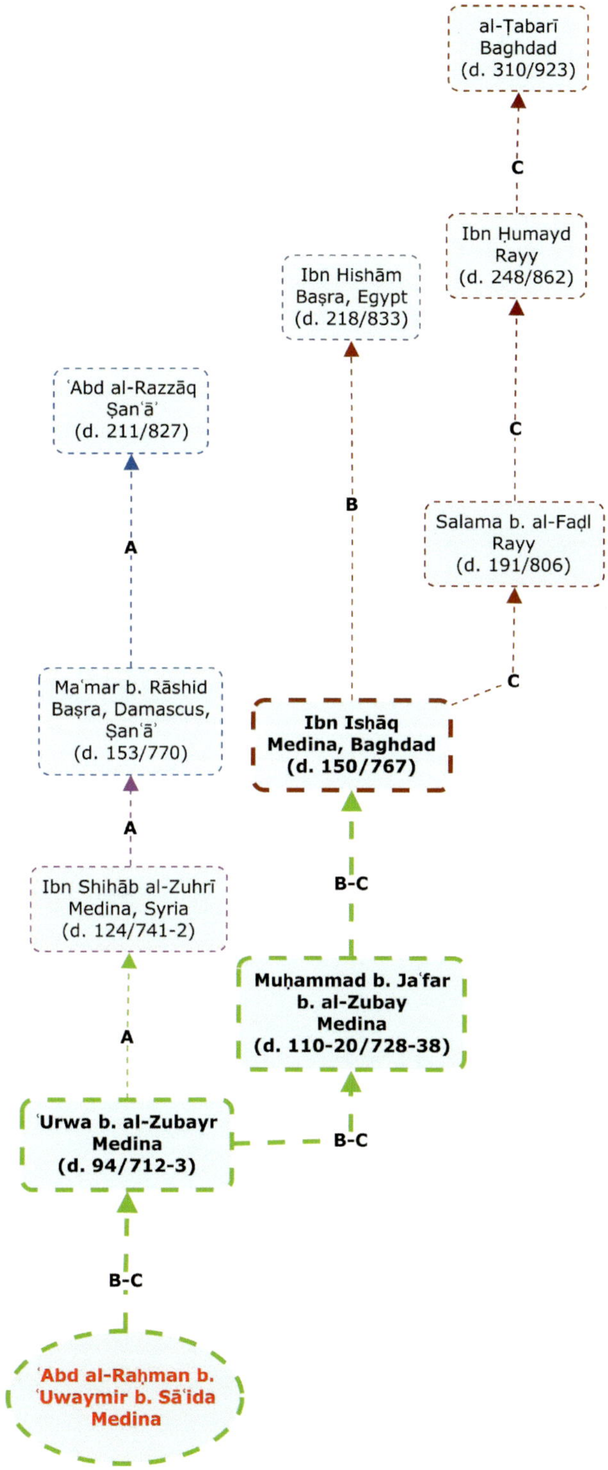

FIGURE 6. *The arrival in Yathrib.*

of the second/eighth century in the spaces where these scholars have been identified. Can we go further back? Several factors would suggest so. In the diagram, Ibn Shihāb al-Zuhrī (d. 124/741–742) appears as an exchanger. Initially a speaker of chains C and D, the motif then goes back to his master ʿUrwa b. al-Zubayr (d. 94/712–713) in chain A. If the attribution of the motif to the companion ʿAbd al-Raḥman b. ʿUwaymir b. Sāʿida is difficult to verify and bears all the traces of a late process of reattribution, we can envisage that the motif was well in circulation at the time when ʿUrwa b. al-Zubayr was teaching in Medina. Furthermore, it is known that ʿUrwa b. al-Zubayr met on several occasions with Caliph al-Walīd (r. 85/705–95/715), who is known to have ordered the city's governor ʿUmar b. ʿAbd al-ʿAzīz to organize the renovation of the Prophet's mosque (Ettinghausen, Grabar & Jenkins-Madina 2001: 24; Munt 2014: 106). The previous year, ʿUrwa b. al-Zubayr had gone with his sons to the caliph's court to pledge allegiance to him (Schoeler 2010). The Medinan scholar had acquired very good relations with his father ʿAbd al-Malik, with whom he potentially even had had a correspondence. It is therefore conceivable that ʿUrwa took an active part in disseminating the account of the foundation of the Prophet's mosque in Medina at a time when al-Walīd was proceeding with great pomp to renovate it. Finally, according to Oleg Grabar and Robert Hillenbrand, the work on the mosque was aimed at extending it to accommodate a growing number of worshippers (Ettinghausen, Grabar & Jenkins-Madina 2001: 24; Hillenbrand 2000: 74). Munt (2014: 124–127) points out that traditions enjoining Muslims to go on pilgrimage to the mosque in Qubāʾ as well as to the Prophet's mosque in Medina are attested in the second/eighth century. We may then suggest that al-Walīd was already hoping to attract Muslims to Medina when he proceeded to extend the mosque, and that propaganda in favour of this type of practice began during his lifetime, at the very end of the first/seventh–early second/eighth century.

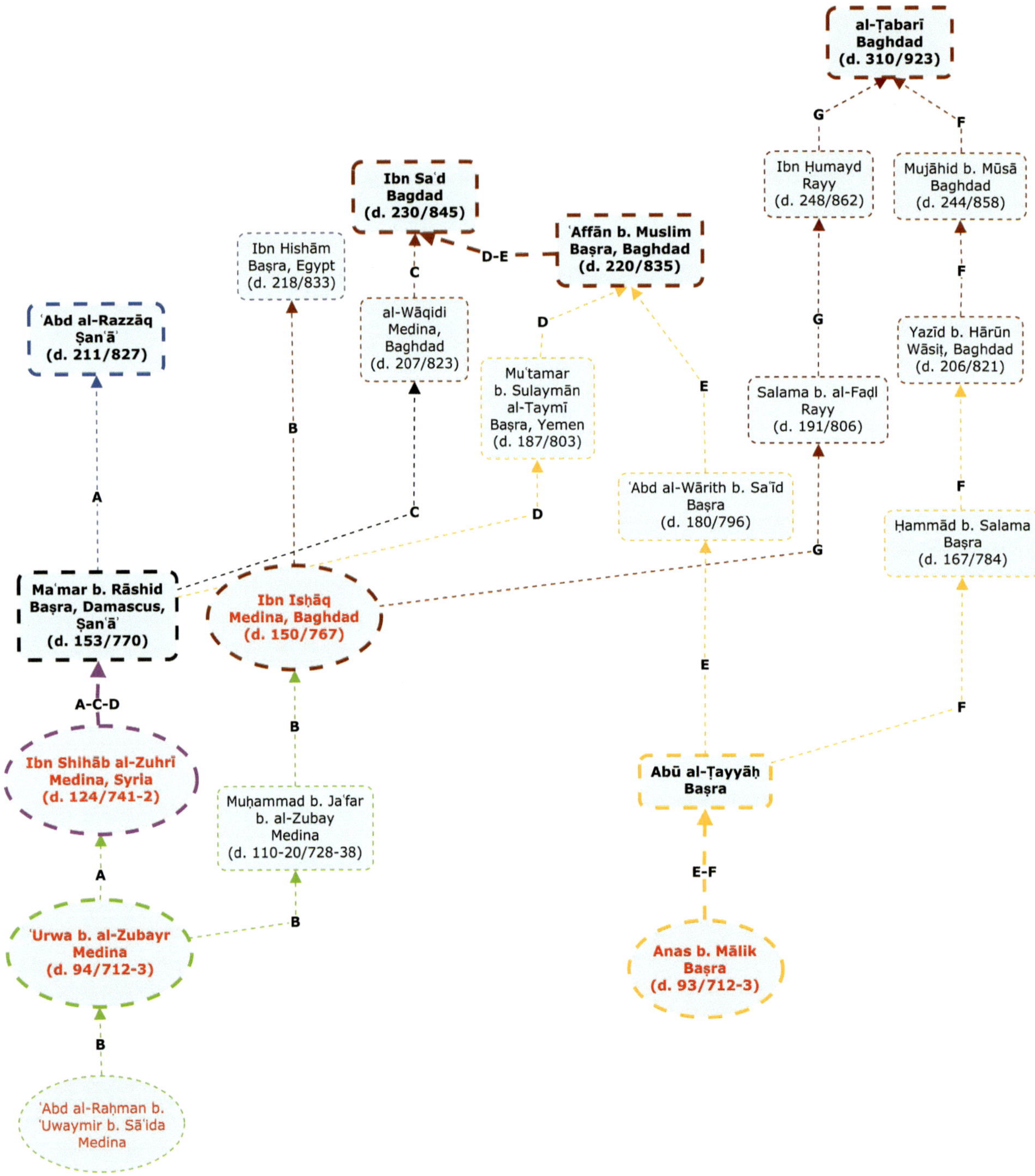

FIGURE 7. *The building of Muḥammad's mosque in Yathrib.*

The persecution of Muḥammad and the *umma*

Surāqa tracks down Muḥammad and Abū Bakr on the coast

At the turn of the second/eighth century, the account of the Hijra was enriched by a number of anecdotes depicting the trials and persecutions suffered by Muḥammad and his companions. The story of the cave already anticipates this trend, which became more pronounced in the following century. A particular anecdote illustrates the situation well. After being deceived by Muḥammad and Abū Bakr, the Quraysh offer a reward of 40 or 100 camels to whoever captures the Prophet and brings him back to Mecca. Surāqa b. Mālik, a Bedouin, consults his divinatory arrows, which twice advise him not to attack. Ignoring these warnings, he sets off in pursuit. On the way, his horse stumbles several times, causing serious falls. Finally, after another fall, he calls Muḥammad and Abū Bakr for help, and once saved, promises not to obstruct them again (ʿAbd al-Razzāq 1973, vii: 392; Ibn Abī Shayba 1989, vii: 343; Ibn Hishām 1987, ii: 130; al-Ṭabarī 1879–1901: 1240–1241).

In Figure 8, chains A and B both go back to Surāqa via his son and grandson. The presence of several members of the same family, a common process in Islamic tradition, suggests disregarding both chains and relying instead on the presence of al-Zuhrī (d. 124/741–742), CL of both chains in the diagram.

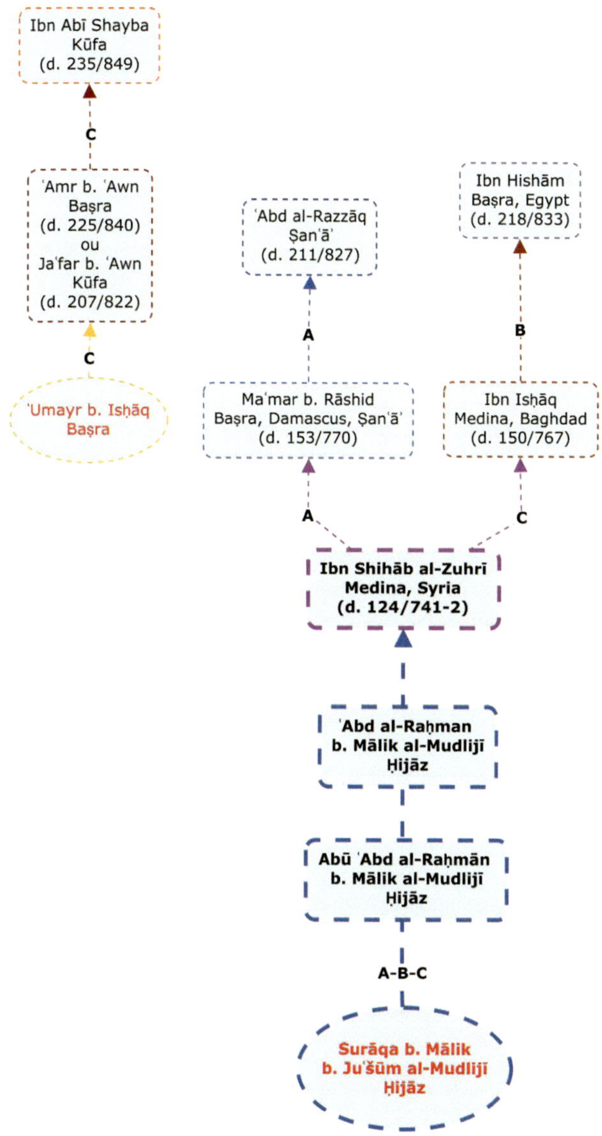

FIGURE 8. *Surāqa tracks down Muḥammad and Abū Bakr on the coast.*

Muḥammad and Abū Bakr escape the Quraysh with the help of ʿAlī

Other accounts emerged even later in the second/eighth century in the Islamic tradition. This is the case of the accounts of the Hijra, in which the Prophet and his companions find themselves persecuted by the Quraysh. The theme of the persecution of prophets is both an inevitability and a major topos rooted in prophetic texts. While persecution puts God's servant to the test, it is also a necessity, as it accompanies him throughout his mission to mankind. Persecution is the mark of the truth of prophecy, the other side of the coin. Once the ordeal is over, the truth of revelation is all the stronger and the sacred text then proceeds to sort people into those who first followed the prophet and those who opposed God's will (Jer. 11: 18–20). The inclusion of this type of motif in the biography of Muḥammad shows from this period onwards a desire to align the history of Muḥammad and the origins of Islam with the biblical model.

A first motive has to do with the plot fomented by the Quraysh against Muḥammad, which decides the latter, with God's permission, to emigrate. In Ibn Hishām's *Sīra*, this episode appears at the beginning of the account of the Hijra. Relentlessly persecuted by the Meccans, Muhammad and Abū Bakr prepare to leave the city. After failing to get the companions closest to Muḥammad to apostatize, the Quraysh meet to discuss the punishment to be inflicted on him. Should he be put in irons, exiled from Mecca, or killed? Through Jibrīl, God informs Muḥammad of the plot being hatched against him. Muḥammad and Abū Bakr decide to go into hiding in the cave of al-Thawr, while ʿAlī takes the Prophet's place and sleeps in his bed to deceive the conspirators. This provides enough time for Muḥammad and Abū Bakr to escape, set out on the road to Medina, and gain a significant advantage over the Quraysh (ʿAbd al-Razzāq 1973, vii: 389–390; Ibn Hishām 1987, i: 480; al-Ṭabarī 1879–1901: 1229–1232).

The majority of the chains in Figure 9 are attributed to Ibn ʿAbbās (d. 67/687), an authority known to serve as a nominee for an immeasurable number of hadiths (Nagel 1967: 56–58; Gilliot 1985: 127–184). The dating of the circulation of the motif could then rest on the presence of Ibn ʿAbbās's *mawlā*, Miqsam (b. Burja) (d. 101/719–720), if the D chain reported by al-Ṭabarī (d. 310/923) were not also broken. The elimination of Ibn ʿAbbās and his *mawlā* leaves only two dating possibilities. The motif may have first appeared in Baṣra under Qatāda b. Diʿāma (d. 117/735). However, given the lack of corroboration of his testimony, it would be safer to refer to Maʿmar b. Rāshid, ICL of chains E and F, whose teaching finds its equivalent in his contemporary Ibn Isḥāq (d. 150/767), CL of chains A and B. Therefore, all these elements lead us to consider that the motif was put into circulation at the end of the first half of the second/eighth century.

Several historians have already cast doubt on the version of the Hijra narrative presented in the Islamic tradition. Muḥammad would not have chosen to emigrate, but could have been exiled from the city and would have had to find refuge in Yathrib. While acknowledging that the departure from Mecca is 'certainly a historical event', Mathieu Tillier and Naïm Vanthieghem agree with Patricia Crone and Michael Cook that the account of the exodus is a late 'dogmatic vision' (Tillier & Vanthieghem 2019: 163; Crone & Cook 1977: 9). An anecdote reported by Ibn Isḥāq, via al-Ṭabarī, might confirm this hypothesis. Learning that the Quraysh were plotting against Muḥammad, the devil — or perhaps just an evil spirit called the *shayṭān* in the story — decided to interfere in their meeting in the guise of Surāqa b. Mālik, a Bedouin from the Najd who was also known in Mecca. Initially, the Quraysh thought of imprisoning him or forcing him into exile. The *shayṭān* then whispered to them to murder and get rid of him once and for all (al-Ṭabarī 1879–1901: 1229). Muḥammad's exile, historically the most likely event, is reduced to a detail of history, a mere proposition of the Quraysh. Instead, Muḥammad is threatened with murder and his fight, fought with God's help, now takes the form of a confrontation against the devil. In this way, the story of the Hijra is reinterpreted as a struggle between good and evil. The city of Mecca is tainted by evil, compelling Muḥammad to abandon it for Yathrib.

The same logic governs the circulation of the episode of the boycott of the Banū Hāshim (*khabr al-ṣaḥīfa*) (Fig. 9). After facing increasing persecution in Mecca, a group of early Muslims, including Jaʿfar ibn Abī Ṭālib, sought refuge in Abyssinia during the first and second Hijra. They were warmly received by the Negus (al-Najāshī), the Christian king of Abyssinia, who granted them protection despite the Quraysh's efforts to convince him to expel them. After learning of the favourable treatment Jaʿfar and his companions had received from the Negus in Abyssinia, the Quraysh decide to prohibit all matrimonial and commercial relations with the Banū Hāshim inside Mecca. Manṣūr b. ʿIkrima is then commissioned to draft a document and hang it inside the Kaʿba. The Banū Hāshim receive no more grain, and the cries of their children are heard on the other side of the mountain for three years. Against the Quraysh, God sends swarms of white ants in response, which consume the document of the boycott on the Kaʿba. Only the name of God (Allāh), inscribed on the document is preserved from the voracity of the ants (Ibn Hishām 1987, ii: 5; al-Ṭabarī 1879–1901: 1189–1191).

Both chains A and B in Figure 10 date to around Ibn Isḥāq (d. 150/767), so the motif came into circulation at the beginning of the Abbasid period, in the mid-second/eighth century. In the narrative of the boycott, persecution is no longer limited solely to the person of the Prophet, but affects the entire first community of believers. Through the theme of persecution, the founding of the *umma* is reinterpreted as a shared experience, bringing Muḥammad's experience closer to that of God's chosen people in the Bible.

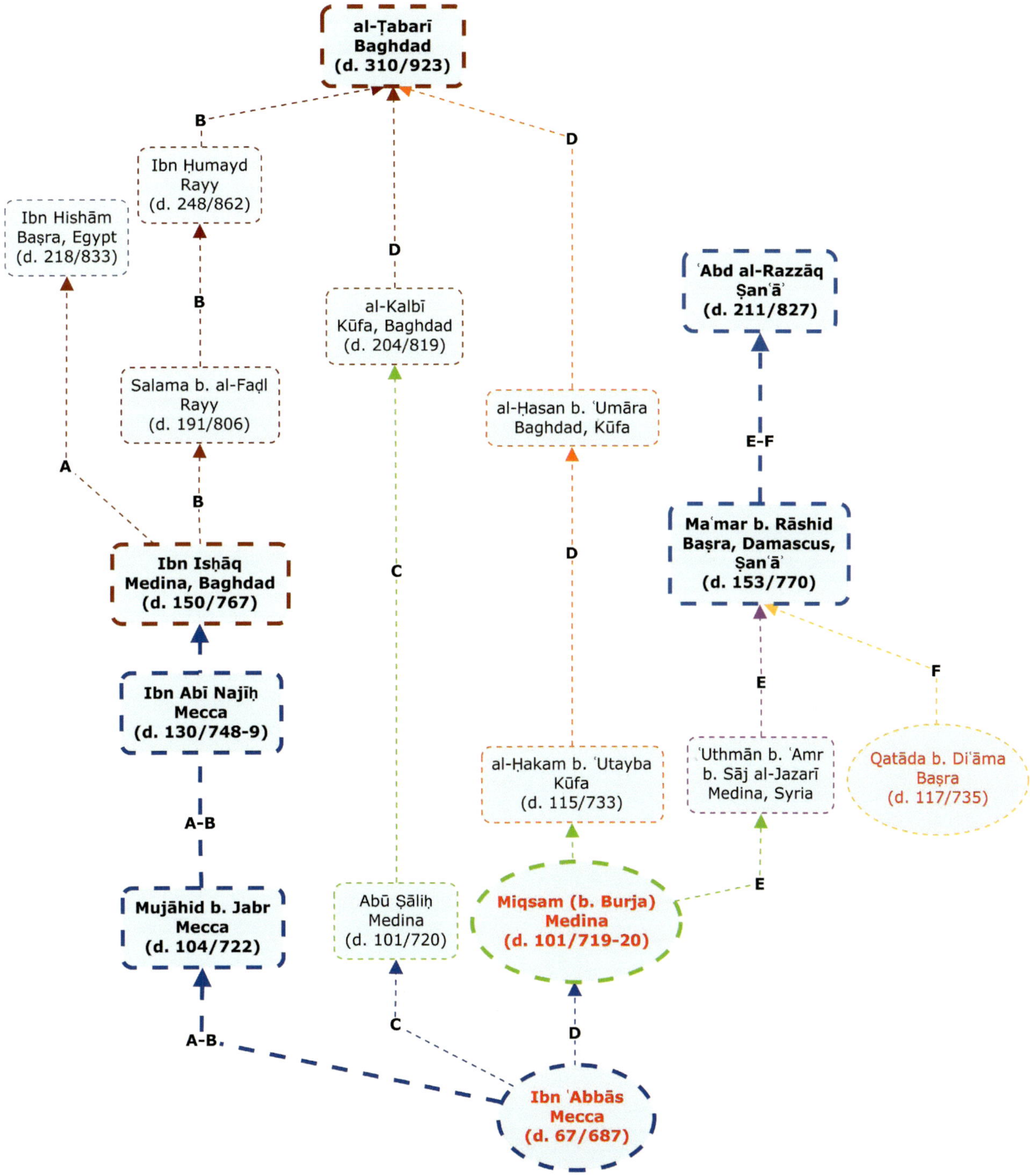

FIGURE 9. *The Quraysh plot against Muḥammad.*

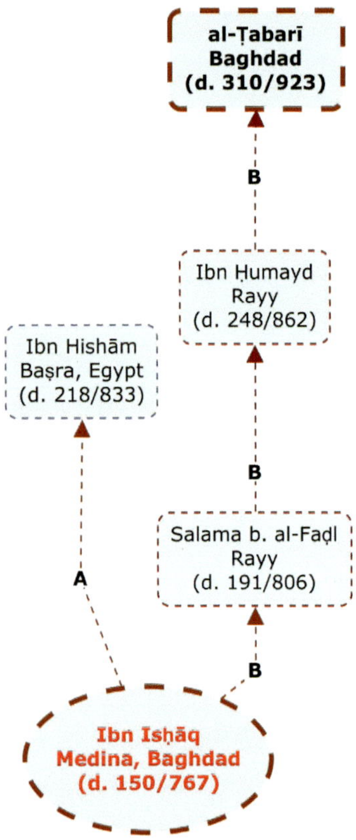

FIGURE 10. *The boycott against the Banū Hāshim.*

The 'constitution' of Medina

A final point concerns the inclusion of the famous 'constitution' of Medina in the *Sīra*. While the aim here is not to provide a new opinion on the authenticity of these documents, it is important to point out that early Muslim scholars make no mention of them until Ibn Isḥāq does himself. Similarly, William M. Watt (1962: 474) writes '[that] apart from a few introductory words, he tells us nothing, neither in what way this document fell to him, nor when, nor how this Constitution came into force'.[8] The same conclusions apply to the fraternization pact. Even in the event that such documents could have been produced by Muḥammad, early Muslim scholars did not consider it important to mention them. Their meaning is not the same for contemporaries and their successors, several generations after they were written. Ibn Isḥāq's setting of these documents therefore tells us more about how Muslim scholars close to the circles of Abbasid power conceived the history of the community's foundation. We can begin by studying the content of the document as reported by Ibn Hishām (1987, ii: 143–144).

The exact title of the document is *Kitābu-hu ṣallā Allāh ʿalay-hi wa-sallam bayn al-muhājirūn wa-l-anṣār wa-muwādaʿat yahūd*, which can be rendered as: 'The document [of the Prophet], may salvation and blessings be upon him, between the *muhājirūn*[9] and the *anṣār*, and the pact with the Jews [of Yathrib]'. The title is probably a creation of Ibn Isḥāq, as the author proceeds to add the *taṣliya*[10] after the name of the Prophet, whereas this formula, almost systematic in historiography, is still unknown on inscriptions that mention Muḥammad at the end of the first/seventh century. Moreover, Ibn Isḥāq makes a strict distinction in the title between the *muhājirūn* and the *anṣār*. This distinction does not appear as such in the text, where reference is made to a 'document between the *muʾminūn* and the *muslimūn*[11] among the Quraysh and [those] of Yathrib'. In this sense, the wording of the title already reveals Ibn Isḥāq's desire to reinterpret the categories rendered in the document, to make them correspond to the groups put forward in the account of the Hijra as reported in the middle of the second/eighth century. Indeed, the heart of the text concerns the founding of a new community made up of these two groups. Between the *muʾminūn*, the *muslimūn* of Mecca and Yathrib, as well as those who follow them and help them in battle, Muḥammad proclaims that they form a single community distinct from (other) people(s) (*inna-hum umma wāḥida min dūn al-nās*). In subsequent articles, Muḥammad also stresses the atmosphere of security (*dhimma*) and peace (*silm*) that must reign between all *muʾminūn*. The discourse of unity displayed here runs completely counter to the discourse professed in the Qurʾān and the most ancient

[8] See also Lecker 2004 for a more complete study of the document.

[9] Mainly understood as the companions who joined Muḥammad in his emigration from Mecca to Yathrib/Medina, the term *muhājirūn* was initially broader. Crone demonstrated that it also encompassed fighters who participated in the early Islamic conquests and emigrated from Arabia to settle in new regions, as discussed in Crone 1994. The debate over the definition of the *muhājirūn* is closely tied to the controversy surrounding the definition of the *sābiqūn* in the Islamic tradition, as explored in de Jarmy 2025.

[10] Invocation of God's blessing on the Prophet.

[11] Respectively believers and Muslims. See Donner 2010 for a discussion on these two terms.

traditions, where the community tends to be subdivided into several factions according to how early they rallied to Muḥammad. Bearing in mind that Ibn Isḥāq's life of Muḥammad is a work compiled under the patronage of the Abbasids (Sellheim 1967: 33), and that this document appears for the first time from his pen, it could be seen as a desire on the part of the caliphs to bring together the previously opposed believers around the same account of the founding of the community. After the Umayyads were overthrown, and in the context of the foundation of a new dynasty seeking legitimacy among the believers, the writing down and dissemination of a new account of the origins of the *umma* could only be welcomed. The content of the Medina document could thus reflect the evolution of Islamic society after the 'Abbasid revolution' and the new aspirations of a social group from which came Ibn Isḥāq himself.

Ibn Isḥāq is also the sole reporter of the fraternization pact between the *muhājirūn* and the *anṣār* in the *Sīra* (Ibn Hishām 1987, ii: 146–147). The document stipulates that Muḥammad assigns each *muhājir* of Mecca a brother (*akh*) from among the *anṣār*. The choice of a brother is supposed to promote good understanding between the two groups and confirms that *muhājirūn* and *anṣār* belong to the same community of believers. Here we find a discourse in favour of unity between two previously opposing factions in Islamic tradition (de Jarmy 2025). Ḥamza, the Prophet's uncle, has Zayd b. Ḥāritha as his brother. Bilāl is paired with Abū Ruwayḥa. Only Muḥammad breaks the rule, as his choice sides with his cousin and son-in-law, ʿAlī b. Abī Ṭālib. We know that ʿUmar II (r. 99–101/717–720) put an end to the *damnatio memoriae* that had befallen ʿAlī since the caliphate of Muʿāwiya (r. 40/661–60/680) (Blankinship 1994: 32). Nonetheless, it was not until the early Abbasid period that references to the character proliferated in *maghāzī* literature. The sudden presence of ʿAlī, presented as Muḥammad's 'brother', could here respond to Shi'ite demands, whose favour the Abbasids were able to curry at the time of the Umayyads' overthrow. Finally, we can dwell on the very special titles given to Muḥammad in the text of the pact. Muḥammad is presented as the 'messenger of the Lord of the [two?] worlds' (*rasūl rabb al-ʿalamīn* [or, *al-ʿalamayn*]), 'the imam of the pious' (*imām al-muttaqīn*), and the 'lord of the messengers [of God]' (*sayyid al-mursalīn*) (Ibn Hishām 1987, ii: 146). The appellation *rasūl rabb al-ʿalamīn* is taken directly from the Qurʾān, where it is attested three times in Sura 7 (*al-Aʿrāf* 7. 61, 67, 104). As for the title *imām al-muṭṭaqīn*, it appears to be derived from the supplication addressed to God in the verse of Sura 25 (*al-Furqān* 25. 74): 'and make us an example for the pious (*wa-jʿalna li-l-muttaqīna imāmān*)'. The title *sayyid al-mursalīn* is not, however, attested in the Qurʾān. This honorific title introduces something radically new. Through this title, Muḥammad is explicitly placed above all other messengers of God. Previously, Muḥammad was placed on equal footing with the other great prophets mentioned in the Qurʾān. In the inscriptions on the Dome of the Rock made in 72/692, Muḥammad and Jesus are both regarded as envoys (*rasūl*, pl. *rusul*) and prophets (*nabī*, pl. *anbiyyāʾ*), as noted by Tillier (2018: 341–365). In the text of the pact, Muḥammad is now placed at the head of the messengers; he completely dominates the hierarchy of prophets. Add to this the fact that the title of *sayyid*, attributed to Muḥammad in the text, is attested among those who claimed descent from the Prophet in the Abbasid period (Bernheimer 2005: 43–69). It could therefore be one of the first traces of the expression of this filiation in the middle of the second/eighth century.

Conclusion

The construction of Hijra narratives thus follows a three-stage evolution in Islamic tradition. The main events were already present in Medina at the end of the first/seventh century, as well as in certain schools of Kūfa and Baṣra. During the first half of this century, Medinese scholars added a series of anecdotes that imbued the narrative with a particular tone, modelling the Hijra on the persecution accounts of the biblical prophets. Ibn Isḥāq, for his part, enriches this narrative by incorporating the 'constitution' of Medina, which he interprets in light of the political and religious issues of his time. In this way, the Hijra becomes not only a historical event, but the founding myth of the *umma*, the 'community of believers', as part of the consolidation of Abbasid power. This narrative process was part of a wider process of religious and political legitimization. The Hijra, beyond its historical dimension, was transformed into a symbolic and structuring narrative that helped to forge the collective identity of Muslims and anchor Medina's central place in the Islamic imagination. The parallel with the biblical prophets serves to reinforce Muḥammad's prophetic status, while inscribing the history of Islam into a continuity with earlier monotheistic traditions.

References

ʿAbd al-Razzāq al-Ṣanʿānī, b. Hammām b. Nafīʿ/ed. H. al-Aʿẓamī. 1973. *al-Muṣannaf.* (12 volumes). Beirut: al-Majlis al-ʿilmī.

al-Balādhurī, Aḥmad b. Yaḥyā b. Jābir b. Dāwūd/ed. S. Zakkār & R. al-Zarkalī. 1996. *Jamāl min ansāb al-ashrāf.* (13 volumes). Beirut: Dār al-fikr.

Berg H. 2003. *Method and theory in the study of Islamic origins*. Leiden/Boston: Brill.

Bernheimer T. 2005. The rise of *sayyids* and *sādāt*: The Āl Zubāra and other ʿAlids in ninth-to eleventh-century Nishapur. *Studia Islamica* 100: 43–69.

Blankinship K.Y. 1994. *The end of the Jihād state: The reign of Hishām Ibn ʿAbd al-Malik and the collapse of the Umayyads*. Albany, NY: State University of New York Press.

Crone P. 1994. The first-century concept of *Hiǧra*. *Arabica* 41/3: 353–387.

Crone P. & Cook M. 1977. *Hagarism: The making of the Islamic world*. Cambridge: Cambridge University Press.

de Jarmy A. 2023. Constructions historiographique et normative des figures du Prophète Muḥammad. Des premières attestations dans les sources au IIIᵉ/IXᵉ siècle. PhD thesis, Sorbonne University, Paris. [Unpublished.]

de Jarmy A. 2025. Who are the *Sābiqūn*? From the Companions of the Tree to the *Muhājirūn*: The story of a controversy and its implications for the *umma* (1st–2nd/7th–8th century). *Der Islam* 102/1: 6–38.

Donner F.M. 2010. *Muhammad and the believers: At the origins of Islam*. Cambridge, MA: Belknap Press of Harvard University Press.

Ettinghausen R., Grabar O. & Jenkins-Madina M. 2001. *Islamic art and architecture. 650–1250*. New Haven, CT: Yale University Press.

Gilliot C. 1985. A 'mythical' portrait of Ibn ʿAbbās. *Arabica* 32/2: 127–184.

Görke A. 2005. Reconstructing the earliest *sīra* texts: The Hiǧra in the corpus of ʿUrwa b. al-Zubayr. *Der Islam* 82/2: 209–220.

Hillenbrand R. 2000. *Islamic architecture. Form, function and meaning*. Edinburgh: Edinburgh University Press.

Ibn Abī Shayba, Abū Bakr ʿAbd Allāh b. Muḥammad/ed. K.Y. al-Ḥawṭ. 1989. *al-Kitāb al-muṣannaf fī l-aḥādīṯ wa-l-athār*. (7 volumes). Riyadh: Maktabat al-Rushd.

Ibn Hishām, Abū Muḥammad ʿAbd al-Mālik/ed. ʿA. Tadmurī. 1987. *al-Sīra l-nabawiyya*. (4 volumes). Beirut: Dār al-Kitāb al-ʿarabī.

Ibn Saʿd, Muḥammad/ed. M. ʿAbd al-Qādir ʿAṭā. 1990. *al-Ṭabaqāt al-kubrā*. (9 volumes). Beirut: Dār al-ʿilmiyya.

Juynboll G. 1993. Nāfiʿ, the *mawlā* of Ibn ʿUmar, and his position in Muslim Ḥadīth literature. *Der Islam* 70: 207–244.

Juynboll G. 1994. Early Islamic society as reflected in its use of *isnāds*. *Le Muséon* 107: 179–185.

Lecker M. 2004. *The 'Constitution of Medina'. Muḥammad's first legal document*. Princeton, NJ: The Darwin Press.

Motzki M. & Schoeler G. 2012. Methods of dating early legal traditions. *Islamic Law and Society* 19: 1–10.

Munt H. 2014. *The Holy City of Medina. Sacred space in early Islamic Arabia*. New York: Cambridge University Press.

Muqātil b. Sulaymān /ed. A.M. Shaḥāṭa 2002. *Tafsīr Muqātil b. Sulaymān*. (5 volumes). Beirut: Dār iḥyāʾ al-turāth al-ʿarabī.

Nagel T. 1967. Die Qisas al-anbiyaʾ. Ein Beitrag zur arabischen Literaturgeschichte. Dissertation zur Erlangung des akademischen Grades Doktor der Philosophie des Fachbereichs Altertums- und Kulturwissenschaften der Universität zu Bonn.

Pavlovitch P. 2020. Dating. Pages 114–133 in D. Brown (ed.), *The Wiley Blackwell concise companion to the hadith*. Hoboken, NJ: Wiley Blackwell.

Schacht J. 1949. A revaluation of Islamic traditions. *Journal of the Royal Asiatic Society* 2: 143–154.

Schacht J. 1979. *The origins of Muḥammadan jurisprudence*. Oxford: Clarendon Press.

Schoeler G. 2010. ʿUrwa b. al-Zubayr. In *The Encyclopaedia of Islam*. (Second edition online). Leiden: Brill. Available at https://doi.org/10.1163/9789004206106_eifo_COM_1305link

Schoeler G. & Görke A. 2008. *Die ältesten Berichte über das Leben Muḥammads: Das Korpus ʿUrwa ibn az-Zubair*. Princeton, NJ: The Darwin Press.

Sellheim R. 1967. Prophet, Chalif und Geschichte. Die Muhammed-Biographie des Ibn Isḥāq. *Oriens* 18: 33–91.

al-Ṭabarī, Abū Jaʿfar b. Jarīr b. Yazīd/ed. M.J. de Goeje. 1879–1901. *Taʾrīkh al-rusul wa-l-mulūk*. (13 volumes). Leiden: Brill.

al-Ṭabarī, Abū Jaʿfar b. Jarīr b. Yazīd/ed. A. Shākir. [n.d.] *Jāmiʿ al-bayān* ʿan *tāʾwīl ayāt al-qurʾān*. (32 volumes). Mecca: Dār al-al-tarbiyya wa-l-turāth.

Tillier M. 2018. ʿAbd al-Malik, Muḥammad and the last judgement: The Dome of the Rock as an expression of Islamic orthodoxy. Pages 341–365 in D. Valérian (ed.), *Les vivants et les morts dans les sociétés médiévales. XLVIIIe Congrès de la SHMESP (Jerusalem, 2017)*. Paris: Éditions de la Sorbonne.

Tillier M. 2022a. Vers une nouvelle méthode de datation du hadith: Les invocations à Dieu dans les inscriptions épigraphiques et dans la sunna. *Der Islam* 99: 337–433.

Tillier M. 2022b. Back to the *isnād*: The prophetization of the sunna: A relative chronology of epigraphic and traditional invocation. *Islamic Law Blog*. Available at https://islamiclaw.blog/2022/01/27/back-to-the-isnad-the-prophetization-of-the-sunna/

Tillier M. & Vanthieghem N. 2019. Recording debts in Sufyānid Fusṭāṭ: A reexamination of the procedures and calendar in use in the first/seventh century. Pages 148–188 in J. Tolan (ed.), *Geneses: A comparative study of the historiographies of the rise of Christianity, Rabbinic Judaism and Islam*. London: Routledge.

Watt W.M. 1962. *Muhammad: Prophet and statesman*. Paris: Payot.

Author's address

Adrien de Jarmy, Department of Arabic studies, University of Strasbourg, 4 rue Blaise Pascal CS 90032, 67 081 Strasbourg, France.
e-mail dejarmy@unistra.fr

Proceedings of the Seminar for Arabian Studies 54 (2025): 88–104

The first excavation season at Shokur: a multi-period fortified settlement between desert and mountains

Francesco Genchi, Nunzia Larosa, Giampiero Tursi, Guido Antinori, Francesco Caputo & Valentina Mili

Summary

The paper presents the results of the first exploration season at Shokur (Dhank), on the western flanks of the Jebel Al Abyad. Shokur is a multiphase fortified settlement originally dated to the Bronze Age. The mound covers an area of more than 1 ha and consists of three terraced areas characterized by a massive external fortification wall, dated to the Early Iron Age, and some internal terracing walls. The data obtained from the extensive archaeological excavation has revealed an imposing fortification wall built in two different phases, which we can date to the Iron Age II, as well as internal rooms consisting of stone walls and intended for production and storage activities. The internal retaining walls delimit terraces composed of mud-brick floors, including the highest, which appears to belong to the original Bronze Age tower. In fact, the material culture has allowed us to identify very clearly the most recent phase of occupation of Iron Age II, characterized by the typical incised storage jars, fragments with a moulded representation of the snake, spouted vessels, and carinated bowls, as well as the recovery of numerous painted fragments of the Wadi Suq phase and some sporadic Umm an-Nar sherds.

Keywords: fortified settlement, south-east Arabia, Iron Age, Wadi Suq, multi-period occupation

Introduction

The Dhank region has been the focus of research efforts (Costa 2006), and in 2004 the site of Shokur was first brought to the attention of the Department of Excavations of the Ministry of Heritage and Culture by G. Weisgerber. Since 2010, the area has been researched by Temple University in Philadelphia, with a project entitled 'The Social, Spatial, and Bioarchaeological Histories of Ancient Oman (SoBO)'. Its aim was to explore the Bronze Age burial landscapes of the Dhank region. The team, led by Kimberly Williams, also carried out fieldwork and surface collections at the Shokur settlement, which is part of a more complex archaeological landscape that also includes the Umm an-Nar cemeteries. The two archaeological areas are currently separated by a modern farm (Williams & Gregoricka 2013).

The settlement of Shokur is located on the western flanks of the Jebel Al Abyad mountain range, in the broad plain of Wādī Dhank, south of the town of Dhank (23°31′54′ north, 56°15′34′ east). The present floodplain of Wādī Dhank is formed of small, braided channels separated by sediment bars and crossed by ephemeral streams. Typical floodplain landforms are present in the area, notably low fluvial terraces of different levels. The original nucleus of the settlement extends over one of the lowest elevations in the area (Fig. 1).

General characterization and morphology of the settlement

The mound with the main evidence has an estimated height of 5 m and a diameter of 83 m, and appears as three semi-distinct tiers (Fig. 2). The lowest tier (T.1) has an irregular morphology, extending to *c.*83–85 m in diameter. It is composed of an irregular boulder arrangement curving clockwise by *c.*280°, from an 'opening' to the north/north-east and extending to the north-west side of the tower, where it connects with the second tier. The stones' outer layer is covered with *c.*40 cm of fine, silty soil, particularly in the western, south-western, and southern sections. This deposit appears to be eroded mud bricks rather than a wind-blown accumulation, as evidenced by the scarcity of artefacts found on this artificial terrace, it having yielded the smallest amount of archaeological material.

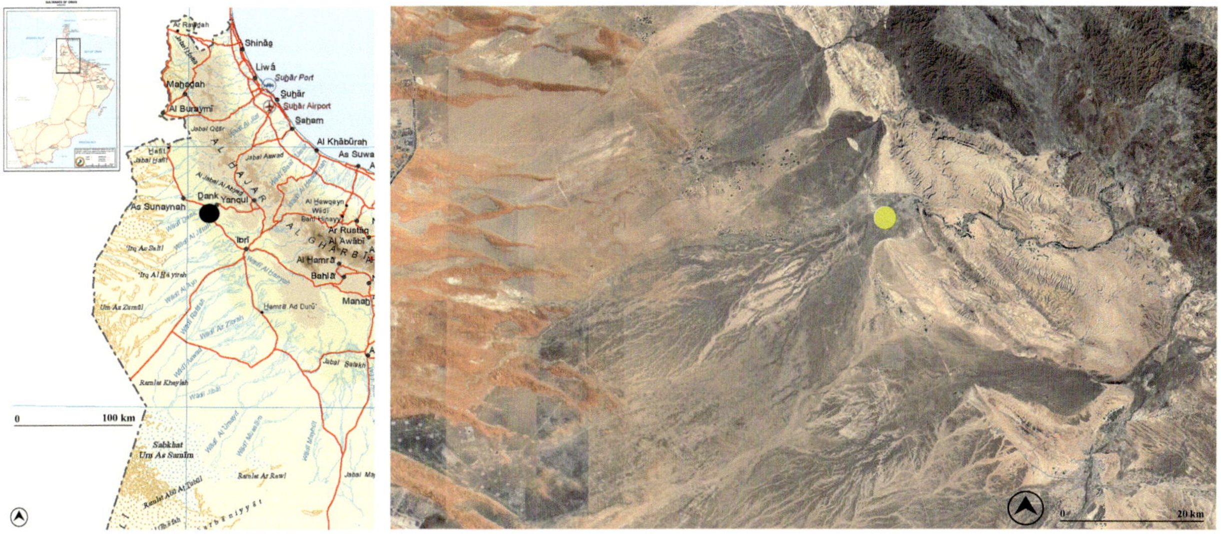

FIGURE 1. *Location of the settlement on a topographic map and detail on a satellite image.*

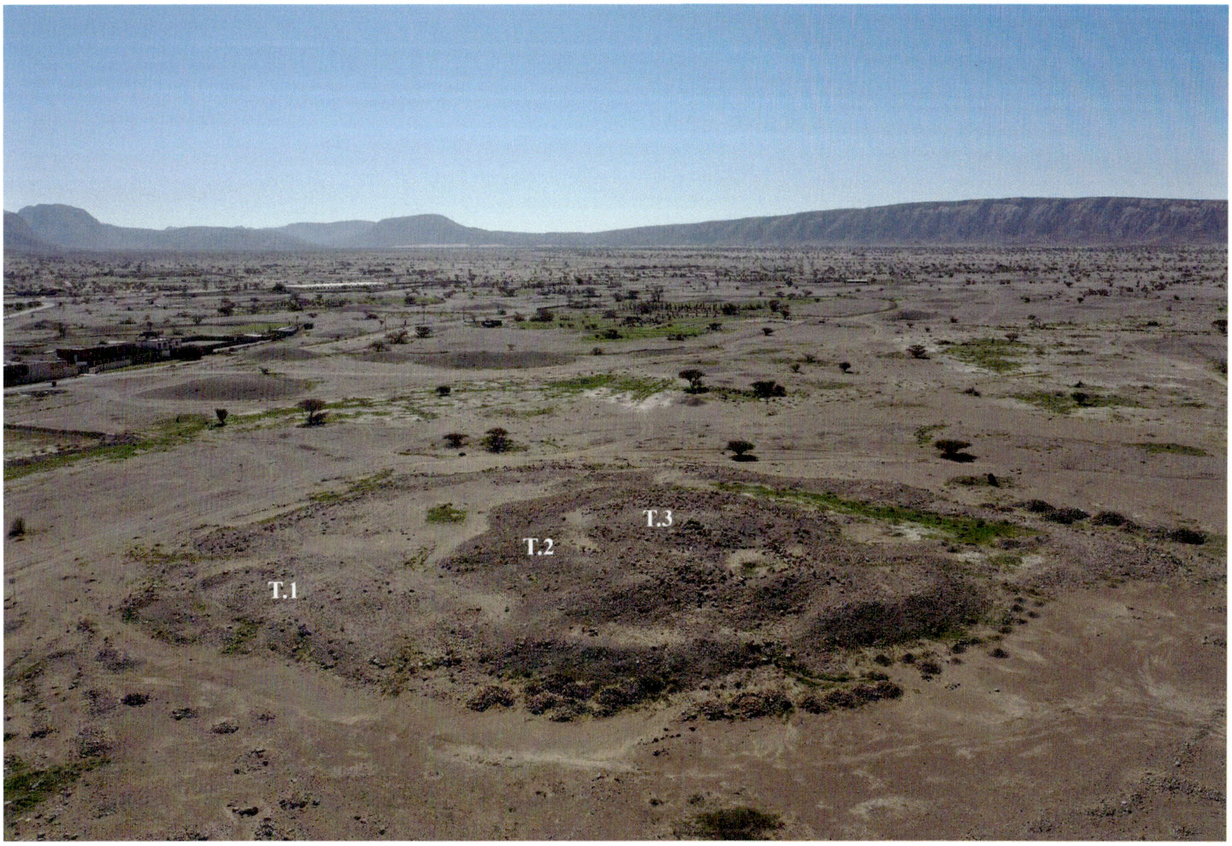

FIGURE 2. *An overview of the Shokur settlement from the north-west showing the terraces.*

Within the outermost stone wall, which surrounds the visible remains of the archaeological site, there are traces of walls that may have been rooms. At the top of this first level, there is a second central tier (T.2). The second terrace, measuring *c.*50 m in diameter and situated slightly off-centre to the north-west, is more than 1 m higher than the first. The outer wall of this terrace consists of small boulders of similar size and rough shape, although only small sections of this wall are currently visible, thus making it difficult to ascertain its precise shape. However, the marked difference in height suggests that much of the stone structure is preserved under debris and sediment. The third terrace (T.3), situated at a slightly off-centre point to the south-west and positioned at an elevation slightly above the second terrace, is believed to represent the original wall of the tower, with a possible Bronze Age foundation. This terrace is composed of medium-sized limestone blocks, measuring *c.*45 × 30 × 30 cm, with up to three courses remaining visible. The stones form a curve which extends for *c.*14 m along the west and south-west sides, enclosing an area of *c.*21.3 m in diameter. The upper terrace (T.3) extends 1 m or more above the middle terrace. Structural remnants of mud-brick walls are discernible at the summit as earthen mounds and stone 'corners', and are probably indicative of fortified watchtowers. The terrace configuration is a substantial, multi-layered mound, encompassing an area of 1.36 ha. The site's defensive configuration is characterized by the presence of at least three walls with the citadel, presumed to be the earliest core of the settlement, situated within the most fortified area. Excavations at the site revealed several phases of occupation, as evidenced by surface finds and collections. The artefacts recovered from Umm an-Nar, Wadi Suq, and notably, a substantial number from the Early Iron Age, suggest that this era represents the settlement's primary developmental phase. The presence of a typical Umm an-Nar tower from the mid-third millennium onwards is highly probable. The site was expanded over the centuries with the addition of another large walled enclosure and further outbuildings. Most of this expansion took place during the Early Iron Age, as evidenced by the substantial archaeological material from this period found in the area. However, an earlier phase of occupation cannot be ruled out.

Survey and topography

A preparatory season in 2022 proved essential before the first archaeological excavation season began the following year. A comprehensive site survey was conducted, resulting in the creation of a digital elevation model (DEM). This model facilitated a detailed understanding of the site morphology and the identification of fortification walls. In the model, the three concentric enclosure walls are shown in different colours, corresponding to the terrace levels (Fig. 3). This preliminary work enabled the determination of the optimum location for opening a long trench, which provided a comprehensive structural layout of the settlement. Specifically, the goal was to investigate an area that intercepted all three walls where the structural remains were best preserved. The southern front of the Shokur mound was identified as the most favourable location for a preliminary site exploration.

The initial trench was planned to be 40 m long and 20 m wide. However, due to the considerable amount of surface ceramics recovered, the trench width was reduced to 10 m, except at the outermost fortification wall where it remained 20 m wide. The excavation trench, designated Area A, was then subdivided into three sectors, corresponding to the three existing walls and terraces encountered (Fig. 4/a):

- Sector I extends from the perimeter wall of the tower and continues for *c.*3 m on the top of the mound, covering the 10 m width of the excavation area. In this sector, a portion of what appears to be the perimeter wall of a Bronze Age tower stands 3 m above the intermediate perimeter wall of Sector II, off-centre to the west of the centre of the mound area. The tower wall consists of medium to large limestone blocks and surrounds an area of *c.*22 m in diameter.
- Sector II extends from the area next to the outer face of the tower wall, continuing down the slope of the mound in three terraced levels. These levels are bordered by sections of stone wall alignments. The outer wall of the second terrace, located further down in Sector II, is an intermediate enclosure wall that probably surrounds a sub-rectangular area around the tower. This area has a diameter of *c.*50 m and rises

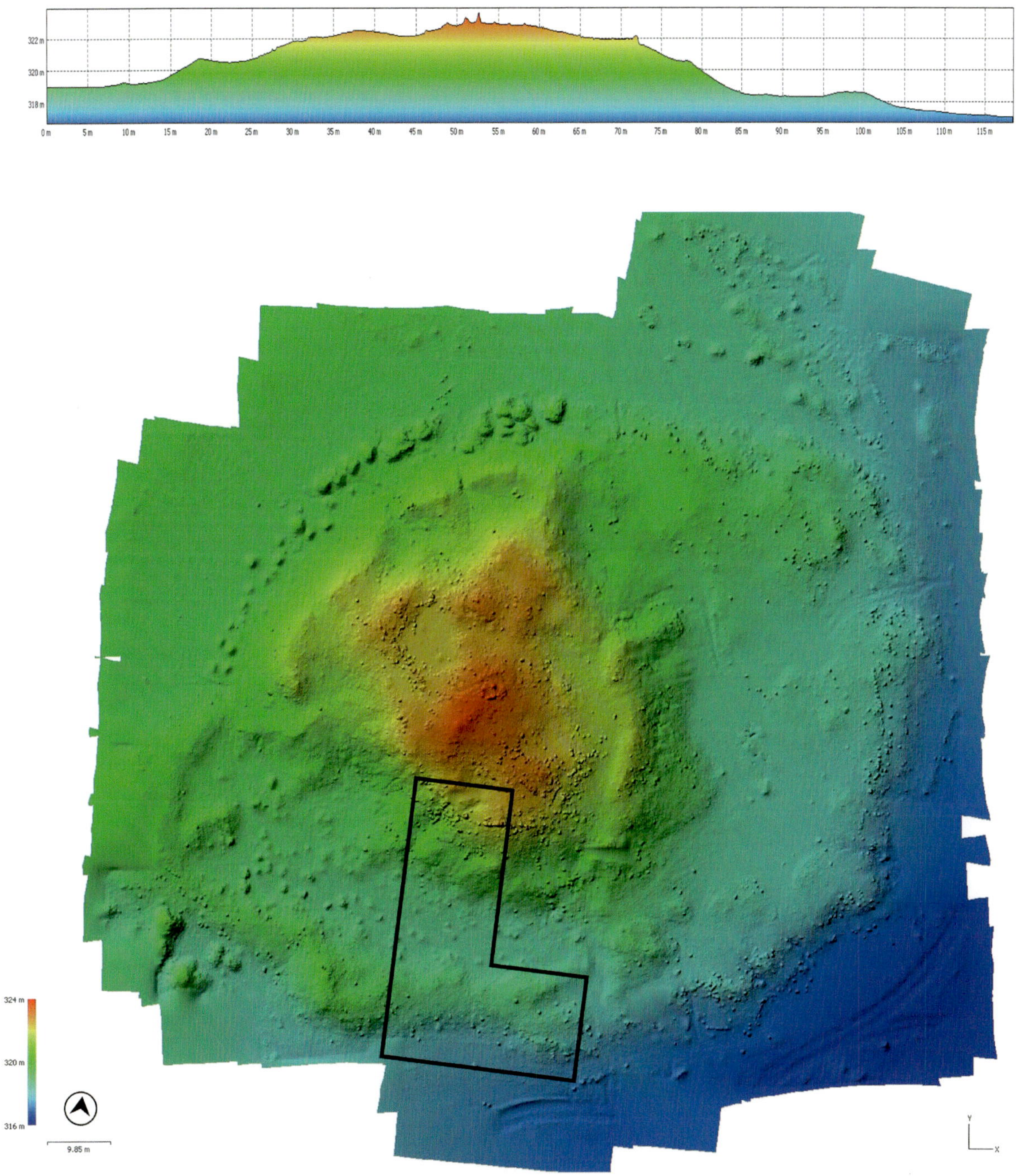

FIGURE 3. *Digital Elevation Model (DEM) and altimetric section of the settlement through aerial image processing.*

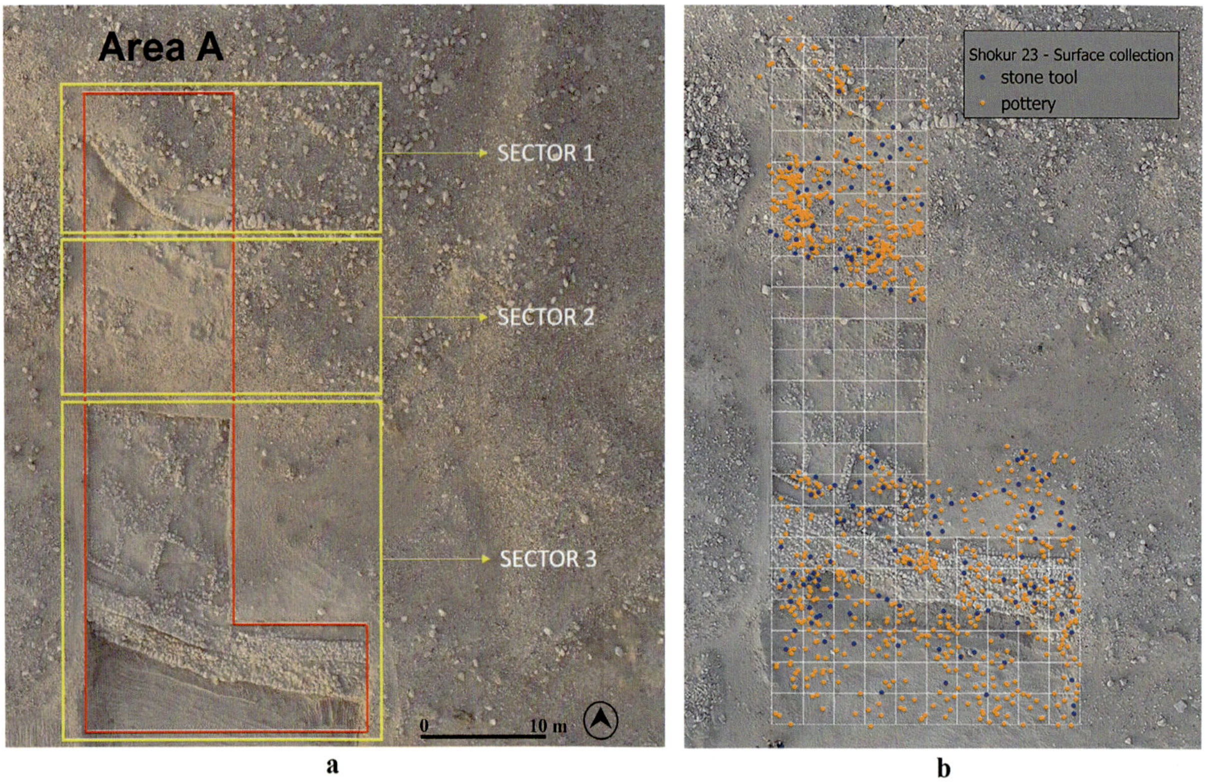

FIGURE 4. **a.** *Area A of the excavation divided into three sectors;* **b.** *a map of the finds distribution after surface collection.*

more than 1 m above the outermost fortification wall exposed in Sector III. The irregular shape of the exposed sections suggests that this wall underwent several phases of construction.

- Sector III comprises the largest portion of Area A and extends from the intermediate boundary wall of Sector II and continues beyond the outer fortification wall of the mound. The sector has only been partially explored, revealing three possible rooms near the enclosure wall and the interior passageway. The outer fortification wall turned out to be the result of the juxtaposition of two massive walls that presumably encircle the entire circumference of the mound over a diameter of *c.*120 m.

The site was surveyed using the total station Topcon GTS-236, and the resulting data were processed in Qgis (QGis.org 2021) to produce scaled plans and maps (Coordinate Reference System: WGS84/UTM zone 40 N). Area A covers 560.369 m^2, with its boundaries delineated in a clockwise direction, starting from the south-eastern corner. The entire mound was then completely covered by a grid of 10 m squares, subdivided into smaller squares of 2 m on each side, oriented north–south. The grid facilitated the identification of structures, archaeological deposits, and the distribution of artefacts during surface collection, as well as stratigraphic excavation. In addition to the grid reference square, the location of each artefact and noteworthy object was recorded with a total station to determine its exact position in space.

As a preliminary step, a systematic collection of archaeological material from the surface of each sector of Area A was carried out (Fig. 4/b). The distribution and density map of the material was obtained by positioning individual finds or clusters of materials, thus showing that the most widespread categories of material are pottery, consisting mainly of large fragments of jars decorated with moulded strings and incisions, and stone lithic tools, represented mainly by grinding stones and anvils. During the 2022 preliminary survey, a complete photographic survey of the mound was obtained using the Phantom IV-Advanced drone. These images were processed using the Agisoft Metashape V. 1.2.6 (Agisoft LLC 2016) to produce a digital elevation model (DEM), contour lines, and a general orthophoto of the settlement.

Results of the archaeological excavation

The main objective of the exploration was to bring to light the archaeological remains of the three tiers of the settlement. The stratigraphic excavation of these three sectors was carried out after the surface collection of artefacts. The surface layer consisted of aeolian and alluvial deposits composed of loose yellowish-grey sandy sediments, mixed with abundant ceramic material and lithic tools.

Sector I

The area circumscribed by the perimeter wall of the tower constitutes the original nucleus of the settlement. The outer face of the imposing wall was exposed to a height of *c.*2 m (Fig. 5). The excavation activities in Sector I were limited, primarily focused on baring the central tower stones subsequent to the collection of surface materials and the removal of aeolian and alluvial sediments. The tower currently stands at a height of 50–80 cm and curves across the entire width of the sector, encompassing the squares from FH 16 in the west corner to EH 5 in the east (Fig. 6). Even though the structure remains only partially exposed, the antiquity of this settlement is substantiated by the abundance of black-painted fine ware pottery fragments attributable to the Wadi Suq phase, as well as the presence of large stone blocks laid in a style characteristic of documented Umm an-Nar structures. The recovery of charred seeds enabled radiocarbon dating, confirming the occupation of the tower at the transition to the second millennium BC (see Fig. 7: FTMC-IC13-4). In the northern limit of Sector I, corresponding to the border of Area A, a compact and uniform clay surface was identified. This

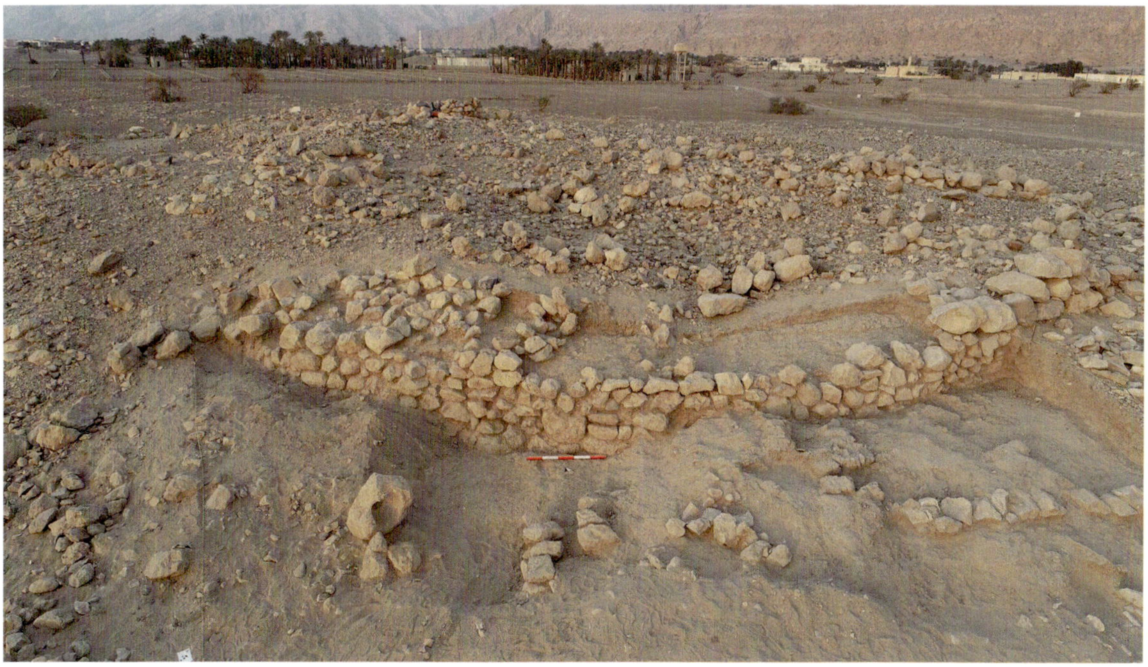

FIGURE 5. *Detail of the exposed portion of the tower at the head of the mound.*

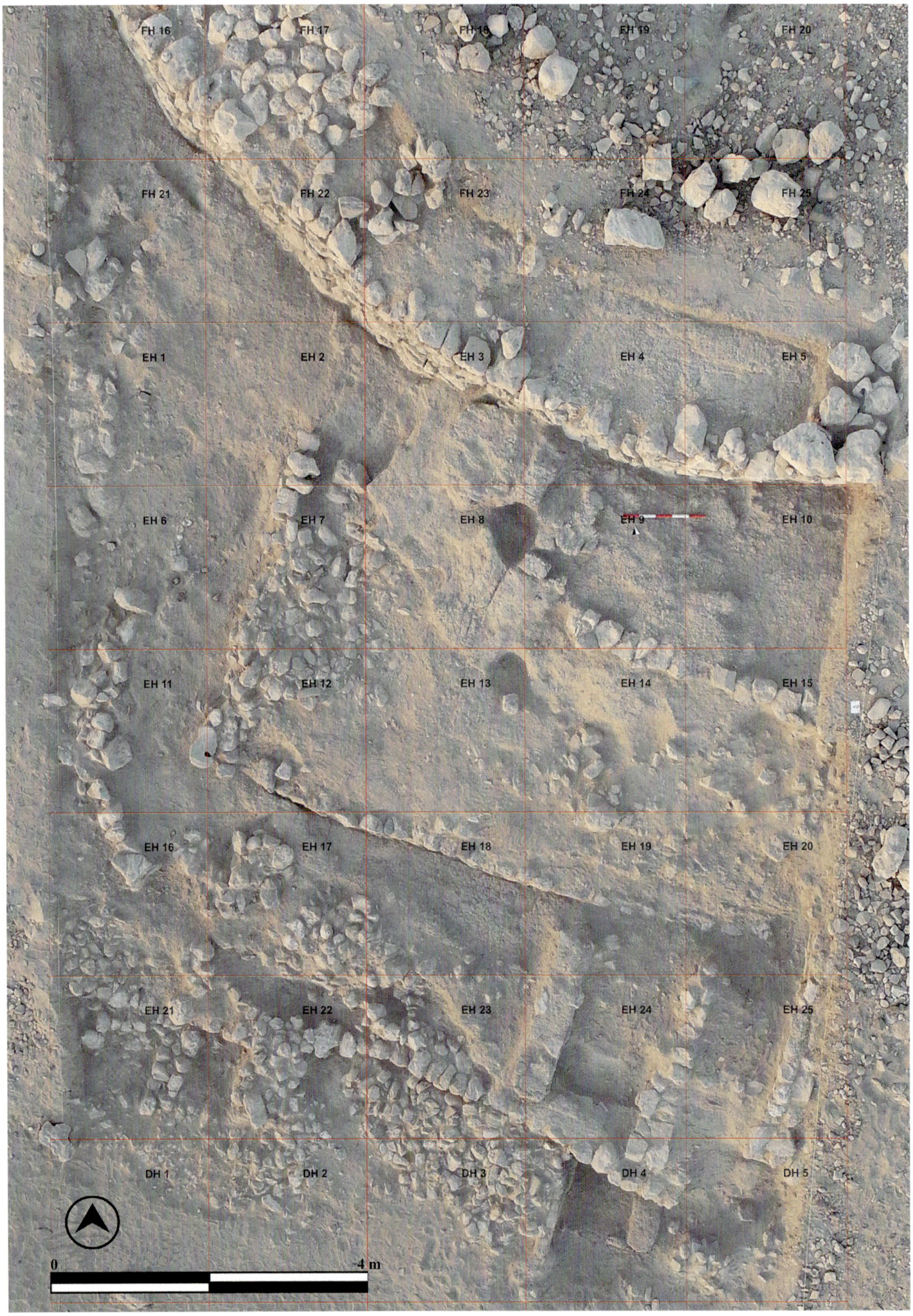

FIGURE 6. *An overview of the terracing walls and the highest circular tower in Sectors II and I respectively.*

surface appears to be a trodden floor situated directly against the tower wall. This discovery thus denotes the cessation of excavation activities in Area 1.

Sector II

Sector II is located between the innermost part of Sector III and the tower situated to the north in the upper section of the mound, which is included in Sector I. Its dimensions are 14 x 10 m and it has a significant elevation disparity due to the presence of three levels of terracing. The archaeological deposit was investigated in two phases, corresponding to the abandonment of the area and the occupation levels, respectively.

Phase 1 is characterized by the cessation of human activity in the area, archaeologically represented by layers of collapses and washout of materials. These layers contain a significant number of ceramic fragments and stone tools across the settlement. Of particular note is the preponderance of painted Wadi Suq pottery compared to Sector III. The removal of surface materials, along with the substantial deposit of aeolian and alluvial origin, has gradually exposed a cluster of collapsed stones in the vicinity of the top wall, accompanied by a substantial clay deposit that extended in an irregular fashion over a considerable portion of Sector II. This evidence of subsidence is most likely attributable to the wall collapse of Sector I, which consisted of a base formed of large stones followed by an elevation of mud bricks. The presence of a clayey layer that extends along the tower, in conjunction with its consistency suggests the occurrence of multiple collapse phases. These, in conjunction with precipitation and flooding, resulted in the erosion of the mud-brick wall and its subsequent destruction.

Phase 2 focuses on the frequency of levels and structural remains thus far identified. These consist of three terraced walls, oriented east–west and parallel to the tower, installed at a modular distance between them on a north–south perspective. The first to be identified is at a depth of 2 m below the tower elevation and is the most modest architecturally, measuring *c*.4 m in length and comprising a single row of stones running in squares EH 9, EH 14, and EH 15 (Fig. 6). Despite its structural austerity, vestiges of the trodden floor have been discerned beneath the various stone and loose mud-brick collapses between it and the tower of Sector I.

The second terracing is aligned with the wall contained in squares EH 1 to EH 20, which extends in a west–east direction for *c*.8 m and encompasses nearly its entire sector in width. At its highest point, the wall was exposed to a height of 50 cm. A thorough examination of the stones that constituted the wall's texture suggested that it was a much more substantial structure, with foundations which appeared to be at a significantly greater depth. It is noteworthy that attached to this wall and covered by a thick layer of clay soil, a floor of well-defined mud bricks was also found, which was related to the terracing.

Near the southern boundary of Sector II, the removal of a cluster of smaller stones unveiled the face of the final and most imposing wall of this Sector. The cluster of smaller stones was presumably utilized to buttress and reinforce the final terracing.

The wall's height is currently recorded at 1 m, with its foundation exhibiting a discernible depth. For *c*.4 m the course of the wall appears to be regular, although it then curves slightly and is interspersed by other collapses. The exploration of this portion of the wall yielded a radiocarbon dating on a charcoal sample, dating the use of this area to the Early Iron Age (Fig. 7: FTMC-IC13-1).

In the south-western part of Sector II, faint traces of structures attributed to Phase 2 have been revealed.

Lab code	Material	Context	Radiocarbon age, BP	2 sigma calibration
FTMC-IC13-2	charcoal	Sect. III (SU 3048)	2969±32	1227–1126 cal BC (63.4%) 1284–1054 cal BC (95.4%)
FTMC-IC13-5	charcoal	Sect. III (SU 3049)	3010±31	1386–1339 cal BC (15.4%)1316–1156 cal BC (75.3%)
FTMC-IC13-1	charcoal	Sect. II (SU 2008)	2934±33	1256–1248 cal BC (1.1%) 1227–1016 cal BC (94.3%)
FTMC-IC13-4	seed	Sect. I (SU 1002)	3508±32	1850–1771 cal BC (55.7%) 1927–1743 cal BC (95.4%)

FIGURE 7. *Table of radiocarbon dates.*

These traces were obscured by topsoil and remnants of clay traces. The structures consist of three parallel south–north walls (in squares EH 24 and EH 25) constructed using a technique that combined stone and mud bricks and creating narrow inner spaces between them. The remains of a final wall structure are distinguished by the dimensions of the stones and their alignment. The feature is close to the western border of the sector, specifically in squares FH 21 to EH 16. It extends for *c.*10 m in a north–south direction, despite its irregular course and the absence of some stones. These stones are notably larger than those of any other exposed walls and are also found at a greater depth. It is conceivable that these stones may, in fact, belong to an earlier structure that predates the organization of the area into terraces. Nevertheless, the limited depth and proximity to the excavation area prevent a precise interpretation. In summary, the wall structures that emerged in Sector II demonstrate a west–east orientation creating three levels of terracing and appear to be associated with later activities. From these walls, other walls diverge towards the north, exhibiting a lighter structure and a mixed technique that incorporates stone and mud bricks. It can be hypothesized that these structures represent internal spaces and subdivisions, although some appear too fragile, consisting of a single row or two medium-sized stones.

Sector III

Sector III is located at the foot of the south-western part of the mound, extending beyond its fortified enclosure wall. The area encompassed by this sector is estimated to be 400 m^2 and is divided into two primary components: the northern portion, measuring 16 x 10 m, and the southern portion, measuring 20 x 12 m. The unit was originally planned to span 20 x 26 m; however, it was narrowed by 10 m behind the area inside the fortification wall due to time and resource constraints.

The investigation in Sector III concentrated on exposing and clearing the substantial enclosure wall, which spanned over 20 m, demarcating the mound boundaries. The wall facade and foundations revealed a height difference of over 2 m between the northern and southern parts. The northern section was found to be relatively flat, with visible architectural remains near the fortification wall and widespread collapse debris.

The surface artefacts recovered included 2294 pottery sherds, primarily of coarse ware, sixty-nine stone tools, including ground stones and anvils, and sporadic fragments of metal and soft-stone vessels. Following a systematic surface collection, the topsoil was removed from the sector, with the last row of squares being excluded to allow passage between Sectors II and III.

Excavation within the fortification wall primarily revealed cultural deposits from collapse and abandonment layers. The architectural structures comprised a double defensive wall and three partially preserved rooms (Fig. 8).

The outer fortification wall, which was exposed over a distance of 20 m, initially exhibited a north-west–south-east orientation before undergoing a curving movement in a west–east direction, thereby forming an arch. Its width varied between 3.5 and 4 m, the result of at least two construction phases. The earliest phase had a width of 1.4–1.5 m, with a core of mixed stones (0.20–0.30 m) and clayey-silt sediment, surrounded by rows of larger stones defining its outer face. A continuous row of stones ran along the inner wall, forming a skirting step that separated the wall from an inner corridor (0.8–0.9 m wide) (Fig. 9).

Two overlaid masonry structures were utilized to reinforce and reface the original enclosure wall. While these additions may represent separate reinforcement phases, the use of a single construction technique cannot be excluded. The later retaining walls employed rubble-core techniques, characterized by irregular rows of medium to large stones (>0.3–0.5 m) and an external row of larger stones (>0.5 m), which refined the facade. The western side of the outermost wall was preserved up to seven rows (2 m high), tapering to 0.5 m on the east.

Further north, adjacent to the wall's inner corridor, three partially excavated rooms and a fourth unexcavated room were identified. Two of these rooms contained hearths, and radiocarbon dates of charcoal samples collected from these hearths were used to date the rooms to the Early Iron Age (see Fig. 7: FTMC-IC13-2, FTMC-IC13-5). It is important to note that the area is poorly preserved, and the northernmost part remains uncleared of collapse. Future seasons aim to explore construction phases and refine the exposed room limits.

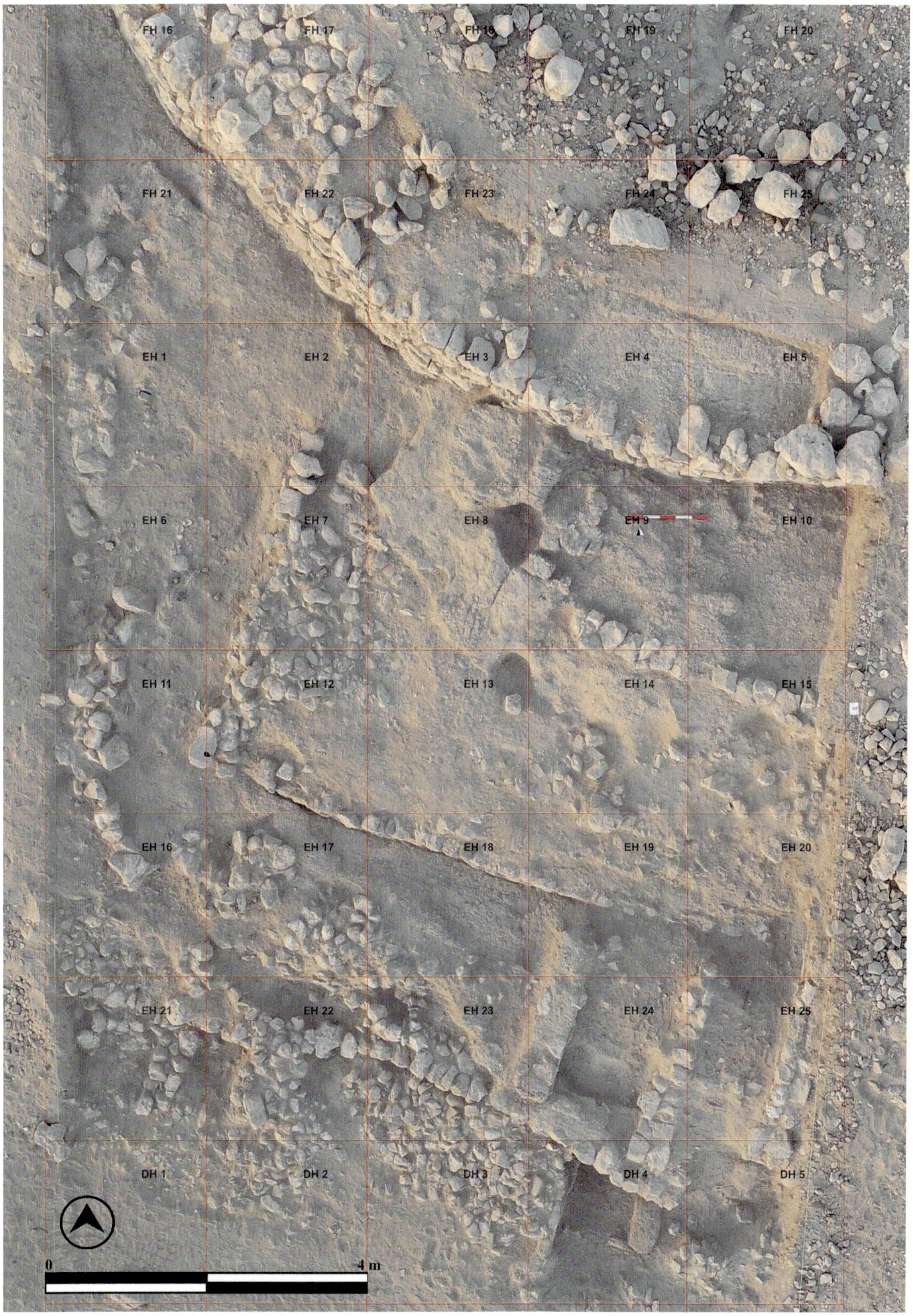

FIGURE 8. *The stone-walled rooms situated side by side in Sector III.*

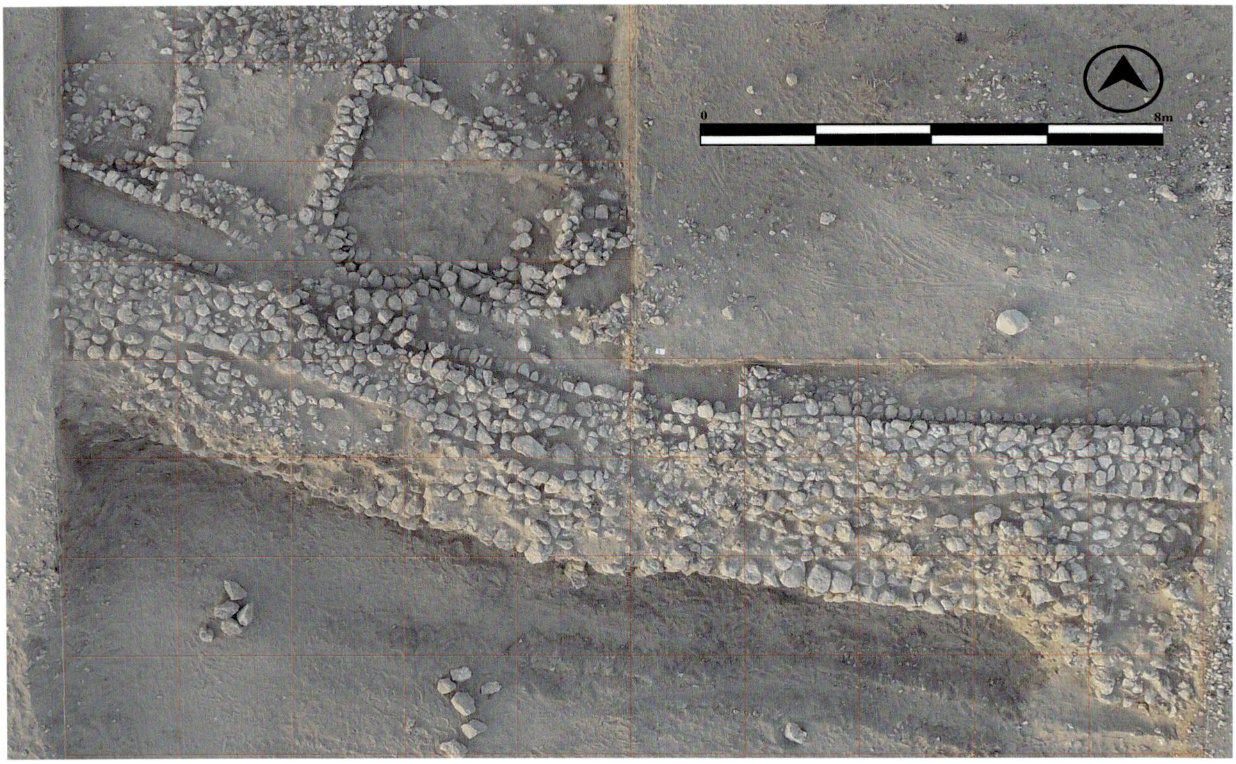

Figure 9. *An overview of the outermost fortification wall included in Sector III.*

Artefact analysis

During the 2023 excavations at Shokur, most of the artefacts collected were ceramic sherds. The percentage of fragments in Sectors I, II, and III was 92%, 96%, and 98% respectively. In contrast, stone tools represented only 4%, 3%, and 2% of the material collected in these sectors. The percentage of other finds in the collected materials of the three sectors is relatively low (0.4%), representing only 3% in Sector I, 0.6% in Sector II, and 0.3% in Sector III.

In the case of ceramics, the sherds were initially processed and classified into two main categories, fine ware and coarse ware. Closer examination revealed various subtypes within these categories, with very few examples of grey ware found among the fine ware and coarse ware categories. In addition, a significant quantity of buff and orange ware was documented, along with a substantial presence of coarse ware. The ceramic sherds were subsequently categorized based on their decorative elements and surface treatments. The analysis of the data revealed that the majority of the fine pottery sherds from all three sectors exhibited slip-decoration and painted surfaces. The presence of painted pottery fragments should be mentioned, predominantly from the surface layers of the three sectors and dating to the Wadi Suq period. The highest concentration of Wadi Suq fragments was identified in Sector II (eighteen fragments), followed by Sector III (six fragments), and Sector I (one fragment). In the case of the coarse sherds, both buff and orange, *c.*65% were found to be undecorated and lacked surface treatments, while about 15% exhibited a slipped surface. However, a wide variety of decorations were observed, with a significant quantitative representation. The most prevalent types of decoration are those exhibiting moulded/slipped, moulded, and moulded/incised features. The quantitative data aligns with the ceramic catalogue of all three sectors, suggesting comparable frequencies of occurrence. Most of the stone tools collected are fragmented, both on the surface and in layers, probably due to the 2023 excavation primarily focusing on the removal of collapsed layers. Grinding stones predominate the lithic finds, along with a smaller number of anvils and other unidentified stone tools. Hammers, mortars, pestles, and whetstones are also present, particularly from Sector III, along with a single spindle from the same sector. Of particular interest is the reuse of both ground and grinding stones in the construction of walls in Sector III, suggesting potential reuse of materials in the local economy.

Excavations in Area A yielded a total of twenty-two shell specimens, with the majority located in Sector III and smaller quantities present in Sector II, primarily from surface contexts (Fig. 11/k–n). However, three specimens were retrieved from layers associated with Room II, and two specimens were obtained from Room III. The presence of gastropods (six specimens) was observed, including *Strombus* sp. (two specimens), *Terebralia palustris* sp. (three specimens), and *Conus* sp. (one specimen). Additionally, a substantial quantity of bivalves was present. The site yielded eleven valves, including *Barbatia* sp. (one), *Callista* sp. (one), *Acrosterigma* sp. (three), *Glycymeris* sp. (one), and *Anadara* sp. (one). Six of these bivalves were identified as shell containers due to the presence of green residues within them. The presence of gastropods in the area is significant, as they typically inhabit marine and lagoon environments that are geographically distant from the site under investigation.

It is of particular interest to note the presence of a pipe and an incense burner among the surface collections of Sector III, although both artefacts are in a fragmentary state. Furthermore, seventeen fragmented pottery lids from Sectors II and III were also found in collapse and abandonment layers. Of particular interest are two fragments of clay animal figurines, one from a collapse layer in Sector II and the other from a surface layer in Room IV, and two stone vessel fragments from a top layer in Room III with reworked bottoms, possibly for reuse as stone tools. Only a few metal fragments and copper/bronze processing waste were found (Fig. 10/o–q). However, it is notable that the highest concentration of metal fragments is found in Sector III, with eight copper/bronze wasters and two generic fragments, but the highest concentration of relevant material was found in Sector III, where there were eight cases of copper/bronze wasters and two generic fragments. In Sector I, there were only two cases of copper/bronze wasters and one generic copper/bronze fragment, and in Sector II, there were three cases of copper/bronze wasters and one malachite fragment. Furthermore, the presence of beads of various sizes, mainly spherical in shape, should be noted (Fig. 11/r).

Regarding the thousands of ceramic fragments, there is no doubt that most of them are representative of the typical phases of the Early Iron Age, with a particular emphasis on Iron Age II. A significant proportion of the fragments pertain to large storage vessels crafted from coarse buff or orange ware and adorned with incised moulded cords or incised motifs, such as zigzags, wavy lines, and net patterns (Fig. 10/d–f). Storage jars are ubiquitous in Early Iron Age settlements, including Tell Abraq (Potts 1991: figs 103–111), Rumeilah (Boucharlat & Lombard 1985: pls 47–48; 52, 54, 55), and Bithnah (Benoist 2013: figs 102–105) for the northern area of the Oman peninsula; and Lizq (Kroll 2012: figs 28–29), Husn Salut (Condoluci, Degli Esposti & Phillips 2018: pls 24, 44, 50–51) for the central area. A diagnostic element that attests to the middle phase of the Iron Age is the moulded snake motif applied to the vessels (Fig. 10/a–c). This motif was prevalent in the Near East during the Iron Age, and in Arabia it has been identified in the cultic areas of sites such as Salut (Avanzini & Phillips 2010; Degli Esposti & Condoluci 2018: pls 5–6) and Mudhmar (Jean, Pellegrino & Gernez 2018: fig. 7) in Oman; and Saruq al-Hadid (Karacic et al. 2017: figs 3–5), Masafi (Benoist et al. 2015: figs 4, 8–9), and Bithnah (Benoist 2007: figs 6, 15; 2013: figs 115–121) in the Emirates, to name the most representative. Other elements that are indicative of the Early Iron Age include black-painted bowls on orange fine pottery and typical painted jars with bridged spouts. The excavation of Sector II/I yielded the oldest pottery, which primarily belongs to the Wadi Suq phase (Fig. 11/a–g,i–j). These fragments, painted in black on an orange or reddish background, can be attributed to globular-bodied jars and beakers. The motifs are those common to the period, including zigzags, chevrons, and bands of parallel wavy lines, which are well known in settlements such as Hili 8 (Cleuziou 1989: pl. 31), Tell Abraq (Potts 1991: figs 49, 51) and Kalba (Carter 1997: fig. 20), and especially in

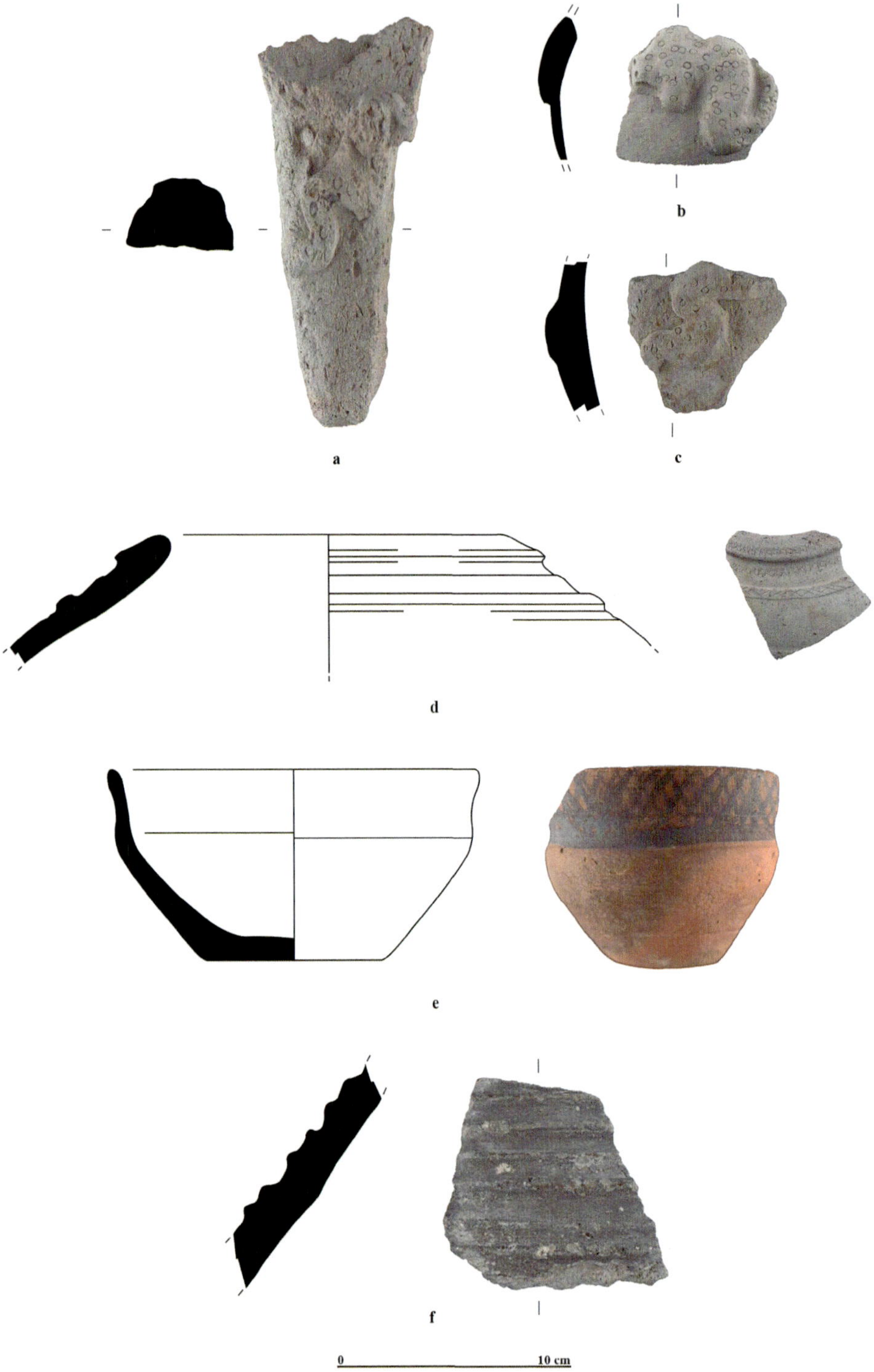

Figure 10. a–c. *Ceramic fragments with moulded snake decoration;* **d.** *engraved storage jar;* **e.** *painted carinated bowl;* **f.** *ribbed storage jar.*

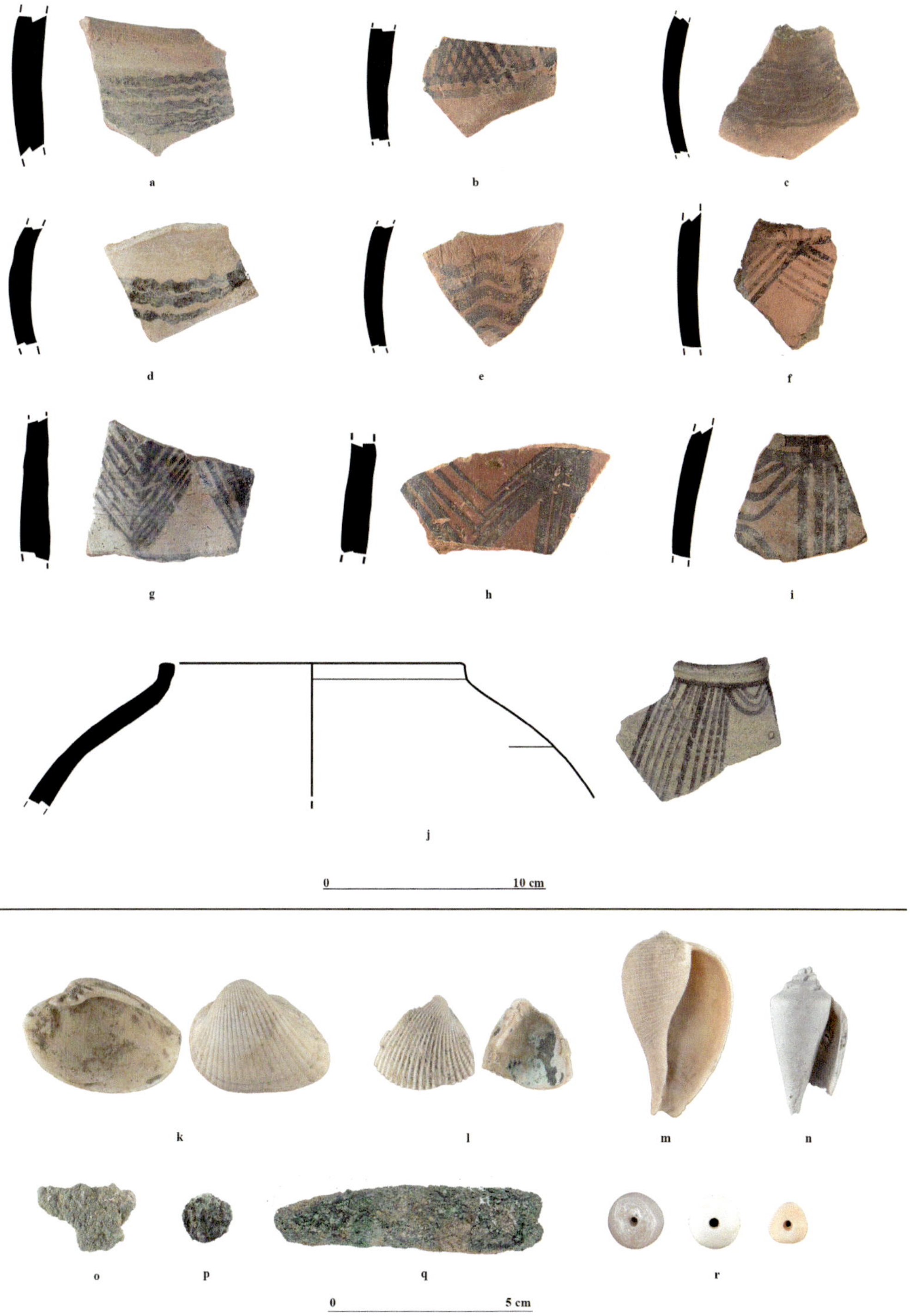

FIGURE 11. **a–g, i–j.** *Fragments painted in brown on an orange or grey background with motifs typical of the Wadi Suq phase;* **h.** *Umm an-Nar fragment painted in black on a red background with a typical banded motif composed of parallel flames;* **k–n.** *specimens of shell;* **o–q.** *metal fragments;* **r.** *various beads.*

graves such as those of Jebel Buhais, BHS 1, BHS 6, BHS 8, BHS 12 (Jasim 2012: figs 8; 44; 53–55; 70–71), Jebel Salut, JS4-G4 (Degli Esposti et al. 2021: fig. 12), Bidya 1 (Al-Tikriti 1989a: pls 63–64), or Shimal SH 99, 102, 103 (Vogt & Franke-Vogt 1987: figs 32; 23–24; 12–13).

However, a fragment painted in black on a red background enables us to hypothesize the origin of the settlement in the Umm an-Nar period (Fig. 11/h). It is a typical banded motif composed of parallel flames well known from the Umm an-Nar phases (Al-Tikriti 1989b: pls 39–40; Frifelt 1991: figs 59, 62–63, 67, 93/1–2, 94–96, 97/1–2, 98, 99/1–2, 100, 101/1; Laursen 2009: figs 1–6; Méry 2002). Moreover, the presence of a large quantity of stone tools in the archaeological layers and on the surface suggests the existence of workshop or production areas. There are numerous anvils, mortars, and grindstones that are possibly related to production activities and reused as building material.

Conclusion

The settlement of Shokur can be considered a fortified centre, occupied between the second and first millennium BC, given the presence of large and powerful walls surrounding a very large area and the probable presence of bastions along the walls. Given the large number of storage jars and stone tools, a very significant expansion must be considered to have occurred in the second half of the second millennium with the construction of production and domestic areas surrounded by the external fortification. Like other Iron Age settlements, such as Bithnah or Muweilah, given the presence of ceramics with the symbol of the serpent there may have been a cult or ritual area inside. The settlement certainly preserves traces of an impressive centre dating back to the Early and Middle Bronze Age, as evidenced by the ceramic fragments of the Wadi Suq phase and the large, squared stones reused for building that belong to the typical structures of the Umm an-Nar phase.

Future research will aim to estimate and verify the continuity of occupation from the Early Bronze Age to the Early Iron Age, as suggested by comparable material culture assemblages and stratigraphic sequences observed at other sites in south-eastern Arabia. For example, the al-Khutm tower has architectural remains and material culture that reveal a sequence of occupation extending from the third to the second millennium BC, to which is added the presence of surrounding buildings attributable to the Early Iron Age (Cattani et al. 2017; Cocca et al. 2019; Cocca, Cattani & Barchiesi 2023). Similarly, sites such as Salut, Hili, and Tell Abraq show evidence of long-term settlement continuity, characterized by pottery and architectural elements from the Umm an-Nar phase, persisting through the Wadi Suq phase and into the Iron Age. These finds support the hypothesis that Shokur originated in the Early Bronze Age and was subsequently expanded, reinforcing the notion of a settlement that maintained its strategic and cultural importance over the centuries. Given its prominent location in the landscape, much like other structures across the Arabian Peninsula, the construction of the Shokur tower was probably tied to the development of the surrounding oasis. In this context, the tower's imposing design served to symbolize the prestige of the community that managed a vital communication route between the desert and the mountains.

The size and location of the site suggest that it may have been a major trading hub, on the inland routes that connected the sea with the mountains and the desert. Proximity to the copper mines of the Hajar mountains (Lehner et al. 2023) and the deposits of soft stones such as chlorite and steatite (Harrower et al. 2016), as well as proximity to the caravan routes (Potts 1988) that came from the desert and reached the interior to exchange and trade or simply to access resources, mark this settlement as a pivotal place for the socio-economic development of the communities of the second–first millennium BC.

Acknowledgements

The authors are grateful to the Ministry of Heritage and Tourism of the Sultanate of Oman for their continued support in this research. They would like to thank the Minister His Excellency Salim bin Mohammed al-Mahruqi, Mr Sultan al-Bakri, Special advisor for Heritage to H.E. the Minister of Heritage and Tourism, and Ali al-Mahruqi, General Director of Archaeology. Thanks also go to La Sapienza University of Rome, which supports our research in Oman, as well as ISMEO (International Association for Mediterranean and Oriental Studies) and MAECI (Italian Ministry of Foreign Affairs and International Cooperation).

References

Agisoft LLC. 2016. AgiSoft PhotoScan Standard (Version 1.2.6) (Software). Retrieved from http://www.agisoft.com/downloads/installer/

Avanzini A. & Phillips C. 2010. An outline of recent discoveries at Salut in the Sultanate of Oman. Pages 93–108 in A. Avanzini (ed.), *Eastern Arabia in the first millennium B.C.* (Arabia Antica – Archaeological and Philological Series, 06). Rome: L'Erma di Bretschneider.

Benoist A. 2007. An Iron Age II snake cult in the Oman peninsula: Evidence from Bithnah (Emirate of Fujairah). *Arabian Archaeology and Epigraphy* 18/1: 34–54.

Benoist A. 2013. *La vallée de Bithnah au cours de l'Age du Fer*. (British Foundation for the Study of Arabia Monographs, 20) (British Archaeological Reports, International Series 2510). Oxford: Archaeopress.

Benoist A., Le Carlier C., Goy J., Degli Esposti M., Armbruster B. & Attaelmanan G. 2015. Snake, copper and water in south-eastern Arabian religion during the Iron Age: The Bithna and Masāfī evidence. Pages 21–36 in M. Arbach & J. Schiettecatte (eds), *Pre-Islamic South Arabia and its neighbours: New developments of research. Proceedings of the 17th Rencontres Sabéennes held in Paris, 6–8 June 2013*. (British Archaeological Reports, International Series 2740). Oxford: Archaeopress.

Boucharlat R. & Lombard P. 1985. The oasis of al Aïn in the Iron Age. Excavations at Rumeilah 1981–1983. Survey at Hili-14. *Archaeology in the United Arab Emirates* 4: 44–73.

Carter R. 1997. Defining the Late Bronze Age in southeast Arabia: Ceramic evolution and settlement during the second millennium BC. PhD thesis, Institute of Archaeology, University College London. [Unpublished.]

Cattani M., al-Lawati H., al-Bakri S., Cocca E., Armigliato A. ... Vinci G. 2017. Excavation at the Bronze Age tower of al-Khutm (Bāt, Sultanate of Oman): A preliminary evaluation of the monument (poster). *Proceedings of the Seminar for Arabian Studies* 47: 51–57.

Cleuziou S. 1989. Excavations at Hili 8: A preliminary report on the 4th to 7th campaigns. *Archaeology in the United Emirates* 5: 61–85.

Cocca E., Cattani M. & Barchiesi F. 2023. Further investigations at al-Khutm Bronze Age monumental tower. Al-Dhahirah region, Oman. *The IASA Bulletin* 30: 22–23.

Cocca E., Vinci G., Cattani M., Armigliato A., Di Michele A. ... Gennuso I. 2019. Al-Khutm Project 2017/2018: A Bronze Age monumental tower (Bat, Oman). *Proceedings of the Seminar for Arabian Studies* 49: 85–96.

Condoluci C., Degli Esposti M. & Phillips C. 2018. A complete sequence for the Early Iron Age of central Oman. Pages 93–109 in A. Avanzini & M. Degli Esposti (eds), *Ḥuṣn Salūt and the Iron Age of southeast Arabia. Excavations of the Italian Mission to Oman 2004–2014*. (Arabia Antica – Archaeological and Philological Series, 15). Rome: L'Erma di Bretschneider.

Costa P.M. 2006. Ḍank archaeological project: A preliminary report. *Proceedings of the Seminar for Arabian Studies* 36: 139–149.

Degli Esposti M. & Condoluci C. 2018. Husn Salut in the Iron Age. Page 33–61 in A. Avanzini & M. Degli Esposti (eds), *Ḥuṣn Salūt and the Iron Age of southeast Arabia. Excavations of the Italian Mission to Oman 2004–2014*. (Arabia Antica – Archaeological and Philological Series, 15). Rome: L'Erma di Bretschneider.

Degli Esposti M., Spano S., Tagliamonte M., Ramorino P., Sasso M. & al-Muzaini W.S.M. 2021. Funerary architecture in the Wadi Suq period and an unusual type of third/second-millennium grave: Initial results from the excavation of prehistoric burials in the Salut Archaeological Park, central Oman. *The Journal of Oman Studies* 22: 73–98.

Frifelt K. 1991. *The island of Umm an-Nar*. i. *Third millennium graves*. (Jutland Archaeological Society Publications 26/1). Aarhus: Aarhus University Press.

Harrower M.J., David-Cuny H., Nathan S., Dumitru I.A. & al-Jabri S. 2016. First discovery of ancient soft-stone (chlorite) vessel production in Arabia: Aqir al-Shamoos (Oman). *Arabian Archaeology and Epigraphy* 27: 197–207.

Jasim S.A. 2012. *The necropolis of Jebel al-Buhais. Prehistoric discoveries in the Emirate of Sharjah*. Sharjah: Department of Culture & Information.

Jean M., Pellegrino M.P. & Gernez G. 2018. New evidence of Iron Age ritual practices in central Oman: 2017 excavations in Muḍmār East, near Ādam. *Proceedings of the Seminar for Arabian Studies* 48: 125–140.

Karacic S., Boraik M., Qandil H. & David-Cuny H. 2017. Snake decorations on the Iron Age pottery from Sarūq al-Ḥadīd: A possible ritual centre? *Proceedings of the Seminar for Arabian Studies* 47: 139–151.

Kroll S. 2012. The early Iron Age fort at Lizq, Sultanate of Oman. Translated and updated by Paul Alan Yule. *Zeitschrift für Archäologie Aussereuropäischer Kulturen* 5:159–220.

Laursen S.T. 2009. The decline of Magan and the rise of Dilmun: Umm an-Nar ceramics from the burial mounds of Bahrain, c.2250–2000 BC. *Arabian Archaeology and Epigraphy* 20/1: 134–155.

Lehner J.W., Dumitru I., Buffington A., Dollarhide E., Nathan S., Paulsen P. ... Harrower M. 2023. Iron Age copper metallurgy in southeast Arabia: A comparative perspective. Pages 1391–1417 in E. Ben-Yosef & I.W.N. Jones (eds), *'And in length of days understanding' (Job 12:12): Essays on archaeology in the eastern Mediterranean and beyond in honor of Thomas E. Levy*. (Interdisciplinary Contributions to Archaeology). London: Springer Nature.

Méry S. 2002. *Les céramiques d'Oman et l'Asie moyenne: Une archéologie des échanges à l'âge du Bronze*. Paris: CNRS Éditions.

Potts D. 1988. Trans-Arabian routes of the pre-islamic period. Pages 127–162 in J.F. Salles (ed.), *L'Arabie et ses mers bordières. I. Itinéraires et voisinages. Séminaire de recherche 1985–1986*. (*Travaux de la Maison de l'Orient*, 16). Lyon: Maison de l'Orient et de la Méditerranée Jean Pouilloux.

Potts D. 1991. *Further excavations at Tell Abraq: The 1990 season*. Copenhagen: Munksgaard.

QGIS.org. 2021. QGIS Geographic Information System. QGIS Association.

Al-Tikriti W.Y. 1989a. The excavations at Bidya, Fujairah. The 3rd and 2nd millennia BC culture. *Archaeology of the United Arab Emirates* 5: 101–114.

Al-Tikriti W.Y. 1989b. Umm an-Nar culture in the northern Emirates: Third millennium BC tombs at Ajman. *Archaeology of the United Arab Emirates* 5: 89–100.

Vogt B. & Franke-Vogt U. 1987. *Shimal 1985/1986. Excavations of the German Archaeological Mission in Ras Al-Khaimah, U.A.E. A preliminary report*. (Berliner Beiträge zum Vorderen Orient, 8). Berlin: Dietrich Reimer.

Williams K.D. & Gregoricka L.A. 2013. The social, spatial, and bioarchaeological histories of Ancient Oman project: The mortuary landscape of Dhank. *Arabian Archaeology and Epigraphy* 24: 134–150.

Authors' addresses

Francesco Genchi, Department of Oriental Studies, Sapienza University of Rome, Scalo S. Lorenzo RM 21, Circonvallazione Tiburtina 4, 00185, Rome, Italy.
e-mail francesco.genchi@uniroma1.it

Nunzia Larosa, School of Humanities, Arts, and Social Sciences, University of New England – UNE, Armidale NSW 2351, Australia.
e-mail larosa.nunzia83@gmail.com

Giampiero Tursi, Fachbereich Geschichts-un Kulturwissenschaften, Institut für Vorderasiatische Archäologie, Freie Universität Berlin, Berlin, Germany.
e-mail giampierotursi@gmail.com

Guido Antinori, Department of Ancient Sciences, Sapienza University of Rome, Piazzale Aldo Moro 5, 00185 Rome, Italy.
e-mail guido.antinori@uniroma1.it

Francesco Paolo Caputo, Independent scholar.
e-mail francescopcaputo@libero.it

Valentina Mili, Independent scholar.
e-mail valentinamili93@gmail.com

Proceedings of the Seminar for Arabian Studies 54 (2025): 105–120

Piecing together the evidence: architecture, inscriptions, and sherds from an early to middle Islamic funerary context in Qurḥ/al-Mabiyāt

Stefanie Janke, Friedrich W. Weigel, Mustafa Ahmad & Arnulf Hausleiter

Summary

Recent archaeological fieldwork in the early to middle Islamic city of Qurḥ/al-Mabiyāt investigated architectural structures within an extramural cemetery. The area is characterized by supposed simple graves, apparently delimited by oval rings or covers of pebbles, while remains of stone walls, brick fragments, and pieces of white plaster indicate the presence of substantial and representative funerary architecture. Excavations by the German Archaeological Institute funded by the Royal Commission for AlUla (RCU) in 2022–2023 uncovered two adjoining architectural units, each confined by enclosure walls and plastered floors surrounding an embedded central structure. Furthermore, the remains show extensive work and elaboration in the form of claddings and superstructures. As the buildings have been looted, investigations concentrated on the architecture, associated fragments of Kufic inscriptions, tenth–eleventh-century AD pottery, and the contextual embedding within the cemetery as part of the city and its built environment. These new findings enable us to develop new perspectives regarding local traditions and early to middle Islamic burial practices in north-western Hijaz and the wider region. The limited number of these monuments at Qurḥ compared with the large number of graves, indicates that a small group of people was treated differently in death, suggesting individual distinctions within the early to middle Islamic society of Qurḥ.

Keywords: Qurḥ/al-Mabiyāt, early to middle Islamic, architecture, pottery, funerary archaeology

Introduction

The ruins of the archaeological site of al-Mabiyāt are located in north-west Saudi Arabia in the Hijaz region (Fig. 1), *c.*19 km south-east of the Old Town of AlUla (al-ʿUlā). Whereas the preserved ruins of the city cover an area of 35 ha, the fenced site covers an area of *c.*100 ha including cemetery areas and flood protection structures, but the archaeological remains are distributed much further afield. The site has been identified as the historical Qurḥ (Nasif 1979), which was described by the tenth-century Arab geographer al-Muqaddasi as the most important city after Mecca in the Hijaz (al-Muqaddasi 1897: 132 [83 in original pagination]). Qurḥ was situated at the crossroads of the ancient Arabian communication network (Frenkel 1996: 181; Young 2011: 90–135; Durand 2019; Fiema et al. 2020a; 2020b; Städtler 2023). These routes maintained their importance for the pilgrimage from Syria and the Levant to the Islamic holy sites of Mecca and Medina (Gilmore et al. 1985; al-Kilabi 2010; Petersen 2012: 9–16, 29–37, 148, 153; al-Ghabban 2019).

Early explorers such as Charles M. Doughty (1921: 161–162)[1] or Antonin Jaussen and Raphaël Savignac (1914: 26) mentioned the site, but never visited it. In 1968, Peter Parr, Gerald Lankester Harding, and John Dayton surveyed al-Mabiyāt briefly and concluded that there is a 'strong possibility' that the settlement was founded during the Umayyad period (Parr, Harding & Dayton 1970: 201, n. 12). The first scientific excavations were initiated in 1984–1985 by the then Department of Antiquities in the area of a residential quarter in the east of the site (Gilmore et al. 1985: 117–121; al-Talhi et al. 1986). Further archaeological and conservation work was carried out by King Saud University from 2004 to 2019, mainly within a larger area with residential buildings in the central northern part of the walled settlement (al-Omeer 2006; al-Muaikel 2011; al-Ghazzi et al. 2018; al-Aboudi et al. 2019; cf. al-Aboudi 2019; 2021).

Between spring 2022 and autumn 2024, the Qurḥ Conservation and Archaeological Project (QCAP)

[1] Doughty asked locals about Qurḥ but its identification with the ruins of al-Mabiyāt seems to have been unknown at the time.

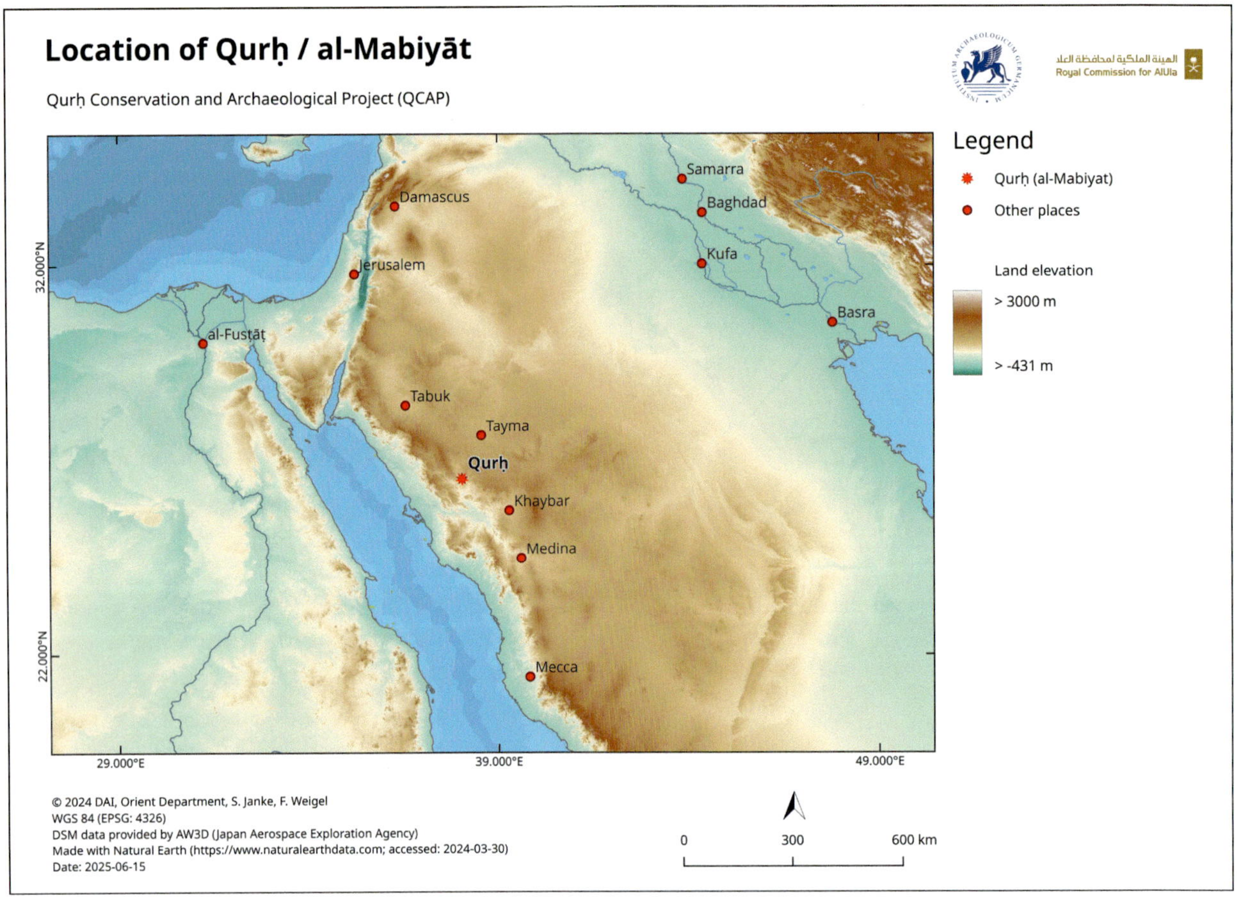

FIGURE 1. *A map with the location of Qurḥ in north-western Hijaz and the surrounding regions (©DAI, Orient Department, S. Janke, F. Weigel).*

conducted five seasons of fieldwork at the site of al-Mabiyāt.[2] The interdisciplinary research at this site operates in the context of the initiative of the Royal Commission for AlUla (RCU) to develop the city and area of al-ʿUlā into a major tourist destination of the Kingdom. An essential part of the initiative is the integration and presentation of historic sites. Qurḥ, in this overall context, is a central pillar in the 'Journey through Time' of the al-ʿUlā oasis. A major aim of the project is to investigate the stratigraphic sequence and the local occupation history by means of archaeological excavations. Furthermore, contexts of different functional and social nature (e.g. residential, production, public/religious) have been investigated by targeted excavations in order to contribute to a more detailed understanding of the settlement. Beyond this, the urban landscape is defined not only by the space occupied by living inhabitants, but also by the surrounding cemeteries. Despite the fact that research was limited to methods that do not disturb potential buried individuals, it became clear from the different types of grave markers and buildings that the cemeteries represent an integral aspect of the sociocultural fabric of the settlement.

[2] Since 2022 the Qurḥ Conservation and Archaeological Project (QCAP) of the German Archaeological Institute's (DAI) Orient Department and the Royal Commission for AlUla (RCU) have been operating at the site of al-Mabiyāt, south of al-ʿUlā. Funded by the latter, fieldwork was carried out between 2022 and 2024. While Stefanie Janke supervised excavations in Area C, Friedrich Weigel is the local field director of the DAI excavations and Mustafa Ahmad is the lead ceramicist of the project. Arnulf Hausleiter is the director and principal investigator of QCAP.

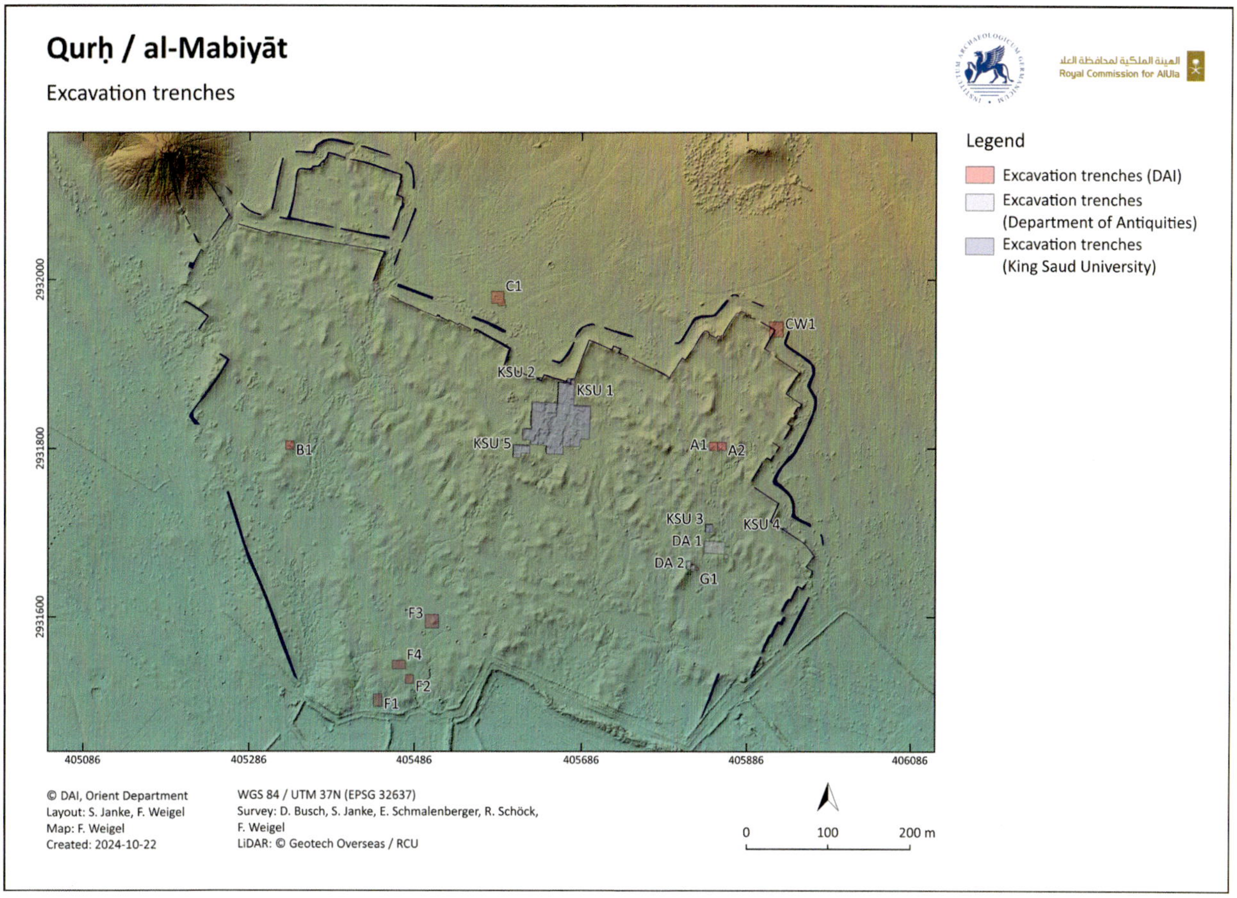

FIGURE 2. *A map of Qurḥ showing DAI excavation areas and previous expeditions (©DAI, Orient Department, F. Weigel).*

Written records about Qurḥ refer to a large market, mining, and local agricultural production (al-Wohaibi 1969: 355, 357, 360–362; Power 2010: 185–189). The new excavations in the western part of the city (Area B) provided archaeological evidence of pottery production — dating to the later occupation phase of the site (eleventh century AD) — in the form of a pottery kiln.[3] In addition to the local ceramics, it was possible to classify imports indicating contacts with Iraq, Syria, Egypt, and China (Gilmore et al. 1985: 116; al-Muaikel 2011: 57, pl. 3.12c; al-Aboudi 2019: 37). Excavations also conducted in other parts of the site, such as Areas A, B, C, CW, F, and G (Fig. 2), combined with the analysis of the pottery and radiocarbon dates, show that apparently the most expansive phase of Qurḥ can be dated to the time between the ninth and eleventh centuries AD. The economic well-being of Qurḥ seems to diminish during the later Fatimid period. A shrinking of the occupied area is indicated, for example, by the change of a residential area within the walled settlement to a site for pottery production (the above-mentioned Area B) as well as the frequent deposition of waste within apparently abandoned houses (see Pollock 1990: 58–59; McMahon 2015) or the installation of *tanānīr* (ovens; sing. *tannūr*) within already partly filled room structures (al-Muaikel 2011: 50, 61). At the end of the twelfth century AD, the site and Wādī al-Qurā seem to have been abandoned with al-Yāqūt stating that no one used the water available there (Wüstenfeld 1869: 54, 81; see Power 2010: 190). This

[3] Pottery production before that time might have taken place in an area 500 m to the east of the walled settlement, indicated by surface remains of kilns and wasters (see al-Muaikel 2011: 42–43).

can be confirmed thus far archaeologically, as material from the subsequent centuries is absent from the site. Whereas chronostratigraphic soundings in various locations in the city (Areas A, F, and G) bear evidence of considerable building activities within this relatively short occupation period (ninth to eleventh century AD), the architecture was founded on a layer of aeolian sand devoid of anthropogenic materials (test trenches in Area A and G) or alluvial deposits (Area F). Although *spolia*[4] and a grave more than 1 m below the aeolian sand may suggest an earlier occupation of Qurḥ, there is as yet no evidence for a pre-ninth-century settlement in al-Mabiyāt. So far, archaeological material indicating such an occupation has only been found at the nearby site 204-44 (Ingraham et al. 1981: 79, pl. 65; Gilmore et al. 1985: 112, 118). These preliminary results are in contrast with Gilmore et al. (1985: 115, 118–121, table 4, pl. 4), who proposed a seventh- to eleventh-/twelfth-century occupation based on their test trench in 'P59'. However, after revisiting the same stratigraphic sequence with a new test trench (Area G) east of 'P59', no material evidence for a seventh-/eighth-century occupation was identified (for similar observations across the site, see Parr, Harding & Dayton 1970: 201, considering, however an Umayyad foundation; al-Omeer 2006: 131; al-Muaikel 2011: 61).[5]

In the period concurrent with the ninth- to eleventh-century occupation of al-Mabiyāt, an extramural cemetery was established north of the city's enclosure. This 'northern cemetery' was investigated in three excavation seasons between 2022 and 2023 in Area C (Trench C1). A burial ground in this area of Qurḥ had already been mentioned by the KSU expedition, which collected examples of gravestones bearing Kufic inscriptions (al-Omeer 2006: pls 10.15–16, 10.17a, 10.25–27; al-Muaikel 2011: 42, 59–61, pl. 3.15e–f). However, al-Omeer's map (2006: pl. 10.21) erroneously located the cemetery within the north-western extension of the city, where no graves are detectible, but there are remains of what was probably a public building. According to observations made in spring 2022, the northern cemetery is bordered to the west and south by the city wall and extends further to the east. The so-called 'Eid' mosque excavated in 1985 (al-Talhi et al. 1986: 58–59) may have had a functional connection to the cemetery or influenced its internal patterning (see Insoll 1999: 173–174). Due to modern surface disturbance and sand drifts in the central area, it is not possible to state with certainty whether this is a single continuous cemetery area or two separate areas.

Area C — The northern cemetery

During the initial survey in spring 2022, two large and apparently anthropogenic but shallow depressions within the cemetery area were identified on the surface *c.*42 m north of the city wall. These depressions were already visible in an orthophotograph taken in 2018 and indicated looting activities recorded by Geotech Overseas and kindly provided by RCU. Their edges were covered with a concentration of deteriorated and fragmentary building materials including several brick fragments, medium-sized fieldstones, and white plaster fragments, suggesting the remains of large architectural structures below. Excavations began in autumn 2022 to clarify their function. After removing the sandy surface and the underlying collapse layers, two rectangular enclosures with central structures were uncovered (Figs 3–4). The north-western enclosure (henceforth Building C-b2) has a slightly trapezoidal shape, measuring 7.65 m (south-west wall) by 8.20 m (north-east wall) by 6.20 m (south-east walls and entrance) by 6.35 m (north-west wall), while the south-eastern enclosure (henceforth Building C-b1), also slightly trapezoidal, measures 5.90 m (north-east walls and entrance) by 6.15 m (south-west wall) by 5.60 m (both north-west and south-east walls). Both buildings share a north-west–south-east orientation and their masonry was mainly constructed using two rows of medium-sized sandstones, between which fragments of bricks were occasionally found. The mortar between the stones was a mixture of clay and sand. On average, only two courses of roughly hewn sandstones were preserved in the masonry of both structures. A test trench opened in the south-west of Building C-b1 suggests that the enclosures were apparently not built on a foundation of other material. The masonry

[4] E.g. a funerary Dadanitic inscription (MA 01650, dated to 27 BC, reading kindly provided by F. Kootstra) reused in an early Islamic stone foundation in Area F, and a funerary Nabataean-Aramaic inscription, dated to AD 280, found reused in a column base by the excavations of King Saud University (al-Muaikel 2011: 59–60, pl. 3.7c, 3.15d).

[5] For the stratigraphic sequence of Qurḥ/al-Mabiyāt based on the DAI excavations, see Weigel, in preparation.

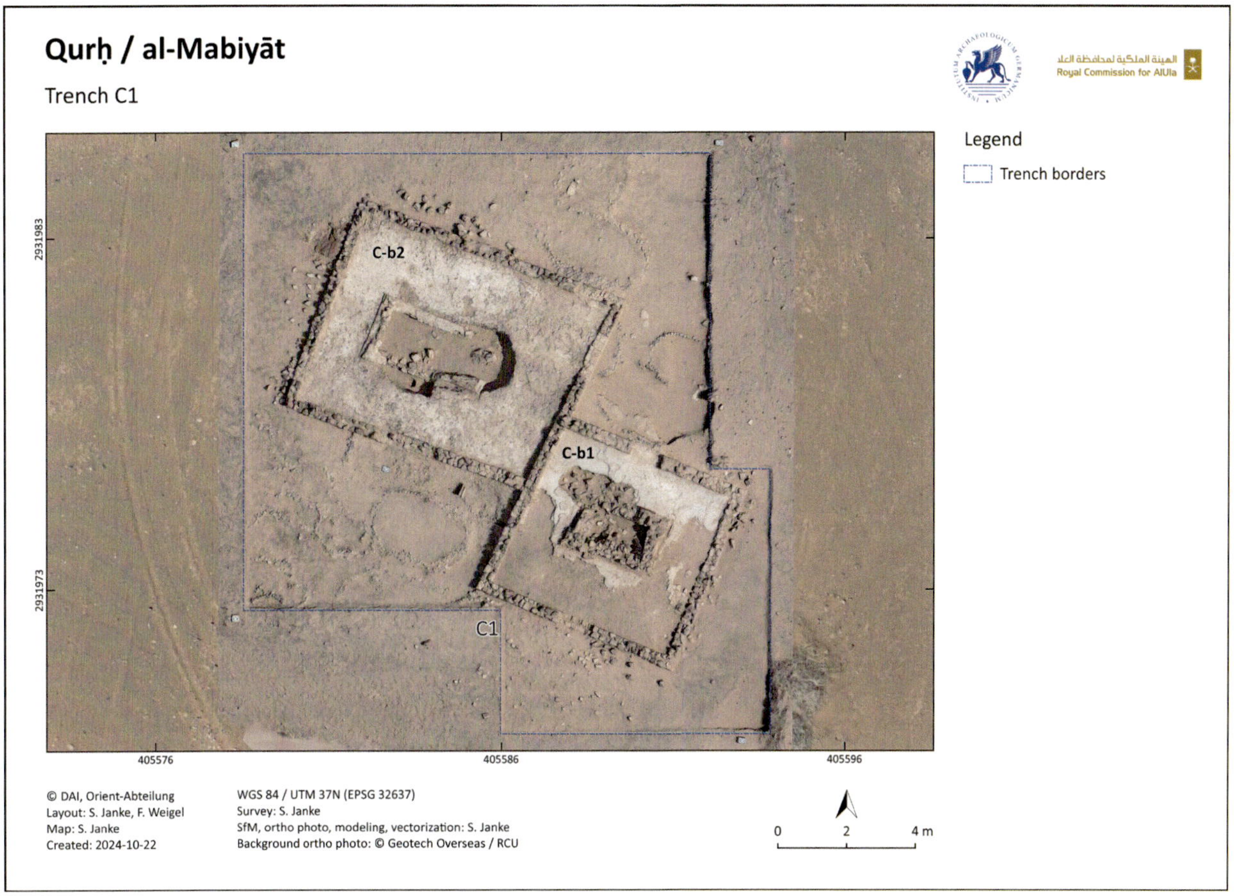

FIGURE 3. *An orthophotograph of Trench C1 (©DAI, Orient Department, S. Janke).*

of each had been coated with white plaster on both interior and exterior faces. Most of the walls have an average width between 0.35 and 0.40 m, except for those of the central structure of Building C-b1 (see below), measuring 0.50–0.60 m including the cladding. The average preserved height of the walls of both buildings ranges between 0.16 and 0.24 m above floor level, with some parts preserved to less than 0.10 m. On the outer face of the south-western wall of Building C-b1, a second layer of plaster was found on top of the first, suggesting that the building had been renovated or maintained. Buildings C-b1 and C-b2 have in common an almost centrally located structure within them, whose north-west–south-east orientation also coincides (Figs 3–4). The central structure of C-b1 measures 2.75 by 1.85 m according to the preserved walls, and that of C-b2 *c.*3.70 by 1.95 m, as can be determined by the preserved edges of the plastered floor. Despite their apparently similar appearance, the two central structures differ in their construction methods.

The structure within C-b1 was built of medium-sized, roughly hewn sandstones, of which two to three layers were still preserved. A layer of clay, 5–7 cm thick, and a layer of white screed, *c.*1 cm thick, lay beneath the lowest layer of stones as a foundation layer for the masonry. The inner face of this smaller structure showed a flat and smoothed surface, whereas the outer face was covered by a thick layer of white mortar, in which originally flat, smoothed reddish flagstones, which served as wall cladding, were embedded. The flagstones were separated from each other by a layer of mortar, which still shows their negative impression (Fig. 5/b–d). In the southern section of the north-west wall, the lower part of one of these flagstones was discovered

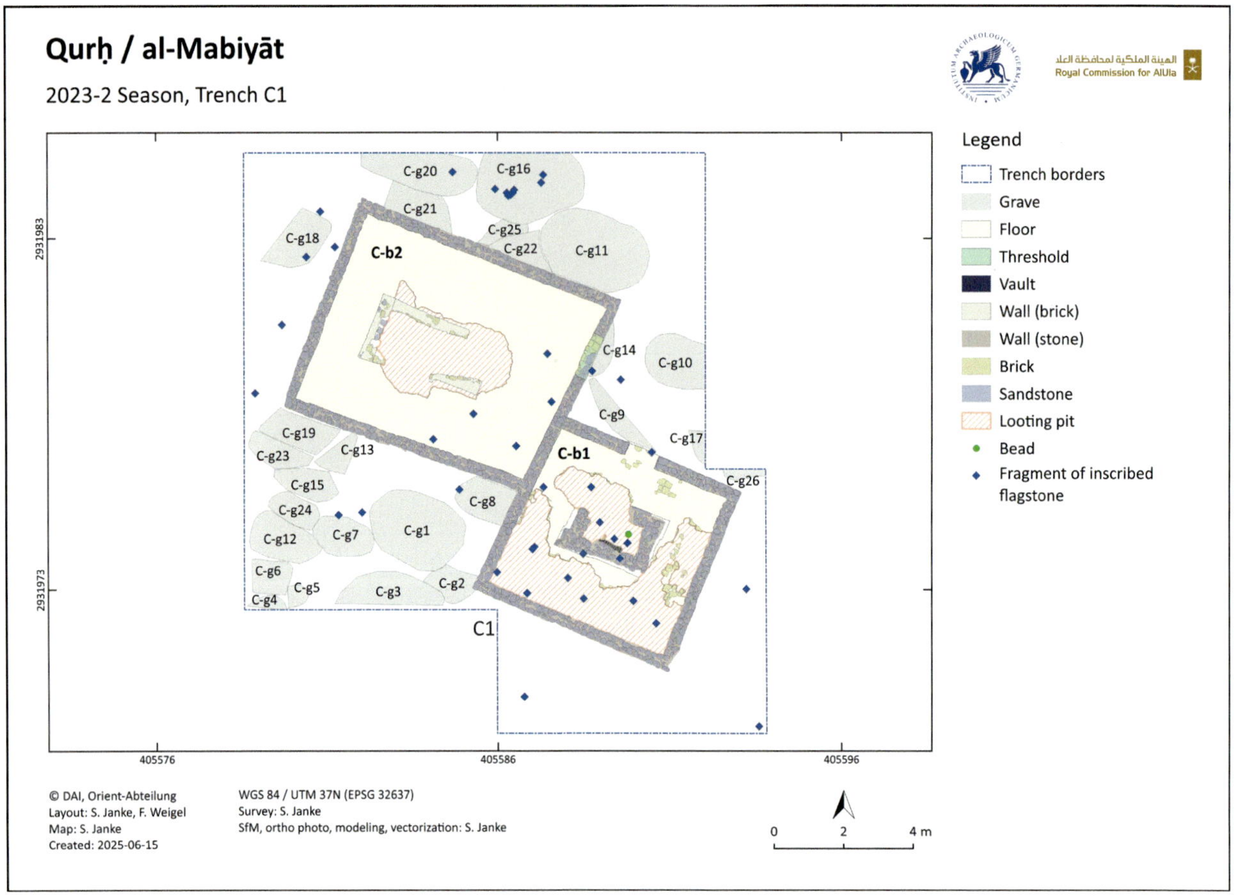

FIGURE 4. *A vectorized plan of Buildings C-b1 and C-b2 with surrounding graves, showing the distribution of inscribed flagstone fragments (©DAI, Orient Department, S. Janke).*

in situ (Fig. 5/c). In the western part of the surviving north-east wall of the small structure of C-b1, an almost complete but very weathered sandstone was found still *in situ* (Fig. 5/b). In the debris layers inside and outside the central structure of C-b1, several fragments of plain as well as inscribed flagstones of varying thickness were found (see Fig. 4). One of these inscribed fragments was lying tilted in the plaster, probably still *in situ*, on the south-west wall (Fig. 5/a). This suggests that the flagstones decorating the outer face of the central structure of C-b1 were at least partially inscribed with Kufic script. The negative impressions in the mortar, in which these were once placed and which extend along the preserved outer wall, are clearly recognizable. A boundary is formed by the surrounding floor, which still preserves a clear-cut edge of the now missing flagstones (Fig. 5/b–d). Compared to the general preservation of the buildings, the selectively missing flagstones suggest an intentional removal.

The central structure of C-b1 was covered by a vault constructed from rectangular bricks held together with a thick layer of mortar. Part of this vault, resting on the second layer of the inner south-west wall, was still preserved (Fig. 6/a). The eastern part was found still *in situ*, whereas the western part may have slipped down a few centimetres. This process could be related to the looting activities that took place inside the central structure as well as in the northern part of it, completely destroying the northern part of the north-east wall and about half of the north-west wall. The looting pit cuts deep into the architecture and underlying deposits (*c.*0.75 m from the floor level) thereby destroying most

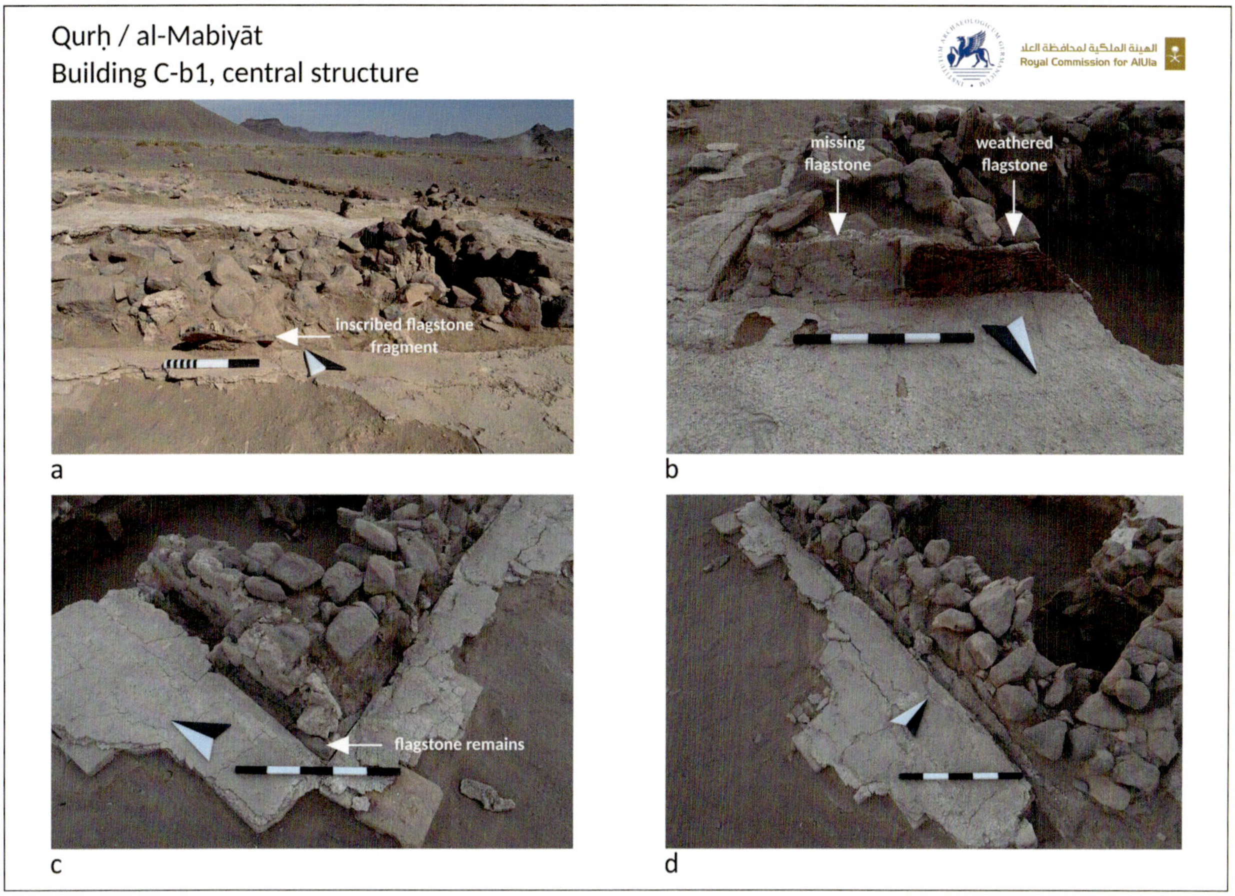

FIGURE 5. *The former flagstone cladding of the central structure of Building C-b1 (details):* **a, b, and c.** *remains;* **b, c, and d.** *negative impressions (Photos ©DAI, Orient Department, S. Janke).*

of the floor in the north-western part of C-b1. Here, the original fill of the central structure, including the grave, was completely removed. Later, the trench was filled with the collapsed building material of the surrounding walls, including medium-sized sandstones, bricks and brick fragments, mortar and plaster fragments, as well as inscribed and plain fragments of red sandstone flagstones. Occasional fragments of pottery and glass, a few animal bones, and charcoal particles were also discovered among the debris. A single cylindrical carnelian bead MA 01511 (Fig. 6/c) was found in the lower part of the trench fill in the eastern part of the central structure.

Coinciding with the overall orientation of the buildings, the central structure of Building C-b2 was built differently (Fig. 7/a). Its surrounding walls were built almost entirely of bricks (Fig. 7/b–c), which do not show a clear pattern of bonding. Three courses of bricks have been preserved on the north-western and north-eastern walls, whereas a collapsed part of the south-east corner (Fig. 7/b, upper centre) shows at least seven courses. Six of them were preserved, and a seventh was indicated by negative impressions within the mortar. The south-east wall had been destroyed by a looting pit cutting through parts of the surrounding floor. This operation removed the complete original fill of the central structure, even undercutting the surrounding walls and floor, eventually leading to their collapse. However, the preserved edges of the surrounding floor enabled us to determine the original extent of the central structure. Plastic items

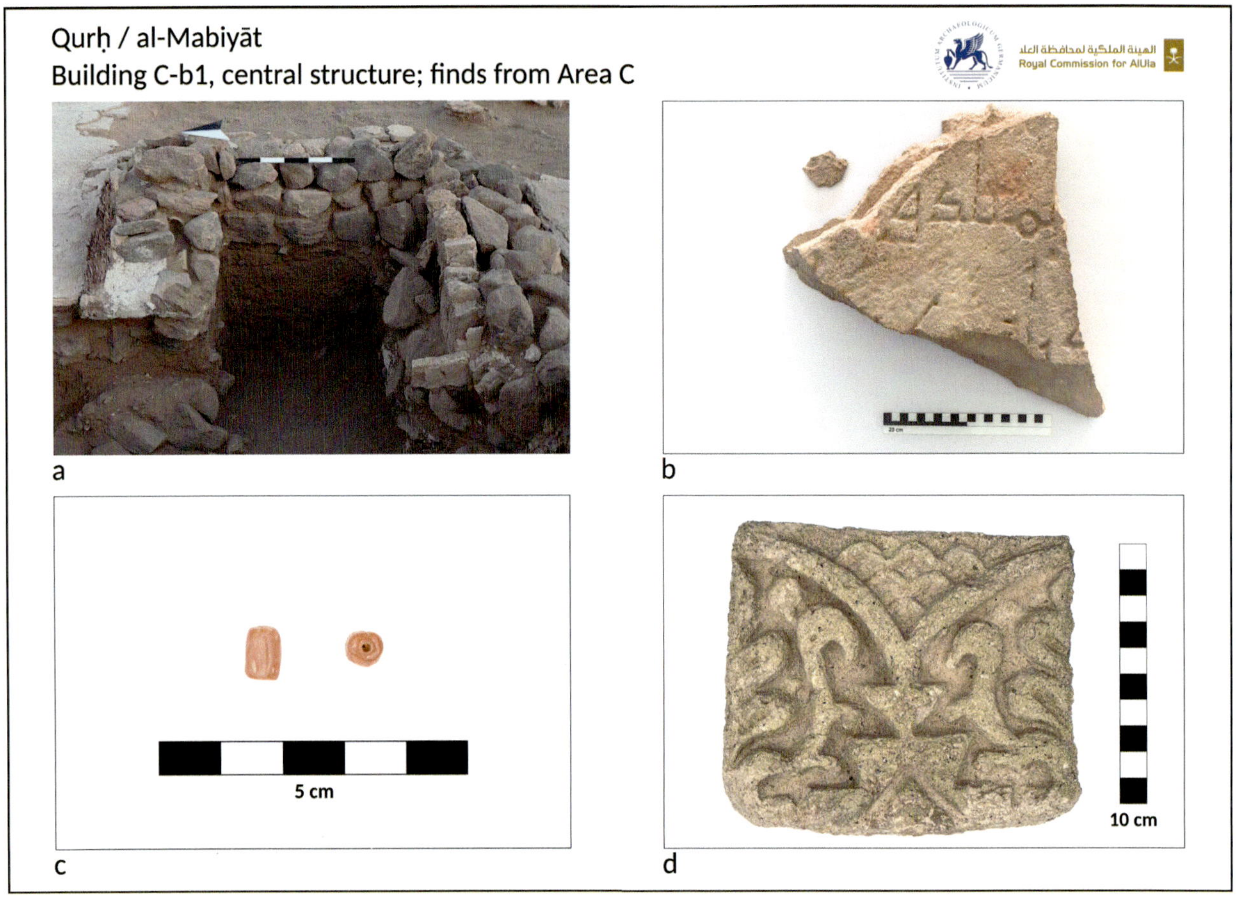

FIGURE 6. a. *The remains of a brick vault (inner right side) in the central structure of Building C-b1 (©DAI, Orient Department, S. Janke);* **b.** *an inscribed flagstone MA 00529 with parts of sura 112 from the lower collapse within the central structure of Building C-b1 (©DAI, Orient Department, L. Dudek);* **c.** *a carnelian bead (MA 01511) found in the collapse of the central structure of C-b1;* **d.** *a moulded brick (MA 00527) decorated with floral motifs from the lower fill of the looting pit of Building C-b2* (**c–d.** *©DAI, Orient Department, T. Rödle).*

found within the loose sand fill of the looting pit suggest a rather recent date for this event. Only the north-western part of the central structure is preserved. The north-west wall had three medium-sized sandstones on top of the brick courses (Fig. 7/c, in the centre of the wall). The use of broken bricks and fragments indicates that building materials might have been reused for the construction of Building C-b2. Although the outer faces were plastered, no indication of a cladding similar to that of the central structure in C-b1 was observed. However, within the lower filling of the looting pit, a moulded brick (MA 00527) with symmetrical floral motifs was found (see Fig. 6/d). Due to its find context, it remains unclear whether it belonged to the original decoration of the structure, was reused as building material, or accidentally fell into the pit. The half palmettes on each side indicate that the brick was part of a larger, probably repetitive frieze. The motif, with its variants, has a long tradition in pre-Islamic south-west Asia and the eastern Mediterranean (Porter 1993; Seidl 2003–2005). It was also prominent in Sasanian visual culture and became widely used in various media in multiple forms and degrees of stylization during the early Islamic period (Dimand 1937; Jenkins 1968; Khazâie 2005).

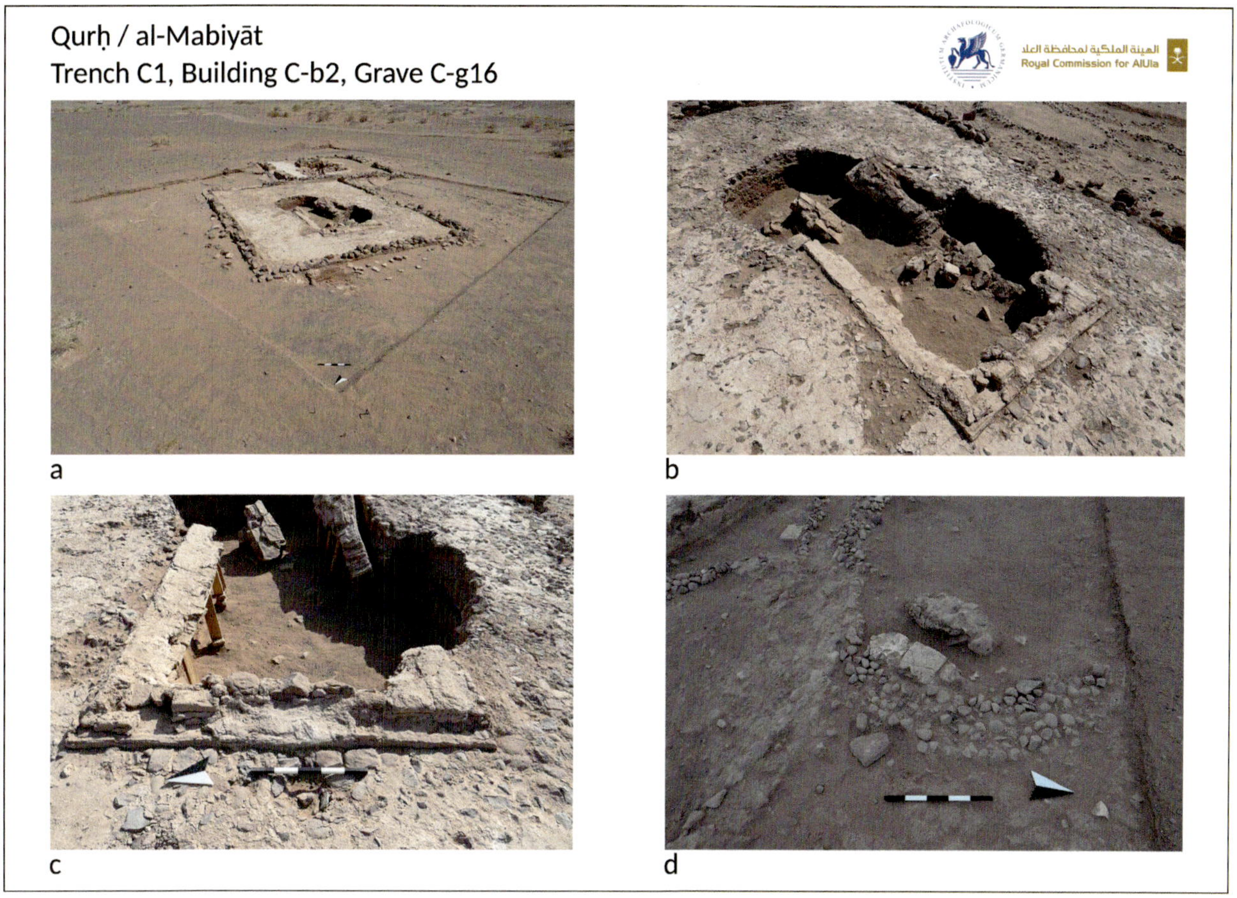

FIGURE 7. **a.** *An overview of Building C-b2;* **b–c.** *details of the central structure of C-b2;* **d.** *detail of grave C-g16 (Photos ©DAI, Orient Department, S. Janke).*

Both buildings also differ in the construction technique of their floors. The floor of the south-eastern Building C-b1 was built with squared bricks which were covered with a finely made, white plaster. In contrast, the floor of the north-western Building C-b2 consists of a layer of pebbles laid into and covered by a hard white plaster. Both buildings can be accessed from an area in front of them. The entrances are situated close to each other (C-b1: to the north-east; C-b2: to the south-east). This and the specific arrangement of this part of the burial ground (see below) may have been an element of the 'internal cemetery patterning' (see Insoll 1999: 173). Furthermore, as the walls of C-b2 abut the original plaster of the walls of C-b1, the latter was built before C-b2.

In the immediate surrounding of both structures, twenty-six graves have been identified (see Fig. 4). They are marked by pebbles laid in an ellipsoid shape (see Fig. 3). None of the graves is oriented towards Mecca, but perhaps the direction was either approximate or influenced by the course of the city wall or the Hajj route passing by the settlement. Whatever the case, this was not due to a lack of ability as the extramural 'Eid' mosque east of the city and other brick structures, possibly also tombs in this area, correctly face towards the qiblah, as is true for the great mosque identified by the DAI excavations in Area F. The stratigraphic relation of the graves to Buildings C-b1 and C-b2 clearly shows that at least some of them were created before the latter. This is most evident in the case of Grave

C-g2, which was cut by Building C-b1, as well as Grave C-g14, which was cut by Building C-b2. Most probably, this grave was covered with sand and not identifiable at the time, as its pebble marking is 0.14–0.18 m below the threshold. It seemingly was not an obstacle to entering C-b2. South of C-b2 and west of C-b1, the lower part of an upright standing gravestone on the western edge of Grave C-g8 was found *in situ*. Building C-b1 was erected partly above its pebble marking The Kufic inscription of the gravestone reads '[...] Muḥammad, the Prophet of God, peace be upon him' (reading kindly provided by M. Ahmad). Other graves such as C-g9 and C-g11 are located directly along the outer walls of both buildings, apparently respecting the existing structures of C-b1 and C-b2 and therefore suggesting a later construction date. The pebble marking of C-g9 is on a similar level to the floor of the entrance of C-b1, which could mean that access to the structure was no longer intended or deliberately obstructed (as walking over graves is usually disapproved of, if these are recognizable). Again, this would suggest that C-g9 was dug after C-b1 and before the collapse of the enclosure wall of C-b1, as its debris covers the former. Furthermore, other graves seemingly cut through earlier ones. This small area uncovered in Trench C1 shows a high degree of dynamism in the occupation of the cemetery, which can be dated to the main occupation phase of the city, as far as can be judged by the pottery (tenth–eleventh century AD).

Some graves bear remains of installations, partly built with pebbles and plaster, others with sandstone and brick fragments to hold the gravestones in an upright position (e.g. Grave C-g16, Fig. 7/d). In some of them, the lower parts of the gravestones were still preserved (e.g. C-g8, with a similar installation on the opposite eastern side of the gravestone). Furthermore, fragments of inscribed flagstones made from sandstone, apparently once belonging to similar gravestones, were found distributed among the graves. A large flagstone with a Kufic inscription, the largest example from C1, was found broken at the north-western corner of Building C-b2. Plaster and mortar remains on the reverse suggest that it was originally installed on a wall. Its exact location, however, is not clear as it was apparently not originally positioned on the spot where it was found, because turning it upright towards the wall of C-b2 would have resulted in the inscription being upside down. It can also not be excluded that the mortar was washed down from the adjacent wall of C-b2. Alternatively, it is conceivable that the object may have been part of a gravestone located further west, where an installation was preserved with remnants of a broken-off gravestone of the same colour. However, the length of the installation appears to be marginally shorter than that of the gravestone. All inscribed flagstone fragments, as far as they are legible, show an Islamic reference such as, for example, MA 00529 (found in the lower part of the collapse of the central structure in C-b1, Fig. 6/b) with parts of the Qurʾān's sura 112 (*al-Ikhlas*, '[He neither] begets n[or is born]'; reading kindly provided by M. Ahmad) preserved. This sura, together with suras 113 and 114, is one of the most frequently quoted in funerary inscriptions, gaining popularity in the tenth century AD (Halevi 2007: 26, n. 33, providing evidence from Egypt), probably because of their apotropaic function and *baraka* (Hillenbrand 1994: 254; Leisten 1998: 87–88). Such inscriptions might have played a role in rites including active recitation at the grave (Halevi 2007: 27–31).

Pottery from Area C

The quantity of pottery recovered from Area C is relatively small compared to other excavated areas at the site, comprising only 8% of the total assemblage. A total of 2892 pottery sherds were collected over the course of three excavation seasons, with 31% being diagnostic sherds and 69% non-diagnostic. These finds were distributed across eighty-one pottery assemblages from seventy stratigraphic units. Analysis of the pottery revealed that the vast majority, 98%, is unglazed, while only a small portion, 2%, consists of glazed ceramics.

While a range of ceramic types and forms were present in the pottery corpus from Area C, one particularly noteworthy feature is the significant quantity of a specific type of pottery labelled as 'grey ware' because of the colour of its fabric. This ware appears exclusively in the form of jars, characterized by a distinct banded rim with a horizontal incised line along the banded outer lip (Fig. 8/1–8). The fabric of the grey ware contains fine to small-sized inclusions of limestone and chaff temper, with its grey to dark grey paste indicating that it was fired in a reduced firing environment. Additionally, body sherds from this ware found in Area C display impressed and grooved decorations, suggesting a degree of stylistic uniformity across this ceramic type.

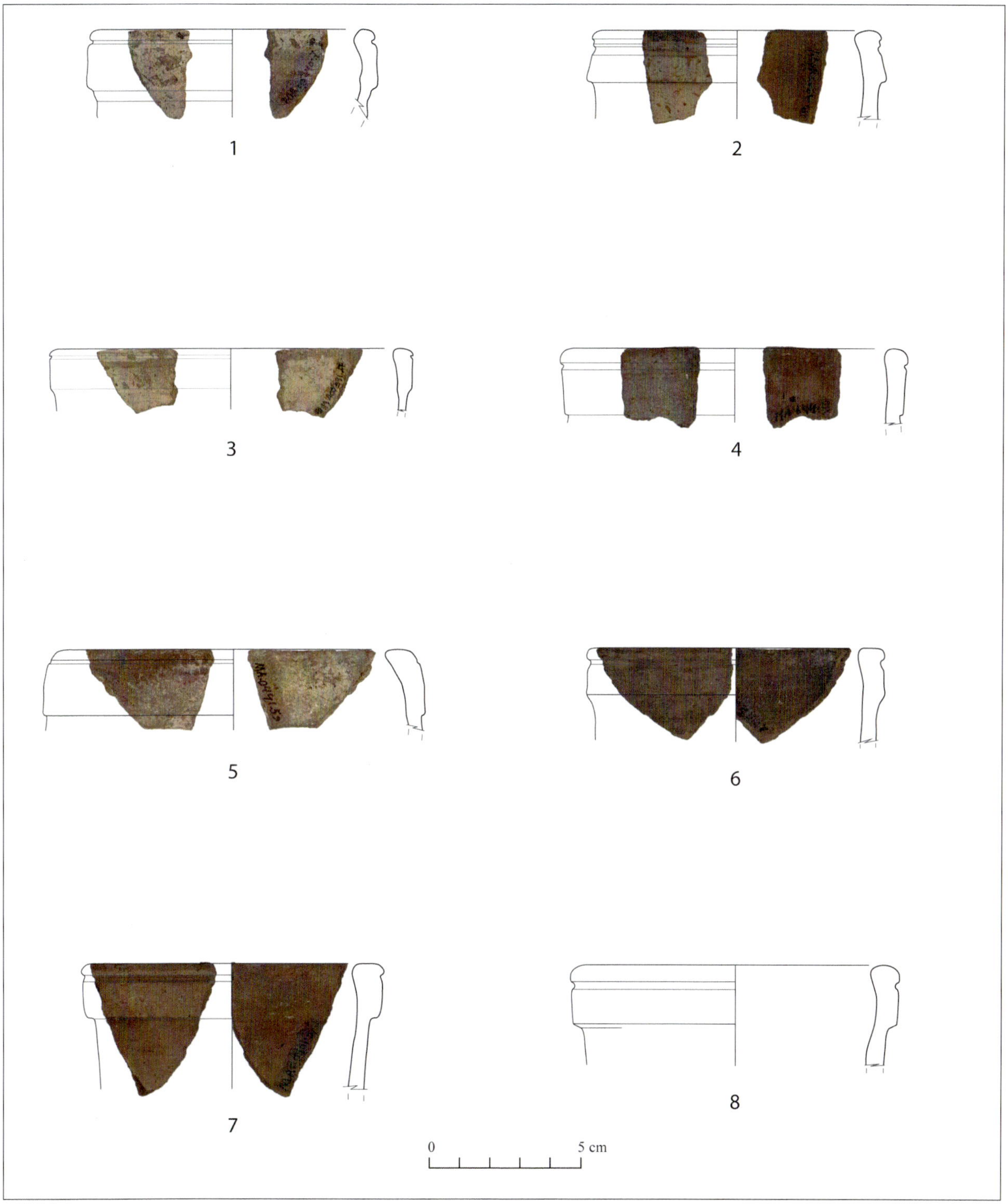

FIGURE 8. *Grey ware from Area C (©DAI, Orient Department; pencil drawings: A. Alsobhi; vector drawings: F. Almehho; photographs: R. Barač; layout: M. Ahmad).*

The prevalence of this grey ware in Area C raises important questions about its function, particularly given that it seems to be limited to one jar form. Its high concentration in this area invites further investigation, especially regarding a potential connection with funerary contexts. Although the specific use of these jars remains uncertain, the dominance of this locally produced ware in such a singular form points to a specialized role that merits closer examination.

A relatively small number of pottery sherds were recovered from contexts over the floor levels in Area C, all unglazed. These unglazed sherds are distinguished by their fabric colours, ranging from greenish-buff to reddish-brown cores with buff or greenish outer surfaces. A small number of glazed sherds were also noted, primarily from the upper stratigraphic layers near the topsoil. These glazed fragments, featuring green, yellow, and turquoise glazes, are probably of local production, as indicated by their fabric characteristics. The style and texture of the glaze application align closely with local ceramic traditions, further supporting the hypothesis of local manufacture. The presence of glazed pottery among the graves and tombs is limited, suggesting that its use was unlikely in such contexts during the early to middle Islamic period in Qurḥ.

No imported pottery was identified in the assemblage from Area C, underscoring the predominance of locally produced ceramics. The pottery collections from Area C, when compared with stratified pottery assemblages from the site, can be dated with relative confidence to the tenth and eleventh centuries. The absence of imported wares, coupled with the strong presence of locally produced grey ware, suggests in particular the unique functional or cultural significance of this area within the settlement. Further analysis of the stratigraphy and the relationship of pottery types to specific architectural features could shed more light on the social dynamics of the site during its occupation.

Discussion

From the ground plan, the presence of inscriptions of religious connotation, and the contemporary surrounding graves, Buildings C-b1 and C-b2 can be interpreted as tombs or commemorative funerary buildings (e.g. *turba*, *qubba*).[6] Similar tombs are known, for example, from the Baqīʿ al-Gharqad of Medina (online reference 1–2; see Leisten 1998: 30, 194–196). Extensive looting of the central structures of both buildings may be a reasonable explanation for the missing buried individuals. However, it cannot be excluded that the structures functioned as cenotaphs dedicated, for instance, to important or respected persons (see examples from the ninth to twelfth centuries in Leisten's catalogue [1998]). The fragmentary state of the inscribed flagstones found in Trench C1, which appears to be the result of deliberate destruction, does not aid in the identification of the buried individuals.

In the area of the northern cemetery, building materials and further remains of pavements have been observed exhibiting a similar orientation to those of C-b1 and C-b2. This finding is supported by the analysis of the orthophotograph from 2018, which suggests that this type of tomb is not a unique occurrence (Fig. 9). However, judging by the multitude and density of graves marked by pebble stones (at least twenty-six of them were identified in Trench C1 only), it seems to be the rarest one. The different types of graves and tombs may reflect distinctions between social groups, rank/status, or wealth, as well as different fashions or diachronic change of funerary customs.

However, these variations might not be interpreted as straightforwardly as it may seem. The persona of the deceased by and for the living community might not correspond directly to their social standing in life (see Hodder 1982: 195–201; Parker Pearson 1982; Insoll 1999: 180). Instead, the focus of analysis may have to be shifted towards tombs and graves as part of the actively employed material culture (see Hodder 1982: 75–85) rather than a simple reflection of social reality. In this sense, their meaning lies in their deliberate construction of social standing and their significance as 'commemorative structures' (in the sense of Grabar 1966) for those alive (Insoll 1999: 176–177).

The Muslim world, although in general consistent in customs of inhumation, 'was and is made up of people, individuals, and communities' (Insoll 1999: 166) that followed different traditions and developed their own interpretation of the rules and ways to lead

[6] On the terminology of Islamic tomb buildings, see Grabar 1966: 9–13; Diez 1986; Leisten 1998: 67–77; 2000.

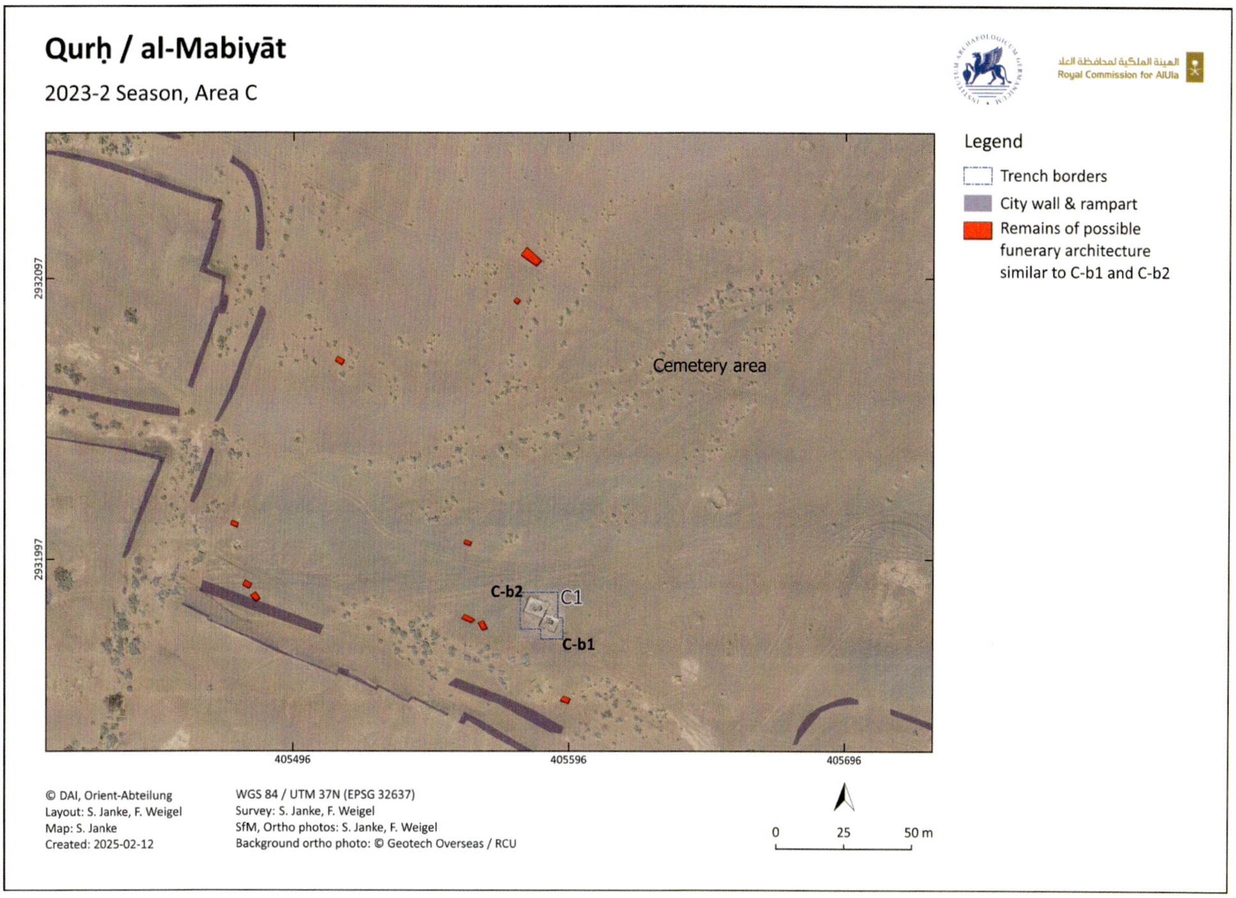

FIGURE 9. *A map of the northern cemetery area of Qurḥ/al-Mabiyāt (Area C) showing the locations of possible funerary structures (©DAI, Orient Department, S. Janke).*

a religious way of life. Despite common funerary rites such as washing the deceased's body, sealing of the body's orifices, perfuming and enveloping the corpse in shrouds or burial garments, an interment within a short time, and the position of the corpse in the grave — laid on the right side with the face towards the qiblah (with varying degrees of accuracy) — a variety of local customs and traditions have always existed (Granqvist 1965: 55–100; Simpson 1995: 241–242, 244–245; Halevi 2007). However, despite these customary ways of treating the dead, the use and acceptability of types of grave markers or commemorative structures have caused controversy among Muslim scholars (Leisten 1990; 1998: 5–25; Halevi 2007: 187–196; Petersen 2019: 252). Alongside these debates, communities developed their own interpretations of rules and recommendations concerning funerary structures (Insoll 1999: 168–169). Among the controversies about prohibition or acceptable forms of commemorative structures, the use of bricks and lime plaster is mentioned in particular — for some scholars their origin in fire carry associations with hell and the drying out of the grave (there is a belief that the dead can still hear, and feel pain and thirst; Leisten 1990: 15–16; 1998: 6, 9). Although funerary structures are often disapproved of by religious authorities, the existence of commemorative monuments and tombs is recorded from the beginning of the early Islamic period (Rāġib 1970; Halevi 2007: 191–192). Their construction became more widespread and common in the Muslim world between the ninth and eleventh centuries AD (Grabar 1966: 41; Leisten 1998: 27–53; Petersen 2019: 252–253).

In the case of Qurḥ, grave markers vary considerably, from rings of stone pebbles to a complete oval-shaped covering of graves with pebbles — both types with or without stone boulders on the shorter ends, and both types with or without inscribed gravestones (see Granqvist 1965: 86; Ibrahim 2001: 99–100, for potential meanings related to gender in other contexts; Simpson 1995: 244–245). In addition, Buildings C-b1 and C-b2 are two examples of several stone and brick structures in the cemetery area of al-Mabiyāt, which apparently differ in size, construction techniques, and degree of elaboration (e.g. claddings, inscriptions, vaults). The high density of graves (26) around Buildings C-b1 and C-b2 might be explained either by social relationships between the buried people or by the incentive to profit from the *baraka* of potentially important persons and protection from disturbance of the graves (Hillenbrand 1994: 262–263, 266; Simpson 1995: 244; cf. Insoll 1999: 173). This applies especially to the graves added after the construction of C-b1 and C-b2. Similar architectural structures have not been observed in another cemetery area located north-west of the settlement. There, pebble stones and stone boulders have been used as grave markings, and fragments of Kufic inscriptions were found (Gilmore et al. 1985: 112). The larger distance from the city suggests that this cemetery may have been used for the interment of non-residents or other social groups (see Simpson 1995: 243–244; Petersen 2019: 254–255).

The frequent occurrence of a particular type of jar made from a specific grey ware in the cemetery is very interesting. This could indicate a specific practice at the burial site, either a funerary rite such as the visiting of graves, often including food consumption (Granqvist 1965: 87–90, 97–100; Grabar 1966: 12; Hillenbrand 1994: 266; Mershen 2004: 175) or offerings for the dead (Insoll 2001: 43) such as libations (Leisten 1998: 6). The breaking of pots might also be a symbolic practice associated with the finiteness of life or with grief (Ibrahim 2001: 112; Mershen 2004: 173, 176). Furthermore, both buildings C-b1 and C-b2 have entrances allowing access to their central (burial) structures, enabling visits and funerary rites at the tombs. This also underlines the fact that the structures were designed for the active participation of those attending the rites during and after the funeral.

Conclusion

Despite the extensive damage to the commemorative structures C-b1 and C-b2 caused by looting, a large amount of information can be recovered by piecing together the evidence. Similar contemporary funerary structures in the Hijaz are very rare and the surviving examples, such as in the Baqīʿ al-Gharqad of Medina, have been subject to various cycles of overbuilding, renovation, dismantling, destruction, and rebuilding during the past centuries. The evidence from Qurḥ, therefore, fills a gap in the knowledge of early to middle Islamic funerary practices in the region. Moreover, the accessibility of the excavated tombs in Area C with their inscriptions, partly citing verses from the Qurʾān, suggests that these funerary structures were built for the deceased as well as for the living. They would thus exemplify an architectural manifestation of active care for the dead. Furthermore, the particular design of these structures indicates that in Qurḥ, local customs for commemorative structures may have developed — as elsewhere in the Islamic world. This might have occurred within or alongside the framework of contemporary religious debates, and in spite of the orthodox rejection of funerary architecture and of certain forms of mortuary practices (Leisten 1990; 1998: 5–25; Halevi 2007: 187–196; Petersen 2019: 252).

References

al-Aboudi A. 2019. The prosperous city of Qurḥ (al-Mabiyat). Pages 94–95 in L. Nehmé, A. Alsuḥaybānī, V. Cassola & N. Bailleux (eds), *AlUla: Wonder of Arabia*. Paris: Institut du monde arabe, Gallimard.

al-Aboudi A. 2021. *The architecture of Qurḥ city in the light of the archaeological exploration of King Saud University: A picture of early Islamic civilization in northwestern Saudi Arabia*. Riyadh: Department of Archaeology, King Saud University.

al-Aboudi A., al-Yousef N., Qaud M. & al-Shammari R. 2019. Preliminary report on the excavation of al-Mabiyat (Qarha), 8th season 2011 AD/1432 AH. *Atlal* 27: 37–46.

Diez E. 1986. Ḳubba. Pages 289–296 in *The Encyclopaedia of Islam*. i. (Second edition). Leiden: Brill.

Dimand M.S. 1937. Studies in Islamic ornament: I. Some aspects of Omaiyad and early ʿAbbāsid ornament. *Ars Islamica* 4: 293–337.

Doughty C.M. 1921. *Travels in Arabia Deserta.* i. (Third edition). London/Boston: Philip Lee Warner & Jonathan Cape.

Durand C. 2019. AlUla, at the crossroads of the ancient Arabian trade routes. Pages 86–89 in L. Nehmé, A. Alsuḥaybānī, V. Cassola & N. Bailleux (eds), *AlUla: Wonder of Arabia.* Paris: Institut du monde arabe; Gallimard.

Fiema Z.T., Nehmé L., al-Talhi D. & Kennedy W. 2020a. The al-ʿUlā–al-Wajh Survey Project: 2013 Reconnaissance season. *Atlal* 28: 112–121.

Fiema Z.T., al-Qanoor N.A., Durand C., Kennedy W., Hassan B.A., Al-Dayel I. & al-Faqeer M. 2020b. The 2016 season of the Al-Wajh — Al-ʿUla Survey Project: Preliminary report. *Atlal* 29: 81–111.

Frenkel Y. 1996. Roads and stations in southern Bilâd Al-Shâm in the 7th–8th centuries. *ARAM* 8: 177–188.

al-Ghabban A.I. 2019. Pilgrimage routes in the region of AlUla. Pages 90–93 in L. Nehmé, A. Alsuḥaybānī, V. Cassola & N. Bailleux (eds), *AlUla: Wonder of Arabia.* Paris: Institut du monde arabe & Gallimard.

al-Ghazzi A., al-Umair A., al-Zahrani A., al-Haddad A., Saleh M., al-Sultan A. ... al-Dhafiri F. 2018. Scientific report on the excavations at al-Mabbiyat (Qarha), sixth season 1430AH/2009 AD. *Atlal* 26: 34–65.

Gilmore M., Ibrahim M., Mursi G. & al-Talhi D. 1985. A preliminary report on the first season of excavations at al-Mabiyat, an early Islamic site in the Northern Hijaz. *Atlal* 9: 109–125.

Grabar O. 1966. The earliest Islamic commemorative structures, notes and documents. *Ars Orientalis* 6: 7–46.

Granqvist H. 1965. *Muslim death and burial: Arab customs and traditions studied in a village in Jordan.* (Commentationes Humanarum Litterarum, 34.1). Helsinki: Centraltryckeriet Helsingfors.

Halevi L. 2007. *Muhammad's grave: Death rites and the making of Islamic society.* New York: Columbia University.

Hillenbrand R. 1994. *Islamic architecture: Form, function and meaning.* Edinburgh: University Press.

Hodder I. 1982. *Symbols in action: Ethnoarchaeological studies in material culture.* Cambridge: University Press.

Ibrahim M.M. 2001. Tombs and their inscriptions from Nizwā and al-Ḥaymalī, Sultanate of Oman. *Proceedings of the Seminar for Arabian Studies* 31: 97–113.

Ingraham M.L., Johnson T.D., Rihani B., Shatla I. 1981. Saudi Arabian Comprehensive Survey Program: Preliminary report on a reconnaissance survey of the Northwestern Province (with a note on a brief survey of the Northern Province). *Atlal* 5: 59–84.

Insoll T. 1999. *The archaeology of Islam.* Oxford: Blackwell.

Insoll T. 2001. Dahlak Kebir: From Aksumite to Ottoman. *Adumatu* 3: 39–50.

Jaussen A. & Savignac R. 1914. *Mission archéologique en arabie II. El-ʿEla, d'Hégra à Teima, Harrah de Tebouk.* Paris: Paul Geuthner.

Jenkins M. 1968. The palmette tree: A study of the iconography of Egyptian lustre painted pottery. *Journal of the American Research Center in Egypt* 7: 119–126.

Khazâie M. 2005. The source and religious symbolism of the arabesque in medieval Islamic art of Persia. *Central Asiatic Journal* 49/1: 27–50.

al-Kilabi H.A. 2010. The pilgrimage road from Syria. Pages 452–461 in A.I. al-Ghabban, B. André-Salvini, F. Demange, C. Juvin & M. Cotty (eds), *Roads of Arabia: Archaeology and history of the Kingdom of Saudi Arabia.* Paris: Somogy Art Publishers.

Leisten T. 1990. Between orthodoxy and exegesis: Some aspects of attitudes in the Shariʿa toward funerary architecture. *Muqarnas* 7: 12–22.

Leisten T. 1998. *Architektur für Tote. Bestattung in architektonischem Kontext in den Kernländern der islamischen Welt zwischen 3./9. und 6./12. Jahrhundert.* (Materialien zur iranischen Archäologie, 4). Berlin: Reimer.

Leisten T. 2000. Turba. Pages 673–675 in *The Encyclopaedia of Islam.* x. (Second edition). Leiden: Brill.

McMahon A. 2015. Waste management in early urban southern Mesopotamia. Pages 19–39 in P.D. Mitchell (ed.), *Sanitation, latrines and intestinal parasites in past populations.* Farnham: Ashgate (Taylor & Francis).

Mershen B. 2004. Pots and tombs in Ibrāʾ, Oman. Investigations into the archaeological surface record of Islamic cemeteries and the related burial customs and funerary rituals. *Proceedings of the Seminar for Arabian Studies* 34: 165–179.

al-Muaikel [=Almaiql] K.I. 2011. Report on the excavations at Qurḥ site (Al-Mabiyyat), second season 1426/2005. *Atlal* 21: 38–62.

al-Muqaddasi/trans. G.S.A. Ranking & R.F. Azoo. 1897. *The best divisions of knowledge of the regions.* Calcutta: Baptist Mission Press.

Nasif A.A. 1979. The identification of Wādī'l-Qurra and the ancient site of al-Mabiyat. *Arabian Studies* 5: 1–19.

al-Omeer A. 2006. Excavations at Islamic site of Qarh (al-Mabbiyat) al-ᶜUlā, first season 1425H/2004 AD. *Atlal* 19: 117–137.

Parker Pearson M. 1982. Mortuary practices, society, and ideology: An ethnoarchaeological study. Pages 99–113 in I. Hodder (ed.), *Symbolic and structural archaeology*. Cambridge: Cambridge University Press.

Parr P.J., Harding G.L. & Dayton J.E. 1970. Preliminary survey in N.W. Arabia, 1968. *Bulletin of the Institute of Archaeology* 8–9: 193–242.

Petersen A. 2012. *The medieval and Ottoman Hajj route in Jordan: An archaeological and historical study*. Oxford: Council for British Research in the Levant (CBRL), Oxbow.

Petersen A. 2019. The archaeology of death and burial in the Islamic world. Pages 241–258 in S. Tarlow & L.N. Stutz (eds), *The Oxford handbook of the archaeology of death and burial*. Oxford: Oxford University Press.

Pollock S. 1990. Political economy as viewed from the garbage dump: Jemdet Nasr occupation at the Uruk Mound, Abu Salabikh. *Paléorient* 16/1: 57–75.

Porter B.N. 1993. Sacred trees, date palms, and the royal persona of Ashurnasirpal II. *Journal of Near Eastern Studies* 52/2: 129–139.

Power T. 2010. The Red Sea during the 'long' late antiquity (AD 500–1000). PhD thesis, University of Oxford. [Unpublished.]

Rāǧib Y. 1970. Les premiers monuments funéraires de l'Islam. *Annales Islamologiques* 9: 21–36.

Seidl U. 2003–2005. Palmette. Page 292 in *Reallexikon der Assyriologie und Vorderasiatischen Archäologie*. x. Berlin: de Gruyter.

Simpson St.J. 1995. Death and burial in the late Islamic Near East: Some insights from archaeology and ethnography. Pages 240–251 in S. Campbell & A. Green (eds), *The archaeology of death in the ancient Near East*. Oxford: Oxbow Books.

Städtler A. 2023. Evaluating ancient Arabia's trade routes with least-cost-path analysis. Pages 21–45 in V.B. Juloux, A. Di Ludovico & S. Matskevich (eds), *The ancient world goes digital*. (Digital Biblical Studies, 6). Leiden: Brill.

al-Talhi D., Ibrahim M., Mursi J.M. & Askubi K. 1986. Excavation at Mabiyyat, second season 1404–1405/1984–1985. *Atlal* 10: 58–63.

Weigel F. (in preparation). A fresh look on Qurh/al-Mabiyat: Developing a new chronostratigraphical model of an early-to-middle Islamic site and its surroundings. *Proceedings of the 14th ICAANE, Lyon, 2-6 June 2025*.

al-Wohaibi A. 1969. The Northern Hijaz in the writings of the Arab geographers, 800–1150. PhD thesis, University of London. [Unpublished.]

Wüstenfeld F. 1869. *Yacut's Geographisches Wörterbuch*. Band 4: ق - ي. Leipzig: F.A. Brockhaus.

Young G.K. 2011. *Rome's eastern trade: International commerce and imperial policy, 31 BC–AD 305*. London: Routledge.

Online references

1. https://upload.wikimedia.org/wikipedia/commons/b/b1/Grave_Ajvaje%28wife%29_nabi_1.JPG (accessed 20 October 2024)
2. https://upload.wikimedia.org/wikipedia/commons/8/82/Baqi_Halimah.jpg (accessed 20 October 2024)

Authors' addresses

Stefanie Janke, German Archaeological Institute, Orient Department, Podbielskiallee 69–71, 14195 Berlin, Germany.
e-mail stefanie.janke@dainst.de

Friedrich W. Weigel, German Archaeological Institute, Orient Department, Podbielskiallee 69–71, 14195 Berlin, Germany.
e-mail friedrich.weigel@dainst.de

Mustafa Ahmad, Goethe-Universität Frankfurt, Institut für Archäologische Wissenschaften Abt. I, Norbert-Wollheim-Platz 1, 60629 Frankfurt am Main, Germany.
e-mail m.ahmad@em.uni-frankfurt.de

Arnulf Hausleiter, German Archaeological Institute, Orient Department, Podbielskiallee 69–71, 14195 Berlin, Germany.
e-mail arnulf.hausleiter@dainst.de

Proceedings of the Seminar for Arabian Studies 54 (2025): 121–137

Exploring the diversity of tomb typology with accompanied burial practices in its socio-economic contexts in the Wadi Suq period (*c.*2000–1600 BC), south-east Arabia

Taichi Kuronuma

Summary

A variety of individual and collective tomb types characterize the Wadi Suq period (Middle Bronze Age) in south-east Arabia. Although previous studies have classified these tombs and their types, the annually increasing number of excavated and surveyed tombs necessitates constant updates to enhance our understanding of regional aspects of mortuary practices. This paper aims to present the latest overview of regional aspects in mortuary practices and discuss their possible socio-economic contexts through the study of 119 sites with cemeteries extracted from publications and relevant open sources. The results indicate that the socio-economic contexts influenced the establishment of cemeteries and the selection of tomb types and burial practices and consequently, affected diverse aspects of Wadi Suq mortuary customs. However, it is also argued that there is no absolute correspondence between the subsistence strategies of social groups and their tomb types or burial practices. Although regional tendencies are generally observable, they probably result from a combination of socio-economic, local environmental, and cultural factors. The diversity of mortuary practices reflects the Wadi Suq people's adaptation to specific topographical and environmental conditions, grounded in a shared ideological and religious foundation.

Keywords: burial practices, Wadi Suq period, tomb typology, socio-economic activities, adaptation

Introduction

The mortuary evidence in the Wadi Suq period (*c.*2000–1600 BC) is characterized by a variety of tomb types (Righetti 2015). The emergence of this diversity marks a transformation in material culture compared to the preceding Umm an-Nar period (*c.*2700–2000 BC), which was associated with a sedentary agricultural society (e.g. Magee 2014) and collective depositions in large circular tombs (Williams 2023). The continuation of collective tomb rites alongside the reintroduction of individual tombs[1] provided binary options in burial practices (Righetti 2015). The distribution of Wadi Suq tombs is characterized by the frequent occurrence of collective tombs in the north-western area of south-east Arabia and the predominance of individual tombs in the eastern area (e.g. Righetti 2015; Döpper 2023). The most likely boundary of these trends follows an axis connecting modern Suhar and Al-Ain, aligned with Wādī al-Jizzi (Figs 1–4) (see Kuronuma, Miki & Kondo 2023). However, the underlying factors behind this pattern have yet to be investigated in detail.

The choice of particular tomb types and burial practices is linked to factors such as social structures and personae (Binford 1971; Brown 1981; Tainter 1978) or religious beliefs (Parker Pearson 1982; 1999). However, given the characteristics of the Wadi Suq period — marked by adaptation to local environmental conditions during the prolonged aridification process from *c.*2200 BC (the 4.2 ka event) (e.g. Parker et al. 2006) — socio-economic perspectives are considered relevant to the diversity of mortuary practices. The significance of local factors, including water availability, has recently been highlighted (de Vreeze, Kennet & Deadman 2024; Döpper 2021). Human adaptations to the environment observed in socio-economic activities can be linked to burial practices. Examining this connection is essential for understanding the diverse aspects of Wadi

[1] Individual and collective tombs in this paper are defined according to Christopher J. Knüsel and John Robb's system (2016: 657). Individual tombs refer to primary depositions with anatomically ordered human remains. Multiple depositions with more than two interments are included if they are simultaneous. In contrast, collective burials involve recurrent depositions over a longer period, often containing commingled remains in anatomically disordered conditions.

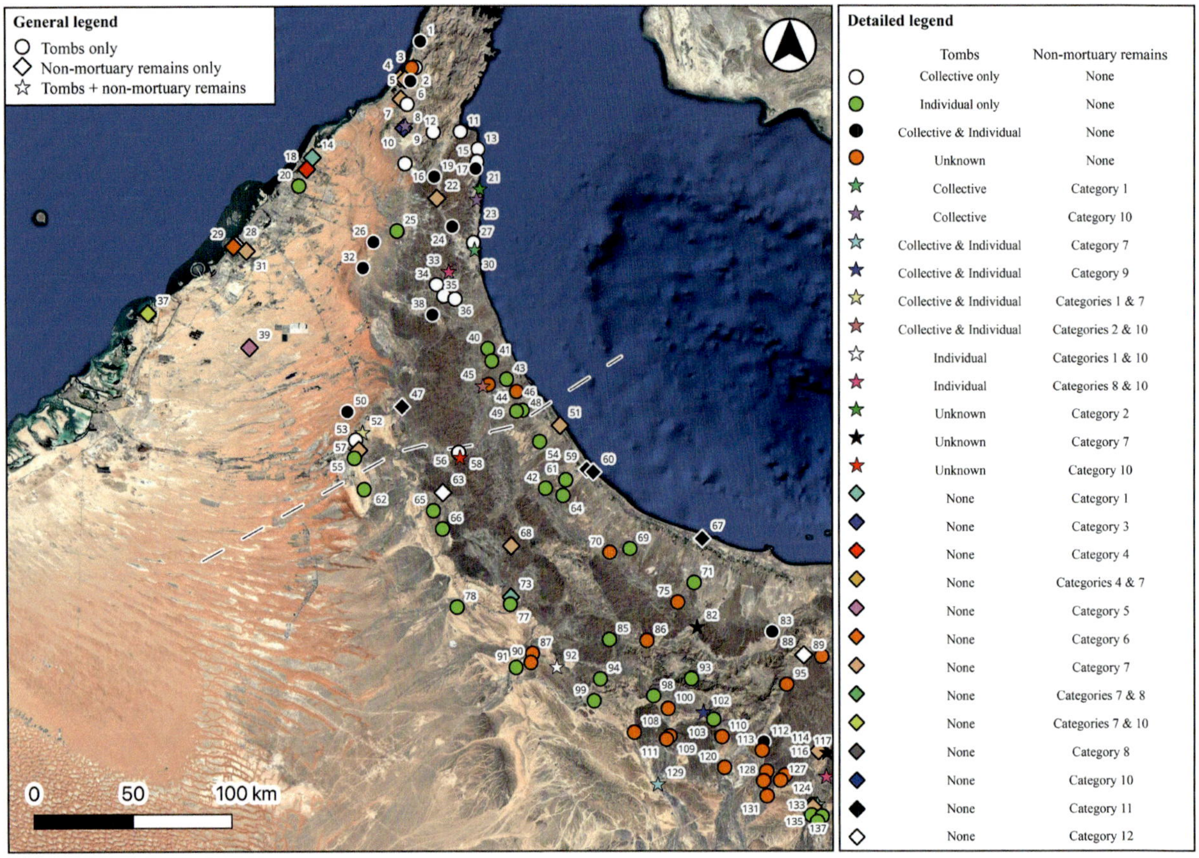

Figure 1. *Distribution of Wadi Suq sites in south-east Arabia. Part I. The north-western area and part of the eastern area. The broken line indicates the border of these areas. Base-map Google Maps, applied with QGIS. The site numbers correspond to those in Figures 3 and 4. Categories mentioned in the legend of the non-mortuary remains correspond to those in Figure 7.*

Suq mortuary customs, including tomb types, burial practices, and site distributions.

To address this issue, an examination covering the whole of south-east Arabia is needed. However, past discussions remain limited to regional levels (e.g. Döpper 2021; Vogt 1998). Furthermore, these discussions lag behind the annually increasing number of excavated and surveyed tombs, leading to the omission of many cemeteries[2] from distribution maps published recently.

In March 2023 the present author published a paper on the regional characteristics of Wadi Suq mortuary practices based on bibliographical surveys, identifying 412 tombs with typological information across sixty-one sites (Kuronuma 2023). The analysis of tomb type distribution, following Righetti's (2015) typology, supports the general argument that collective tombs are more prevalent in the north-western area of south-east Arabia, while individual tombs dominate in the east. However, recent discoveries of collective tombs in the east, such as Salut/Bisya (Condoluci & Degli Esposti 2015; Degli Esposti, Brandolini & Zerboni 2021; Degli Esposti et al. 2018; 2021) and Al-Khashbah (Schmidt & Walter 2021), challenge the previous notion that the more favourable climatic conditions in the north-west (Velde 2009)[3] explain the continued construction of collective tombs. Consequently, the present author proposed that

[2] In this paper, the term 'cemetery' refers to a site with more than one tomb.

[3] A recent interdisciplinary study highlighted the role of karstic aquifers in the north-west, which supported a sustained population during the Wadi Suq period (de Vreeze, Kennet & Deadman 2024).

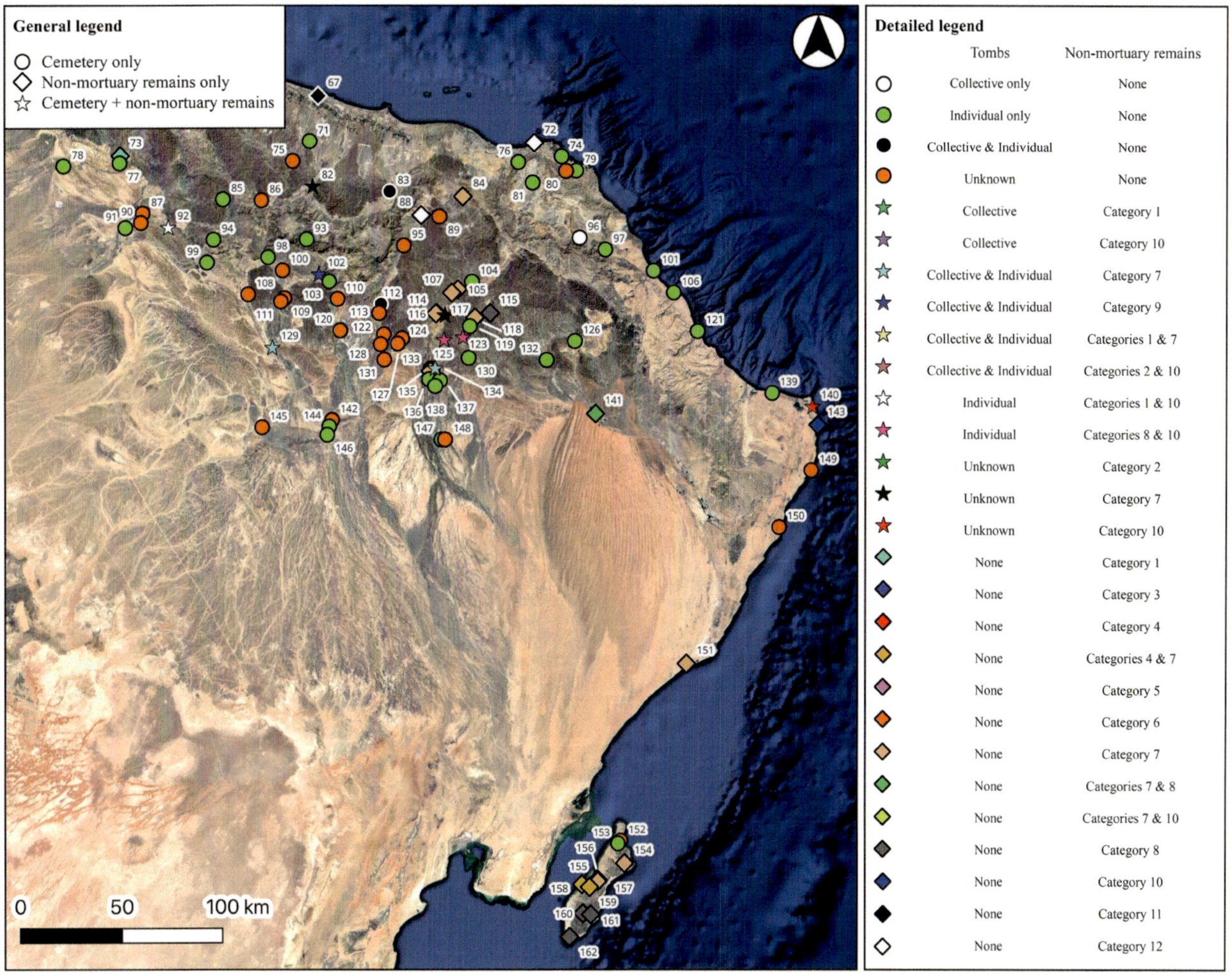

FIGURE 2. *Distribution of Wadi Suq sites in south-east Arabia. Part II. The remainder of the eastern area. Base-map Google Maps, applied with QGIS. The site numbers correspond to those in Figures 3 and 4. Categories mentioned in the legend of the non-mortuary remains correspond to those in Figure 7.*

local environmental conditions influenced the selection of burial practices, and collective tombs may have been constructed in areas with favourable conditions that supported sedentism in the north-west and seasonal sedentism in the east (Kuronuma 2023). Additionally, the author argued that the cultural background for selecting burial practices and tomb types may have been dualistic, reflecting flexible burial practices that adapted to varying environmental and socio-economic conditions (2023). However, this argument requires revision in light of recent field discoveries, and the cultural and socio-economic factors influencing tomb type diversity therefore require further consideration. Based on descriptions extracted from the reports, this paper will comprehensively examine variations in Wadi Suq tombs by assessing their distribution and connections to non-mortuary sites, incorporating recent discoveries.[4]

[4] The description of artefacts and tomb typology is an important factor. However, some cases rely solely on what has been reported. Late Bronze Age tombs were excluded as much as possible.

No.	Name	C	Non-mortuary evidence category												Features
			1	2	3	4	5	6	7	8	9	10	11	12	
1	Ghalilah	X													Tombs
2	Dhayah	X													Tombs
3	Rams	X													Tomb?
4	Julfar / Al-Mataf								X						Artefacts
5	Kush								X						Artefacts
6	Shimail	X													Tombs
7	Bida'								X						Artefacts
8	Qarn al-Harf	X													Tombs
9	Al-Khatt	X										X			Tombs, platform, stone-built structures
10	Nud Ziba				X										Mud-brick building
11	Dibba	X													Tomb
12	Wadi Khabb	X													Tomb
13	Dhadna	X													Tomb
14	Tell Abraq		X												Structures reusing a tower
15	Sharm	X													Tombs
16	Idhn	X													Tomb
17	Bidyah	X													Tombs
18	Al-Hamriya					X									Shell midden
19	Asimah	X													Tombs
20	Mowaihat	X													Tombs
21	Khor Fakkan	X										X			Tombs, stone-built structures
22	Masafi								X						Artefacts
23	Qidfa'	X										X			Tombs, stone-built structures
24	Bithnah	X													Tombs
25	Al-Khudairah	X													Tombs
26	Jebel Faya	X													Tombs
27	Murayshid	X													Tomb
28	Al-Sufouh													X	Ash layers
29	Al-Sufouh 2							X							Hunted camels
30	Kalba	X	X												Tomb, structures reusing a tower
31	Al-Hayl								X						Artefacts
32	Jebel al-Buhais	X													Tombs
33	Wadi al-Hilo	X								X		X			Tombs, stone-built structures
34	Wa'ab	X													Tombs
35	Fashghah	X													Tombs
36	Naslah	X													Tombs
37	Ras Ghanadhah								X			X			Stone-built structures?
38	Jebel al-Yamh	X													Tombs
39	Saruq al-Hadid						X								Pits, artefacts
40	Wadi Hatta	X													Tombs
41	Umm as-Safafir	X													Tombs
42	Dahwa	X													Tombs

No.	Name	C	Non-mortuary evidence category												Features
			1	2	3	4	5	6	7	8	9	10	11	12	
43	Liwa	X													Tombs
44	Wadi Fizh	X													Tombs
45	Wadi al-Zahaimi	X		X								X			Tombs, stone-built structures, structures on slope
46	Suhar Free Zone	X													Tombs
47	Mahadhah												X		Hoard
48	Wadi Suq	X													Tombs
49	Falaj as-Suq	X													Tombs
50	Qarn Bint Sa'ud	X													Tombs
51	Tell ash-Shabul								X						Artefacts
52	Hili and Hili North	X	X						X						Tomb, structures reusing a tower, surface artefact scatter?
53	Qattarah	X													Tombs
54	Batinah Expressway Package 4 Location 5	X													Tombs
55	Al-Ain (National Museum)								X						Artefacts?
56	Al-Wasit	X													Tomb
57	Jebel Hafit	X													Tombs
58	Wadi al-Jizzi	X										X			Tombs, stone-built structures
59	Khor al-Hamam												X		Hoard
60	Mukhailif												X		Hoard
61	Fulayj al-Harth	X													Tombs
62	Mazyad	X													Tombs
63	Ajran													X	Unknown
64	Batinah Expressway Package 4 Location 1	X													Tomb
65	Al-Muraybi	X													Tombs
66	Ayn Bani Sayda near Qumayrah	X													Tombs
67	Hadhib as-Suwayq												X		Hoard?
68	Hayy Ukur								X						Artefacts
69	Batinah Expressway Package 3 Locations 7 and 10	X													Tombs
70	P-11	X													Tombs
71	Wadi Banif	X													Tombs
72	Ras al-Hamra													X	Radiocarbon dates
73	As-Safri near Yanqul		X												Reuse of a tower
74	Bustan	X													Tombs
75	Wadi al-Hawqayn	X													Tombs
76	Bawshar	X													Tombs
77	Al-Jamma	X													Tombs
78	Shokur	X													Tombs
79	Yiti	X													Tombs
80	Yiti West	X													Tombs
81	Al-Berain near Al-Amarat	X													Tombs
82	Al-Tikhah	X							X						Tombs, surface artefacts
83	Wadi al-Ma'awil South	X													Tombs
84	BidBid								X						Artefact?

FIGURE 3. *Wadi Suq sites in south-east Arabia. Part I: nos. 1–84. C = Cemetery.*

Tomb typology — further updates

The most comprehensive classification of Wadi Suq tomb types was established by Righetti (2015), who identified twenty-seven tomb types. This gradually replaced the earlier typologies (Carter 1997; Vogt 1985) and has since been cited in recent studies (e.g. Döpper 2021; Genchi 2023; Gernez, Al-Ghafri & Ciesielski 2023). Righetti's classification is characterized by its variability. The classification criteria focus on aspects such as the number of funerary chambers, their position (either above-ground or subterranean), shape, and other structural features, including the presence or absence of ring walls (Righetti 2015). This variability allows for the addition of new types, enabling my suggestion of eight new types (six individual tomb types: IS1c, IS2c, IG4, IG5, IR1, IR2; and two collective types: CM4e and CM4f) (Figs 5 & 6).[5] The determination of an individual or collective tomb is based on the typological characteristics. The informative quality of funerary practices in the report

[5] Types IR1 and IR2 are omitted from the figures as they have no original structures.

No.	Name	C	Non-mortuary evidence category												Features
			1	2	3	4	5	6	7	8	9	10	11	12	
85	Bilad ash-Shuhum	X													Tombs
86	Yiqa'	X													Tombs
87	Ad-Dariz North	X													Tombs
88	Al-Hob													X	Unknown
89	Al-Nu'aimi / Al-Khobbar	X													Tombs
90	Ad-Dariz South	X													Tombs
91	Wadi Sunaysil	X													Tombs
92	Bat and Al-Khutm	X	X									X			Tomb, structures reusing a tower, stone-built structures
93	Sa'a Sidri	X													Tombs
94	Zammah	X													Tomb
95	Al-Ayn	X													Tombs
96	Manal	X													Tombs
97	Abayah	X													Tombs
98	Wadi Ghul	X													Tombs
99	Qorin as-Sahhaimah	X													Tombs
100	Al-Hamra	X													Tomb
101	Dibab	X													Tombs
102	Wadi Tanuf	X									X				Tombs, cave
103	As-Suwayhirriyah	X													Tombs
104	Siyudian (Al-Jardah)	X													Tomb
105	Rubkah								X						Artefacts
106	Bimah	X													Tombs
107	Khuwisi								X						Artefacts
108	Al-Aqir	X													Tombs
109	Masjid Jame'e in Bahla	X													Tomb
110	Nizwa	X													Tombs?
111	Al-Ghubra near Bahla	X													Tombs
112	Izki	X													Tombs
113	Zukayt	X													Tombs?
114	Mahleya								X						Artefacts
115	Bi'r Kalher									X					Mines, smelting evidence
116	Al-Ghoryeen								X						Artefacts
117	Al-Fulayj (Sharqiya)	X							X						Tombs, artefacts
118	Ar-Rawdhah								X						Artefacts
119	Al-Akhdhar	X													Tombs
120	Manah	X													Tombs?
121	Tiwi	X													Tombs
122	Shafa' North	X													Tombs?
123	Samad ash-Shan and Al-Moyassar	X								X		X			Tombs, stone-built structures, mines

No.	Name	C	Non-mortuary evidence category												Features
			1	2	3	4	5	6	7	8	9	10	11	12	
124	Al-Akal	X													Tombs?
125	Wadi Sahl	X								X					Tombs, mines, smelting evidence
126	Batin	X													Tombs
127	Al-Akal	X													Tombs?
128	Shafa' North	X													Tombs?
129	Salut and Bisya	X							X						Tombs, artefacts
130	Lizq	X													Tomb
131	Shafa' South	X													Tombs?
132	Ibra'	X													Tombs
133	Mukhtru	X													Tombs
134	Al-Khashbah	X							X						Tombs, artefacts
135	BB-28 / Wadi Andam								X						Artefacts. Location uncertain
136	Al-Wafi	X													Tombs
137	Buweiten	X													Tombs
138	Al-Sudairah	X													Tombs
139	Shiya	X													Tombs
140	Ras al-Hadd	X										X			Tombs, stone-built structures
141	Tawi Said								X	X					Artefacts
142	Jebel Mudmar North	X													Tombs
143	Ras al-Jinz											X			Stone-built structures
144	Adam North	X													Tombs
145	Jebel Salakh West	X													Tombs
146	Adam South	X													Tombs
147	Sinaw	X													Tomb
148	Barzaman	X													Tomb
149	Ras al-Kabbah	X													Tomb?
150	Aseelah	X													Tomb?
151	Khuwaymah KHU-1								X						Artefacts
152	Hilf	X													Tombs
153	Sakhrat al-Hadri	X													Tombs
154	Jebel ash-Shabbah								X						Artefacts
155	Marsis								X						Artefacts
156	Sfaiq					X			X						Artefacts, shell middens?
157	Jebel Sfaiq (Safayj)								X						Artefacts
158	Ra's Dahy					X			X						Artefacts, shell middens?
159	Sur Masirah					X			X						Artefacts, shell middens?
160	Wadi Madi									X					Mines, smelting evidence
161	Wadi Khasit									X					Mines, smelting evidence
162	Jebel Suwayr									X					Mines, smelting evidence

FIGURE 4. *Wadi Suq sites in south-east Arabia. Part II: nos. 85–162. C = Cemetery.*

varies. Moreover, most tombs were surveyed rather than excavated and therefore, information on artefacts was considered only when available.

New individual tomb types

Type IS1c is a tomb featuring multiple agglomerated outer ring walls. One example was discovered at Adam South (Gernez 2016).

Type IS2c was discovered at Qorin as-Sahhaimah (Yule 2001; Yule & Weisgerber 1996; Yule et al. 1993) and Wādī Tanuf (Kuronuma, Miki & Kondo 2021). The tombs at Qorin as-Sahhaimah ('Qorin as-Sahhaimah type' by Yule 2001), were classified as Righetti's IS1b by Döpper (2021). Surveys in Wādī Tanuf revealed similar tombs with an above-ground structure (Kuronuma, Miki & Kondo 2021), indicating their incompatibility to IS1 types criteria.

Type IG4 is an above-ground tomb using natural rocks, discovered in Wādī Tanuf (Kuronuma, Miki & Kondo 2021). The substitution of natural materials is observed in the Early Iron Age, but the ceiling and walls, similar to Type IS2c, suggest a possible Wadi Suq date.

Type IG5 corresponds to Yule's 'Ghul type', discovered in Wādī Ghul (Yule 2001). Yule also mentioned a possible example in Qorin as-Sahhaimah (Yule & Weisgerber 1996).

Types IR1 and IR2 are new categories proposed by the present author (Kuronuma 2023), indicating 'reuse' of Early Bronze Age tombs. IR1 refers to the reuse of

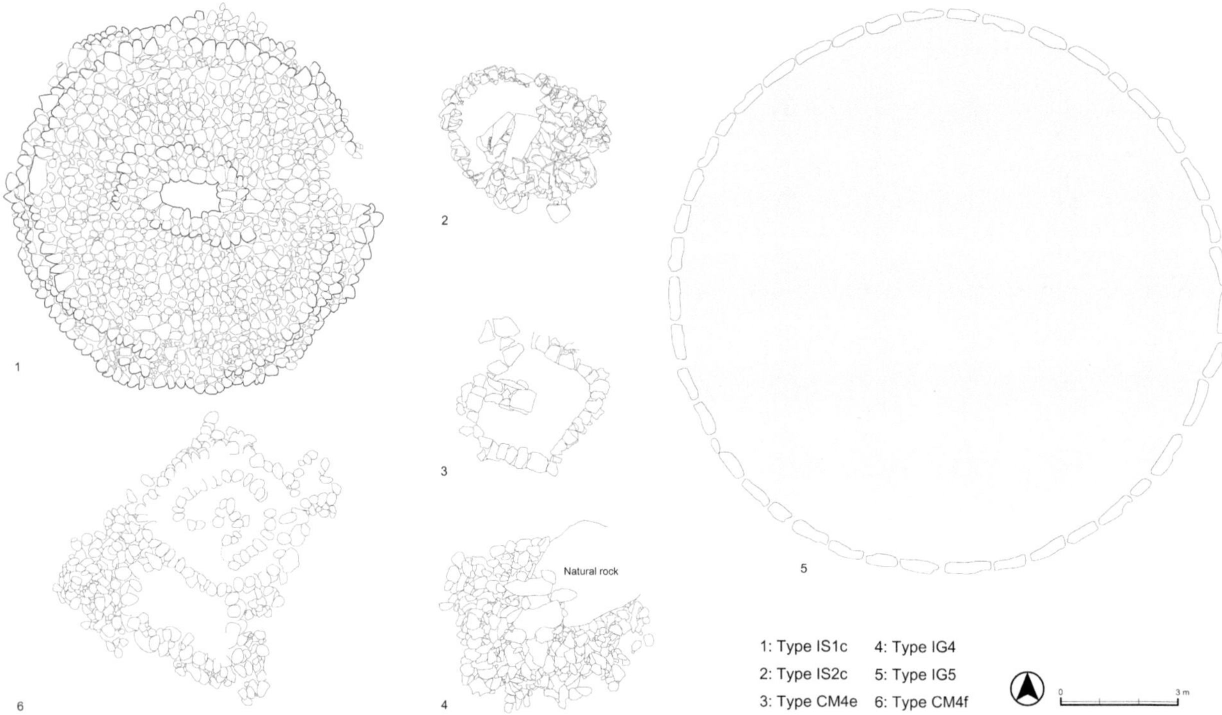

FIGURE 5. *Newly added tomb types (digitally traced by the author):* **1.** *Gernez 2016: fig. 16;* **2.** *Kuronuma, Miki & Kondo 2021: fig. 15;* **3.** *Condoluci & Degli Esposti 2015: pl. 4;* **4.** *Kuronuma, Miki & Kondo 2021: fig. 6;* **5.** *Yule 2001: Tafel 543.* **6.** *Kuronuma et al. 2023: fig. 5.*

Type	Burial type	No. of chamber	Chamber shape	Details of the chamber and other facilities
CM4e	Collective	Single	U-Shape	Half-subterranean, irregular square outline, one short dividing wall
CM4f	Collective	Single	U-Shape?	Annexe to the Southeast, a partial ring wall?, one short dividing wall? Gravel covering on top of the structure
Type	**Burial type**	**Position of chamber**	**Chamber characteristics**	**Details of the chamber and other facilities**
IS1c	Individual	Subterranean	Cist without super structure?	Multiple and condensed ring walls
IS2c	Individual	Subterranean	Cist with superstructure	Without ring walls. Ceil stones are covered with gravels
IG4	Individual	Overground	Cist with superstructure	Convenient use of natural rocks. No gravels for covering the ceil stones
IG5	Individual	Overground?	Unknown	Chamber is unknown. Above-ground structure is covered with gravels
IR1	Individual	Substitution	Substitution of existing chamber	Reuse of Hafit tomb chamber
IR2	Individual	Substitution	Substitution of existing chamber	Reuse of Umm an-Nar tomb chamber

FIGURE 6. *Definition of the suggested new tomb types.*

Hafit tombs, while IR2 refers to the reuse of Umm an-Nar tombs, where a few artefacts were recovered without clear Wadi Suq tomb structures, such as Umm an-Nar Tomb QA1-1 at Ain Bani Sayda near Qumayrah (Rutkowski 2021). IR types probably reflect the labour-saving tendencies of the Wadi Suq period.

New collective tomb types

Two CM4 variants, both featuring a single U-shaped funerary chamber, have recently been published. Type CM4e was reported in Jabal Salut JS2 on the hilltop, with a half-subterranean, irregular rectangular chamber, a dividing wall, and a presumed entrance (Condoluci & Degli Esposti 2015).

Type CM4f was reported at Wādī Tanuf WTN07, featuring an annexe attached to the south-western part of the exterior wall (Kuronuma et al. 2024). This annexe resembles Righetti's Type CM3b (Righetti 2015). However, Type CM4f possibly has a U-shaped funerary chamber, unlike the O-shaped chamber of Type CM3.

These new types of individual and collective tombs can reasonably be expected based on the structural criteria listed by Righetti (2015). Type IS2c fills the gap for a tomb with an above-ground structure without ring walls, while Type CM4f may represent a combination of known structural components. This phenomenon raises expectations for the discovery of more undiscovered variants of tomb types.

Newly reported cemeteries

Newly published cemeteries also contribute to our understanding the distribution of Wadi Suq tombs. On the northern side of the Al-Hajar Mountains, several cemeteries have recently been reported on the floodplains of wadis in Al-Tikhah (Deadman et al. 2022) and in Wādī al-Ma'awil South (Antinori et al. 2023). Possible long-chamber collective tombs and individual tombs were preliminarily reported at the latter site (Antinori et al. 2023), suggesting the potential existence of Righetti's CM2 variants in South Batinah, as seen in other regions in the east, such as Al-Khashbah (Schmidt & Walter 2021) and Izki (Schreiber 2007). This contrasts with the ubiquity of this type in the north-west (Genchi 2023; Kuronuma 2023). The growing number of Wadi Suq cemeteries in South Batinah changes the previous assumption.[6]

On the eastern coastal zone, a Wadi Suq cemetery with probable IS1b type tombs was reported in Bimah (Corrado 2020). Additionally, a Wadi Suq cemetery with possibly IS1b type tombs was reported at Al-Berain in Al-Amarat near Muscat (Yule & Mauro 2019).

On the southern side of the Al-Hajar Mountains, a small cemetery was excavated at Bilad ash-Shuhum, the highest location for Wadi Suq burials, with IS1a and IS2a types (*c.*930 m above sea level [asl]) (Gernez, Al-Ghafri & Ciesielski 2023). This site suggests frequent activity in the Al-Hajar Mountains, as evidenced by the use of caves in Wādī Tanuf (*c.*850 m asl) (Miki et al. 2020; 2022) and the cemetery in Zammah (*c.*700 m asl) (Häser 2003). WTN07 (*c.*640 m asl) in Wādī Tanuf (Kuronuma et al. 2024) is also a newly discovered cemetery, along with the possibly contemporaneous WTN13 cemetery (*c.*700 m asl) (Kuronuma, Miki & Kondo 2021). The recent increase in the discovery of Wadi Suq cemeteries at higher altitudes in the Al-Hajar Mountains adds a new dimension to the Wadi Suq mortuary landscape of interior south-east Arabia, alongside the increasing number of cemeteries in the lower basins.

In the north-west area, several individual tombs on the hilltop were newly reported at the site of Al-Khudairah in the Emirate of Sharjah (del Cerro Linares et al. 2023). Additionally, some possible individual and collective tombs were also reported in Jabal al-Yamh in the Emirate of Dubai (Valente et al. 2022). These discoveries gradually fill the geographical gaps with Wadi Suq tombs and are critical for revising the previous understanding of cemetery distribution.

Updated distribution of tomb types and cemeteries

Wadi Suq burial activities have been confirmed in almost all the accessible terrains, both along the coast and in the interior of south-east Arabia, including the Al-Hajar Mountains (see Figs 1 & 2). These burial activities are geographically more widespread than the preceding Umm an-Nar cemeteries, primarily located in open lowlands (e.g. Giraud & Cleuziou 2009).

A brief observation of the north-west and eastern areas reveals that the situation in the north-west has changed little despite recent discoveries. In contrast, the east has seen more significant change, due to the gradual discovery of collective tombs alongside the dominance of individual tombs. These discoveries alter previous views that advocated contrasting burial customs and cultures between the north-west and the east, prompting a re-examination of the apparent regional differences in burial practices in conjunction with the socio-economic context that forms the background to these cultural activities.

[6] The rescue excavations by the Batinah Expressway at Al-Jamma and Wādī Banif (Genchi & Larosa 2021) and several sites in Packages 3 and 4 (Saunders, Caine & Deadman 2016) have been reported in this decade.

Wadi Suq mortuary evidence and non-mortuary remains

Cemeteries and non-mortuary evidence

The ambiguous application of the term 'settlement' in the archaeology of south-east Arabia has been criticized in studies of the Umm an-Nar period (Swerida 2022). Similar issues arise in studies of the Wadi Suq period, which is characterized by more mobile lifestyles. In this context, the term 'settlement', associated with sedentary and immobile ways of life, is not appropriate. In the present author's overview paper, co-authored with colleagues and based on 120 cemetery and non-cemetery sites from the Wadi Suq period (Kuronuma et al. 2021), one co-author (Takehiro Miki) attempted to classify the non-mortuary evidence into nine categories (Kuronuma et al. 2021: 150–152) (Fig. 7): 1. dwellings around the Umm an-Nar tower; 2. stone-built structures on slopes, slightly raised land, and plateaus, 3. mud-brick buildings; 4. shell middens; 5. stopover places in the desert; 6. places for particular activities, including manufacture and hunting; 7. artefact scatters; 8. copper mines and smelting sites; and 9. cave use. Adding new categories, such as: 10. stone-built structures without reuse of Umm an-Nar towers; 11. hoards; 12. unknown and others, gives a total of twelve categories. These categories can combine more than two. Based on the present author's current dataset of 162 Wadi Suq sites, the site complex with cemetery and non-mortuary evidence is summarized in Figure 8. The details for each site complex are listed in Figures 3 and 4.

A total of 119 cemeteries have been identified out of 162 sites (*c.*73.4 %), indicating their dominance.[7] Of these, seventeen cemetery sites are accompanied by one or two categories of non-mortuary evidence (Figs 9 & 10). Among them, the cemeteries with two categories of non-mortuary evidence are Wādī al-Hilo, Wādī al-Zahaimi, and Hili in the north-western area as well as Bat/Al-Khutm[8] and Samad ash-Shan/Al-Moyassar in the east. Additionally, seventeen cemeteries contain one category of non-mortuary evidence, with a regional breakdown being seven in the north-western and six in the eastern areas. Cemeteries in the north-western area are apparently accompanied with more non-mortuary activities than those in the east. However, one can assume more cemeteries with dismissed non-mortuary activities nearby in both areas.

The non-mortuary evidence accompanying cemeteries includes Categories 1, 2, 7, 8, 9, and 10 (Fig. 10). Categories 7 (artefact scatter) and 10 (stone-built structures without reuse of Umm an-Nar towers) are the most frequently associated activity types. However, the geographical distribution of Categories 7 and 10 differs. Four out of the six sites with Category 7 are located in the eastern area, while six of the seven sites with Category 10 are in the north-west. Cemeteries with Category 7 in the east may reflect the ephemeral nature of Wadi Suq

Category	Definition
1	Dwellings around the Umm an-Nar tower
2	Stone-built structures on slopes, slightly raised land, and plateaus
3	Mud-brick buildings
4	Shell middens
5	Stopover places in the desert
6	Places for particular activities, including manufacture and hunting
7	Artefact scatters
8	Copper mines and/or smelting sites
9	Cave use
10	Stone-built structures without reuse of Umm an-Nar towers
11	Hoards
12	Unknown and others

FIGURE 7. *Definition of the non-mortuary activities.*

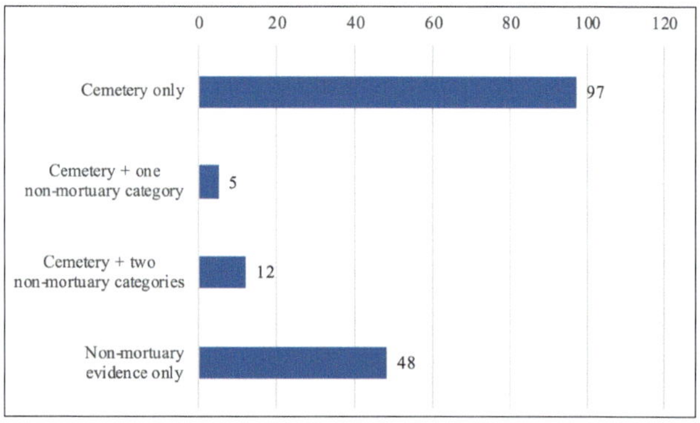

FIGURE 8. *The number of Wadi Suq sites by their site type.*

[7] Due to page limitations, the details and relevant references for these sites can be found on the author's online site distribution map (Kuronuma 2022) and the repository, https://doi.org/10.15026/0002001100

[8] In this study, Al-Khutm is included in the Bat site complex. The inclusion of sites in a complex was determined based on feature distribution rather than strict criteria such as distance.

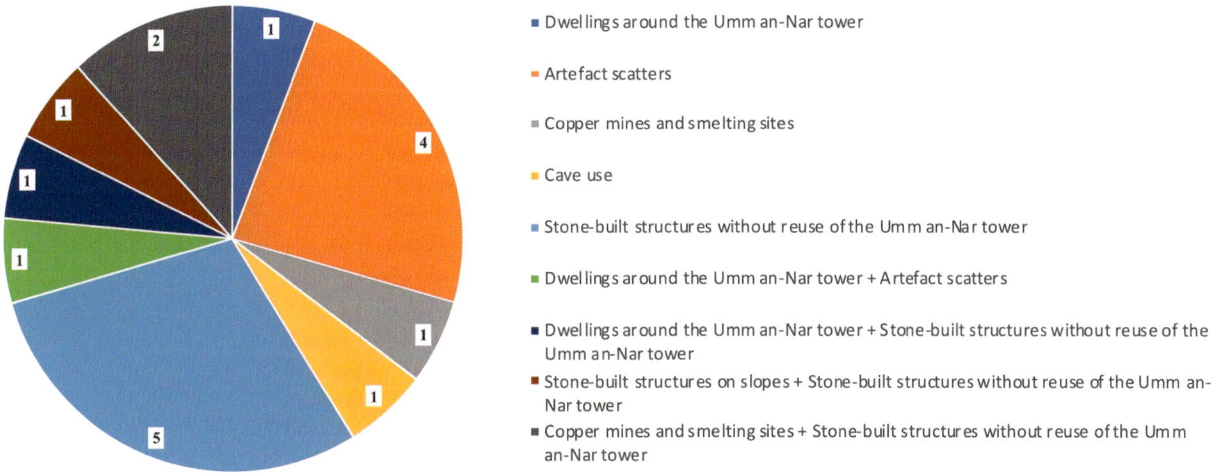

FIGURE 9. *The number of Wadi Suq sites combined with non-mortuary categories.*

No.	Name	Area	Burial type		Non-mortuary evidence					
			Collective	Individual	1	2	7	8	9	10
9	Al-Khatt	NW	X	X?						X
21	Khor Fakkan	NW		X?		X				
23	Qidfa'	NW	X							X
30	Kalba	NW	X		X					
33	Wadi al-Hilo	NW		X				X		X
44	Wadi al-Zahaimi	NW	X	X		X				X
51	Hili and Hili North	NW	X	X	X		X			
57	Wadi al-Jizzi	E		X						X
81	Al-Tikhah	E		X			X			
91	Bat and Al-Khutm	E		X	X					X
100	Wadi Tanuf	E	X	X					X	
116	Al-Fulayj (Sharqiya)	E		X			X			
122	Samad ash-Shan and Al-Moyassar	E		X				X		X
124	Wadi Sahl	E		X				X		
128	Salut and Bisya	E	X	X			X			
133	Al-Khashbah	E	X	X			X			
139	Ras al-Hadd	E		X?						X

FIGURE 10. *A list of Wadi Suq sites with mortuary and non-mortuary evidence. The numbers refer to those given in Figures 1 and 2.*

occupation, as seen in the scarcity of preserved solid stone-built structures. In contrast, Category 10 may suggest a less mobile lifestyle, with seasonal or permanent settlements in the north-west (e.g. Velde 2009; de Vreeze, Kennet & Deadman 2024), although caution is needed when interpreting Category 7. For example, Shimal lacks evidence of permanent settlement but recent surveys to the west of the necropolis have reported artefact scatters with Wadi Suq material (Kdolska & Conolly 2022). This case probably reflects the later destruction of potential residential areas. There are similar cases in the east where Category 7 possibly includes the scatter derived from various original contexts. For instance, examples in anthropogenically modified locations can include former residential areas with permanent structures.

Similar to Category 10, the Wadi Suq cemeteries with Category 1 (dwellings around the Umm an-Nar tower) suggest a less-mobile or seasonal sedentary society. The site complexes exhibiting this combination include Kalba,[9] Hili, and Bat/Al-Khutm, the latter being the only site complex in the eastern area that meets this combination (see Cattani et al. 2024; Cocca et al. 2019;

[9] The collective tomb at Kalba 3 (Phillips 1996) and the tower at Kalba 4 (Carter 1997; Schwall & Jasim 2020), which have traditionally been treated as separate sites, can be considered part of a single site complex due to their relative locations.

Kuronuma, Miki & Kondo 2023; Swerida & Thornton 2019). This combination of mortuary and living spaces probably reflects the socio-economic situation in the north-west, but it also suggests a less intensive sedentary lifestyle in the eastern area.

Less mobile non-mortuary activity is also evident in cemeteries with Category 8 (copper mines and smelting sites), which reflect long-term stays for the procurement and processing of copper. Tombs in this context may be associated with occasional deaths during these stays, resulting in the absence of labour-intensive structures.

Cemeteries associated with Category 2 (stone-built structures on slopes, slightly raised land, and plateaus) require careful assessment. In the cases of Khor Fakkan and Wādī al-Zahaimi, Khor Fakkan can be linked to coastal land conditions (Jasim 2000), reflecting a less mobile socio-economic context, such as a fishing-based, semi-sedentary subsistence strategy, with residential areas situated on higher ground. In contrast, Wādī al-Zahaimi is connected to mobile-oriented activities along the corridor wadi, with a high slope occupation at Site S84 (de Vreeze, Düring & Orijdam 2020).

The cemetery associated with Category 9 (cave use) probably reflects mobility. This pattern is found only in the mountain canyon of Wādī Tanuf (eastern area), where the cave of Mugharat al-Kahf, with Wadi Suq occupation, is situated near the cemeteries on the lower terrace and slope (Miki et al. 2020; 2022). The canyon is probably linked to trans-mountain mobility, indicating a connection between cemeteries and mobile-based, socio-economic activities.

Among the sixty non-mortuary sites which have been confirmed in the present author's literature survey of 162 sites (37 %), evidence of Categories 3, 4, 5, 6, and 11 is not accompanied by mortuary remains. The absence of cemeteries in these categories is not straightforward. For example, Category 5 (stopover places in the desert), such as the case at Saruq al-Hadid, is probably linked to mobility in the desert (Weeks et al. 2018), but any cemeteries remain undiscovered. Similarly, the absence of burials in Category 3 sites (dwellings with mud-brick building) and Category 4 sites (shell middens) is puzzling. The lack of burials in shell middens may reflect the separation of resting places from food-preparation areas, unlike in the Neolithic period (e.g. Bortolini & Munoz 2015). Category 6 (places for particular activities including manufacture and hunting) and Category 11 (hoards) are probably also unrelated to mortuary activities. These results suggest a lack of correlation between cemeteries and specific socio-economic activities.

Furthermore, 102 cemeteries (62.9%) are isolated and not accompanied by non-mortuary evidence. This suggests that Wadi Suq cemeteries were often established in remote locations, far from dwellings and other activities. It is possible that the location of these cemeteries is related to mobile routes or specific places for resting the deceased (see Goldstein 1981; Saxe 1970). It is also possible that the accompanying non-mortuary remains were later destroyed or overlooked, especially if they were ephemeral.

Distributional patterns of the burial practices and tomb types

When we consider the distribution of Wadi Suq tombs in south-east Arabia from a socio-economic perspective, tomb types with non-mortuary evidence, indicative of sedentism and semi-sedentism (such as Categories 1 and/or 10), are associated with both collective and individual tombs in the north-western and eastern areas. However, collective tombs are more frequently found in the north-west (Al-Khatt, Kalba, Qidfa, Shimal, Wādī al-Zahaimi, and possibly Hili).[10] This suggests fixed and stable relationships between tombs and main residential areas, such as oases, as seen in the preceding Umm an-Nar period. Many apparently isolated cemeteries with collective tombs probably lost their associated residential areas with their possible socio-economic context, akin to those with Categories 1 and/ or 10 non-mortuary evidence. Individual tombs in the north-western area can generally also be understood within this mortuary-living relationship.

In contrast, while the above-mentioned view can be extended to the whole of south-east Arabia, cemeteries with Categories 1 and 10 non-mortuary evidence in the eastern area do not currently include collective tombs. For example, in Bat/Al-Khutm, only individual tombs have been confirmed despite its regionally largest-scale

[10] Al-Khatt: CM3a; Kalba: CM4b; Qidfa: CM4d; Wādī al-Zahaimi S66: CM2 variants and IS2 variants; Hili: CM2b and IR2. There are more unspecified tomb types in Al-Khatt. The details of tomb types in Wādī al-Zahaimi are currently unavailable from the publication (Düring et al. 2019).

Wadi Suq site in terms of both mortuary and residential remains (Kuronuma, Miki & Kondo 2023).[11] The absence of collective tombs remains unexplained, but the degree of the fixed relationship between the mortuary and living spheres may be relevant. In the eastern area, this degree could be lower than that in the north-west, possibly suggesting a smaller-scale population or short-term sedentism.

Collective tombs in the eastern area are currently only identifiable by the ephemeral non-mortuary evidence, as seen in Al-Khashbah and Salut/Bisya. These vanished or undiscovered dwellings can also be inferred at sites such as Wādī al-Ma'awil South or Izki. In contrast, the probable collective tomb at Wādī Tanuf WTN07 is associated with stopovers in caves, which are strongly linked to mobility in the Al-Hajar Mountains (Kuronuma et al. 2024). Therefore, while we must take into account the possible biases related to the current state of archaeological investigations and site preservations, the differential socio-economic contexts between the east and north-west should be carefully considered in light of the available archaeological evidence.

The other cemeteries in the eastern area consist of individual tombs. They are distributed across various terrains, suggesting that their construction was related to any presumed socio-economic context.

Unfortunately, the reasons behind the variation in tomb types remain unclear. A chronological difference seems likely. Indeed, as Righetti suggested, there are probably chronological subdivisions within the Wadi Suq period, as evidenced by differences in pottery and other materials (Righetti 2015). However, given that many of the currently identified Wadi Suq tombs lack artefacts or have not been excavated in detail, it is difficult to assess this hypothesis beyond the typological discussions.

The connection between geographical and cultural backgrounds can also provide insight into the distribution of tomb types (e.g. Kuronuma 2023). For instance, long-corridor tombs (Righetti's CM2 series), sometimes over 20 m in length, are primarily found in open, lowland areas (Kuronuma 2023). This may be due to their need for more space, which accommodates the preferred orientation (often north–south) of the tomb's longest axis. In contrast, the CM4 series, with a circular outline, requires less space and has been confirmed not only in wide plains (as seen in the north-western area) but also in more confined locations, such as hilltops, slopes (e.g. Jabal Salut), and narrow terraces inside canyons (Wādī Tanuf). This suggests flexibility in their installation across varied terrains. CM1 and CM3 types may also exhibit such flexibility, although their distributions are more concentrated in the north-west.

Cultural preferences may also influence the biased locations of collective tombs. For instance, CM4b and CM4d types are predominantly found along the eastern coast in the north-western area (Kuronuma 2023; Righetti 2015). A similar phenomenon can be seen in the CP3 type, identified at two nearby sites, Jabal Buhais (Jasim 2012) and Jabal Faya (Jasim & Yusif 2018). The presence of various tomb types at sites like Shimal (Vogt & Franke-Vogt 1987) and Jabal Buhais (Jasim 2012) reflects both cultural preference and the long duration of the site (Kuronuma 2023). Although the sample size is small, these examples may suggest cultural preference within a specific region (2023). However, some types exhibit broader geographical ubiquity, implying that cultural preference is not applicable to all tomb types. It is likely that future discoveries will refine this understanding.

Discussions and conclusions: socio-economic perspectives of Wadi Suq cemeteries and regionally varied tomb types

Aspects of socio-economic contexts, geographical conditions, and cultural preferences are probably closely related to the choice of burial practices (collective or individual) and tomb types in the Wadi Suq period, as modelled in Figure 11.

The apparent regional differences in mortuary customs are probably not indicative of distinct cultural differences. Instead, these regional variations reflect the geographical and climatic conditions that optimized socio-economic practices in each location. For example, the succession of collective tombs linked with sedentism, from the Umm an-Nar to the Wadi Suq period, suggests that wherever the conditions were suitable for sedentary agriculture, collective tombs — closely associated with

[11] Types IS1a, IG1, IG3, IR2. The Wadi Suq tomb types in Bat will be fully published in the future (Kuronuma, forthcoming).

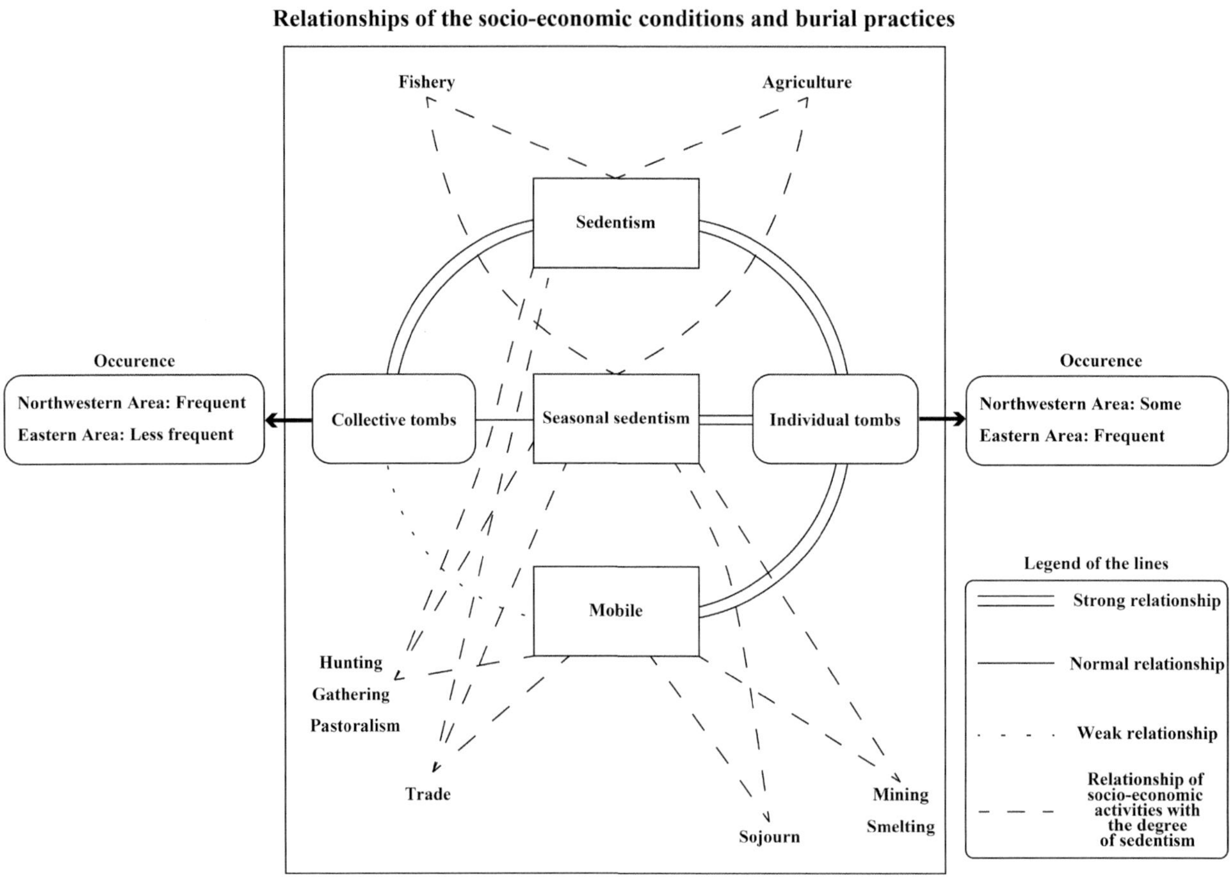

FIGURE 11. *Model of the relationships between socio-economic activities and burial practices.*

sedentism — would have been constructed. The current predominance of Wadi Suq collective tombs in the north-west can be attributed to the favourable land conditions for sedentism, particularly access to water resources (Velde 2009; de Vreeze, Kennet & Deadman 2024).

Conversely, collective tombs could also have been built in the eastern area if the local conditions were favourable (Kuronuma 2023). The gradually discovered collective tombs in the east are probably associated with areas that had sufficient water resources, supporting sedentism or semi-sedentism (see Döpper 2021; Righetti 2015). However, this point is less clear, as evidenced by the small number of sites with solid non-mortuary structures. The relationship between the degree of sedentism and the choice of burial practices may have been weak, especially where only individual tombs are present. Other factors, such as the duration of sedentism at a site, could also have influenced the presence or absence of collective tombs. Nevertheless, it is highly probable that collective tombs will be discovered at open sites where sufficient water was available in the past. The role of collective tombs as monuments may have made them significant as designated places for interring the deceased, independent of nearby dwellings and sedentism. Thus, the possibility of collective tombs beyond sedentary zones should be considered, particularly in more closed topographies, such as mountain interiors where their presence is highly anticipated.

In contrast, individual tombs were more widely distributed across south-east Arabia (Kuronuma 2023; Righetti 2015). Several factors contribute to this pattern: individual tombs require less labour to construct compared to collective tombs, do not require ongoing maintenance, and can be built quickly in response to an unexpected or occasional death. These characteristics align with socio-economic activities of a temporal nature. However, it is important to note that individual tombs have also been found in cemeteries linked to probable sedentary communities, suggesting that they were built to accommodate deaths associated with various socio-economic activities.

Other factors including political, social organizational, or religious may contribute to the apparent difference in tomb types and mortuary practices. The relationship between political structures, social organization, and the variety of tomb types, as well as the choice of burial practices, remains difficult to fully assess in the Wadi Suq period, despite efforts to explore these aspects (e.g. Righetti 2015). There are no clear indications of social stratification or centrally controlled political organization, such as states or chiefdoms, in the Wadi Suq period, making it difficult to evaluate the influence of these factors.

Religious factors, particularly the possible practice of ancestral worship (e.g. Hertz 1907), may help explain the variety in burial customs. This aligns with the nuanced group identity seen in Umm an-Nar mortuary practices (Munoz 2019), which involved the commingling of human remains in collective tombs and associated secondary burial pits (Benton 1996; Munoz 2019; Munoz & Cleuziou 2008; Schmidt 2020; Williams 2023). It is plausible that ancestor worship continued into the Wadi Suq period, especially in relation to collective tombs. In other words, people during the Wadi Suq period may have shared common mortuary customs across south-east Arabia. The regionally distinct tomb types and associated burial practices likely reflect other factors, despite a shared ideological foundation.

To understand Wadi Suq mortuary practices, it is essential to consider the local environmental conditions and socio-economic activities at each site. The people of the Wadi Suq period seem to have selected burial practices and tomb structures based on the specific conditions they faced, all the while adhering to a common mortuary ideological foundation. The distribution patterns of cemeteries and tomb types offer valuable clues about the flexible, adaptive strategies employed by the Wadi Suq people in response to environmental changes, distinguishing their practices from those of the Umm an-Nar period. The dualistic choice between collective and individual tombs according to these principles may have been practised throughout south-east Arabia (Kuronuma 2023).

Additionally, it can be noted that the diversity in Wadi Suq tomb structures can be understood from multiple perspectives. As suggested by Righetti's typology (2015), the various Wadi Suq tomb types are composed of different structural elements, which allowed for numerous combinations and configurations of tomb forms. These varied tomb types emerged from a combination of factors, including the tomb's location, cultural preferences of local communities, and regulations governing mortuary customs, although these remain difficult to specify further due to limitations in available evidence. Future excavations and research aimed at exploring these cultural and societal factors are needed.

The number of Wadi Suq tombs is expected to grow with further discoveries, potentially revealing more collective tombs. By thoroughly researching both the remaining tombs and the faintly visible artefact scatters, an approach to explore the socio-economic contexts behind the establishment of cemeteries, as well as the various tomb types and burial practices, will contribute to a more refined understanding of the burial cultures of the Wadi Suq period.

Acknowledgements

The author would like to thank Dr Romolo Loreto for informing him about the burial discovered at Bimah, and appreciates the invaluable comments from two anonymous reviewers. This study was financially supported by JSPS KAKENHI Grant Numbers JP20J01674 and JP24H00112.

References

Antinori G., Del Bravo F., Genchi F., Di Ludovico A. & Ramazzotti M. 2023. MASPAG 2022 archaeological survey — Methodological perspectives and preliminary results. *Proceedings of the Seminar for Arabian Studies* 52: 1–16.

Benton J.N. 1996. *Excavations at Al-Sufouh. A third millennium site in the Emirate of Dubai.* (Abiel). Turnhout: Brepols.

Binford L.R. 1971. Mortuary practices: Their study and their potential. Pages 6–29 in J. Brown (ed.), *Approaches to the social dimensions of mortuary practices.* Washington, DC: Society for American Archaeology.

Bortolini E. & Munoz O. 2015. Life and death in prehistoric Oman: Insights from Late Neolithic and Early Bronze Age funerary practices (4th–3rd mill. BC). Pages 61–80 in Ministry of Heritage and Culture (ed.), *Proceedings of the Symposium 'The Archaeological Heritage of Oman', (Paris, 7 septembre 2012).* Muscat: Ministry of Heritage and Culture.

Brown J.A. 1981. The search for rank in prehistoric burials. Pages 25–38 in R. Chapman, I. Kinnes & K. Randsborg (eds), *The archaeology of death.* Cambridge: Cambridge University Press.

Carter R. 1997. Defining the Late Bronze Age in southeast Arabia: Ceramic evolution and settlement during the second millennium BC. PhD thesis, University College London. [Unpublished.]

Cattani M., Barchiesi F., Cavazzuti C. & Cocca E. 2024. Bologna University Project in the Sultanate of Oman (2023): Fieldwork activities at Al-Khutm and Ras Al-Hadd. *Alather* 1: 26–35.

Cocca E., Vinci G., Cattani M., Armigliato A., di Michele A. … Gennuso I. 2019. Al-Khutm Project 2017/2018: A Bronze Age monumental tower (Bat, Oman). *Proceedings of the Seminar for Arabian Studies* 49: 85–96.

Condoluci C. & Degli Esposti M. 2015. *High places in Oman. The IMTO excavations of Bronze and Iron Age remains on Jabal Salut.* Rome: 'L'Erma' di Bretschneider.

Corrado L.A. 2020. Il vasellame in pieta dagli scavi italiani de 'L'Orientale' di Napoli a Bimah, Sultanato dell'OMAN. *Newsletter di Archeologia CISA* 11: 125–146.

Deadman W.M., Kennet D., de Vreeze M. & Al-Jahwari N.S. 2022. The nature of third-millennium settlement: The example of al-Tikha (Rustaq) an Umm an-Nar site on the Batinah coast of Oman. *Arabian Archaeology and Epigraphy* 33/1: 49–84.

Degli Esposti M., Brandolini F. & Zerboni A. 2021. 3D digital documentation of archaeological features, a powerful tool for research and dissemination. Case studies from the oasis of Saluut (Sultanate of Oman). *The Journal of Oman Studies* 22: 214–227.

Degli Esposti M., Ramorino P., Spano S. & Tagliamonte E. 2018. Funerary archaeology at Salut (Oman) 2017–2018: Insights on Middle Bronze Age grave's architecture and a possible new type of third millennium grave. *Egitto e Vicino Oriente* 41: 193–210.

Degli Esposti M., Spano S., Tagliamonte E., Ramorino P., Sasso M. & Al Muzaini W.S.M. 2021. Funerary architecture in the Wadi Suq period and an unusual type of third/second-millennium grave: Initial results from the excavation of prehistoric burials in the Salūt Archaeological Park, Central Oman. *The Journal of Oman Studies* 22: 73–98.

del Cerro Linares C., Fernández Rodríguez C., Gómez Sanz P., Alonso García A. & González Martín A. 2023. The Al Khudairah necropolis (Sharjah, UAE). Reflections from the 2023 field season. *Étude et Travaux* 36: 39–56.

de Vreeze M., Düring B. & Olijdam E. 2020. New light on the late Wadi Suq period from the Ṣuhār. *Proceedings of the Seminar for Arabian Studies* 50: 139–154.

de Vreeze M., Kennet D. & Deadman W.M. 2024. Karstic aquifers and climate refugia: A preliminary outline history of water-management strategy in Bronze and Iron Age southeast Arabia. *Open Quaternary* 10/5: 1–16. doi: 10.5334/oq.144

Döpper S. 2021. The Middle and Late Bronze Age in Central Oman: New insights from Tawi Said, Al-Mudhairib and the Wilayat al-Mudhaybi. *Arabian Archaeology and Epigraphy* 32/S1: 313–327.

Döpper S. 2023. *The reuse of tombs in eastern Arabia.* Oxford: Archaeopress.

Düring B.S., Botan S.A., Olijdam E. & Aal J.H.J.M. 2019. The Bronze Age cultural landscape of Wādī al-Zahaimi. *Proceedings of the Seminar for Arabian Studies* 49: 115–127.

Genchi F. 2023. The collective corridor-shaped tombs of the Daba Al Bayaah necropolis (Musandam, Oman): The origin and spread of a funerary structure based on evidence from south-east Arabia. *The Journal of Oman Studies* 24: 19–46.

Genchi F. & Larosa N. 2021. Funerary evidence and reuse practices: The cairn burials at Al-Jamma in the South Batinah foothills (Sultanate of Oman). *The Journal of Oman Studies* 22: 41–72.

Gernez G. 2016. La nécropole d'Adam Sud: Rapport préliminaire. *Revue d'archéologie de l'Orient ancien* Hors-Série 2: 53–72.

Gernez G., Al-Ghafri W. & Ciesielski E. 2023. A Wadi Suq necropolis in the mountains. Rescue excavations at Bilad Ash Shuhum. *The Journal of Oman Studies* 24: 47–77.

Giraud J. & Cleuziou S. 2009. Funerary landscape as part of the social landscape and its perceptions: 3000 Early Bronze Age burials in the eastern Ja'alān (Sultanate of Oman). *Proceedings of the Seminar for Arabian Studies* 39: 163–180.

Goldstein L. 1981. One-dimensional archaeology and multidimensional people: Spatial organization and mortuary analysis. Pages 53–70 in R. Chapman, I. Kinnes & K. Randsborg (eds), *The archaeology of death*. Cambridge: Cambridge University Press.

Häser J. 2003. Archaeological results of the 1999 and 2000 survey campaigns in Wādī Banī ʿAwf and the region of al-Ḥamrāʾ (Central Oman). *Proceedings of the Seminar for Arabian Studies* 33: 21–30.

Hertz R. 1907. Contribution à une étude sur la représentation collective de la mort. *Année sociologique* 10: 48–137.

Jasim S.A. 2000. Second millennium settlement at Khor Fakkan, Emirate of Sharjah, UAE. *Isimu* 3: 145–184.

Jasim S.A. 2012. *The necropolis of Jebel al-Buhais: Prehistoric discoveries in the Emirate of Sharjah, United Arab Emirates*. Sharjah: The Department of Culture & Information, Government of Sharjah.

Jasim S.A. & Yusif E. 2018. Bronze Age tombs from Jebel Faya, Emirate of Sharjah. *Annual Sharjah Archaeology* 15: 10–20.

Kdolska H. & Connolly D. 2022. Mapping the Shimal plain, Ras al-Khaimah: Introducing the Shimal Plain Palm Gardens Project. *Proceedings of the Seminar for Arabian Studies* 51: 201–220.

Knüsel C.J. & Robb J. 2016. Funerary taphonomy: An overview of goals and methods. *Journal of Archaeological Science: Reports* 10: 655–673.

Kuronuma T. 2022. The Bronze–Early Iron Age archaeological sites distribution map in southeast Arabia. https://archaeo-arabia.aa-ken.jp (Accessed 1 November 2024.)

Kuronuma T. 2023. Regional differences in mortuary practices during the Wādī Sūq period in southeast Arabia: Tomb morphology and geographical conditions in the first half of the second millennium BCE. *Journal of West Asian Archaeology* 24: 27–45. [In Japanese with English summary.]

Kuronuma T. (ed.). (forthcoming). Archaeological landscapes through the ages in Bāt, Al-Khutm and Al-Ayn in interior northern Oman. Report of the archaeological investigations by the Bāt Digital Heritage Inventory Project in 2013–2017, 2024.

Kuronuma T., Miki T. & Kondo Y. 2021. A Bronze- and Iron Age cemetery at Wādī Tanūf, Ad-Dākhilīyah: A preliminary report of years 2019–2020 survey. *The Journal of Oman Studies* 22: 99–125.

Kuronuma T., Miki T. & Kondo Y. 2023. The Wādī Sūq landscape at Bāt (Dhahirah Governorate, Oman) and its interregional significance. *Proceedings of the Seminar for Arabian Studies* 52: 205–219.

Kuronuma T., Miki T., Nakashima C.A. & Kondo Y. 2021. Southeastern Arabia during the first half of the second millennium BCE: A review for the study of the Wādī Sūq period. *Journal of West Asian Archaeology* 22: 143–163. [In Japanese with English summary.]

Kuronuma T., Tanabe K., Miki T. & Kondo Y. 2024. Tombs and landscapes in a canyon of the al-Ḥajar mountains. Results of the surveys at WTN07 in the Tanūf District (North-Central Oman), 2022–2023. *Proceedings of the Seminar for Arabian Studies* 53: 104–118.

Magee P. 2014. *The archaeology of prehistoric Arabia. Adaptation and social formation from the Neolithic to the Iron Age*. Cambridge: Cambridge University Press.

Miki T., Kuronuma T., Kitagawa H. & Kondo Y. 2022. Cave occupations in southeastern Arabia in the second millennium BCE: Excavation at Mugharat al-Kahf, North-Central Oman. *Arabian Archaeology and Epigraphy* 33/1: 85–107.

Miki T., Kuronuma T., Kitagawa H., Noguchi A. & Kondo Y. 2020. Bronze Age vessel remains from the cave of Mugharat al- Kahf in the Wādī Tanūf: A preliminary report of the 2017/18 and 2018/19 seasons. *The Journal of Oman Studies* 21: 128–143.

Munoz O. 2019. Promoting group identity and equality by merging the dead: Increasing complexity in mortuary practices from Late Neolithic to Early Bronze Age in the Oman peninsula and its social implications. Pages 21–40 in K.D. Williams & L.A. Gregoricka (eds), *Mortuary and bioarchaeological perspectives on Bronze Age Arabia*. Gainesville, FL: University of Florida Press.

Munoz O. & Cleuziou S. 2008. La tombe 1 de Ra's al-Jinz RJ-1: Une approche de la complexité des pratiques funéraires dans la péninsule d'Oman à l'Âge du Bronze ancien. Pages 627–644 in J.M. Córdoba, M. Molist, M.C. Pérez, I. Rubio & S. Martínez (eds), *Proceedings of the 5th International Congress on the Archaeology of the Ancient Near East*. ii. Madrid: Universidad Autónoma de Madrid.

Parker A.G., Goudie A.S., Stokes S., White K., Hodson M.J., Manning M. & Kennet D. 2006. A record of Holocene climate change from lake geochemical analyses in southeastern Arabia. *Quaternary Research* 66: 465–476.

Parker Pearson M. 1982. Mortuary practices, society and ideology: An ethnoarchaeological study. Pages 99–114 in I. Hodder (ed.), *Symbolic and structural archaeology*. Cambridge: Cambridge University Press.

Parker Pearson M. 1999. *The archaeology of death and burial*. Phoenix Mill: Sutton Publishing Limited.

Phillips C. 1996. Excavations at Kalba 1993–95. *Annual Sharjah Archaeology* 13: 13–31.

Righetti S. 2015. Les cultures du Wadi Suq et de Shimal dans la péninsule omanaise aux deuxième millénaire avant notre ère. Évolution des sociétés du Bronze moyen et du Bronze récent. Thèse de doctorat, Université Paris 1, Panthéon Sorbonne. [Unpublished.]

Rutkowski Ł. 2021. Umm an-Nar soft-stone vessel assemblage from Tomb QA 1-1 (Oman). Based on finds recovered from half the tomb. *Arabian Archaeology and Epigraphy* 32/S1: 213–242.

Saunders B., Caine A. & Deadman W. 2016. *Archaeological rescue excavations on Package 3 and 4 of the Batinah Expressway, Sultanate of Oman*. Oxford: Archaeopress.

Saxe A.A. 1970. Social dimensions of mortuary practices. PhD thesis, University of Michigan, Ann Arbor. [Unpublished.]

Schmidt C. 2020. *Die Bestattungsgruben in Bat*. Oxford: Archaeopress.

Schmidt C. & Walter M. 2021. Die Gräber. Pages 99–232 in C. Schmidt, S. Döpper, J. Kluge, S. Petrella, U. Ochs, N. Kirchhoff ... M. Walter, *Die Entstehung komplexer Siedlungen im Zentraloman: Archäologische Untersuchungen zur Siedlungsgeschichte von Al-Khashbah*. Oxford: Archaeopress.

Schreiber J. 2007. Transformationsprozesse in Oasensiedlungen Omans. Die vorislamische Zeit am Beispiel von Izki, Nizwa und dem Jebel Akhdar. Dissertation zur Erlangung des akademischen Grades Doktor der Philosophie des Fachbereichs Altertums- und Kuturwissenschaften der Ludwig-Maximilians-Universität München. Available at https://edoc.ub.uni-muenchen.de/7548/

Schwall C. & Jasim S.A. 2020. Assessing Kalba: New fieldwork at a Bronze Age coastal site on the Gulf of Oman (Emirate of Sharjah, UAE). *Proceedings of the Seminar for Arabian Studies* 50: 321–332.

Swerida J. 2022. Revisiting 'settlement': A case study of terminology and Early Bronze Age southeast Arabia. *Journal of Anthropological Archaeology* 65: 101382. doi: 10.1016/j.jaa.2021.101382

Swerida J. & Thornton C. 2019. Um An Nar architecture & society at the Bat Settlement Slope, Sultanate of Oman. *The Journal of Oman Studies* 20: 78–111.

Tainter J.A. 1978. Mortuary practices and the study of prehistoric social systems. Pages 105–141 in M.B. Schiffer (ed.), *Advances in archaeological method and theory*. i. New York: Academic Press.

Valente T., Contreras F., Vila B., Fernández A., Lopez D., Mahmud A. ... Zein H.M. 2022. The Jabal al Yamh tombs (Hatta, Dubai, UAE). The architecture, spatial distribution, and reuse of prehistoric tombs in south-east Arabia. *Proceedings of the Seminar for Arabian Studies* 51: 413–431.

Velde C. 2009. The landscape of the Middle Bronze Age in the UAE — Where did people live? Pages 61–74 in National Center for Documentation & Research (ed.), *Proceedings of the international history conference on new perspectives on recording UAE history*. Abu Dhabi: National Center for Documentation & Research.

Vogt B. 1985. Zur Chronologie und Entwicklung der Gräber des späten 4.-2. Jtsd. v.Chr. auf der Halbinsel Oman: Zusammenfassung, Analyse und Würdigung publizierter wie auch unveröffentlichter Grabungsergebnisse. Dissertation, Universität zu Göttingen.

Vogt B. 1998. State, problems and perspectives of second millennium B.C. Funerary studies in the Emirate of Ras al-Khaimah (U.A.E.). Pages 273–290 in D.T. Potts (ed.), *Arabia and her neighbours. Essays on prehistorical and historical developments presented in honour of Beatrice de Cardi*. Turnhout: Brepols.

Vogt B. & Franke-Vogt U. 1987. *Shimal 1985/1986. Excavations of the German archaeological mission in Ras Al-Khaimah, U.A.E. A preliminary report*. Berlin: Dietrich Reimer.

Weeks L., Cable C.M., Franke K.A., Karacic S., Newton C., Roberts J. ... Zein H.M. 2018. Saruq al-Hadid:

A persistent temporary place in late prehistoric Arabia. *World Archaeology* 51: 157–182.
Williams K.D. 2023. *Landscapes of death. Early Bronze Age tombs and mortuary rituals on the Oman Peninsula.* Oxford: Archaeopress.
Yule P.A. 2001. *Die Gräberfelder in Samad al Shān (Sultanat Oman): Materialien zu einer Kulturgeschichte.* Rahden/ Westf.: Marie Leidorf.
Yule P.A. & Mauro F. 2019. Archaeological study visit to the central part of Oman 16.–29.09.2019, Heidelberg University Initiative. Interim report submitted to the Ministry of Heritage and Culture. Ruprecht-Karls-Universität Heidelberg. Available at https://archiv.ub.uni-heidelberg.de/propylaeumdok/4550/
Yule P.A. & Weisgerber G. 1996. Die 14. Deutsche Archäologische Oman-Expedition 1995. *Mitteilungen der Deutschen Orient-Gesellschaft* 128: 135–155.
Yule P.A., Weisgerber G., Kunter M. & Bemmann M. 1993. Wādī Sūq burial structures in the Sultanate of Oman. *Nubica* 3: 379–415.

Author's address

Taichi Kuronuma, Research Institute for Languages and Cultures of Asia and Africa, Tokyo University of Foreign Studies, 3-11-1, Asahi-cho, Fuchu City, 183-8534 Tokyo, Japan.
e-mail taichi.kuronuma@aa.tufs.ac.jp

Proceedings of the Seminar for Arabian Studies 54 (2025): 138–149

The emergence of South Arabian urban societies: the material culture from abroad in context

Romolo Loreto

Summary

The emergence of South Arabian urban societies is a phenomenon that goes hand in hand with the emergence of confederate tribal entities, cities, and circulation of material culture, shaped around the twelfth–eighth century BC. However, the formative process of South Arabian societies and cities, as well as agricultural centres and towns, begins as early as the Bronze Age (third–second millennium BC), between the regions of the Ḫawlān highlands and the pre-desert foothills, where hydraulic technologies were developed.

The available data, looking at the turn of the first millennium BC as well as at the Bronze Age, make it possible better to define the formative process of southern Arabian cities and society. This paper aims — as others have, including de Maigret (2000), Nebes (2001), Sass (2007), Sedov (2005), Mouton & Schiettecatte (2014), Magee (2014), Avanzini (2009; 2016a; 2016b) — to communicate the latest developments and knowledge; furthermore, it intends to uncover those elements of material culture that shed light on the extent to which foreign influence — i.e. from Levantine (Syria-Palestine) and/or Mesopotamian contexts — may have contributed to the creation of urban societies of southern Arabia.

Keywords: southern Arabia, Levant, Mesopotamia, Bronze Age, Iron Age

On the origins of South Arabian historical societies

The emergence of South Arabian kingdoms at the dawn of the Iron Age is a complex phenomenon that goes hand in hand with the emergence of confederate tribal entities, cities, and circulation of material culture, shaped around the twelfth–eighth century BC. However, the formative process of historical South Arabian societies begins as early as the Bronze Age, between the regions of the Ḫawlān highlands and the pre-desert foothills, where hydraulic technologies were developed.

The debate on the genesis of southern Arabian kingdoms goes back to Jacqueline Pirenne (1956; 1974), who dated the beginning of the South Arabian culture to the sixth–fifth centuries BC, denying the validity of the first stratigraphic excavations at Hajār bin Ḥumayd by the American Foundation for the Study of the Man (Van Beek 1969); a hypothesis refuted after the development of archaeological projects in the early 1980s, for example after the 1986 excavation of House A in Yalā/ad-Durayb by Alessandro de Maigret (de Maigret & Robin 1989).

The main economic boost to the development of South Arabian communities was the high skill in hydraulic techniques. Ueli Brunner (1983) pointed out this feature by documenting the strong antiquity of the dam agricultural practice, potentially active since the third millennium BC at Mārib, an early dating confirmed by others (Francaviglia 2000). It was this ability to allow the flourishing of a complex society that, under the pressure of economic and social needs, also contributed to the development of a writing system. In this regard, according to Benjamin Sass (1991; 2005), it is possible that an advanced agricultural civilization existed in southern Arabia as early as the second millennium BC and that this latter period saw the development of the complex socio-economic conditions necessary for the adoption of a writing system.

When discussing the origins of the southern cultures within the wider framework of the central and northern Arabian cultures, with particular regard to the development of trade, de Maigret (2000) suggested a separate development for the southern Arabian kingdoms, the northern Arabian kingdoms, and the Arab nomads. According to him they all originated after migratory movements at the end of the Bronze Age, from north to south, and thus began to develop a trade system only after their maturity (the hypothesis of commercial development as a source of influence for the emerging of the caravan kingdoms is underlined in Shiettecatte 2010 and O'Neill 2020: 163–166). In southern Arabia, the Sabaeans, as well as the Mineans (the Me'units quoted by Tiglath-Pileser III in the northern Sinai), would have originated from the north (Palestine) (Robin & de Maigret 2009).

By considering the linguistic aspect, Norbert Nebes (2001) also proposed, on the basis of the similarities between Proto-Canaanite and Sabaic, a migration from the north, at the end of the Bronze Age, of Proto-Canaanite/pre-Sabaic speakers towards southern Arabia, where there should have been a mixture of the new Sabaean culture with the local substrate formed by peoples speaking archaic Semitic languages. A theory that rests on the fact that such similarities may only be explained by geographic proximity between the two languages in their past. Again, de Maigret (2009) sustained this theory, according to which a migration phenomenon would bring with it not only linguistic traits, but also all those common cultural, socio-economic, and technological traits that were glimpsed in the most varied aspects of southern Arabian societies and material culture.

Along the same lines and suggesting an allochthonous origin, Peter Stein (2013; Kottsieper & Stein 2014) also highlights a close connection between Ancient South Arabian script and Northwest Semitic scripts in Ugarit and Palestine, although the actual genesis of the South Arabian alphabet has not yet been revealed.

Looking at the palaeoenvironmental data and in light of the well-documented local development of southern Arabian agriculture and water management technologies between the Bronze Age and the protohistoric period, Mouton and Schiettecatte (2014) suggested an autochthonous genesis for the southern caravan kingdoms. To them 'South Arabian culture was not based on northern influences' and 'Some of these northern imports may have changed the direction of South Arabian culture, but they were not significant'.

Still referring to the material culture, according to Peter Magee (2014): 'all these examples, although generic parallels between far regions, could suggest that only élite technological traditions could have circulated over such long distances, and that they not necessarily demonstrate allochthonous origins for the emerging of the southern Arabia cultures.'

Regarding the linguistic aspect, Alessandra Avanzini (2016b: 342) was sceptical. According to her, 'The migratory model proposed to explain the linguistic and cultural history of ASA [ancient South Arabia] is oversimplified'. She goes on to state that, 'the Sabaeans formed a part of the Ancient South Arabia culture from its very beginning, and indeed the engine of the creation of the Ancient South Arabia culture'. Nevertheless, although rejecting the migratory model, Avanzini (2016a: 48) believes that on the basis of the material culture, 'South Arabians gained their identity thanks to their contact with the most evolved cultures of the near east' (see also Avanzini 2012). Again, Stein (2020: 338–340) states that the idea of migration of a small group of proto-Sabaeans from north to south is not easily disproved. There are main arguments to put forward against an exogenous origin of the Sabaic language, not just a few isoglosses.

At this stage of research, the statement by Magee is valid and migratory movements proposed to explain complex phenomena usually represent solutions that are too simplified. However, this remains a complex phenomenon where the implications of ancient languages and several other aspects, mentioned but never fully investigated, still await further attention. Therefore, for the sake of a fruitful debate, I wonder what are these 'technological traditions' we are talking about. Quoting de Maigret (2009: 185) in linking the southern cultures with the north: 'I refer to the Mesopotamian influences (sometimes as far back as the 3rd millennium BC) that can be seen in the oldest examples of South Arabian art, and also in the pantheon; I refer to their writing, whose origins are being linked increasingly with the Palestinian world of the late Bronze Age; and I refer especially to the same material culture that is undoubtedly linked (for example in its defensive architecture and pottery) to Syrian-Palestinian cultures of the Iron Age.'

The material culture at the turn of the Iron Age and its foreign influences

Architectural criteria and architectonic materials

The first expression of such 'technological traditions' is architecture, indeed one of the most impressive features of the southern Arabian cities. Similarities in settlements' planning and their fortifications between the South and the Levant during the Iron Age were also highlighted by Jean-François Breton (1998: 136), particularly with regard to the shape and proportions of the settlements themselves, as can be seen in the case of Megiddo compared to al-Bayḍāʾ (ancient Nashq). Also stressed by Breton is the use of the casemate wall technique as well as ashlar masonry, all of these architectural expedients adopted in the Levant since the Late Bronze Age and widely attested from the Iron Age I (twelfth–eleventh centuries BC) (Lapp 1976; Wright 1985: 181–182, figs 317–319). The casemate technique is shared among both the oldest forms of Sabaean temple architecture (eighth century BC) and in the fortifications of the cities of the Awsān kingdom dating from the eighth–seventh century BC, while ashlar masonry had been widespread in southern Arabia since the ninth century BC (Breton 1994: 86–87; 1998: 136–137). Breton (1998: 137) also stressed the strong similarity between the fortification techniques based on the juxtaposition of contiguous buildings, widely attested in southern Arabia throughout the first millennium BC (Breton 1994: 142–152) and in the southern Levant during the Iron Age I (Herzog 1992: 233).

Regarding religious architecture, Alexander Sedov (2005: 74) suggested a derivation of the typical Hadramitic hypostyle sanctuaries from the Levant, returning to a topic he had already addressed regarding the development of agriculture (Sedov 1996). In particular, he compared the Hadramitic temples to the Palestinian temples of the Middle and Late Bronze Age, the so-called 'Monumental Symmetrical Temple' (or 'Syrian Temple' or 'Tower Temple'), since both traditions share a wide monumental podium and two towers flanking the entrance to the temple, designed with one (or more) columned portico supporting the roof of the cella. Although it may seem a random occurrence, the typical southern Arabian hypostyle temples could also be linked to the early Phoenician religious buildings, as attested at Kition in the ninth century BC (Reich 1992: 203).

Moving to the private architecture and within the urban space, de Maigret proposed the derivation of the typical South Arabian tower house from the Palestinian Iron Age four-room house or Israelite house (de Maigret 2005: 107), also well attested at Megiddo, Lachish, or Jericho (Lehmann & Killebrew 2010: 25). Both architectonic traditions share a rectangular stone basement arranged with an axial corridor and lateral aisles, as well as the wall technique based on the articulate composite of a wooden framework filled with mud bricks in the overlying structures, an expedient already attested in southern Anatolia since the middle Bronze Age, such as in the 'Burnt Palace' of Beycesultan (Lloyd & Mellaart 1962: fig. A.5) or in Late Bronze Age Ugarit (Yon 2006: 12, 36).

From a broader perspective, even on the issue of 'urban space' and 'urban planning', in those southern Arabian cities that display not only buildings, but also empty spaces, the latter are regarded as plausible so-called 'market square' or 'ceremonial square'. The aggregating role of squares in the cities of the Near East has been recognized in multiple contexts and periods, for example, in Syro-Hittite (Pucci 2006) and Levantine contexts (Mazzoni 2015; Gilibert 2021), between the Late Bronze Age and the Iron Age. In southern Arabia, the only documented and dated 'market square' is in Tamnaʿ, the capital of Qatabān, where this feature is identified by well-known inscriptions dated to the fourth century BC (de Maigret 2009). Given the trade nature of South Arabian cities, it is safe to assume that such gathering spaces for the fulfilment of 'market' practices existed well before the fourth century BC. Therefore, the apparent randomness in the arrangements of buildings and streets in South Arabian cities stressed by Mouton and Schiettecatte (2014: 206) risks being misunderstood in the absence of extensive excavations. Take for, example, the case of Late Bronze Age Ugarit. Urban planning does not provide for an orthogonal or geometrically homogeneous arrangement of road axes, but as demonstrated by Gilibert (2021), it is possible to identify design criteria according to which the arrangement of buildings and squares responds to the precise needs of representation or symbolic connotations.

Pottery production

A particular class of materials to be analysed is that of the 'carinated bowls' of the neo-Assyrian tradition, defining a class widespread in the Levant and Mesopotamia. This also appears to have spread in the Arabian Peninsula both in the form of imported material (as at Taymāʾ; Tourtet, Daszkiewicz & Hausleiter 2021: 64–65) and in the form of imitation material and thus local production. The latter is mainly attested in Sabaean contexts, with the typical carinated ware of the eighth–seventh centuries BC (e.g. at Yalā, de Maigret 2009: 176; and Mārib, Japp 2005; 2014), and also in Saudi Arabia (at Dūmat al-Jandal, Assyrian Adummatu, and Taymāʾ) and Oman (Assyrian Qade) (Loreto 2020: 292, 299), testifying to the contacts between the Arabian regions and the neo-Assyrian or wider Levantine-Mesopotamian world. In addition, looking to the north (the Levant), among ceramic materials of different Levantine origin in Beersheba, Singer-Aviz (1999) reports several alabaster lids of South Arabian production, in Level II, whose destruction dates back to the Sennacherib campaign of 701 BC. The circulation of materials was also pointed out by Potts (2003) regarding the tributes paid by the *mukarribs* of Sabaʾ to the Assyrian kings.

The southern Arabia trend of imitating *élite* material culture is not limited to the case of pottery. Further similarities are deductible from the texts. According to Erik Frahm, RES 3945, the commemorative inscription of Karibʾīl Watar at Ṣirwāḥ was affected by the neo-Assyrian style at the time of Sennacherib (Frahm 1997; 1999; 2017). Indeed, both the annals of Sennacherib and RES 3945 of Karibʾīl are marked by the same textual division: an introduction with the author's name; a genealogy (not in Sennacherib that rejected his father Sargon II); titling; epithets (relating to the actions of the sovereign in the community, in the cult, and in the function of ruler of the kingdom); eight military campaigns for both; building; commemoration; and date of writing. Also, the typical formula engraved in southern Arabia in the commemorative inscriptions for building constructions 'from the basement to the top' is well attested in neo-Assyrian texts. I wonder if there are more of these similarities in the texts, suggesting that these are not just random occurrences.

Such links at the turn of the seventh century BC are confirmed by the well-known tablet from the kingdom of Sukhu, modern-day Abū Kamāl, close to Mari on the Euphrates, dated to the mid-eighth century BC and referring to the arrival of a caravan from Taymāʾ and Sabaʾ (Robin 1991: 50). This is the earlier textual source for the caravan trade, a topic to be discussed in the near future.

The iconography

Avanzini agrees with de Maigret: 'One of the oldest examples of contact with the outside world, is found in art, testifying a non-episodic, non-superficial but continuous and strong cultural bond between the ASA kingdoms and Mesopotamia' (Avanzini 2016b: 338). The close resemblance between the scenes depicted in the Yemeni so-called Banāt ʿAd engravings and coeval or older Levantine iconography has been repeatedly pointed out (de Maigret 2009: 349–350). For example, Sass demonstrated a Syro-Hittite matrix for the figurative reliefs of the intra-mural temple of as-Sawdaʾ (ancient Nashshān) (Sass 2007). Numerous other examples are known from southern Arabia: the famous Maʿdikarib statue from the Awwam temple of Almaqah (Mārib) with its Levantine trait (Simpson 2002); the *lamassu* model turned into an ibex (Daum 2019: 81); winged genii with aspersorium depicted according to Assyrian/Babylonian models (Bron & Lemaire 2009); episodes of syncretism with the Assyrian society (Caubet, Gajda & Demange 2003); as well as the typical depiction of the sacred tree with animals standing on either side, in mirrored positions (Gerlach 2000; 2004); or the lion model about which Anne Roes (1953) suggested a seventh-century BC Hittite origin (see also ʿAlī ʿAqīl & Antonini 2007: 52).

Apart from these well-known comparisons, de Maigret (2009) suggested a further link regarding the 'ancestors' cult' and its related statuary (Matthiae 2015). Ancestor worship in the Levant meant the dead acquired a new status. Once they made the transition to the afterlife, they lost their personal individuality to gather in collective communities of ancestors, hence they assumed new powers and became objects of veneration. Bronze or stone statues from Qatna, Tell Hazor, Mari, etc. dating from the Middle Bronze Age depict seated figures with their arms folded and stretched forward, or one arm folded on the chest, while clutching votive objects in their hand. De Maigret suggested not only the same intended use but also the same formal model for the so-called ancestor statues from the Yemeni Jawf (de Maigret 2009: 344). This attribution takes shape in light of what Sass demonstrates regarding the Syro-Hittite roots of the decorative patterns from Nashshān.

To conclude this overview on the early centuries of the caravan kingdoms I would say that, as Magee has pointed out, all these fairly abundant elements could still be considered expressions of *élite* fashions, generic parallels between distant regions. If this is the case, they should be episodic or occasional, in other words, deriving from the exploitation of the caravan trade resulting from exchanges among established commercial partners. Nevertheless, the caravan trade, a socio-economic phenomenon well attested during its Minaean management period (from the fifth century BC onwards, as confirmed by both local sources and Greek and Roman authors), is less well documented for the Sabaean management period (eighth–sixth century BC) by biblical quotations, the previously mentioned tablet from Sukhu, the Demirjan 1 from Nashq dated to *c.*550 BC (Bron & Lemaire 2009), and the attestation of plausible southern Arabia names in the archives of Nippur in the years 755–732 BC (Cole 1996: 453–454; Avanzini 2016b: 343). Let us then return to the Bronze Age before the development of the caravan trade, to verify if and to what extent there may already have been contacts over such long distances.

Bronze Age exchange networks

'Caravan trails'

As Laursen and al-Otaibi (2022) recently demonstrated after the excavation of a Dilmunite tomb type from Qaryat al-Fāw, long-distance contacts were well established at the dawn of the second millennium BC by means of the donkey; camels — the desert ships — therefore, were not a prerequisite for long-distance trade and contacts that could already be active in the not yet hyper-arid Bronze Age. Indeed, as many scholars operating both remotely and in the field know well, Bronze Age Arabia is a sort of funerary panorama dotted with turrets, mounds, or generic cairns or pendant tombs revealing precise pathways already systematically exploited since the third millennium BC (Fig. 1).

With the advantage of such a vast dataset, it is possible initially to define two main crossing corridors running from south to north: one from Yemeni Jawf and Najrān to Medina and then Khaybar, al-Ḥā'iṭ, and the Tabūk region; the other cutting north-east from Najrān toward Bi'r Ḥimà and Qaryat al-Fāw and then leading to the Gulf, with Wādī Bisha as a plausible stopover between Qaryat al-Fāw and the Jawf-Medina route.

Regarding Central Arabia, long alignments follow the main cuestas to the west of Jabal Tuwayq and lead to Ḥā'il, providing an almost continuous passage from Yemen through the Najd and then up to the southern Nefud. The latter does not seem to present an insurmountable obstacle: passages are granted to the west, via AlUla, to arrive at the very rich landscape of northern Arabia, revolving around Wādī al-Sirḥān, and linked to Taymā' and Qurayyah to the south-west, and Jordan to the north-west.

Last but not least, the continuation of remote sensing to the Levant and Mesopotamia is providing surprising results. In fact, the abundant funerary evidence unfolds along Wādī al-Sirḥān, although lessening somewhat, and continues along what appear to be well-defined routes across the deserts further north and north-east. In particular, a continuation of this evidence towards the Levant can be followed along a series of palaeolakes up to Palmyra, where dozens of funerary mounds with outer walls and stone alignments have already been surveyed by Morandi Bonacossi and Iamoni (2012).

Toward the Mesopotamian alluvium, even considering the low satellite ground resolution areas, clear evidence of the same tomb types appears in at least two main directions. Coming from Dūmat al-Jandal via Tamriyat, the route diverts along two axes: the first, following the main wadi beds, goes directly to the south of Abū Kamāl (Mari); the second, following a more south-westerly to north-easterly direction goes towards Babylon following a series of parallel wadi alluvia that offer suitable tracks. Typological and functional or symbolic affinity among the several tombs classes is known and further confirmation of the north-eastern display of such tombs toward the Euphrates comes from the 2023 field survey of the University of Qadisiyah in the western Iraqi desert, to the south of Babylon (Johteri 2023).

Undoubtedly, ground-truthing is the only way to define the precise chronology of tens of thousands of such structures, but a general attribution of these funerary elements to the Bronze Age is the most plausible

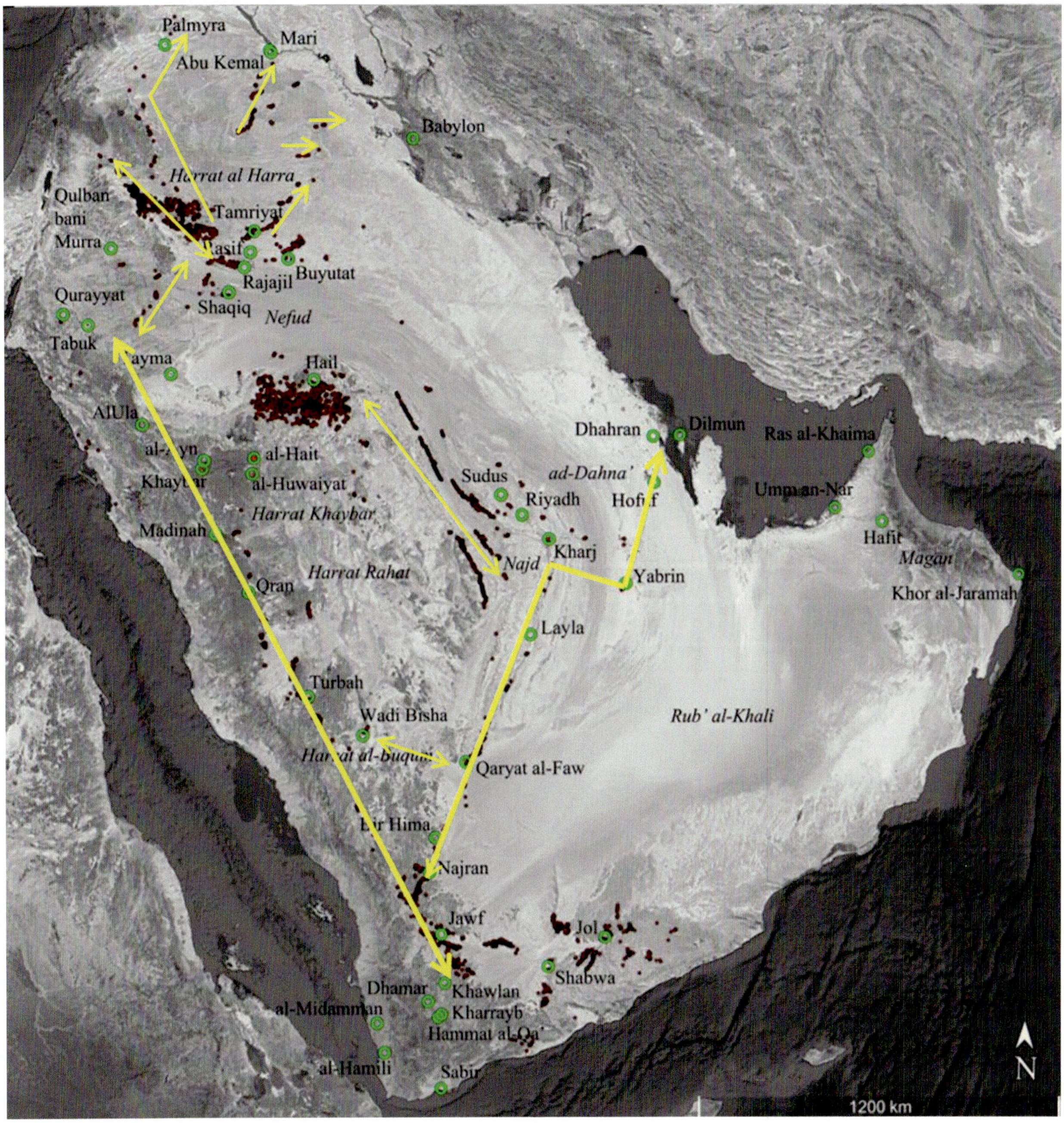

FIGURE 1. *Main trails dotted with funerary evidence in the Bronze Age western Arabian Peninsula (©University of Naples remote sensing laboratory, 2011–2024).*

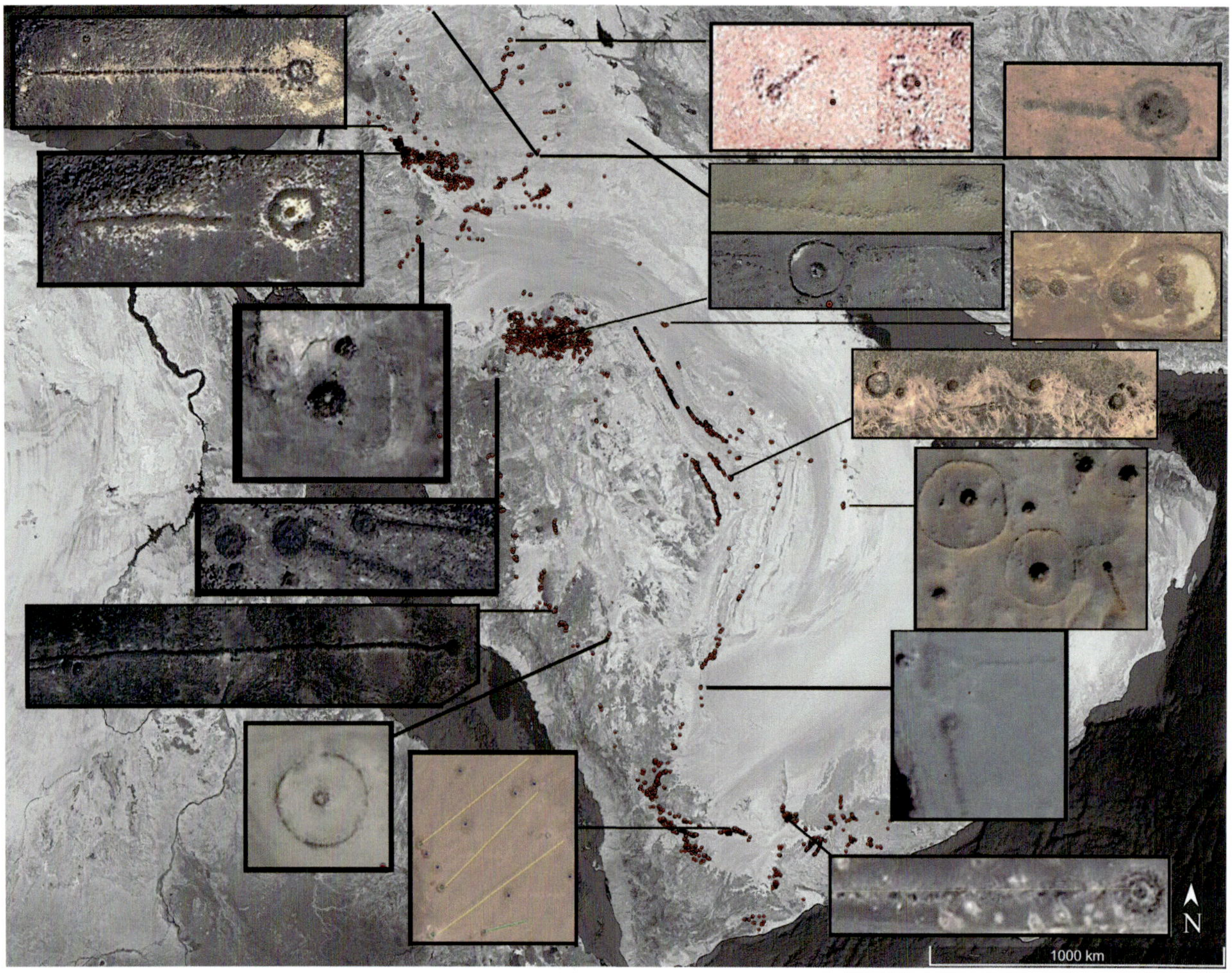

Figure 2. *Examples of mound or turret/circular tombs with alignment and/or outer circular wall from Yemen up to Palmyra/Mari/western Iraqi desert (©University of Naples remote sensing laboratory, 2011–2024).*

in light of the data provided by the excavation of some of them (see esp. Hausleiter et al. 2018; Munoz et al. 2020; Chevalier et al. 2021; Dalton et al. 2022; Hausleiter 2022); even an earlier Chalcolithic to early Bronze Age is possible (Fuji 2016; 2018) as well as an Iron Age reuse (Akkermans et al. 2020). Furthermore, even in a Mesopotamian context, in the territory of the city of Mari such monuments cover the same function as those in Arabian contexts — cultural landmarks along a shared landscape. Indeed, in the texts from Mari (third millennium BC) the funerary tumuli are named *humusūm* or *rāmum* and devoted to the ancestors and their location indicates the zone of control of the tribes (Morandi Bonacossi & Iamoni 2012: 53) (Fig. 2).

As has been stated, thanks to al-Otaibi and Laursen we know that these pathways can be exploited by donkey. When the roads are open, therefore, do the material culture links or 'technological traditions' exist to demonstrate that southern Arabia was connected to the north before the advent of the historical caravan trade?

The Bronze Age material culture

Among the earlier examples of 'technological traditions' there is bronze weaponry, not only fenestrated axes from Taymāʾ linked to Ebla (Hausleiter et al. 2018) but also, in particular, daggers from southern Arabia, from ʿAmrān and the Tihāma (al-Midamman), dating to the second half of the third millennium BC (de Maigret 2000: 297; Giumlia-Mair 2002), which are entirely comparable with the productions of Palestine in the transitional period between the Early and the Middle Bronze Age. Weaponry is also testimony of the contact between central Arabia and Dilmun at the beginning of the second millennium BC (Laursen & al-Otaibi 2022).

Worth mentioning is the case of the earliest Hadramitic pottery documented at Raybūn (1200–800 BC), which exhibits parallels with Late Bronze Age ceramics from Palestine and 'Qurayya Painted Ware', albeit limited to decorative motifs and techniques (Sedov 2003).

Regarding the funerary landscape, so well represented from an architectonic point of view, particularly significant are the anthropomorphic representations of the dead, depicted according to codified rituals visible in the figurative art as well. This is the case in three well-known funerary stelae whose provenance can be traced to the areas of Ḥāʾil and AlUla (Al-Rashid 1970: 57; Steimer-Herbet 2010), as well as the newly discovered stelae from the south, at Jabal Kawkab (Lischi et al. 2024). According to Newton and Zarins (2000) these iconographic elements found strong comparisons with other funerary icons from Bronze Age southern Arabia and, it is now possible to add, northern regions of the Arabian Peninsula. A first match can be identified in the Ḥaḍramawt/Jawl funerary contexts, where engraved stelae depict bearded individuals armed with daggers (Vogt 2000). Conceptual comparisons also come from northern regions, from Qulban Bani Murra and Khirbet Rizqeh (Kirkbride 1960; 1969a; 1969b; Gebel 2010), where anthropomorphic stelae more similar to the three examples discussed here are modelled and not simply engraved.

In the same cultural horizon, reference can be made to Bronze Age statuary — the stone idols from the southern Arabia regions of Jawf and Ḥaḍramawt (de Maigret 2009: 347). Once again it is possible to observe shared representative features as well as symbolic intents: as with stelae, the stone idols reveal anatomies underlying the stone, that is, determined by the type of support chosen, the rigid frontality and verticality of the standing figures, also with arms folded. In this perspective, it might be possible to find a link with the Mesopotamian proto-dynastic sphere (de Maigret 2009), and more specifically the Tarut orant, a local production of the third millennium BC, could be interpreted as a link between these areas, which seem to share a similar concept of the sculptural representation of orants (al-Rashid 1970).

Finally, Newton and Zarins (2000) have already identified a further iconographic trace that testifies to long-distance contacts between the Arabian, Levantine, and Mesopotamian areas — the so-called 'Realistic-dynamic Style' type of rock graffiti attested at Biʾr Ḥimà (Saudi Arabia). In particular, the type of dagger depicted in the hunting scenes reveals the lunette-handled type, also attested in southern Arabian funerary iconographies from Jawl where the lunette is well represented, and bronze weaponry from Levantine and Ur III Early Bronze Age contexts.

Conclusion

On a material culture and an iconographic basis, we observe since the Bronze Age a number of shared elements that trace the precise distribution of the tombs discussed here. This proves that there is no need to wait for the caravan trade to see the arrival of foreign influences, there already was, on a large scale and for a longer period, a deep interconnection among these regions of the Peninsula and the Levant/Palestine and Mesopotamia by means of caravan trails.

Moreover, one of the topics not discussed here is the religion of the South Arabians. The least one can say is that along with the deities only attested in the south (such as Almaqah, the main Sabaean god, or Aranyadaʿ in Nashshān, or Nakraḥ at Yathil) there are also ʿAthtar, Syn, and Wadd, deities well known in the ancient Near East, thus once again proving a complex scenario yet to be fully understood. Should we therefore still address all these 'technological traditions' as generic parallels between distant regions? Should we not recognise that the emergence of southern Arabia historical societies is a phenomenon to be discussed in a broader sense, looking at chronological and spatial issues? Should we not keep in mind that Yemen has still very much to reveal, especially now in light of the huge and extremely fruitful opening of the Kingdom of Saudi Arabia to archaeology that finally allows us to better portray the emergence of the historical southern kingdoms?

References

Akkermans P., Brüning M., Arntz M., Inskip S. & Akkermans K. 2020. Desert tombs: Recent research into the Bronze Age and Iron Age cairn burials of Jebel Qurma, north-east Jordan. *Proceedings of the Seminar for Arabian Studies* 50: 1–18.

ʿAlī ʿAqīl A. & Antonini S. 2007. *Bronzi sudarabici di periodo preislamico*. Rome/Paris: De Boccard-IsIAO.

Avanzini A. 2009. Origin and classification of the Ancient South Arabian languages. *Journal of Semitic Studies* 54/1: 205–220.

Avanzini A. 2012. The Sabaean presence in Jawf in the eighth–seventh centuries BC. Notes on the oldest phase of Ancient South Arabian culture and its relationship with Mesopotamia. Pages 37–52 in G.B. Lanfranchi, D. Morandi Bonacossi, C. Pappi & S. Ponchia (eds), *Leggo! Studies presented to Frederick Mario Fales on the occasion of his 65th birthday*. Wiesbaden: Harrassowitz.

Avanzini A. 2016a. *By land and by sea. A history of South Arabia before Islam recounted from inscriptions*. Rome: L'Erma di Bretschneider.

Avanzini A. 2016b. From south to north in Ancient Arabia. Pages 337–344 in M. Luciani (ed.), *The archaeology of North Arabia. Oases and landscapes. Proceedings of the International Congress held at the University of Vienna, 5–8 December, 2013*. Vienna: Austrian Academy of Sciences Press.

Breton J-F. 1994. *Les fortifications d'Arabie méridionale du 7ᵉ au 1ᵉʳ siècle avant notre* ère. Mainz: P. von Zabern.

Breton J-F. 1998. Les établissements antiques. Pages 127–194 in J-F. Breton, J.C. Arramond, B. Coque-Delhuille & P. Gentelle (eds), *Une vallée aride du Yémen antique. Le wâdî Bayhân*. Paris: Éditions Recherche sur les Civilisations.

Bron F. & Lemaire A. 2009. Nouvelle inscription sabéenne et le commerce en Transeuphratène. *Transeuphratène* 38: 11–29.

Brunner U. 1983. *Die Erforschung der antiken Oase von Mârib mit Hilfe geomorphologischer Untersuchungs methoden*. (ABADY 2). Mainz: P. von Zabern.

Caubet A., Gajda I. & Demange F. 2003. Deux autels de bronze provenant de l'Arabie méridionale, suivi d'un appendice de Mme Françoise Demange sur la technique de fabrication (note d'information). *Comptes rendus de l'Académie des Inscriptions et Belles-Lettres* 147/3: 1219–1242.

Chevalier A., Schiettecatte J., Tzortzis S. & Wermuth É. 2021. The Bronze and Iron Age funerary landscape in Central Arabia. Pages 119–148 in M. Luciani (ed.), *The archaeology of the Arabian Peninsula 2. Connecting the evidence*. (OREA 19). Vienna: Austrian Academy of Science Press.

Cole S.W. 1996. *Nippur IV. The early Neo-Babylonian governor's archive from Nippur*. Chicago: Oriental Institute Publications.

Dalton M., McMahon J., Kennedy M.A., Repper R., Al Shilali S.A., AlBalawi Y. ... Thomas H. 2022. The Middle Holocene 'funerary avenues' of north-west Arabia. *The Holocene* 32/3: 183–199.

Daum W. 2019. The sacrifice of Isaac and its South Arabian parallel, the ritual hunt. Pages 59–83 in J-F. Breton & F. Villeneuve (eds), *La guerre en Arabie antique*. Paris: Geuthner.

de Maigret A. (ed.). 2000. *Yemen. Nel Paese della Regina di Saba*. Milan: Skira.

de Maigret A. 2005. Some reflections on the South Arabian Bayt. *Archäologische Berichte aus dem Yemen* 10: 101–109.

de Maigret A. 2009. *Arabia Felix. An exploration of the archaeological history of Yemen. Foreword by Professor Tony Wilkinson*. London: Stacey International. [Translated from *Arabia Felix. Un viaggio nell'archeologia dello Yemen*. Milan: Rusconi, 1996.]

de Maigret A. & Robin Ch.J. 1989. Les fouilles italiennes de Yalā (Yémen du Nord): Nouvelles données sur la chronologie de l'Arabie du Sud préislamiques. *Comptes rendus de l'Académie des Inscriptions et Belles-Lettres* 133/2: 255–291.

Frahm E. 1997. *Einleitung in die Sanherib Inschriften*. Vienna: Horn.

Frahm E. 1999. Perlen von den Rändern der Welt. Pages 79–99 in K. Van Lerberghem & G. Voet (eds), *Language and cultures in contact: At the crossroads of civilizations in the Syro Mesopotamian realm*. Leuven: Peeters.

Frahm E. 2017. Assyria and the far south: The Arabian Peninsula and the Persian Gulf. Pages 299–310 in E. Frahm (ed.), *A companion to Assyria*. Oxford: Wiley Blackwell.

Francaviglia V. 2000. Dating the ancient dam of Ma'rib. *Journal of Archaeological Science* 27/7: 645–653.

Fuji S. 2016. Wadi Ghubai and Wadi Mohorak sites: Protohistoric burial fields in the Tabuk Province, northwestern Arabia. Pages 115–134 in M. Luciani (ed.), *The archaeology of North Arabia. Oases and landscapes*. Vienna: Austrian Academy of Science Press.

Fuji S. 2018. Bridging the enclosure and the tower tomb: New insights from the Wādī Sharmā sites, north-west Arabia. *Proceedings of the Seminar for Arabian Studies* 48: 83–99.

Gebel H.G. 2010. Untergegangen im Klimawandel. Die paläo-beduinische Kultur von Qulban Beni Murra, Jordanien. *Antike Welt* 6/10: 40–44.

Gerlach I. 2000. Zur Übernahme altorientalischer Motive in die Kunst Südarabiens. Eine reliefierte Bronzeplatte aus dem Jemen. *Baghdader Mitteilungen* 31: 259–295.

Gerlach I. 2004. Un relief en bronze sabéen d'inspiration proche-orientale. *Chroniques Yéménites* 11: 9–35.

Gilibert A. 2021. Verso un metodo per studiare le piazza nel Vicino Oriente antico: Il caso di Ugarit. Pages 135–158 in S. Graziani & G. Lacerenza (eds), *Egitto e Vicino Oriente antico tra passato e futuro*. Naples: UniorPress.

Giumlia-Mair A. 2002. Investigation of a copper-based hoard from the Megalithic site of al-Midamman, Yemen: An interdisciplinary approach. *Journal of Archaeological Science* 29: 195–209.

Hausleiter A. 2022. Tayma, Saudi-Arabien. Funeräre Landschaften, Kontakte und Mobilität in der Bronzezeit Nordwestarabiens (3.–2. Jt. v. Chr.). Die Arbeiten des Jahres 2020. *e-Forschungsberichte des Deutschen Archäologischen Instituts* 1: 1–15.

Hausleiter A., D'Andrea M., Zur A. & al-Hajri Y. 2018. The transition from Early to Middle Bronze Age in northwest Arabia: Bronze weapons from burial contexts at Tayma, Arabia and comparative evidence from the Levant. *Zeitschrift für Orient-Archäologie* 11: 412–436.

Herzog Z. 1992. Settlement and fortification planning in the Iron Age. Pages 231–274 in A. Kempinski & R. Reich (eds), *The architecture of ancient Israel. From the prehistory to the Persian periods*. Jerusalem: Israel Exploration Society.

Japp S. 2005. Selected pottery from the cemetery of the Awām Temple in Marib. Observations on chronology and provenience. *Archäologische Berichte aus dem Yemen* 10: 69–86.

Japp S. 2014. Chronology of Sabean pottery — Some remarks. *Zeitschrift für Orient-Archäologie* 7: 302–323.

Johteri J. 2023. An archaeological survey of the Iraqi Western Desert. *Asor Mesopotamian Fellowship Report*. https://www.asor.org/news/2024/04/mesopotamian-fellowship-report-jotheri

Kirkbride D. 1960. Khirbet Rizqeh. *Revue Biblique* 67: 232–135.

Kirkbride D. 1969a. Ancient Arabian ancestor idols, part I. *Archaeology* 22/2 (April): 116–121.

Kirkbride D. 1969b. Ancient Arabian ancestor idols, part II. *Archaeology* 22/3 (June): 188–195.

Kottsieper I. & Stein P. 2014. Sabaic and Aramaic — a common origin? Pages 81–87 in O. Elmaz & J. Watson (eds), *Languages of southern Arabia*. (Proceedings of the Seminar for Arabian Studies 44, Supplement). Oxford: Archaeopress.

Lapp N.L. 1976. Casemate walls in Palestine and the Late Iron II casemate at Tell el-Fûl (Gibeah). *Bulletin of the American Schools of Oriental Research* 233: 25–42.

Laursen S.T. & al-Otaibi F. 2023. From Dilmun to Wādī al-Fāw: A forgotten desert corridor, c. 2000 BC. *Arabian Archaeology and Epigraphy* 34/1: 63–86.

Lehmann G. & Killebrew A.E. 2010. Palace 6000 at Megiddo in context: Iron Age central hall tetra-partite residencies and the 'Bīt-Ḫilāni' building tradition in the Levant. *Bulletin of the American Schools of Oriental Research* 359: 13–33.

Lischi S., Haquet J., Schiettecatte J. & Prioletta A. 2024. Two anthropomorphic stelae connected with a platform-like structure in the area of Ḥimā (Saudi Arabia): New data from southwestern Arabia. *Arabian Archaeology and Epigraphy* 36. https://doi.org/10.1111/aae.12260

Lloyd S. & Mellaart J. 1962. *Beycesultan*. i. London: The British Institute of Archaeology at Ankara.

Loreto R. 2020. Sulle origini del commercio carovaniero tra la Penisola Arabica e il Vicino Oriente antico.

Pages 287–300 in M. Cammarosano, E. Devecchi & M. Viano (eds), *talugaeš witteš. Ancient Near Eastern Studies presented to Stefano de Martino on the occasion of his 65th Birthday*. Münster: Kasion.

Magee P. 2014. *The archaeology of prehistoric Arabia. Adaptation and social formation from the Neolithic to the Iron Age*. Cambridge: Cambridge World Archaeology.

Matthiae P. 2015. The royal ancestors' cult in northern Levant between Early and Late Bronze Age: Continuity and problems from Ebla to Ugarit. *Bulletin d'Archéologie et d'Architecture Libanaises* (Hors Série 10): 5–32.

Mazzoni S. 2015. Open space around the temples and their ritual use: Archaeological evidence from the Bronze and Iron Age Levant. Pages 118–133 in N. Laneri (ed.), *Defining the sacred: Approaches to the archaeology of religion in the Near East*. Oxford: Oxbow.

Morandi Bonacossi D. & Iamoni M. 2012. The early history of the western Palmyra Desert Region. The change in the settlement patterns and the adaptation of subsistence strategies to encroaching aridity: A first assessment of the desert-kite and tumulus cultural horizons. *Syria* 89: 31–58.

Mouton M. & Schiettecatte J. 2014. *In the desert margins. The settlements process in ancient South and East Arabia*. Rome: L'Erma di Bretschneider.

Munoz O., Cotty M., Charloux G., Bouchaud C., Monchot H., Marquaire C. ... Boschloos V. 2020. Marking the sacral landscape of a north Arabian oasis: A sixth millennium BC monumental stone platform and surrounding burials. *Antiquity* 94/375: 601–621.

Nebes N. 2001. Zur Genese der altsüdarabischen Kultur. Eine Arbeitshypothese. Pages 428–435 in R. Eichmann & H. Parzinger (eds), *Migration und Kulturtransfer. Der Wandel Vorder- und Zentralasiatischer Kulturen im Umbruch vom 2. zum 1. vorchristlichen Jahrtausend. Akten des Internationalen Kolloquiums. Berlin, 23. Bis 26. November 1999*. Bonn: Habel.

Newton L.S. & Zarins J. 2000. Aspects of Bronze Age art of southern Arabia: The pictorial landscape and its relation to economic and socio-political status. *Arabian Archaeology and Epigraphy* 11: 154–179.

O'Neill D. 2020. *The stone and metal miniature repertoire of the Awam Cemetery Marib (Yemen)*. (ABADY 15). Wiesbaden: Reichert.

Pirenne J. 1956. *Paléographie des inscriptions sud-arabes. Contribution à la chronologie et à l'histoire de l'Arabie du Sud antique*. i. *Des origines à l'époque himyarite*. Brussels: Paleis der Academien.

Pirenne J. 1974. Notes d'archéologie sud-arabe, IX: Hajar bin Mumeid. *Syria* 51: 137–170.

Potts D.T. 2003. The *mukarrib* and his beads: Karib'il Watar's Assyrian diplomacy in the early 7th century B.C. *Isimu* 7: 197–206.

Pucci M. 2006. Enclosing open spaces: The organisation of external areas in Syro-Hittite architecture. Pages 169–184 in J. Maran, Juwig C., Schwengel H. & Thaler U. (eds), *Constructing power: Architecture, ideology and social practice*. Hamburg: LIT Verlag.

al-Rashid S.A. 1970. Eine Frühdynastische Statue von der Insel Tarut im Persischen Gulf. Pages 159–166 in D.O. Edzard (ed.), *Gesellschaften im Alten Zweistromland und in den angrenzenden Gebeiten*. Munich: Verlag der Bayerischen Akademie der Wissenschaften.

Reich R. 1992. Palaces and residences in the Iron Age. Pages 202–222 in A. Kempinski & R. Reich (eds), *The architecture of ancient Israel. From the prehistory to the Persian periods*. Jerusalem: Israel Exploration Society.

Robin Ch.J. 1991. *L'Arabie antique de Karib'īl à Mahomet*. Aix-en-Provence: Édisud.

Robin Ch.J & de Maigret A. 2009. Le royaume sudarabique de Maᶜīn: Nouvelles données grâce aux fouilles italiennes de Barâqish (l'antique Yathill). *Comptes rendus de l'Académie des Inscriptions et Belles-Lettres* 153/1: 57–96.

Roes A. 1953. Un grand bronze Hittite trouvé en Arabie. *Syria* 30: 65–71.

Sass B. 1991. *Studia Alphabetica on the origin and early history of the Northwest Semitic, South Semitic and Greek alphabets*. Göttingen: Vandenhoeck und Ruprecht.

Sass B. 2005. *The alphabet at the turn of the millennium. The West Semitic alphabet ca. 1150–850 BCE; the antiquity of the Arabian, Greek and Phrygian alphabets*. (Tel Aviv University Institute of Archaeology Occasional Publications, 4). Tel Aviv: Emery and Claire Yass Publications in Archaeology.

Sass B. 2007. From Maraş and Zincirli to es-Sawdā': The Syro-Hittite roots of the South Arabian table scene. Pages 293–319 in S. Bickel, S. Schroer, R. Schurte & C. Uehlinger (eds), *Bilder als Quellen — Images as sources. Studies on ancient Near Eastern artefacts and the Bible inspired by the work of Othmar Keel*. Göttingen: Vandenhoeck and Ruprecht.

Schiettecatte J. 2010. The Arabian Iron Age funerary stelae and the issue of cross-cultural contacts. Pages 191–203 in L.R. Weeks (ed.), *Death and burial in Arabia and beyond: Multidisciplinary perspectives* (British Archaeological Reports, International Series 2107) (Society for Arabian Monographs, 10). Oxford: Archaeopress.

Sedov A.V. 1996. On the origin of the agricultural settlements in Hadramawt. Pages 67–86 in C.J. Robin & I. Gajda (ed.), *Arabia Antiqua: Early origins of South Arabian states. Proceedings of the First International Conference on the conservation and exploitation of the archaeological heritage of the Arabian Peninsula held in the Palazzo Brancaccio, Rome, IsMEO on 28–30th May 1991.* (Serie Orientale Roma, 70). Rome: Istituto italiano per il Medio ed Estremo Oriente.

Sedov A.V. 2003. Notes on stratigraphy and pottery sequence at Raybūn I settlement (Western Wādī Ḥaḍramawt). *Arabia. Revue de Sabéologie* 1: 173–196; 245–291.

Sedov A.V. 2005. *Temples of ancient Ḥaḍramawt.* Rome: L'Erma di Bretschneider.

Simpson St.J. (ed.). 2002. *Queen of Sheba: Treasures from Ancient Yemen.* London: British Museum.

Singer-Aviz L. 1999. Beersheba — A gateway community in southern Arabian long-distance trade in the eighth century B.C.E. *Tel Aviv* 26: 3–75.

Steimer-Herbet T. 2010. Three funerary stelae from the 4th millennium BC. Pages 166–169 in A.I. Al-Ghabban, B. André-Salvini, F. Demange & C. Juvin (eds), *Routes d'Arabie. Archéologie et histoire du Royaume d'Arabie Saoudite.* Paris: Louvre Éditions.

Stein P. 2013. Palaeography of the Ancient South Arabian script. New evidence for an absolute chronology. *Arabian Archaeology and Epigraphy* 24: 186–195.

Stein P. 2020. Ancient South Arabia. Pages 337–353 in R. Hasselbach-Andee (ed.), *A companion to ancient Near Eastern languages.* (Blackwell Companions to the Ancient World). Hoboken, NJ: Wiley-Blackwell.

Tourtet F., Daszkiewicz A. & Hausleiter A. 2021. Pottery from Tayma: Chronostratigraphy, archaeometry, cultural interaction. Pages 43–88 in M. Luciani (ed.), *The archaeology of the Arabian Peninsula 2 — Connecting the evidence.* (OREA 19). Vienna: Austrian Academy of Science Press.

Van Beek G. 1969. *Hajar bin Ḥumeid. Investigations at a pre-Islamic site in South Arabia.* (Publications of the American Foundation for the Study of Man, 5). Baltimore: Johns Hopkins Press.

Vogt B. 2000. L'Hadramawt nella tarda preistoria. Pages 54–59 in A. de Maigret (ed.), *Yemen. Nel paese della regina di Saba.* Milan: Skira.

Wright G.R.H. 1985. *Ancient building in South Syria and Palestine.* Leiden: Brill.

Yon M. 2006. *The city of Ugarit at Ras Shamra.* Winona Lake, IN: Eisenbrauns.

Author's address

Romolo Loreto, University of Naples L'Orientale, Via Chiatamone, 61/62, 80121 Naples NA, Italy.
e-mail rloreto@unior.it

Proceedings of the Seminar for Arabian Studies 54 (2025): 150–167

Funerary rituals on Qurayyah's painted pottery

Marta Luciani

Summary

Recent discoveries of the Joint Archaeological Project of the Heritage Commission of the Saudi Ministry of Culture and the University of Vienna in the oasis of Qurayyah, north-west Arabia, offer new insights into the symbolic and ritual world of the final Late Bronze Age.[1] Throughout the Bronze and Iron Ages, Qurayyah was a settlement extremely rich in assemblages of bichrome painted pottery. The iconographic analysis of the anthropomorphic themes painted in two-colour chromatism on two exceptional kraters from the funerary complex in Area R reveals the possibility of understanding these figurative motifs not as static but as graphic description of rituals and performances, specifically connected to the burial context. The comparison with contemporary ceramic apparel associated with mortuary settings in neighbouring regions suggests that north-west Arabia shared this tradition with the Greater Levant and the eastern Mediterranean.

Keywords: north-west Arabia, final Late Bronze Age, funerary rituals, Qurayyah Painted Ware, iconography

Introduction

The pottery from Bronze Age Arabia has been known to be decorated with monochrome, bichrome, and occasionally polychrome painting and the overwhelming majority of motifs thus far identified are geometric (Magee 2014). One exception to this rule is the Late Bronze Age pottery formerly known as Midianite (Parr, Harding & Dayton 1970; Parr 1982; Rothenberg 2019) and now called Qurayyah Painted Ware, or QPW (Parr 1988: 73–74). Before fieldwork by the Joint Qurayyah Archaeological Project of the Heritage Commission of the Saudi Ministry of Culture and the University of Vienna started, the single figurative elements attested included occasional depictions of animals (mostly ostriches in the QPW 4 [see Fig. 2] repertoire[2] and quadrupeds such as bull, ibex, and donkey) and four anthropomorphic representations (Intilia 2016: fig. 10). Our current investigations in the oasis have drastically increased the number of both animal and human representations painted on pottery (Luciani 2021a: figs 7c and 8; 2024: fig. 23.7h–i; 23.10–11; 23.13–16) from Late Bronze Age Arabia. However, scholars have not yet developed specific reflections on either meaning or function of these painted scenes. This paper is a first attempt to carry out an iconographic analysis based on the discoveries of the 2023 field season in Qurayyah. Although preliminary, our recent findings have opened the possibility of understanding these depictions as a graphic 'shorthand' for representing celebrations, rituals, and performances, specifically connected to the burial context. Moreover, the custom of painting funerary rituals on large ceramic vessels, or kraters, was widespread in the late second millennium BC in the Aegean and neighbouring regions (Recht & Morris 2021). I propose that the recently unearthed evidence from North Arabia and the southern Levant, notwithstanding clear differences, visibly shares a number of structural commonalities with the Aegean tradition. This suggests that the former may be understood as a part of a larger practice shared in the eastern Mediterranean and the Greater Levant.

The site

Qurayyah is one of the major walled oases in the north-west of the Arabian Peninsula (Fig. 1). It has been

[1] The term 'final Late Bronze Age' in this article denotes the final part (centuries) of the Late Bronze Age. The same applies to the Middle Bronze Age and Iron Age.

[2] Intilia 2016: figs 7–8; Tourtet, Daszkiewicz & Hausleiter 2021: fig. 8i. However, the final MBA-initial LBA pottery from Area A in Qurayyah (QPW 2, see below Fig. 2) already has animal motifs (lion, ibex, and gazelle; Luciani & Alsaud 2018). In Tayma's Early Iron Age pottery, we find birds (Tourtet, Daszkiewicz & Hausleiter 2021: fig. 10a) and anthropomorphic motifs again but they are clearly different, as are the motifs found in Qurayyah's Iron Age pottery — camels, ibex, and birds (Luciani 2023a: fig. 13).

investigated since 2014 in the frame of the Joint Qurayyah Archaeological Project (Luciani 2014; 2023b). During fieldwork conducted over nine seasons, we revealed a walled mega-site extending over 300 ha in total (Luciani 2021b), created thanks to the establishment of a surface water harvesting system that provided sufficient water for irrigation and drinking purposes in an increasingly arid environment (Lüthgens et al. 2023). This foundation is dated to the Early Bronze Age IB[3] (final part of the fourth millennium BC). After its initial establishment, the 'urban' oasis was occupied continuously for over 4000 years without significant gaps throughout the Bronze and Iron Ages until the late Byzantine period (Luciani 2023a).

Without further delving into the different contexts discovered and attesting to multiple phases of the life of the oasis, I would like to emphasize that in Qurayyah, we could successfully single out and establish the chronology of at least seven[4] different contexts with well-stratified pottery assemblages, which are predominantly painted and which may be dated from the final Middle Bronze Age in the seventeenth century cal BC up to the final Iron Age in the sixth century BC and later (Fig. 2).[5] To underscore them as an exclusively Qurayyahite production, we now label these pottery series with the acronym QPW and always add a number, in order to distinguish it from similar-looking pottery found elsewhere in North Arabia and the Greater Levant, and commonly known as QPW, without a number (Intilia 2016). We use the numbers 1–7 for each chronologically distinct assemblage.

In this contribution I will deal with only one of these repertoires, the main assemblage from Qurayyah's Area R (Figs 1 & 3), now called QPW 4 (=ARPW 3-2; see Fig. 2) which is radiocarbon-dated to an interval ranging from the Late Bronze Age to the early Iron Age.

The context

In Area R, we are currently unearthing a large, stone and mud-brick burial complex measuring over 400 m^2 and comprising at least thirteen different architectural units, over twenty different chambers, and two rooms dedicated to a sanctuary (Luciani 2021a). This large multi-chambered compound, radiometrically dated to the thirteen to eleventh century cal BC (earlier skeletal remains) and to the twelfth to the start of the tenth century cal BC (final skeletal remains) yielded several dozen inhumated individuals, both as primary burials but also as curated, secondary interments. In addition to a broad range and very high number of painted vessels, the burial gifts included Egyptian scarabs, iron arrowheads, and two short daggers (18 cm), bracelets and anklets, bronze arm-, finger-, and toe-rings, ostrich eggs, clay figurines (see Fig. 5, bottom left), painted clay pendants (Luciani, forthcoming, b) and thousands of gemstones and other beads. For its location and finds, the Area R compound should be understood as the site of the formal disposal of the bodies of Qurayyah's elite. The pottery assemblage found in this funerary context — **QPW 4** (Fig. 2) — resembles most the Timna Site 200 repertoire; outside Qurayyah it is known generically as QPW (without number), the name currently in use for all Hejazi-looking sherds previously called 'Midianite Pottery' (Parr, Harding & Dayton 1970; Parr 1982; Rothenberg 2019).

The most remarkable discovery in the Area R complex in Qurayyah was made in Unit R-B1 (Fig. 3): a square-shaped yellow mud-brick room (Room 830) with a stone frieze *in situ* depicting a very elaborate scene (Fig. 4, top). From the right it shows a reclining *orante*, a wavy line probably indicating a snake, an upturned ibex, and an upturned perfume burner above a triangular or trapezoidal face. The last-mentioned motif should be identified as the face of a deity — different from the bucrania we find attested in the rock art of Qurayyah's plateau (Alqahtani, al-Sulaimi & Abualhassan, forthcoming) (Fig. 4, bottom). While an overall similarity with later depictions of the head of the Semitic god Ṣalm attested in Tayma is manifest (Luciani 2021a), Qurayyah's relief is significantly more ancient

---

[3] For the designation of the chronological phases I use the terminology in use in the southern Levant (Greenberg 2019; Philip 2008) without necessarily implying that it is always a perfect fit for North Arabia. The Early Bronze Age IB dates (33rd–31st century cal BC) are given by recently measured ^{14}C dates from Area M (Luciani, forthcoming, a).

[4] The number of assemblages refers to those we can identify and date precisely because they come from substantially mono-phase contexts that are radiometrically dated (Luciani 2019; 2023c; 2024). However, some areas of uncertainty remain and will be better understood in the future.

[5] The entire sequence of pottery repertoires is being studied within the frame of the ANAPAN international interdisciplinary project which is funded by the Austrian Science Fund FWF under the international WEAVE scheme, Project no. I6562 (www.fwf.ac.at/en/research-radar/10.55776/I6562).

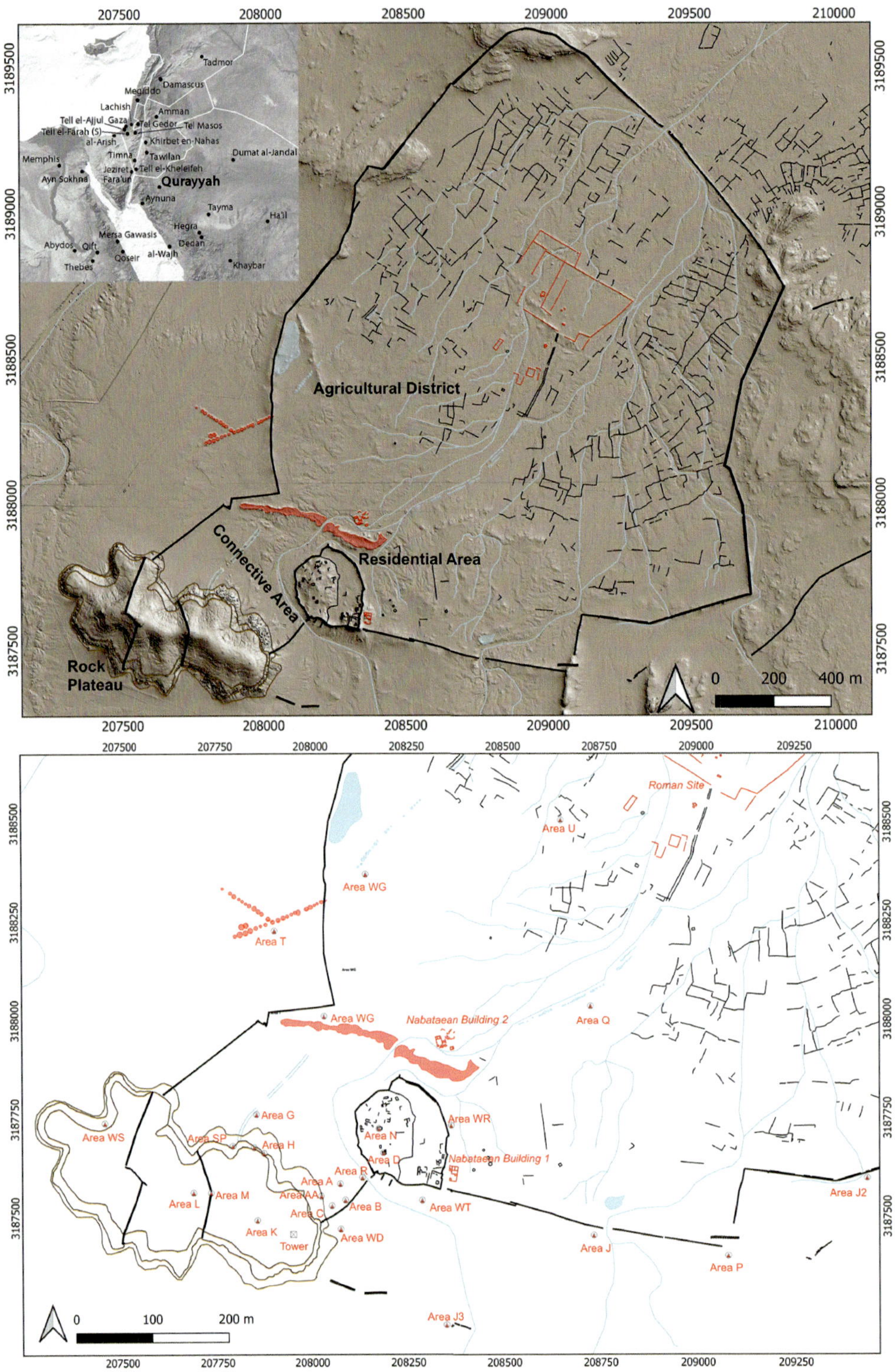

Figure 1. Top: *location of Qurayyah (after Luciani 2021b: fig. 1) and general plan of the site;* **bottom:** *detail of the location of the excavation areas (QGIS: J. Kahl; DEM: A. Uesugi).*

Name	Description	Context	14C Dates / Age	
QPW 1 (SQPW)	(1) Cream-on-red painted, (2) Red-on-orange painted, (3) Barbotine pottery painted over, (4) Red, coarse finger painted, (5) Red painted and grooves, (6) Monochrome painted	**Area A** Phase 5	Late 17th – 15th cent. cal BCE	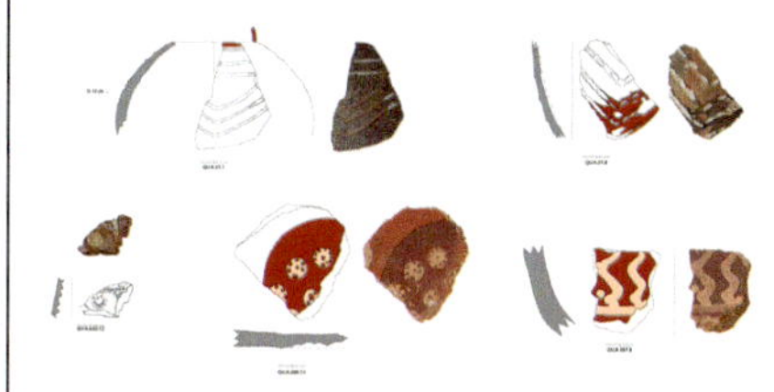
QPW 2 (SQPW)	(7) Fine monochrome and bichrome painted. Figurative animal (lion, ibex, gazelle) and floral motifs. Smoothed	**Area A** Phases 4-3	Late 17th – 15th cent. cal BCE	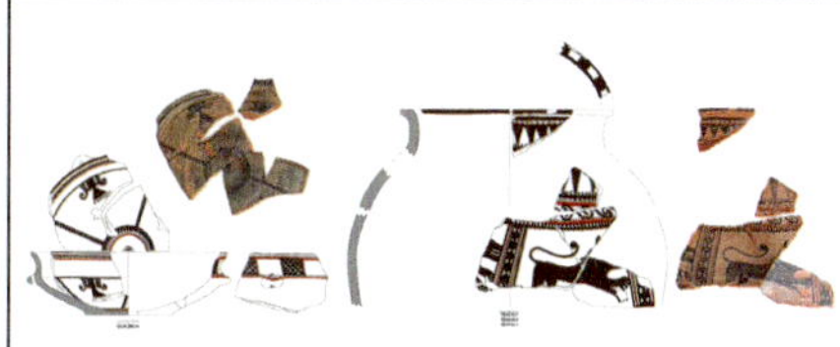
QPW 3 (AAAPW)	Fine bichrome painted, geometric and ostrich motif. Smoothed (=Area **AA** Painted Ware)	**Area AA** **Area M** Phase 5	15th – 14th cent. cal BCE	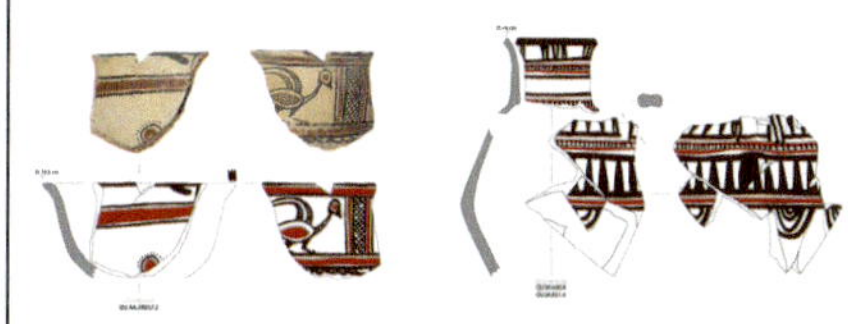
QPW 4 (ARPW 3-2)	Schematic bichrome and monochrome painted, standard jugs and straight-sided bowls (=Area **R** Painted Ware)	**Area R** All units except for R-B4	13th – 11th cent. cal BCE	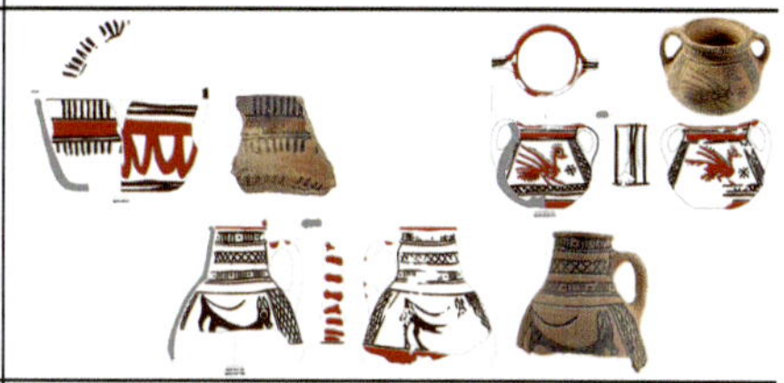
QPW 5 (ARPW 4)	Bichrome painted, mixing QPW 4 and QPW 6 vegetal and geometric motifs (=only from earliest layer Phase 7 of **R-B4** unit)	**Area R** Only unit R-B4 Room 829 Phase 7	10th cent. cal BCE	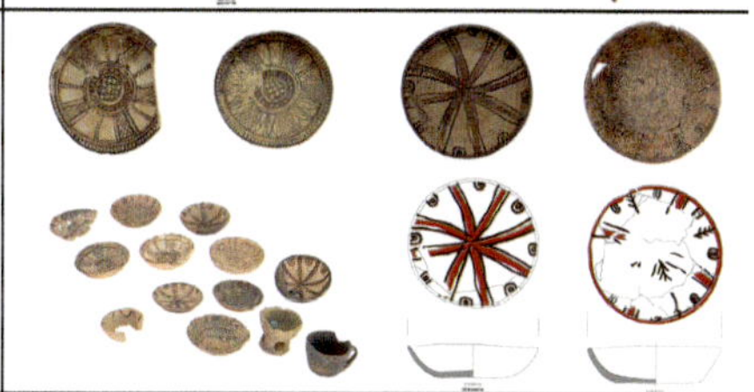
QPW 6 (ADPW 2, AKPW, ARPW 1)	Coarse stroke bichrome and monochrome painted, figurative motifs (animals –camels, ibex and birds– and plants)	**Area D** Phases 15-21	8th – 6th cent. cal BCE	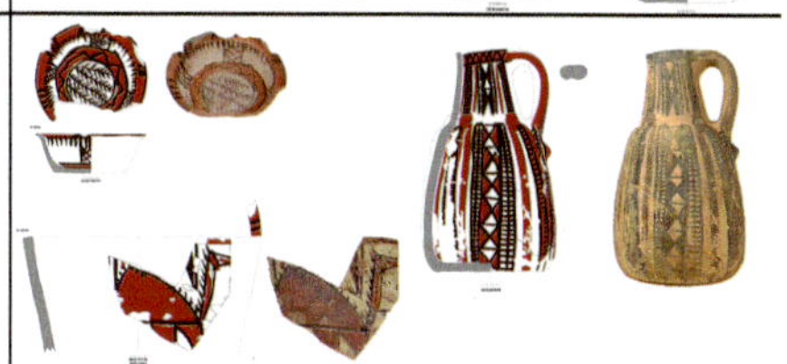
QPW 7 (ADPW 1)	Coarse stroke bichrome and monochrome painted, geometric motifs (esp. triangles)	**Area D** Phases 11-14	Late Iron Age (post 6th cent.)	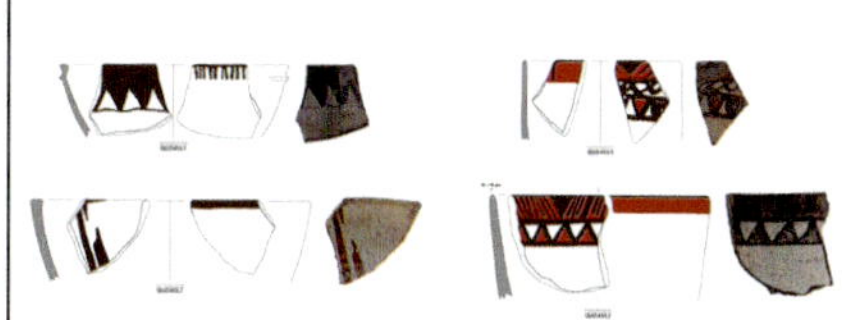

FIGURE 2. *Chronological table listing all the Bronze and Iron Age painted pottery assemblages found in Qurayyah — QPW (Qurayyah Painted Ware) 1–7.*

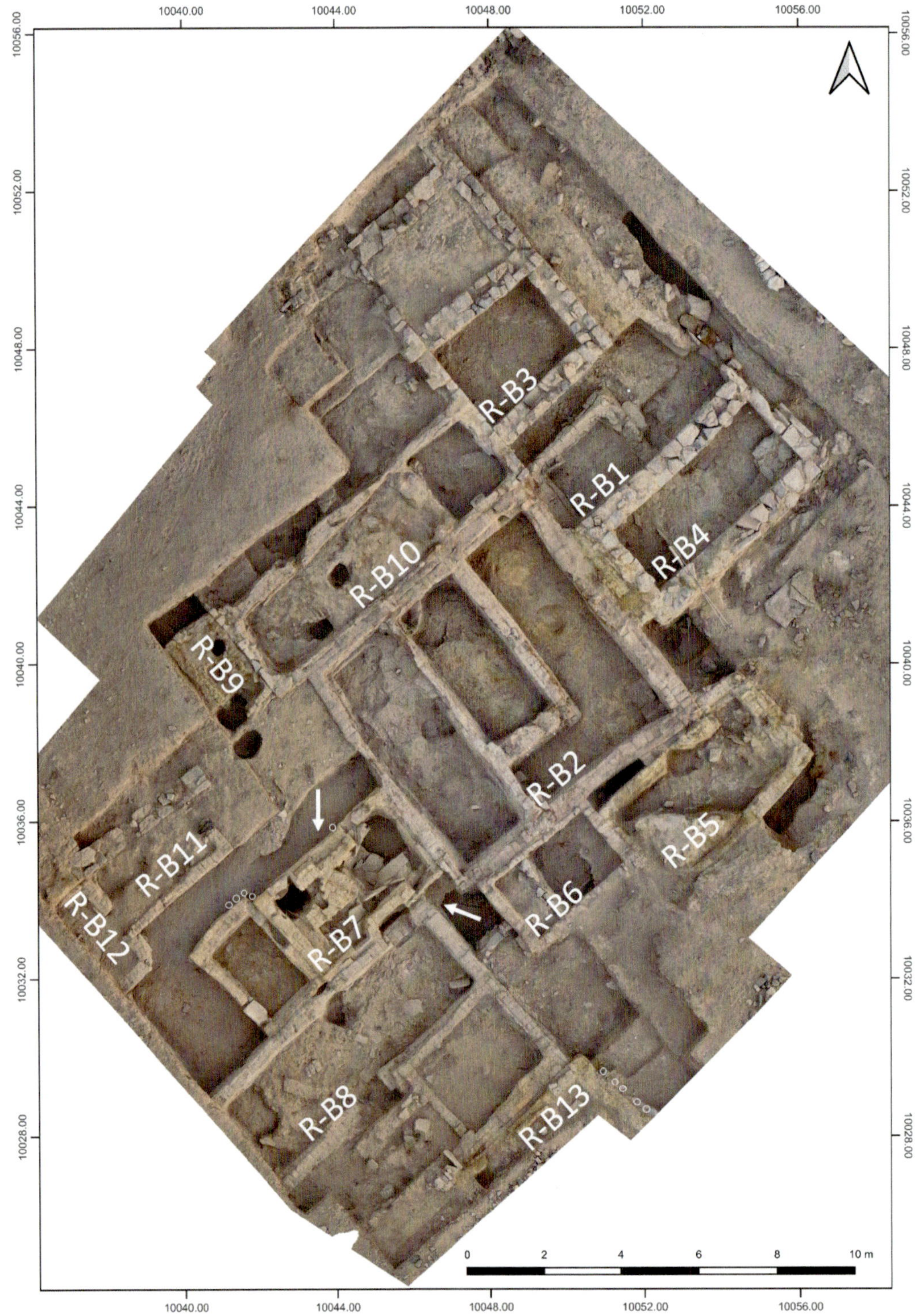

Figure 3. *Orthophoto of Area R at the end of the 2024 field season (photograph F. Spitaler; graphics M. Luciani).*

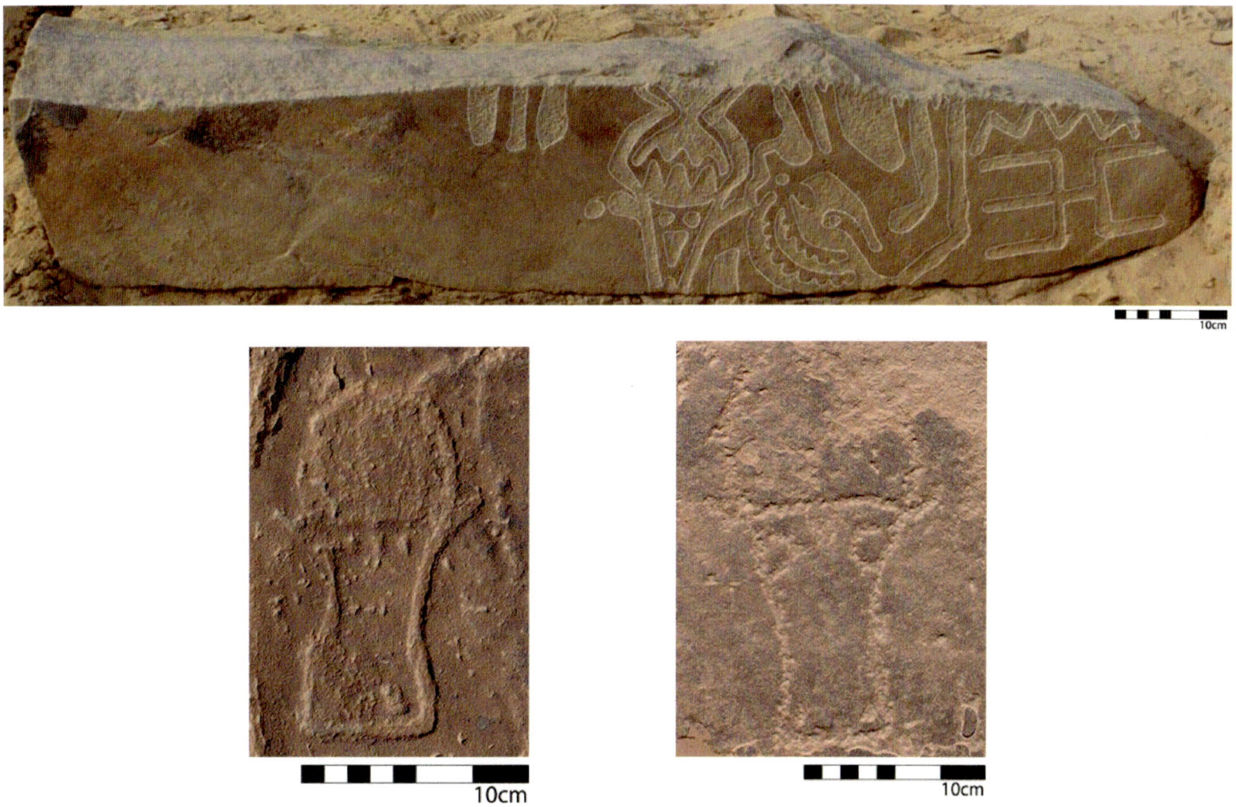

FIGURE 4. **Top:** *stone frieze QU.R.803 (after Luciani 2021a);* **bottom:** *petroglyphs of bucrania from contexts QU.WS.1953 and QU.WS.1967 (photographs and identification after Alqahtani et al., forthcoming).*

than those Iron Age petroglyphs. Since it also lacks epigraphs revealing the deity's name, we cannot be sure that this may in fact have represented a precursor of the god Ṣalm. Possibly, Qurayyah's divine face-type may have been refunctionalized in those Middle Iron Age rock carvings in order to represent the deity Ṣalm. As for the ibex (and the perfume burner), I have discussed elsewhere why they may be represented *tête-bêche* (head to tail) (Luciani 2021a: 281). Moreover, the association of ibex and snake may hint at the 'magical', antivenomous properties of the bezoar goat (Root 2022).

More importantly, I have pointed out that this extraordinary stone frieze proves not only the mastery of Qurayyah's sculptors, but also that they shared with potter-painters a fixed set of iconographic norms in the representations of both animals and cultic paraphernalia such as perfume burners. This is an important indicator of the level of organization and control attained by both masons and potters. The assessed level of coordination together with the sheer size and richness of the pottery assemblage found in this cemetery indicate that in the final Late Bronze Age, the oasis of Qurayyah had become the main producer of a widely recognized, and I would venture as far as to say, iconic, brand of pottery (Luciani, forthcoming, b). Beyond the hundreds of masterfully painted ceramic vessels, three classes of finds, also part of the grave gift, support the hypothesis that the funerary complex in Area R may, in fact, have been the resting place of high-end artisan-potters. Among the finds were: 1) tools for the production of pottery, such as smoothing stones and small mortars for crushing the pigments used for painting the pottery (Fig. 5, top) as well as one hematite stone weight; and 2) the custom of also including ceramic slag and at least one overfired closed-shaped vessel (Luciani 2023a: fig. 11) in the burial kit accompanying the deceased is a constant. Finally, the

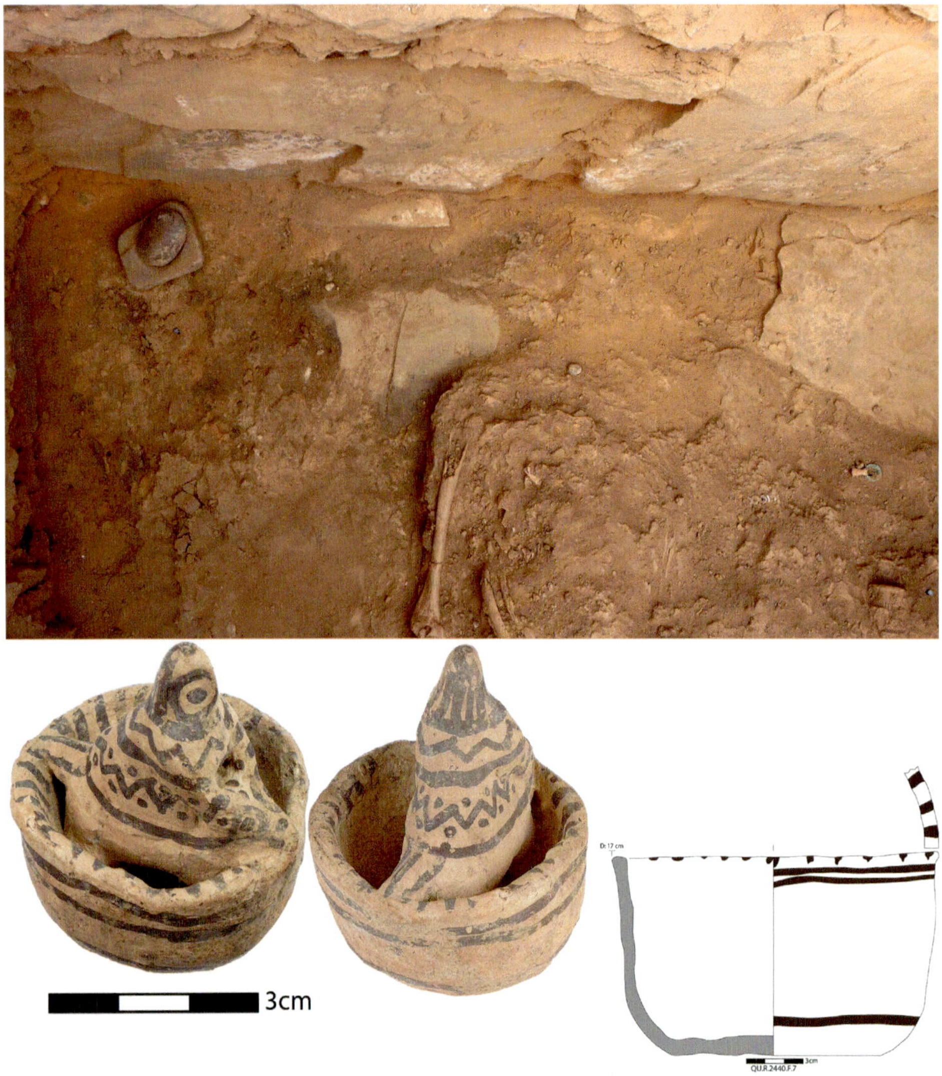

FIGURE 5. **Top:** *small stone mortar with its pestle/smoothing stone QU.R.3490.F.5* in situ, *associated with double inhumation SU 3490 in Room 3218, Unit R-B7 (photograph G. Capasso);* **bottom:** *two views of the monochrome painted miniature clay figurine of a hooded rider in a straight-sided bowl QU.R.2959.F.9 (diam. 4.1 cm; h. 4.7 cm) (photograph C. Bieber) and drawing of straight-sided bowl QU.R.2440.F.7 (graphics D. Klainscek).*

recent discovery among the coroplastic evidence from the burials in unit R-B2 (Room 1493) of 3) a miniature clay figurine (Fig. 5, bottom left) painted with geometric motifs well known from the QPW 4 ceramic assemblage strengthens this interpretation. The figurine represents a person riding a quadruped placed inside a miniature straight-sided bowl. In shape and painted decoration, the miniature bowl looks identical to the life-sized ones (Fig. 5, bottom right) of the QPW 4 series found in the repertoire of the mortuary complex in Area R. It epitomizes the high symbolic value of the QPW 4 ceramic production in the life and afterlife of the oasis.

The assemblage

The repertoire of painted decoration on the QPW 4 vessels is both geometric and figurative. A tally of the attestations of figurative motifs with zoomorphic subject painted on this pottery (Luciani 2021a; 2024) shows a preliminary total of several dozen ostriches, over a dozen bulls and ibexes, five lions, three hyenas, two donkeys, and also including fawn, gerbil, long-tailed shrew, mice, dog, gazelle, fox, spiny-tailed-desert lizard, and many more. Anthropomorphic motifs are less numerous but we now have a total of what could be interpreted as at least ten men and up to four women painted on vessels of the same assemblage. Specifically, two large, barrel-shaped kraters with human representations are the focus of this contribution.

The high investment in time and skilled labour (Rosen 2002; Luciani 2024) put into producing these hundreds of finely decorated vessels is a testament to the high symbolic value of the animal realm and of bichrome painted pottery production in the funerary and cultic world of final Late Bronze Age Qurayyah.

The find context

The kraters each come from one of the two outer areas in front of Unit R-B7 (Fig. 3), a funerary chamber presenting a complex yellow mud-brick construction, which utilized several 2 m-long, thin stone slabs as internal coating and featured canalizations and water basins.

Krater no. 1 (QU.R.2824.F.1) (Fig. 7, above) is complete (h. 28 cm; diam. 18 cm) with the exception of one of the four handles. It was found under the floor of the outer area, outside the south-east corner of the same chamber R-B7.[6] Krater no. 1 was associated with one complete and two fragmentary painted perfume burners, two oversized bowls — one painted on the inside with at least three ostriches — two jugs, one painted with an ibex-and-snake motif and one with an ostrich, a small cup, and an ostrich shell bead.

Krater no. 2 (QU.R.2984.F.4) comes from the area north-west of R-B7. It is an outdoor area in front of the building presenting very well-preserved floors repeatedly laid in different phases. On these strata, in the proximity of the two entrances (south-west and north-east) to R-B7, bichrome painted bowls with one handle and a central passing hole in the bottom, that is, libation bowls, were found *in situ*[7] ready to be used for funerary rites and procedures involving liquids (Fig. 6). With their 20–25 cm diameter they are standard in size, shape, and overall geometric decoration. The extensively painted inner surface, decorated with geometric motifs along the sides of the vessels featured different centrepieces on the base, positioned on the passing hole.[8] Following a suggestion by D. Klainscek (2024: 65), we understand the chequered or criss-cross motifs in this central area of the base to be depictions of carpets.

It is here that krater no. 2 (Fig. 7, bottom) was found broken in large pieces on the floor with the pierced libation bowls. The preserved half of the shoulder (preserved h. 20 cm; diam. 16 cm) features two (different from each other) of the at least four handles characterizing the vessel. Both kraters may be preliminarily described as barrel-shaped, of slightly different size, and with multiple, at times diverse handles. A complete detailed description of the vessels will be presented elsewhere; in this article I focus chiefly on the figurative motifs (Fig. 7), as they help to address and clarify long-standing iconographic questions.

Thus far, by re-analysing published and new evidence (Fig. 8, top), we have concluded that a shirtless male, invariably boasting well-defined pectorals, displayed the hilt (of a dagger?) above a feathered, dome-shaped, short kilt (Klainscek 2024: pl. 9.35b). The

[6] We have yet to complete the excavation and it is possible that in an earlier phase there was an opening here, which was later sealed with mud bricks.

[7] In the case of the north-east entrance a stone niche was constructed to protect libation bowl QU.R.3018.F.1 from the Phase 3 floor. From the same Phase comes a fragment of the same libation bowl type, QU.R.2984.F.3. The complete libation bowl QU.R.2976.F.2 was found in Phase 2 in front of the south-west entrance. While it did not have a complete stone niche, it was leaning on a reddened, small upright stone post. QU.R.2976.41, a fragment of a similar libation bowl, also comes from the same context. There are at least two additional fragments of this bowl typology from two chambers of the adjacent R-B2: from Phase 4 of Room 1493, QU.R.2648.F.2; and from Phase 7 of Room 847 sherd QU.R.2516.23. During the 2024 field season we found an additional four libation bowls extending to the south-west along the outer wall of R-B7 and five along the north-east wall of R-B8, leading to R-B7 and to the location where krater no. 1 was uncovered. All of them were leaning on a small upright stone whose surface was reddened, probably by fire.

[8] Upon closer inspection, D. Klainscek (pers. com., January 2025) remarked that the passing holes were all cut *after* the bowls were painted and fired.

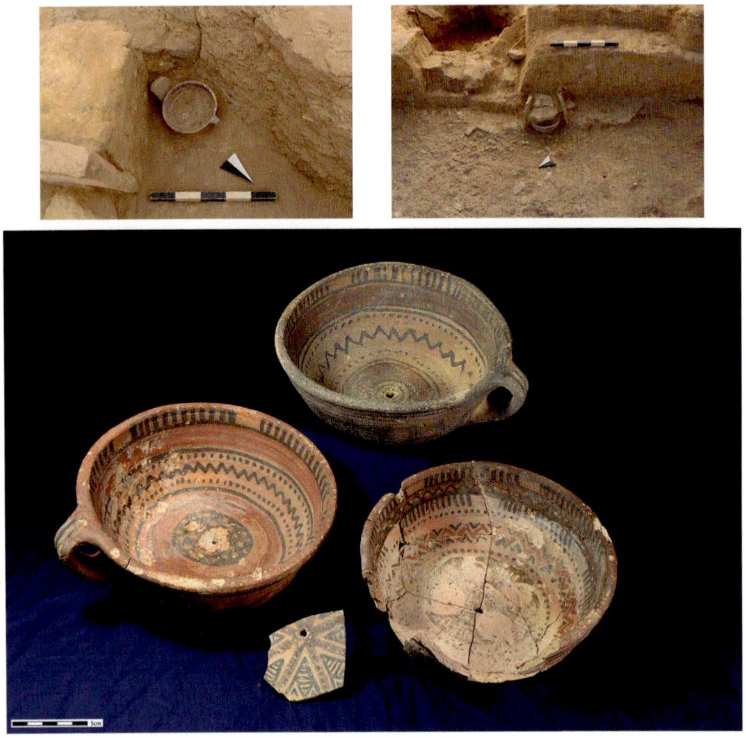

FIGURE 6. Top: *libation bowls QU.R.2976.F.2 and QU.R.3018.F.1* in situ; **bottom:** *the above bowls together with libation bowls QU.R.2984.F.3 and QU.R.2648.F.2 (photographs J. Kahl & E. Weißensteiner).*

head is composed of a central eye and beak-like features, with longer or shorter hair standing up vertically. Both our finds (QU.R.2424.5+; Fig. 8, top) and the one from Barqa el-Hetiye in Jordan (Hauptmann 2007: 152) (Fig. 8, bottom) show that a long set of wavy strands hangs from the man's left side. The Timna Site 200 exemplar, while seeming significantly less elaborate (Rothenberg 1988: fig. 7, nos. 1–2) should be understood as symbolizing the same anthropomorphic motif, because of the identical representation of the head and hair and the position of the arms. However, the iconographic representations on the newly found kraters have opened a totally new perspective.

Krater no. 1 (QU.R.2824.F.1; Fig. 7, top)

Apart from a man, two women and a favoured pin-wheel, 'flower'-motif are also painted in one of the four metopes (Fig. 7, top). The frames of the metope are bichrome, elaborate, and varied. Both women are clad in long robes covering the feet and show off elaborate hairstyles: the second from right exhibits a high pony tail that echoes the conventions of representing notches on ibex horns, ending in tufts that look like a lion's tail. She holds her arms up wider than her coiffure. In the second metope, the woman third from right again sports a notched high pony tail which, here, ends in differently shaped tufts (bull's?). She also adopts a different position, bringing the arms closer to the body and swinging her bull-ponytail in a vast arc. It is not surprising to see in this second metope that her robe is lined with small dots, a diacritic sign we repeatedly see on animal images (Fig. 2, QPW 4, top right: vessel with ostrich; Luciani 2021a; 2024). I have already proposed (Luciani 2021a) to interpret the dotted lines as indicating movement, or water droplets and the shine effect they produce when animals, humans, or objects move. I therefore understand the two metopes on krater no. 1 not as fixed tableaux but as a dynamic sequence of images showing a woman moving. Moreover, the first image of the woman is framed by two four-dotted 'X' symbols. The second image of the woman has a similar symbol on the right-hand side but the one on her left-hand side is a crossed circle surrounded by dots. I propose that the symbol on

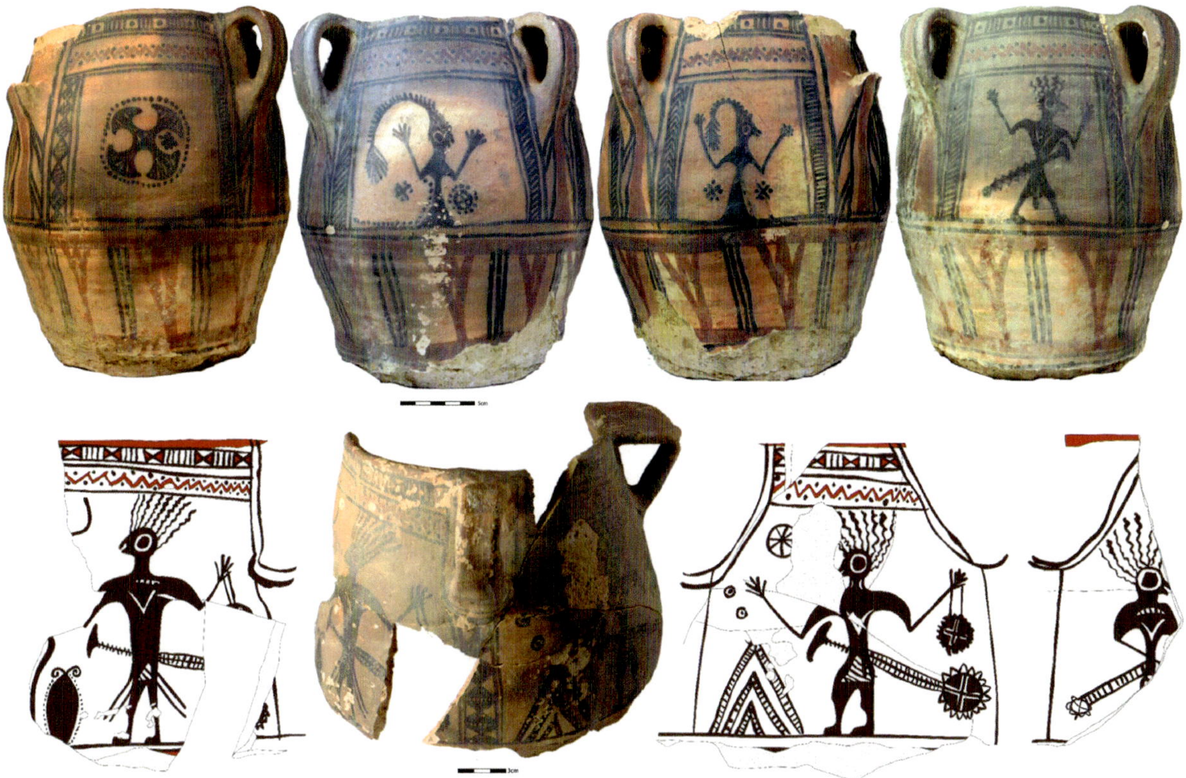

FIGURE 7. Top: *krater QU.R.2824.F.1 (photographs E. Weißensteiner);* **bottom:** *krater QU.R.2984.F.4 (graphics D. Klainscek; photographs E. Weißensteiner).*

her left is nothing other than shorthand for the image found on the third metope (Fig. 7 top, first from left) – a four-petalled pin-wheel 'flower', also surrounded by dots. Interestingly, this four-petalled image also contains a small dotted 'X' symbol.

Even before fully comprehending its meaning, we had noticed that the dotted 'X' symbol is systematically associated with depictions of ostriches (Fig. 2, QPW 4, top right vessel). It is not only attested in Qurayyah but also quite prominently in the Timna Site 200 assemblage (Rothenberg 2019: pl. 4.4.4 nos. 6–8). Last year, one particularly ornate bichrome painted bottle found in Qurayyah revealed that the dotted 'X' symbolizes the bird's spit. Spitting is part of ostriches' habits when they regurgitate food to feed their young, when furious, to convey a message, or to show dominance. They also spit worn-out stones and pebbles that they have used in their gizzards to grind food. The dotted 'X' is therefore one of the shorthand symbols that form part of the accurate graphic 'language' representing the movement and behaviour of animals and humans that we see emerging on the iconography of this pottery manufacture.

If this is true, I propose to explain the dotted 'X' both next to the woman and inside the large four-petalled 'flower' (Fig. 7, top) as a symbolic stand-in for moving ostriches (Fig. 2, QPW 4, top right vessel). The fourth metope of krater no. 1 depicts a man, as usual baring a very muscular torso, with beak-like features and curly hair rising up. Unusually, in this instance the man is stark naked, showing off exaggerated, detailed genitals (Fig. 7, top, right-hand side). The elongated spiked feature departing from his waist is still not entirely clear. Hilts located in that position are normally interpreted as weapons – daggers or swords. However, in this case the supposed sword-scabbard is not only bizarrely spiked, but it terminates with a circular dot.

In summary, I interpret the illustrations in the metopes of krater no. 1 as depicting not static tableaux but moving images (the women, the 'flower', the spitting ostrich symbol) as part of a performance, potentially linked to a funerary ritual. The representation of markedly different anthropomorphic figures, including the emphasis on genitals, indicates that connoting distinct genders participating in the action was of paramount importance.

Krater no. 2 (QU.R.2984.F.4; Fig. 7, bottom)

In the second krater, the man (or men) in the different metopes are not naked but wear different types of kilts. Their hair rises up just as the naked man's on krater no. 1. Two of the figures display a necklace or dress decoration on the upper chest. They, too, have fastened to their waist the hilt of long objects that terminate in circular shapes, this time larger circles, subdivided in quarters, resembling the spokes of a wheel. In two cases it can clearly be seen that a small version of this spoked wheel hangs from the man's left hand. These men, too, are accompanied by additional symbols which, however, remain to be deciphered. Moreover, in the case of krater no. 2 only about half of the vessel's rim and shoulder are preserved. We see three men with different attires but we cannot exclude that in the other half of the vessel at least one man was represented naked, as in krater no. 1. It is possible that the multiple images of the man with diverse kilts and garb — and in one case a modified position of the arms — indicate not distinct individuals but rather the same person changing attire at different phases of the ritual.

Proposed interpretation

Comparison with previously known images of men painted on QPW 4/QPW pottery seems to suggest that the item at the man's waist may not necessarily be a sword or long dagger. In the specimens from Barqa el-Hetiye and Qurayyah (Fig. 8), the hilt does not seem to continue into a dagger. In both cases the lines departing from the waist are shown as soft and wavy. In a large bowl found in Al-ʿUla,[9] at the end of these long, wavy lines is a four-spoked wheel, very similar to those visible on our krater no. 2. On this basis, I would like to propose that we should interpret these wavy/spiked lines as representing the reins of a chariot and the hilt as the device for fastening them at the waist in order to leave the charioteers' hands free. While it is difficult to imagine wheeled chariots in the rugged terrain of the desert, chariot hunting — the quintessential icon of Late Bronze Age upper-class ostentation — was also a cherished motif in the remote deserts of north-west Arabia, as can be observed on multiple rock-art panels. Two examples are particularly significant because they are located at the Wādī Meneʾiyeh mining sites in the southern Negev. Here, in the famous Hathor shrine at Timna Site 200, hundreds of Qurayyah Painted Ware (= QPW 4, Fig. 2) sherds were uncovered, thus testifying to chronological contemporaneity and cultural relations (Rothenberg 2019) with Qurayyah's Area R. Timna Site 25, located close to Site 200, is peculiar. According to Rothenberg (2003), it is the only location in the area with pre-Roman rock engravings. The two very extended tableaux are not only pecked and engraved but also painted in two different colours. Because they are at the entrance of a mine-shaft dated to the Egyptian New Kingdom, Rothenberg (2003: 10) proposed to attribute them to the late second millennium BC, thus perfectly matching Qurayyah's Area R chronology.

The rock-art panels show two vast hunting scenes with ostriches, ibexes, oryxes, and gazelles. In at least five instances, we can identify chariots with four-spoked wheels, driven by two charioteers, who either keep their arms up or hold a bow and arrow or an axe (Fig. 9). In all cases, in order to have the hands free, the reins of the chariot are tied around the waist.

Since the men represented on kraters nos. 1 and 2 also hold their hands up, I propose that the symbol, found on our pottery, of the four-spoked circle connected to their waist with wavy lines may be understood as evocative of chariots' reins in a hunting scene. Moreover, the associated symbol for ostriches — the four dotted Xs mentioned above — should also be seen as an additional reference to hunting, as ostriches are one of the most prized desert prey for both their feathers and their eggs.[10] In addition, the discovery in our burials of at least

[9] Jérôme Rohmer and Shadi Shabo kindly showed it to me during a visit on site. I wish to thank them for allowing me to mention this detail ahead of their publication.

[10] Gorzalczany and Rosen (2022) offer an important update on the role of ostriches and ostrich eggs in archaeological contexts.

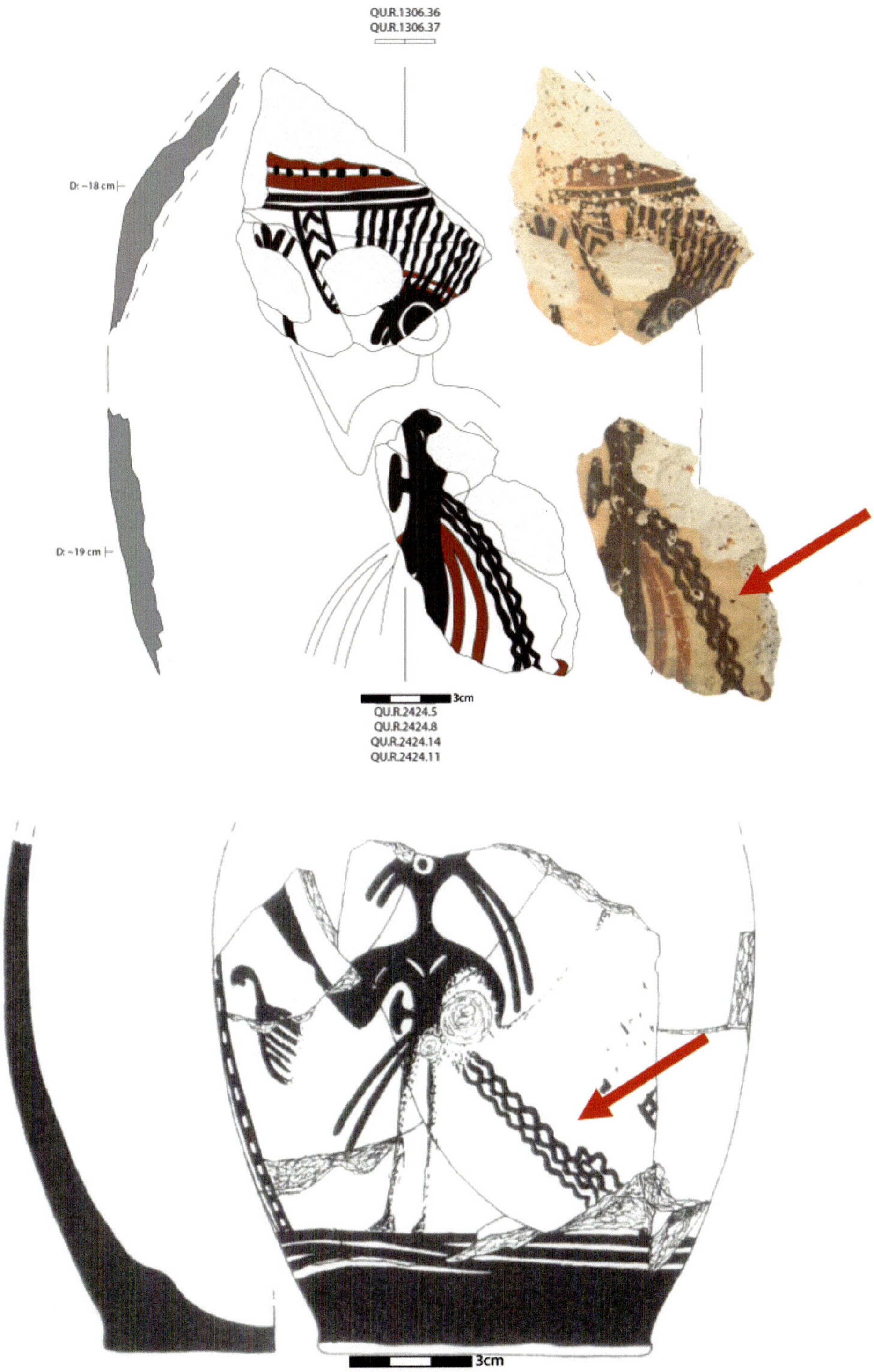

Figure 8. Top: *sherds of closed-shaped vessel (QU.R.1306.36+ and QU.R.2424.5+) with painted anthropomorphic motif (graphics D. Klainscek; photographs E. Weißensteiner);* **bottom:** *base of closed-shaped vessel from Barqa el-Hetiye, Jordan (after Hauptmann 2007: 152).*

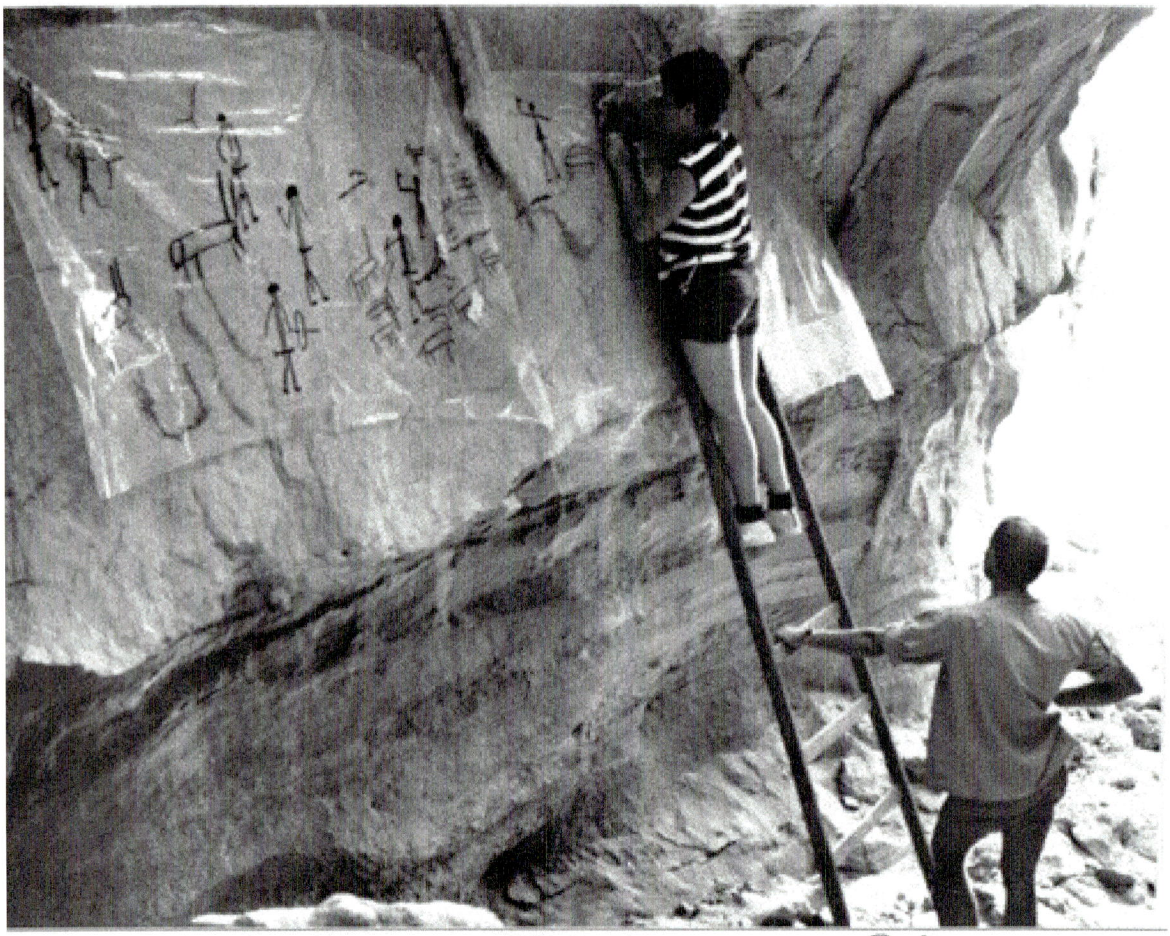

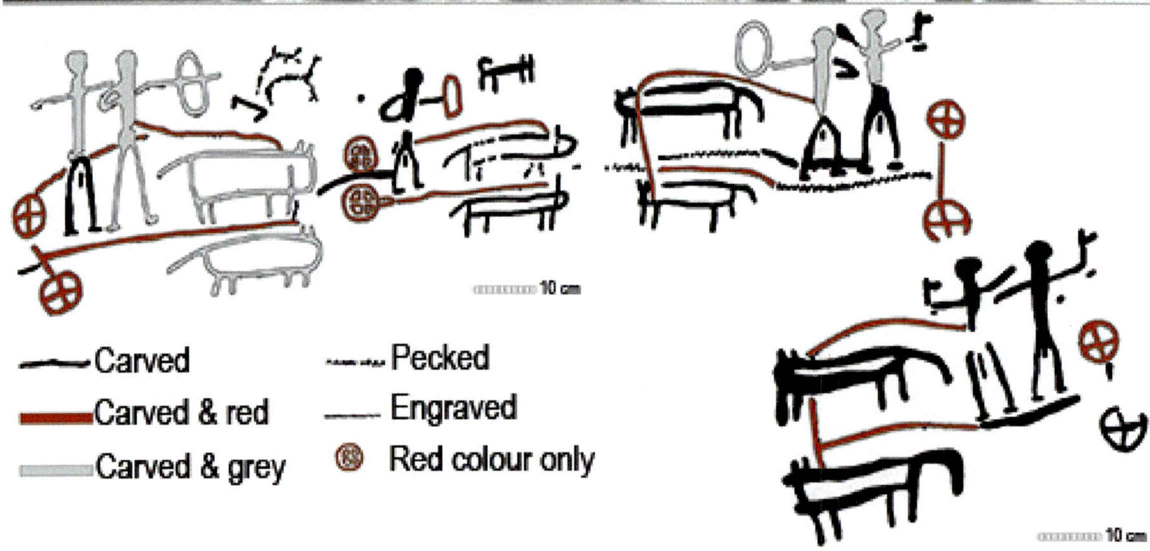

FIGURE 9. Top: *recording the petroglyphs at the entrance of the cave at Timna, Site 25;*
bottom: *drawing of five of the attested chariot hunting scenes (after Rothenberg 1972: 123, fig. 38 & pl. 58).*

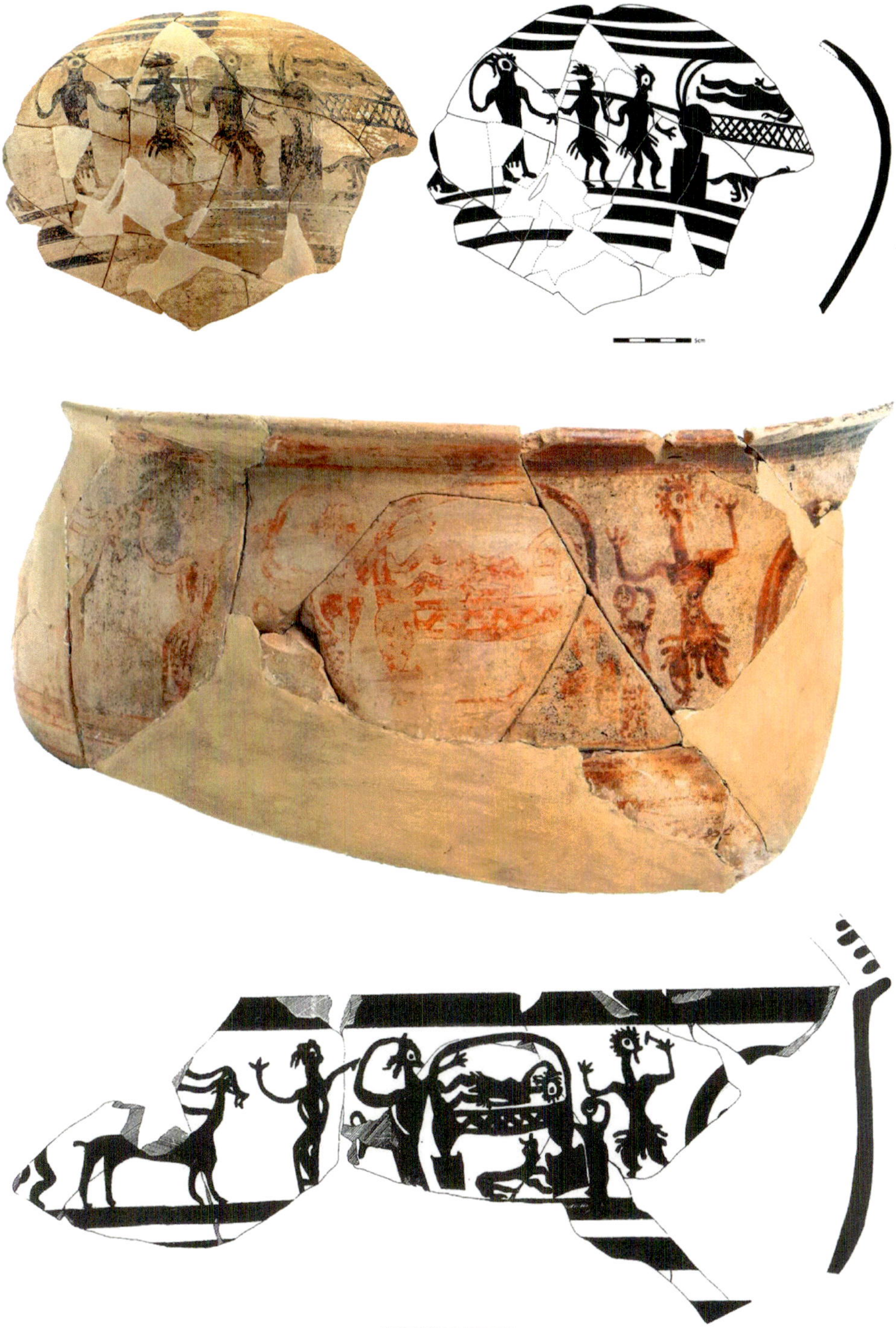

FIGURE 10. **Top:** ekphora *monochrome painted on a krater from Trypes/Kladeos;* **bottom:** prothesis *monochrome painted from a closed-shaped vessel from Aghia Triada, Elis (after Vikatou 2018: 261–262).*

eight specimens of iron arrowheads and spearheads and of large, square nails that could very well be chariot bolts, seems to support this interpretation. Ostrich egg fragments number in the hundreds.

If we accept that the painted motifs discussed above may have referred to processions and/or chariot hunting as an appropriate theme to be painted on kraters that were part of a funerary gift, we are immediately reminded that in this age, in the eastern Mediterranean and Greater Levant hundreds of exemplars of Mycenaean kraters circulated with the chariot depicted as the central subject theme. In Cyprus and the Levant Mycenaean chariot kraters are mostly found in funerary contexts. Recht and Morris (2021: 22) recently pointed out that the entire eastern Mediterranean 'readily understood and widely shared' the notion that horses and chariots were associated with high status and that the chariot scene could refer to both elite hunting and funerary processions. Therefore, while in style and composition Mycenaean chariot kraters look nothing like the Qurayyah ones, the material support (pottery krater) and the theme of a funerary ritual involving hunting ostriches from a chariot may very well be closely related.

Two Aegean vessels, successors of Mycenaean kraters, dated to the final twelfth century BC — a date that overlaps with our Area R kraters — present fitting examples (Fig. 10) of explicitly narrative depictions of two phases of the funerary ceremony. Using Homeric accounts, they have been called *prothesis* and *ekphora* (Vikatou 2018).[11] In the *prothesis* the ceremony is headed by a muscular man, with an axe in his raised hand, wearing a feathered kilt and with exaggerated genitals, the dead body laid out on a bier and two women mourners following with a sacrificial goat. In the *ekphora* two men wearing feathered kilts carry the bier underneath which lies a dog. One woman follows. These younger Aegean vessels feature more stylistic and content similarities with the Qurayyah vessel presented here than with Mycenaean chariot kraters. Visible similarities comprise stylistic and content conventions: the one-eyed head with raised hair, the feathered kilt, and the exposed male genitals. However, exact parallels remain limited. The syntax is also basically different: a narrative developed on an open canvas in the Aegean versus the narrowly defined metopes in Qurayyah. The explicit depiction of the dead body is also not duplicated in Arabia. However, in both cases a naked man and two long-robed women are represented as moving and participating in a procession. A potential reference to a chariot, alluding to the funerary procession (or elite hunting?) may also have been present.

Conclusions

All stylistic and syntax differences notwithstanding, structural and systemic commonalities exist between the Aegean funerary kraters and the contemporary Qurayyahite ones. There is a common practice at the end of the second millennium BC of painting complex figurative scenes on mortuary pottery kraters; of developing elaborate, clearly gendered[12] depictions of humans on exceptional vessels used by the elite and, in spite of Qurayyah's rigid metope-syntax, there is a comparable intention to represent movement and the performative aspects of the ritual, achieved through the use of dotted lines and changing scenes.

Susan Sherratt (1999: 188, 195) writing about Mycenaean chariot kraters highlighted that 'pottery's ability to encapsulate desirable social and cultural values within a readily accessible and expendable medium' could have served as 'aspirational substitute for sub-elites who did not have access to real chariots' (Recht & Morris 2021: 127). Widely imported in the Levant and Cyprus, chariot kraters were incorporated into pre-existing local strategies of feasting in funerary contexts (2021: 122) and used as added value, high-status paraphernalia. In the broader Levant and Syria, Late Bronze Age local vessels painted with anthropomorphic themes are extremely rare[13] and while cultic, they are

[11] For the continuation of this iconography well into the first millennium BC in the Aegean see Vikatou 2018 and Huber 2023 with previous references.

[12] Campbell (2008: 71), although analysing much older (Late Neolithic) pottery holds that, 'Gender representation on vessels was relevant in a context in which identity was something open to negotiation and change. When that ability for identity to be malleable and changeable became more restricted, the need of representing it on ceramics was reduced'. For M. Verhoeven (2002), the depiction of wild animals in ritual contexts 'was a metaphor and mechanism for exerting gender control over society, as well as metaphysically, over nature'.

[13] From Ugarit: one rim of a krater (?) with a hunter holding a deer by the leash fastened to the waist (Caubet 2022) and one mug with the scene of an offering to the god El (Yon 2006: 147); from Tell Brak: one sherd with two standing persons (hunters?) (Mallowan 1947: 244,

not necessarily associated with funerary contexts. Instead, notwithstanding the profound geographic and cultural distance between the Aegean and north-west Arabia, the parallels in the choice of supports (pottery kraters), themes, iconography, and mortuary context likely indicate shared values and habits in funerary practices of local elites, and are evidence of north-west Arabia's role in the interconnectivity at play in the eastern Mediterranean and Greater Levant at the end of the second millennium BC.

Acknowledgements

I am deeply grateful to Dr A. Al-Zahrani, Dr A. Alotaibi, A. Abualhassan, and M. Alahmari of the Heritage Commission of the Saudi Ministry of Culture for over ten years of exemplary cooperation in the Qurayyah Joint Archaeological Project and for permission to publish. I am very happy to acknowledge PhD candidate D. Klainscek, not only for her drawings but for reading an earlier draft of this paper, for so accurately analysing all the pottery in Qurayyah, and always being ready to act as my sounding board — even when she did not share all my interpretations; F. Spitaler for preparing the orthophoto of Area R; J. Kahl for the QGIS plans; C. Blätterbinder for digitizing the pottery drawings; Dr K. Al-Bahloul for commenting on the Ugarit potters; and B. Huber (2023) for discussing his MA thesis with me.

This article was written within the frame of the International WEAVE Project ANAPAN, 'A New Approach to Pottery of Arabia and its Neighbors. Understanding Technology and Commercial Networks in the Greater Levant', funded by the Austrian Science Fund FWF under project no. I6562.

References

Alqahtani M.H.M., Al-Sulaimi M.O. & Abualhassan A.M. (forthcoming). The 2019 epigraphic and petroglyphs survey of Qurayyah's plateau. *ATLAL*.

Campbell S. 2008. Gendered representation and pottery in later Mesopotamian prehistory. Pages 53–76 in D. Bolger (ed.), *Gender through time in the Ancient Near East*. (Gender and archaeology series). Lanham, MD: Altamira Press.

Caubet A. 2022. From Arslan Tash to Ugarit. Remarks on ivory beds, suckling cow and grazing deer. Pages 3–20 and colour plates I–II in D. Wicke & J. Curtis (eds), *Ivories, rock reliefs and Merv. Studies on the Ancient Near East in honour of Georgina Herrmann*. Münster: Zaphon.

Greenberg R. 2019. *The archaeology of the Bronze Age Levant. From urban origins to the demise of city-states, 3700–1000 BCE*. Cambridge: Cambridge University Press.

Gorzalczany A. & Rosen B. 2022. Ostriches and people in archaeological contexts in the southern Levant and beyond. *Levant* 54/1: 29–49.

Hauptmann A. 2008. *The archaeometallurgy of copper — Evidence from Faynan*. Berlin: Springer.

Huber B. 2023. Sepulkrale Ikonographie in spätmykenischer und geometrisch-früharchaischer Zeit. Eine vergleichende Studie. MA thesis, University of Vienna. [Unpublished.]

Intilia A. 2016. Qurayyah Painted Ware: A reassessment of 40 years of research on its origins, chronology and distribution. Pages 172–256 in M. Luciani (ed.), *The archaeology of North Arabia. Oases and landscapes. Proceedings of the International Congress held at the University of Vienna, December, 5th–8th 2013*. (OREA Archaeological Series, 4). Vienna: Austrian Academy of Sciences.

Klainscek D. 2024. Two pottery assemblages from Area R, Qurayyah: A preliminary characterization of the final Late Bronze Age to initial Iron Age ceramics. MA thesis, University of Vienna. [Unpublished.]

Loud G. 1948. *Megiddo II. Seasons of 1935–39*. (Oriental Institute Publications, 62). Chicago: Oriental Institute of the University of Chicago.

Luciani M. 2014. Qurayyah in northwestern Arabia. Archaeological research between Levant and Hejaz, poster presented at the 9th International Congress on the Archaeology of the Ancient Near East, June 9–13, 2014, University of Basel, Switzerland. Page 153 in *Proceedings of the Internal Congresses on the Archaeology of the Ancient Near East*. Wiesbaden: Harrassowitz.

Luciani M. 2019. Qurayyah. Pages 140–155 in A. Capodiferro & S. Colantonio (eds), *Roads of Arabia:*

pl. 48 no. 12); from Ashkelon: a pictorial krater with 'a figure sitting astride a vehicle with one six-spoked wheel, probably representing an abbreviated chariot' (Stager 2006: 174); from Megiddo: the so-called 'Orpheus jug' and the zoomorphic spout with kilted persons holding axes in the raised hands painted on the neck (Loud 1948: pls 76 and 246D).

Archaeological treasures from Saudi Arabia. Catalogue of the Exhibition at Museo Nazionale Romano, Diocletian Baths in Rome. Milan: Electa.

Luciani M. 2021a. Canons of iconography: Water, animals, gods and humans. Pages 277–288 in C. Bührig, M. van Ess, I. Gerlach, A. Hausleiter & B. Müller-Neuhof (eds), *Klänge der Archäologie. Festschrift for Ricardo Eichmann*. Wiesbaden: Harrassowitz.

Luciani M. 2021b. On the formation of 'urban' oases in Arabia: New perspectives from the North West. Pages 89–118 in M. Luciani (ed.), *The archaeology of the Arabian Peninsula 2: Connecting the evidence. Proceedings of the international workshop held at the 10th International Congress on the Archaeology of the Ancient Near East in Vienna on April 25, 2016.* (OREA, 19). Vienna: Österreichische Akademie der Wissenschaften.

Luciani M. 2023a. Qurayyah (al-): Thematic dictionary of ancient Arabia. Online edition 2023. Accessed on 2 March 2024. Available at https://ancientarabia.huma-num.fr/public/dictionary/definition/qurayya-al doi: https://doi.org/10.60667/tdaa-0138

Luciani M. 2023b. Archaeology in the land of Midian. Excavating the oasis of Qurayyah. *Biblical Archaeology Review* 39/4: 32–39.

Luciani M. 2023c. Transitions in material culture of the 2nd millennium BCE: The Middle Bronze to Late Bronze shift seen from northwest Arabia. Pages 53–77 in A. Hausleiter (ed.), *Material worlds: Interdisciplinary approaches to contacts and exchange in the ancient Near East. Proceedings of the workshop held at the Institute for the Study of the Ancient World (ISAW), New York University 7th March 2016*. Oxford: Archaeopress.

Luciani M. 2024. Farther horizons: The Late Bronze Age to Iron Age transition beyond the southern Levant. Pages 555–590 in M.G. Masetti-Rouault, I. Calini, R. Hawley & L. D'Alfonso (eds), *Ancient western Asia beyond the paradigm of collapse and regeneration (1200–900 BC). Proceedings of the NYU-PSL International Colloquium, Paris Institut National d'Histoire et de l'Art, April 16–17, 2019*. New York: Institute for the Study of the Ancient World/New York University Press.

Luciani M. (forthcoming, a). The walled 'urban' oases phenomenon in northwest Arabia – 4th to 2nd millennium BCE. In S.T. Laursen, D. Kennet & L. Weeks (eds), *Bronze Age Arabia*. Brill.

Luciani M. (forthcoming, b). Beyond beauty: Jewelry, brands and the creation of identity in Arabia. In J.S. Baldi, F. Balossi Restelli & P. Fragnoli (eds), *Proceedings of the 13th ICAANE workshop on serializing-standardizing. Paléorient*, Special Issue.

Luciani M. & Alsaud A.S. 2018. The new archaeological joint project on the site of Qurayyah, north-west Arabia: Results of the first two excavation seasons. *Proceedings of the Seminar for Arabian Studies* 48: 165–183.

Lüthgens C., Luciani M., Prochazka S., Firla G., Hoelzmann P. & Abualhassan A.M. 2023. Watering the desert: Oasis hydroarchaeology, geochronology and functionality in northern Arabia. *The Holocene* 33/5: 562–580.

Magee P. 2014. *The Archaeology of prehistoric Arabia. Adaptation and social formation from the Neolithic to the Iron Age*. Cambridge: Cambridge University Press.

Mallowan M.E.L. 1947. Excavations at Brak and Chagar Bazar. *Iraq* 9: 1–87, 89–259, i–iv.

Parr P.J. 1982. Contacts between north west Arabia and Jordan in the Late Bronze and Iron Ages. Pages 127–133 in A. Hadidi (ed.), *Studies in the history and archaeology of Jordan.* i. Amman: Department of Antiquities, Hashemite Kingdom of Jordan/London: Routledge & Kegan Paul.

Parr P.J. 1988. Pottery of the late second millennium B.C. from north west Arabia and its historical implications. Pages 73–89 in D.T. Potts (ed.), *Araby the blest. Studies in Arabian archaeology*. (CNI Publications, 7). Copenhagen: Museum Tusculaneum Press.

Parr P.J., Harding G.L. & Dayton J.E. 1970. Preliminary survey in N.W. Arabia, 1968. *Bulletin of the Institute of Archaeology, University of London* 8/9: 193–242.

Philip G. 2008. The Early Bronze I–III Ages. Pages 161–226 in R. Adams (ed.), *Jordan: An archaeological reader*. London: Equinox.

Recht L. & Morris C.E. 2021. Chariot kraters and horse–human relations in Late Bronze Age Greece and Cyprus. *The Annual of the British School at Athens* 116: 95–132.

Root M.C. 2022. The Arc of the Horn Part I: Ibexes as icons of cultural imperative in early Iranian glyptic. Pages 94–100 in L. Battini (ed.), *Image and identity in the ancient Near East. Papers* in memoriam *Pierre Amiet*. Oxford: Archaeopress.

Rosen S.A. 2002. Invention as the mother of necessity: An archaeological examination of the origins and development of pottery and metallurgy in the

Levant. Pages 11–21 in R. Harrison, M. Gillespie & M. Peuramki-Brown (eds), *Eureka: The archaeology of innovation and science. Proceedings of the twenty-ninth annual conference of the Archaeological Association of the University of Calgary*. Calgary: Archaeological Association of the University of Calgary.

Rothenberg B. 1972. *Timna. Valley of the biblical copper mines*. London: Thames & Hudson.

Rothenberg B. 1988. *The Egyptian mining temple at Timna. Researches in the Arabah 1959-1984. The Arabah Project sponsored by Stiftung Volkswagenwerk*. i. London: Institute for Archaeo-Metallurgical Studies.

Rothenberg B. 2003. Egyptian chariots, Midianites from Hijaz/Midian (northwest Arabia) and Amalekites from the Negev in the Timna mines. Rock drawings in the ancient copper mines of the Arabah — New aspects of the region's history II. *International Association for Mission Studies* 23: 9–14.

Rothenberg B. 2019. Late Bronze Age II/Iron Age IA Midianite pottery. Pages 383–387 in S. Gitin (ed.), *The ancient pottery of Israel and its neighbors from the Middle Bronze Age through the Late Bronze Age*. iii. Jerusalem: Israel Exploration Society.

Sherratt S. 1999. *E pur si muove:* pots, markets and values in the second millennium Mediterranean. Pages 163–211 in J.P. Crielaard, V. Stissi & G. van Wijngaarden (eds), *Complex past of pottery. Production, circulation and consumption of Mycenaean and Greek pottery (sixteenth to early fifth centuries BC). Proceedings of the ARCHON international conference held in Amsterdam, 8-9 November 1996*. Amsterdam: J.C. Gieben.

Stager L.E. 2006. Chariot fittings from Philistine Ashkelon. Pages 169–176 in S. Gitin, J.E. Wright & J.P. Dessel (eds), *Confronting the past. Archaeological and historical essays on ancient Israel in Honor of William G. Dever*. Winona Lake, IN: Eisenbrauns.

Tourtet F., Daszkiewicz M. & Hausleiter A. 2021. Pottery from Tayma: Chronostratigraphy, archaeometric studies, cultural interaction. Pages 43–87 in M. Luciani (ed.), *The archaeology of the Arabian Peninsula 2: Connecting the evidence. Proceedings of the international workshop held at the 10th International Congress on the Archaeology of the Ancient Near East in Vienna on April 25, 2016*. (OREA, 19), Vienna: Ősterreichische Akademie der Wissenschaften.

Verhoeven M. 2002. Ritual and ideology in the pre-pottery Neolithic B of the Levant and South East Asia. *Cambridge Archaeological Journal* 12/2: 233–258.

Vikatou O. 2018. Kontinuitäten. *Prothesis* und *Ekphora* in der Kunst. Pages 260–263 in Badisches Landesmuseum Karlsruhe (ed.), *Mykene. Die sagenhafte Welt des Agamemnon*. Darmstadt: Philipp von Zabern.

Yon M. 2006. *The city of Ugarit at Tell Ras Shamra*. Winona Lake, IN: Eisenbrauns.

Author's address

Marta Luciani, Department of Prehistoric and Historical Archaeology, Franz-Klein-Gasse 1, A-1190 Vienna, Austria.
e-mail marta.luciani@univie.ac.at

Proceedings of the Seminar for Arabian Studies 54 (2025): 168–182

Can community-based participatory research enhance our understanding of Arabian archaeology?

Selin Nugent, Jennifer Swerida, Nora al-Aati, Reilly Jensen & Cindy Srnka

Summary

We examine the scholarly and local implications of integrating traditional fieldwork with participatory approaches in Arabian archaeology through a case study of community outreach and interview research by the Bat Archaeological Project. Our work builds on research from community archaeology with the aim of building collaborations with the Bat community and designing research methodologies around local needs and interests. Bat is of international importance as a UNESCO World Heritage Site with decades of foreign mission-led archaeological research. The community holds the social memory of all archaeological work at Bat, both discoveries and their modes of practice. There is great interest and pride in the research that has taken place, but a feeling of disconnection from the findings. They are also keenly aware of the concerns of preservation and outreach. Based on our findings, we discuss models for local engagement, best practices, challenges, and how engagement can be integrated into scholarly outputs. As foreign scholars, we are in a privileged position to support local learning and opportunities. We argue that formally integrating these approaches into archaeological research in Arabia is timely and presents opportunities to both enhance research rigour and build sustainable community relationships within the region.

Keywords: community research, participatory methods, archaeological research design, outreach, Oman

Introduction

This paper examines the scholarly and local implications of integrating traditional fieldwork with approaches that encourage participation and engagement within the practice and management of Arabian archaeological research, particularly in the context of foreign researcher-led missions. By reviewing prior archaeological practices and the evolving direction of heritage research in the region, we explore how the application of community-based methodologies can reshape archaeological practice. The case study of the Bat Archaeological Project (BAP) serves as a focal point to illustrate the potential of intentionally designed and iterative community engagement. This approach aims not only to broaden the audience and increase local investment in archaeological research but also to shift the research process from one of knowledge extraction to one rooted in inclusivity, respect, and mutual benefit.

Building on lessons from previous seasons' community outreach efforts, BAP trialled a new community heritage research programme during the 2023–2024 field season. This programme was designed systematically to monitor the project's impact on and relationship with the local community in Bat, located in north-western Oman. By incorporating local voices and preferences into both the execution and communication of archaeological research, the project aims to create a more reciprocal and responsive research environment. The data gathered through this programme will inform future engagement initiatives and allow for the continued alignment of archaeological research strategies with local interests and needs. This evolving model of participatory archaeology underscores the need for foreign-led missions to actively and systematically listen to/integrate community members and accordingly to adapt their methods and scholarly communication in ways that foster sustainable, community-centred research.

While there are undeniable challenges and cultural incongruences in implementing such participatory models, this paper contends that the approach taken through BAP has already laid the foundation for intensifying community-led research and engagement in future archaeological practice and heritage management. Rather than concluding with a definitive answer to the question posed in the title of this paper, we call for ongoing dialogue and critical reflection, especially from predominantly Western researchers operating in the region, to ensure that local communities are centred and elevated throughout the research process.

Community-based Arabian archaeology

Our research grew out of dialogues with Oman ministry of Heritage and Tourism partners at Bat, alongside insights from scholarly literature on community-based participatory research (CBPR). Particularly influential is Sonya Atalay's *Community-based archaeology*, which provides a comprehensive framework for conducting research *with*, *by*, and *for* local communities. A participatory approach to archaeology emphasizes knowledge sharing and democratizing the research process with the local community, connected to a research site to ensure more accurate and meaningful findings (Atalay 2012). Additionally, how this research subsequently informs our actions in managing the Bat Archaeological Project draws inspiration from the scholarship of heritage justice, as developed by researchers such as Charlotte Joy (2020) and Veysel Apaydin (2020). The heritage justice framework goes beyond critiquing past heritage practices to consider compensatory mechanisms for past injustices, making it particularly relevant for sites with a long history of foreign-led research, such as Bat, which has been under continuous study by international missions since 1972/1973.

While our research builds upon CBPR literature from diverse international contexts, we recognize that this theoretical framework requires adaptation to the specific cultural contexts of the Arabian Peninsula and the distinct variations between local communities. A critical part of this adaptation involves tailoring participatory approaches to fit regional socio-cultural realities, while still striving to democratize archaeological practice and increase inclusivity. The participatory approach also presents the opportunity to critically assess and address through research management the impact of long-term foreign research on local heritage, an issue particularly pertinent to sites like Bat, which have seen decades of external archaeological influence (Joy 2020).

The cultural context of the Arabian Peninsula is highly diverse, with varying attitudes towards community participation in archaeological research across different countries and regions. Community-based archaeology and outreach by foreign research teams is not new to this area. Notable projects such as the Origins of Doha and Qatar Project (Morgan et al. 2022), Karen Exell and Trinidad Rico's work on Arabian heritage (Exell & Rico 2013; 2014), and Ruth Young's ethno-archaeological study of the Bat mud-brick village (Young et al. 2018; Young 2019) are key examples of Western-led initiatives that have employed community participation and ethnographic methods, dating back to the 2010s.

Despite these efforts, the publication and dissemination of knowledge on community-based archaeology in the Arabian Peninsula remains under-represented in scholarly literature. Few studies explicitly focus on the adaptation of archaeological research to incorporate local perspectives. Even successful community outreach efforts are often under-reported, which presents a challenge for furthering discourse on participatory research in the region. Moreover, as Morgan et al. (2022) point out in their discussion of CBPR integration, achieving wider community buy-in and engagement across the entire research pipeline remains a significant challenge. The very definition of 'local community' can be highly contested, and eliciting public discussion can risk self-censorship or pose dangers to vulnerable groups (Morgan et al. 2022).

In the broader context of heritage and tourism in the Arabian Peninsula, community engagement and the recognition of local communities' value in promoting sustainable social and economic development are becoming increasingly important in national heritage strategies (Freer & Kherfi 2020; Sampieri et al. 2024). Archaeologists working in the region are, therefore, well positioned to contribute critically to these initiatives, drawing from first-hand experiences in community engagement and participatory research practices. This shift emphasizes the importance of incorporating evidence-based approaches that prioritize inclusivity and local agency in shaping the future of archaeological research.

The ability to conduct community-based research is, like any other archaeological work, dependent on navigating support from national governments and openness from communities who may express hesitation in involvement. This research would not have been possible without long-term discussion and the specific socio-political conditions that made documenting the social impact of archaeological heritage of interest to wider stakeholders. We hope by sharing our unique experience at Bat others may be motivated to integrate and document community-based approaches in their archaeological research in the region.

Case study: Bat Archaeological Project

The Bat Archaeological Project (BAP), working within the UNESCO World Heritage Site of Bat, Khutum, and Al-Ayn in north-west Oman, has a long and complex history of foreign-led archaeological missions, deeply embedded in the community's social memory. The site's rich concentration of Early Bronze Age tombs, tower platforms, and domestic settlements has attracted international archaeologists since the early 1970s (de Cardi, Collier & Doe 1976; Frifelt 1976). This section reviews the history of research at Bat, which informs our current approach to community engagement and participatory archaeological practice.

During the 2023–2024 field season, we had the pleasure of welcoming Jens Vellev, a member of the first Danish expedition to Bat, back to the site fifty years after his initial visit. As the expedition photographer, Vellev shared photographs from his time working alongside Karen Frifelt, who led the Danish team's investigations into the funerary and settlement landscape in 1972 (Frifelt 1976; 1985; 2002). Frifelt's work continued until the site's designation as a World Heritage site in 1989. Since then, Bat has continued to be a focus for foreign archaeological teams, with British, German, Japanese, French, and American researchers contributing to the exploration and study of the site (Brunswig 1989; de Cardi, Collier & Doe 1976; Desruelles et al. 2016; Kondo et al. 2016; Schmidt & Döpper 2014; Swerida, Cable & Dollarhide 2020; Swerida, Dollarhide & Jensen 2021; Thornton, Cable & Possehl 2016).

The current Bat Archaeological Project was established in 2007 under the leadership of the late Gregory Possehl. Initially focused on the excavation of the site's Early Bronze Age tower monuments (Thornton, Cable & Possehl 2016), the project has since expanded its research scope to include themes ranging from the Neolithic to the recent past, addressing both micro-archaeological inquiries and broader landscape studies within and beyond the oasis (Böhme & al-Sabri 2011; Cable & al-Jabri 2018; Dollarhide 2019; Swerida 2022; Swerida & Thornton 2019; Swerida, Cable & Dollarhide 2020; Swerida, Dollarhide & Jensen 2021; Swerida et al., in press, a; in press, b).

In 2013, BAP invited Ruth Young to conduct an archaeological and ethnographic study of the Bat mud-brick village and its surrounding community (Young et al. 2018; Young 2019). This project introduced ethnographic methodologies into archaeological research and laid the groundwork for further inquiry into the intersections of archaeology, heritage, and tourism.

In 2020, BAP launched its 'Beyond the Oasis' research objective, seeking to incorporate perspectives from outside the ancient oasis centre into the broader understanding of the site (Swerida et al., in press, a; in press, b). To facilitate this, Assistant Director Reilly Jensen and outreach coordinator Cindy Srnka initiated a programme of outreach activities, including community days, art-based events, and collaborations with local schools. These initiatives have fostered connections with a wide range of stakeholders and have contributed to a growing interest in community engagement at Bat (see preliminary season reports: Dollarhide et al. 2022; Swerida et al. 2023).

The success of these outreach efforts, combined with increased local interest in promoting tourism and economic investment, prompted BAP to develop a new phase of research titled 'Beyond the Oasis and Within the Community.' This initiative, supported by the Oman Ministry of Heritage and Tourism, focuses on deepening community-based research for the future. Bat, a site of immense historical importance, has been continuously researched by foreign archaeological teams for over fifty years. In light of ongoing debates around the decolonization of archaeology, this history invites critical reflection on the often extractive nature of foreign-led research. Such critiques highlight the lack of community engagement, limited knowledge sharing, and the potential strain placed on local resources. Responding to these challenges, BAP has incorporated community-based research and outreach activities into its management practices in an effort to address these wider critiques of archaeological practice. The research questions which guide this research are as follows:

1. How has long-term archaeological research influenced community identity and heritage in Bāt?
2. What are the perceived social, economic, and environmental impacts of long-term archaeological research?
3. How could future research, community outreach activities, and tourism projects improve engagement and support the local community?

This phase has been marked by a series of community engagement efforts, including an interview project conducted during the winter 2023–2024 field season. The project aimed to evaluate the impact of past archaeological research on the community and to gather insights into local perspectives on future research and tourism development. Through a series of interviews with adult residents, participants were asked about their perceptions of past research and their aspirations for the way that archaeology and tourism could shape Bat in the future.

These interviews were designed to help BAP evaluate its community outreach efforts and adapt future research strategies accordingly. By engaging meaningfully and openly with the local community, BAP aims to create a model to show how large-scale international research projects can adopt a participatory and reflective approach that not only advances scientific knowledge but also supports community regeneration efforts. This work underscores the potential of archaeological research to engage with local stories and priorities, ultimately contributing to more sustainable and mutually beneficial outcomes.

Research design and methodology

As a new programme, BAP's community-based research was designed to ease both us and the Bat community into this style of research by continuing outreach activities and conducting interviews with structured and unstructured questions to establish a basic understanding of how our project is perceived and to gauge how the community envisions how archaeologists and the site can better serve their needs. Our community interviews had three primary objectives: 1) to evaluate the cultural (identity, community relations, economic role) impact of long-term archaeological research at the UNESCO World Heritage Site of Bāt (Sultanate of Oman) on local residents; 2) to ensure community stories and priorities are captured in planning for tourism/visitor infrastructure; 3) and to establish a continuous practice of integrating community voices into BAP's archaeological research management.

Participant selection: we aimed to conduct interviews with up to twenty adult residents of the town of Bāt during the course of active excavations (2–15 January). Although not yet a representative sample of the roughly 2500 resident population of Bāt, this project represents the first season of a longer-term project aligning with the aim of working towards a more representative sample during subsequent excavation seasons.

We endeavoured to make the composition of the small participant cohort as representative of different demographic groups as possible. Target participants were full-time residents (in contrast to holiday visitors) who have lived in the town for at least five years, encompassing the period of the recent study conducted by BAP. We aimed to include an equal number of women and men as well as represent younger adults (18–30 years), middle-aged adults (30–50 years), and older adults (50+ years) in order to capture a diversity of perspectives within the community.

Inviting participants: participants were recruited by word of mouth (through existing contacts and neighbours, speaking with walking groups around the site, at Friday gatherings, and sports events) and the distribution of bilingual (English/Arabic) flyers, posted on community boards and social media. To accommodate gendered preferences in recruitment, our male research assistants (J. Burgess and A. Das) supported recruitment at event settings consisting of men, while the two women interviewers (N. Al-Aati and S. Nugent) approached women contacts, neighbours, and walking groups. The adverts provided contact details (email and phone) of the research team so that potential participants could ask questions before committing to an interview. When participants contacted the team, we temporarily collected their contact information (first name, email, or phone) for interview scheduling and consent withdrawal purposes. Study materials, including the Study Invitation Flyer, Participant

عربي		English
أخبرنا عن ارتباطك بـ بات القديمة؟ يرجى أن تشعر بالحرية في مشاركة القصص.	1	Tell us about your connection to old/ancient Bat? Please feel free to share stories.
كيف تعتقد أن البحث الأثري قد أثر أو شكل هوية البلدة؟	2	How do you think archaeological research has influenced or shaped the town's identity?
ما هو فهمك للبحث الأثري المستمر في بات؟	3	What is your understanding of the ongoing archaeological research at Bat?
كيف تشعر بوجود الآثاريين والباحثين في بلدتك؟	4	How do you feel about the presence of archaeologists and researchers in your town?
ما هي الفرص التي تود أن تراها نشأت من البحث الأثري؟	5	What opportunities would you like to see arise from archaeological research?
هل لاحظت أي تغييرات في مجتمع بات بسبب وجود الآثاريين أو مشاريع التراث؟	6	Have you noticed any changes in the Bat community due to the presence of archaeologists or heritage projects?
كيف تفضل أن يتم مشاركة البحث الأثري مع المجتمع؟	7	How do you prefer archaeological research to be shared with the community?
هل ترغب في رؤية المزيد من الفرص لمشاركة المجتمع في تعزيز أو الحفاظ على تراثه الثقافي؟ إذا كان الأمر كذلك، ما الذي قد تكون مهتمًا بالقيام به؟	8	Would you like to see more opportunities for community involvement in promoting or preserving its cultural heritage? If so, what might you be interested in doing?
ما هي تطلعاتك وآمالك لمستقبل علاقة بات مع تراثها الثقافي والبحث الأثري؟	9	What are your aspirations and hopes for the future of Bat's relationship with its cultural heritage and archaeological research?
هل هناك مشاريع أو مبادرات محددة تود رؤيتها في المستقبل؟-	10	Are there specific projects or initiatives that you would like to see in the future?
هل هناك أي أسئلة محددة تود أن تبحثها الأبحاث الأثرية؟	11	Are there any specific questions you would like archaeological research to investigate?
ما هي الموارد والمعلومات التي تود رؤيتها لمجتمع بات في مركز زوار بات المقترح؟	12	What resources and information would you like to see for the Bat community at the proposed Bat Visitor Centre?
هل تود المشاركة في مركز زوار بات عندما يفتح؟ إذا كان الأمر كذلك، ما الذي قد تكون مهتمًا بالقيام به؟	13	Would you like to participate in the Bat Visitor Centre when it opens? If so, what might you be interested in doing?
من تأمل أن يزور موقع بات الأثري؟	14	Who do you hope will visit the archaeological site of Bat?
ما الأجزاء التي تود رؤيتها مفتوحة أو مغلقة للسياح في موقع بات الأثري؟	15	What parts of the Bat archaeological site would you like to see open or closed to tourists?

Figure 1. *Core study questions for all interview participants.*

Information Sheet, Consent Form, and GDPR Privacy Notice, are available to download on an Open Science Foundation (OSF) repository (Nugent 2024).

Interview structure: interviews took place in the Bat office of the Ministry of Heritage and Tourism, in the meeting space of the BAP excavation house, or in a private room/space in the interviewee's home, depending on the preference of the participant. The co-authors conducted interviews, which were approximately 1 hour in length and covered various questions related to perceptions of archaeological research and expectations for future heritage research and tourism projects. Interviewers took hand-written notes and audio recordings on a hand-held recording device (for transcription purposes). The interviews took place in Arabic with a native speaker (N. Al-Aati) leading the interview. In some instances, follow-up discussions took place in English, following the lead of the participant. Some respondents expressed English as a preference for discussing certain topics and we wished to accommodate this communication choice, noting each instance that a language transition took place.

Each interview began by reviewing the objective of the interviews and encouraging open conversation around the themes presented. Structured questions were framed as a starting point to an unstructured dialogue and participants were invited to openly discuss their experiences and thoughts stemming from each question. Interview questions were designed to cover several themes, including: 1) community history and identity; 2) perceptions of archaeological research; 3) economic and social impact; 4) cultural heritage and preservation; 5) collaboration and communication; 6) concerns; 7) community involvement; 8) changing dynamics; 9) hopes and aspirations; and 10) plans for the Bat Visitor Centre. Figure 1 highlights our core study structured questions, asked of all participants. Further questions in our question bank, including tailored follow-up and draft questions are available for download at our OSF repository (Nugent 2024). In order to make questions accessible to all participants, the interviewers took time when asking each question to explain questions in plain language or clarify any concepts according to the needs of each individual participant before they responded with their answer.

Data management: audio recordings of interviews were initially fully transcribed into Arabic and translated into English. Arabic language in transcripts and audio recordings was then reviewed for accuracy before being fully anonymized for coding. All names presented in this paper are pseudonyms.

Analysis and interpretation: interview notes and transcriptions were analysed using NVivo software for coding, labelling, and thematic and content analysis.

Results

Between 2 January and 15 January 2024, we conducted interviews with thirteen Bat residents, including seven men and six women, representing all target age categories (Fig. 2). Response was lower than expected (originally expected to be around twenty respondents). Our recruitment numbers were probably limited due to the brief time available to advertise the project on the ground and the need to build wider awareness of a new interview project. These results represent preliminary qualitative findings, highlighting major themes that emerged across the interviews.

Pseudonym	Gender	Age category	Length
Kaseem	M	Middle	00:36:59
Fiza	F	Middle	00:54:47
Tamir	M	Young	00:34:06
Amima	F	Middle	00:15:21
Ramza	F	Middle	00:32:19
Raza	M	Young	00:28:39
Fadil	M	Young	00:28:39
Yasira	F	Elderly	01:07:24
Jaleelah	F	Middle	01:07:24
Cemal	M	Elderly	00:19:31
Ayra	F	Middle	00:38:23
Haidar	M	Young	00:25:22
Faisal	M	Middle	00:25:22

FIGURE 2. *Anonymized summary of structured interview participants.*

Heritage, identity, and perceptions of archaeological research

Unsurprisingly, given that the town named its championship-winning football team 'The Archaeologists' (Fig. 3), our findings revealed a broad and deep sense of interest and pride in Bat's archaeological heritage. While many residents initially expressed modesty about their knowledge of Bat's ancient past, once engaged they provided rich narratives about the site's tombs, towers, and mud-brick village. Several participants even recalled specific details about material culture unearthed during past excavations, including those from Karen Frifelt's mid-twentieth-century expeditions.

Two areas emerged as particularly significant to the community: the Early Bronze Age funerary monuments

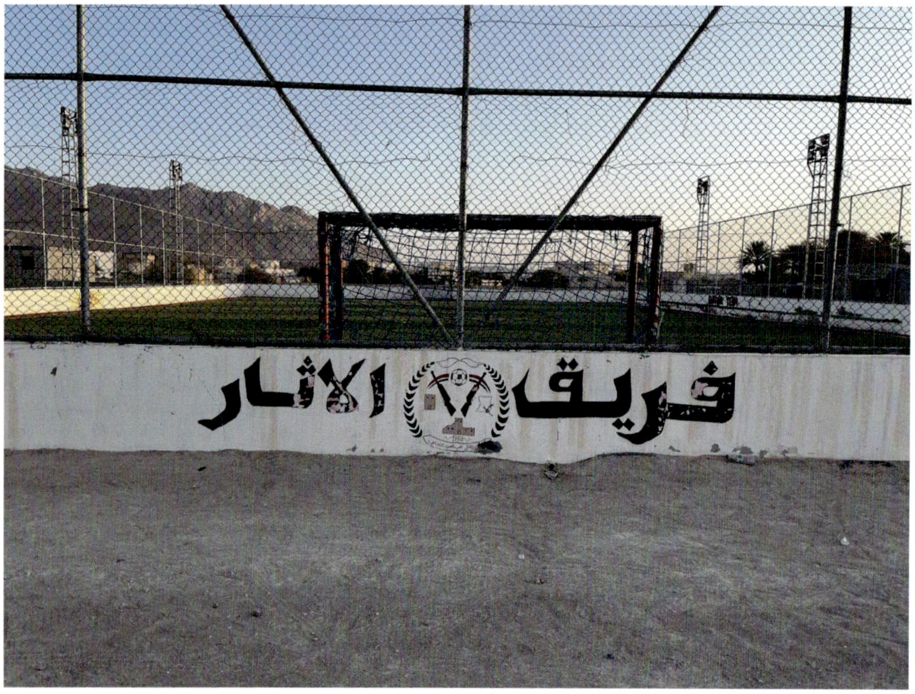

FIGURE 3. *The Bat Archaeologists Football team pitch demonstrates how deeply connected to and knowledgeable of archaeology the community is, through years of archaeological research taking place in their backyard.*

and Ḥiṣn al-Wardi. Residents expressed a strong desire for more focused archaeological research and outreach concerning these sites, indicating their cultural and historical importance to the local community.

Despite this strong connection to Bat's heritage, there was a notable sense of disconnection from the archaeological research itself. Residents felt excluded from past findings and interpretations, a gap attributed to the timing and nature of communication between researchers and the local community. Many remarked that by the time they realized archaeological fieldwork was underway, the researchers were already preparing to depart. This lack of timely engagement led to a sense that archaeological discoveries were happening without their involvement.

In response to these concerns, several recommendations were made. Participants suggested that researchers should engage the community before fieldwork begins, utilizing local communication platforms more familiar to residents. This would allow greater awareness and opportunities for involvement throughout the season, rather than limiting community interaction to post-excavation reports. The importance of having open days or drop-in sessions where residents could visit the site and witness the research in progress was also highlighted.

As one young participant, Tamir, critically noted:

> 'We do hear that every year historical information is being updated, but there isn't that much of a development that makes us feel that there is something new being discovered at Bat.'

This reflects a broader community desire for more accessible and visible engagement with ongoing archaeological work.

Heritage management and outreach

Restoration and preservation emerged as key concerns among participants, particularly regarding the impact of climate change and catastrophic flooding on Bat's archaeological landscape. Of particular focus was the Ḥiṣn al-Wardi, the mud-brick village, where there was a strong desire for support in maintaining community ownership and collective conservation efforts. Residents voiced apprehension about the vulnerability of the

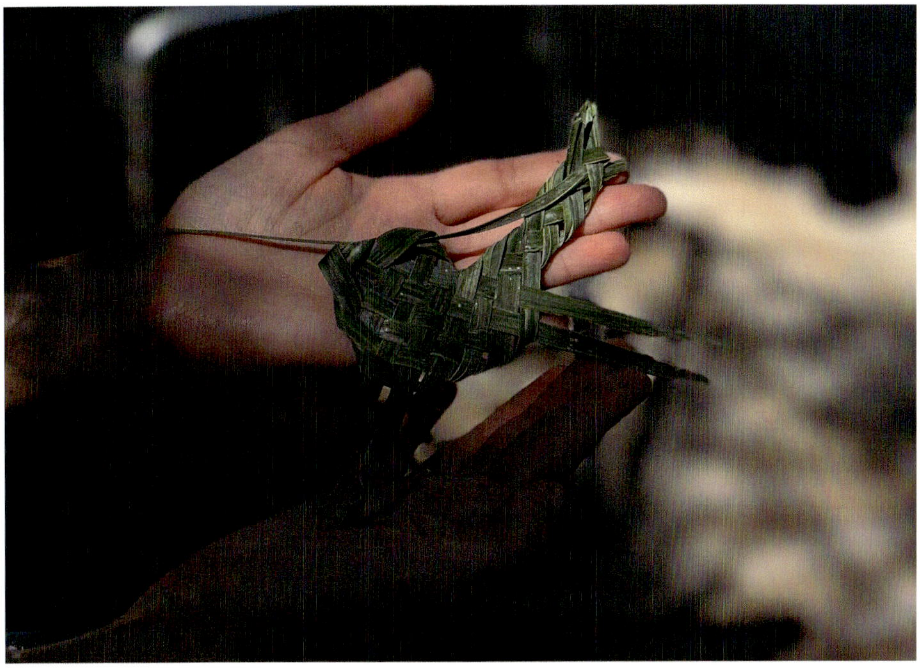

Figure 4. *Residents hoped that preserving and celebrating traditional crafts would be featured alongside ancient heritage as a multi-faceted reflection of Bat community identity within the new Bat Visitor Centre.*

village's structures to environmental forces, with one resident, Ramza, highlighting the issue:

> 'The dust [...] through wind, it collapses if it is strong wind, it collapses [...] and the rain it collapses the same thing. Because they are old, they don't have lots of maintenance, they collapse...'

How preservation would be financed did not arise in conversation and remains an unanswered question, potentially risking the long-term survival of the Ḥiṣn. However, several respondents expressed interest in repairs being undertaken by local contractors who could be trained in mud-brick restoration.

Additionally, participants expressed the importance of preserving intangible contemporary heritage, such as traditional crafts, which they felt had been overlooked in the focus on ancient monumental heritage (Fig. 4). There was a clear call for heritage management efforts to balance the protection of archaeological sites with the preservation of living traditions that are integral to Bat's cultural identity.

Regarding existing outreach opportunities, participants who had engaged with these programmes reported positive experiences and encouraged their continuation. Hands-on activities and experiential learning, particularly for young people, were strongly supported as effective means of engaging the community with their heritage. This feedback underscores the value of interactive and inclusive outreach initiatives in fostering a deeper connection between the local population and the archaeological research conducted at Bat.

Social and economic needs

Economic need and youth education emerged as key concerns regarding how archaeological research at Bat could better serve the community. A recurring topic of discussion was the long-delayed tourism infrastructure, such as the Bat Visitor Centre, which has been a source of anticipation and controversy among local residents. The numerous setbacks in its construction have led to a sense of missed opportunity to attract visitors, who could boost the local economy and improve access to the expansive Bat archaeological landscape through the development of roads, rest areas, and facilities for

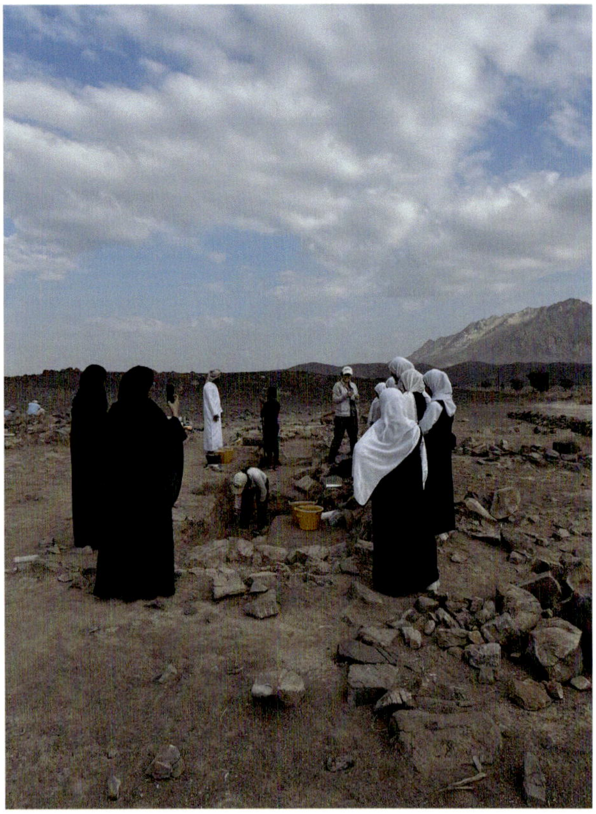

Figure 5. *Students visiting excavations at Rakhat al-Madrh during the 2024 School Day Event.*

both visitors and residents, which was also captured by Benkari's (2018) interviews with the Ministry of Heritage and Culture and Bat residents on the heritage management of the Bat, Khutum, and Al-Ayn World Heritage Site.

Business owners, young people, and parents voiced frustrations that, without a tangible and accessible visitor centre, decades of archaeological research and UNESCO protections might do little to directly benefit the community. Specifically, they highlighted issues such as supporting small businesses, addressing youth underemployment, and influencing educational content in local schools. There was a perception that foreign archaeologists could play a larger role in addressing these needs. Participants noted that instances of archaeologists making a tangible impact were few and far between.

As one resident, Amima, a teacher in Bat, emphasized:

> 'The student should not only study theoretical things. They are not theoretical students. [...] So when we came to the archaeological site, they [archaeologists] did not fall short. Meaning, the archaeologists gave information to the students and their knowledge expanded. They asked with eagerness [...] they witnessed the process of excavation and increased their knowledge, their awareness, and increased their pride [...] and belonging to their homeland.'

Similarly, a young man, Haidar, suggested that archaeologists could contribute by creating job opportunities for the local youth, 'by employing the unemployed youth in assisting the archaeologists in excavating or tidying the archaeological areas.' There was no mention of the impact of archaeologists currently employing adult residents as excavators in the context of economic benefit and it is not clear if this is due to not perceiving this form of employment as beneficial or to a lack of awareness.

Discussion

What do Bat residents teach us about foreign-led archaeological practice? We begin our discussion by emphasizing that our study results are preliminary and part of ongoing longer-term research and we therefore do not wish to make broadly generalized conclusions at this stage. However, our initial findings and their contrast with our approach to the management of the Bat Archaeological Project raise important issues that require further investigation and reflection.

These insights underscore the community's desire for archaeological research to contribute more directly to local socio-economic development, particularly in terms of education, employment, and small business support.

Our interviews were met with an unexpected level of candidness and constructive criticism from the Bat residents. Contrary to expectations that we would face scepticism or polite reserve as a new initiative, we were met with openness and an eagerness to contribute. This challenges initial assumptions that CBPR approaches in this context would require extensive long-term trust-building efforts, especially in a heritage landscape where, as literature suggests, top-down institutional control often prevails (Ataya & Page 2022; Morgan et al. 2022). Although continued trust-building is important, our findings suggest that the local community is already primed for a more active, community-led research role, shifting the onus onto us, as foreign practitioners, to catch up with their desire for involvement. This should serve as an encouraging lesson for other projects facing similar hesitations, demonstrating that perceived barriers to CBPR may potentially not be as insurmountable as initially assumed.

That said, there are challenges ahead. Integrating the perspectives of non-Omanis living in Bat, or those who do not fit neatly into the 'local community' framework, remains complex. This challenge is echoed by other researchers, such as Morgan et al. (2022), who also point to the difficulty of aligning CBPR intentions with local social realities (2022).

Bat residents further remind us of the significant privilege we hold as researchers, benefiting from large funding resources, powerful institutional backing, and valuable skills that we can leverage to uplift the communities whose heritage we study. They explicitly identified the skills and resources they recognize in us, providing a clear opportunity for mutual benefit, as long as we are willing to listen.

Finally, we recognize that much work remains to be done. This is both necessary and encouraging, as it would have been a dull project indeed if we could have wrapped everything up in a single season. The dialogue with the community must not only continue but grow in openness, adapting iteratively as we move forward.

How do we respond as project directors/ researchers?

There has been a long-term commitment to understanding and preserving the archaeology at Bat since 1972. As we entered 2024 we felt it was long overdue that archaeological practice had the disciplinary space to welcome an equal commitment to understanding and supporting the needs and desires of those whose lives and identities have been shaped by the heritage and the culmination of years of scientific research.

As project directors our response to these initial findings is to use this evidence to develop an intentional and organized strategy for specific actions through theory of change. A theory of change is a method that explains how a given intervention, or set of interventions, is expected to lead to a specific change, drawing on a causal analysis based on available evidence (Connell & Kubisch 1998). This approach emerged in the 1990s in social policy as a field in programme design and evaluation and is now widely used by NGOs and those working in development. We feel this is particularly fruitful to integrate into archaeological research management because theory of change is designed to support collective visioning, foster a shared understanding between stakeholders, and bridge thought-styles and different ways of knowing. Further aligning with a long-term field research project, this approach begins not with its intervention but with long-term goals and outcomes and then works backward in time toward the earliest changes that need to occur. In the context of Bat, if our goal is to ensure our work bolsters youth employability or preserves endangered heritage, we need to adjust our current strategies for seeking funding as well as integrate evidence-based advocacy efforts seeking governmental financial support for those initiatives. This means balancing or even shelving some of our academic and professional goals and centring community needs.

Our long-term vision is to transform BAP into a 'living lab' for participatory engagement in heritage. A living lab being a real-life or third space environment for collaborative innovation, which enhances participatory research, fosters local innovation, and promotes sustainable practices (Bergvall-Kareborn & Stahlbrost 2009). We will develop this through continuing and regular formal and informal interviews, integrating community research priorities into season plans, applying for funding with explicit budgeting allocated to community initiatives, providing a variety of outreach activities adapted through regular feedback, and opening field research and training opportunities to anyone who is simply curious and to those who wish to be citizen scientists. One example of this is a project designed to monitor the structural stability and preservation of the Ḥiṣn al-Wardi, which is not only an opportunity to address interest in mud-brick heritage preservation, but also provides the opportunity to teach valuable skills in modelling, data analysis, and risk assessment, which are transferable well beyond the limits of archaeology.

This has been initiated on a small scale using the Penn Museum Director's Field Funds of the University of Pennsylvania, but a larger, more sustainable initiative will require supplementary creative fundraising efforts. Another example includes adapting our communication and outreach plans to host pre-season informational gatherings and informational documents, allowing the community to actively engage with our research in line with their own schedules during our field season. These undertakings address key themes in interview results.

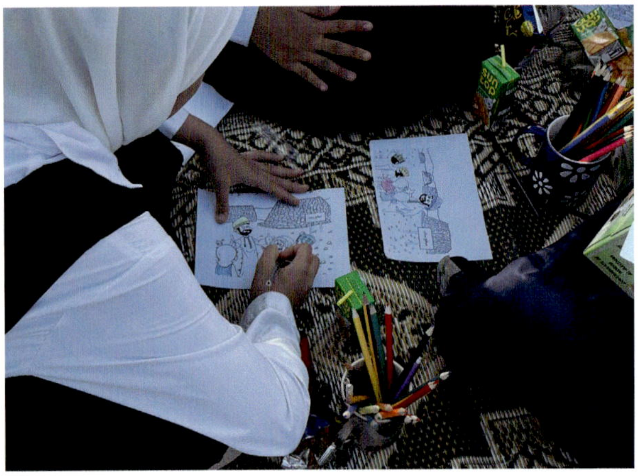

Figure 6. *Students drawing/colouring during their visit to Rakhat al-Madrh during the 2024 School Day Event.*

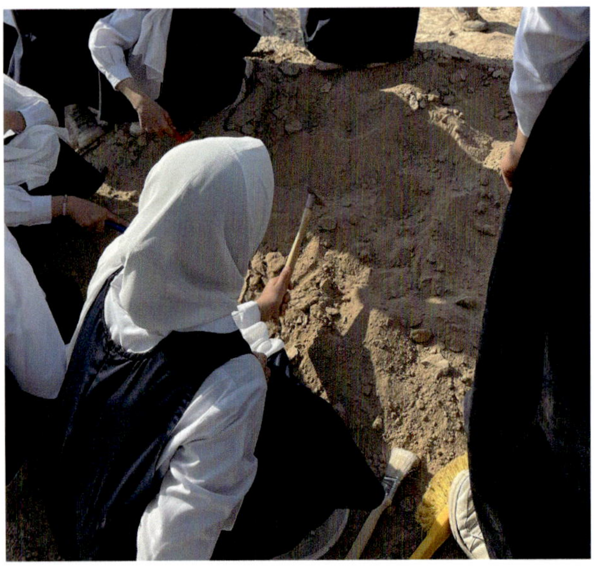

Figure 7. *Students excavating during their visit to Rakhat al-Madrh during the 2024 School Day Event.*

In response to feedback from students and teachers at the event, as well as information from community interviews, we aim to continue developing our contributions for engagement with children in Bat. Providing practical, child-friendly experiences was seen as rewarding and an enjoyable way to learn about history (Figs 6 & 7).

Opportunities and challenges for Arabian archaeology

We return to our broader original question for archaeologists in this region: can community-based participatory research enhance our understanding of Arabian archaeology? While community-centred approaches are gradually being adopted across the Arabian Peninsula, there remains limited literature on the subject compared to other regions. Our ability to conduct community-based studies, much like the rest of archaeological research permission, hinges on support from national governments, which can be hesitant to integrate grassroots approaches into existing institutional approaches to heritage, or from authorities which may not have deemed archaeological projects as relevant mediums for conducting such studies. In many cases, governmental decisions about research permissions are out of our hands as archaeologists. From our experience at the Bat Archaeological Project, this type of study would probably not have been permitted a few years ago and has been possible due to the fortunate confluence of several factors both within and beyond our control. Within our control was the way we interact with government and community representatives, including long-term trust building through engagement activities and informal discussion, flexibility to adapt research proposals to respect local boundaries, and using research dissemination towards supporting community engagement goals set out by national and intergovernmental bodies. Outside our control were public responses to building new tourism infrastructure around the world heritage site and shifts in international and national heritage management policies encouraging more community involvement (see Freer & Kherfi 2020; Sampieri et al. 2024). Beyond the context of Bat, we feel that we are also still missing a critical support system connecting community-based approaches between different international

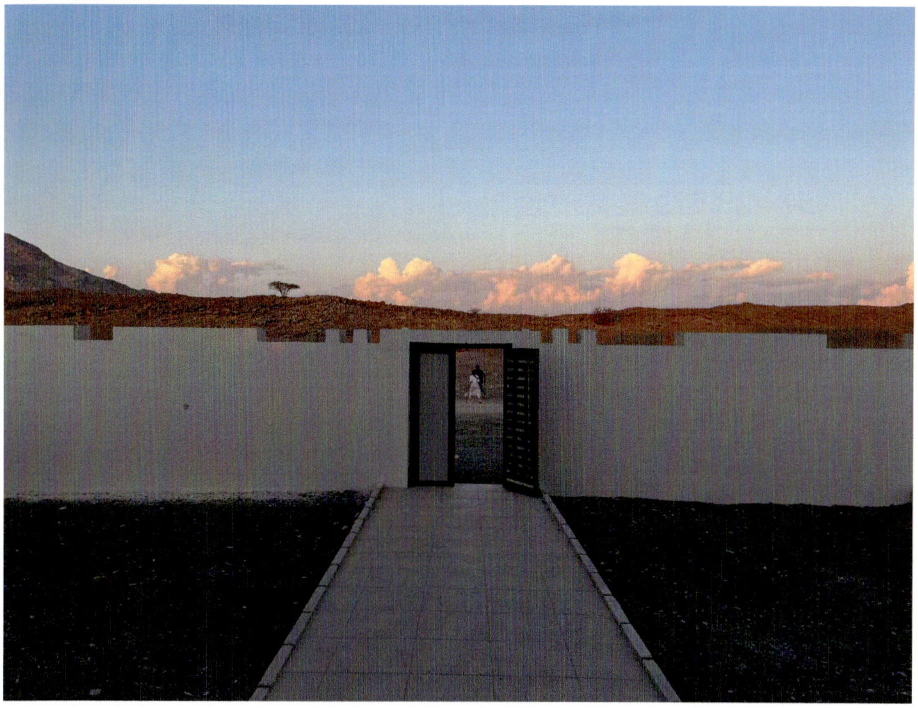

FIGURE 8. *View from the Bat Archaeological Project excavation house facing the Bat necropolis, with children playing football.*

teams working within the region. This lacuna presents an opportunity for the field to grow by expanding its methodologies, sharing best practices, and contributing more actively to global dialogues in archaeology — especially as Arabian archaeology is often under-represented outside conflict-related contexts.

At a recent IASA seminar, concerns were raised about how to safeguard Arabian archaeology amid broader trends in educational policy that devalue the discipline. Our interviews highlight a related issue: we have, perhaps, been too narrowly focused on traditional audiences and lost sight of the wider community (Fig. 8).

CBPR thus offers the promise of a better way of connecting with and expanding our audience and our relevance beyond academic circles. With new audiences come new ways of thinking and the opportunity to break from traditional practice and theoretical frameworks to explore new avenues of research. For sites like Bat, where the history of Western-led excavation has often been extractive, CBPR offers a chance to repair past inequities and co-create a future that benefits both researchers and the local community (Atalay 2012). However, this approach comes with challenges. Although foreign archaeological missions have dominated the region historically, applying CBPR in Arabia requires careful navigation to ensure meaningful community engagement. Furthermore, the double-edged sword of our privilege is that traditional archaeological funding pathways are shifting and narrowing, and community-based projects are often not compatible with traditional funding sources. As a result, the presence of foreign-led missions may (and should) lessen in the upcoming years as locally led teams are well prepared to discover and preserve Arabian heritage. As more Western funders focus on demonstrating societal impact, ongoing international research teams that are embedded within the community are in a prime position to measure and demonstrate these desired outcomes. Community-based research also puts us in a better position eventually to withdraw or step back from research that most certainly could and should be directed by our local colleagues. More reflective and reflexive exercises during excavation field seasons provide tangible evidence of our limitations as international scholars and help us to justify using funds for enhancing and financing local capacities.

There is still more work to be done to recognize CBPR as a core part of practising archaeology, as opposed to an addendum or an extension of heritage management. The seminar, as well as regional publication outlets, constitutes some of the venues where it is essential to establish these dialogues.

Concluding remarks

BAP demonstrates the potential for CBPR to reshape the practice of archaeology in Arabia by fostering deeper connections with local communities. Our experience underscores the value of this approach, not only in generating more robust and inclusive research but also in addressing long-standing challenges of local engagement and representation in archaeological work. By integrating the perspectives of Bat residents, we have been able to gain richer insights into both the heritage of the region and the community's needs and aspirations, which have historically been overlooked.

As foreign scholars, we acknowledge the privileged position we occupy, with access to funding, resources, and international platforms. It is our responsibility to leverage these advantages to support local learning, capacity-building, and opportunities for involvement. BAP has sought to bridge the gap between research and the local community by embedding community voices into its methodology and engagement practices. This not only ensures a more sustainable and mutually beneficial relationship but also enhances the rigour of our work by incorporating local knowledge and perspectives.

The integration of CBPR into Arabian archaeology is a timely opportunity to move beyond extractive research practices toward more collaborative and ethical forms of knowledge production. However, the challenges of implementing CBPR in Arabian archaeology should not be underestimated.

As other projects across the Arabian Peninsula consider similar frameworks, we hope that our experiences at Bat can contribute as a case study to a broader conversation about the future of archaeology in the region. Formalizing these approaches presents an opportunity to advance the field while supporting the long-term sustainability of the communities whose heritage we study.

Acknowledgements

We would like to thank His Excellency Undersecretary for Heritage Affairs, Mr Salim bin Mohammed Al-Mahruqi; Advisor to the Minister of Heritage, Mr Sultan al-Bakhri; Director General of Archaeology and Museums, Ms Yousra al-Subhi; Director of World Heritage Sites, Ms Ibtisam al-Mamari; Director of Excavations and Collections, Mr Ali al-Mahroqi; and Mr Ibrahim al-Maqbali, Ms Samia al-Asmi, and all the staff members of the Department of Excavations and Archaeological Studies, the Ministry of Heritage and Culture, Sultanate of Oman, for their wonderful support of our mission. We are also grateful to the ministry staff members working in the field and offices, particularly to the Ministry of Heritage and Tourism representatives at Bat, in particular Mr Mohammed al-Kaabani, Mr Mohammed al-Essai, Mr Suleiman al-Jabri, Mr Badr al-Badi, and Ms Sumaia al-Marmarri.

Our project was financially supported by the Omani Ministry of Heritage and Tourism, the US National Endowment for the Humanities (grant RFW 279340-21), and the Penn Museum Director's Field Funds of the University of Pennsylvania. Logistical support was provided by Lauren Ristvet and the Near East Section of the Penn Museum, University of Pennsylvania. We are also grateful to our research assistants, Jack Burgess and Achint Das, who supported us in sharing the project with Bat residents.

We are especially grateful to Bat's residents for their hospitality, friendship, and partnership in learning from the region's deep past.

References

Apaydin V. 2020. *Critical perspectives on cultural memory and heritage: Construction, transformation and destruction*. London: UCL Press.

Atalay S. 2012. *Community-based archaeology: Research with, by, and for indigenous and local communities*. Berkeley: University of California Press.

Ataya M. & Page H. 2022. Heritage and community involvement: The case of Sharjah Fort (Al Hisn) Museum. Pages 91–108 in A. Badran, S. Abu-Khafajah & S. Elliott (eds), *Community heritage in the Arab region*. (One World Archaeology). Cham: Springer.

Benkari N. 2018. Archaeological site of Bat-Oman: Management and public perception — Community involvement in archaeological heritage management and planning. *Journal of Cultural Heritage Management and Sustainable Development* 8/3: 293–308.

Bergvall-Kareborn B. & Stahlbrost A. 2009. Living lab: An open and citizen-centric approach for innovation. *International Journal of Innovation and Regional Development* 1/4: 356–370.

Böhme M. & al-Sabri B.A. 2011. Umm an-Nar Burial 401 at Bat, Oman: Architecture and finds. *Arabian Archaeology and Epigraphy* 22: 113–154.

Brunswig R.H. 1989. Culture history, environment, and economy from an Umm an-Nar settlement: Evidence from test excavations at Bat, Oman. *Journal of Oman Studies* 10: 9–50.

Cable C.M. & Al-Jabri S. 2018. The Wadi al-Hijr (Sultanate of Oman) in the third millennium BC. *Arabian Archaeology and Epigraphy* 30/1: 1–15.

Connell J.P. & Kubisch A.C. 1998. Applying a theory of change approach to the evaluation of comprehensive community initiatives: Progress, prospects, and problems. Pages 15–44 in K. Fulbright-Anderson, A.C. Kubisch & J.P. Connell (eds), *New approaches to evaluating community initiatives.* ii. Washington, DC: The Aspen Institute.

de Cardi B., Collier S. & Doe D.B. 1976. Excavations and survey in Oman, 1974–1975. *The Journal of Oman Studies* 2: 101–187.

Desruelles S., Fouache E., Eddargach W., Cammas C., Wattez J., Beuzen-Waller T. ... Murray A. 2016. Evidence for early irrigation at Bat (Wadi Sharsah, northwestern Oman) before the advent of farming villages. *Quaternary Science Reviews* 150: 42–54.

Dollarhide E.N. 2019. *Mapping Magan: The ancient social landscape of north-central Oman.* (PhD thesis, New York University). Ann Arbor, MI: ProQuest Dissertations Publishing.

Dollarhide E.N., Swerida J.L., Jensen R.S. & al-Jassassi A.B.R. 2022. Bat Archaeological Project: Preliminary report of the 2022 season. Report on File, Ministry of Heritage and Tourism, Muscat, Oman. Available at: www.batarchaeologicalproject.com/_files/ugd/b9786c_1ab8ed6821284bfc8453a9f1be39a422.pdf

Exell K. & Rico T. 2013. 'There is no heritage in Qatar': Orientalism, colonialism and other problematic histories. *World Archaeology* 45/4: 670–685.

Exell K. & Rico T. 2014. *Cultural heritage in the Arabian Peninsula: Debates, discourses and practices.* London: Routledge.

Freer C. & Kherfi Y. 2020. Narratives of nationalism in culture and heritage production of the Arabian Peninsula: Bringing the state back in. *International Journal of Middle East Studies* 52/6: 988–1004.

Frifelt K. 1976. Evidence of a third millennium BC town in Oman. *The Journal of Oman Studies* 2: 57–73.

Frifelt K. 1985. Further evidence of the third millennium BC town at Bat in Oman. *The Journal of Oman Studies* 7: 89–104.

Frifelt K. 2002. Bat, a centre in third millennium Oman. Pages 101–110 in S. Cleuziou, M. Tosi & J. Zarins (eds), *Essays on the late prehistory of the Arabian Peninsula.* (Serie Orientale Roma, 93). Rome: Istituto Italiano per l'Africa e l'Oriente.

Joy C. 2020. *Heritage justice.* Cambridge: Cambridge University Press.

Kondo Y., Miki T., Kuronuma T., Hayakawa Y.S., Kataoka K. & Oguchi T. 2016. Concurrent and sustainable development of a local-scale digital heritage inventory through action research at Bat, Oman. *Journal of Cultural Heritage Management and Sustainable Development* 6/2: 195–212.

Morgan C., Carter R., Aziz F.A. & Al Thani M. 2022. Public archaeology and engagement in the Origins of Doha and Qatar Project. Pages 91–108 in A. Badran, S. Abu-Khafajah & S. Elliott (eds), *Community heritage in the Arab region: Values and practices.* Cham: Springer International Publishing.

Nugent S.E. 2024. Beyond the oasis and within the community. Available at: https://doi.org/10.17605/OSF.IO/N5A2Q

Sampieri S., Saoualih A., Safaa L., Martínez de Carnero Calzada F., Ramazzotti M. & Martínez-Peláez A. 2024. Tourism development through the sense of UNESCO World Heritage: The case of Hegra, Saudi Arabia. *Heritage* 7/4: 2195–2216.

Schmidt C. & Döpper S. 2014. German expedition to Bat and Al-Ayn, Sultanate of Oman: The 2010 to 2013 seasons. *Journal of Oman Studies* 18: 187–230.

Swerida J. 2022. House, household, and the Umm an-Nar: Structure SS1 at Bat, Oman. Pages 164–180 in L. Battini, A. Brody & S.R. Steadman (eds), *No place like home: Ancient Near Eastern houses and households.* Oxford: Archaeopress.

Swerida J. & Thornton C.P. 2019. Al-Khafaji reinterpreted: New insights on Umm an-Nar monuments and settlement from Bat, Oman. *Arabian Archaeology and Epigraphy* 30: 1–16.

Swerida J., Cable C.M. & Dollarhide E.N. 2020. Survey and settlement: Preliminary results of the Bat Archaeological Project's 2019 field season. *Journal of Oman Studies* 21: 82–101.

Swerida J., Dollarhide E.N. & Jensen R. 2021. Settlement and chronology in the early Bronze Age of southeastern Arabia: The view from Umm an-Nar period Bat, Oman. *Paléorient* 47/2: 75–96.

Swerida J., Dollarhide E.N., Jensen R.S. & al-Jassassi A.B.R. 2023. Bat Archaeological Project: Preliminary report of the 2022–23 season. Report on File, Ministry of Heritage and Tourism, Muscat, Oman. Available at: www.batarchaeologicalproject.com/_files/ugd/b9786c_7aef4f514ea649c99da4bc9dd6622a49.pdf

Swerida J., Dollarhide E.N., Bryant R.C., Mateiciucová I., Přichystal A., Buffington A. ... Rissman, P. (in press, a). Beyond the oasis: Results from the 2022–23 field season of the Bat Archaeological Project. *Journal of Oman Studies.*

Swerida J., Dollarhide E.N., Fouache E., Engel M., Beuzen-Waller T., Prospereini A. ... Casana J. (in press, b). Cultural and human ecological resilience at Early Bronze Age Bat. *Open Quaternary.*

Thornton C.P., Cable C.M. & Possehl G.L. 2016. *The Bronze Age towers at Bat, Sultanate of Oman: Research by the Bat Archaeological Project, 2007-12.* Philadelphia: University of Pennsylvania Press.

Young R. 2019. *Historical archaeology and heritage in the Middle East.* London: Routledge.

Young R., al-Jassassi A.R., al-Shaqsi S.S.A., al-Jabri S.H., Batchelor O., Dance K. ... Taha S. 2018. Bat Oasis Historical Archaeology Project: Interim report on 2014 field season. *Journal of Oman Studies* 19: 1–18.

Authors' addresses

Selin Nugent, Oxford Brookes University, Centre for AI, Culture & Society, Oxford, OX3 0BP, UK.
e-mail snugent@brookes.ac.uk

Jennifer Swerida, Universiteit Leiden, Faculteit Archeologie, Leiden, 2333 CC, Netherlands.
e-mail j.l.swerida@arch.leidenuniv.nl

Nora Al-Aati, University of Pennsylvania, Department of Anthropology, Philadelphia, PA, 19104, USA.
e-mail nsalaati@sas.upenn.edu

Reilly Jensen, Utah Department of Cultural and Community Engagement, Millcreek, UT, 84106, USA.
e-mail quaffingreilly@gmail.com

Cindy Srnka, University of Pennsylvania, Department of Middle Eastern Languages and Cultures, Philadelphia, PA 19104, USA.
e-mail csrnka@sas.upenn.edu

Proceedings of the Seminar for Arabian Studies 54 (2025): 183–200

A rural perspective on the Umm an-Nar and Wadi Suq periods from Burj Huraiz (northern Oman)

Eric Olijdam, Bleda Düring, Michel de Vreeze & Zoë van Litsenburg

Summary

Despite substantial research on the Umm an-Nar (*c*.2700–2000 BC) and Wadi Suq (*c*.2000–1600 BC), our understanding of rural settlements and their economies during these periods remains limited. Research on the Umm an-Nar period has focused mainly on large sites and monumental towers, and relatively few vernacular buildings have been excavated. Similarly, the few known Wadi Suq-period settlements have provided scant insights into their nature. The discovery of a series of rural settlements in the northern Bāṭinah, particularly the well-preserved vernacular buildings of the Umm an-Nar and Wadi Suq periods at Burj Huraiz in the 2018 season of the Wadi al Jizzi Archaeological Project (WAJAP) survey and subsequent excavations in 2023–2024, have resulted in new and intriguing data. The main results from these excavations are presented here and contextualized, thereby enhancing our understanding of rural settlements in the Umm an-Nar and Wadi Suq periods.

Keywords: Umm an-Nar period, Wadi Suq period, vernacular buildings, rural settlements, economy

Introduction

A focus on sites with monumental towers has dominated the archaeology of settlements in Bronze Age south-east Arabia. By contrast, rural settlements, that is, small settlements of no more than thirty or so buildings and lacking monumental structures (see also Deadman et al. 2022: 33; Squitieri 2024), of the Umm an-Nar and Wadi Suq periods are less well known, due partly to research biases and partly to the characteristics of the sites concerned.

As a result, our understanding of Umm an-Nar buildings remains limited. While the term 'domestic architecture' has been used to refer to all structures in Bronze Age south-east Arabia that are not monumental towers or tombs (Döpper 2018a: 2), we prefer to use the word 'vernacular' as these buildings might have served as workshops, for keeping livestock, for storage, as well as for domestic purposes (see Halperin & Schwartz 2016). Indeed, many buildings for which information is available show mixed and changing uses that include domestic activities, craft activities and metallurgy, or storage. Only a small number of Umm an-Nar-period vernacular buildings have been excavated and published, although many such buildings are known from al-Zībā, al-Gharīyān, al-Ṭīkha, Dahwā, and Zahrah (Costa & Wilkinson 1987: 95–99; al-Jahwari & Kennet 2010; Döpper 2018a; Düring & Botan 2018; Douglas et al. 2021; 2024; Deadman et al. 2022). These sites were predominantly investigated through surveys. While surveys can provide a wealth of information in a cost-effective manner, the data obtained is less informative on issues of chronology, activities, and construction histories. By contrast, excavations are mostly limited in scale, and the results obtained might not be representative for the broader settlement. Therefore, an integrated approach combining data from systematic surveys and excavations is advocated here.

Our understanding of Wadi Suq settlements is even more limited than for the Umm an-Nar, given that only a handful have been attested in south-east Arabia. Climatic deterioration related to the 4.2ka event is commonly believed to have set into motion changes that led to a period of settlement reorganization, which lasted until the end of the second millennium (Magee 2014; de Vreeze, Kennet & Deadman 2024). The paucity of settlements compared to more abundant mortuary evidence has given rise to the hypothesis that the Wadi Suq society was primarily mobile (Cleuziou 1989), except in specific refugia. Even in these refugia, sedentary populations are believed to have been relatively modest (Velde 2009), although more recent analysis suggests sizeable populations (de Vreeze, Kennet & Deadman 2024; Kennet et al. 2025). At present, Wadi Suq settlement evidence derives mainly from small-scale excavations at Khawr Fakkān and Ra's al-Jinz (RJ–1) (Jasim 2000; Monchablon et al. 2003) and limited exposures in tell excavations at Tell Abraq (Potts 1990; 1991), Kalbā' (Carter 1997), and Nud Zībā (Kennet & Velde 1995). Thus, relatively little is known about the nature of Wadi Suq communities and their economies.

The excavation of several Bronze Age vernacular buildings at Burj Huraiz aimed to address some of these lacunae and obtain more information, first, about the nature of Umm an-Nar and Wadi Suq settlements; second, the types of activities that took place in and around these buildings; and, third, possible diachronic changes that can be observed within this site. Before presenting these data, we will briefly summarize the current view on the nature of Bronze Age settlements in south-east Arabia.

Current views on Bronze Age settlements

Umm an-Nar settlements often appear to have consisted of various nuclei or hamlets (Deadman et al. 2022). They vary in size, density, layout, and configuration. It has been suggested that some community members lived permanently in these settlements, while others were frequently on the move (Phillips 2007; al-Jahwari & Kennet 2010; Döpper 2018b; Schmidt 2018; Deadman et al. 2022; Swerida 2022). Tower sites are usually interpreted as regional centres with a hinterland of smaller sites, some of which are described as 'satellite settlements'. Multi-towered settlements appear to have been a class of their own and possibly formed the top tier. This possible settlement system may explain the Mesopotamian terminologies for places and leaders of Magan during the Umm an-Nar period (see Laursen & Steinkeller 2017: 19–25). One of the key questions about Umm an-Nar settlements is how different settlement types were integrated with each other and to what degree they were involved in the production and exchange of copper and other goods.

Further research is crucial to understand a potential hierarchical settlement system more fully. So far, three distinct settlement systems have been identified (Deadman et al. 2022; Swerida 2022). These systems are closely related to ecological settings, particularly hydro-geological conditions. Quintessential Umm an-Nar tower sites are limited to the northern coasts and the 'oasis belt' along the western flank of the al-Ḥajar mountains (Cable & Thornton 2012; Deadman et al. 2022; Döpper 2024). A similar sizeable site is now known along the east flank, at al-Ṭīkha, located in a valley system near Rustāq along the lower reaches of the al-Akhḍar mountains (Deadman et al. 2022).

Apart from this one exception, the Bāṭinah — the most fertile and historically the second most densely populated area in the Sultanate of Oman (Kennet, Deadman & al-Jahwari 2016: 155) — is marked by a general absence of known Umm an-Nar towers beyond al-Ṭīkha and satellite settlements (Deadman et al. 2022; de Vreeze, Kennet & Deadman 2024: figs 1–2). Umm an-Nar towers only reappear at the end of the Bāṭinah plain, at Kalbā', and possibly a little further south. Thus, the Bāṭinah is characterized by 'tower-less' settlements of varying size and complexity. The site of Dahwā, for instance, consists of over sixty buildings and two tombs built from sugar lumps, but lacks towers (al-Jahwari et al. 2018; Douglas et al. 2024). By contrast, settlements in the Ṣuhār hinterlands are smaller, typically have no more than thirty buildings, and lack well-constructed tombs (Düring & Botan 2018; Düring et al. 2019). The difference between the larger and more differentiated Dahwā settlement, which has substantial evidence for metallurgy, and the rural sites in the Ṣuhār hinterlands, is notable. However, it has been suggested that Dahwā consisted of various hamlets, not all of which might have been occupied simultaneously (Deadman et al. 2022: 29), in which case it would not be different in scale from the Ṣuhār hinterland sites. On the other hand, the Dahwā buildings excavated so far reveal prolonged occupational histories, from the start of the Umm an-Nar period to its very end (al-Jahwari et al. 2018; Douglas et al. 2024), which appears to contrast with the shorter lifespans exhibited for the three settlements in our research area.

The site of Burj Huraiz

During the WAJAP surveys of the Ṣuhār hinterlands (2014–2018), a series of well-preserved Bronze Age and Iron Age settlements and cemeteries in the Wādī Fizḥ/ Wādī al-Zahaimi corridor were documented (Düring &

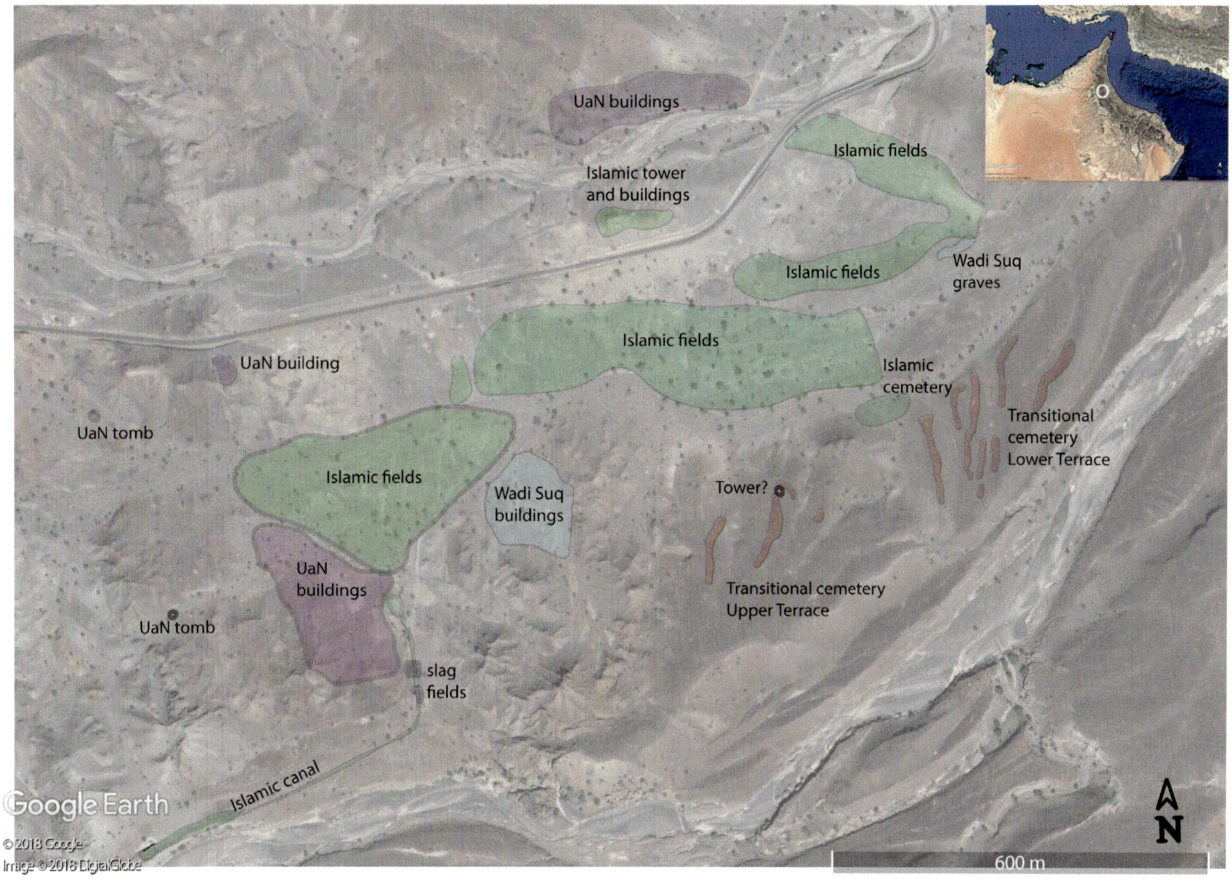

FIGURE 1. *An overview of the archaeological components of Burj Huraiz (WAJAP Site 66/73).*

Botan 2018; Düring, Olijdam & Botan 2017; de Vreeze, Düring & Olijdam 2020; Düring 2022). During the final season, a small valley north of Wādī al-Zahaimi was explored. Near the late Islamic tower of Burj Huraiz, we found a cluster of archaeological remains that include the late Islamic tower and hamlet of Burj Huraiz and an associated sophisticated irrigation and field system. Further elements of the site comprise a small Wadi Suq-period cemetery and an extensive cemetery provisionally dated to the Umm an-Nar/Wadi Suq transition (see Düring et al. 2019 for further details). Finally, Site 66/73 contains settlement remains dating to the Bronze Age. These consist of a substantial Umm an-Nar settlement (dated *c.*2200–2000 BC) and a much smaller Wadi Suq settlement (dated to the earlier part of *c.*2000–1600 BC) (Düring et al. 2019).

The Umm an-Nar settlement at Site 66/73 (Burj Huraiz) comprises about thirty structures, partially concentrated in a central cluster with some structures spread further across the landscape. The Wadi Suq settlement consists of seven small buildings in close vicinity, except for Building 58, which is located about 300 m north of the others. The two settlements are close but spatially distinct, with the Wadi Suq habitation located east of the Umm an-Nar settlement (Fig. 1). All Bronze Age buildings are located on slightly raised terrain bordering the flat area where the late Islamic field systems are constructed. Finally, in one part of the site there is a substantial concentration of heavily processed slag. This is cut in two by the main canal of the late Islamic irrigation system, which suggests that the slag concentration is most likely of Bronze Age date.

The excellent levels of preservation of the Bronze Age buildings at Burj Huraiz warranted targeted excavations in order to add chronological and contextual resolution to the data obtained from the surface survey. During the 2023 and 2024 seasons, we excavated six 5 x 10 m trenches, following a site-wide grid. These trenches were placed over Bronze Age buildings of relatively small size with suspected substantial archaeological deposits. In the end, two trenches were excavated in the Umm an-Nar settlement and four in the Wadi Suq sector of the sites, as these had much shallower deposits.

Of the 2543 sherds unearthed in the course of the excavations, mostly small body sherds, 1167 can be attributed to the Umm an-Nar and 930 to the Wadi Suq (Fig. 2).[1] Late Umm an-Nar ceramics dominate the assemblages from the Umm an-Nar in trenches AO18 and AS25. These ceramics can be compared closely to the later Umm an-Nar phases at Hīlī (see below) and to the late Umm an-Nar ceramic assemblage from al-Ṭīkha (Deadman et al. 2022: 58–60). Small quantities of late Umm an-Nar pottery are found in all four trenches in the Wadi Suq sector of the site: AV61, BP08, BQ04, and BQ06 (Fig. 3). These assemblages are mainly of early Wadi Suq date in terms of fabric, surface treatment, and decoration (see de Vreeze 2016; 2025), and a few similar sherds were also found in AO18 and AS25. The results indicate a transition from the Umm an-Nar to the Wadi Suq period at Burj Huraiz.

Our preliminary analysis of the assemblage further suggests chronological differences between the excavated trenches. Trench AS25 was probably occupied slightly later in the Umm an-Nar than AO18, and AV61 has the earliest Wadi Suq assemblages, with those from trenches BP08, BQ04, and BQ06 somewhat later and possibly continuing into the middle Wadi Suq period based on fabrics and decoration more akin to these phases (as further developed in de Vreeze 2016; 2025; de Vreeze et al. 2020: 145–150). The occupation history of the settlement sequence is consistent with the extensive transitional cemetery located directly to the east and the small Wadi Suq cemetery nearby (Düring et al. 2019).

[1] A total of 276 handmade, coarse-tempered, poorly fired fragments from the Wadi Suq buildings have been identified as Iron Age I (c.1300–1000 BC). These bowls and jars are closely related to the Late Bronze Age/Iron Age I traditions in the north (Pellegrino et al. 2020; 2023). This assemblage will be reported on in a separate paper.

The Umm an-Nar settlement

Based on data from the 2018 survey, the Umm an-Nar buildings range in size from 30 to 400 m^2. Three types of buildings can be distinguished — small buildings (one or two rooms of modest size), large buildings (multi-room buildings), and compounds (large walled-courtyard buildings). These three types have discrete size ranges (Fig. 4). Conceivably, they served different functions, with small buildings serving as primarily domestic units, large buildings having additional functions for production or storage, and compounds possibly serving to shelter livestock or engage in open-air craft activities. One possible analogy for the compounds are the walled-courtyard buildings that were common in the Bāṭinah until fairly recently (Costa 1985a; 1985b: pl. 4). Large buildings at other sites usually have evidence of craft activities or were used as warehouses, for example at Dahwā and the site of Umm al-Nār (Frifelt 1995; al-Jahwari et al. 2018; Kluge 2018). Our investigations focused on two of these complex buildings whose excavation could be managed with the limited resources at our disposal. Trench AO18 is located over Building 33, which is subdivided into four spaces; trench AS25 is situated over Building 4, of which we exposed an L-shaped cluster of rooms (Fig. 5).

Based on observations from the 2018 survey and excavations elsewhere in Oman, for example at al-Zībā (Schmidt 2018), we expected to find relatively shallow stone walls that served as the basis for a loam or brushwood superstructure (Düring et al. 2019: 117–118). However, the buildings in trenches AO18 and AS25 had walls preserved to a substantial height of up to 60 cm, suggesting that these were not the stone foundations for a superstructure made of other materials. Within the excavated rooms, substantial amounts of collapse deposits consisting of stones and disintegrated loam mortar were found, which indicates that the original height of the stone-built walls was at least double what we excavated, possibly even matching the stature of a Bronze Age person of around 1.70 m (Méry et al. 2004: 171). In addition to the collapse deposits, various occupation deposits were found. In Building 33, pottery clusters of semi-complete vessels were sandwiched between collapse deposits, indicating that pots might have stood on a shelf, were hung from the ceiling, or placed on the roof.

	Umm an-Nar	Umm an-Nar/ Wadi Suq	Wadi Suq	Iron Age I	Iron Age II	Late Islamic
Trench						
AO18	548	2	12			1
AS25	588	1	48			
AV61	3		122	3	1	
BP08	17		324	217		
BQ04	9		150	21		
BQ06	2	1	274	35	2	

FIGURE 2. *An overview of the chronological classification of the ceramic sherds retrieved from the 2023 and 2024 excavations at Burj Huraiz.*

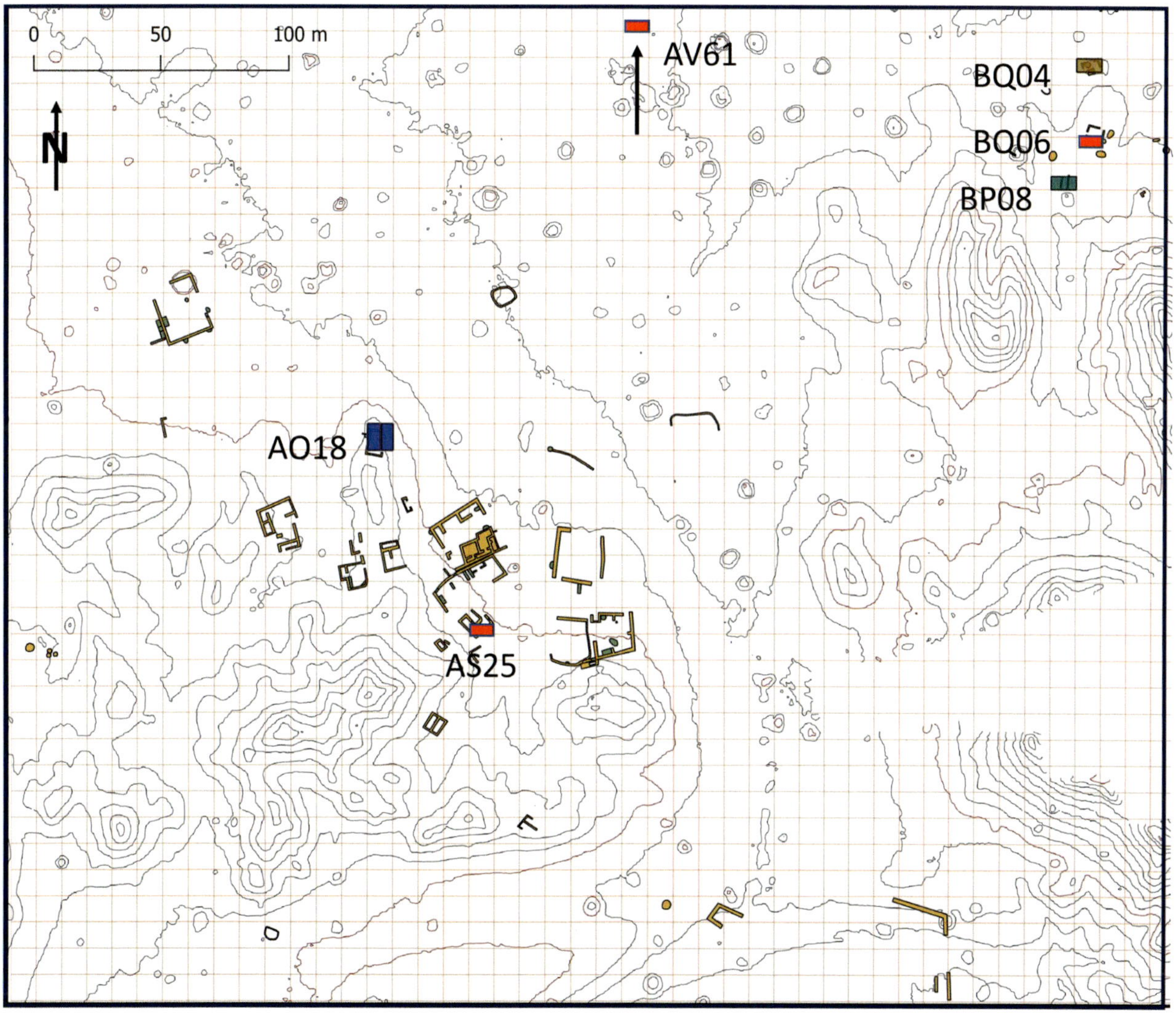

FIGURE 3. *An overview of the trench locations in the 2023 and 2024 excavations at Burj Huraiz.*

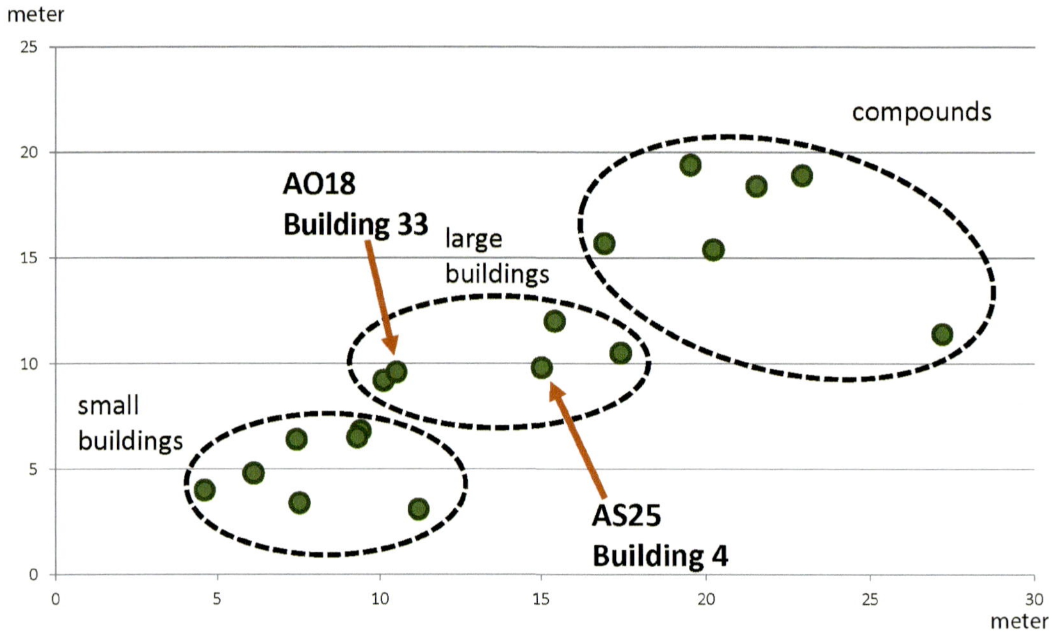

FIGURE 4. *Size distribution of the Umm an-Nar buildings at Burj Huraiz (produced by E. Olijdam).*

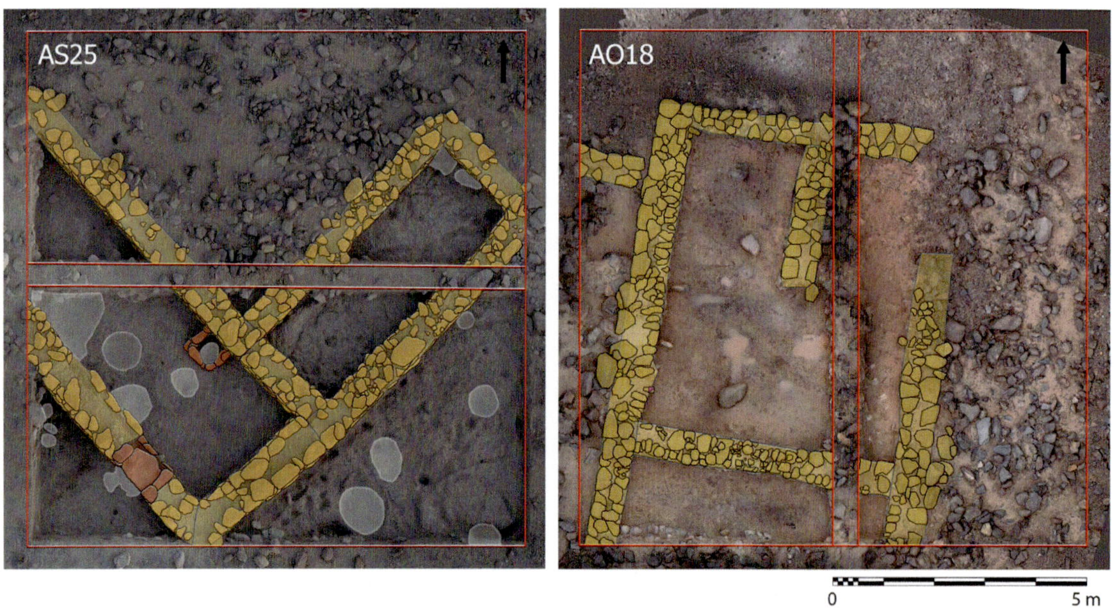

FIGURE 5. *Plan of Building 4 in Trench AS25 and Building 33 in Trench AO18 (produced by R. Hartman).*

All walls are double-faced with a rubble-and-mud core. They are constructed of unworked stones that were retrieved from the direct surroundings. There is a diversity of masonry styles, even within the same structure. Walls can be made of large flat stones placed on their sides (see Fig. 6/wall U27) or of smaller, roughly similar-sized stones placed in horizontal layers (see Fig. 6/wall U13). Both techniques share the rubble-and-mud core and use copious amounts of loam mortar. The diversity highlighted in the two excavated Umm an-Nar buildings from Burj Huraiz suggests that various people were involved in their construction and building traditions did not adhere to a standardized method or require specialized knowledge (but see Azzarà 2020 for a different perspective). Instead, the building styles suggest the existence of localized traditions. Buildings 4 and 33 both show evidence of several building and phases of use.

Building 33 contained animal bones, pottery, and soft-stone vessel fragments directly overlying the modified bedrock floor. Building 4 showed various installations underneath the layers of collapse, including a silo and several fire installations that were located both inside and outside the building. In addition to large amounts of ash and charcoal, these fire pits contained clusters of angular stones. Most fire pits were repeatedly used, as manifested in successive deposits of ash and rocks. Since neither charred seeds or bones nor prills or slag fragments were found, they were most likely used for food processing, for example, for smoking meat and/or fish or heating food in flat-based cooking pots (which we did not encounter in our excavations, but which are known from Dahwā). Five AMS radiocarbon dates derive from charcoal samples from four of these pits (Fig. 7). Four samples cluster tightly between 3800 and 3760 BP; all five provide a range of 2200–2000 cal. BC, which is in accordance with the ceramic dating.

Artefacts

The Umm an-Nar ceramics consist predominantly of vessels made of Sandy ware that is well-known from late Umm an-Nar layers at Hīlī 8, and which could originate from the al-ʿAyn Oasis or from central Oman (Méry 2000; Douglas et al. 2021: 207).[2] The vessel typology compares well to late Umm an-Nar vessels from Hīlī 8, al-Ṭīkha, al-Muyassir, and al-Zībā (Fig. 8). Small jars in semi-fine wares, painted with simple wavy lines, were also found. Black-on-Red Fine ware is attested in smaller numbers. Medium-sized storage jars and smaller vessels, mainly from trench A018, show reduced cores indicative of a change in firing conditions, as has been attested for the latest Umm an-Nar wares at al-Ṭīkha (Deadman et al. 2022).

Black-Slipped jars are the most common imported vessel type, with eighty sherds. Most are of the red micaceous variety, most likely pointing to an Indus origin. Preliminary investigation suggests the existence of several fabric groups that might be linked to different workshops and production centres. Only one sherd is non-micaceous and presumably a local Omani product. One of the micaceous Black-Slipped jars has a post-firing graffito consisting of two, possibly three, Indus signs. Besides Black-Slipped jars, two Grey ware sherds from south-eastern Iran or southern Baluchistan have been recovered.

Additional evidence for a late Umm an-Nar occupation derives from a fragment of a soft-stone vessel. Although it has a slightly larger diameter, this beaker is identical in shape, decoration, stone type, and carving technique to one of the Iranian imported pieces from Hīlī North Tomb A, the last monumental tomb in Hīlī, and was almost certainly produced in the same workshop (Fig. 9).[3] The indigenous soft-stone vessels (cups, bowls, and beakers) also correlate with a late Umm an-Nar date.

Ecofacts

The poor preservation of botanical and faunal remains at Burj Huraiz limits our understanding of agricultural practices and animal management. Despite systematic flotation of all floor deposits and ashy contexts, few carbonized botanical remains were retrieved. The regular occurrence of grinding stones does point to the possible preparation of plant foods. At present, only *Ziziphus* is identified among the macrobotanical remains, perhaps indicating the consumption of this fruit (C. Bakels, internal report September 2024). Thus,

[2] Chemical and petrographic analysis is planned to study the potential local production and origin of the ceramics.

[3] Details and a thorough discussion about this intriguing fragment will be provided in a separate report.

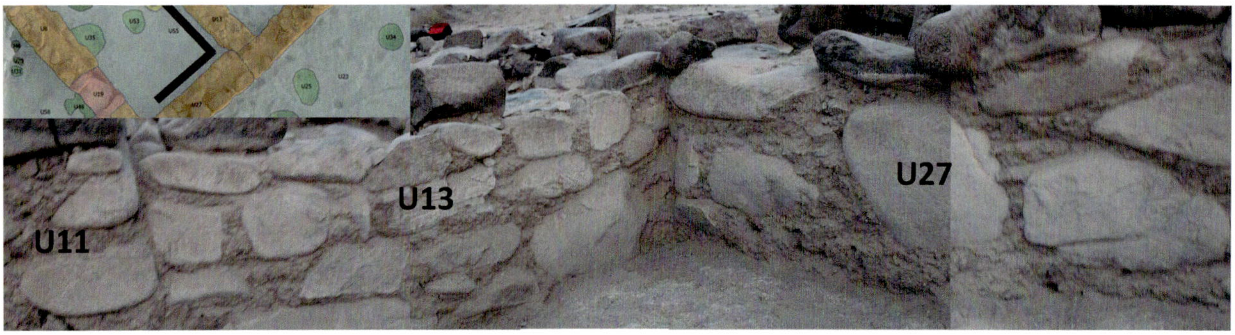

FIGURE 6. *An image of three walls that form part of Building 4.*

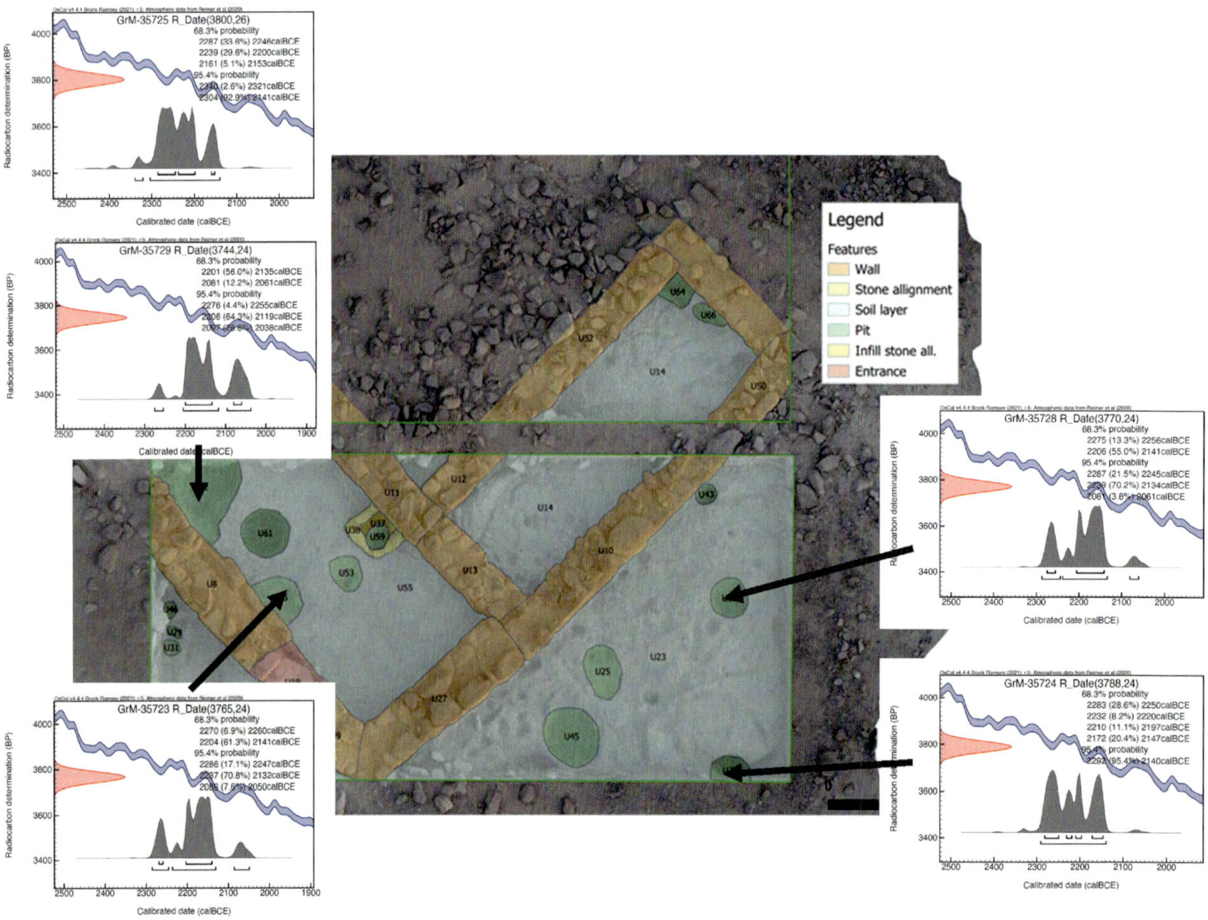

FIGURE 7. *AMS dates obtained from Trench AS25 with their calibrations.*

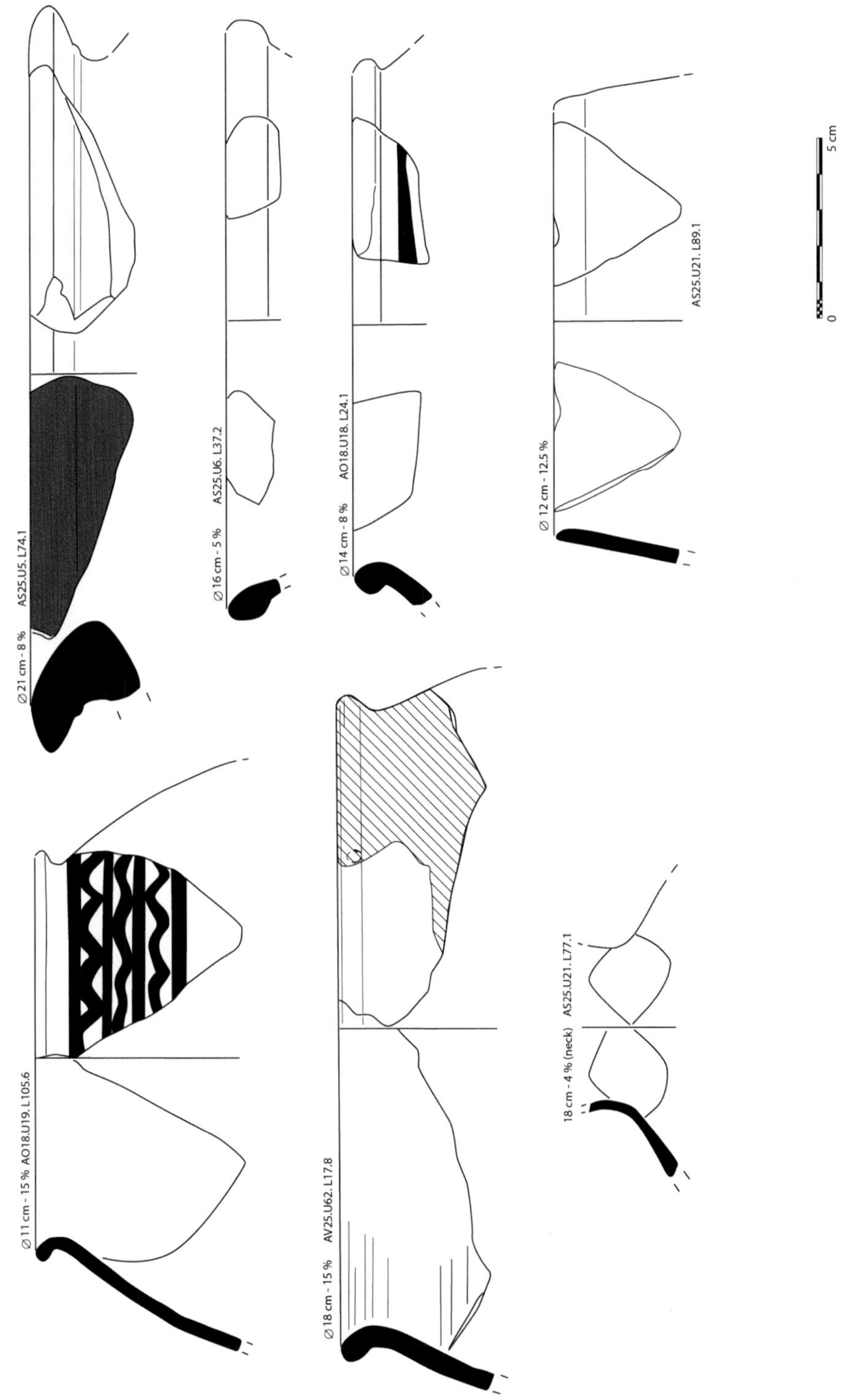

Figure 8. *Selected Umm an-Nar pottery from Trenches AO18 and AS25 (drawings by M. de Vreeze).*

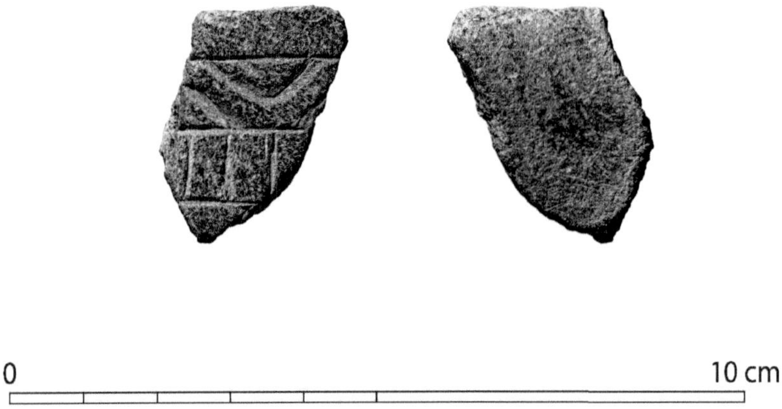

Figure 9. *Imported soft-stone vessel fragment from Trench AS25.*

we lack direct evidence of crop cultivation at Burj Huraiz. At the nearby Umm an-Nar site of Zahrah, a possible Bronze Age dam was found that may have been used to trap runoff water, which was located in a small wadi drainage (Costa & Wilkinson 1987: 98–99). A very similar landscape is found at Burj Huraiz, but subsequent irrigation farming in the late Islamic era, accompanied by the remodelling of the arable fields to make them suitable for irrigation, has obscured earlier uses of the landscape.

Faunal remains were retrieved but are scarce and fragmented, making identification challenging. Pending ongoing examination and given what we know from inland Umm an-Nar sites, these remains should probably be attributed to small ruminants — predominantly, if not exclusively, caprids (Uerpmann & Uerpmann 2008; 2018; Suryanarayan et al. 2024). If this were the case, the large-walled compounds in the settlement might have been linked to animal husbandry.

Fish remains were found from the flotation of surfaces and pits. These are mainly vertebrae but also include cranial bones, such as premaxillae. Two fish taxa have been identified — sardines and a species of emperor. This indicates fishing strategies that relied on near-shore fishing, as emperors predominantly live in coastal waters near rock formations and also venture into mangroves (Lidour et al. 2023). The nearest mangrove is located on the coast of Liwaʾ, nearly 20 km from the site.

Craft industries

Two slag concentrations are located south-east of the Umm an-Nar buildings. Individual fragments are generally between 5 and 10 cm. Areas with the highest density consist of tiny pieces of crushed slag. Fragments with well-formed flow ripples are commonplace. Both concentrations are heavily processed, and slag remains were crushed to be (re)smelted to extract as much remaining copper as possible. While these slag concentrations indicate copper production at a larger scale than anything encountered at other Umm an-Nar sites in our research area, the production was probably still relatively modest. Minute amounts of slag were retrieved from the two buildings, prills were absent, and furnace fragments were small and rare.

The discovery of a nodule of carnelian and shell taxa such as *Dentalium* and *Pinctada*, including a possible bead, indicate some form of production of beads or other personal ornaments. Moreover, on the interior of two valves of Anadara, coloured substances are attested, presumably remnants of cosmetics. The green substance has been identified via portable XRF as malachite and the yellow as possibly goethite (D. Braekmans, internal report November 2024). Other intriguing finds include four pieces of ochre and a grinding stone with a discoloured surface due to the processing of ochre.

Two of the four soft-stone bowl fragments from AS25 are made of a blueish-grey stone rather than the dark-grey stone commonly used for Umm an-Nar bowls, like those from AO18. Likewise, the rim fragment of a beaker is made of a dark-grey stone rather than a blueish-grey stone. This material reversal for the most common Umm an-Nar shapes is notable. Possibly, this indicates further local production. Another possibility is that the fragments date to the terminal phase of the Umm an-Nar period, when production became more experimental, heralding some of the developments of the Wadi Suq period. These two options are, of course, not mutually exclusive. Although no evidence of soft-stone production has yet been identified at Burj Huraiz, it is attested on WAJAP Site 84 (Wadi Suq period) and Site 74 (Iron Age II period), both located nearby in the Wādī Fizḥ/Wādī al-Zahaimi corridor (Düring et al. 2019).

Exchange

The Harappan and Iranian ceramics and the Iranian soft-stone vessel represent imported pieces and suggest that the late Umm an-Nar community living at Burj Huraiz was connected to broader exchange networks. However, these long-distance networks were probably less important than local and regional connections. Regional connections are manifested in the ceramics. Umm an-Nar Fine Red ware appears to have been produced in a few unlocated centres somewhere in the northern al-Ḥajar mountains (Méry 2000: 122). Domestic pottery is dominated by a Sandy ware, for which the most likely source is the al-ᶜAyn Oasis, although additional production sites, possibly even located near Burj Huraiz, might have existed. Given its proximity to the major route towards the Buraimi/al-ᶜAyn oasis, it is highly probable that these connections indicate movement through the Wādī al-Jizī corridor and might be connected to seasonal copper working. The fish remains indicate connections to the nearby coast. It is unclear if this involved inhabitants of the Burj Huraiz settlement or whether it was obtained through exchanges with other communities, such as those occupying the settlement at Site 63/Fizḥ 1 (Düring & Botan 2018) or more mobile groups. Although the on-site copper production at the settlement does not indicate it reached an industrial scale, it probably exceeded domestic demands. This would fit a model in which Burj Huraiz was one of several sites in a network of small-scale copper production sites.

The Wadi Suq settlement

Four trenches have been excavated in the Wadi Suq settlement, each measuring 5 x 10 m, and positioned over well-preserved buildings. The buildings are small, single-roomed rectangular structures of fairly standardized dimensions, *c.*6 x 3 m (Fig. 10). Where entrances are attested, they are located in the long walls, often off-centre. Renovations were observed in all four buildings, indicating several phases of use of these structures.

The interior width of the inner room does not exceed 2.5 m. The stone walls have two outer faces and a rubble-and-mud core. As such, they are similar to the Umm an-Nar walls, yet they are more modest in width — the stones used are smaller, and the wall facing is much less regular. Most exposed walls are made of horizontally placed stones, either parallel to the wall or perpendicular to it; one of the original walls of Building 37 consists of large boulders placed on their side, with the flat side facing inwards. In some cases, where the buildings were sunken into the bedrock, only an interior wall face was present.

Contrary to the Umm an-Nar buildings, walls are typically preserved only one or two courses high. Combined with the fact that we encountered significantly less collapse deposits, this suggests that these walls did not stand higher than three to four courses. Moreover, there are no indications of mud or mud-brick superstructures, which would have left more loamy deposits. This suggests a light superstructure made of branches and fabrics. Two buildings yielded chunks of clay with impressions of straight wooden sticks that may be linked to this type of lightweight and ephemeral superstructure (Fig. 11).

Deposits inside the buildings were shallow, usually not more than 10 cm deep, and devoid of constructed floors, clear installations, or occupational deposits. It is possible that most activities during the Wadi Suq period took place outside the buildings. This is supported by various pits in the outdoor areas, either against the exterior walls or in the immediate vicinity. None of these pits showed evidence of burning. Additionally, most finds were found outside the buildings, such as a soft-stone vessel lid and a copper ring.

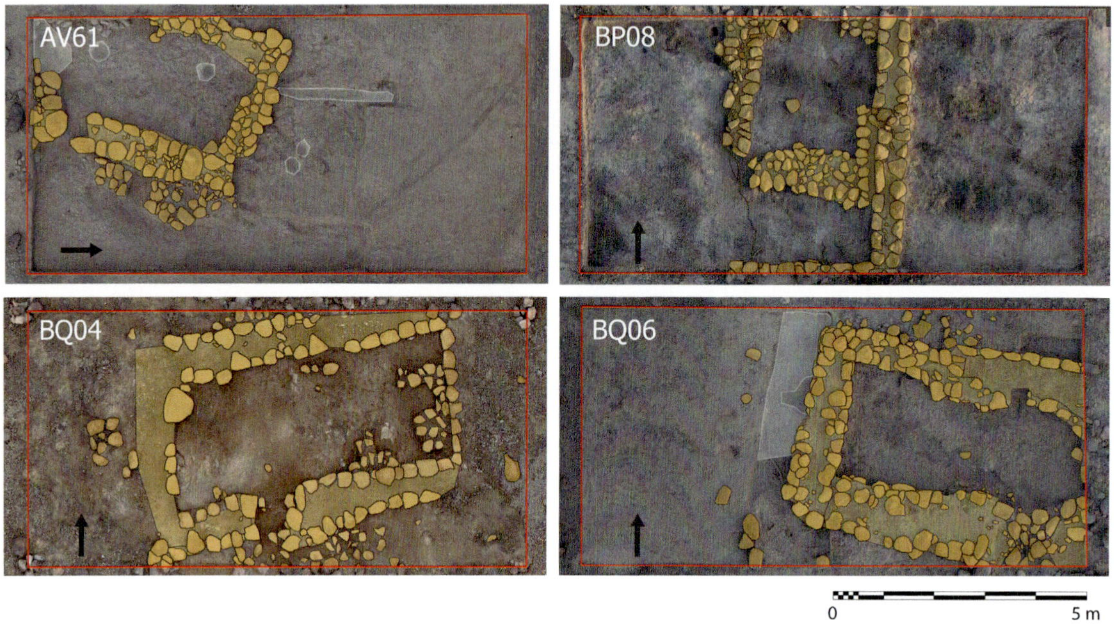

FIGURE 10. *Plans of Building 58 in Trench AV61, Building 37 in Trench BP08, Building 44 in Trench BQ04, and Building 39 in Trench BQ06 (produced by R. Hartman).*

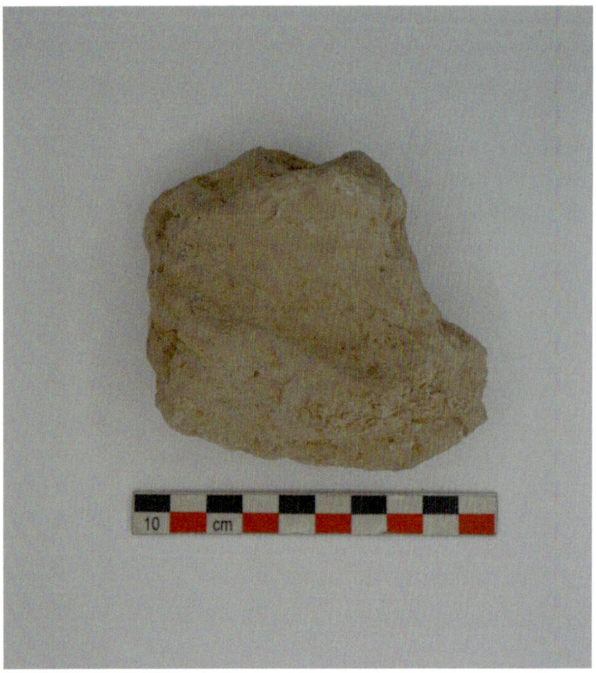

FIGURE 11. *A piece of clay building material displaying an impression of a wooden stick (S73_BQ06_U5_L29).*

Due to the paucity of information about Wadi Suq settlements, comparison with other sites is limited. Our small, single-roomed buildings can be contrasted with the larger, multi-roomed buildings at Raʾs al-Jinz and Khawr Fakkān (Jasim 2000; Monchablon et al. 2003). Published photographs from Khawr Fakkān clearly show walls that are preserved to a considerable height, presumably because these buildings were constructed on a steep slope, thereby cutting into the rock outcrop to create a platform for the interior rooms. By contrast, walls from free-standing buildings appear to be preserved only one or two courses high.

Artefacts

The Wadi Suq ceramic assemblage comprises a wide range of storage jars, bowls, beakers, and spouted jars, the latter often quite fragmented (Fig. 12: spouted jar middle right, BQ04_U1_L2.3 & BQ04_U1_L1.1). Although various fabrics are represented, a slightly gritty Sandy ware (WS.1) dominates. This fabric is prevalent in early Wadi Suq assemblages and can be considered a continuation of Umm an-Nar household industries (as

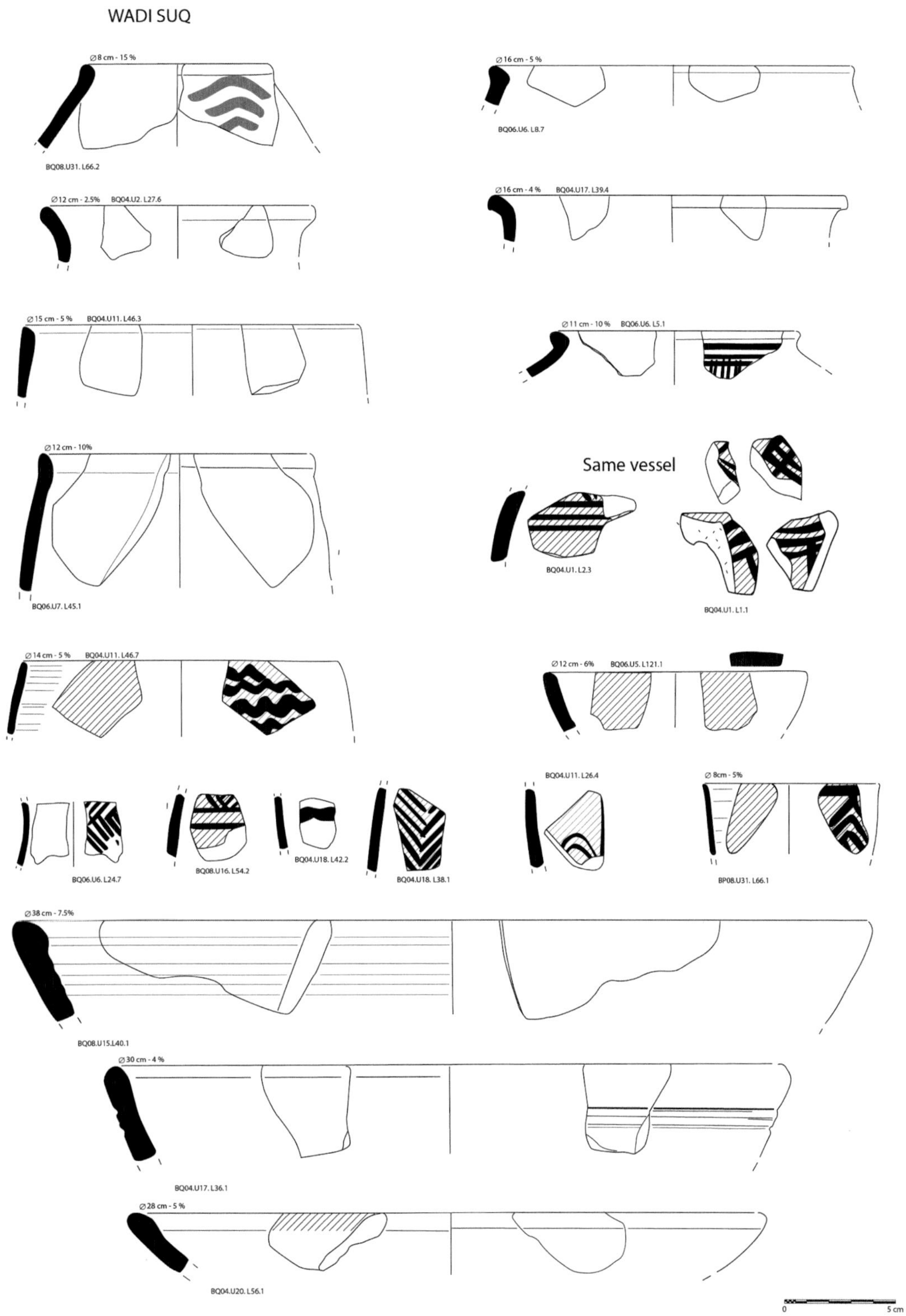

FIGURE 12. *Selected Wadi Suq pottery from Trenches AV61, BP08, BQ04, and BQ06 (drawings by M. de Vreeze).*

also discussed for al-Ṭīkha: Deadman et al. 2022: 58–60). An early Wadi Suq date is typologically congruent with the bowls and beakers with straight rims, globular jars with rim spouts, and medium-sized jars. The most common decorative patterns — combinations of thin wavy lines — are very much in line with those attested in the early Wadi Suq assemblage of Phase III at Hīlī 8 (Cleuziou 1989; de Vreeze 2025). Vessels with painted decorations, such as groups of chevrons and loops, also fit earlier decorative schemes (de Vreeze 2016).

Slightly later (middle) Wadi Suq wares, characterized by a denser vegetal temper, are also attested, predominantly in Building 39 in trench BQ06. This could suggest that the Wadi Suq settlement possibly remained in use for up to two to three centuries. Of the buildings we excavated, Building 39 appears to have been occupied the longest.

Rare imports might include Late Harappan wares, but this needs to be confirmed by future petrographic and chemical analysis. An early second-millennium Barbar sherd from Dilmun was already reported from the surface of Building 39 (Düring et al. 2019: 125, fig. 11).

Ecofacts

We have limited botanical and faunal data for the Wadi Suq buildings due to poor preservation. However, these buildings yielded significant quantities of shells, almost exclusively *Terebralia palustris*. Even though there are no shell mounds anywhere on or near the site, their ubiquity in our excavations indicates they were almost certainly a major food source. This signals a radical break in the diet, as only a few *Terebralia* were found in the Umm an-Nar buildings excavated. The fragmented shells display specific breaking patterns, suggesting they were methodically processed for consumption (cf. Müller Garcia & Nebelsick 2024). The nearest source for *Terebralia* is the Liwaʾ mangrove, nearly 20 km from the site. Their ubiquity at Burj Huraiz fits the idea that *Terebralia* consumption, and its transportation across the region, became a major component of subsistence strategies during the Wadi Suq period (de Vreeze, Kennet & Deadman 2024: 10).

By contrast, the Wadi Suq buildings yielded only a few fish remains. One is the vertebra of a cartilaginous fish, either a ray or a shark. It is likely from the Wadi Suq period, but it may date to the Iron Age I horizon of the building. Animal bones are also virtually unattested, with one notable exception — a goat deposition in BQ06. The context might be Wadi Suq, although there is again the possibility that it belongs to the Iron Age I period. Unfortunately, the deposition was found against the exterior of the southern wall in a pit within a pit. While still largely anatomically aligned, the remains represent an incomplete specimen, as two feet and most of the skull were missing. The young goat appears to have been deposited with the legs up and the head down.

Carbonized plant remains have not been attested in the samples. Only indirect inferences can, therefore, be made about possible (on-site) agricultural practices. Significant quantities of grinding stones are found in all four buildings; Building 37 in trench BP08 stands out because of the large number of grinding stones. Most fragments come from collapse deposits, while others were found *in situ* in the lower courses, indicating they were incorporated into the walls, particularly those that seem to be later additions or refurbishments. This confirms that they are Wadi Suq in date or older. Many more grinding stones can be seen on the surface in the immediate surroundings of the Wadi Suq buildings, where the final occupants probably left them, possibly during the Iron Age I period. A late Islamic field system is located north-east of the Wadi Suq hamlet and contains a background noise of Wadi Suq ceramics (including an Indus import). It is unclear, however, which activity these represented during the Wadi Suq period.

Craft industries

In contrast to the Umm an-Nar buildings, there are indications of possible copper processing near the Wadi Suq buildings in the form of small pieces of slag, pounding stones, and crushing stones. Furthermore, furnace fragments and several small amorphous and rounded fragments of copper were found. Pounding stones and crushing stones also occur in significant numbers in between the buildings. Although this evidence is all indirect, and no primary evidence for metallurgy was found, the fact that more evidence was found in these Wadi Suq buildings at some distance from the slag concentrations and much less in the Umm an-Nar buildings located nearer to these concentrations may be significant. This may be explained by suggesting that copper processing at Burj Huraiz started during the Wadi Suq period, not before. Another, more likely possibility is that Umm an-Nar copper processing occurred away from the buildings, suggesting a stricter spatial division. This might have changed during the Wadi Suq period when craft activities were conducted on a seasonal basis near the intermittently used ephemeral buildings. The few metal objects that were retrieved during the excavations include two rings/earrings, one object resembling a hook, and two perforated flat blunt objects, all of which are no larger than a few centimetres in length. Three of these objects can be plausibly assigned to the Wadi Suq and two to the Umm an-Nar.

Exchange

Evidence of coastal exploitation is much more prevalent in the Wadi Suq sector of the site. The importance of *Terebralia* in the diet might suggest that members of the Burj Huraiz community procured these in person from the nearby coast. Furthermore, the size of the settlement and presumably its community was significantly reduced during the Wadi Suq period. Reliance on the mangrove for food may have been a means of diversifying food supplies, along with pastoralism, (opportunistic) agriculture, fishing, collecting, and craft production (cf. de Vreeze, Kennet & Deadman 2024: 10). The possible Harappan sherds, if confirmed, would indicate a continuation of the involvement of the Indus Civilization known to have lasted in south-east Arabia until *c.*1900 BC. Another indicator of long-distance exchange is the Barbar sherd retrieved during the 2018 survey. It seems that this tiny community remained connected to the larger world. As mentioned above, the slightly gritty Sandy ware dominates the early Wadi Suq domestic pottery and evolved from the Umm an-Nar period Sandy ware, which was predominantly produced in the al-ʿAyn Oasis. This perhaps suggests continuing contacts between Burj Huraiz and communities in the al-ʿAyn Oasis.

The Burj Huraiz settlements in context

Excavations at Burj Huraiz were undertaken to obtain new evidence on rural settlements of the Umm an-Nar and Wadi Suq periods, which are not well investigated, in order to shed more light on the nature of this type of settlement and its associated economies.

There are marked differences between the Umm an-Nar and Wadi Suq settlements. The Umm an-Nar settlement consists of about thirty buildings, which vary in size, complexity, and the types of activities that occurred within them. In contrast, Wadi Suq buildings are more standardized and consist exclusively of small, single-roomed structures. The size of the settlement is also much smaller, even though preliminary chronological evaluation suggests both settlements were in use for about 200 years.

Differences between the substantial Umm an-Nar settlement and a more ephemeral Wadi Suq settlement are mirrored by the level of sophistication of the buildings excavated. Umm an-Nar buildings are well constructed, have more substantial walls, and considerable deposits of collapse, suggesting that they were originally stone-built structures. By contrast, the walls of the Wadi Suq buildings stand only one or two courses high and lack substantial collapse deposits, suggesting their superstructure was made of organic materials. Within these buildings virtually no evidence of domestic activities was found, and most pit features were found outside the buildings.

These differences support a distinction between a more substantial Umm an-Nar settlement, which could point to a more sedentary occupation within a well-integrated settlement system, and a more ephemeral Wadi Suq settlement, which might have been used on a seasonable basis, as indicated by the buildings that probably had organic superstructures and the increased importance of molluscs in the diet. This pattern of reduced occupation at previous Umm an-Nar sites is also attested at other sites (such as Bāt, Raʾs al-Jinz, and al-Ṭīkha), albeit not at the level of detail presented here for Burj Huraiz.

Given the strong evidence of continuity in the pottery, these substantial changes appear to have happened in a very short period of time. Similarly, the evidence from the transitional cemetery indicates it remained in use early into the Wadi Suq period (Düring et al. 2019), a clear sign of social continuity. Another indication suggesting members of the same community continued to use the site is the construction method of the buildings. All Umm an-Nar and Wadi Suq buildings have a thick layer of mortar between the bedrock and the lowest course of stones. Combined with using unworked stones, this specific construction method appears to be typical for Burj Huraiz as it is unreported elsewhere. Given such continuities, it is remarkable that the Umm an-Nar and Wadi Suq settlements are spatially separated, which suggests a deliberate choice on behalf of the Wadi Suq community.

Despite the highlighted differences, both periods show evidence of craft activities, most likely at a household scale. There is evidence for the site's continuing inclusion in regional and long-distance exchange networks, as manifested by imports from the al-ʿAyn Oasis and across the sea (Indus, south-eastern Iran/southern Baluchistan, and Dilmun). At the same time, craft activity and evidence of imports are much more prominent at sites such as Dahwā and Raʾs al-Jinz, indicating that we are perhaps dealing with a different, more rural, type of settlement and economy.

With ongoing further analyses, the evidence from Burj Huraiz is starting to demonstrate how occupation shifted within the context of a single settlement from the Umm an-Nar to the Wadi Suq period (*c.*2000 BC). The Late Umm an-Nar habitation continued into the Wadi Suq period with a shift of focus — a change in architecture to more ephemeral structures and nuances in the relation between space and daily activity, probably related to a gradual but profound change in lifestyle.

Acknowledgements

The Wadi al-Jizzi Archaeological Project (WAJAP) is a collaboration between Leiden University and the Department of Heritage and Tourism. The 2023 and 2024 excavation seasons were made possible through a Beatrice de Cardi Award granted by the Society of Antiquaries of London, alongside funding from the Faculty of Archaeology at Leiden University. We are grateful for the help and support of Sultan al-Bakri, Ali al-Mahrooqi, Ismail al-Rowahi, Samiya as-Shaqsi, Ibrahim al-Kaabi, and Ajjoub al-Balushi, as well as long-time friends Nasser al-Hosni and Seif Abu Said. The fieldwork was carried out by Bleda Düring (2023–2024), Rita Kremer (2023–2024), Eric Olijdam (2023–2024), Zoë van Litsenburg (2023–2024), Noah Melton (2023–2024), Lidwien Meulenkamp (2023–2024), Maxence Bailiff (2023), Attiat Gamal (2023), Lois van den Oever (2023), Suzanne van Beek (2024), Irini Biezeveld (2024), Ruben Hartman (2024), Annelijn Vermaes (2024), and Ajjoub al-Balushi (2024).

References

Azzarà V.M. 2020. Modelling the built environment: Spatial patterns, siting techniques and layout works of non-monumental architecture in Early Bronze Age eastern Arabia. *Arabian Archaeology and Epigraphy* 31: 301–326.

Cable C.M. & Thornton C. 2012. Monumentality and the third-millennium 'towers' of the Oman peninsula. Pages 375–399 in S.G. Abraham, P. Raczek & U.Z. Rizvi (eds), *Connections and complexity. New approaches to the archaeology of South Asia.* Walnut Creek, CA: Left Coast Press.

Carter R. 1997. Defining the Late Bronze Age in southeast Arabia: Ceramic evolution and settlement during the second millennium BC. PhD thesis, University College London. [Unpublished.]

Cleuziou S. 1989. Excavations at Hili 8: A preliminary report on the 4th to the 7th Campaign. *Archaeology in the United Arab Emirates* 5: 61–87.

Costa P.M. 1985a. The Baṭinah and its built environment. *Journal of Oman Studies* 8/2: 109–116.

Costa P.M. 1985b. The palm-frond house of the Baṭinah. *Journal of Oman Studies* 8/2: 117–120.

Costa P.M. & Wilkinson T.J 1987. The hinterland of Sohar. Archaeological surveys and excavations within the region of an Omani seafaring city. *Journal of Oman Studies* 9: 10–238.

Deadman W.M., Kennet D., de Vreeze M. & al-Jahwari N.S. 2022. The nature of third millennium settlement: The example of al-Tikha (Rustaq) an Umm an-Nar site on the Batinah coast of Oman. *Arabian Archaeology and Epigraphy* 33: 49–84.

de Vreeze M. 2016. The social significance of ceramic change at the start of the Wadi Suq period. Rethinking ceramic continuity and change based on recent evidence from the tombs at Qarn al-Harf. *Proceedings of the Seminar for Arabian Studies* 46: 63–80.

de Vreeze M. 2025. *The Wadi Suq ceramics from Qarn al-Harf: Tracing social change through technical developments in ceramics during the early 2nd millennium BC. Qarn al-Harf excavations II.* Oxford: Archaeopress.

de Vreeze M., Düring B.S. & Olijdam E. 2020. New light on the late Wadi Suq period from the Ṣuhār hinterlands. *Proceedings of the Seminar for Arabian Studies* 50: 141–155.

de Vreeze M., Kennet D. & Deadman W.M. 2024. Karstic aquifers and climate refugia: A preliminary outline history of water-management strategy in Bronze and Iron Age Southeast Arabia. *Open Quaternary* 10/5: 1–16.

Döpper S. 2018a. Introduction. Pages 1–6 in Döpper 2018c.

Döpper S. 2018b. Al-Zebah and its position in the regional settlement pattern of central inner-Oman. Pages 87–96 in Döpper 2018c.

Döpper S. (ed.). 2018c. *Beyond tombs and towers. Domestic architecture of the Umm an-Nar period in Eastern Arabia.* (Arabia Orientalis, 4). Wiesbaden: Harrassowitz.

Döpper S. 2024. *Landmarks of identity. Bronze Age towers of the Oman Peninsula.* (The Archaeological Heritage of Oman, 13). Oxford: Archaeopress/Muscat: Ministry of Heritage and Tourism.

Douglas K.A., al-Jahwari N.S., Hesein M. & de Vreeze M. 2024. A ritual building from the Umm an-Nar settlement, Dahwa 7 in al-Batinah Plain, northeast Oman. *Arabian Archaeology and Epigraphy* 35/1: 17–40.

Douglas K.A., al-Jahwari N.S., Méry S., Hesein M. & Williams K.D. 2021. Umm an-Nar settlement pottery from Dahwa 7 (DH7), northern al-Batinah, Oman. *Arabian Archaeology and Epigraphy* 32/S1: 198–212.

Düring B.S. 2022. Beyond dots with dates: A landscape approach to the Sohar Hinterlands. *Arabian Archaeology and Epigraphy* 33: 170–177.

Düring B.S. & Botan S. 2018. The Early Bronze Age settlements of the Sohar Hinterlands: Scratching the surface. Pages 17–27 in Döpper 2018c.

Düring B.S., Olijdam E. & Botan S.A. 2017. New Iron Age funerary data from collective graves in Wādī Fizḥ, northern Oman. *Proceedings of the Seminar for Arabian Studies* 47: 75–91.

Düring B.S., Botan S.A., Olijdam E. & Aal H.J.M. 2019. The Bronze Age cultural landscape of Wādī al-Zahaimi. *Proceedings of the Seminar for Arabian Studies* 49: 115–127.

Frifelt K. 1995. *The island of Umm an-Nar.* ii. *The third millennium settlement.* (Jutland Archaeological Society Publications, 26/2). Aarhus: Aarhus University Press.

Halperin C.T. & Schwartz L.E. 2016. The archaeology of vernacular architecture in the Pre-Columbian Americas. Pages 17–36 in C.T. Halperin & L.E. Schwartz (eds), *Vernacular architecture in the Pre-Columbian Americas.* New York: Routledge.

al-Jahwari N.S. & Kennet D. 2010. Umm an-Nar settlement in the Wadi Andam (Sultanate of Oman). *Proceedings of the Seminar for Arabian Studies* 40: 161–172.

al-Jahwari N.S., Douglas K., al-Belushi M. & Williams K.D. 2018. Umm an-Nar settlement at Dahwa (DH1), Oman: Preliminary results of the archaeological investigation, 2014–2016. Pages 29–49 in Döpper 2018c.

Jasim S.A. 2000. Second millennium settlement at Khor Fakkan, The Emirate of Sharjah, UAE. *Isimu* 3: 145–184.

Kennet D. & Velde C. 1995. Third and early second-millennium occupation at Nud Ziba, Khatt (U.A.E.), *Arabian Archaeology and Epigraphy* 6: 81–99.

Kennet D., Deadman W.M. & al-Jahwari N.S. 2016. The Rustaq-Batinah archaeological survey. *Proceedings of the Seminar for Arabian Studies* 46: 155–168.

Kennet D., Caine A., Weeks L. & Velde C. 2025. *Southeast Arabia at the dawn of the second millennium. The Bronze Age collective graves of Qarn al-Harf, Ras al-Khaimah (UAE).* London: Oxbow Books.

Kluge J. 2018. The domestic architecture of Umm an-Nar island. Pages 7–15 in Döpper 2018c.

Laursen S. & Steinkeller P. 2017. *Babylonia, the Gulf Region, and the Indus: Archaeological and textual evidence for contact in the third and early second millennium BC.* (Mesopotamian Civilizations, 21). Winona Lake, IN: Eisenbrauns.

Lidour K., Beech M.J., Eddisford D., Phillips C.S., Schwall C. & Jasim S.A. 2023. A Bronze to Iron Age fishing economy at Kalbāʾ 4 (Emirate of Sharjah, United Arab Emirates). *Arabian Archaeology and Epigraphy* 34: 44–62.

Magee P. 2014. *The archaeology of Prehistoric Arabia. Adaptation and social formation from the Neolithic to the Iron Age.* Cambridge: Cambridge University Press.

Méry S. 2000. *Les céramiques d'Oman et l'Asie moyenne. Une archéologie des échanges à l'Age du Bronze.* (CRA Monographies, 23). Paris: CNRS.

Méry S., McSweeney K., Al Tikriti W.Y. & van der Leeuw S. 2004. New approaches to a collective grave from the Umm An-Nar period at Hili (UAE). *Paléorient* 30/1: 163–178.

Monchablon C., Crassard R., Munoz O., Guy H., Bruley-Chabot G. & Cleuziou S. 2003. Excavations at Ra's al-Jinz RJ-1: Stratigraphy without tells. *Proceedings of the Seminar for Arabian Studies* 33: 31–47.

Müller Garcia I.D.L.F. & Nebelsick J.H. 2024. Morphology and taphonomy of the Gastropod *Terebralia Palustris* from an Iron Age site in the Arabian Peninsula. *Facies* 70: 13.

Pellegrino M.P., Méry S., Benoist A., Costa S. & Charbonnier J. 2020. Ceramic exchange in the northern UAE during the Late Bronze Age: Preliminary results of macroscopic and petrographic analyses. *Proceedings of the Seminar for Arabian Studies* 50: 259–273.

Pellegrino M.P., Charbonnier J., Benoist A., Decruyenaere D., Lidour K., Degli Esposti M. & Hamel A. 2023. Insights on the Late Bronze Age economy in south-eastern Arabia. Self-sufficiency and exchanges in Masafi–5. Pages 157–181 in P. El Fadi, M. Gannon, K.A. Shohof & T. Al Ghoul (eds), *Advances in UAE archaeology. Proceedings of Abu Dhabi's archaeology conference 2022.* (Archaeopress Archaeology). Oxford: Archaeopress/Abu Dhabi: Department of Culture and Tourism – Abu Dhabi.

Phillips C. 2007. The third-millennium tombs and settlement at Mowaihat in the Emirate of Ajman, U.A.E. *Arabian Archaeology and Epigraphy* 18: 1–7.

Potts D.T. 1990. *A prehistoric mound in the Emirate of Umm al-Qaiwain, U.A.E. Excavations at Tell Abraq in 1989.* Copenhagen: Munksgaard.

Potts D.T. 1991. *Further excavations at Tell Abraq. The 1990 Season.* Copenhagen: Munskgaard.

Schmidt C. 2018. The Umm an-Nar settlement of Al-Zebah. Pages 71–86 in Döpper 2018c.

Squitieri A. 2024. Assyrian conquest and ruralization: Unveiling territorial dynamics in the provinces of Magiddû and Samerina. *Levant* 56: 239–258.

Suryanarayan A., Degli Esposti M., Méry S., Stronlin L., Mazuy A., Moraleda-Cibrían N. ... Regert M. 2024. Domestic food practice and vessel-use at Salūt-ST1, central Oman, during the Umm an-Nar Period. *Arabian Archaeology and Epigraphy* 35: 41–60.

Swerida J. 2022. Revisiting 'settlement': A case study of terminology and Early Bronze Age Southeast Arabia. *Journal of Anthropological Archaeology* 65: 101382.

Uerpmann M. & Uerpmann H-P. 2008. Animal economy during the Early Bronze Age in south-east Arabia. Pages 465–485 in E. Villas, L. Gouichon, A.M. Choyke & H. Buitenhuis (eds), *Archaeozoology of the Near East VIII.* (Travaux de la Maison de l'Orient et de la Méditerranée, 49). Lyon: Maison de l'Orient.

Uerpmann M. & Uerpmann H-P. 2018. Animal economy in an early oasis settlement. Pages 254–255 in D. Frenez & R. Garba (eds), *In the shadow of the ancestors. The Prehistoric foundations of the early Arabian civilization in Oman.* (Second expanded edition). Muscat: Ministry of Heritage and Culture/Oxford: Archaeopress.

Velde C. 2009. The landscape of the Middle Bronze Age in the UAE — Where did people live? Pages 61–74 in *Proceedings of the international history conference on new perspectives on recording UAE history.* Abu Dhabi: National Centre for Documentation and Research.

Authors' addresses

Eric Olijdam, Faculty of Archaeology, Leiden University, Adriaan Butijnweg 1, 4411 BT Rilland, The Netherlands.
e-mail olijdam@zeelandnet.nl

Bleda S. Düring, Faculty of Archaeology, Leiden University, Einsteinweg 2, 2300 RA Leiden, The Netherlands.
e-mail B.s.during@arch.leidenuniv.nl

Michel de Vreeze, Lower Mount Joy, South Rd, Durham DH1 3LE, UK.
e-mail micheldevreeze@gmail.com

Zoë C.A.N. van Litsenburg, Faculty of Archaeology, Leiden University, Einsteinweg 2, 2300 RA Leiden, The Netherlands.
e-mail ZoevLitsenburg@outlook.com

Proceedings of the Seminar for Arabian Studies 54 (2025): 201–212

The onomasticon of the Himaitic and Ancient South Arabian inscriptions from Ḥimā: a comparative overview and insights into their cultural and linguistic layers

Alessia Prioletta

Summary

The ever-growing corpus of inscriptions from Ḥimā recorded and digitized by the MAFSN mission provides an extremely rich onomastic repertoire of over 23,800 personal names. The majority of these inscriptions are written in the Himaitic-Thamudic script, while the rest are in the monumental South Arabian script. Several hundred texts are carved in Arabic script, while a few others are in other Semitic and non-Semitic scripts (Nabataean, Nabataeo-Arabic, Syriac, and Greek).

This study provides a comparative overview of the onomasticon of the first two categories, focusing on the typological features of proper names, including their structure, linguistic patterns, and theophoric elements. Archaic onomastic traits, such as the use of mimation and names derived from verbal roots, are examined alongside the distribution of names invoking both North and South Arabian deities. The corpus also displays phonological and morphological features unique to the region or associated with North Arabian languages.

This research identifies significant differences in name types and linguistic patterns between the different script traditions and script sub-varieties used in the region. Such script variation also correlates with certain formulaic expressions and linguistic features. The onomastic data therefore seem to converge on the idea that the area of Ḥimā was a complex ethnolinguistic landscape in which different populations interacted, perhaps through different historical periods.

Keywords: onomasticon, Himaitic, Ancient South Arabian, inscriptions, onomastic typology

Introduction: overview of the corpus and methodology

The ever-expanding corpus of inscriptions and graffiti recorded and digitized by the French-Saudi Archaeological and Epigraphic Mission to Najrān (MAFSN) in the area of Ḥimā now surpasses 20,000 items. Three quarters of these texts are written in the local variety of Thamudic script, labelled Himaitic (HIM) (Robin & Gorea 2016; Prioletta 2018). The last quarter is carved in monumental Ancient South Arabian script (ASA) (Prioletta 2022a). A few hundred texts are carved in a mixed South Arabian and Himaitic script.[1]

Throughout twelve seasons of investigations, the MAFSN mission surveyed a substantial part of the desert macro-area around the village of Ḥimā, but several sectors have yet to be recorded. However, it is reasonable to assume that this ratio between ASA and HIM inscriptions also applies to the areas that remain unexplored to date.

A preliminary hypothesis is that in addition to its use by ancient South Arabian travellers from Yemen, the South Arabian alphabet was also used by settled populations in the oases of Najrān and Qaryat al-Fāw. This is evidenced by the presence of local lineages from these cities in ASA graffiti. Conversely, the pastoralist communities inhabiting the desert margins of these oases appear to have used the Himaitic-Thamudic alphabet.

This paper presents a non-exhaustive comparative overview of the onomasticon of both kinds of documents, for two main reasons. Firstly, research on Thamudic inscriptions from the southern Arabian Peninsula has greatly progressed recently but is still in its infancy, and the domain of onomastics is clearly an extremely rich field to explore, given that the overwhelming majority of data are made up of proper names. Secondly,

[1] A few hundred texts are carved in Arabic script, while a few others are in other Semitic and non-Semitic scripts (Nabataean, Nabataeo-Arabic, Syriac, and Greek).

a contrastive approach between these two sub-corpora is fundamental in order to identify possible areal distribution patterns of the various onomastic typologies. This could help us gain a better grasp of the cultural profile of the social components that produced these texts.

The research conducted by Christian Robin on various areas of the Himaitic onomasticon revealed significant insights that enabled him to formulate hypotheses regarding the authors of the graffiti from Ḥimā (Robin & Gorea 2016; Robin et al. 2022). He noted, for example, that the distribution of theonyms in the theophoric names of both documentations is rather similar, with a predominance of North Arabian or pan-Semitic deities. Based on this evidence, Robin argued that the people who carved the graffiti belonged to the same local population and worshipped the same deities, regardless of the type of script they used.

Our research aims to pursue these pioneering studies, adopting a somewhat different approach aimed at testing new historical and linguistic hypotheses. Prior to presenting the results of our data analysis, it is also necessary to clarify a number of points. To begin with, our recent research has revealed that the Thamudic-Himaitic script is not graphically uniform, as it consists of two main varieties. The majority of these inscriptions, including over 10,000 texts, are carved in a Thamudic script known for its formal aesthetics, large characters, and angular design. Previously labelled 'formal', 'geometric', or 'ostentatoire', this script has been reclassified by the present author as Common Himaitic due to its widespread use in Ḥimā and surrounding areas. In addition, *c.*1500 inscriptions exhibit distinctive characteristics such as smaller letters and curved, serpentine strokes. To differentiate this script from earlier classifications such as 'informal' or 'cursive', it is designated Curvilinear Himaitic.[2] In addition, we should also stress that the sub-corpus in ASA script is particularly difficult to untangle as far as the origin of the authors of the graffiti is concerned. Only when the content offers some historical or linguistic data are we able to determine whether the author was an inhabitant of the nearby oases or rather someone from southern Arabia (Prioletta 2022a).

Lastly, it is pertinent to provide a brief overview of the data collection and analysis methods employed in this research. The onomastic corpus was processed by digitizing the inscriptions in a custom-built Information System using Filemaker Pro™, designed for the internal use of the MAFSN to manage the extensive dataset. The epigraphic records include transcriptions and translations of each text, along with their linguistic, grammatical, and palaeographic features. Among the documented attributes, the onomastic content is captured in two distinct fields. The first, 'Onomastic formula', describes whether a text consists of one or multiple juxtaposed names, and whether it includes an explicit patronymic or lineage name introduced by the words *bn* ('son') and *ḏ* ('he of'). The second field, 'Name structure', details the composition of each name, specifying whether it is a simple or sentence name, its reconstructible pattern, and whether it is theophoric, among other characteristics. The data were then exported to Excel for quantitative and comparative analysis. The study is therefore based on unpublished material, as only a few hundred ASA and HIM graffiti have been published so far (notably in Robin et al. 2022).[3] However, a project for the online publication of the corpus on available platforms is in progress, with plans for implementation in 2026.

Some general aspects of the corpus

In light of the multifaceted ethnic and cultural nature of our onomasticon and the significant numerical disparity between the aforementioned sub-corpora, we will now present the figures and outline the most salient elements of the corpus.

The collection counts to date just over 23,800 personal names, of which 63% are in Himaitic. First of all, we observe that the most represented typological category of proper names in the two corpora is by far that of simple or one-word names. Two-word names, on the other hand, occur eight times less than one-

[2] In addition to the preliminary results published in Prioletta 2018, our current research on Himaitic graffiti has been presented in a number of workshops and seminars, although these remain unpublished. An article focusing specifically on the Himaitic alphabet and its sub-varieties is in preparation.

[3] This volume contains the complete corpus of graffiti found in the ʿĀn Jamal sector, including 339 ASA inscriptions, 193 HIM inscriptions, and thirty-one Arabic inscriptions. References to these texts and to other relevant examples published in other publications are given throughout the text and in the tables.

word names.[4] Following on from this, two other, quite predictable observations can be made: on the one hand, slightly more than two thirds (68%) of the one-word names are found in the Himaitic graffiti. On the other, nearly half of the two-word names (47%) occur in the ASA inscriptions, and this despite the fact that the latter are largely outnumbered by Himaitic graffiti.

Sentence names are known to be typical of the most archaic stage of West Semitic and are extensively attested in the Amorite onomasticon (Streck 2000). Conversely, simple names represent the bulk of some first-millennium Semitic cultures, such as those of central and northern pre-Islamic Arabia (Amaldi 1989). Subsequently, this class of simple names becomes characteristic of the Islamic Arabic onomasticon, where sentence names containing theophoric elements referring to the pagan heritage are almost entirely replaced by compound names that conform to Islamic tradition and values, specifically those containing the name *Allah* and its epithets (Schimmel 1989).

Typologically archaic features and their possible origins

Mimation

The first one is the use of the final -m morpheme, or mimation.[5] This morpheme again characterizes the proper names of Early West Semitic, although remnants of it have also been detected in Ugaritic and biblical Hebrew names (Layton 1990: 155–197). In the Arabian Peninsula, mimation is a typical feature of Ancient South Arabian proper names. Mimation is suffixed to one-word names and only exceptionally to compound names.[6]

Common HIM	ANA
bgrm (MNS02.02 no. 61)	*bgr*
bhs^{2}m (SHI01.55 no. 01)	*bhs^2*
ġlbm (SSA02.136 no. 15)	*ġlb*
hnʾm (SSA04.03 no. 29)	*hnʾ*
ns^{1}ʾm (UNK01.04 no. 27)	*ns^{1}ʾ*
qs^{1}rm (GRZ05.16 no. 79)	*qs^{1}r*
s^{1}ʿdm (GRZ07.13 no. 13)	*s^{1}ʿd*

FIGURE 1. *Pairs of personal names attested in Himaitic (HIM) and other Ancient North Arabian (ANA) corpora, highlighting the presence of the -m morpheme in the Himaitic forms.*

In the onomasticon of Ḥimā, mimation is a minor feature, as it concerns 11% of the corpus. However, it is noteworthy that *c.*50% of the instances of mimated names are observed in Himaitic graffiti. This relatively high percentage may reasonably be explained as an areal feature shared by Himaitic and ASA, which distinguishes this southern variety of Thamudic from the other Ancient North Arabian epigraphic corpora produced in the nomadic milieu (Fig. 1).[7]

One striking observation, however, is that mimation is more characteristic of common script, while it is practically unknown in curvilinear script. Only seventy-five out of 1500 occurrences of mimated names are found in curvilinear script.[8] This disproportion cannot only be ascribed to the quantitative contrast between these two corpora, nor to the distribution of the different onomastic classes in each corpus, as one-word names also largely prevail over sentence names in the curvilinear script corpus. This distinctive feature

[4] Two-word names were conceived as a broad category that includes sentence or compound names, but also defined names (name and article). The latter, when they contain three elements, have been grouped under the category of three-word names, which currently comprises less than fifty items.

[5] One should distinguish between the enclitic particle -m (which is invariably followed by a vowel) and the authentic mimation, representing the vestige of the morpheme -m that was distinctive of proto-Semitic nouns in unbound state following the case vowel in singular and plural feminine. Despite the presence of these two morphemes in specific morpho-syntactic positions, it is often challenging to distinguish between them in the absence of vocalization (see Layton 1990: 155).

[6] In compound names, mimation can occur after *ʾl* in nominal sentence names, such as in the Ugaritic *ʿbdʾilm* as opposed to *ʿbd ʾil*, both to be translated 'servant of God/El' (Layton 1990: 163).

[7] The names presented in the tables may occur multiple times across different corpora. The occurrences in the ASA and ANA corpora were sourced from the DASI and OCIANA databases, and no sigla for individual texts have been provided, as these references are easily searchable in their respective databases. As for the ASA and Himaitic texts from Ḥimā containing the names studied here, references have been provided throughout the text and in the tables to the publications where relevant examples were previously published.

[8] Examples of mimated names in the curvilinear script are *Ḏʾbm* (JFR01.06 no. 4), *S^{2}hrm* (MRY01.27 no. 6), and *Whbm* (JFR01.36 no. 20).

a

YFʿL-NAMES[1]	*YHFʿL*-NAMES[2]
yʾmr (HAB01.66 no. 07)	*yhḏkr* (GRZ05.14 no. 44)[3]
yʿml (SMA01.14 no. 15)	*yhfrʿ* (JFR01.14 no. 02)
ygmd (MNS02.05 no. 19)	*yhġṯ* (HAB01.20 no. 07)
yhrg (SHI01.122 no. 07)	*yhkbr* (ZGT01.02 no. 13)
yḫld (SSA02.153 no. 07)	*yhqm* (HJB01.01 no. 13)
ynʿm (HQN01.57 no. 54)	*yhs¹mʿ* (SHA01.05 no. 29)
ynṣfn (KSM01.05 no. 07)	*yhṯb* (SHI01.41.04)
yrfʾ (SSA04.21 no. 14)	*yhwgd* (JFR01.81 no. 01)
ys²gb (GDY01.66 no. 02)	*yhyṯʿ* (JFR06.18 no. 01)

b

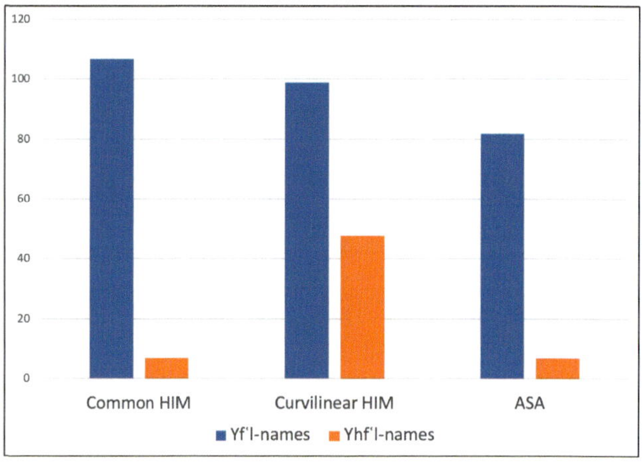

[1] see Prioletta, in preparation: table 14; [2] see Prioletta, in preparation: table 15; [3] see Prioletta 2018: fig. 8.

FIGURE 2. a. *Examples of* yfʿl *and* yhfʿl *names in curvilinear Himaitic; some of them are also attested in common Himaitic;* b. *distribution of* yfʿl *and* yhfʿl *names by type of script and script variety.*

thus necessitates a comprehensive investigation, which we intend to undertake in the future with the aim of providing a compelling historical and linguistic explanation.

Yfʿl- and *yhfʿl*-names

By contrast, the curvilinear corpus comprises a comparatively high percentage of other typologically archaic names, such as those based on verbs in the prefix-conjugation, either in the G-stem (*yfʿl*) or the C-stem (*yhfʿl*). One third of the *yfʿl* names are in curvilinear script and, quite exceptionally, forty-six of the sixty names based on the *yhfʿl* pattern are also in this script (Fig. 2).

It is important to recall that both typologies appear in the ASA onomasticon (Bron 1991)[9] while in the ANA corpora, it is particularly the *yfʿl* names that are well attested; the *yhfʿl* names, on the other hand, are rarer in northern Arabia.[10]

Theophoric names[11]

Theophoric names make up 6.7% of the entire corpus,[12] and about half of the occurrences (45%) are found in ASA texts, which proportionally signifies a considerably high correlation of this type of name with ASA script. There are, however, some differences in the distribution of the theonyms used.

The most attested theophoric names in Himaitic are by far elistic names, based on the theonym -*ʾl*- (Fig. 3) (e.g. Robin & Gorea 2016: pl. 7 [*ʾlgrm*]). The theophorous element *ʾl* appears most often at the end of the name. While some of them are well attested in both the ANA and ASA onomasticon (*ʾws¹ʾl*, *Bnʾl*, *Mʿdʾl*, *Wddʾl*, *Whbʾl*), others only appear in ANA (*ʾmrʾl*, *Yms¹kʾl*).[13]

[9] A sub-category of the *yfʿl* names are theophoric names based on PC + divine name. In his study, Bron observed that these nouns and the roots they are based on are common between ASA and Hebrew. Furthermore, he noted that although they are found across the four ASA languages, in Sabaic they are typical of the early phase of the language.

[10] In the Dadanitic corpus on OCIANA (accessed October 2024), only two examples of *yhfʿl* names are attested: *Yhḏkr* and *Yhḏfm*. Additional *yhfʿl* names have been identified in Thamudic epigraphic material not yet available online. We are grateful to one of the anonymous reviewers for bringing this to our attention.

[11] Giovanni Mazzini contributed substantially to this section. He and the present author are preparing a study focusing on the stock of theophoric names within the Himaitic onomasticon.

[12] A list of the theophoric names found at Ḥimā, along with specific examples and references to the publication, can be found in Robin et al. 2022: 101–102.

[13] Despite the fact that they are formed from well-known roots, none of these three names is found in the DASI database (accessed February 2025). In OCIANA (accessed February 2025), *ʾmrʾl* is attested forty-five times, *Yms¹kʾl* twice.

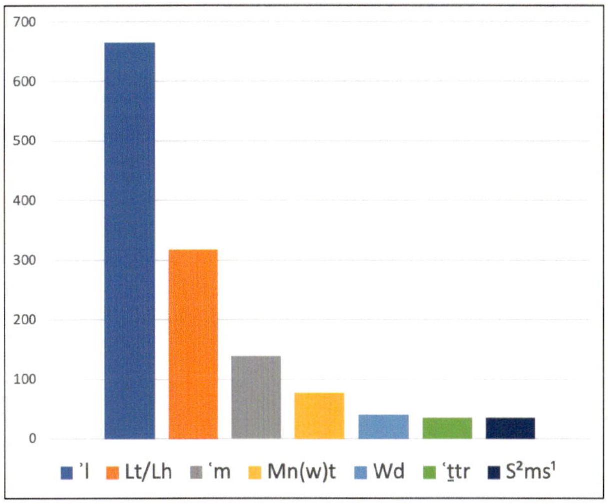

FIGURE 3. *Distribution of theonyms in the onomastic corpus from Ḥimā.*

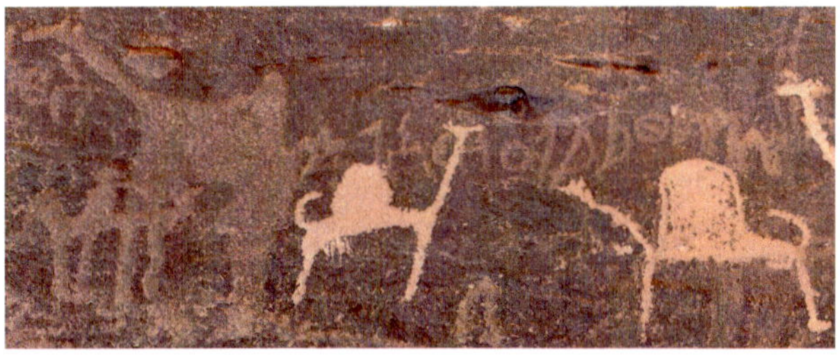

FIGURE 4. *The graffito JFR01.13 no. 4 reading* [.]lm wdd lʿḏrʾl. *The beginning of the author's name is covered by a camel drawing.*

A remarkable name attested three times in the curvilinear corpus is *lʿḏrʾl* (Fig. 4).[14] This name is known from the ASA inscriptions as the name borne by two kings of Muhaʾmir; the tribe settled in the area of Najrān between the eighth and second centuries BC (Robin 2024).[15] The variant *ʿḏrʾl* is attested twice in the graffiti in ASA script, and is also common in the Ancient North Arabian corpora,[16] where theophores derived from the root *ʿḏr* are well attested.[17] As this root is again typical of the early Semitic onomasticon, being especially documented in Amorite personal names,[18] its occurrence in both the northern and southern pre-Islamic corpora is indicative of a shared trait, suggesting the presence of an archaic onomastic layer in the Arabian Peninsula.[19]

Names based on appellatives usually used as theophorous elements, such as common Semitic kinship nouns (*ʾb* 'father', *dd* 'paternal uncle', *ʿm* 'paternal grandfather', and so forth; Kogan 2012: 234–236) are found across the two sub-corpora. One highly interesting trend concerns the *ʿm*-noun (Fig. 5). This may appear as the first or second element of sentence names. In ASA onomastics, where *ʿm*-based names are quite common (Bron 1994), names with *ʿm* in the second position are especially typical of Qatabanic, and it is generally believed that in this case it more likely refers to the main deity of this kingdom.

On the other hand, a name such as *ʿmʾl*, which is relatively common throughout the Ḥimā corpus and is largely attested in both the Ancient South Arabian and the pre-Islamic North Arabian onomasticon, is again an Arabian relic of early West Semitic, to be compared to Amorite Am-mu-e-el, /ʿAmmu-ʾel/ 'the paternal grandfather is God'. It should be noted, however, that apart from *ʿmʾl* and other names shared between Himaitic and ASA inscriptions, such as *ʿmḏhr*, *ʿmydʿ*, and *ʿmyṯʿ*, the majority of the *ʿm*-names are correlated with the Himaitic curvilinear sub-corpus. Given the fact that

[14] In the graffito JFR01.13 no. 4 the name is preceded by the word *wdd*, and so it is unlikely that *Lʿḏrʾl* should be parsed *l-ʿḏrʾl* (assuming therefore an initial *l-* particle). For ASA names composed of a preposition and a theonym or theophoric element, see Hazim 1994. The name *Lʿḏrʾl* is listed on p. 370.

[15] A king named *Lʿḏrʾl* was already known from the Sabaic inscription RES 3943. A more recent king with this name is the author of an inscription from Najrān and published in Robin, Ghabbān & Saʿīd 2014: 1070–1073, fig. 20.

[16] The name has sixty-seven occurrences, the vast majority of which are found in Safaitic (OCIANA, accessed October 2024).

[17] The root *ʿḏr* is used in both simple and compound names; *ʿḏr* and *ʿḏrʾl* are the most common names of the former and latter category, respectively (OCIANA, accessed October 2024).

[18] Interesting parallels in Amorite onomastics are *Ya-aḫ-za-ar-DINGIR* (with the variants *Ya-aḫ-za-ar-i-il*; *Ya-dar-DINGIR*) to be interpreted *Yaʿḏar-ʾel* 'God/Ilu has helped' (Streck 2000: 159) and *La-aḫ-si-ru-um* / *Laʿaḏirum*/ (2000: 201).

[19] This is corroborated at the lexical level by the fact that while the root *ʿḏr* in West Semitic signifies 'to help', in ASA languages, where the verb is attested in the D-stem, *ʿḏr* developed a distinct meaning, such as 'to follow, to pursue' (Sabaweb, accessed October 2024). The occurrence of this name therefore indicates an earlier linguistic phase in the Arabian Peninsula when *ʿḏr* retained the same meaning as in Northwest Semitic. It should be noted that the *hapax ḫāziru* 'helper' occurs in the Akkadian of Mari as a result of the Northwest Semitic lexical influence (Gelb et al. 1956: 166). See Bron 1991 for other Amorite parallels in ASA onomastics. The occurrence of Amorite onomastics in the Arabian Peninsula, particularly in Ancient South Arabian inscriptions, many centuries after its disappearance in Mesopotamian cuneiform sources, is a well-established fact also among Assyriologists (Glassner 2000).

ASA	Common HIM	Curvilinear HIM
ʿmʾl	*ʿmʾl* (MRY04.01 no. 1)	
		ʿmʿhr (HAB01.80 no. 1)
ʿmḏḫr	*ʿmḏḫr* (JFR01.42 no. 1)	
	ʿmhll (ZGT03.12 no. 2)	*ʿmhll* (HAB01.35 no. 4)
ʿmkrb		
ʿmrtʿ		
ʿms^{1}mʿ		*ʿms^{1}mʿ* (SSA01.116 no. 4)
ʿms^{2}bm		*ʿms^{2}bm* (MWQ02.01 no. 30)
		ʿmwql (SHI01.110 no. 4)
		ʿmwth (JFR01.28 no. 9)
ʿmydʿ	*ʿmydʿ* (MNS02.03 no. 3)[1]	
ʿmyṯ	*ʿmyṯʿ* (GRZ05.02 no. 50)	*ʿmyṯ* (HAB01.110 no. 17)

[1] see an example of this name in Prioletta 2018: fig. 7.

Figure 5. *Distribution of some* ʿm- *theophoric names by type of script and script variety.*

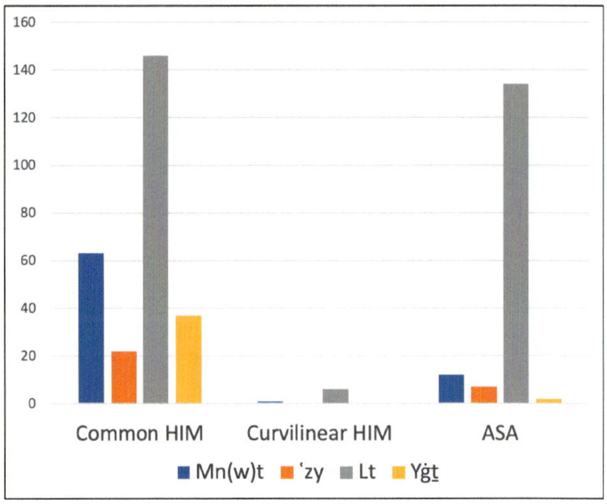

Figure 6. *Distribution of North Arabian theonyms by type of script and script variety.*

names in common Himaitic script represent 84% of the total number of Himaitic names, it is striking to observe that only twenty examples of *ʿm*-names are found in this script, as opposed to twenty-four in the curvilinear script variety.

A distinct typology of theophoric names comprises those invoking North Arabian deities, such as ʿUzzā, Lāh/Lāt, Manāt, Kahl, and Yaġuṯ (Fig. 6) (e.g. Robin & Gorea 2016: pls 1 [*mrʾlʿzy*, *grmlt*], 7 [*ʿmyġṯ*], 20 [*hnʾyġṯ*], 27 [*grmyġṯ*]; Prioletta 2018: fig. 11 [*ʿbdyġṯ*]). These names are typologically 'recent' in contrast to the more archaic theophores formed with elements such as *ʾl*, *ʾb*, *ʿm*, etc. As Robin et al. (2022: 52–53) observe, this category is widely attested in both ASA and Himaitic inscriptions, reflecting a different structuring of divine reference within personal names. However, the Himaitic sub-corpus in curvilinear script also stands out in this regard, as names invoking these deities are virtually unknown.[20]

The typological features outlined above may have two possible explanations, one being that they may reflect an influence from ASA onomastic practices, given the prominence of similar elements in inscriptions from southern Arabia.[21] In this view, their presence in Ḥimā could be understood within a broader framework of linguistic diffusion and cultural exchange rather than as isolated relics of early Semitic. The differentiation between the common Himaitic and curvilinear Himaitic scripts in the attestation of these names further suggests that either chronological strata or varying degrees of exposure to ASA traditions played a role in shaping the corpus. Alternatively, these archaic traits may be rooted in deeper layers of early Semitic, particularly West Semitic, traditions. Rather than being the result of direct borrowing, they could indicate a broader linguistic continuity within the Arabian Peninsula. Future research will aim to determine whether these features represent deep-rooted Arabian naming traditions or the outcome of sustained contact with the southern Arabian kingdoms.

[20] Among these, one can only mention *ʾlkhl* (JFR06.02 no. 13), *ʾblt* (e.g. JFR01.08 no. 1), and *Hnlt* (SMA01.31 no. 1). However, the last two are not completely certain, as they may be based on the *fʿlt* pattern.

[21] One reviewer suggested that these names may result from direct contact with Sabaic culture, where such features are well attested. While plausible, these elements would more likely reflect a broader linguistic and cultural continuum shared by neighbouring South Arabian states, shaped by long-standing regional interactions.

North Arabian features

The onomasticon of the inscriptions from Ḥimā also contains names with a number of phonological and morphological features which are very rare or completely unknown to the ASA onomastic tradition, and which may rather be associated with one or more languages belonging to the North Arabian linguistic background. Moreover, as these features are again shared between the two sub-corpora, when they are found in ASA inscriptions they indicate with little doubt that the origin of their bearers is to be sought in the local oases rather than in southern Arabia. Interestingly, many of these features — but not all of them — are also found in the written languages attested in the region, namely in the non-onomastic material detected in Himaitic graffiti as a result of our recent research (Prioletta 2022b), and in 'Sabaeo-Arabic' from a geographically larger area, including the city of Haram and other sites of the Yemeni Jawf, in addition to Najrān and Qaryat al-Fāw (Robin 2023).

s^3 > s^1 sound change

One main phonological feature is the sound change concerning the s-phonemes, by which the etymological s^3 merged with s^1. We therefore encounter names such as *Qs¹mt*, from the root QS³M (see Robin & Gorea 2016: pl. 10 for the name *qs¹mm*), or names such as *Ws¹ln*, from the root WS³L (Fig. 7).

HIM	ASA
qs¹mm (SHI.01.33 no. 3)	*qs³mm*
qs¹mt (SHI.01.100 no. 15)	*qs³mt*
qs¹mʾl (SAD02.01 no. 1)	*qs³mʾl*
ws¹ln (SSA0.2173 no. 3)	*ws³ln*

FIGURE 7. *Pairs of Himaitic and Ancient South Arabian personal names highlighting the* s^3 > s^1 *sound change in the Himaitic forms.*

ḏ > *z*

While the interdentals are retained in Himaitic and in the other local languages, there are traces of the merger of the voiced interdental *ḏ* with the correspondent dental *z* in names such as *Zʾbm* or *Zhbm*.[22] Not surprisingly, these examples concern the graffiti in Himaitic script alone and not the ASA inscriptions (Fig. 8).

HIM	ASA
zʾb (SMA06.61 no. 08)	*ḏʾb*
zʾbm (SSA01.149 no. 04)	*ḏʾbm*
zhbm (SMA01.26 no. 15)	*ḏhbm*

FIGURE 8. *Pairs of Himaitic and Ancient South Arabian personal names highlighting the* ḏ > z *sound change in the Himaitic forms.*

at > *ah* sound change

In the same way as the other languages of pre-Islamic Arabia, those spoken in this area of southern Arabia did not undergo the sound change *at* > *ah* of the feminine ending morpheme, which is productive in Classical Arabic, even though not systematically. Nevertheless, the corpus might include some names in which the final -*h* could reflect this sound change. Some examples of such names are found in Dadanitic.[23] The presence of pairs such as *ʾws¹h* (as opposed to *ʾws¹t*), *ʾrmh* (vs. *ʾrmt*), *ʿḏrh* (vs. *ʿḏrt*), or *Ḏkrh* (instead of *Ḏkrt*) could speak in favour of this hypothesis (Fig. 9). On the other hand, the final -*h* could also be interpreted as the singular suffixed pronoun referring to the god.[24]

[22] In northern Arabia, this sound change is found in Taymanitic (Kootstra 2016: 73) and Thamudic C (Al-Jallad 2018: 27). In onomastics, this kind of opposition can therefore be seen in names such as Safaitic *Ḏʾb* as opposed to Taymanitic *Zʾb* (see Kootstra 2017: 255–256).
[23] As also highlighted in Kootstra 2017: 256.
[24] I thank Ahmad Al-Jallad for bringing this to my attention.

HIM	ANA/ASA
ʿḏrh (GRZ07.03 no. 03)	*ʿḏrt*
ḏkrh (GRZ07.11 no. 08)	*ḏkrt*
s^{1}*bnh* (SHI01.74 no. 02)	*s*^{1}*bn*

FIGURE 9. *Pairs of Himaitic and Ancient South Arabian or Ancient North Arabian personal names highlighting the* t > h *sound change in the Himaitic forms.*

Spelling of glides

Another interesting feature to examine using a contrastive method in the Ḥimā onomasticon is the spelling of glides. An investigation of some of the most frequently used weak radical roots — namely ʾWS^{1}, QYS^{1}/QWS^{1}, TYM, and ZYD as well as the divine names *Mnwt* and *ʿzy* — identified approximately 380 relevant names. The first notable finding is that in just over 57% of these names, the glides are not written (221 names). Secondly, 72% of these instances are names carved in Thamudic or in mixed script (Fig. 10). This aligns with a broader tendency observed across the ANA corpora, where diphthongs are generally not represented in the script, especially in medial position.[25]

As the same name is often attested with both spellings, it appears that the plene spelling is generally used in ASA inscriptions and the defective spelling in Thamudic ones. Among the sentence theophoric names, examples include *ʾs*^{1}*mnwt* vs. *ʾs*^{1}*mnt*,[26] *Qys*^{1}*mnt* (cf. JML-G-90 (Robin et al. 2022: 328) vs. *Qs*^{1}*mnt*, *S*^{1}*ʿdmnwt* vs. *S*^{1}*ʿdmnt*, *Tymʾl* vs. *Tmʾl*, and *Tymlt* (e.g. Robin & Gorea 2016: pl. 11) vs. *Tmlt*. The percentage expressing the correlation between spelling and script increases when it comes to the root ZYD, where 88% of the plene writings are ASA inscriptions — exemplified by pairs such as *Zydʾl* vs. *Zdʾl*, *Zydlt* (cf. JML-D-58 [Robin et al. 2022: 214]) vs. *Zdlt*, *Zydm* (cf. JML-E-19 [Robin et al. 2022: 235]) vs. *Zdm* (see the name *Zdn* in Robin & Gorea 2016: pl. 19), *Zydmnt* vs. *Zdmnt* (e.g. Robin & Gorea 2016: pl. 24), etc. Again, quite remarkably, this class of names is simply unknown in the corpus in curvilinear script.

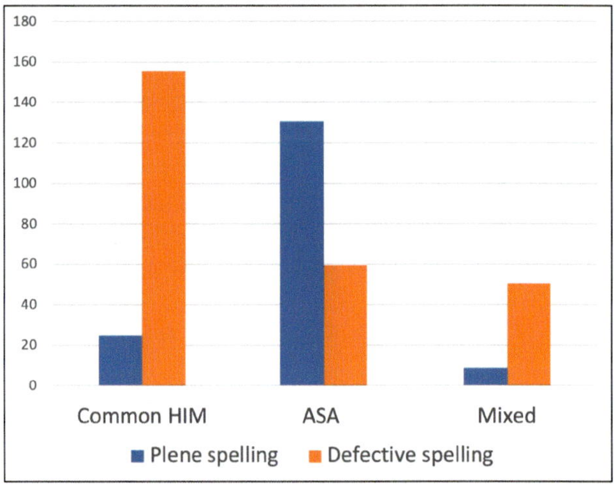

FIGURE 10. *Distribution of plene and defective spellings of glides by type of script.*

The definite article

One previously acknowledged main morphological feature of the Ḥimā onomasticon is the prefixed definite article, similar to some of the languages from North Arabia (Robin & Gorea 2016: 327). The corpus comprises about ninety names, 60% in Himaitic common script and only one example confidently attributed to curvilinear script. These names exhibit all the allomorphs attested in North Arabia, namely those based on the *h*- morpheme (*h-*, *hn-*), as well as the *ʾl*-article that becomes typical of Classical Arabic (al-Jallad 2018). It is important to note that the *ʾl*-article is by far the most prevalent form, accounting for 70% of all occurrences. Conversely, the *hl*-article is by far the most common of the *h*-forms,[27] representing 78% of all examples (Fig. 11).[28]

[25] The present study does not intend to delve into the complex subject of the phonological treatment of diphthongs and triphthongs and their reflection in orthography. It is now established, for example, that diphthongs were preserved phonetically but not represented graphically in Safaitic (Al-Jallad & Al-Manaser 2016).

[26] See also the name *ʾws*^{1}*lt* (with plene spelling of the root ʾWS^{1}) in the ASA graffito JML-D-45 (Robin et al. 2022: 208).

[27] The *hl*-form is virtually unknown in North Arabia. Traces of the *hl* article can be found in names such as the Dadanitic *Hlʾs*^{1} (JSLih 067) and *Hlḥyt* (JaL 052 c), and the Safaitic *Hlḥr* (BES15 782). Note, however, that the *hl-* article is found in the Dadanitic inscription JSLih 071 together with the *hn-* and the *ʾl-* forms. There are about sixty-seven occurrences of names based on a pattern *hfʿl*. It is likely, however, that most of these are based on verbal phrases.

[28] These figures, however, may be biased by the over-representation of the tribe name *ʾl-ʾs*^{1}*d*/*hl-ʾs*^{1}*d*.

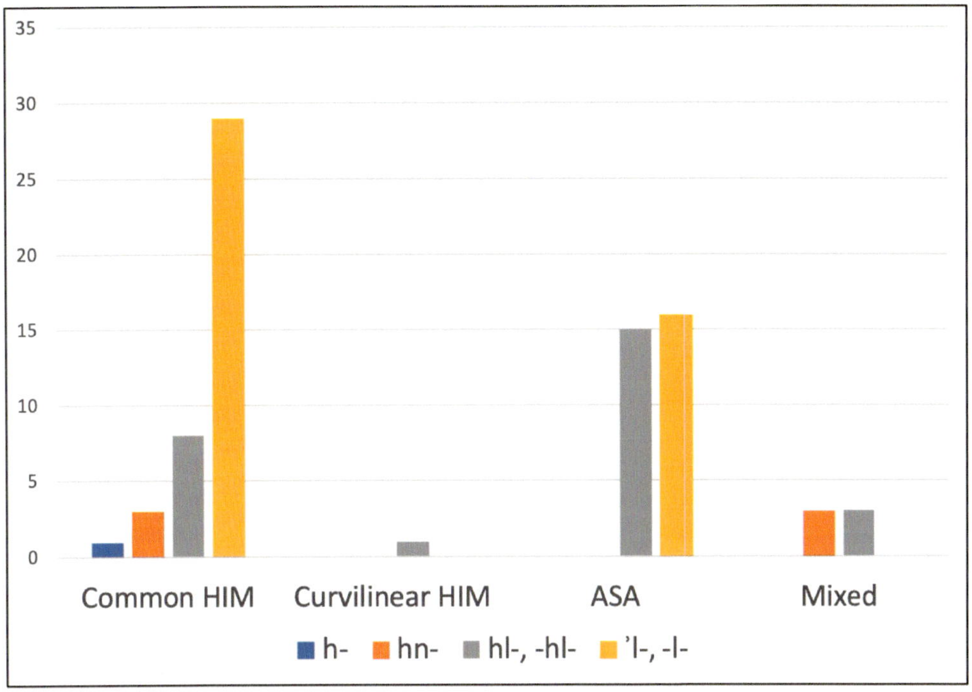

FIGURE 11. *Distribution of the different forms of the definite article by type of script and script variety.*

The article-names may be made up of two words (e.g. *ʾl-ʾs*^{1}*d*), or be three-word names usually composed of a word followed by a divine name or divine epithet that is preceded by the definite article (e.g. *ʿbdlʿzy*[29]). The onset of the *al*-article is only retained in the script at the beginning of the name, whereas it is regularly assimilated in the medial word position.[30]

As regards the assimilation pattern of the article codas *n* and *l*, there is no useful evidence for the *ʾl*-article,[31] but the available examples of the *hn*-article before non-laryngeals (*hnḏkr*, *hnfrʿ*) and of the *hl*-article before coronals (*hls*^{1}*mʿ*, *hls*^{1}*ḥb*, *hlṣʿdm*) demonstrate that neither of them is assimilated to the following consonant.

Taken together, these phonological and morphological features demonstrate clear connections between the Ḥimā onomasticon and the North Arabian linguistic traditions. Their parallels with forms attested in Safaitic, Dadanitic, or the various Thamudic corpora as well as in the broader linguistic continuum of North Arabia, underscore the diversity of linguistic influences in the region and the interaction between local and external naming conventions.

Conclusions

In light of the evidence presented, it is reasonable to conclude that the Ḥimā onomasticon is a composite corpus with multiple layers reflecting both chronological and typological distinctions. The distribution of features across different scripts and naming conventions suggests that these layers correspond to different linguistic and cultural influences over time, resulting from historical processes of interaction and settlement.

---

[29] See JML-D-20 (Robin et al. 2022: 197). Graffito JML-F-4 attests the variant *ʿbdhlʿzy* (2022: 246).

[30] Cf. theophoric names such as *ʿbdlqys*^{1}, *Mrʾlqs*^{1} or the various ones based on the *ʿzy* theonym (such as *Grmlʿz*, *Mrʾlʿz(y)*, *Tmlʿz(y)*, *Whblʿz*). On *Mrʾlʿz* and *Tmlʿz*, see already Robin & Gorea 2016: 327.

[31] However, one may speculate that the hundreds of occurrences of names apparently formed on the *ʾfʿl* pattern may well include names with the *ʾl* article, where the *l* is assimilated to the following consonant. One such case could be the name *ʾḏkr*, which occurs three times in the corpus and may be paired with the variant *hnḏkr*. Interestingly, although the root ḎKR is well attested in the ANA onomasticon, neither *ʾḏkr*/*ʾlḏkr* nor *hnḏkr* are attested as proper names in these corpora (OCIANA, accessed December 2024).

It is evident that the authors of the inscriptions in the South Arabian script bear names that are more closely aligned with the onomastic practices of South Arabia. This can be attributed to two main factors: first, their origin from that society, as in the case of South Arabian merchants or military troops; and second, cultural contact or political and economic dominance, as seen in the urbanized communities of Najrān and Qaryat al-Fāw, which, whether for commercial, military, or political reasons, looked to South Arabia as a cultural model. When securely recognizable, these names conform to the orthographic conventions established by the scribal centres of southern Arabia, particularly in the use of mimation and the spelling of glides. However, they also display grammatical features that may reflect a closer linguistic reality.

Indeed, the onomastic data support the findings of ongoing linguistic research into the languages expressed by the scripts used in the region.[32] The evidence suggests that Himaitic graffiti reflect significant internal linguistic variation, which correlates with script variety. Notably, the corpus of texts in curvilinear Himaitic script exhibits onomastic peculiarities that align with distinct linguistic traits compared to the graffiti in common Himaitic script.[33]

The different layers within the Ḥimā onomasticon may also correspond to different historical periods. The typologically archaic features — such as mimation, certain verbal patterns, and theophoric elements — could plausibly be linked to a broader West Semitic continuum spanning the Levant and the Arabian Peninsula in the second millennium BC. If so, these features may represent deeper linguistic continuities rather than local borrowings from ASA traditions. In contrast, other features, particularly those associated with North Arabian languages — including phonological shifts, the use of the definite article, and specific orthographic tendencies — appear to be more recent, reflecting linguistic developments that took place in the first millennium BC and later.

Overall, the data suggest that Ḥimā was inhabited in antiquity by diverse populations with distinct linguistic and cultural backgrounds. These populations expressed themselves through a regional onomastic tradition that, while exhibiting blending, also maintained distinct differences. Their settlement in the region may have occurred at different times, contributing to the linguistic and cultural complexity observed in the corpus.

Future onomastic and linguistic studies will further test these research hypotheses and refine our understanding of the historical and linguistic dynamics that influenced the Ḥimā epigraphic corpus.

Acknowledgements

This research was carried out within the framework of the cooperation agreement between the Saudi Heritage Commission (Ministry of Culture) and the Centre National de la Recherche Scientifique (CNRS). We gratefully acknowledge the financial support provided by the ANR AAPG 2019 funding call to the project ALMAS 'Ancient and Modern Languages of South Arabia. A cross-disciplinary approach to a linguistic area', which made this study possible.

The author would also like to express her sincere thanks to Ahmad Al-Jallad, Giovanni Mazzini, and the two anonymous reviewers for their valuable insights and thoughtful comments on the text.

[32] The temptation to use onomastic data as direct evidence for the underlying language of the name bearers is even greater in the case of a poorly attested and still poorly understood language such as Thamudic-Himaitic. In order to avoid the well-known potential risks associated with such an approach, the onomastic data will be analysed contrastively in parallel with the linguistic evidence from the graffiti, serving as a distinct but complementary corpus. The debate among Amorite specialists between maximalists and sceptics as to whether onomastics should be used to reconstruct the language is well known (see O'Connor 2004: 462–463). Among the representatives of the first category, Gelb (1962) was convinced that personal names, being innovative, could provide a correct picture of the ethno-linguistic situation of a given area, in contrast to place names, being conservative, reflecting an earlier situation. On the other hand, a conservative approach to the use of proper names to infer cultural practices and linguistic reality in the epigraphy of North Arabia is found in Macdonald (1999).

[33] The corpus of curvilinear Himaitic graffiti exhibits distinct characteristics, particularly in its textual formulas. These include the *w* and Proper Name formula, the *l ṯhy ʿn* and Proper Name blessing formula, as well as the infrequent use of affection, grieving, and yearning formulas — more commonly found in standard Himaitic script. Linguistically, this variety is marked by the verb *yqr* ('to carve') instead of *wqr*, the use of the 1st- and 2nd-person endings in *-k* (as in ASA), and the presence of III-y verbs rather than III-w forms typical of common Himaitic. The curvilinear graffiti has been systematically analysed by the author in an article soon to be submitted for publication.

Sigla

The following sigla refer to inscriptions found by the MAFSN in different areas of the Ḥimā region:

GDY	Shaᶜīb Ghuḍayyayn
GRZ	al-Gharaziyyāt
HAB	Malāzim Ḥāba
HJB	Fardat al-Ḥijāb
HQN	Shiᶜb al-Ḥuqūn
JFR	Wādī al-Jufra
JML	ᶜĀn Jamal
KSM	Khashm al-ᶜĀn
MNS	Jibāl al-Minshāf
MRY	al-Murayrā
MWQ	Mawāqiᶜ
SAD	Jabal Saᶜad
SHA	Barqāʾ ash-Shaᶜ
SHI	Najd Saḥī
SMA	Jabal aṣ-Ṣammāʾ
SSA	Wādī Shasᶜāʾ
SYB	Fardat Shaybān
UNK	ʾUmm ᶜUnayk
ZGT	Shaᶜīb aẓ-Ẓāghaṭ

References

Amaldi D. 1989. Les noms de personnes dans la poésie préislamique. Pages 71–88 in A. Avanzini (ed.), *Problemi di onomastica semitica meridionale.* (Seminari di orientalistica, 1). Pisa: Giardini editori e stampatori.

Bron F. 1991. Les noms propres sudarabiques du type '*yfᶜl* +nom divin'. Pages 86–91 in *Études sud-arabes; recueil offert à Jacques Ryckmans.* Louvain-la-Neuve: Institut Orientaliste de Louvain.

Bron F. 1994. Remarques sur l'onomastique sudarabique archaïque. Pages 62–66 in N. Nebes (ed.), with the collaboration of R. Richter, I. Kottsieper & M. Maraqten, *Arabia Felix Beiträge zur Sprache und Kultur des vorislamischen Arabien Festschrift Walter W. Müller zum 60. Geburtstag.* Wiesbaden: Harrassowitz.

Gelb I. 1962. Ethnic reconstruction and onomastic evidence. *Names* 10/1: 45–52.

Gelb I.J., Jacobsen T., Landsberger B. & Oppenheim A.L. (eds). 1956. *The Assyrian Dictionary Volume 6 Ḫ.* Chicago: Oriental Institute of the University of Chicago.

Glassner J-J. 2000. L'onomastique 'amorrite' dans la péninsule Arabique. Pages 123–127 in L. Milano, S. de Martino, F.M. Fales & G.B. Lanfranchi (eds), *Landscapes, territories, frontiers and horizons in the Ancient Near East Papers presented to the XLIV Rencontre assyriologique internationale Venezia, 7–11 July 1997.* Padua: Sargon srl.

Hazim R. 1994. Ein Typus altsüdarabischer theophorer Namen. Pages 95–101 in N. Nebes (ed.), with the collaboration of R. Richter, I. Kottsieper & M. Maraqten, *Arabia Felix Beiträge zur Sprache und Kultur des vorislamischen Arabien Festschrift Walter W. Müller zum 60. Geburtstag.* Wiesbaden: Harrassowitz.

Al-Jallad A. 2018. What is Ancient North Arabian? Pages 1–43 in D. Birnstiel & N. Pat-El (eds), *Re-engaging comparative Semitic and Arabic studies.* (Abhandlungen für die Kunde des Morgenlandes, 115). Wiesbaden: Harrassowitz.

Al-Jallad A. & al-Manaser A. 2016. New epigraphica from Jordan II: Three Safaitic-Greek partial bilingual inscriptions. *Arabian Epigraphic Notes* 2: 55–66.

Kogan L. 2012. Proto-Semitic lexicon. Pages 179–258 in S. Weninger (ed.), in collaboration with G. Khan Michael, P. Streck & J.C.E. Watson, *The Semitic Languages.* (Handbücher zur Sprach- und Kommunikations-Wissenschaft, 36). Berlin/Boston: De Gruyter Mouton.

Kootstra F. 2016. The language of the Taymanitic inscriptions & its classification. *Arabian Epigraphic Notes* 2: 67–140.

Kootstra F. 2017. The Taymanitic onomasticon. *Arabian Archaeology and Epigraphy*: 254–263.

Layton S.C. 1990. *Archaic features of Canaanite personal names in the Hebrew Bible.* (Harvard Semitic Monographs, 47). Leiden: Brill.

Macdonald M. 1999. Personal names in the Nabataean realm. A review article. *Journal of Semitic Studies* 44/2: 251–289.

O'Connor M. 2004. The onomastic evidence for Bronze-Age West Semitic. *Journal of the American Oriental Society* 124/3: 439–470.

Prioletta A. 2018. New research on the Thamudic graffiti from the region of Ḥimā (Najrān, Saudi Arabia). Pages 53–69 in M.C.A. Macdonald (ed.), *Languages, scripts and their uses in Ancient North Arabia, papers from the Special Session of the Seminar for Arabian Studies held on 5 August 2017*. (Proceedings of the Seminar for Arabian Studies, Supplement 48). Oxford: Archaeopress.

Prioletta A. 2022a. The inscriptions in Ancient South Arabian script from Ḥimā: A preliminary historical and cultural appraisal. *Proceedings of the Seminar for Arabian Studies* 51: 271–282.

Prioletta A. 2022b. Les inscriptions en thamoudéen de la région de Ḥimà (Arabie saoudite): description linguistique, analyse comparative et aréale. MA thesis, Université Sorbonne Nouvelle/Inalco — Institut national des langues et civilisations orientales. [Unpublished.]

Prioletta A. (in preparation). The curvilinear script: A graphic, linguistic, and historical overview of a newly identified minor variety of Himaitic.

Robin C.J. 2023. *Le vieil arabe de Najrān: Une variété archaïque de la langue arabe dans la région de Najrān vers le début de l'ère chrétienne*. (Association Semitica & Classica). Paris: Geuthner.

Robin C.J. 2024. *Najrān en Arabie. La ville des 200 martyrs chrétiens: Histoire et archéologie antiques et médiévales*. (Documenta Coranica, 5). Leiden: Brill.

Robin C.J. & Gorea M. 2016. L'alphabet de Ḥimà (Arabie séoudite). Pages 310–375 in I. Finkelstein, C.J. Robin & T. Römer (eds), *Alphabets, texts and artifacts in the ancient Near East. Studies presented to Benjamin Sass*. Paris: Van Dieren.

Robin C.J., Al-Ghabbān A.I. & Al-Saʿīd S.F. 2014. Inscriptions antiques récemment découvertes à Najran (Arabie séoudite méridionale): Nouveaux jalons pour l'histoire de l'oasis et celle de l'écriture et de la langue arabes. *Comptes rendus de l'Académie des Inscriptions et Belles-Lettres*: 1033–1127.

Robin C.J., Schiettecatte J., al-Saʿīd S.F., Arbach M., Charloux G. & Dridi H. 2022. *Une halte dans la steppe. Les gravures rupestres de ʿĀn Jamal près de Ḥimà (région de Najrān, Arabie saoudite) — A stop-over in the steppe. The rock carvings of ʿĀn Jamal near Ḥimà (Region of Najrān, Saudi Arabia)*. Paris: Académie des Inscriptions & Belles-Lettres.

Schimmel A. 1989. *Islamic names*. Edinburgh: Edinburgh University Press.

Streck M.P. 2000. *Die Amurriter. Die onomastische Forschung Orthographie und Phonologie Nominalmorphologie*. (Das amurritische Onomastikon der altbabylonischen Zeit, Band 1). Münster: Ugarit.

Author's address

Alessia Prioletta, CNRS — UMR 8167 Orient & Méditerranée, 27 rue Paul Bert, 94204 Ivry-sur-Seine cedex, France.
e-mail alessia.prioletta@cnrs.fr

Proceedings of the Seminar for Arabian Studies 54 (2025): 213–229

Muʿtariḍ Community Mall: more insights into the development of the hydraulic, agricultural, and funerary landscapes of al-ʿAyn (UAE)

Peter Sheehan, Nour Al Marzooqi, Mohammed Khalifa & Malak Al Ajou

Summary

Excavations carried out in 2023 for a major commercial construction project along the north-western edge of Muʿtariḍ Oasis produced important new evidence for the origins and development of the hydraulic, agricultural, and funerary landscapes of al-ʿAyn.

The multi-period palimpsest presented by the site includes at least one monumental Umm an-Nār (2600–2000 BC) tomb, located nearly 10 km to the south of the nearest known parallels at Hīlī. The Bronze Age funerary landscape to which this tomb belongs is overlain by an extensive and complex Iron Age (1300–300 BC) field system, with a network of channels feeding coherent groups of tree pits and plots and providing further evidence of the scale, extent, and diversity of Iron Age agriculture in al-ʿAyn. Deep sections provided by 4 m+ excavations for underground car parks immediately to the north and west of the preserved archaeological landscape have shown the relationship between the natural geomorphology of the site and the Iron Age hydraulic and agricultural systems.

The Iron Age agricultural landscape here is preserved beneath 1–2 m-deep deposits of wind-blown sand overlain by late Islamic earthen structures that were in turn abandoned and then buried by the formation of aeolian dunes. These structures include several walls forming part of a field system around the western edge of Muʿtariḍ Oasis, as well as more fragmentary remains of a fortified house or defensive tower and a well-preserved mosque.

Subsequent agreement between the developer and DCT (Department of Culture and Tourism) Abu Dhabi to preserve parts of these three key elements *in situ* within a 3000 m^2 area of the plot provides a significant opportunity for future presentation of the site and increased public engagement with ongoing archaeological investigations by DCT Abu Dhabi into the development of the oasis landscape of al-ʿAyn.

Keywords: al-ʿAyn, oasis landscape, archaeological monitoring, Iron Age agriculture, Umm an-Nār tombs

Introduction — recent insights into the development of the oasis landscape of Al Ain

Since 2010 the Historic Environment Department of DCT Abu Dhabi has been engaged on an ongoing landscape archaeology project focused on understanding the formation processes at work in the origins and development of the oasis landscape of al-ʿAyn (Power & Sheehan 2012). Over the past five years the overall aims of this project have been greatly accelerated by archaeological monitoring and detailed documentation of several large-scale construction and infrastructure projects, each of which has presented a distinct range of opportunities and challenges and thrown new light on different aspects — hydraulic, agricultural, and funerary — of the landscape of al-ʿAyn. These projects have increasingly come to function as archaeological evaluations of different areas of the city, and they are helping to define research questions, inform further fieldwork, and aid in the cultural resource management of the historic environment.

This paper will focus on the most recent of these projects, archaeological monitoring during 2023 of excavations for the Muʿtariḍ Community Mall (hereafter, MCM) (Fig. 1). Approaching the archaeology of the oasis landscape is a dynamic process of iterative recontextualization, in which understanding of the whole is informed by reference to the individual parts and the individual parts by reference to the whole. The paper will thus begin with a brief recap of the major new insights gained between 2019 and 2023. The basis of the outline chronology proposed here is a comparison of the

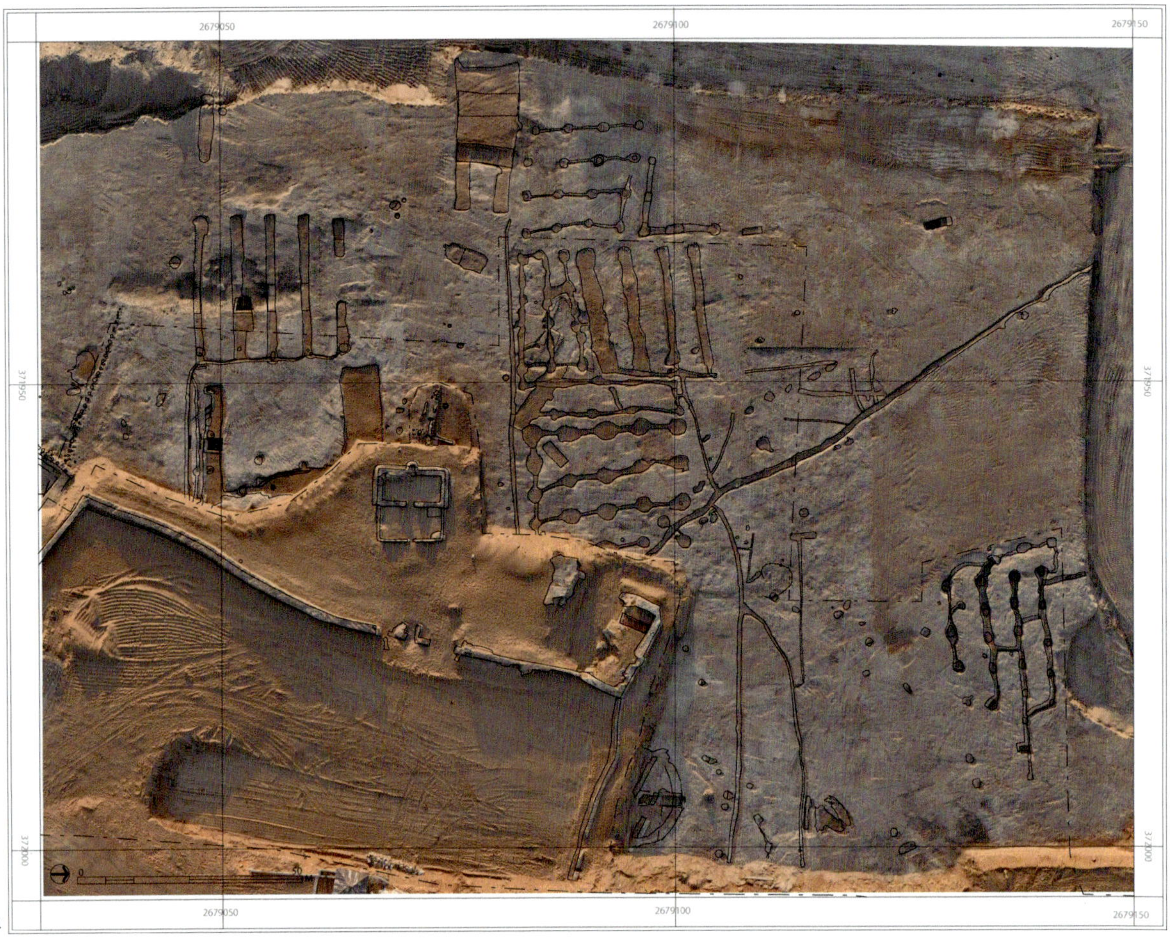

a

b

Phase	Description of deposits and features	Interpretation	Suggested date
0	Natural grey marl becoming more compact and gravelly after 500 mm	Natural	–
1	Large stone-built structure(s) cut into grey marl	Umm an-Nār tomb(s)	2600–2200 BC
2	Channels and pits cut into grey marl	Iron Age (IA) Agriculture	1100–300 BC
3	Clean orange wind-blown sand filling Iron Age pits and channels	Abandonment post-IA	-
4	Light brown compact sand layer with features 0.4 m deep	Industrial activity?	PIR/early Islamic?
5	Clean orange wind-blown sand	Abandonment post-PIR/EI	-
6	Earthen structures built on wind-blown sand	Late Islamic occupation	LI AD 1650–1900
7	Clean orange wind-blown sand, deeper along east of site	Abandonment	Post 1900
8	Modern debris and mixed deposits 0.50 m deep	Dumps	Modern

FIGURE 1. **a.** *A CAD survey overlaid on a UAV image of the MCM site during excavation in 2023, highlighting the three key elements of this multi-period landscape, with late Islamic earthen structures defining the edge of the largely unexcavated orange sand deposits along the east of the site, and beyond this and at a lower level the network of channels and tree pits forming the Iron Age field system. The partially explored Umm an-Nār tomb is at the bottom centre of the image;* **b.** *a table showing the sequence of main deposits and activities on the MCM site.*

diagnostic pottery from the site with published Bronze Age, Iron Age, and late Islamic ceramic assemblages from other sites in al-ʿAyn and the region, along with two ^{14}C dates taken from key contexts (Magee 1996; Benoist 2000; Power, Benoist & Sheehan 2019; Power 2015; Cleuziou, Méry & Vogt 2011).

Archaeological work at Al Ain Museum (hereafter, AAM), initially from 2019 to 2020 and resuming from 2023 to 2024, has produced a wealth of new information on various aspects of the ancient landscape. Deep excavation over the half-hectare area of the proposed museum basement provided evidence for the sedimentary dynamics of the site and revealed approximately 200 deeply cut features. These included the shafts (*thuqb*) of several shallow Iron Age *aflāj* (sing. *falaj*) (utilizing a shallow water table with an irregular or seasonal flow) crossing the site from east to west, as well as at least one south–north *dawudi*-type *falaj* tapping a stable and perennial water source in the form of a deep aquifer. We have suggested that the introduction of this type of 'true' *falaj* was associated with the creation of the first sunken *bustan*-type oases towards the end of the Iron Age or in the late pre-Islamic (PIR) period. Both at AAM and elsewhere in al-ʿAyn there is evidence that the early Islamic period (AD 700–1100) saw repairs to this type of *falaj* carried out with the red bricks typically associated with this period in the region. New evidence from AAM for the funerary landscape of al-ʿAyn was provided first by the discovery of an elite stone PIR tomb in 2019 and subsequently in 2023 by the discovery of a number of individual graves dating to the same period (Sheehan et al. 2022; in press).

From 2020 onwards, archaeological monitoring of a major ongoing project by Al Ain Municipality to install storm water lines in the old *shaabiyāt* housing areas of the city has so far yielded evidence of around sixty separate *aflāj* of various depths and alignments in more than 150 different locations (Sheehan et al. 2024). This work has provided important new insights into the chronology of the different *falaj* types and the dynamics of their creation, use, and ultimate abandonment. It has also presented the opportunity to explore and record in plan substantial areas of Iron Age field systems watered by some of these *aflāj*. Monitoring of excavations for new storm water lines in the Kuwaitat area of al-ʿAyn town centre in 2022 produced evidence for the ancient funerary landscape in the form of more than twenty individual graves with well-preserved grave-goods at the eastern edge of a PIR cemetery (Sheehan et al. 2023a).

In 2021 archaeological monitoring of the Oman Border Fence project (hereafter, OBF) provided a series of deep sections through the ancient landscape totalling 11.5 km in length. Here the sedimentary sequence included deep deposits of compact sand overlying two distinct phases of an extensive Iron Age agricultural landscape. The first of these extends for at least 1 km from south to north and is characterized by a regular layout of deep intersecting channels with shallower rills branching off to water neat rows of individual, mostly square, tree pits. These pits have been provisionally dated to the Iron Age based on the associated ceramic assemblage from their fills, their stratigraphic position sealed beneath the overlying sand deposits, and the general absence of later intrusive material. A second and less extensive phase of Iron Age agricultural activity is marked by surviving 'islands' of the earlier arrangement of tree pits and channels that have been cut by deeper and roughly rectangular basins. The project also produced important evidence for the interrelation between the agricultural and funerary aspects of a multi-period inherited landscape, including a large 25 m+ long stone-built Late Bronze Age collective tomb incorporating Umm an-Nār ashlars, which was then reused in the Iron Age when it seems to have formed the focal point of an extensive cemetery at the southern limit of the Iron Age agricultural landscape described above (Sheehan et al. 2023a).

Mutaredh Community Mall (MCM) — background and progress of the works

The MCM site occupies a 25000 m^2 plot at the north-west corner of Muᶜtariḍ Oasis. It thus lies approximately midway between two main seasonal water courses, Wādi al-ʿAyn and Wādi al-Jīmī, both originating in the foothills of the Hajar mountains and flowing broadly east to west at a distance of *c.*4 km apart. Muᶜtariḍ Oasis is part of the southern group of al-ʿAyn oases (the others are al-ʿAyn and Muwaijᶜī) and covers an area of *c.*24 ha. Like the rest of the al-ʿAyn group, in its present form it is an artificially watered sunken basin supporting intensive palm cultivation within

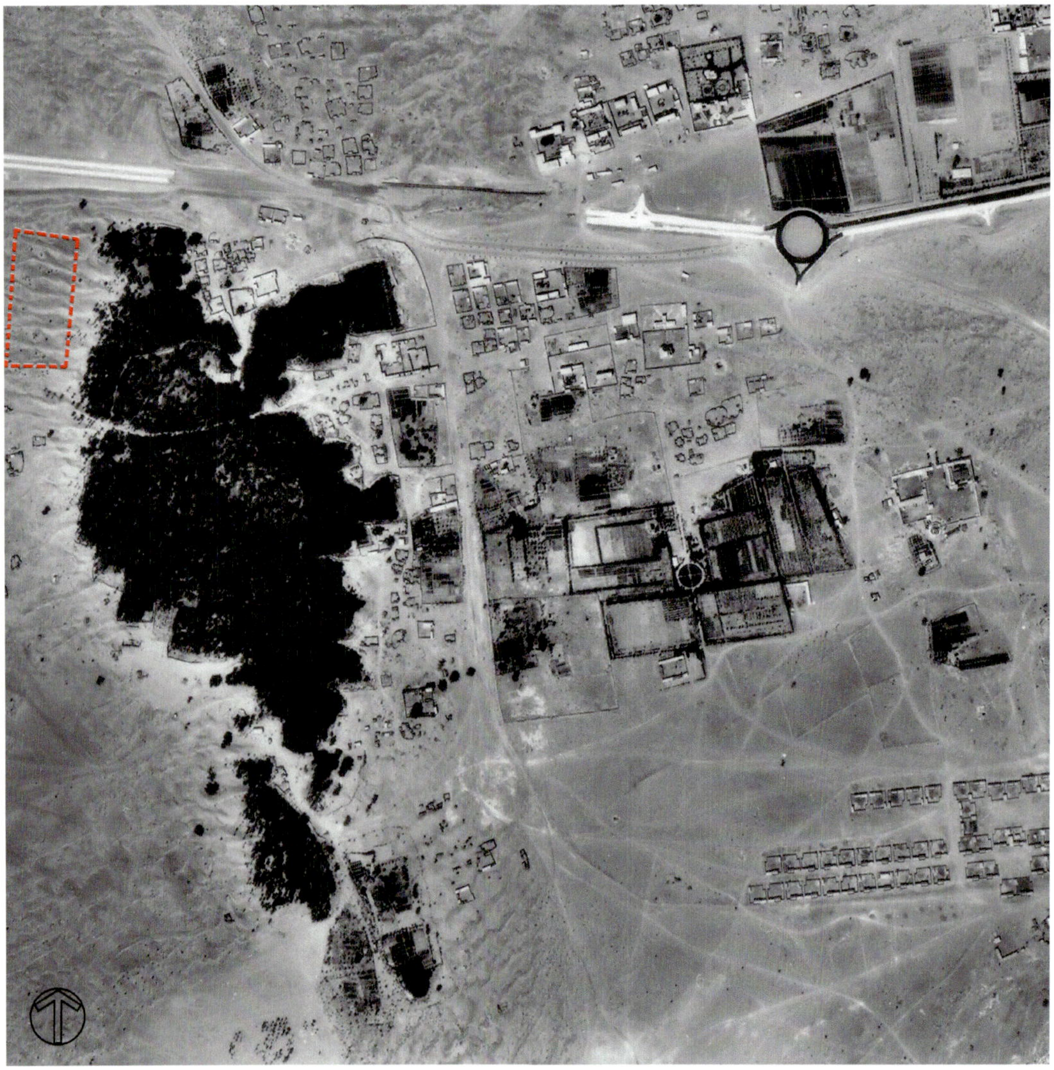

Figure 2. *A 1968 RAF aerial photo of Muᶜtariḍ Oasis, with the location of the MCM site highlighted, showing the extensive area of wind-blown sand dunes along the western edge of the oasis.*

numerous individually owned plots. Archaeological information for the Muᶜtariḍ area is limited, with the nearest investigated sites being the Shaikh Khalifa Grand Mosque site 1 km to the north-east, investigated by DCT between 1999 and 2001 and again from 2011 to 2014 (al-Tikriti et al. 2015), and Qaṣr Al Muwaijᶜī, 1.4 km to the west, excavated between 2009 and 2011 (Power & Sheehan 2011a). Some limited archaeological investigations have also taken place at several of the historic earthen buildings dating from the late Islamic period that are found at various points around the edge of the oasis (Al Tawalebah & Al Haj 2018).

Oral histories indicate that the area was formerly known as *hayy al-nudood*, a reference to the high mounds or dunes that lay along the western edge of the oasis. A 1968 RAF aerial photo of Muᶜtariḍ Oasis shows the site at that time still covered by these deep aeolian sand dunes (Fig. 2), while a desktop review of satellite imagery for the plot over the past twenty years indicates various episodes of planting and material storage, culminating in November 2022 with the clearance of trees from the eastern edge of the site ahead as part of the preparations for the MCM project. The site lies within the buffer zone of the Muᶜtariḍ Oasis component of the UNESCO World Heritage Site, and the design of the building in relation to its oasis setting was carefully developed in coordination with urban planners and architects from DCT Abu Dhabi and Al Ain Municipality to enhance the World Heritage Site and minimize the visual impact of the development on the views of the oasis.

Planning for mitigation of the archaeological impact of the proposed underground car park had been less comprehensively developed, but monitoring of initial test trenches by the contractor along the northern and western edges of the site in December 2022 revealed a sequence of mixed modern deposits of loose sand and mixed debris over clean orange wind-blown sand, with the depth of the latter substantially greater towards the eastern edge of the site. These loose surface sand deposits in turn overlie a narrow band of more compact grey silty natural conglomerate of the type previously noted in the sedimentary sequence from the AAM and OBF projects. The very loose surface deposits found across the site made archaeological monitoring of test trenches and supervision during subsequent machine excavation a challenging process.

The late Islamic landscape — fields and buildings along the western limits of Muᶜtariḍ Oasis

Mass excavation for the MCM building began in January 2023, proceeding from east to west across the site. Removal of the deep deposits of orange wind-blown sand along the eastern edge of the site very quickly revealed an intact archaeological sequence represented initially by several surviving earthen structures. These included substantial boundary walls, apparently forming the limit of a field system around the western edge of Muᶜtariḍ Oasis, as well as the partial remains of a fortified house or defensive tower and a small but well-preserved mosque, very similar in size and form to the mosque from the Shaikh Khalifa Grand Mosque site, dated there to the early Islamic period (al-Tikriti et al. 2015).

At the MCM site, however, the mosque and the other earthen structures belong to the late Islamic (AD 1650–1950) oasis landscape. The earthen walls, with remains of a gateway through them leading to the mosque beyond, seem to mark the limit of fields around the oasis similar to those shown in historic archive photographs of various al-ʿAyn oases. A late Islamic date for these structures is also suggested by associated ceramic finds, the shallow footings of the structures on wind-blown sand, and the similarity of materials and method of construction between these buildings and others preserved around the edge of the historic Muᶜtariḍ Oasis, in particular the house of Shaikh Ahmed Bin Surūr, some 500 m away at the south-west corner of the oasis, that was similarly buried in wind-blown sand until it was excavated by DCT Abu Dhabi in 2005. The substantial preservation of earthen buildings in both these areas is an indicator of how rapidly these deep aeolian sand deposits can form. Like the other earthen buildings, the mosque was built over deep deposits of clean wind-blown sand that overlie ephemeral features, perhaps representing an intermediate PIR/early Islamic occupation, that is in turn separated from the underlying Iron Age agricultural landscape by further wind-blown sand deposits. Excavation was initially suspended over the *c.*3000 m^2 defined by these earthen buildings (Area 3 in Fig. 3). Following discussions between the developer and the DCT team they were subsequently included, together with other key elements of the multi-period landscape discussed below, within the area of the site to be preserved *in situ* for further investigation and presentation (see Fig. 10).

The Iron Age hydraulic and agricultural landscape

To the west and north of Area 3, archaeological monitoring and cleaning following the machine clearance of deep overlying sand deposits continued, revealing the second major element in this cultural landscape, a complex system of Iron Age irrigation channels watering arrays of tree pits and basins cut into the natural subsoil and covering an area of more than 4000 m^2 (Fig. 4).

The initial division of these agricultural features into Areas 1 and 2 was based on a difference in the ceramic

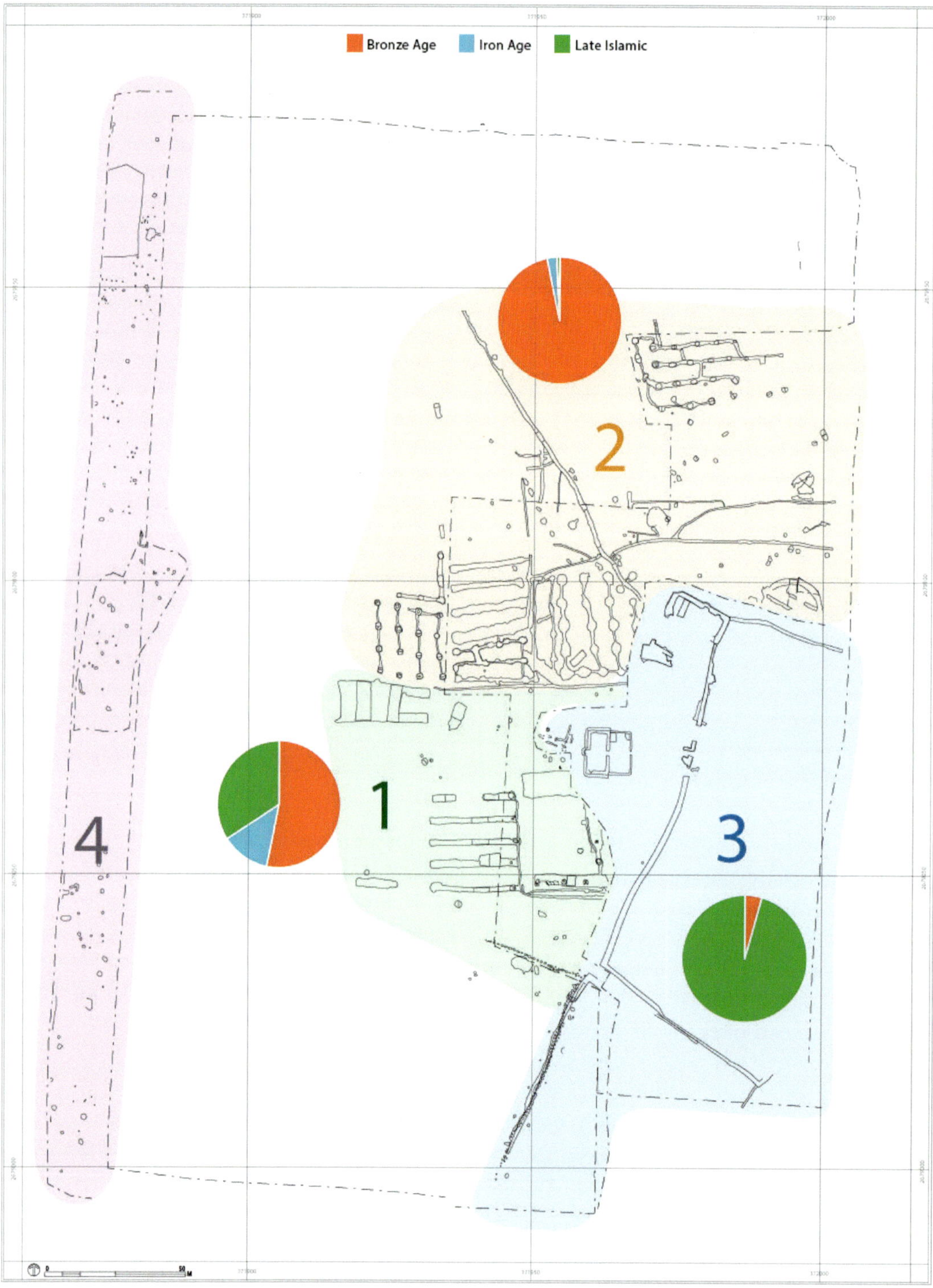

Figure 3. *A plan of the site showing the different excavation areas 1–4, with preliminary pie charts indicating the proportions of the different ceramic assemblages found in Areas 1–3.*

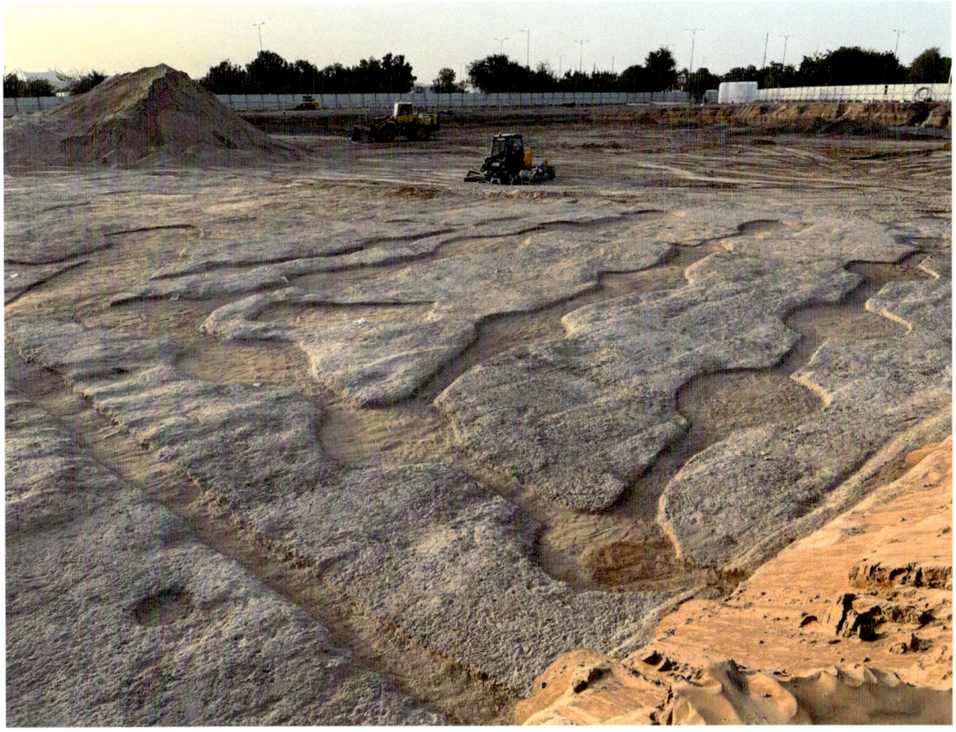

FIGURE 4. *Progress of the works in Area 2, with a detail of the arrangement of Iron Age channels and tree pits revealed during the monitoring of machine excavation. The pits and channels in the foreground were later seen to form part of Plot I, discussed below.*

finds assemblage, with greater quantities of late Islamic wares in Area 1 contrasting with almost exclusively Bronze and Iron Age material in Area 2 (see Fig. 3). The differences in the finds from each area may be due to the uneven topography and variable depth of the sand dunes on which the overlying late Islamic occupation took place. Preliminary quantification indicates that the ceramic assemblage from the MCM site is dominated by Bronze Age wares (up to 90% of the ceramic assemblage from the site), with much of this assemblage having been redeposited either during previous destruction episodes or during the tree removal and machine excavation for the MCM project. The division into Areas 1 and 2 also initially reflected a different morphology of cut features (parallel rows of tree pits in Area 2 versus long rectangular vegetable beds in Area 1), but the subsequent identification of rectangular beds in both areas and the similar east–west orientation of all these cut features (quite distinct from that of the overlying late Islamic field walls) strongly suggests they form different but complementary units of the same agricultural system.

Machine excavation and construction traffic over the soft sand deposits overlying the Iron Age pits and beds generally truncated at least the upper 200 mm of these features, with the depth of truncation increasing as excavation continued towards the west and north. The continuation of similar cut features to those recorded in plan was noted in both the north and north-east sections at the edge of the site. Notwithstanding the increased truncation towards the west, the impression that Areas 1 and 2 lie close to the original western limit of this agricultural system is supported by the absence of similar channels and tree pits during subsequent excavation of Area 4 (see Fig. 3). This westward extension of the additional project footprint was intended partially to compensate the developer for the loss of Area 3. The soft sand deposits overlying the natural soil in Area 4 were carefully excavated under archaeological supervision, and no truncation of the interface with underlying features and deposits took place.

Within the Iron Age agricultural system recorded in Areas 1 and 2 we were able to identify not just the arrangement of the main irrigation channels, but also at

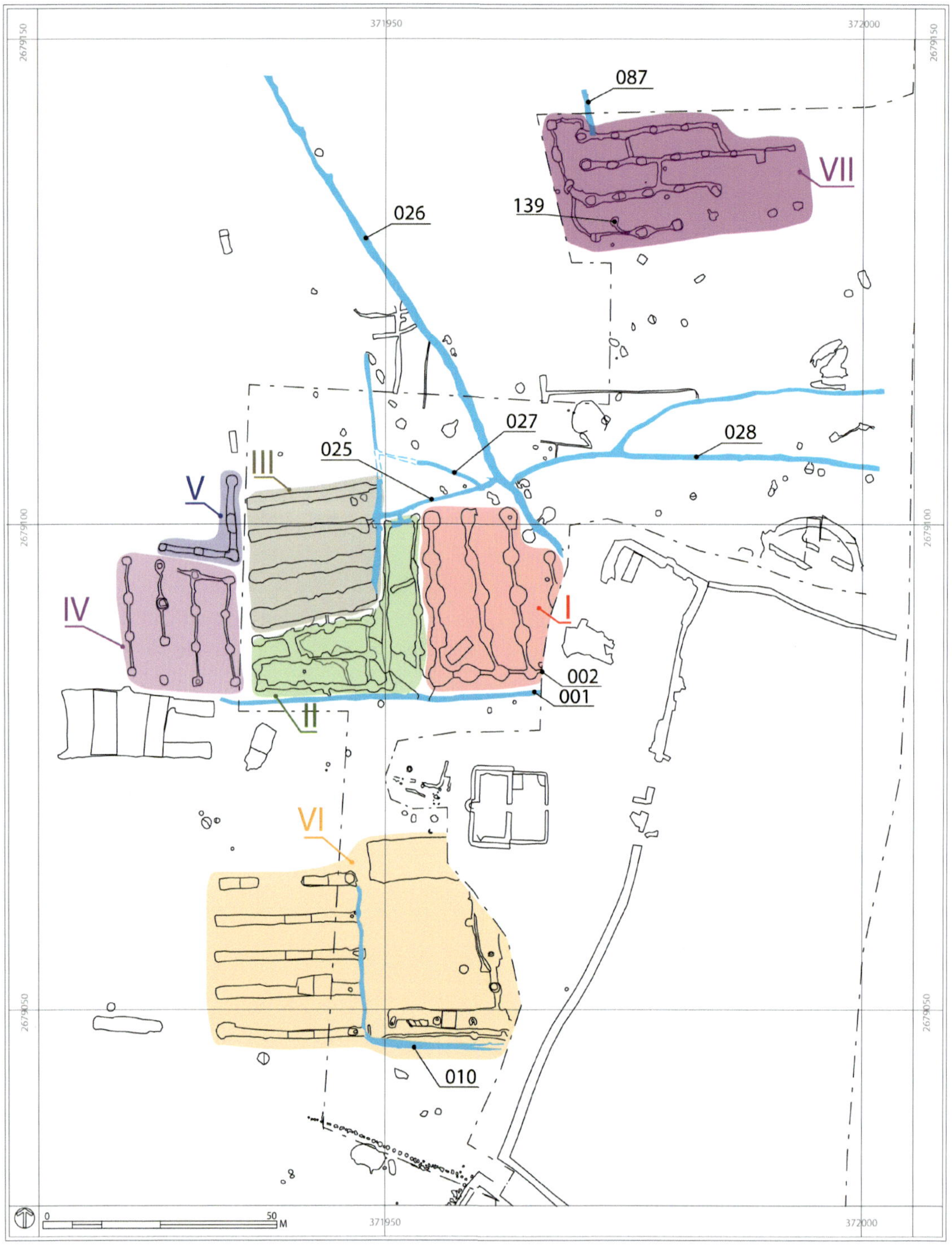

Figure 5. *Plan of the site showing (numbered) the main and subsidiary channels and other features mentioned in the text, as well as garden 'plots' (numbered here I–VII) that were watered in sequence based on the size and shape of the pit or bed and the plants being grown in it.*

least seven separate and distinct gardens or plots (Plots I–VII), with each of these watered by secondary channels in a sequence clearly related to the speed and direction of flow and the volume of water provided to each plot, that in turn was based on the size and shape of the tree pits or beds and the type of plant being grown. Both the general scope and the individual details of this complex agricultural system as well as the regular arrangement of a primary channel with subsidiary channels feeding separate plots, evidence of root balls in the tree pits, and broken pottery used to regulate the water flow, find close parallels in the Iron Age cultivation area (ICNA, Irrigation Channel Network Area) excavated by the Spanish team since 2009 at Al Madam 2 (AM2), located in the central plain of the Emirate of Sharjah (Fernandez & Del Cerro 2024).

The main channels and the agricultural plots

The principal water supply to the agricultural areas was provided by a substantial V-shaped linear channel (LNR 026), *c.*0.8 m wide and up to 1.2 m deep that was traced in plan for more than 60 m from where it emerges from below the unexcavated north-east corner of Area 3 and continues towards the north-west. North of this point it was not recorded in plan due to the truncation of the archaeological deposits, but the distinctive shape of this channel was recorded in the south-facing section of the site, confirming that it continues beyond the MCM plot. It is worth remarking that the orientation of this main channel is very similar to at least three of the *aflāj* recorded at the Shaikh Khalifa Grand Mosque site (al-Tikriti et al. 2015).

Excavation of the fill of the main channel to its sloping base confirmed the direction of flow and indicates it was partially fed by a subsidiary channel (LNR 028) flowing from east to west that was perhaps intended to recuperate surplus flow from irrigated areas to the east (a similar deep channel collecting surplus water from irrigated areas was also recorded at the OBF). From this main channel a secondary one (LNR 025) branches off to the west to water Plots II and III. Another subsidiary channel (LNR 001) running from east to west supplies Plots IV and V and possibly marks a division between a mixed group (I–V) of five similarly sized plots (each *c.*200 m^2, total 1000 m^2) and the mainly long and rectangular beds and basins found in the single larger plot VI (*c.*1000 m^2) to the south, which are watered by another subsidiary east–west channel (LNR 010) emerging from beneath Area 3.

Plot I covers a roughly rectangular area of *c.*200 m^2 and contains a coherent group of eighteen tree pits, each presenting as ovoid or circular cuts between 1.4 and 2 m in diameter, linked by 300 mm-wide channels and arranged in three roughly north–south parallel rows, with a fourth row to the east only partially revealed at the edge of excavation (Figs 4 & 5). Excavation of one of these rows showed that these channels and the bases of each tree pit gradually step down from south to north. This row is watered by a channel (LNR 002) that enters one of the tree pits at the south-east corner of the plot. The deeper level of this incoming channel compared with a shallower outflow channel in the north of the same tree pit shows the direction of flow and indicates that the tree pits were watered in sequence, with the water filling each pit and then overflowing to the next. The size of these pits, their square profile at a lower level, and the small holes dug at the bottom of each pit for drainage into the underlying gravel all find parallels with similar Iron Age tree pits from the OBF and Falaj Al Mazmi (south of Hīlī Oasis, hereafter FAM) and suggests these were for substantial trees, perhaps palms (Sheehan et al. 2023a; 2023b; 2024)

Plot II is a similar size (*c.*185 m^2) but forms an L-shape with eighteen noticeably smaller pits indicating the cultivation of smaller plants or bushes arranged in both north–south and east–west rows. The plot was watered via a T-shaped junction from a subsidiary channel (LNR 025), and this junction is marked, as noted in several other locations, by stones and potsherds used to temporarily dam these inlet channels and thus allow water to flow on to the neighbouring Plot III. This is another roughly square plot of *c.*200 m^2 consisting of four east–west rectangular beds each about 12 m long and 1 m wide, with a preserved depth of 0.6 m. One of these beds showed evidence of its inflow channel having been temporarily blocked with potsherds, while regular arrangements of darker patches within the sandy fill indicated possible plant locations.

Plot IV was more truncated than those further to the east but covers an area of *c.*170 m^2 and consists of sixteen medium-sized and roughly square tree pits arranged in

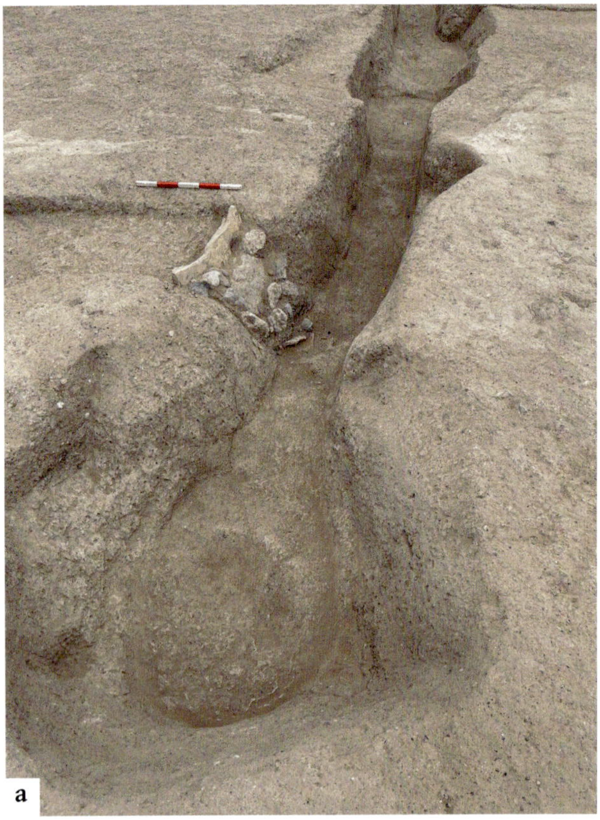

a

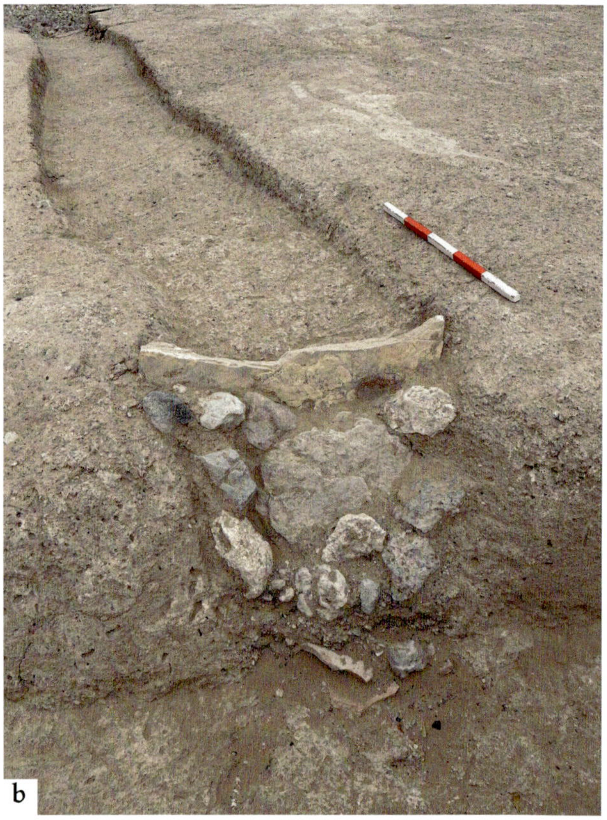

b

Area	Sample reference	Type of sample	Radiocarbon age BP	Lab code	Calibrated radiocarbon age BC	IRMS δ13C
2	MCM23/Context 129, Sample 08/03/23, firepit	Charred material	2730 +/- 30 BP	Beta - 660080	928–810 cal BC (95.4%)	-24.6
2	MCM23/Context 135, Sample 08/03/23, burnt patch	Charred material	3690 +/- 30 BP	Beta - 660081	2147–2012 cal BC (82.8%) 2001–1975 cal BC (6.8%) 2197–2170 cal BC (5.8%)	-25.6

c

Figure 6. a. *An array of tree pits in Plot VII supplied by channel (LNR 087);* **b.** *detail showing the final blocking of the channel with stones and potsherds. The Iron Age II sherds used provide a* terminus post quem *for the end of the field system and a poignant reminder of the farmer who never returned;* **c.** *a table of radiocarbon dates from MCM.*

four parallel north–south rows. Plant locations are again marked by looser sand at the centre of the fill and/or a central depression for drainage in the base of the pit. Plot V was even more heavily truncated but appears to have had a similar arrangement, possibly watered by a continuation of the channel (LNR 027) branching off from the subsidiary channel (LNR 025).

South of this group of five roughly 200 m² plots, Plot VI covers a bigger overall area of *c.*1000 m², and contains a group of long and narrow east–west vegetable beds like those of Plot III, here watered by another east–west channel (LNR 010). In this area there are also several substantially deeper sunken basins that have been cut down through the underlying gravel layers, with

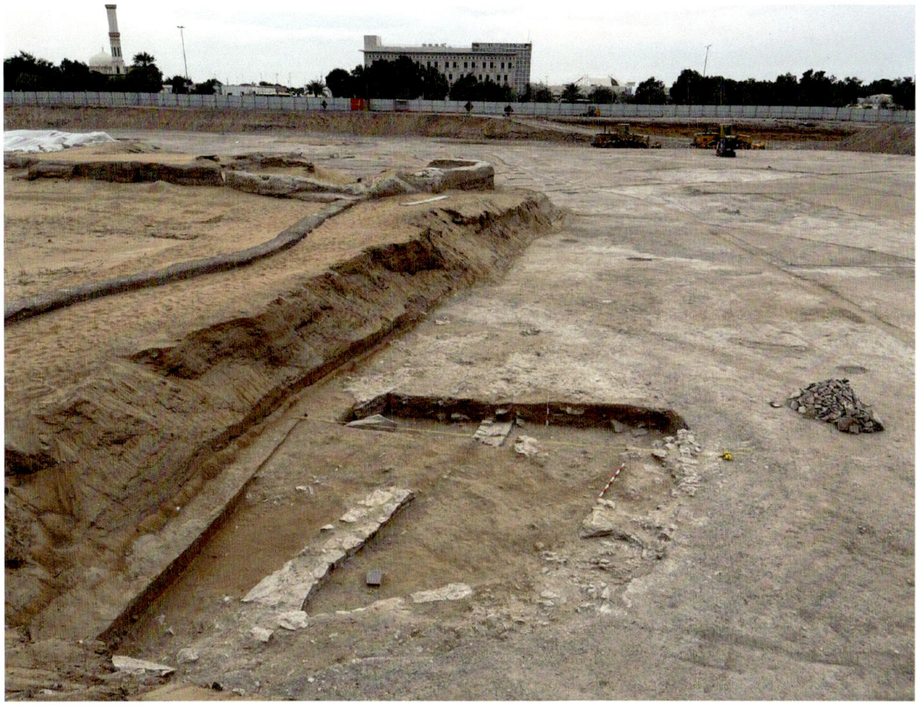

FIGURE 7. *View looking east during initial investigation of the Umm an-Nār tomb, showing the deep deposits of wind-blown sand overlying the robbed tomb on which the late Islamic field walls and other structures were built.*

individual tree pits linked by channels cut into the floor of the basin. These deeper basins may represent a second phase of more concentrated Iron Age activity, or they may simply have been intended to maximize the benefits of subsurface flows within the deeper gravel deposits (perhaps representing a former wadi course?) in this part of the site.

Plot VII lies towards the more truncated north-east corner of the excavated area, *c.*30 m north of the group of Plots I–V. Although the arrangement of twenty-four individual tree pits arranged in four parallel east–west rows shares the same general orientation, it may represent a separate farm or group of plots. In any case this plot appears to have been supplied with water by a channel from the north (LNR 087) that preserves another human touch with its final and rather poignant blocking of the channel still *in situ* (Fig. 6). This is composed of stone slabs mixed with large sherds of broken Iron Age II ceramics and provides a *terminus post quem* for the abandonment of this plot. The lower undisturbed fill of the channels and tree pits excavated in Plot VII produced similar Iron Age II ceramics. The tree pits here are similar in size to Plot II, with excavated examples showing a square profile at the lower level. The southernmost row of tree pits in Plot VII is linked by a short channel to an oval cut (CUT 129) filled with burnt stones, a distinctive type of feature that was noted previously, also in an Iron Age agricultural context, at the OBF. Radiocarbon dating of charred material from this MCM pit provided a date of 928–810 cal BC (2 sigma), consistent with an Iron Age II dating.

A Bronze Age funerary landscape

Excavation along the eastern edge of the site immediately north of Area 3 revealed a large circular cut feature filled with stone fragments, which on closer inspection and excavation of a small test trench was revealed to be a monumental Umm an-Nār tomb (Fig. 7). The initial test trench produced fragments of soft-stone vessels and relatively large quantities (220 sherds — or nearly 14% — of a total Bronze Age assemblage of 1360) of Bronze Age decorated, fine and miniature wares, all types often found in burial contexts (Cleuziou, Méry & Vogt 2011). Human bone, burnt and otherwise, was also present in significant quantities, but in the absence of a bio-archaeologist on the team, excavation was discontinued and the tomb covered and backfilled. The southern half of the tomb extends under the deep wind-blown sand deposits in Area 3 and so remains unexcavated, but it is clearly a large circular stone structure *c.*11 m in (external) diameter, with an outer wall *c.*1 m thick laid in a trench cut into the underlying natural soil. The remains of three east–west walls can be seen to divide the internal space into four separate compartments. Only the lowest courses of stone blocks forming the exterior circuit of the tomb survive, as the tomb was dismantled and heavily robbed out down to the contemporary ground level in antiquity, presumably for its building stone but perhaps initially also for the grave-goods it may have contained. The date of this destruction remains unclear but is likely to account for the extensive spread of Bronze Age ceramics throughout Areas 1 and 2. The presence of a late Islamic field wall built on the deep sand deposits overlying the robbed tomb suggests the robbing pre-dates the most recent phase of activity on the site. Finds of burnt bone and grave-goods, probably derived from an upper level of the tomb during its destruction, appear similar to those recovered during excavation by the French Archaeological Mission in the early 1980s of what appears to be its closest parallel in both form and presumed date, Hili North Tomb A, currently located in the grounds of Hili Fun City *c.*10 km to the north (Cleuziou, Méry & Vogt 2011).

The presence of burnt bone and funerary objects inside the tomb may be linked to relatively frequent patches of burning found in Area 2, some of which clearly pre-date and are cut by the Iron Age channels. Similar features, identified as fireplaces forming part of an occupational layer and associated with a largely intact Wadi Suq jar, were found at the Shaikh Khalifa Grand Mosque site (al-Tikriti et al. 2015). At MCM, radiocarbon dating of charred material (context 135) taken from a patch of burning that had later been cut by a channel linking tree pits in Plot I provided results consistent with an Umm an-Nār date.

Conclusions

The discovery of a monumental Umm an-Nār tomb on the western edge of Muʿtariḍ Oasis invites a major re-evaluation of evidence for the Bronze Age landscape of al-ʻAyn, and its southern part in particular, that will include a review of the evidence from the nearby Shaikh Khalifa Grand Mosque site, reused Umm an-Nar ashlars from the OBF, and isolated discoveries at other locations in the town centre. More evidence will be provided when excavation of the MCM Umm an-Nār tomb resumes, as well as by future investigations of the rising ground to the east of the site which appears to be a mound on which Muʿtariḍ Oasis is set. The nature of the Umm an-Nār tomb (and perhaps others within a wider cemetery around it) and its possible continuation as a sacral and/or territorial marker in the later Iron Age agricultural landscape analogous with the situation recorded at the OBF, is another possible avenue of future research.

The next stage of fieldwork on the site will also have the opportunity to explore, under more controlled excavation conditions, the loose sand deposits within Area 3 where the complete archaeological sequence from the Bronze Age to the late Islamic period remains intact. The decision to preserve Area 3 *in situ* has already provided the opportunity for a ground penetrating radar (GPR) and magnetometry survey of the site by a team from the Earth Science Department of Khalifa University (Fig. 8). This has allowed us to compare the geophysical data from this survey with visible results in adjacent already excavated areas, and initial 3D results from this geophysical survey have indicated both the likely continuation of the Iron Age agricultural features and the possible presence of further stone structures similar to the Umm an-Nār tomb beneath the sands of Area 3 (Santos-Assunção et al. 2024).

The very large (*c.*4000 m^2) area of agricultural landscape revealed at Muʿtariḍ also represents another major step forward in understanding both the nature and extent of the area under cultivation in al-ʻAyn during the Iron Age. These new insights into the scale and techniques of agriculture and water management in an arid environment are important not only for our understanding of the development of the oasis landscape of al-ʻAyn, but also for the wider context of agriculture in south-east Arabia both past and present (Córdoba 2016; Charbonnier et al. 2017; Purdue et al. 2019). The different plot sizes, the position and shape of the various types of tree pits and beds, and the arrangement of channels all point to the diversity of plants being grown within a drought-resistant regime focused on the careful control and maximizing of the available water resources. It also underlines the point that Iron Age agriculture was clearly about more than growing palm trees. Further specialist analysis of the

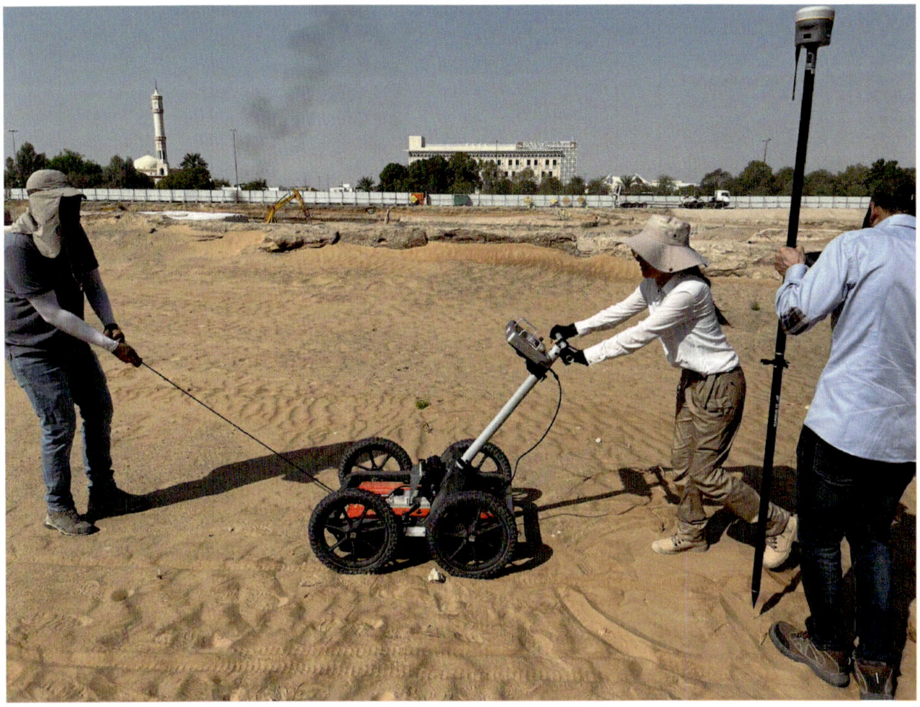

FIGURE 8. *The team from the Earth Science Department of Khalifa University carrying out ground penetrating radar (GPR) survey in Area 3. The survey indicated the likely presence of more stone tombs in this area.*

extensive soil samples taken from the site, together with archaeobotanical data recovered during the processing of these samples, will help to further define our view of the practice of agriculture and its place within the rhythms of daily life.

The scale, morphology, and orientation of the agricultural features at Muʿtariḍ all find close parallels with the extensive Iron Age agricultural landscape, covering an area of at least 100 ha and consisting of more than one phase, that has been recorded at various locations (OBF, FAM, the Bayt BinʿĀtī in Qaṭṭāra) around the northern group of al-ʿAyn oases (Hīlī, Qaṭṭāra, Jīmī) (Sheehan et al. 2023b; Power & Sheehan 2011b). For the southern group (Muwaijʿī, Muʿtariḍ, al-ʿAyn), the recent evidence from MCM, AAM, and the central areas of Murabba and Kuwaitat (Sheehan et al. 2022; 2024), supplemented by previous observations from the Shaikh Khalifa Grand Mosque (al-Tikriti et al. 2015) and Muwaijʿī (Power & Sheehan 2011a), all add to the growing picture of a similarly extensive but still largely unexplored Iron Age field system, watered from shallow surface sources and wadis flowing westwards across the modern border with Oman. The next steps will be to attempt a synthesis of the archaeological evidence from all these sites with geoarchaeological and archaeobotanical data, which we hope will provide a fuller understanding of the agricultural base upon which Iron Age 'civilization' in al-ʿAyn and the wider region was founded.

At MCM the focus of activities for DCT Abu Dhabi has now shifted to the ongoing management of the site and future presentation of a core area containing three major elements — the late Islamic earthen buildings, a representative area of Iron Age agriculture, and the Umm an-Nār tomb. Pending a resumption of archaeological investigations and future interpretation measures, this has so far involved careful reburial and the construction of conservation shelters. Areas of Iron Age agriculture beyond this core will be preserved *in situ* beneath the building by locating the piled foundations in such a way as to avoid these features (Fig. 10). Planning for the future presentation of the site will also begin to focus on how it can be protected against the elements and integrated within its setting between the new building and Muʿtariḍ Oasis, an approach that has already been successfully employed in recent years with other areas of the ancient landscape presented in the Archaeological Basement at Qattara Arts Centre and in the new archaeological galleries at Al Ain Museum.

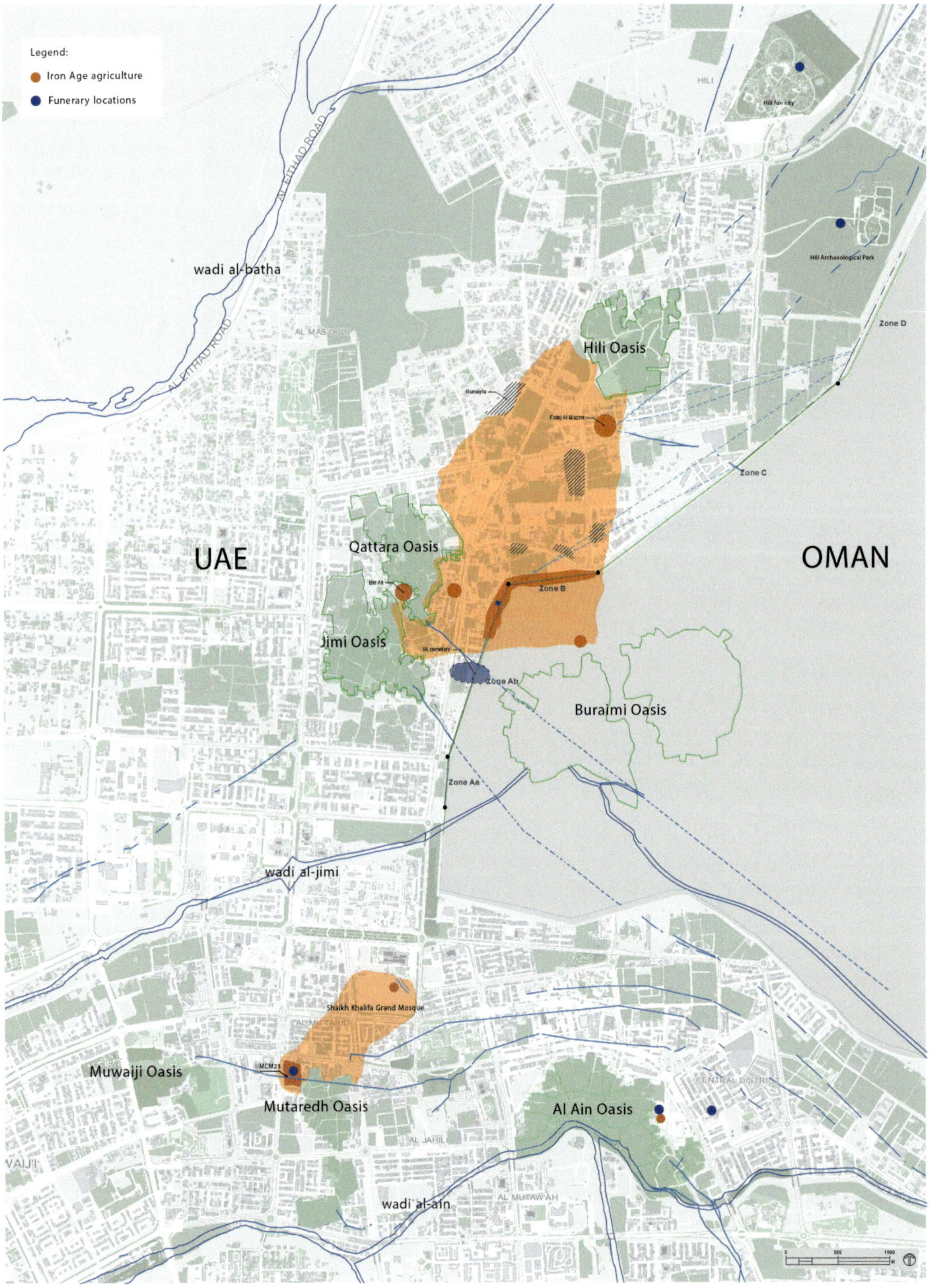

FIGURE 9. *A plan of al-ʿAyn showing the extent of Iron Age field systems based on recent archaeological observations, with recorded locations of* aflāj *and known locations of the funerary landscape, as well as previously identified locations of Iron Age settlement (hatched).*

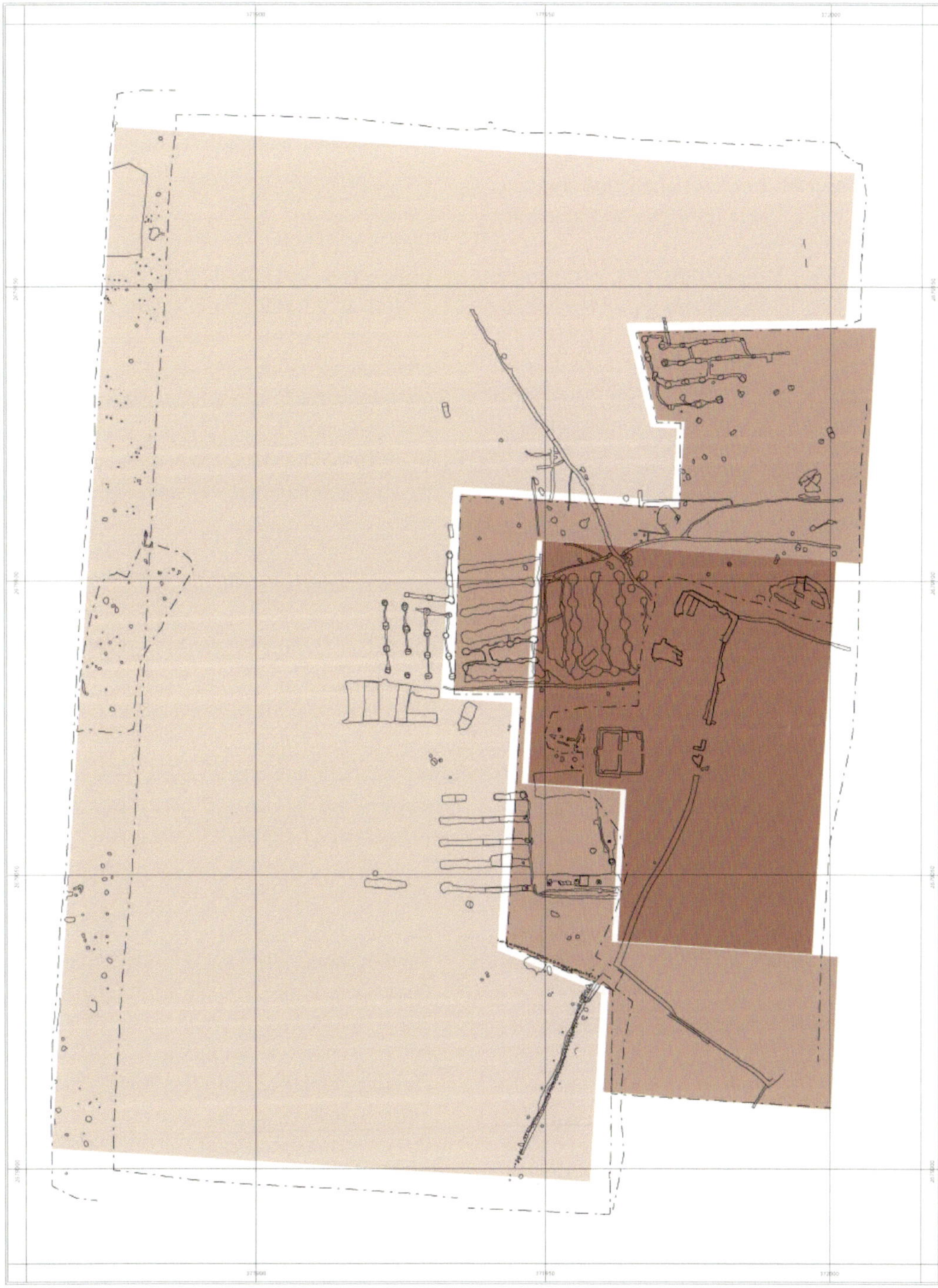

FIGURE 10. *A plan of the MCM site showing (from dark to light): areas of the archaeological site preserved for further investigation and presentation; parts to be preserved* in situ *beneath the building; parts to be preserved by record only.*

Acknowledgements

We would like to thank the MCM developer, Nayel Al Shamsi, Chairman of Nael General Contracting LLC, his representative Tamer Gabr, and the project consultants Arak Engineering for their continuous support and assistance during the project and for their forbearance with delays and major changes to the scope and schedule of a major construction project.

From the DCT side the major archaeological results from this site have once more demonstrated the value of the development control procedures implemented by the Historic Environment Department to protect the historic environment in all its aspects. We are grateful for the unstinting support and assistance from all our colleagues in the Department.

Our thanks also to Diana Francis, Sonia Santos-Assunção, and their team from the Earth Science Department at Khalifa University, and to Geotech3D and Al Mayedy Production & Aerial Shot.

References

Benoist A. 2000. La céramique de l'Age du Fer en péninsule d'Oman. Thèse de doctorat, Université de Paris I, Panthéon-Sorbonne. [Unpublished.]

Benoist A., Degli Esposti M., Charbonnier J. & Power T.C. 2021. al-Madam and the Archaeology of the Falaj in South East Arabia. Pages 165–182 in A.J.D. Monedeor, C.C. Linares, F.J.V. Ruiz de Toledo & F.L.B. Gallardo (eds), *Nomina in aqua scripta. Homenaje a Joaquín María Córdoba Zoilo*. Madrid: Universidad Autónoma de Madrid.

Charbonnier J., Purdue L., Calastrenc C., Régagnon E., Sagory T. & Benoist A. 2017. Ancient agricultural landscapes in Southeast Arabia: Approach and first results of an archaeological, geo-archaeological, and spatial study of the Masāfī Palm Grove, Emirate of Fujairah. Pages 45–65 in W.Y. al-Tikriti & P.A. Yule (eds), *Proceedings of Water and Life in Arabia conference 14th–16th December, 2014*. Abu Dhabi: Abu Dhabi Tourism and Culture Authority.

Cleuziou S., Méry S. & Vogt B. 2011. *Protohistoire de l'oasis d'al-Aïn. Travaux de la Mission archéologique française à Abou Dhabi (Émirats arabes unis): Les sépultures de l'âge du Bronze*. (British Archaeological Reports, International Series 2227). Oxford: Archaeopress.

Córdoba J.M. 2013. New perspectives about Iron Age and the oasis culture in the Oman peninsula. Two conclusive seasons at al Madam (Sharjah, UAE). *Isimu* 16: 139–152. Available at https://revistas.uam.es/isimu/article/view/3181/3376

Fernandez C. & Del Cerro C. 2024. Cultures, technologies and environment on the Oman peninsula: Recent discoveries and some hypotheses about the falaj system in Al Madam, Sharjah, UAE. Pages 271–292 in Zayed National Museum (ed.), *Advances in UAE archaeology. Proceedings of Abu Dhabi's Archaeology Conference 2022*. Abu Dhabi: Department of Culture and Tourism.

Magee P. 1996. The chronology of the south-east Arabian Iron Age. *Arabian Archaeology and Epigraphy* 7/2: 240–252.

Power T. 2015. A first ceramic chronology for the late Islamic Arabian Gulf. *Journal of Islamic Archaeology* 2/1: 1–33.

Power T.C. & Sheehan P.D. 2011a. The Qaṣr al-Muwaijʿī: *Diwān of the Āl Nahayyān in the al-ʿAin/Buraimi Oasis*. *Liwa: Journal of the National Center for Documentation & Research (Abu Dhabi)* 3/5: 26–41.

Power T.C. & Sheehan P.D. 2011b. The Bayt Bin ʻĀti in Qaṭṭāra oasis: A prehistoric industrial site and the formation of the oasis landscape of al-ʻAyn (UAE). *Proceedings of the Seminar for Arabian Studies* 41: 267–282.

Power T.C. & Sheehan P.D. 2012. The origin and development of the oasis landscape of al-ʻAyn (UAE). *Proceedings of the Seminar for Arabian Studies* 42: 291–308.

Power T., Benoist A. & Sheehan P. 2019. An Iron Age ceramic sequence from the Bayt Bin Ati, al-Ain, UAE. *Arabian Archaeology and Epigraphy* 30: 75–102.

Purdue L., Charbonnier J., Régagnon E., Calastrenc C., Sagory T., Virmoux C. ... Benoist A. 2019. Geoarchaeology of Holocene oasis formation, hydro-agricultural management and climate change in Masafi, southeast Arabia (UAE). *Quaternary Research* 92/1: 109–132.

Santos-Assunção S., Ali M., Ali M.Y., Francis D., Sheehan P. ... Iqbal M.A. 2024. Identification of subsurface archaeology at Mutaredh, United Arab Emirates, using ground penetrating radar. *Frontiers of Earth Science* 12: 1450518.

Sheehan P.D., Power T.C., Karacic S. & Costa S. 2022. Al Ain Museum: An ancient landscape beneath the carpark. *Proceedings of the Seminar for Arabian Studies* 51: 353–369.

Sheehan P.D., Khalifa M., Al Ajou M. & Al Marzouqi N. 2023a. Secrets of the *shaabiyat:* Recent developments in the archaeology of the (urban) oasis landscape of Al Ain. Pages 293–306 in Zayed National Museum (ed.), *Advances in UAE Archaeology. Proceedings of Abu Dhabi's Archaeology Conference 2022.* Abu Dhabi: Department of Culture and Tourism.

Sheehan P.D., Khalifa M., Al Ajou M., Al Marzooqi N., Van Bellegem M., Ferreira A. ... David-Cuny H. 2023b. The Oman Border Fence Project 2021: A journey through the hydraulic, agricultural, and funerary landscapes of al-ʿAyn. *Proceedings of the Seminar for Arabian Studies* 52: 323–337.

Sheehan P.D., Khalifa M., Al Ajou M., Al Marzooqi N., Al Merri J. & Power T.C. 2024. *Aflāj* discoveries in al-ʿAyn — exploring and documenting the network of shafts and tunnels recently revealed below the streets of the modern city. *Proceedings of the Seminar for Arabian Studies* 53: 262–277.

Sheehan P.D., Al Marzooqi N.N., Khalifa M. & Al Ajou M. (in press). Beyond the carpark: Further insights into the development of the oasis landscape from the new Al Ain Museum. *Proceedings of the DCT Archaeology Conference December 2023.*

Al-Tawalebah D. & Al Haj A.A. 2018. The residence of Ibn Suroor Al Dhahri in Al Mutaredh Oasis in Al Ain. *Liwa: Journal of the National Center for Documentation & Research (Abu Dhabi)* 19: 33–52. [In Arabic.]

Al-Tikriti W., Al Neyadi M., Tawalbeh D., Al Nuaimi A.R., Al Kaabi A. & Omar W. 2015. Filling a blank: New excavations at an early Islamic site at Oud Al Toba/ Muataredh in al-ʿAyn, UAE. *Proceedings of the Seminar for Arabian Studies* 45: 371–384.

Authors' addresses

Peter Sheehan, DCT Abu Dhabi, Historic Environment Department, Abu Dhabi Department of Culture and Tourism, Al Ain, Abu Dhabi, UAE.
e-mail peter.sheehan@dctabudhabi.ae

Nour Al Marzooqi, DCT Abu Dhabi, Historic Environment Department, Abu Dhabi Department of Culture and Tourism, Al Ain, Abu Dhabi, UAE.
e-mail NMarzooqi@dctabudhabi.ae

Mohammed Khalifa, DCT Abu Dhabi, Historic Environment Department, Abu Dhabi Department of Culture and Tourism, Al Ain, Abu Dhabi, UAE.
e-mail mohamed.khalifa@dctabudhabi.ae

Malak Al Ajou, DCT Abu Dhabi, Historic Environment Department, Abu Dhabi Department of Culture and Tourism, Al Ain, Abu Dhabi, UAE.
e-mail MAjou@dctabudhabi.ae

Proceedings of the Seminar for Arabian Studies 54 (2025): 230–246

An Iron Age artefact hoard discovered at Saruq al-Hadid-53 archaeological site, Dubai, UAE: a preliminary study

Mariam A. Al Suwaidi, Joseph W. Lehner & Bader M. Al Ali

Summary

This article presents archaeological findings from the site of Saruq al-Hadid-53 (SAR.53), focusing on a significant hoard uncovered during the 2018–2019 excavation season. The hoard, consisting of over 100 artefacts, mostly copper alloy vessels and tools, was discovered in a circular pit. It represents a novel practice at the site and is consistent with an emerging pattern of wealth storage or deposition noted across south-eastern Arabia during the Iron Age. The variety of tools discovered, including axes and ladles, reflects the multifaceted daily life of the inhabitants. Decorative motifs on the artefacts reflect advanced craftsmanship and cultural interactions, linking them to broader regional traditions. Radiocarbon dating places the site within the Iron Age II (eighth–seventh century BC). Comparisons with other regional hoards highlight the interconnected nature of ancient metallurgical traditions, situating SAR.53 within wider networks of copper production and exchange in south-eastern Arabia.

Keywords: Saruq al-Hadid, Iron Age II, hoard, vessels and tools, copper alloy

Introduction

Saruq al-Hadid is situated at the fringes of the Rub' al-Khali desert on the southern border of Dubai in the United Arab Emirates (Fig. 1). Characterized as a site with long-term, persistent, and seasonal occupation stretching from the Neolithic to the early Islamic period (Weeks et al. 2019a), archaeological evidence at Saruq al-Hadid has a strong expression of Bronze and Iron Age ritual economy and craft production (Weeks et al. 2023). Since its discovery in 2002 (Herrmann, Casana & Qandil 2012; Weeks et al. 2019a), numerous research projects have been carried out at the site by different teams. These include the Jordanian team (Al-Khraysheh & An-Nashef 2007; Nashef 2010), the Saruq al-Hadid Archaeological Research Project (SHARP) (Cable 2015; 2016; 2017), the Polish Mission from the University of Warsaw (Wygnańska et al. 2022), the German Mission (Ihde 2017), the archaeological consultant company Sanisera Archaeological Institute (Contreras Rodrigo et al. 2017; Valente et al. 2020), Tübingen University (Müller & Bloom 2019), the University of Seville, and the University of Sydney, alongside continuous work by the local archaeological teams. Collectively, the investigations have spanned over two decades and primarily focused on the main site Saruq Al-Hadid-7 (SAR.7), which is characterized by a significant quantity of copper slag and metal artefacts (Contreras Rodrigo et al. 2017: 60; Casana, Herrmann & Qandil 2009: 39; Herrmann, Casana & Qandil 2012: 50; Karacic et al. 2018: 23; Potts 2009: 3; Valente et al. 2020: 170–185; 2023: 11). SAR.7 provides exceptional evidence of persistent occupation from the Bronze Age to the early Islamic period (Karacic et al. 2018: 24; Valente et al. 2020: 177; 2023: 16; Weeks et al. 2017: 53; 2019b: 2). Intensive use of the site occurred predominantly during the Iron Age, for which most evidence of metal production was found (Herrmann, Casana & Qandil 2012: 60–66; Soriano et al. 2018: 1–9; Valente et al. 2020: 182; 2023: 11; Weeks et al. 2017: 44; 2019a), including evidence of smelting, refining, artefact production, and recycling (Valente et al. 2020; Weeks et al. 2023). Research on metal production debris and metal artefacts from SAR.7 demonstrates that copper smelting was a dominant component of the upper deposits at the site. Evidence for refining, metalworking, and recycling has been found, suggesting that these technological practices were key to the site's importance. Additionally, objects made from different materials such as ceramics, stones, and metal such as iron, copper, bronze, and gold (Weeks et al. 2017: 32–57; Soriano et al. 2018: 2–9), in addition to extensive evidence of human-environment interactions (Bernáldez-Sánchez et al. 2024; Roberts et al. 2018; Weeks et al. 2017), show that the site was the focus for many different activities and consumption practices linked to ritual economy. The chronological framework at SAR.7 developed by the SHARP team provides the comprehensive understanding of the occupational sequences at the site (Weeks et al. 2019a).

While most of the work has focused on the main site, SAR.7, investigations of other areas, particularly Saruq Al Hadid-53 (SAR.53), have been limited. Located east of SAR.7, SAR.53 is of significant interest due to its potential density of Iron Age occupation and well-preserved, stratified deposits of charred botanical materials. Extensive evidence of metal consumption and deposition patterns also appears to be prevalent, evinced in particular by the recent discovery of a large hoard of metal artefacts. The artefacts recovered here offer an exceptional opportunity to enhance our understanding of Iron Age material culture and metal consumption. This paper provides an overview of the excavation of the hoard at SAR.53, including a description of the site, its archaeological and environmental context, and a summary of excavations. The stratigraphic sequence is presented along with the artefacts discovered, with a discussion focusing on their decoration and craftsmanship. The paper also provides a chronological framework and suggests the relationships between SAR.53 and other areas within Saruq al-Hadid.

Archaeological and environmental setting

Situated within the site boundaries of Saruq al-Hadid, SAR.53 is located *c.*540 m east of SAR.7 (see Fig. 1). SAR.53 was first described by archaeological surveys conducted by the Jordanian, American, and local teams in the surrounding areas of the Saruq Al-Hadid and the site of al-Ashoosh (Qandil 2003; Casana, Herrmann & Qandil 2009: 31). Through the course of the surveys, over fifty-eight archaeological sites were discovered, most of which are small surface sites (Al Kassem et al. 2024: 2, Fig. 1). Since these sites are located near the Saruq al-Hadid archaeological site, they were numbered consecutively and collectively referred to as Saruq Al-Hadid. SAR.53 may have functioned as a potential auxiliary site within Saruq al-Hadid, although this relationship merits further study.

Defined by an area measuring 600 x 600 m, the site is situated in a region which is characterized by severe climate conditions, high temperatures, and the presence of high sand dunes as well as scarce vegetation. The climate in this desert area is extreme, with summer temperatures that can reach 50°C (122°F) and mild but very dry winters. The area around SAR.53 contains patches of active 15–20 m-high seif dunes with interdune regions, where deflated archaeological deposits are discernible. The sand dunes are organized into wide bands (termed *draa*) in this part of the desert. Some *draa* are oriented west–east and appear to originate from another set of *draa* oriented south-west–north-east. This topography may have played a role in preserving the site, as wind-blown sand has gradually buried and shielded many of the artefacts left behind.

Overview of excavations at SAR.53

SAR.53 was discovered in 2007 during surveys aimed at defining the boundaries of Saruq al-Hadid. Surface investigations revealed scattered fire-altered sandstone cobbles and slabs, compact and dense deposits of charcoal and ash intermixed with animal bone, and Iron Age pottery sherds. Test excavations of the site revealed distinct layers. The uppermost layer comprised a later accumulation of natural sand deposits. Beneath this, a stratified deposit was found containing ash, charcoal, and fire-altered stones associated with pottery sherds and faunal remains. At the lowest level, *c.*2–3 m below ground surface, a compact layer of gypcrete was encountered, marking the basal zone of the stratigraphy at the site. Among the notable artefacts discovered at this basal zone was a fragmented soft-stone bowl with geometric engraving, similar to those found on stoneware during the Iron Age (Boraik 2019: 163).

Excavations were discontinued until 2015–2016 and 2018–2019. In 2015–2016, a single 10 x 10 m square (Area T) was excavated to prevent sand slides and gather comprehensive information about the site's formation. This excavation revealed eight layers and reached a depth of 3.2 m to the gypsum bedrock. In 2018–2019, a total of nineteen squares, each measuring 5 x 5 m, were excavated (Areas T and O). Four squares

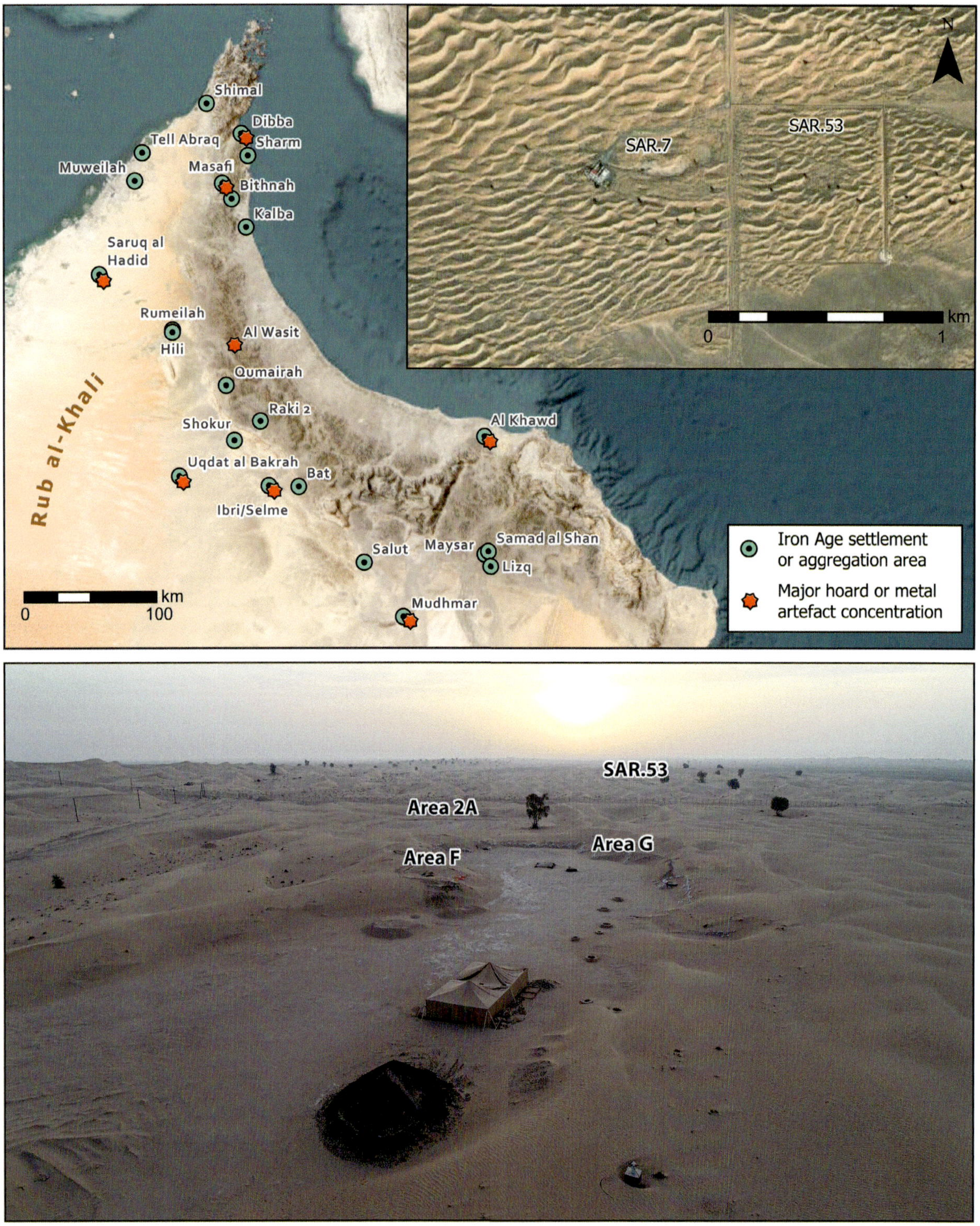

FIGURE 1. *The location of Saruq al-Hadid in relation to the Iron Age sites mentioned in the text and an aerial overview of the site. Inset: the location of SAR.53 relative to SAR.7.*

(T.X5, T.X6, T.Y5, T.Y6) were dug during the 2015–2016 season, and excavation continued with fifteen squares (O.Z5, O.Z6, O.Z7, T.Z6, T.Z5, T.W5, T.W6, T.W7, T.X7, T.Y7, T.Z7) in the 2018–2019 season. Of these, two squares (T.Z5, T.Z6) were previously partially excavated in 2015–2016, and re-excavated and cleaned in 2018–2019, and a further four squares were opened (T.Y8, T.Z8, O.Z8, O.U11), where only the upper layers were excavated (Fig. 2). Before the 2018–2019 excavation season, a weathered globular Iron Age II (first millennium BC) jar with handles and indications of a spout was uncovered by the wind on the surface of square T.W5.

Stratigraphy and material culture at SAR.53

The excavations revealed several layers of ash, charcoal, and fire-altered rock bracketed by layers of wind-blown sand. The successive laminations of charcoal, ash, and wind-blown sand at SAR.53 appear to represent a large mound of detritus measuring at least 20 x 30 m, although the actual size of the mound is at present unknown. Six stratigraphic layers, all dating to the Iron Age II period, are distinguished by these changes in laminations and wind-blown sand. While the presence of wind-blown sand is consistent with short periods of disuse or changes in activity, in this region they can accumulate rapidly over the course of a year. Commonly interspersed among these layers are hearths with concentrations of fire-altered rock and charcoal (see Fig. 2). The sequence of archaeological deposits represents a unique archive of events and activities that have so far not been observed at Saruq al-Hadid, as SAR.7 consists of several horizons with a well-described absolute chronology extending from the third millennium BC to the first millennium AD (Weeks et al. 2019a; Alkhalid et al. 2024).

Archaeological materials in these layers include distributions of fragmented and complete small ceramic bowls and animal bone typically associated with the hearths. Many of the pottery vessels are red-slipped (Fig. 3) and consistent with Iron Age periodization (Magee 1996; 2014). Discrete finds of copper alloy tools, including awls, daggers, fishing hooks, arrowheads, hoes of different sizes, and axe heads, collectively point towards a pattern of discard not dissimilar to SAR.7. Further discrete finds include fragmentary iron blades, carnelian beads, and fragments of soft-stone vessels.

Beneath these layers, *c.*2–3 m below the surface, lies the natural gypsum bedrock. The bedrock serves as the foundational layer upon which subsequent human activities took place. Evidence of extensive anthropogenic modifications is observed through the presence of large pits excavated into this layer, possibly functioning as furnaces or kilns. A total of approximately thirty-six pits of varying dimensions were documented, with diameters ranging from 50 cm to 2.75 m and depths varying from 15 to 47 cm. These features contained fire-altered sandstone fragments and were filled with ash and charcoal, indicating repeated high-temperature combustion. We hypothesize that these are associated with charcoal production.

Found in a large pit (90 cm diameter, 50 cm deep) in Layer 2 in Area T, squares Z7–Z8, a large intentionally deposited hoard of over 100 objects was recovered *c.*40 cm below the surface (Fig. 4). Described in detail below, the stratigraphic context of this hoard is sealed by laminated strata of charcoal, ash, and stone comprising Layer 1. Unlike discrete finds found in distributions in SAR.7, this context and assemblage is unique in its composition of curated, deposited, and buried objects.

Absolute chronology

The absolute chronology of the stratigraphic sequence at SAR.53 is presently underway, but preliminary results derived from six wood charcoal samples collected during the 2018–2019 field season provide an indication of the chronological sequence (Figs 5 & 6). The determinations reported here come from hand-picked wood charcoal from sections of squares T-Z6 and T-Z8 (samples 1 and 6–8), the context abutting the hoard (sample 9), and an intact ashy charcoal fill from a pit cut into the underlying gypcrete in square T-Y6 (sample 10) (Fig. 5). These samples come from contexts which effectively bound the hoard deposit and thus provide a reasonable estimation of its absolute age. We note, however, the problems associated with using wood charcoal to determine absolute ages because of the so-called 'old wood effect', which may result in an earlier estimation of calendrical age given the long growth periods of tree species (Schiffer 1986).

Unmodelled calibrated ages provide a maximum date range of 895–422 BC (95.4% probability) of the entire archaeological deposit. This range is influenced

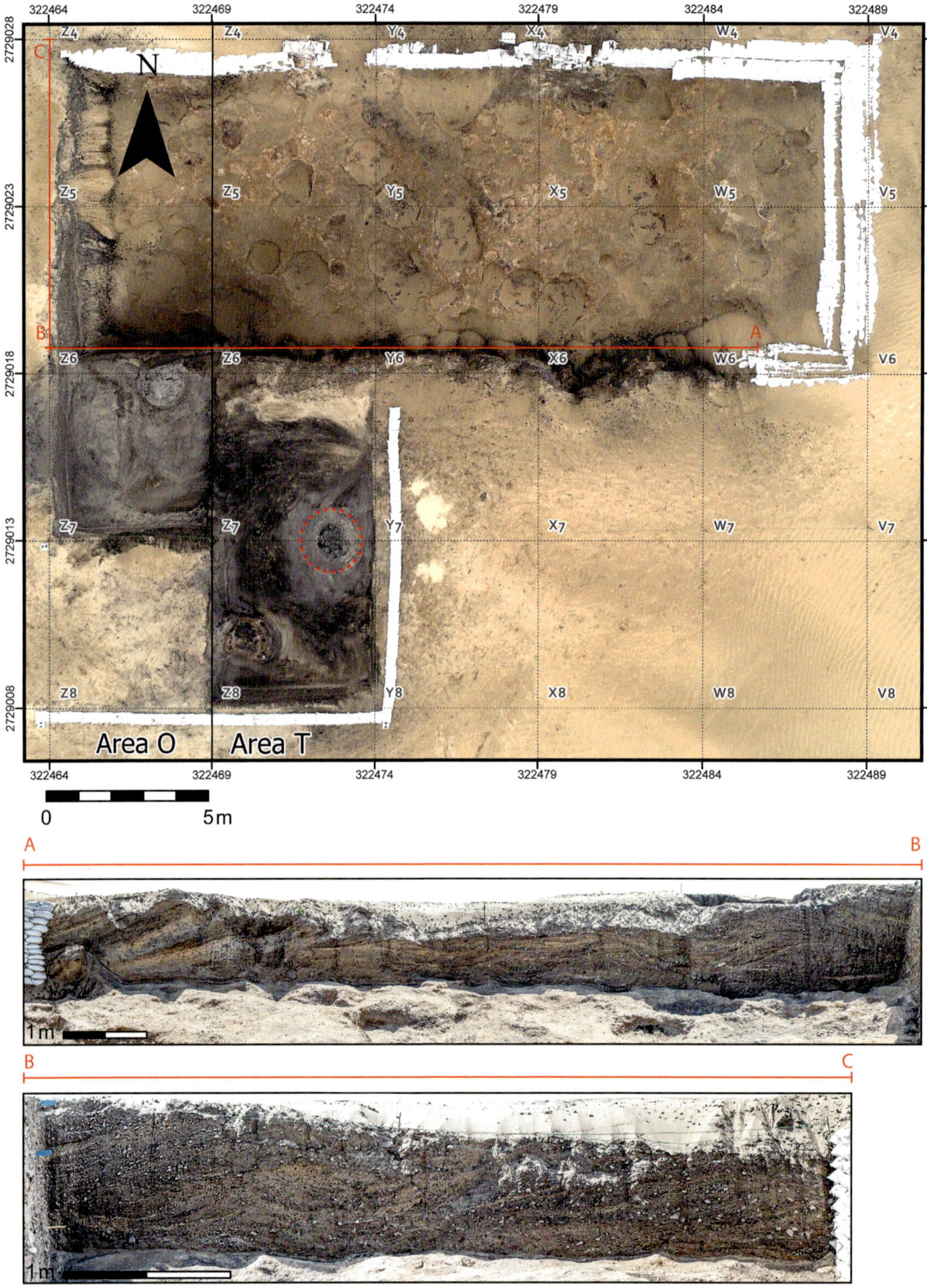

FIGURE 2. *An overview of 2018–2019 Area T/O excavations at SAR.53 and photographs of stratigraphic sections (note the different scales of the photographs);* **A–B.** *north section O-Z7 to T-W7;* **B–C.** *west section O-Z6 to O-Z5 (section photographs courtesy A. Zuber of the Sanisera Archaeology Institute).*

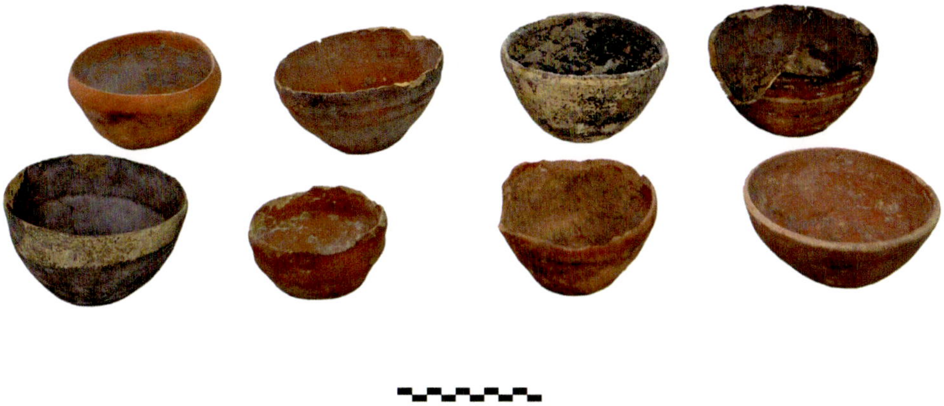

Figure 3. *Typical red- and brown-slipped ceramic bowls from Area T/O excavations at SAR.53.*

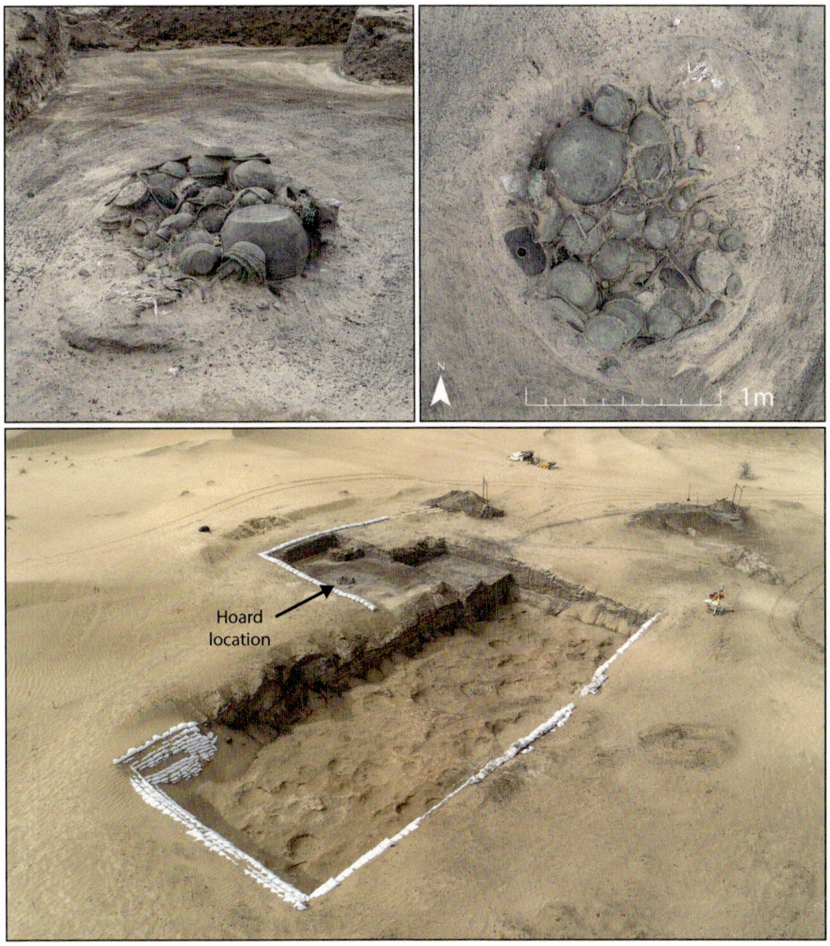

Figure 4. *The metals hoard discovered in Area T squares Z7/Z8.* **Top:** *oblique photograph facing south and plan view of the hoard;* **bottom:** *south-west aerial view of the excavation trenches at SAR.53 Area T/O.*

Sample No.	Sample Lab No.	Area - Square No.	Dated materials	Layer	$\delta^{13}C$(‰)	Conventional ^{14}C age BP	Calibrated age BC (2σ)	Absolute elevation (masl)
1	Beta - 528409	T–Z6	Wood charcoal, unidentified	1	-25.4	2540 ± 30	796–740 (37.2%) 694–662 (15.4%) 648–547 (42.8%)	104.09
9	Beta - 528413	T–Z8/Z7	Wood charcoal, unidentified	2	-24.8	2620 ± 30	827–772 (95.4%)	103.84
6	Beta - 528410	T–Z8	Wood charcoal, unidentified	2	-9.6	2470 ± 30	766–465 (93.4%) 436–422 (2.1%)	103.02
7	Beta - 528411	T–Z8	Wood charcoal, unidentified	3	-10.3	2540 ± 30	796–740 (37.2%) 694–662 (15.4%) 648–547 (42.8%)	102.56
8	Beta - 528412	T–Z8	Wood charcoal, unidentified	5	-9.8	2550 ± 30	801–744 (47.4%) 690–664 (13.1%) 645–550 (34.9%)	102.07
10	Beta - 528414	T–Y6	Wood charcoal, unidentified	6	-10.3	2640 ± 30	895–874 (5.5%) 836–776 (90.0%)	101.31

Notes: Calibrated using OxCal v4.4.4 (Bronk Ramsey 2009); IntCal20 atmospheric data (Reimer et al. 2020). Pretreatment for all samples: acid/alkali/acid. All samples hand-picked from context.

FIGURE 5. *A table showing radiocarbon ages and calibrated dates from SAR.53 Area T.*

by substantially higher standard deviation of the younger calibrated ages of samples 1 and 6–8 which are clearly affected by the Hallstatt plateau in the calibration curve. While further samples are required for advanced modelling of the radiocarbon ages, the stratigraphic control of the samples provides a relative ordering of events from the top to the bottom of the sequence. Modelling provides a provisional range of calendrical dates that is narrowed with a mean top date of 713±69 BC (2σ) and a bottom date of 821±37 BC (2σ) over a total deposit depth of 2.8 m. Assuming old wood ages are not influencing earlier ages, this possibility provides evidence that supports a comparatively rapid accumulation of materials over the course of *c.*50–200 years.

More specifically regarding the dating of the hoard, sample 9 is most closely associated with the hoard and has a modelled date of 794±18 BC. This date is somewhat earlier although within the error ranges of samples 1 and 6 which bracket the hoard stratigraphically (modelled dates of 761±38 BC and 740±40 BC respectively), suggesting that the date of sample 9 may be affected by heartwood or other old wood effects.

These data confidently place the hoard context and depositional sequence so far recovered in SAR.53 within Horizon I at SAR.7, which is defined by several radiocarbon determinations from the central and north-east sectors (Area F/G and Area 2A) (Contreras Rodrigo et al. 2017: 64; Weeks et al. 2019a: 1066–1069). Present evidence from SAR.7 supports a range of 1200–800 BC for the major industrial phase of metal production, including exceptional evidence ranging from primary smelting and copper refining to artefact production and recycling (Valente et al. 2020; Weeks et al. 2023). While it is tempting to link the hypothesized charcoal production activities in SAR.53 to the fuel requirements associated with the intense pyrotechnological activities in SAR.7, the overlapping ages place the activities at SAR.53 at the very end of the major industrial phase. Industrial activities are known from Horizon I, with evidence from directly dated metallurgical production residues, although present data are more consistent with a more periodic and less intensive production strategy (Weeks et al. 2019a: 1066).

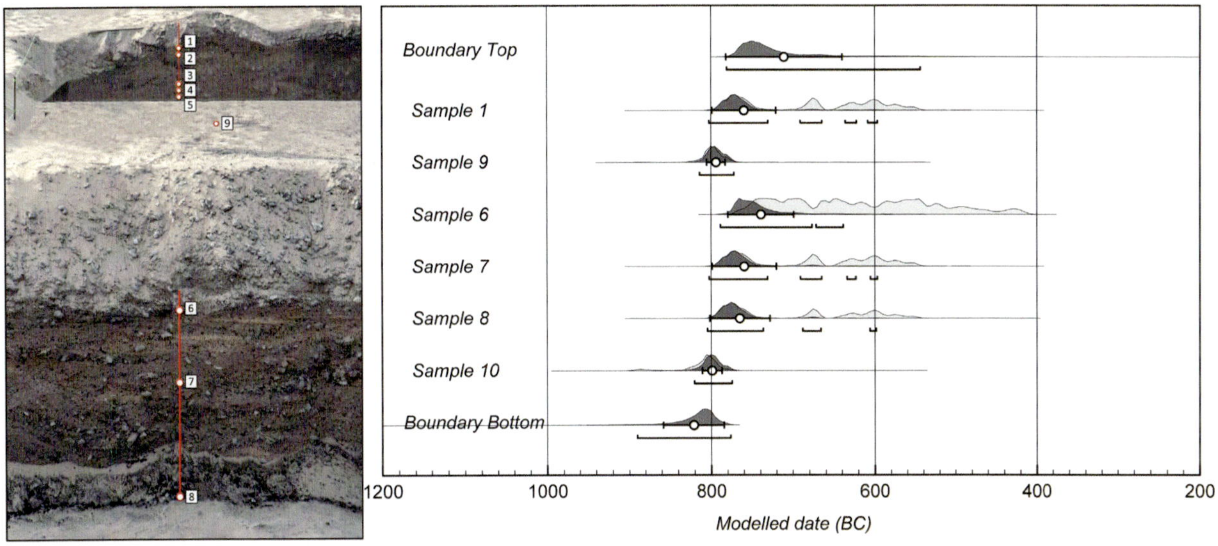

FIGURE 6. *Southern sections of T Z-6 and Z8 indicating the location of hand-picked wood charcoal samples. Sample 9 was collected in the same stratum and in proximity to the hoard. The location of sample 10, not shown here, was from the bottom of a pit carved into the basal gypcrete layer in T-Y6. Modelled and unmodelled probabilities, mean model age, and 95.4% probability estimate of the radiocarbon dates are shown on the chart on the right.*

The metal hoard

The hoard contains over 100 artefacts, mostly copper alloy vessels, tools, pan weights, axe heads, mirrors, plates and ladles, cumulatively weighing more than 47 kg. The ancient inhabitants may have intentionally stored their tools and vessels as a means of safeguarding them during periods of absence, possibly in response to mobility constraints. In this context, the deliberate concealment or deposition of objects may have served as a practical strategy to reduce the burden of transport while ensuring their preservation for future use. The burial of the artefacts may have also been tied to ceremonial practices or religious rituals related to the ritual deposition of wealth or other status markers. The copper alloy vessels were placed upside down, suggesting they were buried to prevent damage. The vessels and bowls also show signs of burning, which suggests that they were used several times.

Artefact classification and description

Of the 102 objects catalogued in the hoard (Fig. 7), ninety-five (or 93% of the total) are made of copper or copper alloy. The majority of the copper alloy objects are finely raised vessels (Fig. 8) produced mainly of sheet metal, including mostly bowls with flared and incised rims, and many with incised decorations on the interior bottom of the vessels. One of the largest of this class of vessel has a volume of several litres and was accompanied with a vessel with scores of perforations in the bottom meaning that it probably served as a strainer. A pedestaled and stemmed cup with rows of circular decoration on the outer surface is anomalous in its presence in the hoard; it was probably produced using lost-wax casting technologies rather than the more common raising and working of sheet metal. Other objects include pan scales, hoes, ladles, and cast axe heads (Fig. 9). Five mirror-like tools with a handle attached to a flat disc were also found (Fig. 9). The mirror found in Qidfa' 1 in Fujairah in a multi-period tomb (Wadi Suq–Late Bronze/Early Iron Age) (Al Tikriti

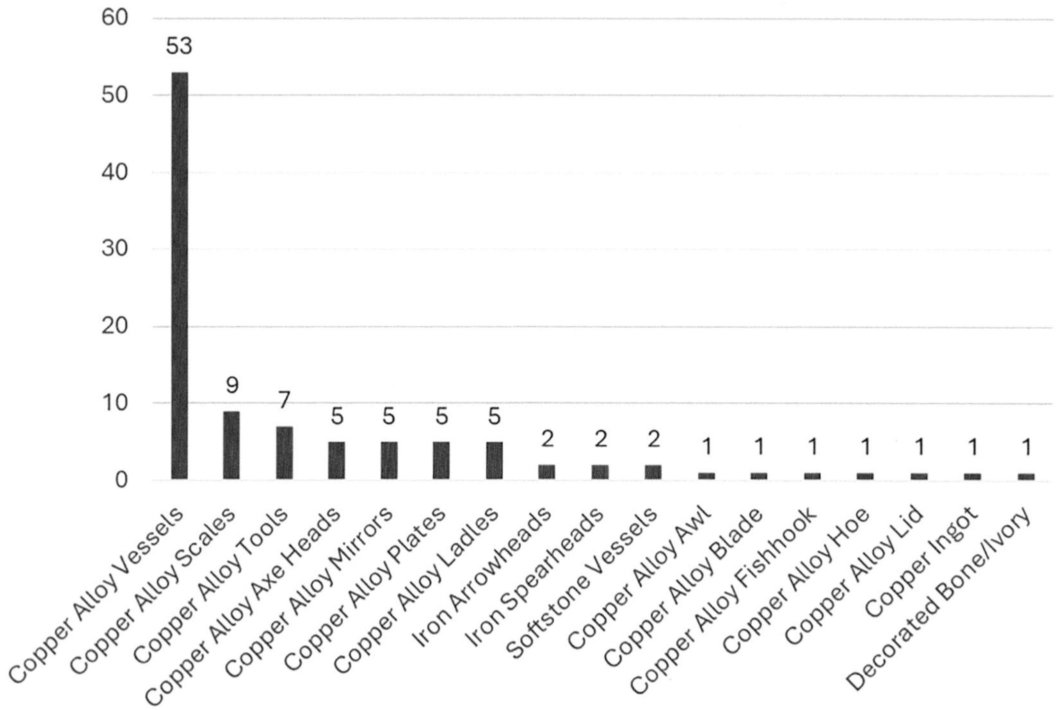

FIGURE 7. *The number of complete objects from the SAR.53 hoard by general classification.*

2022) is a strong parallel to these objects. Another object has an elongated handle topped with a crescent-like shape (Fig. 9); its function is at present unknown.

Some of these tools may be linked to charcoal production. Among these, copper alloy axes and adzes (Fig. 9) are noteworthy for their solid and sharp cutting edges. It is possible these tools were used for felling tree trunks, a necessary step in the charcoal-making process. The use of well-sharpened implements would have been essential for efficiently cutting timber before burning.

The excavations also yielded several bronze hoes of various sizes, with one hoe found among the artefacts hoard. Copper alloy hoes at Saruq al-Hadid are oval with a circular hole at the top for the wooden handle. Similar examples have been revealed at several sites in south-eastern Arabia, but not in as large a number as at Saruq al-Hadid, where both large and small hoes have been found. Their proximity to kilns strongly suggests they were crucial to charcoal production; possibly used to shovel charcoal around the kilns.

Additionally, three copper alloy ladles were found in the hoard. Similar examples have been found at other sites in south-eastern Arabia, including Muweilah (Magee 1998), indicating their widespread use throughout the Iron Age. A large ladle with a snake head handle, which may have borne symbolic or ceremonial significance, was found (Fig. 10). Additionally, nine copper scale-pans of different sizes were found among the hoard; they have almost flat circular plates and are perforated with three to four holes below the edge in several places. Some of these scales are decorated with incised motifs.

In addition to the copper alloy objects, two iron arrowheads and two spearheads were recovered. Two complete soft-stone vessels with incised decoration consistent with Iron Age II decoration were found, including a small cup and spouted vessel with incised

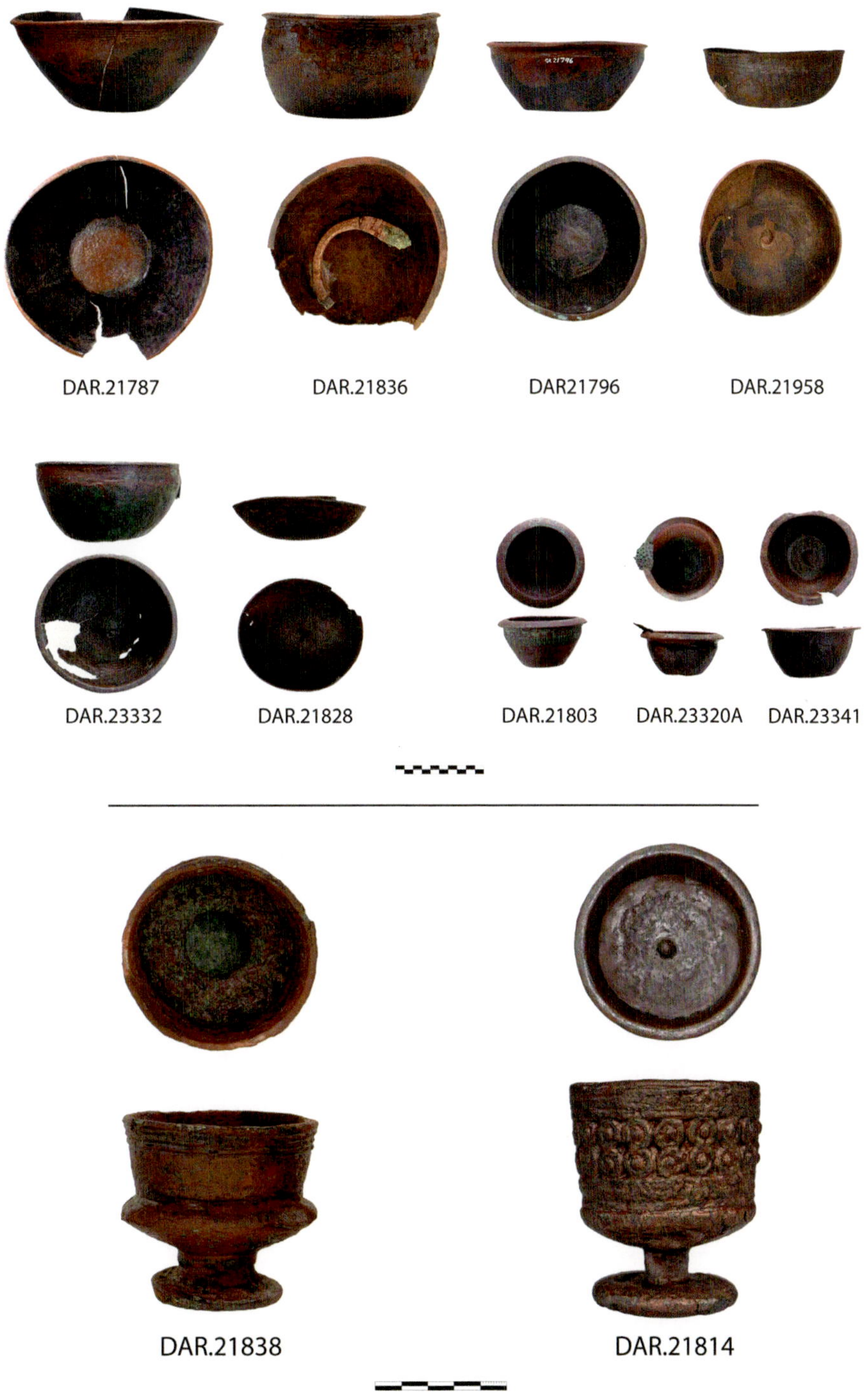

FIGURE 8. *A selection of complete or near-complete copper alloy vessels from the assemblage. The range of vessel types includes large bowls, cups, and chalices.*

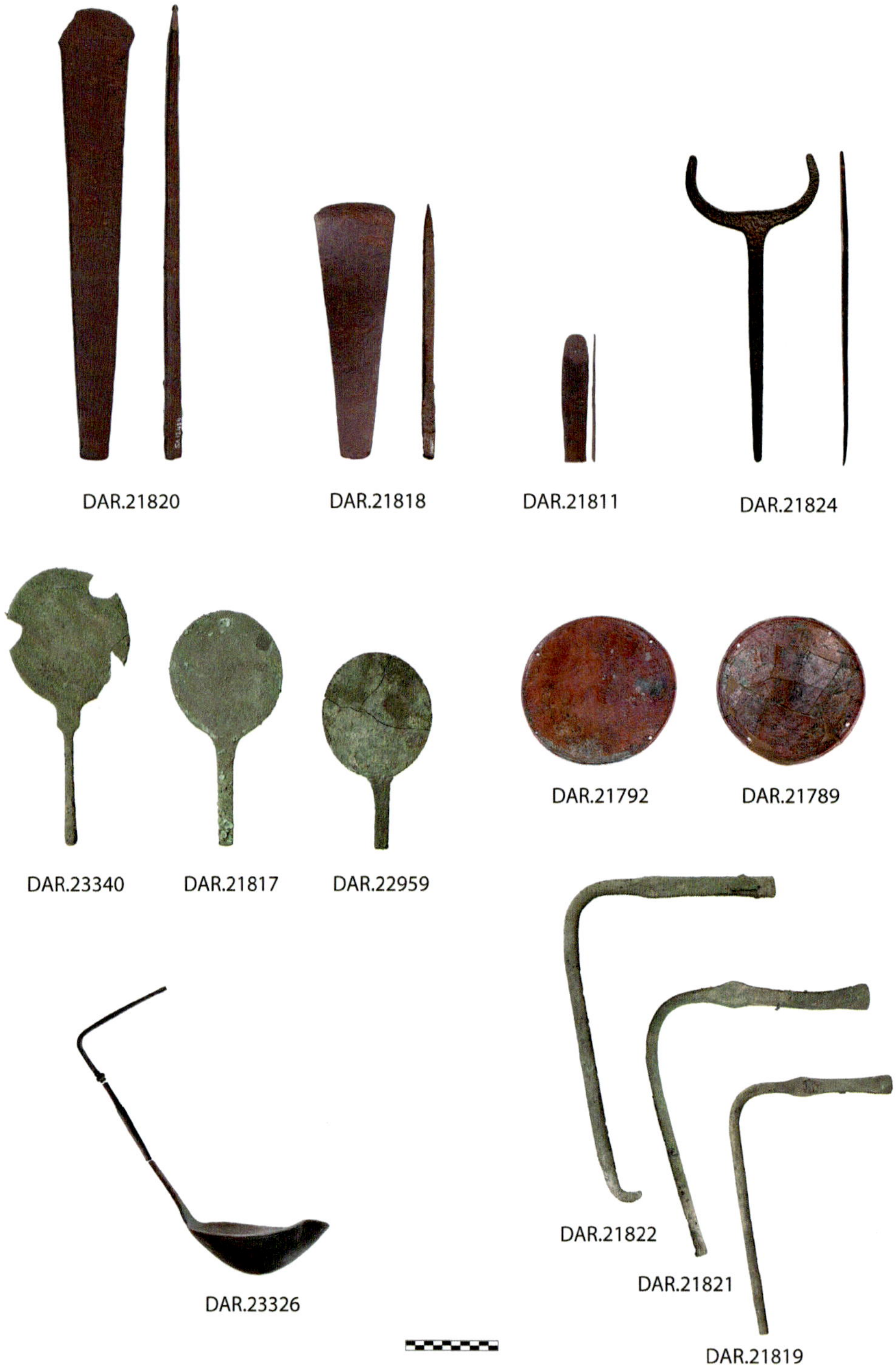

FIGURE 9. *A selection of complete copper alloy tools and other objects from the assemblage. These include exceptionally large axe heads or chisels, a potential pre-form, a two-pronged artefact, mirrors, and objects of unknown function.*

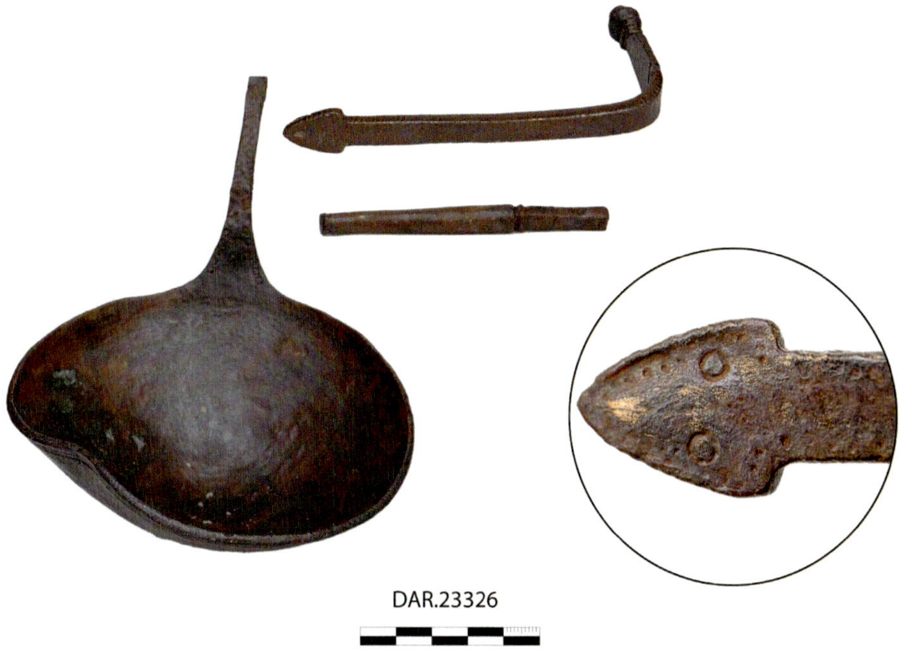

FIGURE 10. *A copper alloy ladle with detail of a handle finial with a punched and incised snake decoration.*

lines forming rhombic shapes. The only object produced of animal bone or ivory is a small rectangular piece, possibly a handle, decorated with circular holes. Many fragments of vessels and other objects were also found.

Decorations on the discovered artefacts

Most of the copper alloy artefacts discovered in the hoard were intricately decorated, reflecting the industrial skill of ancient inhabitants during the Iron Age. The decorations executed on the hoard items can be divided into two types: geometric and floral. Triangles and circular motifs are meticulously incised on the interior bottom of several copper bowls. These decorative elements consist of either finely incised horizontal lines or a series of small concentric circles, as exemplified by one of the goblets (see Fig. 8), which demonstrates remarkable craftsmanship. A comparable motif has been identified on a Neo-Assyrian gypsum alabaster relief from Nimrud, specifically within the central palace, dated to the seventh century BC (Graff 2016: 202, fig. 9). Another distinct category of decoration consists of floral motifs, which are incised on the interior base of several bowls. Strong parallels can be drawn with patterns found on worked shell objects from the Saruq Al-Hadid and Dibba sites, particularly rosette motifs and pointed star designs (Weeks et al. 2019b: 3–13, figs 2–10) (Fig. 11). Similar motifs are also present in Neo-Assyrian imagery from the Northwest Palace at Nimrud (Weeks et al. 2019b: 15–17, figs 11–12). The rosette motif, often featuring twelve or more petals, has its origins in the Middle and Neo-Assyrian periods (Albenda 2020: 73), where it frequently appeared in artistic and material culture associated with religious and royal contexts. In these instances, the rosette is commonly interpreted as a symbol of the goddess Ishtar, reflecting its broader iconographic and symbolic significance in Mesopotamian tradition. Another comparative example is a bowl in the Metropolitan Museum collections, which is decorated in the centre with a rosette around a raised point, encircled by two series of incised lines (Muscarella 1988: 381, 501). Bowls of this type are known

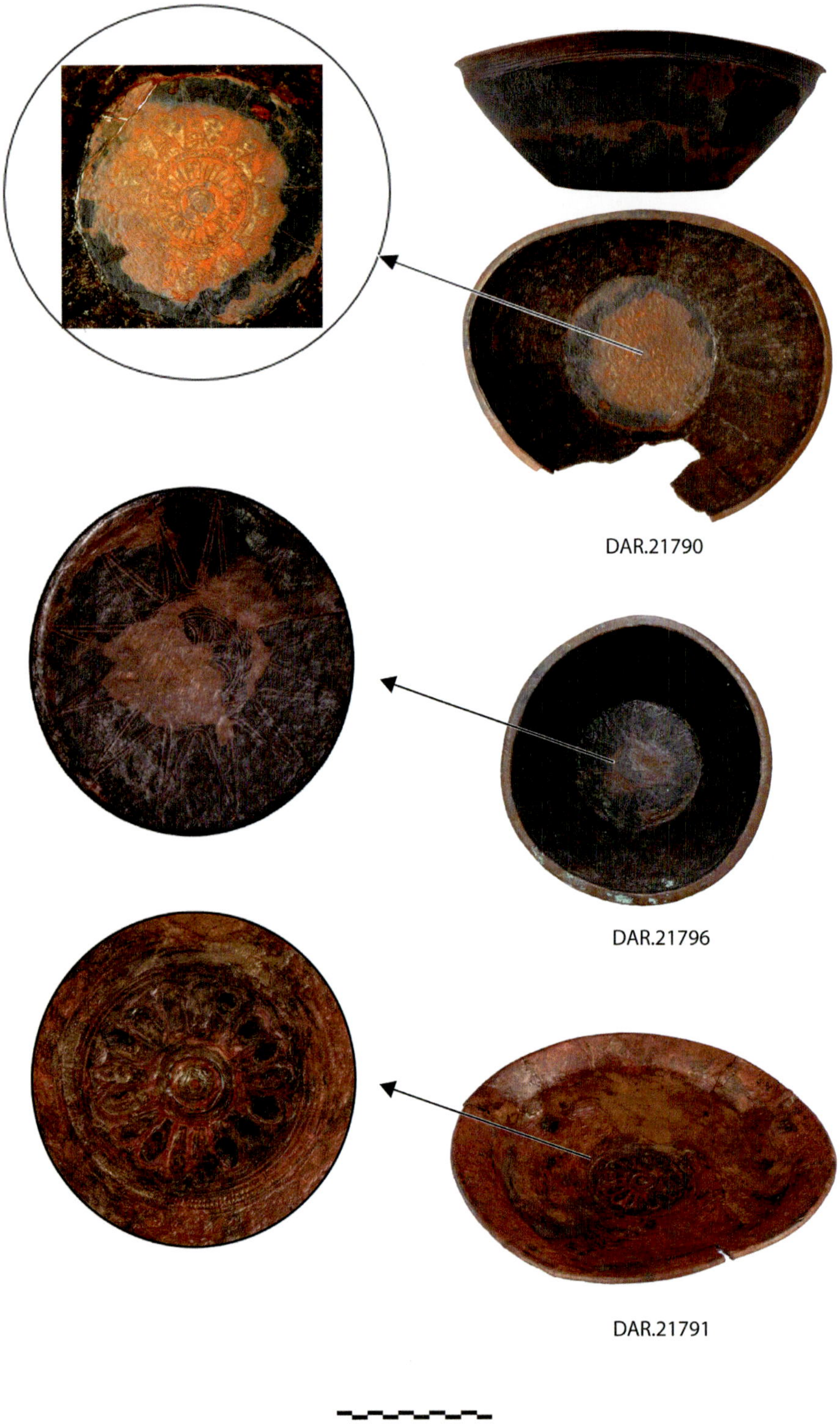

FIGURE 11. *Details of three vessels from SAR.53 with incised rosette decorations.*

from Assyria and the Levant (Aruz et al. 2016: 20–22, 26; figs 8–10, 16), each varying slightly in size, shape, and decoration, indicating that variety was desired. Collectively, these patterns serve as evidence of the artisanal traditions and cultural interactions between different communities in the wider region. At Saruq al Hadid, these ornamental elements indicate that the ancient inhabitants placed significant emphasis on embellishing both utilitarian and ceremonial objects, reflecting an artistic tradition integrated into daily and ritual practices.

Comparisons with metal hoards in south-eastern Arabia

Three other metal hoards in south-eastern Arabia — Masafi in Fujairah, the ʿIbrī/Selme hoard, and the Al-Khawḍ hoard (see Fig. 1) — provide broader contextual parallels for the Saruq Al-Hadid assemblage. At Masafi, ingots were found in two pottery jars in Iron Age II building contexts (Benoist et al. 2023:18). The ʿIbrī/Selme hoard, uncovered at Dar al-Salām Farm north-east of the ʿIbrī pass, is considered one of the largest known ancient metal hoards in the Near East (Yule 2015). The hoard was not recovered through systematic excavation but was instead unearthed during gardening activities (Yule 2015). This assemblage consists of 508 metallic artefacts, with metal vessels comprising approximately three-quarters of the deposit. The collection includes axes, daggers, vessels, and bangles, among other objects. Many of the metal vessels exhibit evidence of intentional folding, suggesting they were compacted for transport or prepared for recycling in kilns (Yule 2015: 133–139). Another important and comparable metal hoard is the Al-Khawḍ assemblage, identified in the eastern part of the Sultanate of Oman and dated to the Early Iron Age. The Al-Khawḍ hoard comprises a diverse array of metallic artefacts, including arrowheads, axes/adzes, bangles, daggers, knives, vessels, razors, spearheads, rings, swords, and tweezers, illustrating a wide range of metallurgical production and utilization in the region (Al-Jahwari et al. 2021). Together these hoards exhibit both similarities and distinctions in their composition, depositional contexts, and possible function.

Conclusion

The excavations at Saruq Al Hadid-53 (SAR.53) revealed a complex stratigraphy characterized by continuous deposits of ash and charcoal that accumulated in a short period of time. Radiocarbon dates situate the site within the Iron Age II period (eighth–seventh century BC). The discovery of several hearths, fragmented Iron Age vessels, and animal bone in these deposits reflects domestic practices. The existence of several large pits within the bedrock rich with charcoal may have functioned as furnaces or kilns linked to charcoal production. The discovery of a rich collection of deposited copper alloy artefacts including vessels, tools, and weaponry in a sealed context is particularly significant. A comparison with other regional hoards hints at a broader shared pattern of metal hoarding practices among ancient societies during the Iron Age. Additionally, the motifs and ornamentation found on the recovered artefacts suggest shared artisanal traditions and cultural influences across the wider Near East. The discoveries at SAR.53 represent unique evidence of activities that have so far not been observed at Saruq al-Hadid, and provide a means to explore metal hoarding practices during the Iron Age in south-eastern Arabia in more detail in the future.

Acknowledgements

We deeply appreciate the support of Muna Faisal Algurg, CEO of the Dubai Culture and Arts Authority — Culture & Heritage Sector, which enabled the inclusion of this paper at the 57th Seminar for Arabian Studies. We would like to express our sincere gratitude to our colleagues involved in the excavations and restoration for their dedication and hard work. The 2018–2019 excavation work was supervised by Dr Mansour Boraik. Our heartfelt thanks go to Eng. Bader Al Ali, Noora Abdul Ghani Al Khoori, and Dr Maria-Paola Pellegrino. We are also grateful to photographer/surveyor Jamal Safi for providing the essential photographs. Finally, we extend our thanks to the Spanish International School for their cooperation in sending samples for site dating; their assistance has been crucial to our research.

References

Albenda P. 2020. The royal Assyrian rosette. *Nouvelles Assyriologiques Brèves et Utilitaires* (N.A.B.U.) no. 1 (March): 73–75.

Alkhalid M., Alkassem A., D'Auria A., Naime Y., Reize F., Alsuwaidi M. ... Ali B.A. 2024. Archaeological excavations at Sarūq al-Ḥadīd — 2022–2023 season: Stratigraphy and new absolute chronological sequence of Area G. *Arabian Archaeology and Epigraphy* 35/1: 71–102.

Aruz J., Killebrew A.E., Collins P. & Gansell A. 2016. Pages 1–361 in J. Aruz & M. Seymour (eds), *Assyria to Iberia: Art and culture in the Iron Age*. (First edition). New York: Metropolitan Museum of Art.

Benoist A., Hamel A., Le Carlier de Veslud C., Degli Esposti M. & Goy J. 2023. Iron Age metalworking at Masafi -1? A reconsideration of the metal hoards discovered in the collective buildings. *Études et Travaux* 36: 11–37.

Bernáldez-Sánchez E., García-Viñas E., Seco-Álvarez M., Ramos-Soldado J.L., Boraik M., Youssef Y.A. ... Ferrer-Albelda E. 2024. Wild and domesticated fauna in desert regions of the Near East: The case of Saruq al-Hadid (UAE). *Near Eastern Archaeology* 87/3: 194–208.

Boraik M. 2019. *Season 2018/2019 report*. Antiquities Department Archive, Dubai Municipality. [Unpublished report.]

Bronk Ramsey C. 2009. Bayesian analysis of radiocarbon dates. *Radiocarbon* 51/1: 337–60.

Cable CM. 2015. Excavation results. Pages 327–398 in L. Weeks (ed.), Saruq al-Hadid Archaeological Research Project: Interim report 1. [Unpublished report for Dubai Municipality.]

Cable CM. 2016. Excavations. Pages 1–38 in L. Weeks (ed.), Saruq al-Hadid Archaeological Research Project: Interim report 2. [Unpublished report for Dubai Municipality.]

Cable CM. 2017. Excavations. Pages 1–118 in L. Weeks (ed.), Saruq al-Hadid Archaeological Research Project: Interim report 3. [Unpublished report for Dubai Municipality.]

Casana J., Herrmann J.T. & Qandil H.S. 2009. Settlement history in the eastern Rub al-Khali: Preliminary report of the Dubai Desert Survey (2006–2007). *Arabian Archaeology and Epigraphy* 20: 30–45.

Contreras Rodrigo F., Vila B., Albarracín P., Bukhash R.M., Al Abbar S.O., Radwan Karim M.B. & Zein H.M. 2017. Excavations in Area 2A at Sarūq al- Hadīd: Iron Age II evidence of copper production and ceremonial activities. *Proceedings of the Seminar for Arabian Studies* 47: 57–66.

Graff S.B. 2016. *The art of the elephant and its consequences*. Pages 194–203 in J. Aruz & M. Seymour (eds), *Assyria to Iberia: Art and culture in the Iron Age*. (First edition). New York: The Metropolitan Museum of Art.

Herrmann J.T., Casana J. & Qandil H.S. 2012. A sequence of inland desert settlement in the Oman peninsula: 2008–2009 excavations at Saruq al-Hadid, Dubai, UAE. *Arabian Archaeology and Epigraphy* 23: 50–69.

Ihde CA. 2017. Sarouq Al-Hadid 2016/17 final report. German mission. November 1st 2016–April 30th 2017. [Unpublished report submitted to Dubai Municipality.]

Al-Jahwari N.S., Yule P.A., Douglas K.A., Pracejus B., Al-Belushi M.A.K. & ElMahi A.T. (eds). 2021. *The Early Iron Age metal hoard from the Al Khawd area (Sultan Qaboos University), Sultanate of Oman. (The Archaeological Heritage of Oman)*. vii. Oxford: Archaeopress.

Karacic S., Weeks L., Cable C., Méry S., Al Ali Y., Boraik M. ... MacDonald B.L. 2018. Integrating a complex late prehistoric settlement system: Neutron activation analysis of pottery use and exchange at Saruq al-Hadid, United Arab Emirates. *Journal of Archaeological Science: Reports* 22: 21–31.

Al Kassem A., Groucutt H.S., Reize F., Alsuwaidi M.A., Al Ali B.M.A. & Boraik M. 2024. Neolithic arrowheads and Bronze Age industry at Saruq al Hadid, UAE. *Journal of Archaeological Science: Reports* 57: 1–15.

Al-Khraysheh F. & An-Nashef K. 2007. *Dubai: Civilization and progress throughout three thousand years. Five seasons of joint archaeological excavations between the Emirate of Dubai and the Hashemite Kingdom of Jordan at Sarouq al-Hadeed*. Dubai: Department of Tourism and Commerce Marketing, Government of Dubai, UAE. [In Arabic.]

Magee P. 1996. The chronology of the south-eastern Arabian Iron Age. *Arabian Archaeology and Epigraphy* 7: 240–252.

Magee P. 1998. Cultural interaction and social complexity in the southeast Arabian Iron Age. *Iranica Antiqua* 33: 135–142.

Magee P. 2014. *The archaeology of prehistoric Arabia. Adaptation and social formation from the Neolithic to the Iron Age*. (Cambridge World Archaeology). New York: Cambridge University Press.

Müller M. & Blum S.W.E. 2019. Excavation at Saruq Al-Hadid (Emirate of Dubai, UAE): Interim report of the Tübingen Mission (2018/2019). Universität Tübingen. [Unpublished report.]

Muscarella O.W. 1988. General objects. Pages 381–382 and no. 501 in O.W. Muscarella, *Bronze and iron: Ancient Near Eastern artifacts in the Metropolitan Museum of Art*. New York: The Metropolitan Museum of Art.

Nashef K. 2010. Sārūq al-Hadīd: An industrial complex of the Iron Age II period. Pages 213–226 in A. Avanzini (ed.), *Eastern Arabia in the first millennium BCA*. (Arabia Antiqua 6). Rome: L'Erma di Bretschneider.

Potts D.T. 2009. Urartian and Assyrian echoes at Saruq al-Hadid (Emirate of Dubai) *Liwa* 1/2: 3–9.

Qandil H. 2003. Survey and excavations at Saruq al Hadeed, 2002–2003. Pages 120–138 in P. Hellyer & M. Ziolkowski (eds), *Proceedings of the first annual symposium on recent palaeontological & archaeological discoveries in the Emirates (Al Ain, 2003). Emirates Heritage* i. Al Ain: Zayed Center for Heritage and History.

Reimer P.J., Austin W.E.N., Bard E., Bayliss A., Blackwell P.G., Bronk Ramsey C. ... Talamo S. 2020. The Intcal20 Northern Hemisphere radiocarbon age calibration curve (0–55 Cal Kbp). *Radiocarbon* 62/4: 725–757.

Roberts J., Weeks L., Cable C., Fillios M., Al Aali Y.Y., Radwan M.B. & Zein H. 2018. The role of wild terrestrial animals in late prehistoric societies of south-eastern Arabia: New insights from Saruq al-Hadid. *Arabian Archaeology and Epigraphy* 29/2: 115–134.

Schiffer M.B. 1986. Radiocarbon dating and the 'old wood' problem: The case of the Hohokam chronology. *Journal of Archaeological Science* 13/1: 13–30.

Soriano I., Perea A., Escanilla N., Contreras Rodrigo F., Al Ali Y.Y., Boraik Radwan M. & Zein H. 2018. Goldwork technology at the Arabian Peninsula. First data from Saruq al Hadid Iron Age site (Dubai, United Arab Emirates). *Journal of Archaeological Science: Reports* 22: 1–10.

Al Tikriti W.Y. 2022. *Qidfa' 1: Excavation of a late prehistoric tomb, Fujairah Emirate, United Arab Emirates*. Oxford: Archaeopress.

Valente T. 2023. Copper metallurgy at Saruq al-Hadid (Dubai, UAE). MA thesis, Faculty of Arts and Humanities of the University of Porto. [Unpublished.]

Valente T., Contreras F., Mahmud A., Boraik M., Karim R., Al Mansoori M.S. & Zein H. 2020. Five seasons of excavations in areas 2A and G of Saruq al Hadid (Dubai, UAE): Iron Age II evidences of copper production, workshop area and ceremonial activities. *Isimu* 23: 169–195.

Weeks L., Cable C., Franke K., Newton C., Karacic S., Roberts J. ... Zein H. 2017. Recent archaeological research at Saruq al-Hadid, Dubai, UAE. *Arabian Archaeology and Epigraphy* 28/1: 31–60.

Weeks L., Cable C.M., Karacic S., Franke K.A., Price D.M., Newton C. ... Zein H. 2019a. Dating persistent short-term human activity in a complex depositional environment: Late prehistoric occupation at Saruq al-Hadid, Dubai. *Radiocarbon* 61/4: 1041–1075.

Weeks L., David-Cuny H., Avanzini A., Lischi S., Genchi F., Caputo F. ... Boraik M. 2019b. Worked and decorated shell discs from southern Arabia and the wider Near East. *Arabian Archaeology and Epigraphy* 30/2: 213–238.

Weeks L., Valente T., Franke K., Contreras F., Radwan M.B. & Zein H. 2023. Iron Age copper production and the 'ritual economy' of Saruq Al-Hadid (Dubai, UAE). Pages 239–270 in P. El Fadi, M. Gannon, K. Al Shohof & T. Al Ghoul (eds), *Advances in UAE Archaeology: Proceedings of Abu Dhabi's archaeology conference 2022*. Oxford: Archaeopress.

Wygnańska Z., Bagi O., Rądkowska J., Zych I., Rempel S., Juchniewicz K. & Radwan M.B. 2022. Reconstructing a changing landscape of human activities in the Iron Age II at Saruq al-Hadid (Dubai). *Proceedings of the Seminar for Arabian Studies* 51: 449–464.

Yule P.A. 2015. The ʿIbrī/Selme hoard from al-Ẓāhirah Province — 30 years after. Pages 133–140 in *Proceedings of the symposium 'The archaeological heritage of Oman', UNESCO, Paris, 7 September 2012*. Muscat: Ministry of Heritage and Culture, Sultanate of Oman.

Authors' addresses

Mariam Ali Al Suwaidi, Chief Archaeologist, Antiquities Department, Dubai Culture and Arts Authority, PO Box 115222, Dubai, United Arab Emirates.
e-mail Mariam.alsuwaidi@dubaiculture.ae

Joseph W. Lehner, Discipline of Archaeology, School of Humanities, A18 Brennan Maccallum, The University of Sydney, Sydney, NSW 2006, Australia; Vere Gordon Childe Centre, Faculty of Arts and Sciences, The University of Sydney, Sydney, NSW 2006, Australia.
e-mail joseph.lehner@sydney.edu.au

Bader Mohamed Al Ali, Director of Antiquities Department, Antiquities Department, Dubai Culture and Arts Authority, PO Box 115222, Dubai, United Arab Emirates.
e-mail bader.alali@dubaiculture.ae

Proceedings of the Seminar for Arabian Studies 54 (2025): 247–262

The production of Bahlā Ware in the context of late Islamic Oman

Jelena Živković, José Cristobal Carvajal López, Irini Biezeveld & Stephanie Döpper

Summary

Among glazed Arabian Gulf wares, Bahlā Ware stands out as one of the most documented objects of consumption at sites in Oman, the UAE, Qatar, and Bahrain from the sixteenth to the early twentieth century. Previous scientific studies of Bahlā Ware from UAE and Qatar formed the basis for understanding its production technology and provenance, as well as the unique composition of its lead-barium glaze. This paper presents the new results of petrographic and chemical analyses of thirty-two Bahlā samples from Oman, contributing to a better understanding of the compositional variability of ceramics, the provenance of raw materials, and techniques used for the application of lead-barium glazes. The compositional match between samples of Bahlā Ware from Oman, the UAE, and Qatar reveals the exploitation of the same geological source of raw materials over several centuries. Previous research has associated this source with the ophiolitic geological formation in Oman. The results of chemical analysis of glazes confirmed that the Omani samples were also coated with a lead-barium glaze of the same type as reported for UAE and Qatar.

Keywords: Bahlā Ware, late Islamic ceramic production, provenance, lead-barium glaze

Introduction

Bahlā Ware is a major class of late Islamic glazed pottery local to the Gulf, with well-documented findings reported from Oman (Biezeveld & Düring 2020: 206; Döpper 2022: 161; Costa & Wilkinson 1987), the United Arab Emirates (Power 2015: 10–11; Živković et al. 2019), Qatar (Carvajal López et al. 2019; Carter 2011: 37; Petersen et al. 2010: 48; Bystron 2019: 43; Garlake 1978a: 174; 1978b: 167), Bahrain (Carter & Naranjo-Santana 2011: 90–91), and Iran (Priestman 2005: 269–270). This ware consists of bowls, dishes, and storage jars coated with monochrome glazes of brown, green, and yellow colours (Fig. 1), which were used for food consumption, transportation, and storage. Their wide distribution and significant quantities at urban, rural, coastal, and inland sites across the Gulf highlights their importance for archaeological interpretations of socio-economic networks between the sixteenth and early twentieth centuries. The provenance of Bahlā Ware has been a subject of long-lasting debate, with either Khunj in Iran or Bahlā in Oman being considered as centres of production (Kennet 2004: 54; Priestman 2005: 270; Whitcomb 1975: 129; Carter 2011: 37).

Recent studies of Bahlā Ware using archaeological science methods have shed new light on questions of provenance, production technology, and potting traditions in the Gulf (Živković et al. 2019; Carvajal López et al. 2019). The consistency of mineralogical compositions of Bahlā samples from al-Ain and Doha indicated a common origin of raw materials used for the production of this particular type of ceramic. Research showed that this source of calcareous raw materials lies in the zone of the ophiolitic geological formation in Oman, likely within the boundaries of the town of Bahlā (Živković et al. 2019: 4707). This result ruled out Khunj as a production centre, at least for Bahlā Ware used on the Arabian side of the Gulf.

Additionally, the study of technology used in the production of these vessels showed an unexpected complexity concerning the composition of their glazes. The Bahlā glaze is of a lead-barium type unknown elsewhere in the Islamic World (Živković et al. 2019: 4706). The key components of this glaze are lead and barium sulphates that were naturally mixed in minerals, and as such extracted for the glaze preparation. Not only is this a very specific process, but sulphidic minerals containing barium also have poor fluxing properties and their use in the glaze preparation often requires more energy. As other seemingly less complex glazing technologies, such as the use of lead oxides associated with monochrome lead glazes, were available at the time,

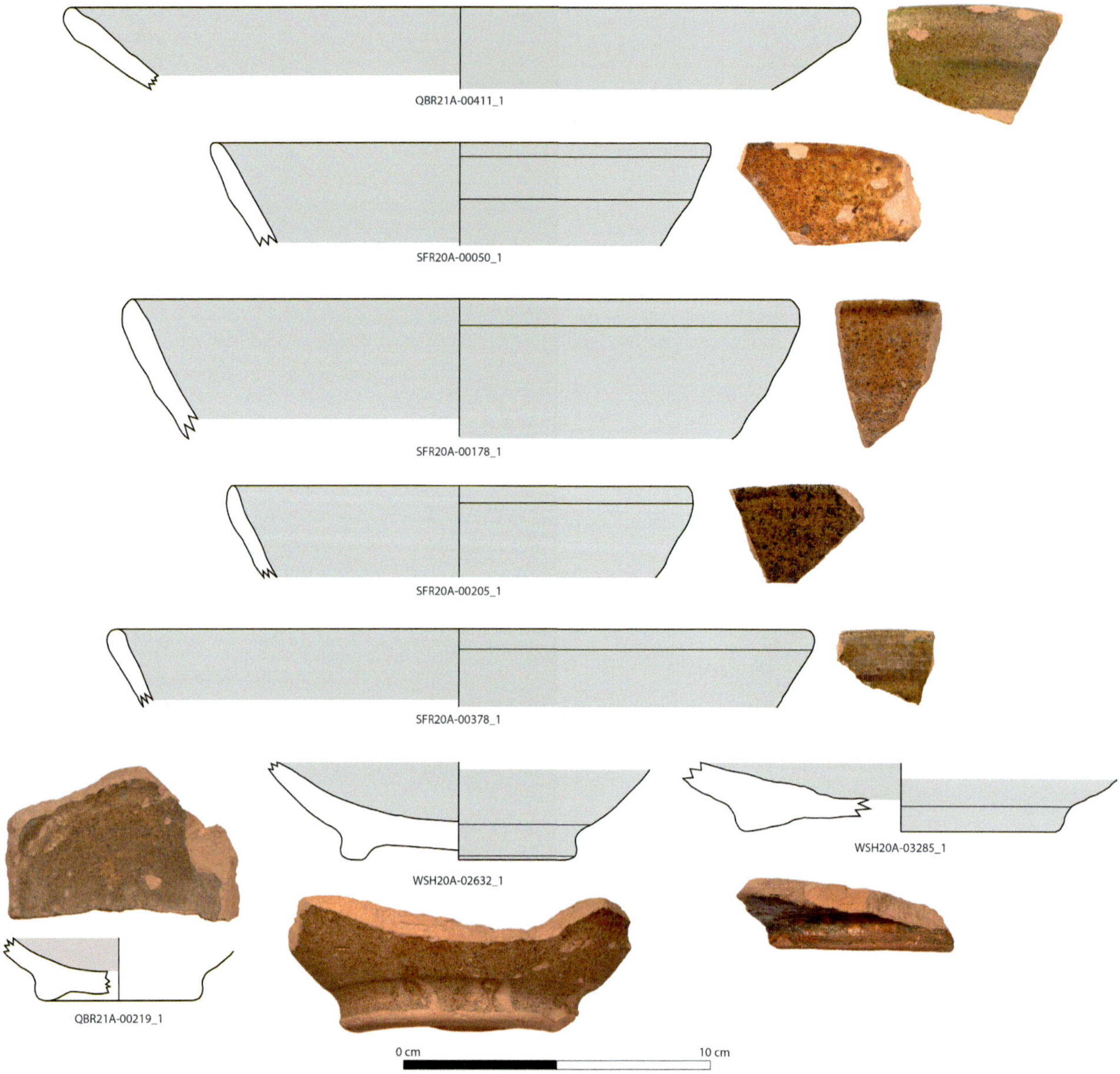

FIGURE 1. *Bahla Ware from Oman. Bowls: QBR21A-00411_1: surface find from Al-Qabrayn; SFR20A-00050_1, SFR20A-00178_1, and SFR20A-00378_1: surface finds from Safrat al-Khashbah; bases: QBR21A-00219_1: surface find from Al-Qabrayn; WSH20A-02632_1 and WSH20A-03285_1: surface finds from Al-Washhi.*

it is possible that the use of sulphidic minerals in glaze preparation was strongly embedded in the technological choices in producing Bahlā Ware, although we cannot pinpoint what the cultural significance of these choices were. Nevertheless, they were repeated and became a pattern of long-term exploitation of raw materials used for the production of both ceramic bodies and glazes, successfully transmitted as the know-how of a characteristic technological tradition within the Omani potting community.

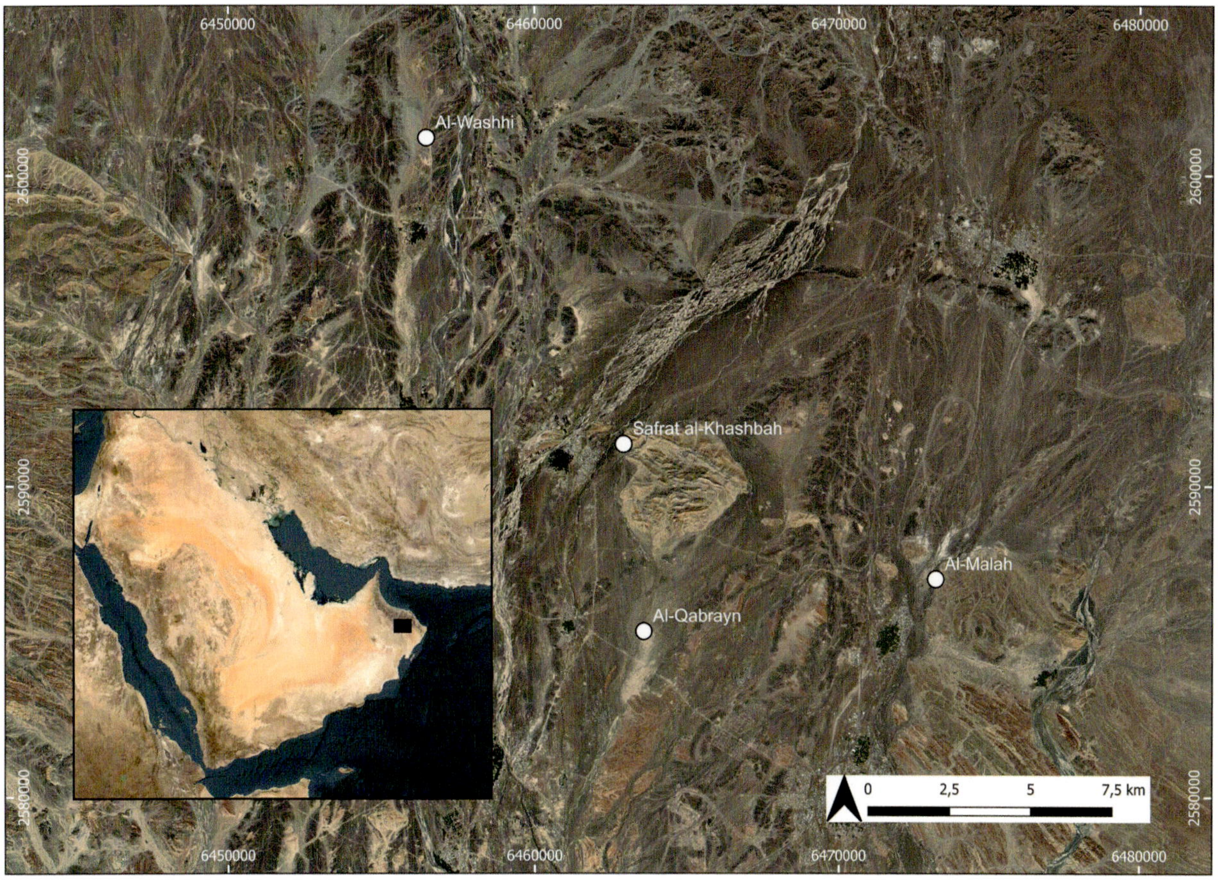

FIGURE 2. *A map showing the archaeological sites in Oman included in this study (basemap: ESRI).*

This study seeks to further characterize the production technology and knowledge of the provenance of Bahlā Ware by presenting the results of petrographic and chemical analyses of thirty-two samples of this ware recovered from rural settlements in northern Oman. The goal is to explore the compositional variability and investigate whether there are possible centres of production, other than those discussed in the context of the assemblages from al-Ain and Doha.

Archaeological background

As part of the project 'The abandoned mudbrick settlements of central Oman: between romanticization and neglect', funded within the Lost Cities framework of the Gerda Henkel Foundation, four late Islamic settlements — Al Malah, Safrat al-Khashbah, Al-Washhi, and Al-Qabrayn — were surveyed and partially excavated between 2020 and 2022 (Biezeveld 2023). They are all located in the Wilayat of Al-Mudhaybi in the governorate of Al-Sharqiyah North in the Sultanate of Oman (Fig. 2).

Al-Malah is a rectangular mud-brick settlement surrounded by a wall with a freestanding tower in the centre of the settlement. The tower has its entrance on the first floor, which is common in central Oman (Bonnenfant, Bonnenfant & al-Harthi 1997: 118). Al-Malah was described by the British traveller J.G. Lorimer (1908: 1767) as a deserted town with 600 date trees in the oasis. Radiocarbon dates from test trenches excavated at the site have yielded dates in the eighteenth and nineteenth centuries, with only

	Trench	Lab Code (MAMS)	Sample Name	14C Age [yr BP]	±	δ13C AMS [‰]	2σ cal. CE	Material
Al-Malah	1	56324	MLH22A-01008	111	18	-35.3	1691–1921	charcoal (Acacia)
	1	56325	MLH22A-01009	273	18	-29.7	1524–1792	palm mat
	2	56326	MLH22A-01017	131	17	-28.5	1682–1938	charcoal (indet.)
	2	56327	MLH22A-01022	98	17	-24.9	1694–1917	charcoal (indet.)
Safrat al-Khashbah	2	56328	SFR22A-00014	215	17	-32.2	1647–1950	charcoal (indet.)
	2	56329	SFR22A-00024	141	18	-31.9	1673–1944	charcoal (Acacia)
	3	56330	SFR22A-00056	140	18	-25.7	1674–1943	palm mat
	3	56331	SFR22A-00057	150	17	-29.3	1670–1950	charcoal (Acacia)
	3	56332	SFR22A-00064	162	17	-26.9	1667–1950	charcoal (Acacia or Prosopis)
Al-Washhi	2	56333	WSH22A-00028	224	19	-25.9	1642–1800	charcoal (Phoenix dactylifera stem)
	1	56334	WSH22A-00053	186	18	-29.9	1661–1950	date pit
	1	56335	WSH22A-00059	328	18	-29.6	1494–1638	charcoal (Acacia or Prosopis)
	2	56336	WSH22A-00064	246	18	-24.0	1639–1797	charcoal (Phoenix dactylifera)
Al-Qabrayn	1	56342	QBR22A-00072	130	18	-25.6	1682–1937	charcoal (indet.)
	1	56346	QBR22A-00158	215	18	-29.5	1647–1950	charcoal (Phoenix dactlyfera stem)
	1	56347	QBR22A-00169	131	20	-20.2	1680–1940	charcoal (Phoenix dactlyfera petrole)
	2	56348	QBR22A-00199	220	18	-26.5	1644–1945	date pit

Figure 3. *Radiocarbon dates from archaeological sites. The ^{14}C ages are calibrated to calendar ages using the IntCal20 data set and the Oxcal software. Charcoal was determined by L. Proctor.*

one exception dating back to the seventeenth century (Fig. 3). The archaeological finds, such as glass bangles and a late nineteenth-century coin minted by Sultan Faisal Bin Turkee fall within this dating range.

Safrat al-Khashbah was briefly described by Al-Jahwari (2008: 472, site CS.5.8) and Schmidt et al. (2021: 240–242). It is located 1 km from the modern-day village of Al-Khashbah and consists of twenty-five buildings and a large field system. Radiocarbon dates have a rather wide range, between the eighteenth and twentieth centuries (Fig. 3), as does the retrieved pottery, which includes Chinese Blue and White as well as modern coffee cups.

Al-Washhi is not as well preserved as the other sites; there are no mud-brick remains and only the foundations of the buildings can be seen. It thus seems likely that this site was abandoned in a period before the other sites. It lies 2.5 km north of the modern village of Al-Washhi and consists of ten buildings, including the foundations of a tower. Based on radiocarbon dating and finds collected during survey and excavation, the settlement was in use between the seventeenth and nineteenth centuries (Fig. 3). The whole area was covered with slag, indicating intensive copper processing.

Al-Qabrayn differs from the other sites in being a fort-like structure surrounded by a large field system, and a handful of scattered buildings in the field system. The fort consists of two towers that are located across from each other. The towers are equipped with shooting holes and the entrance was probably on the first floor, as can be seen at other towers in the region. During the survey, various coins were collected, including a quarter Anna of the East India Company from AD 1832, as well as a coin from 1299 AH (AD 1881–1882). Radiocarbon dates are available from excavations in the fortified area, and their dates range between the seventeenth to eighteenth and the eighteenth to twentieth centuries (Fig. 3).

More than 6000 sherds were collected from both the excavation and the survey, with *c.*3700 diagnostic sherds from the survey and 325 diagnostic sherds from the excavations. The majority of these sherds are medium coarse and coarse ware with lower numbers of comb-impressed pottery, porcelain, and more than 500 Bahlā Ware sherds (409 from Al-Washhi, 97 from Al-Malah, 66 from Al-Qabrayn, and 48 from Safrat al-Khashbah). From the latter, thirty-two sherds (10 from excavation contexts, 22 surface material collected during the surveys) were chosen for scientific analysis. The selection favoured recognizable forms (rim and base sherds) and sherds from excavation contexts. It also aimed for an approximate equal distribution of the samples across the four sites (9 sherds from Al-Qabrayn, 8 sherds from Al-Malah, 8 sherds from Al-Washhi, and 7 sherds from Safrat al-Khashbah) (Fig. 4).

Methodology

The scientific analysis of ceramics carried out in this study consisted of three methods. Ceramic petrography and wavelength dispersive X-ray fluorescence (WD-XRF) analysis were used for the compositional characterization of ceramic bodies and their provenance determination. All thirty-two samples were subjected to petrographic analysis while a sub-set of twenty-eight samples was studied with WD-XRF analysis. Scanning electron microscopy with energy dispersive spectrometry (SEM-EDS) analysis was used for the characterization of chemical composition of glazes and their application methods. After obtaining the results from the petrographic and chemical analyses of the ceramics, a sub-set of fifteen samples containing well-preserved glazes of a range of colour tones and thickness were subjected to SEM-EDS analysis.

This methodology is compatible with that of previous scientific studies of Bahlā Ware from al-Ain (Živković et al. 2019) and Doha (Carvajal López et al. 2019), which enables the comparative analysis of production technology and provenance.

Ceramic petrography

Thin sections of the selected ceramics were prepared in the laboratories of the School of Archaeology and Ancient History at the University of Leicester, UK (the thin sections were then analysed on a microscope with a polarizer, a ZEISS AXIOSCOPE 5 POL, in the same laboratories). This analysis enables the identification of rocks and minerals, as well as patterns in the way in which they are grouped, and optical characteristics of the ceramic matrix in which they are embedded (all of which is known as 'texture'). All these elements are indicative of technological choices taken by the potter when selecting and mixing the clays ('clay recipes') and when firing them. The methodology of analysis and grouping of ceramic thin sections that was followed is well developed in the works of I. Whitbread (1995: 365–396; 2001) and P. Quinn (2022).

Elemental analysis of ceramics (WD-XRF)

Samples for the WD-XRF analysis of ceramics were submitted to the Fitch Laboratory of the British School at Athens. The analysis was carried out on a BRUKER S8 TIGER with a 4kW Rh X-ray tube instrument. The instrument measures twenty-six elements: Na, Mg, Al, Si, P, K, Ca, Ti, Fe, V, Cr, Mn, Co, Ni, Cu, Zn, Rb, Sr, Y, Zr, Ba, La, Ce, Nd, Pb, and Th. The custom calibration of the instrument was based on forty-three certified reference materials (for details see Georgakopoulou et al. 2017: 187). Two certified reference materials — CRMs: PMS and GSR-1 — were analysed together with the samples in order to monitor the instrument performance (Georgakopoulou et al. 2017).

Prior to pulverizing the samples and the preparation of glass beads, glazes were removed and the ceramic surface was cleaned with a tungsten-carbide drill. Glass beads were prepared as a mixture of 1 g of the pulverized and ignited sample and 6 g of a mixture of lithium metaborate/lithium tetraborate with lithium bromide as a non-wetting agent. Despite the cleaning, high contents of main elements found in glazes — Pb, Ba, and Cu — show the persistent contamination of

	Code FITCH	Code Thin Section	Label	Building	Room	Context	Unit	UTM WGS 84 40N East	UTM WGS 84 40N North
Al-Malah	MAL001	BAHIB 08	MLH22A-00328	MLH-0016	MLH-PD	surface	MLH-A-Fs0041	618150.61	2502710.75
	MAL002	BAHIB 26	MLH22A-00196	MLH-0009	MLH-IC	surface	MLH-A-Fs0027	618150.34	2502678.31
	MAL003	BAHIB 15	MLH22A-00454	MLH-0019	MLH-SB	surface	MLH-A-Fs0050	618156.58	2502735.93
	MAL004	BAHIB 21	MLH22A-01020	MLH-0016	MLH-PB	trench 2	MLH-A-Fs0087	618155.04	2502704.38
	MAL005	BAHIB 28	MLH22A-00335	MLH-0017	MLH-QA	surface	MLH-A-Fs0042	618148.91	2502704.43
	MAL006	BAHIB 32	MLH22A-00345	MLH-0017	MLH-QB	surface	MLH-A-Fs0043	618151.76	2502707.11
	MAL008	BAHIB 20	MLH22A-0103 (sorted from MLH22A-01019)	MLH-0016	MLH-PB	trench 2	MLH-A-Fs0087	0	0
	MAL008	BAHIB 27	MLH22A-0103 (sorted from MLH22A-01019)	MLH-0016	MLH-PB	trench 2	MLH-A-Fs0087	0	0
Safrat al-Khashbah	SFR001	BAHIB 09	SFR20A-00015	SFR-0001	SFR-AD	surface	SFR-A-Fs0004	608654.63	2506565.18
	SFR002	BAHIB 31	SFR20A-00205	SFR-0014	SFR-NB	surface	SFR-A-Fs0057	608665.64	2506634.57
	SFR003	BAHIB 17	SFR20A-00378	field system	-	surface	SFR-A-Fs0079	608473.75	2506512.41
	SFR004	BAHIB 25	SFR20A-00178	threshing platform	-	surface	SFR-A-Fs0048	608660.76	2506657.01
	SFR005	BAHIB 12	SFR20A-00050	SFR-0003	SFR-CB	surface	SFR-A-Fs0010	608653.78	2506583.11
	SFR006	BAHIB 22	SFR20A-00072	SFR-0004	SFR-DE	surface	SFR-A-Fs0018	608672.90	2506568.08
	SFR007	BAHIB 24	SFR20A-00071	SFR-0004	SFR-DE	surface	SFR-A-Fs0018	608672.48	2506569.63
Al-Washhi	WSH001	BAHIB 18	WSH20A-01906	WSH-0009	WSH-IC	surface	WSH-A-Fs0029	602605.57	2515632.33
	WSH002	BAHIB 19	WSH20A-01932	WSH-0009	WSH-ID	surface	WSH-A-Fs0030	602609.35	2515635.24
	WSH003	BAHIB 29	WSH20A-03209	WSH-0008	WSH-HH	surface	WSH-A-Fs0034	602609.61	2515627.27
	WSH004	BAHIB 05	WSH20A-02632	WSH-0010	WSH-JC	surface	WSH-A-Fs0040	602600.57	2515627.21
	WSH005	BAHIB 07	WSH20A-03285	WSH-0010	WSH-JI	surface	WSH-A-Fs0047	602603.81	2515634.09
	WSH006	BAHIB 30	WSH20A-00055	WSH-0002	WSH-BB	trench 1	WSH-A-Fs0003	602612.02	2515802.77
	WSH007	BAHIB 03	WSH22A-00066 (sorted from WSH20A-00047)	WSH-0002	WSH-BB	trench 1	WSH-A-Fs0003	602614.67	2515805.66
	WSH007	BAHIB 04	WSH22A-00066 (sorted from WSH20A-00047)	WSH-0002	WSH-BB	trench 1	WSH-A-Fs0003	602614.67	2515805.66
Al-Qabrayn	QAB001	BAHIB 13	QBR21A-00219	QBR-0001	QBR-AS	surface	QBR-A-Fs0017	609295.20	2501098.49
	QAB002	BAHIB 10	QBR21A-00009	QBR-0001	QBR-AB	surface	QBR-A-Fs0002	609297.15	2501113.23
	QAB003	BAHIB 06	QBR21A-00630	field system	-	surface	QBR-A-Fs0038	609316.41	2500747.90
	QAB004	BAHIB 11	QBR21A-00411	QBR-0006	QBR-FA	surface	QBR-A-Fs0026	609415.99	2500938.60
	QAB005	BAHIB 23	QBR21A-00228	QBR-0001	QBR-AS	surface	QBR-A-Fs0017	609292.10	2501100.57
	QBR001	BAHIB 14	QBR22A-00281 (sorted from QBR22A-00192)	QBR-0001	QBR-AI	trench 2	QBR-A-Fs0064	0	0
	QBR002	BAHIB 16	QBR22A-00279 (sorted from QBR22A-00022)	field system	-	surface	QBR-A-Fs0041	0	0
	QBR003	BAHIB 01	QBR22A-00280 (sorted from QBR22A-00056)	QBR-0001	QBR-AS QBR-AR	trench 1	QBR-A-Fs0055	0	0
	QBR003	BAHIB 02	QBR22A-00280 (sorted from QBR22A-00056)	QBR-0001	QBR-AS QBR-AR	trench 1	QBR-A-Fs0055	0	0

FIGURE 4. *A list of pottery samples and their find contexts.*

ceramic bodies caused by diffusion of these elements from the glaze (Živković et al. 2024: table CHEM 1). For the statistical treatment of WD-XRF data, therefore, these elements were excluded. Additionally, Th was excluded because the high concentrations of Pb affect its accuracy, as measured with the Fitch WD-XRF setup (Georgakopoulou et al. 2017). P_2O_5 was also disregarded because of its association with diagenetic contamination of ceramics (Freestone, Meeks & Middleton 1985).

A principal component analysis (PCA) was used to examine relationships between the twenty-one elements. The chemical data were transformed to logratios prior to the PCA.

Chemical analysis of glazes (SEM-EDS)

The SEM-EDS analysis of glazes was carried out at the Archaeological Science Laboratories of the Cyprus Institute. SEM instrument Zeiss EVO 15 that operates with an attached EDS (Oxford Instruments Ultim Max EDS with a 65 SSD detector) was used. The analysis was run in high vacuum conditions, at an accelerated voltage of 20 kV, working distance 8.50 mm, process time 4, and acquisition time 30s live time. The microstructure of glazes was studied using the backscatter image mode.

Corning Glass Standard C was analysed together with the archaeological samples to monitor the instrument's performance (Brill 1999: 542). The accuracy was measured in comparison to the recently published certified values of Corning glasses (Adlington 2017). The difference between the means of the certified values and those measured in this research (estimated as ((xcert – xmeas)/xmeas) x 100) were below 9.1% for Na_2O, MgO, Al_2O_3, SiO_2, K_2O, CaO, Fe_2O_3, CuO, Ba, and PbO, except for TiO_2 where it is 21.6% and CoO where it is 17.6%. The precision, estimated as relative standard deviation (RSD) is within 6.5% for the major elements. For TiO_2 and CoO, RSD is 17.6% and below.

Bahlā glazes are heterogeneous and for their study a case-specific methodology has been developed (see Živković et al. 2019). Clear areas of the glaze matrix were analysed using x800 magnification and area scans of *c.*135 x 45 µm that were selected in the middle of the glaze layer. In samples with completely crystallized glazes (BAHIB_05 and 24), the bulk compositional analysis included various inclusions. The same magnification and the size of area scans were used for glaze bulk analysis as for glaze matrix analysis. For some samples, both types of glaze compositional analyses were documented. Inclusions were separately analysed using spot analysis. The study of application methods required measurements of three additional areas. The bulk analysis of ceramic bodies was carried out using x300 magnification and area scans of 368 x 280 µm. The layer of glaze above the interface (glaze/low) was analysed using x800 magnification and area scans of *c.*50 x 15 µm. The layer of ceramic body below the interface (ceramic body/up) was analysed using x400 magnification and area scans of *c.*255 x 65 µm.

Results

The full set of results of the analysis discussed in this article can be consulted in the associated database (Živković et al. 2024).

The mineralogical and petrological composition of ceramics

The petrographic analysis of the samples indicates that they all belong to the same group (Figs 5 & 6), which is defined by several characteristics. One of them is an abundance of sedimentary components, mainly micritic limestone (as in Fig. 6/B and C) and clay pellets (as in Fig. 6/A and C). They also include a component of mafic and ultramafic detritic rocks, some of them metamorphosed to serpentinite (Fig. 6/A–D). The other element is the texture of the matrix, which is slightly inhomogeneous and with a level of optical activity that indicates a relatively stable maximum firing temperature reached across all the samples (examples of this inhomogeneity and variation in the matrix can be seen in Fig. 6/A–D). This fabric matches very well the composition of the Limestone and Serpentinite Fabric of the Bahlā Ware from al-Ain (Živković et al. 2019) and Fabric 7 from Doha (Carvajal López et al. 2019). Of these two, the former contains inclusions consistent with the geological composition of the ophiolitic mountain in Oman, including those found around the town of Bahlā, home to ceramic production workshops in the past (Živković et al. 2019: 4707). Fabric 7 in Doha is considered essentially the same in terms of composition and provenance. This is also the case with the fabric described in this paper. The geological

Fabric name (unique)	Textural characteristics	Main inclusions	Technological implications
Limestone-rich sedimentary fabric with serpentinite	Low number of pores (1–5%) and abundant inclusions (20–40%). Poorly sorted (close- to single-spaced in some samples, open-spaced in others), weakly to moderately aligned inclusions, unimodal grain-size distribution.	TF1 (clay pellet) (Predominant-Common, high to neutral optical density; <3.6 mm); micritic limestone (Dominant-Common; <1.4 mm); TF2 (calci-mudstone) (Frequent-Common, diffuse boundaries, low optical density; <2 mm). Other inclusions in the coarse fraction include serpentinite (Few), pyroxene, serpentinised amphibole (Very Few) and recrystallised quartzite (Very Rare). In the fine fraction there is monocrystalline quartz and micritic limestone (Dominant-Common), serpentinite and birefringent minerals (Common-Few), plagioclase feldspar and chert (Few) and amphibole (Very Few).	The wide variability of the fabric in the abundance of inclusions in its fine fraction and in the abundance of limestone and TFs suggests that the fabric was produced in a range of workshops in a same area and with the same basic technical traits over a period of time, rather than of a single workshop well localized in time. The mafic rocks documented are detrital in a sedimentary deposit from which the clay was collected. The elements of the fine fraction are abundant enough to suggest that there is no levigation process. The relatively relevant appearance of TFs suggests a possibility of clay mixing, in particular of a purer darker clay that would form the clay pellets and twirls, but more experiments would be required to test this (it must be noted that if there is clay mixing, then the recipe would include only a very small part of the purer clay). The lack of widespread optical activity suggests a high equivalent temperature of firing, and the similarities of the colours of the matrix suggest a very uniform atmosphere. All this speaks again of a very standardized way of production.

FIGURE 5. *Description of the petrographic fabric identified in the assemblage studied in this paper. This is a simplified version of the fabric description published on the online database by Živković et al. (2024: Petrographic fabric document).*

background (which includes fragments of ophiolites) is the same for all. It is true that some minor differences can be noted between the descriptions, but these point mainly to possible variations in the technological process of manufacturing, which may be caused by the technological choices of different artisans. Among the variations noted, there are wide ranges of the frequency of inclusions across different samples, which may indicate the use of different quarries or slightly different clay recipes. The relative abundance of clay pellets in some samples could be interpreted as clay mixing in some cases, but there is no definite evidence to support the use of this technological process at this stage. To be sure, the observed variation does not show regular patterns on which sub-categories or groups can be made. For this reason, in the present analysis the fabric has been maintained as a single group until more samples of Bahlā Ware and more targeted analysis can be undertaken. In the future, the potential different technical choices should be explored to determine if they are significant enough to define different fabrics or sub-fabrics to be considered under the term 'Bahlā Ware'.

The chemical composition of ceramics

The results of WD-XRF analysis show that all samples of Bahlā Ware from Oman form a single chemical cluster, suggesting a common origin of raw materials used for its production (Živković et al. 2024). This is calcareous pottery characterized by varying contents of CaO (5.6–17.8 wt%), which is related to the uneven distribution of limestone as observed by petrography. Among trace elements, a relatively high variability is measured for Sr (229–660 ppm), Cr (423–718 ppm), and Mn (392–690 ppm). Sr is related to CaO in calcareous ceramics while Cr can be associated with serpentinite (Quinn 2022: 387), which is another rock identified petrographically. The variability of these elements can therefore be explained by the natural heterogeneity of raw materials.

The PCA plot shown in Figure 7 illustrates the matching compositions of Bahlā ceramics from Oman

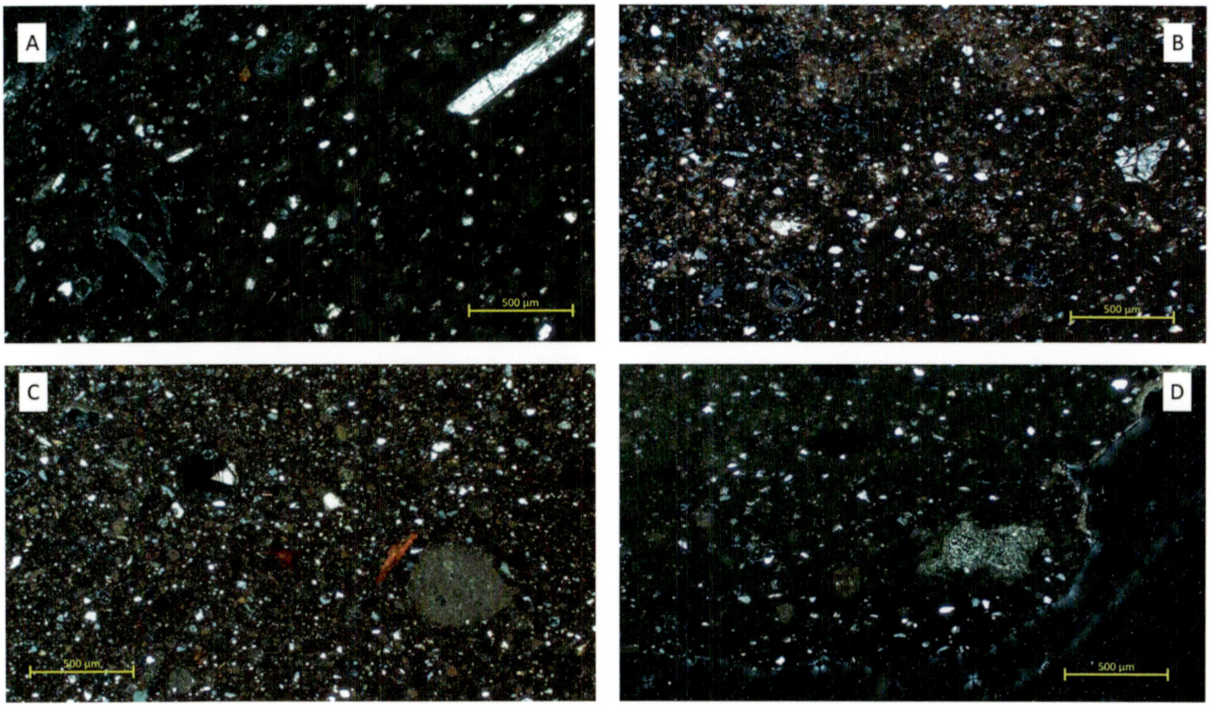

FIGURE 6. *Microphotographs of several samples, all in crossed polars.* **A.** *Sample 1, showing a burnt clay pellet on the lower left side and a birefringent mineral, probably a serpentinized amphibole, in the upper right corner;* **B.** *Sample 13, showing a more calcareous matrix with micritic limestone and quartz in the fine fraction. To the right of the image a serpentinized amphibole is very clear;* **C.** *Sample 7, showing a very calcareous matrix over which a larger grain of micritic limestone (centre right) and a burnt clay pellet (centre left, slightly towards the top) can be seen. Between them there are some orange fragments of serpentinite;* **D.** *Sample 20, showing a relatively clean matrix with some TFs and a relatively large fragment of a serpentinized mafic rock (images taken from the online database published by Živković et al. (2024: Petrography micro-images).*

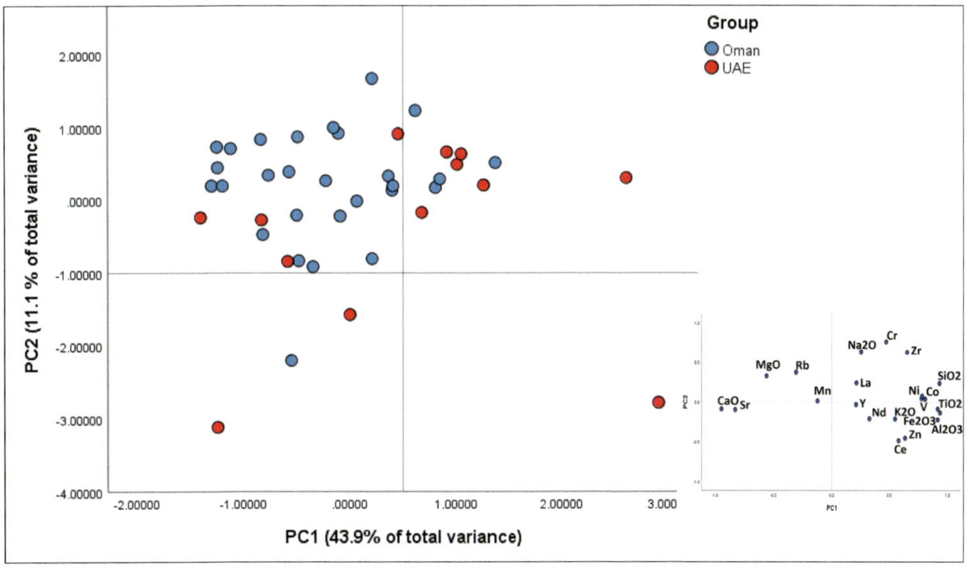

FIGURE 7. *Scatter-plot of the first two principal components and plot of loadings derived from principal component analysis of the WD-XRF elemental data treated as log ratios, showing all Bahlā samples from Oman and the C1 cluster of Bahlā samples from al-Ain (Živković et al. 2019: 4703). Excluded elements are P_2O_5, Cu, Ba, Pb, and Th.*

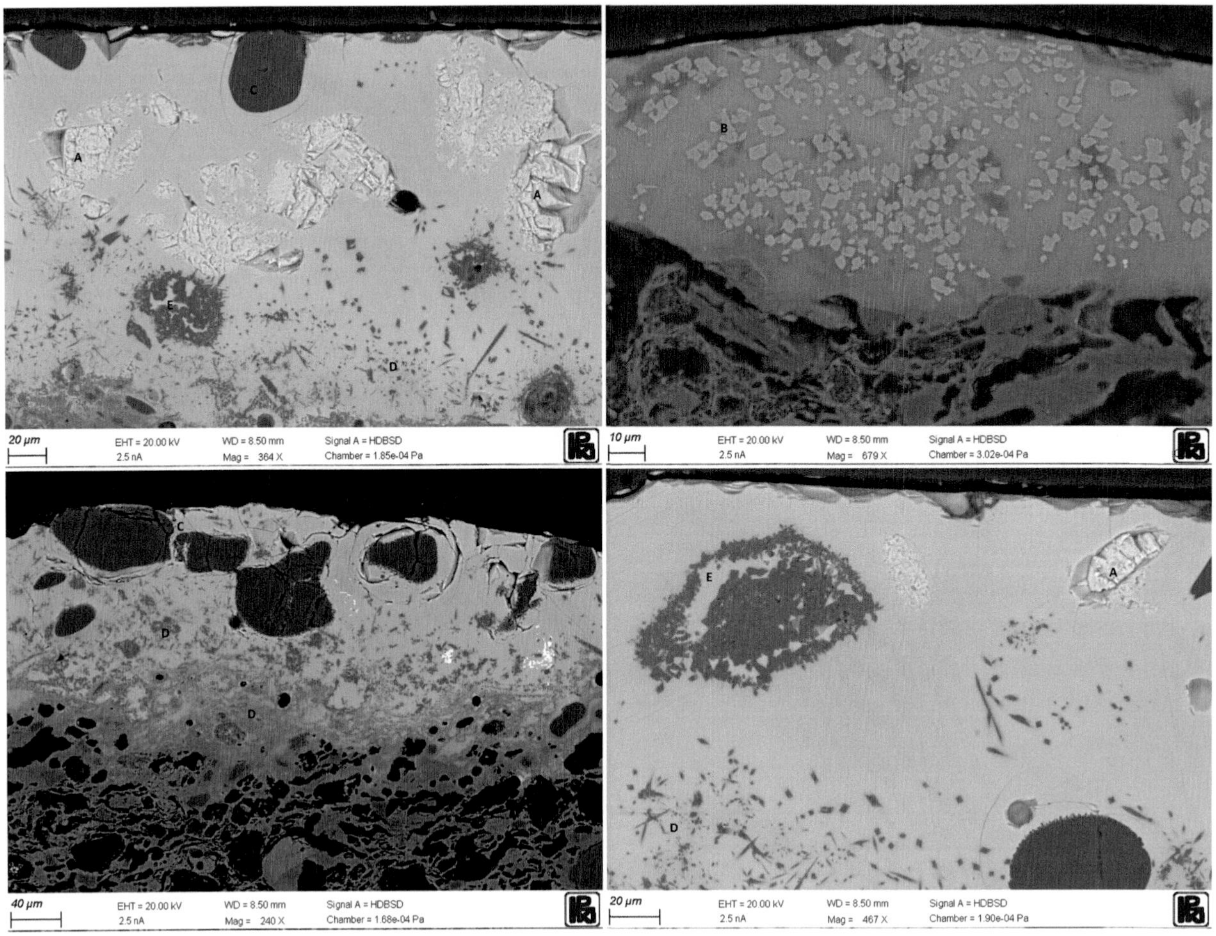

Figure 8. *SEM photomicrographs of Bahlā lead-barium glazes taken in the backscatter mode. Visible inclusions are non-dissolved baryte (A), iron oxides (B), quartz (C), crystals of the ceramic-glaze interface (D), and Ca-rich pyroxenes floating in the glaze (E). Top left BAHIB_04; top right BAHIB_15; bottom left BAHIB_09; bottom right BAHIB_04 (images taken from the online database published by Živković et al. [2024: SEM-EDS figures]).*

and the C1 cluster of Bahlā ceramics from al-Ain (Živković et al. 2019: 4702–4703). Comparisons with samples from Doha are not possible here because chemical data from that site have not yet been published. Two samples from al-Ain — B114 and B195 — visible on the right side of the PCA plot, stand out because of the lower content of CaO and the variability of several trace elements related to it, as explained by Živković et al. (2019: 4703). In both groups, the variability of CaO, Sr, Cr, and Mn is observed, which can be taken as a characteristic of raw materials used for the production of Bahlā Ware.

The chemical composition of glazes

The SEM photomicrographs show that the thickness of Bahlā glazes varies between 80 and 250 µm (Fig. 8). The glaze layer contains various inclusions. The most common are those of non-dissolved barium-sulphate or baryte ($BaSO_4$) that ranges in size from small (2 x 9 µm) to large (50 x 25 µm) sub-angular lumps, both easily identifiable by their bright colours in the backscattered mode (Fig. 8/A). They have a scattered distribution throughout the glaze layer. Another type of bright-colour

Sample		Na_2O	MgO	Al_2O_3	SiO_2	K_2O	CaO	TiO_2	FeO	NiO	CuO	BaO	PbO
BAHIB_02 (5)	mean	1.5	0.8	1.2	56.1	5.4	3.2	–	14.1	–	–	12.5	5.1
	stand. dev.	0.1	0.1	0.1	1.4	0.2	0.3	–	1.7	–	–	1.0	0.3
BAHIB_04 (5), interior	mean	0.6	1.4	2.5	43.6	1.3	3.1	–	5.1	–	–	4.7	37.8
	stand. dev.	–	–	0.2	1.0	0.1	0.2	–	0.2	–	–	0.4	0.5
BAHIB_04 (4), exterior	mean	0.6	1.9	2.7	44.5	1.5	3.6	–	5.4	0.8	–	4.8	34.2
	stand. dev.	0.0	0.2	0.1	1.3	0.1	0.3	–	0.2	0.2	–	2.1	0.7
BAHIB_06 (5), interior	mean	2.8	1.9	2.5	52.0	6.3	3.1	–	13.1	–	–	16.3	2.2
	stand. dev.	0.1	0.2	0.3	1.0	0.1	0.3	–	1.2	–	–	1.0	0.2
BAHIB_06 (4), exterior	mean	1.7	1.6	2.7	45.2	4.5	3.1	–	11.1	–	0.2	11.5	18.5
	stand. dev.	0.2	–	0.1	1.0	0.2	0.1	–	0.4	–	–	0.3	0.5
BAHIB_08 (5)	mean	1.3	1.6	2.7	52.9	2.0	5.6	–	10.9	–	–	20.9	2.1
	stand. dev.	0.1	–	0.3	0.6	0.1	0.3	–	0.5	–	–	0.3	0.1
BAHIB_09 (5)	mean	0.9	2.0	2.6	51.1	1.6	6.1	–	6.4	–	0.9	20.9	7.5
	stand. dev.	0.1	0.1	0.1	1.0	0.1	0.3	–	0.3	–	0.2	1.0	0.4
BAHIB_10 (5)	mean	1.6	1.0	1.2	54.1	5.0	1.8	–	13.0	–	0.5	13.0	8.9
	stand. dev.	0.1	0.1	0.3	2.8	0.5	0.3	–	1.5	–	0.1	1.6	0.8
BAHIB_11 (6), interior	mean	1.8	1.3	1.2	54.9	3.8	3.6	–	10.7	–	2.1	14.4	6.2
	stand. dev.	0.1	0.1	0.1	1.1	0.3	0.4	–	0.6	–	0.2	1.0	0.1
BAHIB_11 (3), exterior	mean	1.5	1.3	1.5	55.1	3.5	3.1	–	10.8	–	1.2	14.4	7.7
	stand. dev.	0.1	0.1	–	3.1	0.2	0.3	–	1.7	–	0.1	1.0	0.6
BAHIB_12 (5)	mean	1.8	1.3	1.4	51.4	4.2	4.0	–	15.8	–	0.2	18.2	1.8
	stand. dev.	0.1	0.1	0.1	0.9	0.1	0.1	–	0.8	–	–	0.4	–
BAHIB_14 (5)	mean	0.2	0.9	1.8	34.0	0.5	2.3	–	4.6	–	–	3.7	52.1
	stand. dev.	–	–	0.2	0.4	0.0	0.1	–	0.1	–	–	0.1	0.5
BAHIB_15 (5)	mean	1.5	1.1	1.4	56.4	4.7	3.7	–	13.4	–	–	9.4	8.5
	stand. dev.	0.1	0.1	0.3	1.5	0.7	0.9	–	1.5	–	–	2.0	0.7
BAHIB_25 (5), interior	mean	1.8	0.8	1.1	54.9	4.5	2.6	–	13.0	–	0.4	15.2	5.8
	stand. dev.	0.1	0.1	0.3	2.0	0.3	0.6	–	1.9	–	–	1.0	0.3
BAHIB_25 (3), exterior	mean	2.0	1.3	1.3	54.4	5.5	3.5	–	11.8	–	0.4	14.2	5.6
	stand. dev.	–	0.1	0.3	1.4	0.3	0.4	–	0.4	–	–	1.0	0.3
BAHIB_26 (5)	mean	2.8	1.8	2.4	50.8	4.8	6.4	–	12.9	–	–	16.2	1.8
	stand. dev.	0.1	0.1	0.3	1.1	0.2	0.4	–	0.5	–	–	0.4	0.1
BAHIB_28 (5), interior	mean	1.9	1.8	1.9	58.4	4.8	5.4	0.4	11.7	–	–	12.9	0.8
	stand. dev.	0.1	–	0.3	0.6	0.1	0.5	–	0.8	–	–	0.2	0.1
BAHIB_28 (3), exterior	mean	2.2	1.5	2.4	57.7	4.7	6.4	0.5	10.6	–	–	13.4	0.6
	stand. dev.	–	0.2	0.4	0.8	0.1	0.3	–	0.9	–	–	0.6	0.1
BAHIB_29 (5)	mean	0.6	0.7	1.2	38.5	3.0	2.9	–	11.3	–	–	5.7	36.1
	stand. dev.	–	–	0.1	1.1	0.2	0.3	–	0.8	–	–	0.4	0.8
BAHIB_32 (5)	mean	1.7	1.6	2.0	57.6	3.2	4.6	–	11.6	–	–	16.4	1.3
	stand. dev.	–	–	0.1	0.7	0.1	0.1	–	0.8	–	–	0.4	0.1

FIGURE 9. *The chemical composition of glaze matrices (areas without inclusions) determined through SEM-EDS. The number in parenthesis denotes the number of area measurements taken on the SEM-EDS for each sample. All values are normalized to 100 wt%; '–' stands for below detection limits (table taken from the online database published by Živković et al. [2024: table SEM 1]).*

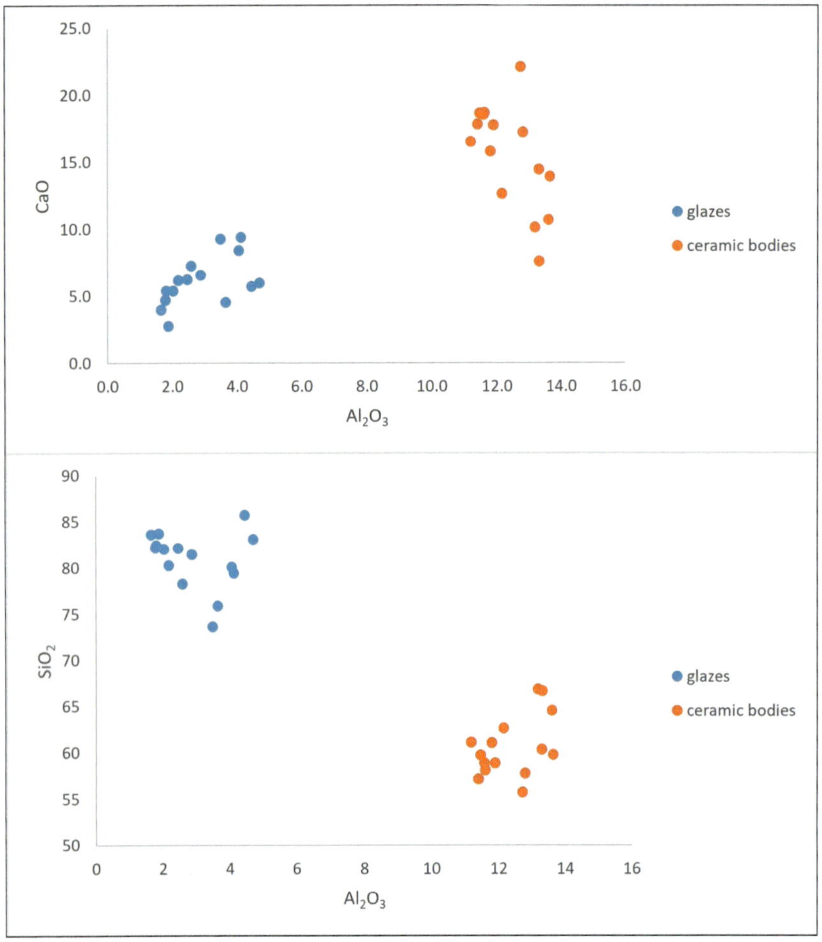

FIGURE 10. *Scatter plot showing the comparison between glazes and ceramic bodies of Bahlā Ware based on the chemical compositions determined through SEM-EDS. Excluded oxides are PbO, BaO, CuO, and FeO and remaining compositions were normalized to 100 wt%.*

inclusion is non-dissolved iron oxide (FeO is > 96 wt%) that was used for colouring the glaze (Fig. 8/B). These inclusions have rounded to sub-rounded shapes (*c.*5 x 5 μm) and appear densely clustered. Furthermore, coarse inclusions of quartz (max. 70 x 50 μm) are randomly scattered through the glaze (Fig. 8/C). A crystalline phase formed at the ceramic-glaze interface in some cases extends to include all layers of the glaze (Fig. 8/D). It is characterized by dark-colour inclusions of sub-angular shapes (*c.*3 x 3 μm) that are clustered together and appear floating in the glaze (Fig. 8/E). Compositionally, these are Ca-rich pyroxenes ranging between diopside ($CaMgSi_2O_6$) and hedenbergite ($CaFeSi_2O_6$), as already described by Živković et al. (2019: 4703).

Bahlā glazes are of the lead-barium type (Fig. 9). Looking at values measured for the glaze matrix, Bahlā glazes are characterized by a negative correlation between lead oxide, PbO (0.6–52.1 wt%) and barium oxide, BaO (3.7–20.9 wt%), which shows their natural mineralogical association. Glazes also contain varying contents of silica, SiO_2 (34.0–58.4 wt%), calcium oxide, CaO (1.8–6.4 wt%), sodium oxide, Na_2O (0.2–2.8 wt%), and potassium oxide, K_2O (0.5–6.3 wt%). More consistent values were observed for magnesia, MgO (0.7–2.0 wt%) and alumina, Al_2O_3 (1.1–2.7 wt%). The main colourant is iron oxide, FeO (4.6–15.8 wt%), that was deliberately added and, in some cases, not entirely dissolved in the glaze (BAHIB_02, 12, 15, 25). Green glazes also show the presence of copper oxide, CuO (0.2–2.1 wt%).

For the reconstruction of the glaze application methods, elements associated with glazes — PbO, BaO, CuO, and FeO — were excluded and the remaining composition was normalized to 100 wt% for the comparison with the ceramic body (as explained by Tite et al. 1998: 249–250). FeO was also excluded from the ceramic body composition because its value in the glaze

Sample	Area of analysis	Na_2O	MgO	Al_2O_3	SiO_2	K_2O	CaO	TiO_2	FeO	CuO	BaO	PbO
BAHIB_02	glaze/middle/matrix	1.5	0.8	1.2	56.1	5.4	3.2	–	14.1	–	12.5	5.1
	glaze/low/matrix	1.4	0.8	3.1	58.6	6.0	2.6	–	12.7	–	10.1	4.6
	c. body/up	0.7	6.3	11.5	51.6	2.1	22.3	0.8	4.8	–	–	–
	c. body/middle	1.1	6.2	10.9	56.6	1.8	17.7	0.6	5.2	–	–	–
BAHIB_04	glaze/middle/matrix	0.6	1.4	2.5	43.6	1.3	3.1	–	5.1	–	4.7	37.8
	glaze/bulk	0.6	2.2	4.3	45.4	1.6	5.3	–	4.9	–	4.6	31.0
	c. body/up	1.4	6.0	12.8	59.8	2.7	7.8	0.8	6.1	–	–	2.4
	c. body/middle	1.4	6.3	12.8	60.7	2.2	10.0	0.7	6.0	–	–	–
BAHIB_12	glaze/middle/matrix	1.8	1.3	1.4	51.4	4.2	4.0	–	15.8	0.2	18.2	1.8
	glaze/low/matrix	1.6	1.3	2.9	53.6	5.4	3.3	–	14.2	0.2	16.0	1.6
	interface	1.5	3.4	5.4	59.4	5.6	6.5	0.4	9.3	–	7.6	0.8
	c. body/up	0.9	7.2	12.9	53.9	3.0	15.7	0.6	5.7	–	–	–
	c. body/middle	1.0	7.6	11.1	57.6	1.6	14.9	0.6	5.7	–	–	–

FIGURE 11. *The chemical composition of different layers of samples determined through SEM-EDS, showing the gradual diffusion of elements. 'Glaze/middle' stands for the middle part of the glaze layer; 'glaze/low' for the layer of glaze located above the interface ('interface' refers to the ceramic-glaze interface); 'c. body/up' for the layer of ceramic body situated below the interface; and 'c. body/middle' for the middle part of the ceramic body. All values are normalized to 100 wt%; '–' indicates below detection limits (table taken from the online database published by Živković et al. [2024: table SEM 4]).*

is higher than in the body. The remaining compositions of ceramic bodies were also normalized to 100 wt%. The consistent differences between the composition of the glazes and the ceramic bodies suggest that the glaze recipe included the mixture of lead/barium compound and silica (Fig. 10).

The methodology used for studying firing methods of lead glazes proposed by Tite et al. (1998) and Molera et al. (2001) cannot be applied with certainty in this case, because the reaction between barium and lead in relation to archaeological ceramics is yet to be fully understood through laboratory experiments. However, some observations, indicative of the reaction between the ceramic body and the glaze during the firing process, can be outlined. First, the thickness of the ceramic-glaze interface varies significantly across the analysed assemblage. Some samples (BAHIB_06, 10, 11, 15, 25) have no visible interface while others (BAHIB_04, 05, 08, 09, 24, 26) have a thick one that covers approximately half of the glaze layer or more (see Fig. 8). While the former is more indicative of double-firing, the latter is associated with a single-firing regime, but this also depends on the cooling rates and the composition of the ceramic body (Molera et al. 2001: 1126–1127). Furthermore, when high-lead glazes are applied over raw calcareous ceramic bodies, the reaction results in the creation of Ca-rich pyroxenes in the glaze that appear to float away from the interface (2001: 1126). These crystallites are detected in the Bahlā glaze, as described above.

Another parameter to be considered is the diffusion of elements from the glaze (Pb/Ba) to the ceramic body and from the ceramic body to the glaze (Al, K, Ca). In all cases, PbO and BaO show a gradual decrease of values as measured from the middle to the lower part of the glaze layer located above the interface (Fig. 11). In only three samples, PbO is detected in the upper part of the ceramic body, situated below the interface (0.9–2.4 wt%), while the same can be said for BaO in one case only (0.2 wt%). Looking at a reverse pattern of diffusion, the content of Al_2O_3 is consistent in layers of middle and upper ceramic body, but then gradually drops in the lower part and the middle part of the glaze. Alkalis

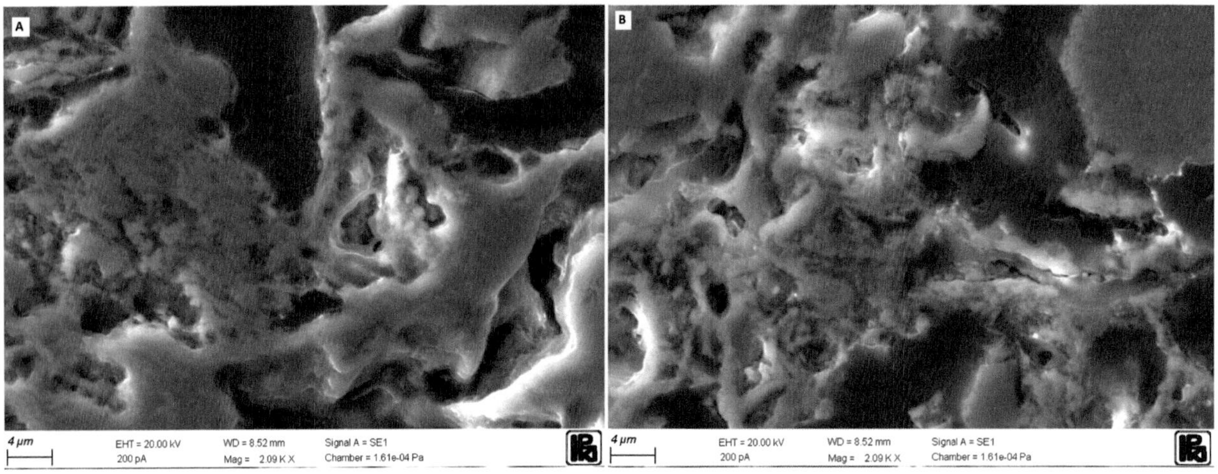

Figure 12. *SEM photomicrographs taken in the scanning electron mode of lead-barium glazes showing initial vitrification and areas of more extensive vitrification. Both A and B belong to BAHIB_08 (images taken from the online database published by Živković et al. [2024: SEM-EDS figs]).*

(Na_2O+K_2O) do not follow this pattern; their contents vary across different layers.

The gradual diffusion of elements and the scarce presence of PbO in the upper part of the ceramic body are indicative of double firing. This interpretation could be supported by the lack of the ceramic-glaze interface in several samples. On the other hand, the appearance of crystalline phases, both at the interface and Ca-rich pyroxenes in the glaze, would support the single-firing regime for many of the analysed samples.

The high-resolution SEM images, taken in the secondary electron mode, were also used for the study of ceramic body vitrification, which is indicative of approximate firing temperature (Quinn 2022: 409). The results show initial vitrification accompanied by areas of extensive vitrification, which is consistent with an approximate firing temperature range between 750 and 800°C (Fig. 12). This is in line with the petrographic observation of the matrix activity.

Discussion

This analysis of Bahlā Ware samples recovered from multiple sites in Oman confirms that their provenance is the same as those from assemblages in al-Ain and Doha, and is indicative of the spread of this important late Islamic pottery type. Raw materials used for the production of Bahlā Ware found at sites in the Oman peninsula and Qatar came from one source exploited in the range of the ophiolitic mountain. The production centre was probably in the town of Bahlā, but this is yet to be confirmed through a comparison between samples of archaeological pottery, kiln wasters, and geological clays.

Both petrographic and chemical data show that Omani samples are consistent with the Limestone Serpentinite fabric from al-Ain and all Bahlā samples from Doha. The variability observed in al-Ain's eighteenth-century assemblage, in which a few samples were described as outliers that have different compositions of ceramic bodies and glazes (Živković et al. 2019), was not attested in Oman. This variability therefore remains to be further investigated in the future.

The results of this study confirm the existence of a distinct technological tradition of pottery making in late Islamic Oman. This tradition is defined by the consistency in the exploitation of calcareous clays and the preparation of lead-barium glaze from sulphidic minerals, suggesting the successful transmission of this technical knowledge and skills from one generation of potters to the next. The workshop or workshops that produced Bahlā Ware played an important role in the regional trade network for several centuries.

Acknowledgements

This paper is dedicated to the memory of Myrto Georgakopoulou (1976–2022), a beloved colleague and friend. She was an invaluable member of the teams working on the scientific analysis of Bahlā Ware from al-Ain and Doha and had planned to contribute to this study of Omani samples. Although illness cut short her work, we remain deeply grateful for her expertise.

The archaeological fieldwork from which the sherds were analysed was made possible by funding from the Gerda Henkel Foundation (AZ 05/LC/19) under the Lost Cities framework. We are grateful to the School of Archaeology and Ancient History of the University of Leicester for infrastructural support; the A.G. Leventis Foundation for funding the glaze analysis; Noémi Müller, Evangelia Kiriatzi, and Zoe Zgouleta for the chemical analyses conducted at the Fitch Laboratories of the British School at Athens; Thilo Rehren for his support in the use of the SEM-EDS instrument at the Archaeological Science Laboratories of the Cyprus Institute; Judith López Aceves for the preparation of thin sections at the University of Leicester; and Giulia Fogarizzu for the preparation of polished blocks at the Cyprus Institute.

References

Adlington L.W. 2017. The Corning archaeological reference glasses: New values for 'old' compositions. *Papers from the Institute of Archaeology* 27/1: 1–8.

Biezeveld I. 2023. Re(dis)covering the recent: Surveying settlements and society in central Oman from the 17th to the 20th centuries. *Arabian Archaeology and Epigraphy* 34/S1: S107–S121.

Biezeveld I. & Düring B.S. 2020. Pre-oil globalization in a rural community: The late Islamic village of Sahlat in the Suhar Region. *Journal of Islamic Archaeology* 7/2: 199–219.

Bonnenfant P., Bonnenfant G. & al-Harthi S.H. 1997. Architecture and social history at Mudayrib. *Journal of Oman Studies* 3: 107–135.

Brill R. 1999. *Chemical analysis of early glasses.* ii. *Tables of analyses.* New York: The Corning Museum of Glass.

Bystron A.M. 2019. Pottery from al-Zubārah, Qatar: Reference collection and ware typology. *Proceedings of the Seminar for Arabian Studies* 49: 33–50.

Carter R. 2011. *Ceramics of the Qatar National Museum. Report on behalf of the Qatar Museums Authority.* Oxford: Oxford Brookes University.

Carter R. & Naranjo-Santana J. 2011. *Muharraq Excavations 2010.* Oxford: Oxford Brookes Archaeology and Heritage.

Carvajal López J.C., Giobbe M., Adeyemo E., Georgakopoulou M., Carter R. ... al-Na'īmī F. 2019. Production and provenance of Gulf wares unearthed in the Old Doha Rescue Excavations Project. *Proceedings of the Seminar for Arabian Studies* 49: 51–67.

Costa P.M. & Wilkinson T.J. 1987. The hinterland of Sohar. Archaeological surveys and excavations within the region of an Omani seafaring city. *Journal of Oman Studies* 9: 1–238.

Döpper S. 2022. Walk the line: The 2020 field season of the al-Mudhaybi Regional Survey. *Proceedings of the Seminar for Arabian Studies* 51: 157–167.

Freestone I.C., Meeks N.D. & Middleton A.P. 1985. Retention of phosphate in buried ceramics: An electron microbeam approach. *Archaeometry* 27/2: 161–177.

Garlake P.S. 1978a. Fieldwork at al-Huwailah, Site 23. Pages 172–189 in B. de Cardi (ed.), *Qatar Archaeological Report. Excavations 1973.* Oxford: Oxford University Press.

Garlake P.S. 1978b. An encampment of the seventeenth to nineteenth centuries on Ras Abaruk, Site 5. Pages 164–171 in B. de Cardi (ed.), *Qatar Archaeological Report. Excavations 1973.* Oxford: Oxford University Press.

Georgakopoulou M., Hein A., Müller N. & Kiriatzi E. 2017. Development and calibration of a WDXRF routine applied to provenance studies on archaeological ceramics. *X-Ray Spectrometry* 46/3: 186–199.

Al-Jahwari N.S. 2008. Settlement patterns, development and cultural change in northern Oman peninsula: A multi-tiered approach to the analysis of long-term settlement trends. PhD thesis, Durham University. [Unpublished.]

Kennet D. 2004. *Sasanian and Islamic pottery from Ras al-Khaimah. Classification, chronology and analysis of trade in the western Indian Ocean.* Oxford: Archaeopress.

Lorimer J.G. 1908. *Gazetteer of the Persian Gulf.* ii. *Geographical and statistical.* London: British Library.

Molera J., Pradell T., Salvado N. & Vendrell-Saz M. 2001. Interactions between clay bodies and lead glazes. *Journal of the American Ceramic Society* 84/5: 1120–1128.

Petersen A., Grey T., Rees C. & Edwards I. 2010. Excavations and survey at al-Ruwayḍah, a late Islamic site in northern Qatar. *Proceedings of the Seminar for Arabian Studies* 40: 41–53.

Power T. 2015. A first ceramic chronology for the late Islamic Arabian Gulf. *Journal of Islamic Archaeology* 2/1: 1–33.

Priestman S.M.N. 2005. Settlement and ceramics in southern Iran: An analysis of the Sasanian and Islamic periods in the Williamson Collection. MA thesis, University of Durham. [Unpublished.]

Quinn P.S. 2022. *Thin section petrography, geochemistry & scanning electron microscopy of archaeological ceramics.* Oxford: Archaeopress.

Schmidt C., Döpper S., Kluge J., Petrella S., Ochs U. ... Walter M. 2021. *Die Entstehung komplexer Siedlungen im Zentraloman Archäologische Untersuchungen zur Siedlungsgeschichte von Al-Khashbah.* Oxford: Archaeopress.

Tite M.S., Freestone I., Mason R., Molera J., Vendrell-Sanz M. & Wood N. 1998. Lead glazes in antiquity — methods of production and reasons for use. *Archaeometry* 40/2: 241–260.

Whitbread I.K. 1995. *Greek transport amphorae, a petrological and archaeological study.* Oxford: The British School at Athens.

Whitbread I.K. 2001. Ceramic petrology, clay geochemistry and ceramic production — from technology to the mind of the potter. Pages 449–459 in D.R. Brothwell & A.M. Pollard (eds), *Handbook of archaeological sciences.* Chichester: John Wiley & Sons.

Whitcomb D. 1975. The archaeology of Oman, a preliminary discussion of the Islamic periods. *The Journal of Oman Studies* 1: 123–157.

Živković J., Carvajal López J.C., Döpper S. & Biezeveld I. 2024. *Bahla ware from Central Oman: Petrological and chemical information on bodies, chemical information on glazes.* DIGITAL.CSIC. doi: https://doi.org/10.20350/digitalCSIC/16704

Živković J., Power T., Georgakopoulou M. & Carvajal López J.C. 2019. Defining new technological traditions of late Islamic Arabia: A view on Bahlā Ware from al-Ain (UAE) and the lead-barium glaze production. *Archaeological and Anthropological Sciences* 11: 4697–4709.

Authors' addresses

Jelena Živković, The Institute of Archaeology, Kneza Mihaila 35/IV, 11000 Belgrade, Serbia; The Cyprus Institute STARC, 20 Konstantinou Kavafi Street, 2121 Nicosia, Cyprus.
e-mail j.zivkovic@ai.ac.rs

José Cristóbal Carvajal López, Institute of Heritage Sciences (INCIPIT) - Spanish Council of Scientific Research (CSIC), Edificio Fontán, Bl. 4, Cidade da Cultura, Monte GAiás s/n 15707 Santiago de Compostela, Spain; School of Archaeology and Ancient History, University of Leicester, University Road, Leicester, LE1 7RH, UK.
e-mail josecristobal.carvajal-lopez@incipit.csic.es

Irini Biezeveld, Drents Museum, Brink 1–5, NL-9400 AC Assen, The Netherlands.
e-mail i.biezeveld@drentsmuseum.nl

Stephanie Döpper, Ancient Near Eastern Studies, University of Würzburg, Residenzplatz 2, Tor A, 97070 Würzburg, Germany.
e-mail stephanie.doepper@uni-wuerzburg.de

Proceedings of the Seminar for Arabian Studies 54 (2025): 263–263

Focus session 'Zaydi governance in Yemen between legal theory and political practice'

Introduction

The focus session 'Zaydi governance in Yemen between legal theory and political practice', a selection of papers from which are published in these *Proceedings*, was generously hosted by the 57th Seminar for Arabian Studies. The goal of the session was to explore the intersection of legal theory and political practice in the formation of Yemeni Zaydi political institutions. Central to this conversation was the figure of the Zaydi imam, particularly his role in formulating the legal framework of the pre-modern Zaydi state. Contributions stressed different aspects of this function. Ebrahim Mansoor's article discusses how a fifteenth-century imam — Aḥmad Ibn al-Murtaḍā — shaped the Zaydi legal tradition for centuries to come through the composition of a legal work, *Kitāb al-Azhār*. Kerstin Hünefeld's article demonstrates that in the nineteenth century debates on what could appear rather narrow topics — such as the question of the forced conversion of Jewish orphans — continued to rely on legal reasoning from previous centuries while also infusing the discussion with a politicized exploration of the nature of the Zaydi imamate. Papers read at the Seminar but not published in this volume touched on other dimensions of this theme. Johann Heiss and Eirik Hovden in their complementary papers discussed the theory and practice of selecting an imam through a close study of the manner of this selection (examination, *imtiḥān*) and people involved in decision-making. Clarck Membourou Moimecheme discussed how medieval Zaydi imams sought diplomatic relations with Mecca and Medina to affirm their position of leadership in Yemen.

All the published contributions shed light on an under-studied but transformative period of Yemen's Zaydi history — the fifteenth to the sixteenth century. In this period, under the pressure of regional geopolitics and internal change, Zaydi imams and their supporters reformed the functioning of the imamate and updated the legal and political theories that underpinned it. This is particularly evident in the case of Aḥmad Ibn al-Murtaḍā, discussed by Ebrahim Mansoor, and of his grandson, imam Yaḥyā Sharaf al-Dīn. The latter's attempts to innovate the Zaydi political system through the appointment of an heir is discussed in Ekaterina Pukhovaia's contribution. These transformations continued to influence the development of the Zaydi political system up to the twentieth century, as Kerstin Hünefeld shows.

Finally, all contributions highlighted the rich variety of sources available to the historian of Yemeni Zaydism, be it legal texts, histories, biographies, or documents. The close readings offered by the authors of the contributions to the focus session provide a wide-ranging view of the ways in which Zaydi legal thinking was influenced by political practice and vice versa.

Ekaterina Pukhovaia

Proceedings of the Seminar for Arabian Studies 54 (2025): 264–272

Dhimma governance and the Zaydī *madhhab* spectrum: the forced conversion of Jewish orphans, its Islamic legal background, and political relevance

Kerstin Hünefeld

Summary

This paper discusses two fatwas from the reign of the Qāsimid imam al-Manṣūr ʿAlī b. ʿAbbās (r. 1189–1224/1775–1809) concerning the forced conversion of Jewish orphans to Islam. It examines the legal opinions of four authors regarding whether it is permissible, forbidden, or even considered a religious obligation (*wājib*) to 'remove' (*intazaʿa*) minor *dhimmī* orphans from their non-Muslim surroundings and raise them as Muslims. These authors are Ḥusayn b. ʿAbdallāh al-Kibsī (d. 1223/1808), Muḥammad b. ʿAlī al-Shawkānī (d. 1250/1834), ʿAbdullāh b. Muḥammad al-Amīr (d. 1242/1826), and Ibrāhīm b. ʿAbd al-Qādir b. Aḥmad al-Kawkabānī (d. 1223/1808).

The Islamic sources cited by all four authors to support their opposing opinions include both Sunnī and Zaydī texts. This paper, however, looks beyond the binary conception of the two schools juxtaposed against one another. Specifically, it aims to identify a third group within the central Yemeni legal sphere that advocates for orphan 'removal', referencing the practice of imam Sharaf al-Dīn Yaḥyā (d. 965/1558) as a precedent. Based on the analysis of the two fatwas and their political-historical background, towards the end of the article a brief reference will be made to the role of imam Yaḥyā Ḥamīḍ al-Dīn (d. 1367/1948) regarding the forced conversion of Jewish orphans that took place within his realm.

Keywords: late medieval–modern Yemen, Zaydiyya, 'Sunnisation of Zaydism', Qāsimid state, anti-Qāsimid opposition

Introduction

The majority of sources referring to the practice of forced conversion of Jewish minor orphans to Islam and their removal from their remaining family environment are Jewish-Yemeni ones from the twentieth century. Research focusing on this practice (see e.g. Gaimani 2004; Eraqi-Klorman 2001; Parfitt 1998; Klein Franke 1984), however, was unable to clarify the exact legal basis for that practice and with it the role of the then acting Zaydī imam and Yemeni king al-Mutawakkil Yaḥyā b. Muḥammad Ḥamīd al-Dīn (r. 1904–1948) in enforcing or preventing it.[1] While Shlomo Dov Goitein vaguely ascribed the practice of forced orphan conversion to the 'Shiites of Yemen' (Goitein 1976: 77–78), more recent research attributed it to 'neo-Sunnī' or 'traditionist' thought (both terms introduced by Haykel 2003) or, even more concretely, to Muḥammad b. ʿAlī al-Shawkānī (Haykel 2003: 126; Tobi 1990: 119–120). However, neither of them had the opportunity actually to access and study the relevant texts and hence they were unable to prove their assessments. This article fills that research gap. Introducing two fatwas from the Yemeni manuscript archive, Dār al-Makhṭūṭāt in Ṣanʿāʾ, it analyses the Islamic legal background of the practice and provides an initial assessment of the broader political agendas of their authors vis-à-vis the acting imam.

[1] Although the practice is reported to have taken place during his realm, he is not mentioned as a driving force by Jewish sources (see e.g. Qoraḥ 5753/1993: 157). On the contrary, it is most likely that he himself was challenged on this practice by oppositional actors from within the Zaydī spectrum (Hünefeld 2011; 2023a: 171–173). For a differing assessment, see Ariel 2010 and Eraqi-Klorman 2001. For an overview of the respective research literature, see Hünefeld 2023a: 167–178. Regarding earlier Jewish sources, there is a poem by Shalom Shabazi (d. *c.*1720) that speaks of 'stealing orphans' (Nini 1991: 22). For an overview on Jews in Zaydī *fiqh* see Hünefeld 2023b.

Two fatwas from the Dār al-Makhṭūṭāt in Ṣanʿāʾ

The earlier treatise (MS 2392) is entitled *Baḥth fī man māta abawāhū min aṭfāl al-yahūd* ('Study on Jewish orphans').[2] It was written around the year 1209/1794,[3] copied in 1349/1930–1931 by Muḥammad b. Qāsim b. Aḥmad Abū Ṭālib (d. 1320/1902–1902), and includes three opinions: an opening question by Ḥusayn b. ʿAbdallāh al-Kibsī (d. 1223/1808),[4] an answer by Muḥammad b. ʿAlī al-Shawkānī (d. 1250/1834),[5] and a comment by ʿAbdullāh b. Muḥammad al-Amīr (d. 1242/1826).[6] The second treatise (MS. 3859) is entitled *Ḥujjat al-aʾimma fī intizāʿ al-ṭifl idhā māta abawāhu min ahl al-dhimma* ('the imams' justification for removing *dhimmi* orphans'). It was written in 1216/1802 by Ibrāhīm b. ʿAbd al-Qādir b. Aḥmad al-Kawkabānī (d. 1223/1808)[7] and copied in 1355/1936 from an earlier copy made in 1251/1835.[8]

As the dates indicate, the two fatwas — whose authors will be discussed below — were issued during the second half of the Zaydī-Qāsimid imamate in Yemen (1006–1289/1597–1872) that consolidated after the withdrawal of the Ottomans (1045/1635), and from the turn of the eighteenth to nineteenth century — at the time when the fatwas were written — developed into a patrimonial state that extended over the whole of south-west Yemen and remained in control for over a century (on the Qāsimid imamate see Pukhovaia 2021; Klarić 2007; Haykel 2003).[9]

While each author indirectly adopts a more general stance on the legitimacy of the Qāsimid state, the fatwas specifically address the legal status of minor *dhimmī* orphans in this world (*al-aḥkām al-dunyawiyya*), particularly Jewish ones as Jews constituted the only local *dhimmī* community. More specifically, they debate whether, after the death of their parents (or fathers) and while the children are still minors, it is permissible, forbidden, or even considered a religious obligation (*wājib*) to 'remove' (*intazaʿa*) these *dhimmī* orphans from their non-Muslim surroundings and raise them as Muslims.[10]

The fatwas in light of the 'Sunnisation of the Zaydiyya'

Drawing on additional sources, each of the four authors refers to both the *fiṭra* hadith[11] transmitted by Aḥmad Ibn Hanbal (d. 241/855) and included in the major Sunnī hadith collections, and a passage from Ibn al-Murtaḍā's (d. 840/1436–1437) *Kitāb al-Azhār*, to this day one of the principal works of Zaydī jurisprudence.[12]

This is less contradictory than it might seem at first glance. Beginning with Muḥammad b. Ibrāhīm al-Wazīr (d. 840/1436; on him, see Wilmers 2018), Zaydī scholars increasingly referred to Sunnī sources to strengthen their arguments. Some scholars and their works, such as the aforementioned *Kitāb al-Azhār* and Ibn Miftāḥ's

[2] MS 2392, fos. 1r–5r, Dār al-Makhṭūṭāt, Ṣanʿāʾ, al-Maktaba al-Gharbiyya (Western Library).

[3] One of the authors refers to that year. It is uncertain, however, whether the text was written in the same year or shortly afterwards. The immediate reasons for engaging with the legal question at this particular point will be examined in another article. In his introduction, al-Kibsī briefly mentions the emergence of Jewish orphans in the Thulā/Kawkabān region following an unspecified extinction of the local Jewish population (*fanāʾ fī yahūd al-maḥal*), see MS 2392, fo. 1v.

[4] For his short biography, see al-Shawkānī 1427/2006: 255–256; Zabārah 1348/1929–1930: 380–382; and al-Akwaʿ 1416/1995: 4.1789.

[5] This treatise should not be confused with another by Muḥammad b. ʿAlī al-Shawkānī on the judgement of *dhimmī* children in the afterlife, entitled *Baḥt fī aṭfāl al-kuffār*. For the latter, see al-Shawkānī 1423/2002: 2.685–701. For his biography, see Haykel 2003: 18–23.

[6] Whereas the parts containing al-Kibsī's and al-Shawkānī's opinions are almost identical with another version of the text that was published in al-Shawkānī's *fatāwā* collection (1423/2002: 10. 4979–4993), the published version includes neither the opinion of al-Amīr nor the introduction. For al-Amīr's biography, see Zabārah 1348/1929–30: 97–100; al-Akwaʿ 1416/1995: 4.1858–1859; and al-Shawkānī 1427/2006: 273–274.

[7] For his short biography, see Zabārah 1348/1929–1930: 11–16; al-Shawkānī 1427/2006: 48–49.

[8] The copyist names and the location are not mentioned.

[9] For the periodization of the early Qāsimid imamate I follow Pukhovaia 2021.

[10] This legal argument is closely linked to the theological discussion concerning the eligibility of minor non-Muslim orphans to enter Muslim paradise upon dying as minors. The second issue discussed in the fatwas is whether Jewish orphans raised as Muslims can inherit from their non-Muslim parents. A separate article by me, examining this connection in further detail, is in preparation.

[11] The Arabic word *fiṭra* may be translated as 'a way of being created' (Adang 2000: 393), 'natural constitution', 'condition of religious innocence' (Stande der religiösen Unschuld)' (Jon Hoover and Joseph van Ess cited in Bosanquet 2020: 326 n. 7), or 'original human disposition' (Wilmers 2018: 89). In one of its variants, the *fiṭra* hadith cites the prophet as having said: *mā min mawlūd illā yūlad ʿalā-l-fiṭra fa-abawāhu yuhawwidānahu wa-yunaṣṣirānahu wa-yumajjisānahu* ('Every child is born into the *fiṭra*; it is their parents who make them a Jew, a Christian, or a Zoroastrian'; my translation). For an overview on the different versions from Muslim's *Ṣaḥīḥ* (*kitāb al-qadr, bāb maʿnā kull mawlūd yūlad ʿalā-l-fiṭra wa-ḥukm mawt aṭfāl al-kuffār wa-awlād al-muslimīn*) see Adang 2000: 394 n. 11.

[12] The *Kitāb al-Azhār* is included within Ibn Miftāḥ's *Sharḥ al-Azhār* as the *matn*, from which I subsequently cite.

(d. 877/1472) comparative commentary, the *Sharḥ al-Azhār*, remained Zaydī in their scholarly affiliation while occasionally referencing Sunnī hadith. Other scholars, however, who also came from a Zaydī background, developed a 'traditionist', 'neo-Sunnī' (Haykel 2003), or proto-Salafi approach that fully relied on Sunnī sources and gradually opposed the teachings of the Zaydī school, while they simultaneously served the political institution of the Zaydī state.[13] The peak of this latter development is represented by Muḥammad b. ʿAlī al-Shawkānī (Haykel 2003), one of the authors of the first fatwa (MS 2392). He was appointed chief judge of the Qāsimid imamate in 1209/1794, the same year in which the fatwa was written. Serving in this position until his death in 1834, al-Shawkānī later wrote a comprehensive refutation of *Kitāb al-Azhār*, titled *al-Sayl al-Jarrār* (al-Shawkānī 2000). The Zaydī perspective within the Sunnified spectrum, as well as the Zaydī outright opposition to the extreme form of 'Sunnisation' advocated by al-Shawkānī, has yet to be studied in greater detail.[14]

Regarding the fatwas discussed here, there are two major lines of argumentation. Muḥammad al-Shawkānī and ʿAbdullāh al-Amīr represent the traditionist, neo-Sunnī or proto-Salafi position. In contrast, Ḥusayn al-Kibsī and Ibrāhīm al-Kawkabānī take a Zaydī stance; however, it has yet to be established which specific current within Zaydism their views reflect.

Opinions and sources against the 'removal' (*nazʿ*) of minor *dhimmī* orphans

Al-Shawkānī unambiguously rejects the 'removal' of *dhimmī* orphans from their family environment, stating that it contradicts the (Sunnī) sources.[15] He either ignores or deconstructs any potential consistency in the Zaydī sources mentioned by al-Kibsī, which will be discussed further below. Instead, al-Shawkānī refers to the practices of the Prophet, his companions, and the 'pious predecessors' (*al-salaf al-ṣalih*), none of whom are reported by the sources to have interfered in internal Jewish matters and, therefore, are not known to have raised Jewish orphans as Muslims. He further asserts that no such instruction is implied in the *fiṭra* hadith (*lā yadull ʿalā dhālik al-maʿnā*).[16]

ʿAbdullāh b. Muḥammad al-Amīr supports al-Shawkānī's arguments. In addition to referencing the *Salaf*, he cites the Prophet's biography, particularly his interactions with Jews in Yathrib/Medina and Khaybar, as evidence that all relevant role models upheld the principle (also conveyed in a hadith) that *dhimmī* children should be treated like their parents (*wa-ammā al-aḥkām al-dunyawiyya fa-qad ʿulim min sīratihi* [...] *muʿāmalatuhum muʿāmalat abāʾihim*) and, thus, should be granted security and the right to continue practising their religion.

Sources supporting the 'removal' (*nazʿ*) of minor *dhimmī* orphans within the context of the Zaydī *madhhab* spectrum

In his letter to Muḥammad al-Shawkānī, Ḥusayn al-Kibsī addresses two possibilities. One rejects the practice of 'removal' with reference to Sunnī sources, which al-Shawkānī refers to in his answer. The other supports the 'removal' of minor *dhimmī* orphans with reference to Zaydī sources. This paper focuses on some of these Zaydī sources and explores their political stance towards the Qāsimid state.

As a significant Zaydī reference that advocates for the removal of Jewish orphans from their surroundings, al-Kibsī mentions the practice of imam al-Mutawakkil Sharaf al-Dīn Yaḥyā (d. 965/1558), who ruled from various towns around Ṣanʿāʾ during the sixteenth century, before the first Ottoman administration of Yemen (1538–1635) and the imamate of the Qāsimid dynasty (1598–1872) (Pukhovaia 2021). According to al-Kibsī, imam Sharaf

[13] Both of these developments form part of what is described as the 'Sunnisation of the Zaydiyya' (coined by Cook 2000: 247–251; further developed by Haykel 2003), a topic that still requires further research (Wilmers 2018; Hovden & Mansoor 2023). For al-Shawkānī's influence on modern Salafism, see Haykel 2024.

[14] While Haykel (2003: 148) refers to them as 'strict Hādawīs,' this terminology has been challenged more recently (Hovden 2019: 144–145; Hünefeld 2023a: 21–24). However, a more appropriate terminology has yet to be developed.

[15] This contradicts the assessment of Haykel (2003: 126), who attributed the legal opinion promoting the forced conversion of Jewish minor orphans to Muḥammad al-Shawkānī and Tobi (1990: 119–20). As mentioned above, however, neither of them had access to the text of al-Shawkānī's fatwa, but were only aware of its title.

[16] In doing so, he implicitly agrees with Hajar al-ʿAsqalānī (d. 1449), who, according to al-Kibsī, took the view that this only points to a matter of fact (*al-bayān mā huwa fī nafs al-amr*) but does not provide any concrete directive regarding the judgement and treatment of children (*aḥkām fī'l-dunya*) in this world. See MS 2392, fo. 2r.

al-Dīn dispatched messengers throughout the country to seize Jewish children whose parents had died (*baʿath fī bilād li-yaqbiḍu man māt abawāhu min ṣibyān al-yahūd*) to raise them as Muslims (see MS 2392, fo. 2r). This is recorded in one of the imam's biographies as an event of the year 936/1530, which is the earliest hitherto known date for that practice.[17]

Following al-Kibsī's opinion, imam Sharaf al-Dīn's practice constitutes the legitimate practical implementation of a passage from the *Kitāb al-Azhār* which, while not explicitly referring to *dhimmī* orphans, states that among other cases, a child is legally considered Muslim when found within Islamic territory without their parents (*bi-kawnihi fī dārinā dūnahumā*). The passage continues, stating that a minor whose religious affiliation is unclear should be legally treated according to the territory in which they are found (*wa-l-multabis yuḥkam bi-l-dār*).[18] This, in al-Kibsī's opinion, is not only in accordance with the practice of imam Sharaf al-Dīn but also with the *fiṭra* hadith transmitted by Ibn Hanbal, or rather Ibn Qayyim al-Jawziyya's (d. 751/1350) interpretation of it (Bosanquet 2020: 340–344; Friedmann 2003: 112–113; for an overview, see Hünefeld 2023a: 179–180) which, however, he does not state explicitly.[19]

Despite his irritation with the conflicting assessments of the different Sunnī and Zaydī sources, al-Kibsī concludes that it is better to follow the mentioned Zaydī sources and therefore approves the 'removal' of minor Jewish orphans from their remaining family environment (*fa-ẓaharnī ṣaḥḥāt nazʿ al-sabī*) (see MS 2392, fo. 2v). As for the question of whose responsibility and obligation it is to carry out or order the 'removal', he refers to the one who granted them a *dhimma* contract (*wa-wujūbihi ʿalā man ṣalaḥ lahu*) in the first place and before the death of the parents which clearly, although indirectly, refers to the reigning Zaydī imam (Hünefeld 2023a: 116–119).[20]

However, this opinion, supported by specific Zaydī sources, does not reflect the Zaydī majority view of the late Qāsimid imamate, during which the fatwas were written. The main commentary on the cited *Kitāb al-Azhār*, the *Sharḥ al-Azhār*, for instance, does not interpret the passage in this way and offers no practical directive to search for *dhimmī* orphans and 'remove' them from their family environment (Ibn Miftāḥ 1464/2019: 9.603). This includes the notes, glosses, and *madhhab* signs that were added to the *matn* (*Kitāb al-Azhār*) and the *Sharḥ al-Azhār* up until the mid-eighteenth century (Hovden 2019: 170–171; Messick 2018: 65–70), a process associated with the Qāsimid imamate (Hovden & Mansoor 2023). Moreover, the *Sharḥ al-Azhār* as a multi-layered text corpus does not refer to the practices of imam Sharaf al-Dīn, who was a pre-Qāsimid imam from a different dynasty and, from a Qāsimid perspective, was not regarded as a leading role model. So, how can this non-mainstream Zaydī opinion be further defined?

The second fatwa (MS 3859) by Ibrāhīm b. ʿAbd al-Qādir b. Aḥmad al-Kawkabānī does not explicitly refer to the first one but seems to allude to its discussion indirectly. Al-Kawkabānī strongly advocates the forced conversion of minor *dhimmī* orphans and asserts that removing them from their 'infidel' environment constitutes a 'religious duty' (*wujūb intizāʿ aṭfāl al-dhimmiyīn idhā māta abāʾihim wa-ummahātihim*), as it aligns with what 'our imams have stated' (*qawl aʾimmatinā*). Like al-Kibsī, al-Kawkabānī also refers to the practice of imam Sharaf al-Dīn. As an additional reference for the obligation of *intizāʿ* (*ḥujjatinā ʿalā wujūb al-intizāʿ*), he points to Qurʾān 30. 30 and the *fiṭra* hadith. As proof that the correct interpretation of *fiṭra* is Islam, he refers to Ibn Ḥajar al-ʿAsqalānī, albeit ignoring the latter's assessment that it does not provide any directive regarding the judgement and treatment of minor *dhimmī* orphans (see MS 2392, fo. 42r, n. 16 above) in this world. He dismisses the narrative that the 'pious predecessors' (*al-salaf al-ṣāliḥ*) did not interfere with internal Jewish matters and, therefore, did not raise Jewish orphans

[17] For the passage in imam Sharaf al-Dīn's biography, see al-ʿUlufī, *Sīrat al-imām al-Mutawakkil Yaḥyā Sharaf al-Dīn*, MS ZA 561-01, fo. 156r. I am grateful to Ekaterina Pukhovaia for directing me to this source.

[18] See Ibn Miftāḥ 1464/2019: 9.603 (*kitab al-siyar, faṣl fī bayān al-ridda*).

[19] Tobi (1990: 119–20) refers to possible Hanbalī influences on the practice of the forced conversion of minor *dhimmī* orphans but is not aware of the differing assessments of Ibn Qayyim al-Jawziyya and his teacher Ibn Taymiyya (d. 728/1328) on that matter, the latter of whom rejected this interpretation (Bosanquet (2020: 340–344).

[20] See MS 2392, fo. 2v. The first to refer to a possible 'religious obligation' of the 'Shiites of Yemen', in other words the Zaydīs, to forcibly convert Jewish minor orphans to Islam and remove them from their remaining family environment, was Goitein, who described them as 'sectarians, who have their own interpretation of the law' without providing any references (1976: 77–78). In an earlier article, he stated that this practice contradicts commonly accepted Islamic law. He speculated that there may be a connection to the *fiṭra* hadith as transmitted by Bukhārī (Goitein 5698/1929–1930: 91 n. 11).

as Muslims by arguing that 'the absence of [practical] evidence does not imply the absence of obligation' (*ʿadam al-wujūd inna lā yadull ʿalā ʿadam al-wujūb*) (see MS 2392, fo. 38v–39r). Al-Kawkabānī also cites the aforementioned passage from the *Kitāb al-Azhār*, stating that a child should be treated according to the *dār* in which they are found. To reinforce his support for *intizāʿ* ('removal'), he cites additional Zaydī texts, including the *Athmār al-Azhār*.

The *Athmār al-Azhār* is an alternative, earlier, and abbreviated commentary on the *Kitāb al-Azhār*, written by the same imam al-Mutawakkil Yaḥyā Sharaf al-Dīn, who is cited as a precedent for practising *intizāʿ*. However, the *Athmār al-Azhār* does not explicitly advocate the 'removal' of minor *dhimmī* children either. It only expands on the words of the *Kitāb al-Azhār* by emphasizing that a child is considered Muslim when found in Islamic territory, regardless (*muṭlaqan*) of whether their parents are deceased or absent (Sharaf al-Dīn 1442/2021: 274).[21] However, as no further clarification is given, this may also concern their legal status in the afterlife (*al-aḥkām al-ākhira*) and the possibility of entering Muslim paradise if they die as minors. It could also pertain to situations where the children are found without surviving family or means of support. In such cases, the passage could be interpreted as the legal basis for caring for these children by fully integrating them into Muslim society, an interpretation seemingly adopted in the twentieth century by imam al-Mutawakkil Yaḥyā Ḥamīd al-Dīn (Hünefeld 2023a: 218–221; Nini 1991: 19). Regarding the lack of a clear directive within the *Athmār al-Azhār* and the fact that al-Kawkabānī cites additional *fiqh* works associated with the rule of imam Sharaf al-Dīn (Hovden & Mansoor 2023), it seems likely that in doing so, he was less interested in their specific content than on reinforcing the authority of the Sharaf al-Dīn imamate's legal tradition as a whole.[22]

Finally, al-Kawkabānī turns to the matter of 'legal guardianship' (*wilāyā*) and states that it must be left neither to an unbeliever (*kāfir*) nor to a sinful (*fāsiq*) Muslim. If the parents die, he states, the *wilyāya* must be passed on to the imam (*fa-idhā mātā fa-walīhu al-imām*). He then takes his statement one step further and argues that it is not permitted to prevent minor *dhimmī* orphans from being taken away and to leave them among the 'unbelievers' (*fa-lā yajūz tark aṭfāl ahl al-ḏimma ʿan al-intizāʿ wa-tabqīyatuhum bayn ẓahrānay al-kuffār*) (see MS 2392, fo. 44v).

Political implications and the authors' positions vis-à-vis the Qāsimid imamate

To understand the political dimension of this legal discussion, we must clarify what it means to recognize the *dhimma* governance of the pre-Qāsimid imam, Sharaf al-Dīn Yaḥyā, as legally valid during the reign of the Qāsimids.

Al-Kawkabānī's final words seem like an indirect critique of the reigning imam al-Manṣūr ʿAlī b. ʿAbbās (r. 1189–1224/1775–1809), who is not reported to have enforced the 'removal' of minor Jewish orphans in the sources discussed here.[23] This policy aligns with the fact that imam al-Manṣūr ʿAlī was the first of the three Qāsimid imams under whom Muḥammad al-Shawkānī served as chief judge when traditionist or 'neo-Sunnī' thought was propagated by the state (Haykel 2003). Indeed, the opinions of the two 'neo-Sunnī' scholars, al-Shawkānī and al-Amīr included in the first fatwa (MS 2392), strictly reject the imam's interference in inner-Jewish matters, referencing the practice of the Prophet and the *salaf al-ṣāliḥ*.

Against this background, it appears that beyond addressing the specific legal question of what to do with minor *dhimmī* orphans, al-Shawkānī and al-Amīr used the legal discussion for an additional purpose: by identifying imam al-Manṣūr's *dhimma* governance of

[21] *Muṭlaqan* is explained in the *Athmār al-Azhār*'s footnotes.

[22] Additionally, al-Kawkabānī cites the commentary of al-Qāḍī Muḥammad b. Yaḥyā Ibn Bahrān (d. 957/1550), titled *Taftīḥ al-Qulūb*, the *Kitāb al-Wābil* by ʿImād al-Dīn Yaḥyā b. Muḥammad al-Miqrāʾī (d. 990/1582), and the *Bayān al-Shāfī* by Yaḥyā b. Aḥmad b. ʿAlī Ibn al-Muẓaffar (d. 875/1470–1471). These references will be analysed in more detail in another article. For further research on the legal tradition associated with the Sharaf al-Dīn imamate, see the forthcoming works by Ebrahim Mansoor.

[23] Citing R. Ḥayyim Ḥibshūsh, Nini (1991: 18) writes that the 'decree was revived in the latter days of the imam al-Manṣūr ʿAlī ibn ʿAbbās in 1809', which largely corresponds to the composition dates of the fatwas discussed here (1209/1794 and 1216/1803). While the sources discussed in this article make no mention of imam al-Manṣūr initiating orphan conversion, however, Ḥibshush relates that imam al-Manṣūr ordered the seizure of Jewish orphans to be made servants at his sons' newly built palaces. Nini points out that this is an isolated account. For an English translation of Ḥibshush's mention of the forced conversion of Jewish orphans, see Verskin 2019: 150 and 184. Verskin does not investigate the role of imam al-Manṣūr any further. The matter will be examined in a separate article.

non-interference in internal Jewish affairs as legitimate and aligned with the mentioned Islamic sources, they also positioned themselves in relation to the late Qāsimid imamate, aiming to strengthen the legitimacy of the reigning imam while reinforcing their own authority as scholars within the ruling elite of the state.

Ḥusayn al-Kibsī, and even more so Ibrāhīm al-Kawkabānī, do the exact opposite. By presenting the pre-Qāsimid Imām Sharaf al-Dīn Yaḥyā's *dhimma* policy as ideal and in line with their interpretation of the sources, they implicitly challenge the legitimacy of Imām al-Manṣūr, who appears to fall short of fulfilling the religious duties expected of a legitimate Zaydī imam. In doing so they take a critical, if not oppositional, stance against the Qāsimid state. This assessment aligns with the biographies and genealogical background of the two authors.[24]

A few years after the fatwas were written, Ḥusayn al-Kibsī became involved in the riots against the Qāsimid state in 1796 and 1802 (Haykel 2003: 167–179). In 1222/1807, the last year of imam al-Manṣūr's reign he joined his relative Ismāʿīl b. Aḥmad al-Kibsī (d. 1250/1834, referred to as 'al-Mughallis')[25] and some members of the Āl Abū Ṭālib in migrating (*hijra*) from Ṣanʿāʾ to escape the sphere of 'unjust rule' and to establish a short-lived counter-imamate in al-Rawdha, an incident referred to as the 'Revolution of the Kibsīs' (*thawrat al-Kabāsiyya*) in the biographical lexica (*tarājim*) (see al-Shawkānī 1427/2006: 255; Zabārah 1348/1929–1930: 381; al-Akwaʿ 1416/1995: 4.1789; on the al-Kibsī family, see vom Bruck 2020). Shortly after, he even proclaimed himself as imam (*wa-kāna ṣāḥib al-tarjama anna yadʿū ikā nafsihi*) (see al-Shawkānī 1427/2006: 256) and died in prison after the rebellion was put down by order of imam al-Manṣūr ʿAlī.[26]

For his part, Ibrāhīm b. ʿAbd al-Qādir al-Kawkabānī was himself a direct descendant of imam Sharaf al-Dīn Yaḥyā.[27] He belonged to the Āl Shams al-Dīn of Kawkabān who, alongside the Āl Mutahhar branch and as descendants of imam Sharaf al-Dīn, became known as the 'Princes' or 'Lords' (*aṣḥāb*) of Kawkabān that the central government recognized. During the sixteenth and seventeenth centuries, the different branches of the family took varying positions towards the Qāsimid state, sometimes supporting it and sometimes standing in opposition to it (Pukhovaia 2023). Research indicates they formed a local political elite until at least the nineteenth century.[28]

Conclusion and outlook

As the analysis of the two fatwas and the historical context of their composition has shown, the Islamic legal basis for the forced conversion of Jewish orphans, or more precisely, the 'removal' (*nazʿ*) of minor *dhimmi* orphans from their remaining non-Muslim environment, does not go back to 'neo-Sunnī' legal scholars such as Muḥammad b. ʿAlī al-Shawkānī and ʿAbdullāh b. Muḥammad al-Amīr. Instead, this practice was identified as legitimate and even described as a 'religious obligation' on the imam by the authors Ḥusayn al-Kibsī and Ibrāhīm al-Kawkabānī, both of whom explicitly refer to Zaydī sources to strengthen their arguments.

However, this legal debate cannot simply be explained as a binary juxtaposition between the 'neo-Sunnī' — or proto-Salafī — and the Zaydī school of thought or *madhhab*. Firstly, all four scholars refer to both Sunnī hadith and a passage from the *Kitāb al-Azhār*, which remains one of the authoritative works for the Zaydī *madhhab* to this day. They just interpret these sources in different ways, and in the case of al-Kibsī and al-Kawkabānī, refer to additional Zaydī sources, such as the practice of imam al-Mutawakkil Sharaf al-Dīn Yaḥyā and the legal works associated with his reign. Al-Shawkānī and al-Amīr ignore all those additional sources. Secondly, the cited Zaydī mainstream source, the *Kitāb al-Azhār*, which itself reflects a certain degree of 'Sunnisation', does not provide a concrete directive to search for and 'remove' minor *dhimmī* orphans from their non-Muslim surroundings. This practice is reported for the pre-Qāsimid imam

[24] A subsequent article will analyse the biographical literature in more detail.

[25] For his short biography, see Zabārah 1348/1929–1930: 259–261.

[26] The latter detail is only mentioned in the *tarājim* by al-Shawkānī and Zabārah, the latter citing al-Shawkānī.

[27] For a family tree of imam Sharaf al-Dīn's descendants, see Brinkmann (2022: 366).

[28] Pukhovaia 2023 covers the history of the 'Lords of Kawkabān' from the fifteenth to the seventeenth century and therefore does not refer to Ibrāhīm al-Kawkabānī.

Sharaf al-Dīn Yaḥyā and pointed out as legitimate by al-Kibsī and al-Kawkabānī.

Instead of viewing the issue as a binary dispute between the 'neo-Sunnī' and Zaydī *madhhab*, we must consider the political dimension and recognize the existence of three legal schools rather than just two: firstly, a Zaydī mainstream and 'middle ground' represented by the *Sharḥ al-Azhār* as a multi-layered text corpus, which is associated with the Qāsimid state and reflects a moderate stage of Sunnisation while remaining distinctly Zaydī; secondly, the neo-Sunnī — or proto-Salafī — late teachings of Muḥammad b. ʿAlī al-Shawkānī who, despite serving as Chief Judge of the Qāsimid state, adopts an increasingly critical stance against Zaydī law and political theory; and thirdly, a Zaydī school that lies outside the legal and intellectual spectrum of the Zaydī middle ground and adopts an oppositional stance against the Qāsimid state. Regarding the two fatwas analysed in this paper, this latter group is represented by Ḥusayn al-Kibsī, who later joined a rebellion against the Qāsimid state and even proclaimed himself an anti-imam, and by Ibrāhīm al-Kawkabānī, a direct descendant of imam Sharaf al-Dīn, who sought to reinforce the authority of the state, legal tradition, and dynasty of Sharaf al-Dīn Yaḥyā through his legal argumentation.

Apart from understanding the political context in which the two fatwas were written at the turn of the nineteenth century in order to challenge the legitimacy of the Qāsimid state from one side and to strengthen it from the other, their analysis can be used to draw lessons about Mutawakkilite Yemen; more precisely, on the role of imam al-Mutawakkil Yaḥyā Ḥamīd al-Dīn, a descendant of the Qasimids, in the forced conversion of Jewish orphans during the twentieth century. As in the eighteenth and nineteenth centuries, the forced conversion of Jewish minor orphans in the twentieth century was probably initiated by oppositional actors associated with the political agendas of non-Qāsimid Sayyid families or individuals among them. While this issue requires further research to be resolved, the initial suspicion falls on imam Sharaf al-Dīn's descendants, the 'Princes of Kawkabān', as well as the Bayt al-Kibsī and Bayt al-Wazīr. Prominent members of these families, such as ʿAbdullāh b. Aḥmad al-Wazīr and Ḥusayn b. Muḥammad al-Kibsī (both executed in 1367/1948) had been involved in the political opposition against imam Yaḥyā Ḥamīd al-Dīn since the late 1930s and were among the driving forces behind the coup d'état and imam Yaḥyā's assassination in 1367/1948 (Hünefeld 2023a: 75–76).

Acknowledgements

This paper was written during my postdoctoral fellowship at the Martin Buber Society of Fellows and with the support of a stipend from the Shmuel Badihi Foundation, both at the Hebrew University of Jerusalem.

References

Primary sources

al-Kawkabānī, Ibrāhīm b. ʿAbd al-Qādir b. Aḥmad. Ḥujjat al-aʾimma fī intizāʿ al-ṭifl idhā māt abawāhu min ahl al-dhimma ('The imams' justification for removing dhimmi orphans'), MS 3859, fos. 38r–47v. Written in 1216/1802. Dār al-makhṭūṭāt, Ṣanʿāʾ, al-Maktaba al-Gharbiyya (Western Library).

al-Shawkānī, Muḥammad b. ʿAlī. Baḥth fī man māta abawāhū min aṭfāl al-yahūd ('Study on Jewish orphans'), MS 2392, fos. 1r–5r, including opinions by Ḥusain b. ʿAbdallāh al-Kibsī and ʿAbdallāh b. Muḥammad al-Amīr. Written in *c.*1209/1794. Dār al-makhṭūṭāt, Ṣanʿāʾ, al-Maktaba al-Gharbiyya (Western Library).

Al-ʿUlufī. Sīrat al-imām al-Mutawakkil Yaḥyā Sharaf al-Dīn (vol. 2). ZA 561-01. Imam Zayd Cultural Foundation. Accessible via the Omani Ministry of Religious Endowments and Religious Affairs website.

Secondary sources

Adang C. 2000. Islam as the inborn religion of mankind: The concept of *fiṭra* in the works of Ibn Ḥazm. *Al-Qantara* 21/2: 391–410.

al-Akwaʿ I. 1416/1995. *Hijar al-ʿilm wa-maʿāqiluh fi-l-Yaman*. (6 volumes). Beirut/Damascus: Dār al-fikr al-muʿāṣir.

Ariel A. 2010. A reconsideration of Imam Yahya's attitude toward forced conversion of Jewish orphans in Yemen. *Shofar: An Interdisciplinary Journal of Jewish Studies* 29/1: 95–111.

Bosanquet A. 2020. *Minding their place: Space and religious hierarchy in Ibn Qayyim's* Aḥkām ahl al-dhimma. Leiden: Brill.

Brinkmann S. 2022. From Iran to Kawkabān: The transfer of Sunnī ḥadith to Zaydī Yemen: A case study of Ms. Vienna, Cod. Glaser 30. Pages 347–384 in H. Ansari & S. Schmidtke (eds), *Yemeni manuscript cultures in peril*. Piscataway, NJ: Gorgias Press.

Cook M. 2000. *Commanding right and forbidding wrong in Islamic thought*. Cambridge: Cambridge University Press.

Eraqi-Klorman B-Z. 2001. The forced conversion of Jewish orphans in Yemen. *International Journal of Middle East Studies* 33/1: 23–47.

Friedmann Y. 2003. *Tolerance and coercion in Islam: Interfaith relations in the Muslim tradition*. New York: Cambridge University Press.

Gaimani A. 2004. The 'Orphans' Decree' in Yemen: Two new episodes. *Middle Eastern Studies* 40: 171–184.

Goitein S.D. 5698/1929–1930. Ḥayim Ḥabshush we-sifro ḥizayon Teman. Pages 89–96 in Y.L. Magnes, J.N. Epstein & F.J. Baer (eds), *Sefer Magnes: Qoveṣ meḥqarim me-et anše ha-universitah ha-ʿivrit*. Jerusalem: ḥevrah le-hozaʾat sefarim ʿal-yad ha-universitah ha-ivrit.

Goitein S.D. 1976. *Jews and Arabs: Their contact through the ages*. (Revised second edition). New York: Schocken Books.

Haykel B. 2003. *Revival and reform in Islam: The legacy of Muḥammad al-Shawkānī*. Cambridge: Cambridge University Press.

Haykel B. 2024. Muḥammad b. ʿAlī sh-Shawkānī. Pages 1–16 in G. Tamer (ed.), *Qurʾānic hermeneutics in the 19th and 20th century*. iv. Berlin/Boston: De Gruyter.

Hovden E. 2019. *Waqf in Zaydī Yemen: Legal theory, codification, and local practice*. Leiden: Brill.

Hovden E. & Mansoor E. 2023. A short history of Zaydī Fiqh. *Leiden Arabic Humanities Blog*. (Zaydī Studies Series, University of Leiden, 15 April). Accessed 6/10/2024. www.leidenarabichumanitiesblog.nl/articles/a-short-history-of-Zaydī-fiqh

Hünefeld K. 2011. The imām is responsible for me before God! — The dimension of protection (dhimma) granted by Imām Yaḥyā to the Jews of Yemen. Pages lxxxii–cii in A. Oettinger & D. Bar-Maoz, *Mittuv Yosef: Yosef Tobi Jubilee Volume*. ii. *The Jews of Yemen: History and culture*. Haifa: University of Haifa.

Hünefeld K. 2023a. *Dhimma im Kontext des Zaiditischen Jemen. Imam Yaḥyā Ḥamīd Al-Dīn (1869–1948), Die Juden: Jüdinnen von Sanaa und die Aushandlung islamrechtlich legitimierter Regierungsführung*. Berlin: De Gruyter.

Hünefeld K. 2023b. Zaydī *fiqh* and the Jews of Yemen. *Leiden Arabic Humanities Blog*. (Zaydī Studies Series, University of Leiden, 2 June). Accessed 6/10/2024. www.leidenarabichumanitiesblog.nl/articles/Zaydī-fiqh-and-the-jews-of-yemen

Ibn Miftāḥ, ʿAbdullāh Abū l-Ḥasan/ed. I.M. b. al-Muaʾayyadī. 1464/2019. *Kitāb al-Muntazaʿ al-muḫtār min al-Ğait al-midrār al-mufattiḥ li-kamāʾim al-Azhār fī fiqh al-aʾimma al-aṭhār* (*Šarḥ al-Azhār*). (9 volumes). Ṣaʿda: Maktabat ahl al-bait.

Klarić T. 2007. Untersuchungen zur politischen Geschichte der Qāsimidischen Dynastie (11./17. JH.). Dissertation zur Erlangung des Doktorgrades der Philosophie an der Georg-August-Universität Göttingen.

Klein-Franke A. 1984. The orphans: Their flight and their immigration to Eretz Israel — A study of a rescue operation. Pages 85–111 in S. Gamliel, M. Caspi & S. Avizemer (eds), *Yemenite paths*. Jerusalem: The Shalom Research Center. [In Hebrew.]

Messick B. 2018. *Sharīʿa scripts: A historical anthropology*. New York: Columbia University Press.

Nini Y. 1991. *The Jews of the Yemen, 1800–1914*. Chur: Harwood Academic Publishers.

Parfitt T. 1998. The imam, the orphans and the Jews. Pages 160–69 in A.D. Crown (ed.), *Noblesse oblige: Essays in honour of David Kessler OBE*. London: Vallentine Mitchell.

Pukhovaia E. 2021. Between sultans and imams: The state and political elites in Yemen (late 15th–middle of 17th century). PhD thesis, Princeton University. http://arks.princeton.edu/ark:/88435/dsp013f462858k

Pukhovaia E. 2023. The Lords of Kawkabān and the transformation of the state in early modern Yemen (15th–17th centuries). *Journal of the Economic and Social History of the Orient* 66/3–4: 289–317.

Qora, ʿA./ed. M. Qoraḥ 5753/1993. *Sa'arat Teiman: A history of Yemenite Jews, their costumes, and ancestral traditions*. Jerusalem: Privately printed. [In Hebrew.]

Sharaf al-Dīn Y. 1442/2021. *Athmār al-Azhār fī fiqh al-āʾimma al-aṭhār*. Preface by I.M. al-Muʾayyadī. Ṣaʿda: Maktabat ahl al-bayt.

al-Shawkānī, Muḥammad b. ʿAlī/ed. Ḥ. Ḥallāq 1461/2000. *Al-Sayl al-jarrār al-mutadaffiq ʿalā ḥadāʾiq al-Azhār*. (3 volumes). Damascus: Dār Ibn Kathīr.

al-Shawkānī, Muḥammad b. ʿAlī/ed. Abū M. Ḥallāq. 1423/2002. *Kitāb al-fatḥ al-Rabbānī min fatāwā al-imām al-Shawkānī*. (10 volumes). Ṣanʿā': Maktabat al-jīl al-jadīd.

al-Shawkānī, M./ed. M. Ḥallāq 1427/2006. *Al-Badr al-Ṭāliʿ Bi-Maḥāsin Man Baʿd al-Qarn al-Sābiʿ*. (2 volumes). Damascus/Beirut: Dār Ibn Kathīr.

Tobi Y. 1990. Conversion to Islam among Yemenite Jews under Zaydī rule — The position of Zaydī law, the imam, and Muslim society. *Peʿamim* 42: 105–126. [In Hebrew.]

Verskin A. 2019. *A vision of Yemen: Travels of a European Orientalist and his native guide, a translation of Hayyim Habshush's travelogue*. Stanford: Stanford University Press.

vom Bruck, G. 2020. al-Kibsī family. *Encyclopaedia of Islam Three Online*. Leiden: Brill. https://referenceworks.brill.com/display/db/ei3o

Wilmers D. 2018. *Beyond schools: Muḥammad b. Ibrāhīm al-Wazīr's (d. 840/1436) epistemology of ambiguity*. Leiden: Brill.

Zabārah M. 1348/1929–1930. *Nayl Al-Waṭar min tarājīm rijāl a-Yaman fī l-qarn al-thālith ʿashar*. (2 volumes). Cairo: al-Maktaba al-ṣalafiyya.

Author's address

Kerstin Hünefeld, Independent researcher, The Hebrew University of Jerusalem.
e-mail kerstinhuenefeld@gmail.com

Proceedings of the Seminar for Arabian Studies 54 (2025): 273–280

The Yemeni Zaydi school of law: a brief history of its textual tradition (third/tenth–tenth/sixteenth century)

Ebrahim Mansoor

Summary

Scholarly interest in Zaydism began in the late nineteenth century, with most research concentrating on its political and social history. In contrast, Zaydi law (*fiqh*) remains comparatively underexplored, with many aspects still awaiting systematic analysis. This paper offers a brief history of the Yemeni Zaydi school of *fiqh* (the *madhhab*), focusing on the development and significance of the famous Zaydi legal text *Kitāb al-Azhār*. It examines the processes of codification and canonization that shaped the text's authority and influence, while also pointing out related areas that warrant further research.

Keywords: Yemen, Zaydism, Zaydi *fiqh*, *madhhab*, *Kitāb al-Azhār*

Introduction

Zaydism, a branch of Shīʿī Islam, initially emerged as a political movement following the failed rebellion of Zayd b. ʿAlī in Kūfa in 122/740 (Haider 2014: 189–215). Zayd, a descendant of the Prophet through ʿAlī b. Abī Ṭālib, was martyred during this uprising. His followers, who came to be known as the Zaydis in his honour, continued to advocate for his cause under the leadership of other members of the Prophet's family (imams). More than a century later, the Zaydis began to develop a distinct theological identity closely tied to their political ideals (Madelung 1965). Concurrently, a body of legal thought attributed to early Zaydi imams began to take shape and was progressively enriched over the subsequent centuries. By the early fifth/tenth century, this corpus of legal opinions had coalesced into the Zaydi school of law (*madhhab*).

From the mid-third/ninth century, the Caspian region (in what is now northern Iran) served as the primary centre of Zaydism until its gradual shift to Yemen in the mid-sixth/twelfth century.[1] Following this relocation, the Zaydi legal tradition experienced substantial development. One of the most significant developments in this trajectory was the composition of *Kitāb al-Azhār*, a succinct 'code-like' text authored in the early ninth/fifteenth century by the famous Zaydi scholar Aḥmad b. Yaḥyā b. al-Murtaḍā (d. 840/1436–1437). This work has maintained its authority and canonical status within the Zaydi legal *madhhab* up to the present day. By examining Zaydi *fiqh* both before and after *Kitāb al-Azhār*, this paper sheds light on the processes of codification and canonization within the Zaydi *madhhab*, thereby revealing broader dynamics underlying the formation and transmission of the Zaydi legal authority.

This paper is structured in two main sections. The first section traces the origins and early development of Zaydi *fiqh* up to the ninth/fifteenth century, offering the necessary historical and scholarly context for understanding the codification of *Kitāb al-Azhār*. The second section examines the canonization of *Kitāb al-Azhār* and its enduring influence on the later legal tradition of the Zaydi *madhhab*.

Towards codification (ninth–fourteenth century)

Given its strong association with modernity, the applicability of the term 'codification' to premodern Islamic legal texts has been questioned by some scholars. However, referring to such texts as 'codes' need not

[1] Compared to the other Muslim communities, the Zaydi community in Yemen is relatively small. It primarily exists in a small geographical area in the northern highlands of the country, predominantly inhabited by a tribal population.

suggest that they conform to the same criteria as modern legal codes,[2] nor that they serve as precursors to early modern legal systems (Hovden 2024: 11; Burak 2019). In the context of Islamic legal history, a legal code can be understood more broadly as a compilation, collection, or enumeration of legal rules that, having gradually acquired authoritative status, are systematically arranged into a concise, coherent, and comprehensive textual form (Hovden 2024: 17; Kooria, forthcoming).

The Zaydi legal *madhhab* is grounded in the opinions and principles of five key imams — a familial cluster centred on Imām al-Hādī ilā l-Ḥaqq, along with his grandfather, uncle, and two sons, Muḥammad and Aḥmad (Haykel & Zysow 2012: 340). Their genealogical connection to the Prophet endowed them with exceptional authority among their followers. During the third/ninth century, their *fatāwā* — legal responses issued in reply to specific queries — were compiled by their students, marking an early effort toward the textual consolidation of Zaydi *fiqh*. This process gave rise to what can be considered the first legal canon of the Zaydi tradition. Because of their foundational role, these imams came to be known in Zaydi sources as *al-muʾassisūn* ('the founders'). The direct transmission and explicit articulation of their legal opinions, whether expressed by the imams themselves or preserved in written form, also led to their designation as *ahl al-naṣṣ* or *ahl al-nuṣūṣ* ('the people of texts').[3]

A key feature of the legal corpus of the *ahl al-naṣṣ* was its limited scope, as it did not offer comprehensive coverage of all areas of *fiqh*. In the fourth/tenth century, a second generation (*ṭabaqa*) of Zaydi scholars emerged in the Caspian region. Among the most prominent figures of this group were Abū l-ʿAbbās Aḥmad b. Ibrāhīm al-Ḥasanī (d. *c.*352/963) and his students, Aḥmad b. al-Ḥusayn al-Hārūnī (al-Muʾayyad bi-llāh, d. 411/1020) and his brother Yaḥyā b. al-Ḥusayn al-Hārūnī (al-Nāṭiq bi-l-Ḥaqq, d. 424/1033). These scholars became known as the *mukharrijūn* because of their practice of *takhrīj* — an analogical process by which they extrapolated legal rulings from the foundational opinions and principles of the *ahl al-naṣṣ* (Haykel & Zysow 2012: 340–341; Ansari & Thiele 2022: 9; Hallaq 2001: 43–56; Jackson 1996: 91–96). Through the systematic application of *takhrīj*, the *mukharrijūn* played a pivotal role in expanding the legal corpus of the *ahl al-naṣṣ*.

Because *takhrīj* was often carried out independently by multiple scholars, the legal opinions derived through this method frequently diverged, leading to internal contradictions (*khilāf*). As a result, it was not uncommon for a single Zaydi imam from the *ahl al-naṣṣ* to be attributed multiple, and sometimes conflicting, legal positions. This phenomenon of *khilāf* became a defining characteristic of the Zaydi legal textual tradition and persisted for centuries.

Beginning in the seventh/thirteenth century, Yemen emerged as the primary centre of the Zaydi *madhhab*, following the large-scale transfer of legal texts from the Caspian region, which later declined as the intellectual hub of Zaydism. This shift gave rise to a third *ṭabaqa* of Zaydi scholars in Yemen, succeeding the *ahl al-naṣṣ* and the *mukharrijūn*. The principal activity of this Yemeni scholarly generation was to address and harmonize the internal contradictions found within the imported Caspian legal tradition by selecting or validating one opinion as the predominant position of the *madhhab* (henceforth the *madhhab*-opinion). The method employed in this evaluative process is described in Zaydi sources as *mudhākara* (Yaḥyā b. al-Ḥusayn 2022: 1:449), a hermeneutical procedure analogous to *taṣḥīḥ* and *tarjīḥ* in the broader Islamic legal tradition (Hallaq 2001: 133–155; Al-Azem 2017: 143–147). The Yemeni scholars who engaged in this practice became known as the *mudhākirūn*. Among the most prominent figures in this group were al-Amīr ʿAlī b. al-Ḥusayn (d. *c.*650/1252), Yaḥyā b. al-Ḥasan b. al-Baḥaybiḥ (d. *c.*730/1330), ʿAlī b. Yaḥyā al-Wishalī (d. 787/1386), and al-Ḥasan b. Muḥammad al-Naḥwī (d. 791/1389). Collectively, the *mudhākirūn*, alongside the *ahl al-naṣṣ* and *mukharrijūn*, came to constitute a tripartite structure of legal authority within the Zaydi *madhhab*.

While the *mudhākirūn* played a crucial role in validating the *madhhab*-opinion, they did not eliminate legal plurality altogether. Less authoritative or secondary opinions continued to accompany the *madhhab*-opinion within their legal writings. Indeed, the *mudhākirūn* often presented these divergences in a comparative format, sometimes even broadening the scope of *khilāf* by incorporating opinions from non-Zaydi legal traditions. Within this comparative framework, the *madhhab*-opinion they endorsed typically served as the central

[2] A code is the product of the 'codification' process, but the latter can also refer to both the product and the process.

[3] The literal translation of this phrase is 'people of texts'; texts do not mean books in this context, but rather the direct written statements or opinions of these imams.

point of comparison. This approach reflects an effort to move toward codification while preserving the discursive richness and interpretive openness characteristic of the Zaydi legal tradition.

The rise of *Kitāb al-Azhār*

By this stage, the *mukhtaṣar* genre — concise legal manuals intended for basic teaching and judicial practice — was still scarcely represented within the Zaydi legal tradition. In contrast to the writings of the *mudhākirūn*, which were primarily composed in the genres of *khilāf* (comparative legal analysis) and *shurūḥ* (commentaries), *mukhtaṣar* works aimed to streamline and standardize legal rulings, significantly reducing internal plurality (Fadel 1996; Ibrahim 2015; Oberauer 2022). The emergence of this genre marked a pivotal development in the movement towards codification within the Zaydi *madhhab*.

In the early ninth/fifteenth century, the prominent Zaydi scholar Aḥmad b. Yaḥyā Ibn al-Murtaḍā (d. 840/1436–1437) identified the absence of a *mukhtaṣar* within the Zaydi legal tradition of his time as a significant impediment to students' ability to learn and memorize the *fiqh* of *Ahl al-Bayt* (the Prophet's family). In response, he undertook the composition of a *mukhtaṣar* that, in his view, would be widely circulated among students and facilitate both memorization and accurate transmission of legal knowledge (Ibn al-Murtaḍā 1690: fo. 2a). This statement underscores the explicitly educational aim of Ibn al-Murtaḍā's text, which he titled *Kitāb al-Azhār fī fiqh al-aʾimma al-aṭhār* (Ibn al-Murtaḍā 2013).

According to the biographical account of Ibn al-Murtaḍā, *Kitāb al-Azhār* was based on an earlier work he had compiled during his formative studies of *fiqh*. In that earlier compilation, he collected the contradictory opinions he encountered in the writings of the *mudhākirūn*. However, when composing *Kitāb al-Azhār*, Ibn al-Murtaḍā deliberately set aside these contradictions and included only those legal positions that had been validated by the *mudhākirūn* (al-Ḥasan 1653: fo. 123). He presented the validated opinions in a systematic, concise, and coherent sequence, separated only by *wa* ('and') (Hovden 2019: 159). This methodological shift underscores his intention to produce a more unified and authoritative legal text.

To demonstrate the type of content included in *Kitāb al-Azhār*, consider the legal issue of *zawjat al-mafqūd* — a woman whose husband is missing, and whose status (alive or dead) remains unknown. The central legal question concerns whether, under this condition of uncertainty, she may lawfully remarry. According to the explicit opinion of Imām al-Hādī ilā l-Ḥaqq (*naṣṣ*), a *zawjat al-mafqūd* is not permitted to remarry unless there is *yaqīn* (certainty) regarding her husband's death, divorce, or apostasy (al-Hādī ilā l-Ḥaqq 2023: 328). While this opinion has come to form the *madhhab*-opinion as validated by the *mudhākirūn*, they disagreed over what constitutes sufficient grounds for establishing such certainty.

In *al-Tadhkira al-fākhira* (al-Naḥwī 2006), the aforementioned al-Ḥasan b. Muḥammad al-Naḥwī begins his discussion of this issue by presenting the *madhhab*-opinion, which holds that certainty must be established either through *tawātur* (multiple transmissions) or the testimony of *shahīdān ʿadlān* (two trustworthy male witnesses). He then compares this position with a less authoritative opinion that permits reliance on the testimony of a *khabar ʿadl* (a single trustworthy narrator). This alternative opinion was originally derived through *takhrīj* by al-Muʾayyad bi-llāh and was later upheld by influential Zaydi jurists such as Qāḍī Jaʿfar (d. 573/1177) and Imām al-Manṣūr ʿAbdallāh b. Ḥamza (d. 614/1217). In *Kitāb al-Azhār*, however, Ibn al-Murtaḍā disregards this minority opinion and includes only *tawātur* and *shahāda kāmila* (an equivalent term for *shahīdān ʿadlān*) as legitimate means for establishing certainty in the case of the *zawjat al-mafqūd* (Ibn al-Murtaḍā 2013: 95). This selective approach reflects a deliberate narrowing of legal options in the interest of standardization and codification.

The conservatism of *Kitāb al-Azhār*

Ibn al-Murtaḍā adopted a notably conservative approach in the composition of *Kitāb al-Azhār*. He limited the content of the work to legal opinions that had been validated by the *mudhākirūn* and attributed specifically to Imām al-Hādī ilā l-Ḥaqq. This 'conservatism' should not be understood in its modern political sense, but rather as a methodological commitment to preserving a particular selection of rulings grounded in traditional sources, while deliberately excluding more recent or innovative opinions. Ibn al-Murtaḍā adhered strictly and consistently to this approach throughout the text, even when he personally disagreed with many of the opinions he chose to include.

In the case of the *zawjat al-mafqūd*, for instance, when the woman is unable to meet the evidentiary requirements of *tawātur* or *shahāda kāmila*, al-Naḥwī first cites the opinion of Imām al-Hādī's son, Muḥammad. According to this view, if the wife cannot establish *yaqīn* through either method, she must wait for a period equivalent to her husband's natural lifespan, which is set at 120 years. Ibn al-Murtaḍā, however, expressed disagreement with the *mudhākirūn* over the literal application of this 120-year waiting period. He argued that the duration was not a legal requirement in itself, but rather a means by which the wife might come to believe that her husband is no longer alive. Once such a belief arises, he maintained, the waiting period becomes unnecessary and immediately stops. He writes:

> وأعلم أن المذاكرين يزعمون أنه متى مضى العمر الطبيعي جاز لها أن تزوج ولو لم يحصل لها ظن بموته وهو ضعيف من وجهين أحدهما أنه لا وجه لتربصها هذه المدة إلا ليحصل لها الظن بموته، لأنه لا دليل على تحديد المدة من كتاب ولا سنة رأسا ...

> 'Note that the *mudhākirūn* claim that once the husband's natural lifespan has passed, she is permitted to remarry even if she has merely developed a suspicion of his death. This is weak for two reasons. The first is that there is no justification for her to wait such a lengthy period except to arrive at a suspicion of his death, as there is no evidence from either the Qur'ān or the Sunnah specifying this duration' (Ibn al-Murtaḍā 1690: fo. 386b).

Furthermore, Ibn al-Murtaḍā criticized the *takhrīj*-based opinion of the aforementioned ʿAlī b. Yaḥyā al-Wishalī. According to the *madhhab*-opinion, the completion of the husband's natural lifespan serves merely as a *qarīna* (pl. *qarāʾin*; circumstantial indicators) of his death. Al-Wishalī, however, extended the use of *qarāʾin*, arguing that a wife could rely on any such indicator to establish the termination of the marriage — whether by death, divorce, or apostasy — rather than limiting its application solely to death, as prescribed by the *madhhab*-opinion. In this line of reasoning, recognizing the husband's handwriting in a divorce document, for example, could constitute a valid *qarīna* indicating divorce. Ibn al-Murtaḍā rejected this interpretation and questioned the attribution of such a view to al-Muʾayyad bi-llāh, stating:

> فلا وجه لما حكاه الفقيه علي عن المؤيد بالله أنه يعمل بالقرائن على الإطلاق، فأما تخريجه له عن مسألة الكتاب بالطلاق فضعيف وذلك لأنه قد شرط أن يكون فيه أمارة صحيحة والأمارة الصحيحة هناك هي أن يكون لزوجها خط تعرفه ...

> 'There is no basis for what the jurist ʿAlī has reported from al-Muʾayyad bi-llāh that he accepted indicators [*qarāʾin*] in an unrestricted sense. As for his *takhrīj* from the case of the divorce document, it is weak, because al-Muʾayyad bi-llāh explicitly stipulated that the indicator must be reliable [*amāra ṣaḥīḥa*]. In that specific context, the reliable indicator is that her husband has a known handwriting' (Ibn al-Murtaḍā 1690: fo. 387a).

Several interconnected factors may help explain the conservative nature of *Kitāb al-Azhār*. One plausible interpretation is that Ibn al-Murtaḍā sought to defend the traditional Zaydi *madhhab* against the growing influence of the Sunni-oriented current. Over the centuries, Zaydi scholars engaged extensively with the Sunni legal and hadith literature, often incorporating Sunni texts into the Zaydi curriculum (Ansari & Schmidtke 2017: 171–180). Moreover, close readings of the Zaydi legal texts from this period reveal frequent citations of Sunni hadith collections. However, this engagement was largely instrumental: rather than adopting Sunni doctrines wholesale, Zaydi scholars typically employed Sunni hadith selectively, using them to reinforce already established Zaydi legal opinions (Haykel 2003: 9).

Recent scholarship has identified a shift occurring in the early ninth/fifteenth century — precisely around the time *Kitāb al-Azhār* was composed — marked by a heightened Sunni influence on the Zaydi *madhhab*. This phenomenon has often been described through the framework of the 'Sunnisation of Zaydism' (Cook 2010: 247; Haykel 2003: 10–11; Wilmers 2018: 9), a term that refers to the gradual adoption of Sunni doctrines by certain Zaydi scholars. In this context, the conservative orientation of *Kitāb al-Azhār* may be interpreted not merely as pedagogical or traditionalist, but as a conscious response to this reformist, Sunni-influenced trajectory — a textual effort to reaffirm and codify the distinctiveness of Zaydi legal identity.

Building the canon (fourteenth–sixteenth century)

The applicability of the Western term 'canonization' to the study of the Islamic textual tradition remains a subject of scholarly debate. However, when applied specifically to legal traditions, the term may be usefully understood in a more focused sense. In this context, canonization refers to the process by which a particular rule — or more commonly, a collection of rules — is declared to be canonical, meaning that it is recognized as authoritative by a specific community or legal authority (Hovden 2024: 17).

The afterlife of *Kitāb al-Azhār* suggests that Ibn al-Murtaḍā's conservative project had a lasting impact on the broader Zaydi community and its legal tradition. Beyond its use as a textbook in educational contexts, *Kitāb al-Azhār* became the subject of numerous commentaries, authored not only by scholars closely associated with Ibn al-Murtaḍā but also by those beyond his immediate intellectual circle (Mansoor 2025). This widespread scholarly engagement reflects the recognition of *Kitāb al-Azhār* as the canonical legal text of the Zaydi *madhhab*.

The most renowned commentary on *Kitāb al-Azhār* is *al-Muntazaʿ al-mukhtār min al-ghayth al-midrār al-mufattiḥ li-kamāʾim al-Azhār* — commonly known as *Sharḥ al-Azhār* — authored by ʿAbdallāh b. Abī al-Qāsim Ibn Miftāḥ (d. 877/1472). The reasons for the widespread recognition and enduring authority of *Sharḥ al-Azhār* remain a subject of scholarly inquiry. The Zaydi historian Ibn Abī l-Rijāl implicitly attributed the commentary's success to a special intellectual and spiritual affinity between Ibn Miftāḥ and Ibn al-Murtaḍā. He recounts a dream in which Ibn Miftāḥ saw Ibn al-Murtaḍā using an iron shovel to fill holes in a piece of land, after which Ibn Miftāḥ took the shovel and continued the task himself. This symbolic imagery portrays Ibn Miftāḥ as the natural successor to Ibn al-Murtaḍā — one entrusted with the transmission, refinement, and elaboration of his canonical work (Ibn Abī l-Rijāl 2004, iii: 119).

From this period onwards, scholarly engagement increasingly centred on *Sharḥ al-Azhār*, particularly through the genre of *ḥawāshī* (marginal glosses). These *ḥawāshī* functioned as a multi-authored, interpretive layer written around the margins of *Sharḥ al-Azhār*. Rather than composing new, independent commentaries, scholars interacted with *Kitāb al-Azhār* by commenting on it indirectly through its authoritative commentary. Structurally, this created a three-tiered textual apparatus: *Kitāb al-Azhār* as the *matn* (base text), *Sharḥ al-Azhār* as the first layer of commentary, and the *ḥawāshī* as a third, marginal layer. Over time, this marginal commentary tradition itself became increasingly standardized and, in certain instances, attained a degree of canonicity in its own right (Hovden, forthcoming). The *matn* or base text remained remarkably stable over time, with any changes eventually relegated to the status of *ḥawāshī*. In what follows, I examine two notable attempts to change elements of the *matn*.

Hidāyat al-afkār

In 907/1501, the prominent Zaydi scholar Ibrāhīm b. Muḥammad al-Wazīr (Ṣārim al-Dīn, d. 914/1508), a descendant of the same family branch as Muḥammad b. Ibrāhīm al-Wazīr — who is widely regarded as the first Zaydi scholar to advocate the Sunni-influenced legal reform — composed a *mukhtaṣar* entitled *Hidāyat al-afkār ilā maʿānī l-Azhār* (al-Wazīr 1645; *Ṭabaqāt*, 1: 80–89). In this *mukhtaṣar*, Ṣārim al-Dīn articulated his own legal opinions, diverging in key respects from those presented in *Kitāb al-Azhār*. A notable example appears in his treatment of *zawjat al-mafqūd*, where he accepted the testimony of a single trustworthy witness as sufficient grounds to dissolve the marriage (al-Wazīr 1645: fo. 46b). As previously discussed, this position stands in direct contrast to the *madhhab*-opinion codified in *Kitāb al-Azhār*.

There appears to have been considerable interest in copying *Hidāyat al-afkār*, particularly during the eleventh/seventeenth century. A survey of manuscript collections reveals seven copies in the online library of Muʾassasat al-Imām Zayd and three in the British Library (al-ʿAmrī 2006: 278–80; Rieu 1894: 236–237),[4] all dating between 1001/1593 and 1102/1690. Several of these manuscripts contain *ḥawāshī*, indicating a degree

[4] The numbers given to the manuscripts in the library of Muʾassasat al-Imām Zayd are as follows: ZA: 019-04, ZA: 108-06, ZA: 129-06, ZA: 265-05, ZA: 375-05, ZA: 482-05, ZA: 639-05.

of scholarly engagement with the text. Despite this interest, however, *Hidāyat al-afkār* does not appear to have achieved the same level of prominence as *Kitāb al-Azhār*, particularly when comparing the number of extant manuscript copies of both works from the same period.[5] This disparity suggests that while *Hidāyat al-afkār* was received with some enthusiasm, it ultimately failed to challenge the canonical status of *Kitāb al-Azhār*.

Athmār al-Azhār

In 941/1555, Ṣārim al-Dīn's student — and the grandson of Ibn al-Murtaḍā — Imām Yaḥyā Sharaf al-Dīn b. Shams al-Dīn (r. 912/1506–965/1558) composed another *mukhtaṣar* titled *Athmār al-Azhār fī fiqh al-aʾimma al-aṭhār* (Shams al-Dīn 2021; al-Mufaḍḍal 2012). In this work, Imām Yaḥyā Sharaf al-Dīn introduced a number of substantive revisions to the legal positions found in *Kitāb al-Azhār*. Regarding the issue of the *zawjat al-mafqūd*, for example, he made two notable changes.

The first change relates to the 120-year waiting period requirement. On this specific issue, Imām Yaḥyā Sharaf al-Dīn aligned with his grandfather's own opinion that the prescribed duration is not inherently binding, but rather functions as a means to cultivate the wife's belief that her husband is no longer alive (Ibn al-Murtaḍā 1690: fo. 387b). Ibn al-Murtaḍā articulated this opinion in his works *al-Ghayth al-midrār* and *al-Baḥr al-Zakhkhār*, while reserving *Kitāb al-Azhār* for the *madhhab*-opinion. In contrast, Imām Yaḥyā incorporated this interpretation directly into *Athmār al-Azhār*, making his dissenting position explicit and visible within the *mukhtaṣar* itself (Shams al-Dīn 2021: 95).

The second change concerns the use of *qarīna* in establishing the termination of a marriage. As noted earlier, Ibn al-Murtaḍā had expressed strong reservations about al-Wishalī's *takhrīj*-based opinion, which permitted the use of any *qarīna*, not just the expiration of the husband's natural lifespan, as evidence for death, divorce, or apostasy. In *Kitāb al-Azhār*, Ibn al-Murtaḍā omitted al-Wishalī's view altogether, preserving only the *madhhab*-opinion, which restricts the use of *qarīna* to death alone and excludes its applicability in cases of divorce or apostasy. By contrast, in *Athmār al-Azhār*, Imām Yaḥyā Sharaf al-Dīn not only diverged from his grandfather's position but also explicitly incorporated and endorsed al-Wishalī's opinion (Shams al-Dīn 2021: 95).

These two examples of change — among ten changes introduced by Imām Yaḥyā Sharaf al-Dīn only in the chapter on *nikāḥ* (marriage) — demonstrate a marked shift away from the strict conservation of canonical consensus towards a more open assertion of alternative views within the main legal text. By endorsing his grandfather's view, Imām Yaḥyā shifted the focus from a rigid temporal requirement to a more subjective assessment, thereby reshaping how this particular ruling might be interpreted and applied. Moreover, by adopting al-Wishalī's *takhrīj*, which allows for a broader range of conjectural indicators in all cases of marital termination, he reinforced the case for greater flexibility in legal reasoning, particularly in contexts characterized by uncertainty. These revisions underscore an important moment of contestation in the process of canonization, reflecting both continuity and resistance within the Zaydi legal tradition.

With the rise of *Athmār al-Azhār*, scholarly attention began to shift towards this new *mukhtaṣar*. Among the most notable commentaries on the text were *al-Wābil al-mighzār* by Yaḥyā b. Muḥammad al-Muqrāʾī (d. c.990/1582) and *Taftīḥ al-qulūb* by his teacher Muḥammad b. Yaḥyā b. Bahrān (d. 957/1550). However, there are indications that Imām Yaḥyā Sharaf al-Dīn actively promoted an enthusiastic reception of his *mukhtaṣar*. Evidence also suggests that he imposed restrictions to ensure that judges adhered to *Athmār al-Azhār*, thereby reinforcing its authority within the Zaydi legal tradition (Mansoor 2025).

Following Imām Yaḥyā's death in 965/1558, the momentum behind *Athmār al-Azhār* came to a complete stop. The changes he introduced were gradually absorbed into the *ḥawāshī* tradition surrounding *Kitāb al-Azhār*, rather than displacing it. This transition paved the way for the renewed prominence of *Kitāb al-Azhār* and from around 1600 onwards, scholarly attention once again coalesced around it through the medium of marginal commentary. Since that time, *Kitāb al-Azhār* has retained its position as the canonical legal text of the Zaydi *madhhab*, a status it continues to hold to this day.

[5] For a survey on the number of manuscript copies produced for *Kitāb al-Azhār* during this period, see Hovden, forthcoming.

Conclusion

This article has traced the historical development of the Zaydi legal *madhhab*'s textual tradition through the lenses of codification and canonization. In the first section, we examined how the early legal opinions of the *ahl al-naṣṣ*, the expansion of that corpus through *takhrīj* by the *mukharrijūn* and the evaluative work of the *mudhākirūn*, gradually laid the groundwork for codification. This culminated in the composition of *Kitāb al-Azhār* by Ibn al-Murtaḍā in the early ninth/fifteenth century — a concise and conservative *mukhtaṣar* that deliberately sought to present a unified body of rulings grounded in the legal views of Imām al-Hādī ilā l-Ḥaqq.

The second section shifted focus to the canonization of *Kitāb al-Azhār*, exploring how its reception evolved through layers of commentary, especially the pivotal *Sharḥ al-Azhār* and its accompanying *ḥawāshī*. While challenges to its authority emerged, most notably through *Hidāyat al-afkār* and *Athmār al-Azhār*, these reformist interventions although briefly influential, ultimately failed to displace *Kitāb al-Azhār* from its canonical position. By the early eleventh/seventeenth century, scholarly attention had returned to *Kitāb al-Azhār*, and the tradition of marginal commentary helped reinforce its enduring authority.

Taken together, these developments illustrate how the conservative codification project of Ibn al-Murtaḍā gradually gave way to the canonization of his text *Kitāb al-Azhār*. The authority of *Kitāb al-Azhār* was not only a function of its textual content but also of how it was received, interpreted, institutionalized, and defended over time. Its persistence as the central legal reference in the Zaydi *madhhab* underscores the complex interplay between legal reasoning, textual transmission, and communal authority in the making of Islamic legal canons.

The attempt to explain the conservative nature of *Kitāb al-Azhār* as a response to the emergence of the Sunni-influenced Zaydi reformists in the early ninth/fifteenth century, while plausible, risks oversimplification if the text is not studied within its own intellectual context. Further research is therefore needed better to understand the conservative orientation of *Kitāb al-Azhār* and its relationship to the emerging Sunni trend. One promising avenue of inquiry is to trace the lives and work of the Zaydi scholars who were allegedly influenced by Sunnism, compile their legal writings, and systematically compare them with *Kitāb al-Azhār*. Such a comparative analysis would help reconstruct the formation of the Zaydi legal canon, offering a more detailed picture of which legal rules became canonical, and how — through which processes, actors, and modes of transmission — they entered the canon.

Acknowledgements

This paper builds on my PhD research and was previously presented at the 57th Seminar for Arabian Studies. I would like to thank Eirik Hovden, Christian Mauder, and Jan Thiele for their continued supervision and guidance. I would also like to thank Kerstin Hünefeld and Johann Heiss for their collaboration and insights before and during the Seminar. I am especially thankful to Ekaterina Pukhovaia for her assistance and feedback on this paper. All errors are my own.

References

Al-ʿAmrī Ḥ.ʿA. 2006. *Maṣādir al-turāth al-Yamanī fī l-Maktaba al-Birīṭāniyya*. Damascus: Dār al-Fikr.

Ansari H. & Schmidtke S. 2017. The literary-religious tradition among seventh/thirteenth-century Yemenī Zaydīs (I): The formation of Imām al-Mahdī li-Dīn Allāh Aḥmad b. al-Ḥusayn b. al-Qāsim. Pages 159–192 in H. Ansari & S. Schmidtke, *Studies in medieval Islamic intellectual traditions.* (Resources in Arabic and Islamic Studies). Atlanta, GA: Lockwood Press.

Ansari H. & Thiele J. 2022. Zaydite ḥadīth literature and thought. Available at https://digital.csic.es/bitstream/10261/262083/1/Ansari-Thiele-preprint.pdf

Al-Azem T. 2017. *Rule-formulation and binding precedent in the maḏhab-law tradition: Ibn Quṭlūbuġā's commentary on the compendium of Qudūrī*. Leiden: Brill.

Burak G. 2019. Codification, legal borrowing and the localization of 'Islamic law'. Pages 389–399 in K.A. El Fadl, A.A. Ahmad & S.F. Hassan (eds), *Routledge handbook of Islamic law.* London: Taylor & Francis/Routledge.

Cook M. 2010. *Commanding right and forbidding wrong in Islamic thought*. Cambridge: Cambridge University Press.

Fadel M. 1996. The social logic of *taqlīd* and the rise of the mukhtaṣar. *Islamic Law and Society* 3: 193–233.

Al-Hādī ilā al-Ḥaqq, Yaḥyā b. al-Ḥusayn. 2023. *al-Aḥkām fī al-ḥalāl wa al-ḥarām*. Ṣaʿda: Maktabat Ahl al-Bayt.

Haider N. 2014. *The origins of the Shīʿa: Identity, ritual, and sacred space in eighth-century Kūfa*. New York: Cambridge University Press.

Hallaq W. 2001. *Authority, continuity and change in Islamic law*. New York: Cambridge University Press.

Al-Ḥasan b. Aḥmad, b. Yaḥyā al-Murtaḍā. 1653. Hādhihi sīrat al-Imām al-Mahdī li-dīn Allāh Aḥmad b. Yaḥyā al-Murtaḍā. MS. Princeton University Library.

Haykel B. 2003. *Revival and reform in Islam: The legacy of Muḥammad al-Shawkānī*. Cambridge: Cambridge University Press.

Haykel B. & Zysow A. 2012. What makes a Maḏhab a Maḏhab: Zaydī debates on the structure of legal authority. *Arabica* 59: 332–371.

Hovden E. 2019. *Waqf in Zaydī Yemen: Legal theory, codification and local practice*. Leiden: Brill.

Hovden E. 2024. Understanding and framing change in Islamic law: Potentials and possible pitfalls of the concepts of canonization and codification. *Oxford Journal of Law and Religion* 12/3: 289–313.

Hovden E. (forthcoming). Canonising the code: The authorisation and authorship of Shurūḥ and Ḥawāshī on the *Kitāb al-Azhār* under the early Qāsimī dynasty in Zaydi Yemen (ca. 1600–1700 CE). *Arabica*.

Ibn Abī l-Rijāl, Aḥmad b. Ṣāliḥ b. Muḥammad. 2004. *Maṭlaʿ al-budūr wa-majmaʿ al-buḥūr fī tarājim rijāl al-Zaydiyya*. Ṣaʿda: Markaz Ahl al-Bayt li-l-Dirāsāt al-Islāmiyya.

Ibn-al-Murtaḍā, Aḥmad b. Yaḥyā. 1690. Kitāb al-Ghayth al-midrār al-mufattiḥ li-kamāʾim al-Azhār. MS. Staatsbibliothek zu Berlin.

Ibn al-Murtaḍā, Aḥmad b. Yaḥyā. 2013. *Matn al-Azhār fī fiqh al-Aʾimma al-aṭhār*. Ṣanʿāʾ: Maṭābiʿ al-Ṣafwa.

Ibrahim A.F. 2015. The codification episteme in Islamic juristic discourse between inertia and change. *Islamic Law and Society* 22: 157–220.

Jackson S.A. 1996. Taqlīd, legal scaffolding and the scope of legal injunctions in post-formative theory muṭlaq and ʿāmm in the jurisprudence of Shihāb al-Dīn al-Qarāfī. *Islamic Law and Society* 3: 165–192.

Kooria M. (forthcoming). 'If al-Ghazālī is a Prophet, the Wajīz is His Miracle': Abū Ḥāmid al-Ghazālī's codification of Shāfiʿī law. *Arabica*.

Madelung W. 1965. *Der Imam al-Qāsim ibn Ibrāhīm und die Glaubenslehre der Zaiditen*. Berlin: Walter de Gruyter & Co.

Mansoor E. 2025. The Yemeni Zaydi school of law: A study of its scholarly and textual history. PhD thesis, University of Bergen. [Unpublished.]

Al-Mufaḍḍal, Muḥammad b. Ibrāhīm b. 2012. *al-Sulūk al-dhahabiyya fī khulāṣat al-sīra al-Mutwakkiliyya*. Jiddah: Maktabat al-Malik Fahd al-Waṭaniyya.

Al-Naḥwī, al-Ḥaṣan b. Muḥammad. 2006. *al-Tadhkira al-fākhira fī fiqh al-ʿitra al-ṭāhira*. Ṣanʿāʾ: Markiz al-Turāth wa-l-Buḥūth al-Yamanī.

Oberauer N. 2022. Canonization in Islamic law: A case study based on Shāfiʿī literature. *Islamic Law and Society* 29: 123–208.

Rieu C. 1894. *Supplement to the catalogue of the Arabic manuscripts in the British Museum*. London: The British Museum.

Schmidtke S. 2012. The history of Zaydī studies. An introduction. *Arabica* 59: 185–199.

Shams al-Dīn, Yaḥyā Sharaf al-Dīn. 2021. *Athmār al-Azhār fī fiqh al-Aʾimma al-aṭhār*. Ṣaʿda: Maktabat Ahl al-Bayt.

Al-Wazīr, Ṣārim al-Dīn Ibrāhīm b. Muḥammad. 1645. Hidāyat al-afkār ilā maʿānī al-Azhār. Maktabat al-Imām Zayd, ZA: 639-02.

Wilmers D. 2018. *Beyond schools: Muḥammad b. Ibrāhīm al-Wazīr's (d. 840/1436) epistemology of ambiguity*. Leiden: Brill.

Yaḥyā b. al-Ḥusayn. 2022. *Kitāb al-ṭabaqāt fī dhikr faḍl al-ʿulamāʾ wa-ʿilmihim wa-muṣannafātihim al-maʿrūf bi-ism al-mustaṭāb*. Ṣanʿāʾ: Markiz al-Turāth wa-l-Buḥūth al-Yamanī.

Author's address

Ebrahim Mansoor, Department of Foreign Language, Faculty of Humanities, University of Bergen, Harald Hårfagres gate 1, 5007 Bergen, Norway.
e-mail ebrahimansor@gmail.com

Proceedings of the Seminar for Arabian Studies 54 (2025): 281–285

Transfer of power in the Sharaf al-Dīn imamate (912–980/1506–1573): theory and practice

Ekaterina Pukhovaia

Summary

The tension between the meritocratic principle underlying Zaydi political theory that prevented the formation of dynasties, and the practical need to stabilize the transfer of power between rulers was constant throughout the pre-modern history of the Zaydi imamate. The demand for a stabilized transfer of power became particularly strong when the imamate expanded its territory and developed a broader support base. This article analyses the development of dynasticism in Zaydi Yemen by focusing on a unique document from the period of rule of Imām al-Mutawakkil ʿalā-llāh Yaḥyā Sharaf al-Dīn (d. 965/1557), the first Zaydi imam to rule over both Upper and Lower Yemen. The document contains a will (*waṣīyah)* composed during the plague of 933/1527. It demonstrates how the Zaydi political elite sought to ensure hereditary transfer of power. The paper contextualizes this unique document, preserved in a single manuscript of a biography (*sīrah*) of imam Yaḥyā Sharaf al-Dīn, in the broader context of sixteenth-century political transformation in Yemen.

Keywords: Yemen, Zaydism, political theory, dynasty, elites

Introduction

The Zaydi imamate was founded in northern Yemen by Imām al-Hādī ilā-l-ḥaqq Yaḥyā (d. 298/911). Throughout its millennium-long history it underwent significant political transformations, ranging from territorial expansion and contraction to the restructuring of the institution of the imamate itself under the Qasimid dynasty (Haykel 2003). One transformation that appears of particular importance to the changing architecture of the Zaydi imamate is the practice of succession. Classical Zaydi theory made no provisions for a hereditary transfer of power and prohibited it, insisting instead on a meritocratic method of leader selection, in which a candidate-imam issued a call to the imamate (*daʿwah*). At the same time, the socio-political development of the Zaydi state necessitated stability in moments of transition. To approach this topic the paper analyses how the question of transfer of power and succession was addressed in the Sharaf al-Dīn imamate (912–980/1506–1573), the last pre-Ottoman Zaydi state in Yemen. This Zaydi polity integrated territories that were traditionally in Sunni (Shāfiʿī) hands, thus disposing of larger economic revenue and a more diverse population than its predecessors. In such a setting, questions of power transfer became more urgent to resolve than ever before.

Previous attempts to form a dynasty

A table of contents from *Tatimmat Kitāb al-ifādah fī tārīkh al-aʾimmah al-sādah*, a collection of biographies of Yemeni Zaydi imams, provides a clear overview of succession in the imamate from the eleventh to the sixteenth century (al-Ḥibshī: f. 48a). An attentive reader will notice that, with a few exceptions, sons rarely followed fathers as imams (Pukhovaia 2017: 181–182). This information is confirmed in other Yemeni Zaydi sources (al-Zuḥayf 2002). Despite this historical record, there were multiple attempts to form Zaydi dynasties throughout the history of the imamate in Yemen. Families of descendants of the Prophet, *sādāh* (sing. *sayyid*), who were the only group eligible to lead the Zaydi imamate, repeatedly sought to concentrate power in their hands. In fact, descendants of Imam al-Hādī ilā-l-ḥaqq consistently held power in the Yemeni Zaydi imamate in the first century of its existence (al-Zuḥayf 2002: 632–664). As the Yemeni Zaydi imamate strengthened and survived against all odds, competition for the imamate increased and dynastic transmission of power became more difficult to sustain.

This trend seems to have intensified from the thirteenth century onwards, a period that ushered increased bureaucratization of the Zaydi imamate in response to competition from the Sunni powers in South Yemen, including the Rasulids and the Tahirids. The greater involvement of tribal and *sayyid* elites in the developing Zaydi state led to increased competition for the position of imam and resulted in a decrease of successful dynastic power transfers in the Zaydi imamate between the thirteenth and sixteenth centuries. It is in this period that we witness the rise of powerful *sayyid* clans: the Banū Ḥamza, who were descendants of Imam al-Manṣūr ʿAbdallāh b. Ḥamza (d. 614/1217), the Banū al-Wazīr, and the al-Muʾayyadī family based in Ṣaʿdah.

Sharaf al-Dīn history and historiography

Imam al-Mutawakkil Yaḥyā Sharaf al-Dīn came to power in 912/1506. He spent the next three decades expanding the Zaydi imamate beyond its geographical constraints of the northern highlands. This expansion became possible after the Egyptian Mamluk invasion of Yemen in 1517 that removed the Tahirid dynasty from power (Serjeant 1983: 68–69). With their gunpowder weapons, previously unseen in Yemen, the Mamluks changed the balance of power in the region. However, 1517 was also the year in which the Egyptian Mamluk sultanate was conquered by the Ottomans. As a result, shortly after their conquest, the Mamluks found themselves stranded in Yemen (Serjeant 1983: 68–69). Imam Yaḥyā Sharaf al-Dīn, who located in the vicinity of Sana'a, in the region of Ḥajjah, stepped into this vacuum of power. With the Tahirids removed and some of the defeated Mamluks joining his army, he held the biggest political and military force in Yemen at the time. Not only the territorial expansion, but also the institutional development of this period made a break with the patterns of preceding Zaydi imams. This is especially visible in the way this imam approached the question of power transfer.

Until recently our knowledge of this early modern imamate's history has been based on sources compiled more than a century after these events, including the biography (*sīrah*) of the imam written by Imam Yaḥyā Sharaf al-Dīn's descendant Ibn al-Mufaḍḍal (d. 1085/1674) (Ibn al-Mufaḍḍal 2012). This biography is in fact an abridgement of at least four previously unstudied sources contemporaneous with Imam Yaḥyā Sharaf al-Dīn, compiled by court historians in the circle of the imam. With these new sources we can revise the events of Sharaf al-Dīn's history, particularly the question of succession.

The will of Imam Yaḥyā Sharaf al-Dīn

Al-Murhibī's incomplete biography of the imam is one of the recently discovered biographical sources on the early Sharaf al-Dīn imamate. It contains a unique document that does not survive in any other sources -- a will (*waṣīyah*) of Imam Yaḥyā Sharaf al-Dīn, written in 933/1527 (al-Murhibī: 250a–268b). That year Yemen was hit by an epidemic (*ṭāʿūn*) (Ibn Luṭfallāh 2003: 75). The will appears to have emerged as a political and legal solution to this situation of crisis. Uniquely to Zaydi historiography, it contains provisions to appoint an heir to the imam. Wills composed by other imams survive, but examples from the medieval period tend to deal with questions of piety, rather than political appointments (al-Ḥusaynī 1992, iii: 151–153).

The text introducing the will of Imam Yaḥyā Sharaf al-Dīn and the will itself cite the epidemic as the cause of its composition (al-Murhibī: 248b–249b, 264a). One can accept this reasoning, especially considering memories of the devastating epidemic (*ṭāʿūn*) of 840/1436, during which Imam Yaḥyā Sharaf al-Dīn's paternal grandfather, Imam al-Mahdī Aḥmad Ibn al-Murtaḍā, died (al-Zuḥayf 2002: 1091). It is not impossible that Yaḥyā Sharaf al-Dīn saw this as the right moment to put in place reassurances for his family and his elites that the state and its institutions would remain intact. There is, however, at least one other possible explanation for the motivation behind this document. In 929/1523 the opponent of Imam Yaḥyā Sharaf al-Dīn, Imam al-Nāṣir Ḥasan b. ʿIzz al-Dīn al-Muʾayyadī of Ṣaʿdah, died (al-Zuḥayf 2002: 1376, 1379). Immediately after his death, even though his son Majd al-Dīn issued his call to the imamate (*daʿwah*) and received support from the Ṣaʿdah elites, the validity of the Muʾayyadī family's claim to rule was open to question. Imam Yaḥyā Sharaf al-Dīn could have seen in this situation an opening to affirm the validity of his own family's claim to power. Simultaneously, he also needed to define what made his arrangements for dynastic transfer of power different from those of the Muʾayyadī family. These complex motivations probably informed the composition of the will.

Imam Yaḥyā Sharaf al-Dīn anticipated resistance to this document and approached the framing of his innovative ideas in a cautious way. Half of the will deals with topics of property, the foundation of family *waqf* (charitable endowment), and the separation of the property of the imam as a person from state property (al-Murhibī: 252a–260b). This section is followed by the 'political' section (al-Murhibī: 260b–263a). It opens with a description of the functions and responsibilities of the will's executioner (*wāṣī*). The document then deals with the question of eligibility for the imamate. Here, Imam Yaḥyā Sharaf al-Dīn appears as an innovator of Zaydi political theory as he introduces, in addition to the classical categories of the fully eligible imam (*sābiq*) and a 'placeholder imam' (*muḥtasib*), a new category of ruler, the 'competent person' (*ṣāḥib al-ṣalāḥīyah*). This type of ruler, according to the will, is a person apt in affairs of the state, including civil administration and war. The term itself is an innovation, even though it appears linked to the notion of public interest (*maṣlaḥah*). Following this theoretical intervention that is supported by opinions from Zaydi scholars and a broad reference to the Shāfiʿī school, Imam Yaḥyā Sharaf al-Dīn argues that his age is characterized by the absence of the *sābiq* and *muḥtasib* categories, and therefore only the 'competent person' chosen by the imam can become the next ruler. He then names his eldest son al-Muṭahhar as his heir and *ṣāḥib al-ṣalāḥīyah* (al-Murhibī: f. 263a).

The will proceeds to explain the mechanism of power transfer and the contours of the state led by a *ṣāḥib al-ṣalāḥīyah* (al-Murhibī: ff. 263a–265b). It seeks to lay the foundation for a stable political regime. To this end, Imām Yaḥyā Sharaf al-Dīn stressed two themes. One focused on the consultative relationship (*iʿtimād*, reliance and approval) between the ruler and the elite. As such, the document acts as a guarantee that al-Muṭahhar and the Sharaf al-Dīn elite will support each other. It mentions that al-Muṭahhar respects his father's advisors – the imam states 'I am convinced he will easily accept what the nobles will order' (*atayaqqanu minhu suhūlata qubūli mā yaʾmuru bihi ʾl-fuḍalāʾ*). The second theme Imām Yaḥyā Sharaf al-Dīn sought to address was that of potential sources of instability. Central among those were competition between siblings and the possibility that the imam's chosen heir would die in the epidemic. Therefore, the will guarantees that the brothers of al-Muṭahhar will support him and, should he die, will take his place. It is this concluding provision that indicates the family-centred character of power transfer that the imam envisioned.

At the same time, the will avoided open discussion of the fact that it was in essence laying a legal foundation for a dynasty. The text presents the new type of heir as a category of ruler who is not an imam. It also records criticisms of the decision in the form of questions (*masāʾil*) that the imam responded to (al-Murhibī: 266a). Finally, Imam Yaḥyā Sharaf al-Dīn appears not to be envisioning the continuation of his state beyond the generation of his sons (al-Murhibī: 265b).

Imam Yaḥyā Sharaf al-Dīn's will illustrates how the institutional development of the newly expanded Zaydi state necessitated a revision of foundational political principles. The new Zaydi state, with a vast Sunni population and access to trade routes, had become richer than its predecessors. This meant that the question of what defined this polity as a Zaydi state became more acute, not least with the existence of an alternative -- the Ṣaʿdah imams of the Muʾayyadī family. The will can be seen as part of this response, an explanation of the envisioned developmental path of the Zaydi imamate. The focal point of this development was the increased political role of the elites, who were recognized as the guarantors of power transfer from the imam to his sons and as the only group invested with the power to decide on the next imam.

Consequences of the 933/1527 will

Although the 933/1527 will has survived only as a single copy, which one could take as a sign of irrelevance, the attempt at restructuring the Zaydi state and formulating dynastic principles that it recorded had far-reaching consequences.

Al-Muṭahhar continued his rise to the pinnacle of power in the years following the composition of the document. He led most of his father's military campaigns, ranging from southward expeditions to Zabīd and Aden to clashes with the Ismāʿīlis of Ḥarāz and the conquest of the northern regions around Ṣaʿdah. His importance in the Sharaf al-Dīn imamate is reflected in his titles -- Fighter in the Path of God (*mujāhid fī sabīl allāh*), Pride of the World and of the Faith (*fakhr al-dunyā wa-ʾl-dīn*), Conqueror for Truth (*al-nāṣir li-l-ḥaqq*) (al-Zurayqī: 3a). Eventually, his rise to power led to conflicts with his father. The tension seems to have intensified after the conquest of Ṣaʿdah and was probably related to the integration of more conservative Zaydi circles into the Sharaf al-Dīn imamate.

In 948/1541 Imām Yaḥyā Sharaf al-Dīn revised his will. He chose a different son to become heir, claiming that he was more eligible. In response, al-Muṭahhar rose against his father in revolt. This led to a protracted succession crisis in the Sharaf al-Dīn imamate. During this crisis al-Muṭahhar succeeded in keeping his political status. In 953/1546 the imam revised his decision that led to the conflict and offered a compromise. As a result, the imamate was divided into dominions between his sons (al-Sharafī: 33a). After this succession crisis, the imam and his son reached a reconciliation and al-Muṭahhar received the approval (*riḍā*) of his father to rule (al-Sharafī: 31a). The dominions of descendants of the imam survived the Ottoman conquest of Yemen in the sixteenth century; his descendants continued to play a role in Yemeni politics well into the nineteenth century (Pukhovaia 2023). The succession crisis of 948–953/1541–1546 showed that the power of the 933/1527 will continued to shape politics and expectations of leadership in the Sharaf al-Dīn imamate two decades after its composition.

Epilogue

It appears that the echoes of Imam Yaḥyā Sharaf al-Dīn's political innovations continued to affect Zaydi politics in the next century. This is particularly apparent in relation to the history of the Sharaf al-Dīn imamate in the early Qasimid period (1006–1054/1597–1644) following the expulsion of the Ottomans from Yemen. Aḥmad al-Sharafī, a scholar and contemporary of the first Qasimid Zaydī imams, recorded many details on the Sharaf al-Dīn state and the question of succession. Several copies of Imam Yaḥyā Sharaf al-Dīn's 953/1546 will were produced for members of the Qāsimid family, showing a lasting interest in this innovative attempt to form a dynasty. It is not unlikely that the Sharaf al-Dīn precedent informed the way the early Qasimid imamate was shaped.

While the Qasimid circles were busy uncovering details of the Sharaf al-Dīn imamate, their contemporaries from the descendants of Imam Yaḥyā Sharaf al-Dīn were on a mission to suppress this information. Ibn al-Mufaḍḍal, in his biography of his illustrious ancestor did not mention either the 933/1527 or the 953/1546 will. Another historian, ʿĪsā b. Luṭfallāh, who was a grandson of al-Muṭahhar, also ignored this information in his chronicle. He does not mention the writing of the 933/1527 will in his discussion of the events of that year and ignores the start of the succession crisis in 948/1541 about which we know from other sources (Ibn Luṭfallāh 203: 75, 111). Both historians no doubt had access to al-Murhibī's unique manuscript but chose to ignore it. The decision to rewrite the history of their ancestors indicates that the solutions Imam Yaḥyā Sharaf al-Dīn devised for the Zaydi polity remained controversial, even a century after his lifetime. Despite this controversy, however, they need to be acknowledged as an important innovation of Zaydi political thinking. Further study of their long-term impact on the development of the Qasimid imamate is a desideratum.

Acknowledgements

The preparation of this article has received funding from the European Union's Horizon 2020 research and innovation programme under the Marie Skłodowska-Curie grant agreement no. 101023803. I thank the participants of the focus session 'Zaydi Governance' at the Seminar for Arabian Studies for their comments and suggestions.

References

Ancient sources

Al-Murhibī, Ṣalāḥ b. Dāwud. *Sīrat al-imām al-Mutawakkil ʿalā llāh Yaḥyā Sharaf al-Dīn.* MS Imam Zayd b. ʿAlī Cultural Foundation ZA 561-01.

Al-Ḥibshī, Yaḥyā b. ʿAlī. *Tatimmat al-ifāda fī tārīkh al-aʾimma al-sāda.* MS Berlin Staatsbibliothek Glaser 37, ff. 48a–110a.

Al-Sharafī, Aḥmad b. Muḥammad. *Al-Laʾālī al-muḍīʾa fī aʾimmat al-zaydīyah.* MS Biblioteca Ambrosiana Nuovo Fondo D.545.ar.

Al-Zurayqī, Ḥasan b. Muḥammad. *Sīrat mawlānā amīr al-muʾminīn al-imām al-aʿẓam Sharaf al-Dīn Yaḥyā b. Shams al-Dīn.* MS Vienna Österreichische Nationalbibliothek Glaser 39.

Secondary literature

Haykel B. 2003. *Revival and reform in Islam: The legacy of Muhammad al-Shawkānī*. Cambridge: Cambridge University Press.

al-Ḥusaynī S.A. 1992. *Muʾallafāt al-zaydīya*. (3 volumes). Qum: Maṭbaᶜat Ismāᶜīlyān.

Ibn Luṭfallāh, ᶜĪsā/ed. I.b.A. al-Maqḥafī. 2003. *Rawḥ al-rūḥ fī mā ḥadatha baᶜd al-miʾah al-tāsiᶜah min al-fitan wa-l-futūḥ*. Sana'a: Markaz ᶜAbbādī li-l-dirāsāt wa-l-nashr.

Ibn al-Mufaḍḍal, Muḥammad b. Ibrāhīm/ed. Z.b.A. al-Fuḍayl. 2012. *Al-Sulūk al-dhahabīyah fī khulāṣat al-sīrah al-mutawakkilīyah*. Jeddah: Maṭbaᶜat al-mafāhīm.

Pukhovaia E. 2017. A Zaydī multitext manuscript from the Glaser Collection (Staatsbibliothek zu Berlin): MS Glaser 37. *Shii Studies Review* 1: 175–193.

Pukhovaia E. 2023. The lords of Kawkabān and the transformation of the state in early modern Yemen (15th–17th centuries). *Journal of the Economic and Social History of the Orient* 66: 289–317.

Serjeant R.B. 1983. The post-medieval and modern history of Sanaa and the Yemen, ca.953–1382/1515–1962. Pages 68–107 in R.B. Serjeant & R. Lewcock (eds), *Sanaa: An Arabian Islamic city*. London: World of Islam Festival Trust.

al-Zuḥayf, Muḥammad b. ᶜAlī b. Yūnus Ibn Fand/ed. ᶜA.ᶜA. al-Wajīh & Kh.Q.M. al-Mutawakkil. 2002. *Maʾāthir al-abrār fī tafṣīl mujmalāt jawāhir al-akhbār wa yusammā al-lawāḥiq al-nadīyah bi-l-ḥadāʾiq al-wardīyah (Sharḥ Bassāmat al-sayyid Ṣārim al-dīn al-Wazīr)*. (3 volumes). Amman: Muʾassasat al-imām Zayd b. ᶜAlī al-thaqāfīyah.

Author's address

Ekaterina Pukhovaia, Leiden University, Faculty of Humanities, Leiden Institute for Area Studies, PO Box 9500, 2300 RA Leiden, The Netherlands; Utrecht University, Department of Philosophy and Religious Studies, Janskerkhof 13, 3512 BL Utrecht, The Netherlands.
e-mail e.pukhovaia@hum.leidenuniv.nl; e.d.pukhovaia@uu.nl

Proceedings of the Seminar for Arabian Studies 54 (2025): 286–296

Titles of papers read at the Seminar for Arabian Studies held at the Institut national d'histoire de l'art, Paris, 27–29 June 2024

NB All papers published in this volume of the *Proceedings* are in *italics.*

South East Arabia — Bronze & Iron Age

Matteo Faraoni, Valentina M. Azzarà & Alexandre P. De Rorre	Tracing Ancient Pathways: A Landscape Archaeological Survey of Settlements and Routes in Coastal Omani Sharqiyah
Sara Pizzimenti, Khaled Douglas, Nasser Al-Jahwari & Mohammed Hussein	The Omani-Italian Archaeological Expedition at Al Tikha: Preliminary Report of the 2023–2024 Archaeological Campaigns
Khaled Douglas, Nasser Al Jahwari & Mohamed Hesein	A unique Early Bronze Age Building from Al-Ghoryeen, Oman
Peter Sheehan, Mohammed Khalifa, Nour Al Marzooqi & Malak Al Ajou	Mutaredh Community Mall — more insights into the development of the hydraulic, agricultural and funerary landscapes of al-ʿAyn (UAE)
Ali Abdu Rahman Al Meqbali, Daniel Eddisford, Sam Botan, Michel de Vreeze, Dominic Tomasi, Abdullah Al Yammahi, Abdullah Khalfan Al Kaabi & Dia Al Tawalbeh	Hili 14 and its role within Iron Age society
Michele Degli Esposti, Maria Paola Pellegrino, Federico Borgi, Francesca Barchiesi & Rania Hussein Kannouma	Tell Abraq After the Bronze Age: Results from the 2023 Field Season
Eugenio Bortolini, Antonino Vazzana, Francesca Seghi, Sara Facciani, Elisa Brener, Sara Bernardini, Sara Silvestrini, Dennys Frenez, Federico Lugli, Alberto Urcia & Stefano Benazzi	Exploring the funerary archaeology of Halban, Batinah South Governorate, Sultanate of Oman
Francesco Genchi, Nunzia Larosa, Giampiero Tursi, Guido Antinori, Francesco Caputo & Valentina Mili	The first excavation season to Shokur (Dhank, Oman): a multi-period fortified settlement between desert and mountain
Lloyd Weeks, Adrian Parker, Lesley Gregoricka, Susanne Lindauer, Melanie Fillios, Cemre Üstünkaya, Caitlin D'Gluyas, Amanda Dusting & Guy Hazell	A new programme of field research at Shimal, Ras al-Khaimah (UAE): Exploring human adaptations across the second millennium BCE

Islamic archaeology

Stephen McPhillips, Guillaume Chung-To, Kévin Guadagnini, Guillaume Charloux, Munirah AlMushawh, Charlotte Faiers & François Guermont	Settlement change and continuity through the Islamic period in the Khaybar Oasis
Karol Juchniewicz, Sami Nawar, Otto Bagi, Dan Socaciu, Agnieszka Bystroń, Karol Ochnio, Pawel Rongies & Olga Wasilewska	Uthman bin Affan mosque in Jeddah
Stefanie Janke, Mustafa Ahmad, Friedrich Weigel & Arnulf Hausleiter	*Piecing together the evidence: Architecture, inscriptions and sherds from an early Islamic funerary context in Qurḥ/al-Mabiyat*
Abdullah Alzahrani	Mining Site Project: Excavations in al-Maʿmalah and al-ʿAblāʾ, southwest Saudi Arabia
Peter J. Brown, Ajab Al-Otibi, Mashael Al-Dughailbi & Mishal Al-Khudaydi	New discoveries from the pilgrim way-station at al-Aqiq, Taif Governorate, Makkah Province, Saudi Arabia
Mohamed Enab	An Architectural, Documentary, and Archaeological Study of Models of Ottoman Citadels on Al ṭarīq Al-Sulṭānī, between Al-Madīnah and Mecca

Late Antique Arabia

Bertrand Riba, Jérôme Rohmer, Elora Chambraud, Paul Picavet & Louise Purdue	A newly identified Late Antique settlement in the al-ʿUlā oasis. New insights on the occupation, material culture, agricultural practices and religion of Late Antique northwest Arabia
Julie Bonnéric, Abdelkareem Alhebeshan, Yann Béliez, Léa Buttard, Julie Clerc, Lukasz Miechowicz, Rémi Perrogon & Pierre Thiolas	Excavations at the centre of the early Islamic monastery of al-Qusur: results of the 2019, 2022 and 2023 campaigns
Timothy Power, Michele Degli Esposti, Robert Hoyland, Rania Hussein Kannouma, Seth Priestman, Teresa Nicolosi & Mohamed al-Marri	Continued Work at a Nestorian Monastery and Sasanian-Period Settlement on Sīnīya Island, Umm al-Quwain
ʿAwaḍ Abdullah Saʿad Ibn Naḥee	Syriac Sources for the History and Civilization of the Arabs and Arabia, 3rd–13th century CE (SSHCAA)

Urban Dynamics

Agnieszka Lic	Urban generative processes and morphology of Early to Middle Islamic settlements in Eastern Arabia
Apolline Vernet, Aljohara Almodarra & Marek Z. Barański	*Connected units in the Old Town of AlUla and their social significance*

South Arabian Epigraphy

Alessia Prioletta & Giovanni Mazzini	The onomasticon of the inscriptions from Ḥimā
Irene Rossi	Studying Minaean society through a digital prosopography approach
Justine Potts	The 'confession' inscriptions of ancient South Arabia: a diachronic study

Animal, Plants, Diet

Akshyeta Suranarayan, Sophie Méry, Arnaud Mazuy, Nuria Moraleda, Joan Ribes & Martine Regert	Organic residue analysis of Ubaid vessels in the eastern Gulf: preliminary results from Akab and Umm al-Quwain 2
Olivia Munoz & Kaïna Rointru	Early Bronze Age Agriculture in the Hajjar Foothills: Insights from Bisya Population Oral Health (3000–2500 B.C.E., Oman)
Elena Maini & Francesco Genchi	The role of animals in the afterlife. The case of the human/animal primary depositions of corridor-shaped tomb LCG-2 at Dibbā al-Bayah (Musandam – Sultanate of Oman)
Vladimir Dabrowski, Jérôme Rohmer, Ibrahim al-Mshabi, Fabien Lesguer, Guillaume Chung-To & Marie Laguardia	How to supply a large urban population in the desert during Antiquity? Archaeobotanical multi-proxy analyses on the caravan city of Thāj
Laura Strolin, Jacqueline Studer, Wael Abu-Azizeh, Saeed Alahmari, Melissa Kennedy, Jane McMahon & Hugh Thomas	Comparative study of Neolithic animal deposits found in the mustatils of the AlUla region (Saudi Arabia)

Heritage and Community Building

Selin Nugent, Jennifer Swerida, Nora Al-Aati & Reilly Jensen	*Beyond the Oasis and Within the Community: can community-based participatory research enhance our understanding of Arabian Archaeology?*

Astrid Kensinger & Shaima Sherif — Activating Heritage Sites through Embodied Intangible Heritage and Community Engagement

Trevor Marchand, Abdulhakim al-Sayaghi, Sabina Antonini de Maigret, Cristina Muradore & Ester Lopardo — Recovery & Conservation in (Post)Conflict Ṣanʿāʾ: challenges & learnings

South East Arabia, Prehistory and Protohistory

Knut Bretzke, Frank Preusser & Adrian Parker — The youngest Paleolithic at Jebel Faya and the Arabian Standstill hypothesis

Alžběta Danielisová, Maria Pia Maiorano, Dominik Chlachula, Roman Garba, David Daněček & Jiří Šneberger — Investigating the Neolithic of South-Central Oman between Duqm and Nafun (South-Central Oman)

Michel de Vreeze — The multicultural nature of Umm an-Nar society, and what happened to it?

South East Arabia, Landscape and Communities

Valentina M. Azzarà & Alexandre P. De Rorre — Coastal Crossroads: Rethinking Nomadism versus Sedentism Dynamics in Oman Early Bronze Age Communities

Bleda During, Michel de Vreeze & Eric Olijdam — *A Rural Perspective on the Umm an-Nar and the Wadi Suq Periods from Burj Huraiz (northern Oman)*

Louise Purdue, Sophie Costa, Hatem Djerbi, Gourguen Davtian, Julien Charbonnier, Alain Carré, Linda Herveux, Aline Garnier, Derek Kennet, Anne Benoist & Claude Rouvier — A long-term history of oasian landscapes in Southeast Arabia — assessment from the oases of Ras al Khaimah, Masafi and Rustaq

South East Arabia, Material Culture

Tracey Cian — Iron Age Snake Figurines in south-eastern Arabia: A Critical Reassessment

Jennifer Swerida — Pottery making in the first oases: comparison between Bat and Bisya domestic and funerary assemblages

Jelena Živković, José Cristobal Carvajal López, Irini Biezeveld & Stephanie Döpper — *The production of Bahlā Ware in the context of Late Islamic Oman.*

South East Arabia, Funerary Practices, Physical anthropology

Jaime Ullinger & Lesley A. Gregoricka	Dental Health in the Umm an-Nar and Wadi Suq
Lesley A. Gregoricka & Jaime Ullinger	Biogeochemical evidence for site use and continuity among Umm an-Nar and Wadi Suq communities at Shimal
Taichi Kuronuma	*Regional differences or duality: Reconsideration of the mortuary customs during the Wadi Suq period through geospatial analyses*

Special session

Late Antique Arabia (4th–8th cent.): a changing landscape

Dominik Fleitmann, John Haldon, Raymond S. Bradley, Stephen J. Burns, Hai Cheng, R. Lawrence Edwards, Christoph C. Raible, Matthew Jacobson & Albert Matter	Hydroclimate during the emergence of Islam in late Antique Arabia
Guillaume Chung-To, Guillaume Charloux & Jérôme Rohmer	Northwest Arabia during Late Antiquity: crisis or transformation? A reassessment of the archaeological evidence (4th–8th century AD)
Robert Hoyland	Christianity and the expansion of East Syrian monasticism in East Arabia (6–8th cc. CE)
Philip Wood	Nasrids and Jafnids as sponsors of Christianity
Ilkka Lindstedt	Pre-Islamic Arabic Christian poets and the religious landscape of Western Arabia
Iwona Gajda	Religions of Ancient South Arabia from polytheism to monotheism (4th–6th century CE)
Laila Nehmé	Religious continuity and variability in Northwest Arabia, 200–600 CE
Ahmad Al-Jallad	The Ḥigāzī Paleo-Arabic Inscriptions and the Context of the Quran
Imar Koutchoukali	Legitimacy and authority in late pre-Islamic and early Islamic South Arabia: the case of the Yuʿfirids and the Manāḫids
Simon Pierre	The ‘Entry’ of Iyād into Tanūkh. Invasion, Migration, and Integration in Late Antique North-Eastern Arabia

Pleistocene and Holocene Dynamics

Matthew Meredith-Williams, Roman Garba, Yamandu Hilbert, Lee Arnold, Ash Parton, Mathieu Duval, Dominik Chlachula, David Alsop & Nick Sutton	Out of Africa and into Oman: Palaeolithic Survey
Caroline Mougne, Anaïs Marrast, Pierre Lozouet, Philippe Béarez & Jean-François Berger	Exploitation and use of marine invertebrates at the Neolithic site of Sur-Masirah 10 (Sultanate of Oman)
Katharine E. Schmitt, Conrad Schmidt, Lucas Proctor, Tara Beuzen-Waller, Susanne Lindauer, Julia Unkelbach, Dana Pietsch & Bernd R. Schöne	The potential of snails as climate and environmental archives in dryland environments: new perspectives from Oman
Arnulf Hausleiter, Julia Schönicke, Alina Zur, Patrick Keilholz, Markus Huber & Anna Nilges	Between heavy rain events, groundwater recharge and water supply: a first geo-hydrological assessment of the Saq district of the AlUla oasis
Laurent Lespez, Louise Purdue, Hatem Djerbi Amaury Fernandes, Eric Andrieux, Jean François Girard, Gourguen Davtian, Ségolène Saulnier-Copard, Sophie Costa, Alain Carré, Claude Rouvier & Valentina Villa	Environmental dynamics in northwestern Arabia during the Holocene: fluvial, wetland and dune archives in the AlUla oasis
Rémy Crassard, Diaa Albukaai, Kathleen Dupinay, Marylise Marmara, Benjamin Mutin, Jacques Élie Brochier, Sylvain Colin, Bruno Depreux, Hervé Monchot, Victoria Reina, Séverine Sanz Laliberté, Guillaume Charloux & Munirah Almushawh	The Neolithic and Chalcolithic occupation of Khaybar, Saudi Arabia

North-West Arabia, Mustatils and Funerary practices

Melissa Kennedy, Laura Strolin, Anas Abahussain, Adel Alqaibari, Naif Alshehri, Jane McMahon & Hugh Thomas	New Insight into the Neolithic Mustatil Tradition: First Evidence from the Harrat Khaybar, Saudi Arabia
Hugh Thomas, Daniel Franklin, Lauren Swift, Fahad Bagdadi, Jane McMahon & Melissa Kennedy	Contextualising the Bronze Age Funerary Landscapes of AlUla and Khaybar
Marta Luciani	*Funerary Rituals on Qurayyah's Painted Pottery?*

North-West Arabia, oasian landscape

Guillaume Charloux, Noisette Bec-Drelon, Modwene Poulmarc'h, Kévin Guadagnini, Diaa Albukaai, Rémy Crassard & Munirah Almushawh	The sedentarization process in North-west Arabia during the Bronze Age: new evidence at Khaybar and other regional oases
Charlène Bouchaud, Elora Chambraud, Vladimir Dabrowski, Munirah Almushawh, Abdulrahman Alsuhaibani, Guillaume Charloux, Rémy Crassard, Xavier Desormeau, Louise Purdue & Jerôme Rohmer	The field of possibilities: Early crops in north-western Arabia
Jérôme Rohmer & Abdulrahman Alsuhaibani	3000 years of settlement in one of the main ancient north-Arabian oases: Dadan, from the Bronze Age to the Early Islamic Period

Ancient South Arabia

Romolo Loreto	*The emerging of South Arabian urban societies at the dawn of the Iron Age: the material culture from abroad*
Juan de Lara	The Art of Qaryat al-Faw: A Reassessment and Contextual Analysis
Silvia Lischi	Beyond Sumhuram: Defining the South Arabian Influence over Khor Rori (Dhofar, Sultanate of Oman)
Amgad E.M. Abdulmughni & Mohammed A. Atbuosh	*The Yemeni Mummies: Investigative Report*

Trade and Interconnectivity

Jaafar Jotheri, Rajwan Almayali, K.A. Hopper, Daniel Lawrence, Abdullah Al-Khrayfawee, Abbas Hadrawi, Raheem Alabdan, John A. Webb & Rodd J. Fensham	Where east meets west: The historical relevance of the springs on the Abu-Jir lineament, the Arabian Desert in Iraq
Sara Quaggio	Metallurgical Synergy: Copper trade, unveiling technological exchange in Southeastern Arabia (4th–3rd millennium BC)
Walter D. Ward	Evidence for the commercial connections between the Red Sea, Arabia, and the later Roman province of Third Palestine

Daniele Zampierin	Sailing to and from Khor Rori. The pottery assemblage from Khor Rori (Oman) as testing ground for models of the western Indian Ocean trading routes between the 5th c. BCE and the 5th c. CE
Maria Paola Pellegrino, Francelin Tourtet, Cassandra Furstos, Nolwenn Guedeau, Anne Leschallier de Lisle, Yasmin Kanhoush & Julien Charbonnier	Made elsewhere: what do imports reveal about the evolution of cultural practices in Al-Ula (Hejaz) during the Islamic period?

Late Antique and Early Islamic History

Werner Daum	*Abraha's Cathedral in Ṣanʿāʾ and the Great Mosque: Material and Spiritual Continuity*
Adrien de Jarmy	*From the Oath Under the Tree to the Hijra: Evolving Narratives of the Umma's foundation*
Zacharie Mochtari de Pierrepont	Taqī al-Dīn al-Fāsī and the emirate of Mecca: toward the sharifisation of the sharifate (7th–9th/13th–15th centuries)?

Varia (Coinage, Surveys, Pottery)

Bader Mohamed Al Ali, Mansour Boraik Radwan & Mariam Ali Al Suwaidi	*Iron Age Metal Hoard discovered at Saruq Al Hadid-53 Archaeological Site, Dubai-UAE*
Dhaifallh bin Thaár al-Otaibi	Al-Shu'aybah Hoard Coins: A Comprehensive Study from Salvage to Cataloguing
Doralice Klainscek	'Midianite' Pottery from Timna and Qurayyah: A Novel Assessment
Jaafar Ben Nasr, Faisal Aljibrin & Faysal Lemjidi	Rock art and funerary monuments in Jabal al Qahar — Al Reeth (Saudi Arabia)
Risa Tokunaga, Ajab Alotibi, Majed Dahash & Muzhira Alqahtani	*Epigraphic Survey in Yanbuʿ, Saudi Arabia: First Season (2023)*

Focus session 'Zaydi governance in Yemen between legal theory and political practice'

Johann Heiss	Legitimating the rule: The examination of an imam
Eirik Hovden	Shifts in the Zaydi theory of appointing the imam (ca. 1400–1500 CE)

Kerstin Hünefeld	*Dhimma Governance and the Zaydi Madhhab Spectrum: The forced conversion of Jewish orphans, its Islamic-legal background, and political relevance for Qāsimī and Mutawakkilī Yemen*
Ebrahim Mohammed Abdulwahid Mansoor	*Restricting Judicial Discretion in Medieval Zaydism (1348–1558)*
Ekaterina Pukhovaia	*Transfer of power in the Sharaf al-Dīn imamate (912–980/1506–1573): theory and practice*
Clarck Jr Membourou Moimecheme	Power, Lineage, and Submission in the 13th Century: Sources and Historiography of the Relationship between the Emir of Mecca and the Zaydi Imam of Yemen

KEYNOTE ADDRESS

The Society of Antiquaries of London, Beatrice de Cardi Keynote Lecture

Martina Müller-Wiener & Martin Gussone	More than the Lakhmid capital — The late heyday of al-Hira in the early Islamic period

POSTERS

Carmine Andrea Falco	Down to the river. A geoarchaeological analysis of Wadi al'Uayli and its river basin in the Harrat al-Harrah (KSA)
Amer Alhadi & Bader Alshammari	Initiative to Antigraffiti from Archaeological Sites
Barak Al-Hasinah & Amjaad Alsaedi	Project Ancient Water Systems in Al-Kharj & Al-Aflaj in Riyadh Province, Saudi Arabia
Yasuhisa Kondo, Naima Benkari, Kengo Hayashi, Hideyuki Ōnishi, Yohei Kondo, Mikio Koshihara, Naoyuki Matsumoto, Kazuma Yamao, Yoshiko Takubo & Taichi Kuronuma	A community-based living heritage management project in Salalah, Oman
Yasuhisa Kondo & Taichi Kuronuma	Archaeological survey of the Northern Musandam, Oman: Introduction to a new project
José C. Carvajal López	Stone vessels from Yughbī (Qatar). Connections of an Early Islamic site between the 660s and the 770s
Lucas Proctor, Maria Pia Maiorano, Jakez Moreau & Tara Beuzen-Waller	A Neolithic campsite near Al-Khashbah, Oman: two seasons of research at KHS-A

Risa Tokunaga & Abdulelah Altarib	A Pre-Islamic Bilingual Inscription of ʿAlaqān, Northwest Saudi Arabia
Yamandú H. Hilbert & Patrick Schmidt	Mechanical testing of Boswellia sacra gum (Frankincense): in search of the Prehistoric Adhesives of South Arabia
Kantaro Tanabe, Yasuhisa Kondo, Taichi Kuronuma & Takehiro Miki	Three-dimensional documentation of fortresses in Oman
Paige Paulsen	Movement potential: Modeling and assessing the accessibility of the landscape of Southeast Arabia
Fabien Lesguer, Elora Chambraud, Régine Hunziker-Rodewald, Sterenn Le Maguer-Guillon, Hervé Monchot, Paul Picavet, Shadi Shabo, Abdulrahman Alsuhaibani & Jérôme Rohmer	From the emergence to the abandonment of an urban district in the oasis town of Dadan through 2500 years of occupation
Fausto Mauro & Stephanie Döpper	Decoding Late Iron Age tomb reuse patterns in Sharqiyya North, Oman
Jerome Kahl	'The Silent Guardians'. Petroglyphs of weapon-bearing figures in Arabia: a perspective from Qurayya
Guido Antinori, Martin Sauvage, Ahmad al Tamimi & Ayoub Al Oufis	The towers of Bisya. An inventory of the Early Bronze Age monumental sites in the vicinity of Bisya, Oman
Théo Mespoulet, Ludivine Audebert, Josselin Pinot, Ayoub Al Oufi & Mathilde Jean	'The Largest tower in Oman'. Recent excavations in the Al Dhabi 2 monumental site (Bisya)
Zainab Salmin, Mansour Boraik, Bader Al Ali, Vijo Poulose & Thies Thiemann	Soil corrosivities at Saruq Al-Hadid and Al-Qusais archaeological sites in Dubai (UAE), and its effects on the buried metal objects – comparative study
Elora Chambraud, Charlène Bouchaud, Vladimir Dabrowski, Alexia Decaix, Jérôme Rohmer, Fabien Lesguer, Josselin Pinot, Bertrand Riba, Alexia Rosak, Sebastiano Lora & Mathilde Lenoir	Fruitful desert: preliminary results of the archaeobotanical study of Dadan (NW Saudi Arabia)
Jean-François Breton	Evolution religieuse et architecturale d'Al-Bayda (Jawf, Yemen). Nouvelles recherches de la mission archéologique française au Yemen